Table of Contents

Northern BC
Regions 5, 6 &7

Fishing Mapbooks

"With their guides you will be an expert on the lake even before you get there."

~ Fishing4Fools.com

"...Mussio Ventures gets a big two thumbs up from this angler!"

~ Richard A. Cuffe

"The absolute best selling fishing guides in the store."

~ George Chenge, Angling Specialties

come see us at

www.backroadmapbooks.com

British Columbia
Total Area... 944 735 km^2
Population...4 113 487
Capital...Victoria
Largest City...Vancouver
Highest Point...Mount Fairweather
4 663 meters (15 299 ft)
Tourism info...1.800.HELLO.BC
www.hellobc.com

Acknowledgements

Published by:

Mussio Ventures Ltd.
Unit 106- 1500 Hartley Ave,
Coquitlam, BC, V3K 7A1
P. (604) 521-6277 F. (604) 521-6260
E-mail: info@backroadmapbooks.com
www.backroadmapbooks.com

Backroad Mapbooks

DIRECTORS
Russell Mussio
Wesley Mussio
Penny Stainton-Mussio

ASSOCIATE DIRECTOR
Jason Marleau

VICE PRESIDENT
Chris Taylor

COVER DESIGN & LAYOUT
Farnaz Faghihi

COVER PHOTO
Allcanadaphotos.com

CREATIVE CONTENT
Russell Mussio
Wesley Mussio

PROJECT MANAGER
Andrew Allen
Marie Plavetic

PRODUCTION
Shaun Filipenko
Karen Lo
Justin Quesnel
Dale Tober
Jonathan Wang

SALES / MARKETING
Jason Marleau
Chris Taylor

WRITER
Trent Ernst

Library and Archives Canada Cataloguing in Publication

Ernst, Trent
Northern BC fishing mapbook [cartographic material] : region 5, Cariboo, region 6, Skeena, region 7, Omineca & Peace / Trent Ernst.

Includes index.
ISBN 978-1-897225-56-1

1. Fishing--British Columbia, Northern--Maps. 2. Fishing--British Columbia, Northern--Guidebooks. 3. British Columbia, Northern--Bathymetric maps. 4. British Columbia, Northern--Guidebooks. I. Title.

G1172.N62E63E76 2009 799.109711'8 C2009-900460-7

Printed in Canada

Acknowledgement

We would like to thank everyone for their support and encouragement to resurrect the Fishing Mapbook series. This book is a collaboration of many organizations and people and is intended to be a resource that can and will be used by all anglers in BC. First off, this is a big thank you to the Freshwater Fisheries Society of BC, in particular Brian Chan. Then there is Trent Ernst. He took over the writing and research of the lakes and streams and has really learned to fish out impressive information. Of course we can not forget the helpful team of mappers, editors and graphics people at Backroad Mapbooks. These are the people who pieced everything together in such a convenient, yet comprehensive package. Thank you Andrew Allen, Farnaz Faghihi, Shaun Filipenko, Karen Lo, Jason Marleau, Marie Plavetic, Justin Quesnel, Chris Taylor, Dale Tober, Jonathan Wang.

When doing our research, we had to consult numerous people who live and play in the area. Many times we were looking for the owner of a store, but got someone who was much more knowledgeable. We apologize when we forgot to ask your names.

Here are some of the people who have helped us, though:

First and foremost, we'd like to thank Jack Simpson, whose knowledge of fly-fishing around Williams Lake is encyclopedic, and Doug Porter in Alexis Creek, who is equally as knowledgeable on the Chilcotin Lakes. Rob Seaton at Northwest Escapes, Ltd. filled us in on most of the lakes along the Cassiar Connector, as well as a bunch around Terrace.

Gary Hill knows about all there is to know about fishing the Atlin area, and promised to take us out to all the best spots next time we make it up there. Steve at Oscar's Source for Sports was our contact in Smithers. While they have a bit of a bias towards river fishing there, they also helped point us in the right direction for the lakes, too.

Larry and Chad at Northern Troutfitters Fly and Tackle shop in Prince George basically filled us in on all the lakes in the Omineca Region. If you need to know something about fishing around Prince George, that's the place to go. Brenda Hiebert at Beaver Point Lodge on Tchesinkut Lake told us all we needed to know and more about fishing on that lake. Paul Ron was our go-to guy for information on lakes in the Peace. He works at Backcountry in Fort St. John.

Finally, Noel Gyger has probably forgotten more about fishing the Skeena area rivers than most guides ever learn. He spends most of his days booking for other guides in the area, but he still does some guiding himself.

The maps and charts used in this book were built by the talented artists here at Backroad Mapbooks. However, we had to source Fisheries for the templates for the Lake Depth Chart Maps as well as Geogratis and the Ministry of Sustainable Resources for the source data for the overview maps.

Also a special thanks goes out to our advertisers for supporting the product line as well as helping out with information for the book, and they are: Backcountry, Barkerville BC, Camping & RVing BC Coalition, Freshwater Fisheries Society, Quesnel Chamber of Commerce, Screamin' Reel (Donex Pharmacy), South Cariboo BC, Surplus Herby's, Wells BC.

Finally we would like to thank Allison, Devon, Jasper, Nancy, Madison and Penny Mussio for their continued support of the Backroad Mapbook Series. As our family grows, it is becoming more and more challenging to break away from it all to explore our beautiful country.

Sincerely,

Russell and Wesley Mussio

Disclaimer

The lake charts contained in this book are not intended for navigational purposes. Uncharted rocks and shoals may exist. Mussio Ventures Ltd. does not warrant that the information contained in this guide is correct. Therefore, please be careful when using this or any source to plan and carry out your outdoor recreation activity. Also note that travelling on logging roads, trails and waterways is inherently dangerous, and you may encounter poor road conditions, unexpected traffic, poor visibility, and low or no road/trail maintenance. Please use extreme caution when travelling logging roads, trails and waterways.

Please refer to the British Columbia Freshwater Fishing Regulations for closures and restrictions. Salmon and steelhead anglers should also visit http://www.env.gov.bc.ca/fw/fish/regulations/ or www.pac.dfo-mpo.gc.ca/recfish/default_e.htm before heading out. It is your responsibility to know when and where closures and restrictions apply.

Help Us Help You

A comprehensive resource such as Fishing Mapbooks for Northern BC could not be put together without a great deal of help and support. Despite our best efforts to ensure that everything is accurate, errors do occur. If you see any errors or omissions, please continue to let us know.

All updates will be posted on our web site: www.backroadmapbooks.com

Please contact us at:
Mussio Ventures Ltd.
Unit 106- 1500 Hartley Ave,
Coquitlam, BC, V3K 7A1

Email: updates@backroadmapbooks.com
P: 604-521-6277 toll free 1-877-520-5670
F: 604-521-6260 , www.backroadmapbooks.com

Welcome

Welcome to the first edition of the Northern BC Fishing Mapbook. This book is the latest in our continuing quest to produce the perfect fishing guide. It is basically an evolution of the former Cariboo edition of the former Fishing BC series but a whole lot bigger and better. In addition to the much expanded area of coverage, anglers will now note that it includes the more popular rivers and streams in the area. The north is well known to be home to some of the best trout, steelhead and salmon rivers in the world. Less obvious, but just as important is the fact that many of the write-ups have been expanded to provide even more detailed fishing information. Everything has been tweaked, updated, and simply made better, to help you find the perfect fishing experience.

Of course, different people have different definitions of what defines the perfect fishing experience. Some people love fast and furious action. They would rather snag 100 small fish in a day than spend time waiting around for the big one. Others would rather sit patiently waiting for The One. Some people prefer bar fishing for salmon, sitting with a dozen other anglers and shooting the breeze; catching a fish is almost secondary to the experience. Still others enjoy the pure fly-fishing experience, standing knee deep in a fast flowing mountain stream searching for trout, and the experience is sullied somehow if there is another angler within 5 kilometres. As a result, there is a vast diversity in the lakes and rivers we present here.

Northern BC is a vast area, and this book covers well over half the province, from the 100 Mile House area all the way north to Atlin Lake, which spills over into the Yukon. The lakes and rivers span the province, some rivers draining into the Pacific Ocean, others flowing east into Alberta. It is an area of raw beauty and some of the most remote locations in BC. It encompasses the awesome Coast Mountains, the Chilcotin Plateau, the Cariboo and Northern Rocky Mountains and even a chunk of prairie on the east side of the Rockies.

To compliment the surroundings, there is an abundance of lakes, both large and small, allowing fishermen of all ages to enjoy a successful outing. Whether you are an ardent fly fisherman or prefer the old fashion bait and bobber, there is surprisingly good lake fishing very close to the urban centres.

The Cariboo is notorious for its excellent lake fishing even during the hot summer months. The prolific fly hatches, nutrient rich environment and clear, crisp water make this area a fantastic lake fishing destination. Another unique thing about many of the lakes in the area is the lack of people fishing. There are literally thousands of lakes to discover and it is quite easy to find a lake all to yourself. The incredible fishing, peace and quiet and stunning scenery makes this an ideal family fishing and camping destination.

The Skeena Region is an area dominated by its rivers. While we have listed some of the best fishing lakes from this area, expect to get a few odd looks if you ask at a local tackle shop about lake fishing. In a land where 6 kg (12 lb) steelhead are the average and where Chinook salmon can get to 15 kg (30 lbs) and more, it seems a bit odd to some to fish a lake for a 0.5 kg (1 lb) rainbow. But taking a feisty rainbow with a light rod on a surface fly can be every bit as exciting as fighting a monster Chinook.

As you get farther north and east, the fishing season gets shorter and shorter, as the ice-free season gets shorter and shorter. Lakes in the Omineca and Peace, especially those lakes farther north, are extremely susceptible to over fishing. You will also find fish in the north that you don't find anywhere farther south, like the pretty Arctic grayling.

Since a lot of the lakes require you to weave your way through a maze of backroads, we recommend you pick up a copy of the *Cariboo Chilcotin Coast* and the *Northern BC Backroad Mapbooks*. These books have detailed maps along with descriptions on everything from camping areas to other fishing opportunities. They are the perfect compliment to the Fishing Mapbook series.

Northern BC
Regions 5, 6 &7

History

The Fishing Mapbook Series evolved from research done when creating the Backroad Mapbook Series. The authors and researchers really enjoy exploring and fishing new lakes but didn't always know where to start. After stumbling across the depth charts for a few lakes, they learned how to read a lake a lot quicker and have been able to fish that much more effectively.

In their travels, they get a chance to explore a lot of new lakes and streams. The visual information provided in the depth charts and river maps help the researchers find the best place to fish time and time again. They figured if they found these charts that useful, other anglers would too.

Mussio Ventures Ltd. was not the first company to see the value of depth charts. Other companies were producing individual lake charts and selling them for a premium. In typical entrepreneurial fashion, Russell and Wesley Mussio took it one step further. Rather than selling individual charts, they put several lakes in a single book and added valuable information on everything from directions and facilities to fishing tips and stocking information. They also priced the book reasonably.

Today, the series have evolved into even bigger books and now cover the more popular streams in the area. Working with key people in the industry has also helped gain more valuable insight into fishing the various lakes and rivers covered in each book.

Russell & Wesley Mussio - Founders of Backroad Mapbooks

Legend - Regions 5, 6 & 7

Regional Boundaries

Conservation Officer Service District Offices

Bella Coola: .....(250) 982-2421	Terrace:............(250) 638-6530
100 Mile House:(250) 395-5511	Mackenzie: ......(250) 997-6555
Quesnel: ....(250) 992-4212	Prince George: (250) 565-6140
Williams Lake: .(250) 398-4569	Vanderhoof: .....(250) 567-6304
Atlin: ....(250) 651-7501	Chetwynd:........(250) 788-3611
Burns Lake: .....(250) 692-7777	Dawson Creek:(250) 784-2304
Dease Lake: ....(250) 771-3566	Fort Nelson:.....(250) 774-3547
Q.C. City:.........(250) 559-8431	Fort St. John:...(250) 787-3225
Smithers: ....(250) 847-7266	

Lake Chart Classifications:

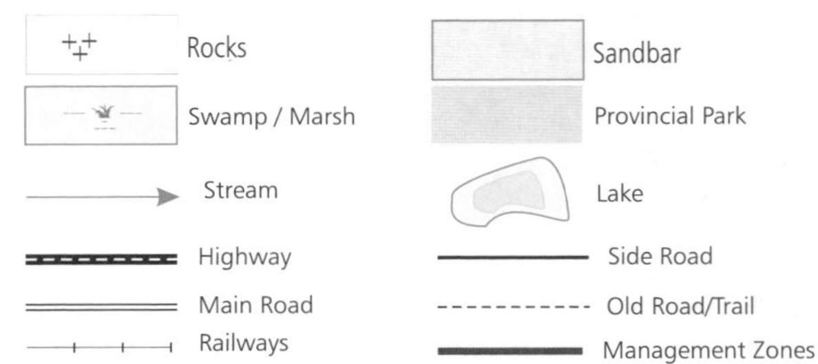

Recreational Activities and Miscellaneous

Wheelchair
Parking
Swimming
Paddling
Hiking
Boat Launch
Biking
Picnic Area
Dock/Wharf
Beacons
Waterfall
Lodge / B&B
Resort
Anchorage
Viewpoint
View
Community
Dam

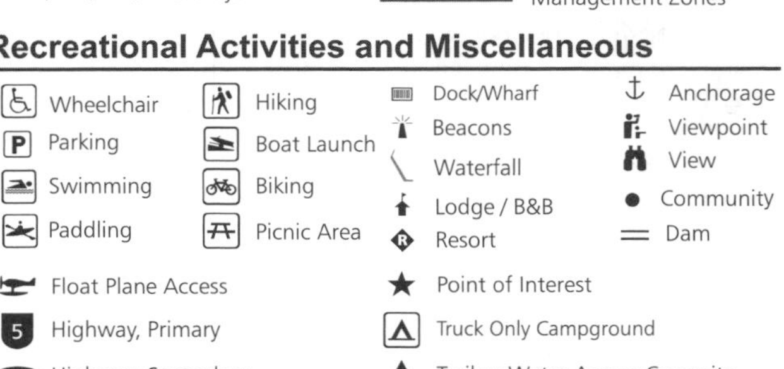

Regions 5, 6 & 7- Cariboo, Skeena, Omineca & Peace

Fish and Wildlife Regional Office (Cariboo)

Williams Lake: 400-640 Borland St.,V2G 4T1, 250-398-4530

Fish and Wildlife Regional Office (Skeena)

Smithers: Bag 5000, 3726 Alfred Ave.,V0J 2N0, 250-847-7260

Fish and Wildlife Regional Office (Omineca)

Prince George: 4051-18th Ave.,V2N 1B3, 250-565-6135

Fish and Wildlife Regional Office (Peace)

Fort St. John: Rm 400, 10003-110th Ave.,V1J 6M7, 250-787-3411

Overview Key - Regions 5, 6 & 7

Top 20 Hot Spot Lakes

1. Atlin Lake
2. Babine Lake
3. Charlie Lake
4. Charlotte Lake
5. Chaunigan Lake
6. Chief Gray Lake
7. Chilko Lake
8. Dragon Lake
9. Dugan Lake
10. Francois Lake
11. Fraser Lake
12. Hobson Lake
13. Lakelse Lake
14. Morchuea Lake
15. Morice Lake
16. Natadesleen Lake
17. One Island Lake
18. Quesnel Lake
19. Sapeye and Bluff Lake
20. Tzenzaicut Lake

Top 5 Hot Spot Rivers

1. Chilko River
2. Dean (Lower) River
3. Muskwa River
4. Peace River
5. Skeena River

How to use this Mapbook

Fish Species

The book begins with a rather elaborate section on the main sportfish species in the region. In it we give pointers on how to identify and fish for these sometimes elusive fish. These tips should not be overlooked, as they are an accumulation of many years of personal experience and research. Of course there are many anglers out there that know a lot more than we do, but few sources put it all together in such a convenient, compact package. Whether you are new to the area or new to fishing or have fished these holes for years, we guarantee that following these tips will help you find more fish.

The Lakes (Bathometric Charts)

The lake fishing section of this book features all of the favourites as well as some of those lesser known lakes that can produce that lifetime fishing memory. With so many lakes to choose from, the task was indeed a challenge to try to get that right mix in our book.

Similar to this book's predecessors, Fishing BC Cariboo, we have highlighted many of the better lakes with depth charts. These charts, if read properly will help you pinpoint the likely areas on a lake to start fishing. These charts show the contours of the lake and help readers figure out where the shoals, drop-offs, hidden islands or basically any sort of water structure that will likely hold fish is located. Reviewing these charts before visiting the lake for the first time could reveal where to find the fish. At the very least, they will help you know where to start fishing.

We have also included the fish species and whether they are stocked or not for each listing. In some cases we even tell you how and what to fish with. If there are no fishing tips included under the individual listing, you can refer to the front or back of the book to refresh yourself on tactics and fly patterns of the prominent species in that lake. Of course, when you get to the lake and there are other anglers there do not be shy to ask where to fish and what to use. Most people are more than willing to help out.

Rivers & Streams

The river or streams section is new to the series, but follows the similar pattern of including fish tips, access and facilities for each stream that is highlighted. Of course, the river maps are a popular feature that include fishing pools and popular access points where possible.

Fishing Tips & Techniques

Near the back of the book this is another excellent resource to refer to. In this section, we give pointers on how to fish using the various lake and stream fishing techniques, as well as some useful fishing tips. Constant referral to this section will help anglers new and old to the sport.

Overview Map and Index

There are also handy planning tools such as the Overview Map and an Index. If you know the waterbody you are planning on visiting, you simply turn to the lakes or river section and find the listing you are interested in. Alternatively, you can look it up in the index to see what page it is listed on.

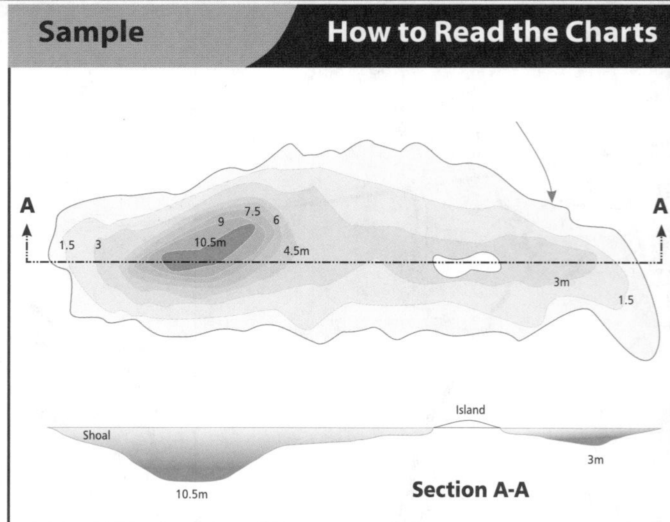

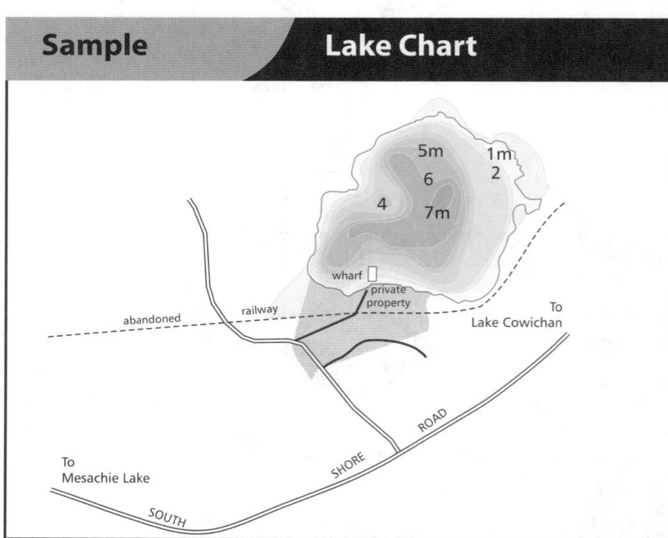

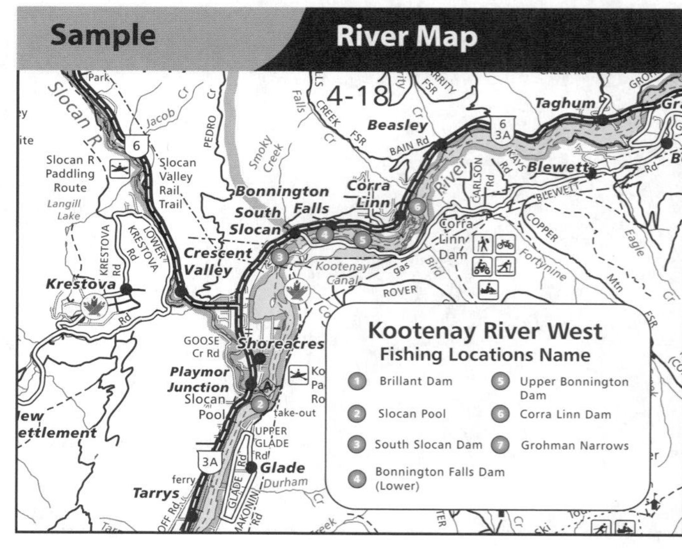

Fish Species

Northern BC has a good variety of species of fish and some of the most important salmon and steelhead runs in the world. The breadth and variety of fish species that can be found here is a testament to how good the fishing can be. We have listed the main sportfish found in the region, along with tips on how and when to fish for each species.

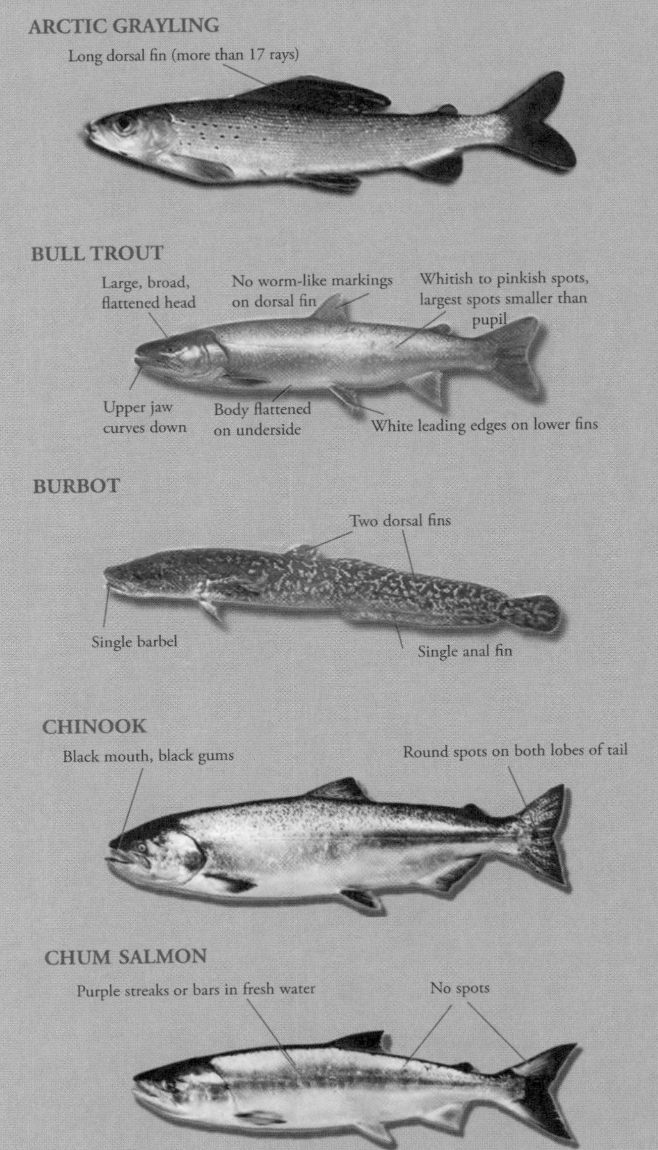

Arctic Grayling

The Arctic grayling is a salmonoid and is found in cold water lakes and rivers, especially in the northernmost parts of the province. They are omnivorous and often quite ravenous as they have an extremely short ice-free period when they can feed. They average about 30–40 cm (12–15 in), although some can get bigger. They are a beautiful fish with a sail-like dorsal fin and are often multi-coloured, with purple, silver, gold, lavender, green, pink and other colours, sometimes in spots and sometimes in an iridescent sheen. Their diet consists of insects, invertebrates, minnows, fish eggs and whatever else they can find. They will rise to a dry fly quite willingly. Typical rainbow trout techniques usually work for grayling. In rivers like the Murray and the Peace, they are usually found near seams in the water, where fast moving water and slow moving waters meet. They will usually wait in the slower moving water for food to wash or swim past and then dart out to feed.

Bull Trout & Dolly Varden

Bull trout and Dolly Varden are the often confused members of the char family. Both are recognized by their pinkish spots on the body, but bull trout have larger heads. Dollies are more common in coastal areas, while bull trout are usually found further inland. They can reach up to 6.5 kg (14 lbs) in bigger lakes and the sea run stream version of the Dolly Varden have been known to top 9 kg (20 lbs). These fish spawn in the fall and are not known for their great fighting ability. Feeding primarily on insects, eggs and small fish, they prefer cold water and grow slowly.

Try trolling a green or orange Flatfish or Krocodile lure or fishing the creek mouths with bait balls (a large cluster of worms and hook). Also, jigging with a bucktail and flasher in the winter or spring near a large creek mouth can be very successful. Fly fishers should try a larger leech pattern or streamer patterns, while spincasters can try silver coloured spoons.

Due to significant declines in their population, tough regulations have been imposed on both species to avoid over fishing.

Burbot (Ling Cod)

Burbot or ling cod are a large bottom feeder that used to be a common sportfish. Over fishing has drastically affected the numbers and size and many lakes are now catch and release only for this tasty fish. They are an ugly fish that is easily recognized by their large mouth and long brown body with sharp fins. Jigging near creek mouths can produce the odd cod to 4 kg (10 lbs) in the larger water bodies. However they are most frequently caught through the ice. In some lakes in the north, it is possible to fish for burbot using a set line. Check your regulations.

Chinook

Chinook are the largest of the Pacific Salmon. They can reach an impressive 27 kg (60 lbs) on occasion. They are found in rivers like the Bella Coola and Atnarko and in the Skeena drainage. Casting or drift fishing with cured roe into deep holes seems to be the most effective method. If trout are cleaning the hook of bait, switch to lures, wool (white, red or pink) or flies. Lures of choice include a Kitimat spoon or Spin-N-Glos. The fly angler will need heavy gear and fast sinking lines with short strong tippet to get down to the deep holes. Shooting heads allow increased line control and help maintain a drag-free drift. Patterns mixing bright and dark colours seem to be most effective. Woolly Buggers, Egg Sucking Leeches or Marabou Eggs dead drifted are equally good.

Chum

Chum can be found in most rivers from late September until late November. Often referred to as dog salmon, they prefer fast, shallow water and colour quickly when they enter freshwater. They are the second largest Pacific Salmon, averaging 5–9 kg (12-20 lbs). Flies such as a '52 Buick (a small, green shrimp imitation) work well. However, many anglers prefer big Marabou flies (green, pink or orange). Beadheads help vary the presentation. Fly-fishing works best by leaving the fly dead or by a slow steady retrieve. You will need heavy gear to fish these strong, acrobatic fish. Alternatively, float fishing with pink worms or bottom bouncing wool or lures with pink in them can also be very effective.

Coho

Coho are the most prized of all river run salmon. These silver fish are identified by their white mouths and spots on their tail and their acrobatic nature makes them a joy to catch. They average 2-5 kg (5-10 lbs). On most rivers, you can use lighter line, while smaller floats and lighter weights are essential since Coho are easily spooked. Look for them to run quickly from the deep pools and structure when the water raises and clarity of the river is reduced.

Coho can be caught by drift fishing wool or bait (salmon eggs or roe). Spincasters should try size 4 or 5 spinners (Blue Fox or Mepps) cast upstream and worked through slower edges of pools. Spoons such as Gibbs Ironhead, Pen

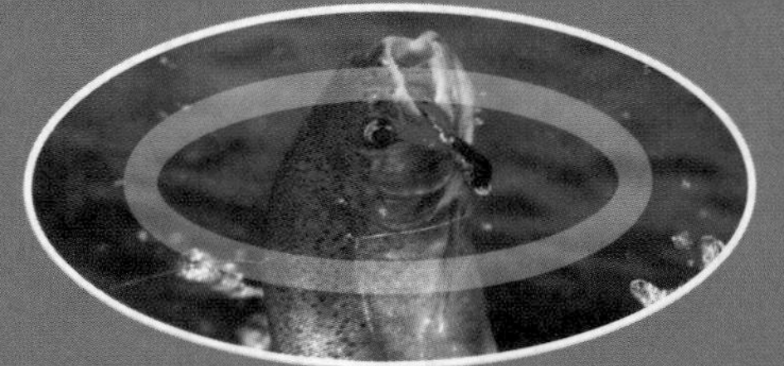

Fish Species

COHO

CUTTHROAT TROUT

EASTERN BROOK TROUT

KOKANEE

LAKE TROUT

Tac's BC Steel and a Little Cleo with 2/0 hook are other popular spincasting gear. Coho will only chase moving flies, Rolled Muddlers and Harrison Fiords are local favourites. Working with a size 4 to 8 gold or silver Muddler Minnow, Mickey Finn or beaded Woolly Bugger can also be dynamite. Try olive colours on bright days and brighter colours on darker days.

Cutthroat Trout

Cutthroat get their name from the red slash under their jaw. You will find both resident and sea-run cutthroat in rivers and lakes. Cutthroat are predatory fish, feeding extensively on small fish such as kokanee, sculpins and sticklebacks. If baitfish aren't present, they will survive quite nicely on insects. They are usually found in the 25–50 cm (10–20 in) range. The most productive times of the year to fish for cutthroat are during the salmon fry migration from March through May and the stickleback spawn in July through September. A fly imitating a baitfish is a good choice when baitfish are present. Muddler Minnow or Wool Head Sculpin are two such patterns to try. Cast around the drop-off areas as the cutthroat tend to cruise the near shore area in search of baitfish.

Sea-run cutthroat run in schools, chasing spawning salmon. In the spring they feast on the salmon fry. Look for feeding activity and cast across the current slightly downstream. Fly anglers should use a floating line with a long leader and weighted fly. During the fall, they'll grab salmon eggs or anything close. Attractor patterns, such as Woolly Buggers and sparkle leeches are good bets in winter when food is scarce.

Eastern Brook Trout

Brook trout are actually char that were first introduced into BC in the early 1900s. They are found in many of the cooler streams and smaller mountain lakes, as they can survive harsher conditions than other trout. Easily identified by the large number of speckles (they are also called speckled trout), they are good fighters and very tasty. Brookies feed on insects and shrimp. They are attracted to small lures such as the Panther Martin, Mepps, Vibrax, Kamlooper and Krocodile and will respond to a lake troll tipped with worms, leeches, insects or Powerbait. Even though brook trout will take a dry fly, subsurface flies generally work better. A dragonfly or damselfly nymph or a black leech pattern trolled or retrieved near the lake bottom often brings success. The Werner Shrimp pattern is another good fly to try, along with muddlers, Woolly Buggers and Clouser minnows. A slow retrieve seems to be the most effective. They are also a popular fish for ice fishing, as they typically remain quite active through the winter.

Kokanee

Kokanee (a word that means 'red fish') are actually landlocked sockeye salmon. They are easily recognizable by their slim silver bodies and forked tail. Kokanee turn a brilliant red when they spawn in the late summer. In the plankton-rich interior lakes, they can reach 3 kg (5 lbs), though that is rare. Kokanee are usually caught using similar techniques as you would use for rainbow trout. One of the most popular means of fishing for kokanee is trolling a Willow Leaf with a short leader and a Wedding Band and maggot. Troll as slow as possible and in an "S" pattern so your line, will speed up or slow down and change depths as you round the bend. This entices the fish to bite. Trolling with one ounce of weight or less, which takes the lure to 5–15 m (15 to 45 ft), is the most productive. An exciting alternative is to try to catch kokanee on a fly. In the spring, chironomids and mayflies can yield surprising results. Unlike rainbow, kokanee school, so if you have found one, chances are you've found a bunch.

Lake Trout

Lake trout are another misnamed char. They are only found in large, deep and cold lakes. They grow very slowly but often reach sizes in excess of 10 kg (25 lbs), since they live longer than most other fish species. Fish to 3 kg (5 lb) are quite common. Lakers are a fall spawning fish and are recognized by their forked tail, long head and large snout as well as an abundance of spots. These fish stay near the surface during the early spring and late fall when the water temperatures are cold. In the summer, the fish retreat to the depths of the lake so it is best to troll deep during summer months.

Lake trout are not great fighters; however, they do have a lot of mass and there's something special about catching a fish that big. Trolling silver spoons or spinners, which imitate the fish's main food source, the minnow is the most effective method to catch lakers. Ice fishing can also be quite effective, although the big lakes rarely freeze. During winter, lakers can be found closer to the surface and they readily hit small spoons tipped with minnows.

Pink Salmon

Pinks are the smallest of the Pacific Salmon and rarely reach over 2.5 kg (5 lbs). Also known as humpies, they develop a large, prominent hump and hooked mouth in freshwater. Pinks fade quickly in freshwater, so it is best to fish them closer to the estuary to find bright, hard fighting fish. They are the perfect fish to learn how to fly-fish with due to their preference for shallow water with medium currents. They return every two years. The peak of the run usually occurs in early September. Fly-fishing for pinks has become very popular. Getting them to bite, as opposed to fowl hooking them, requires drifting a fly or lure dead slow allowing it to bump along the bottom. Use anything with pink in it.

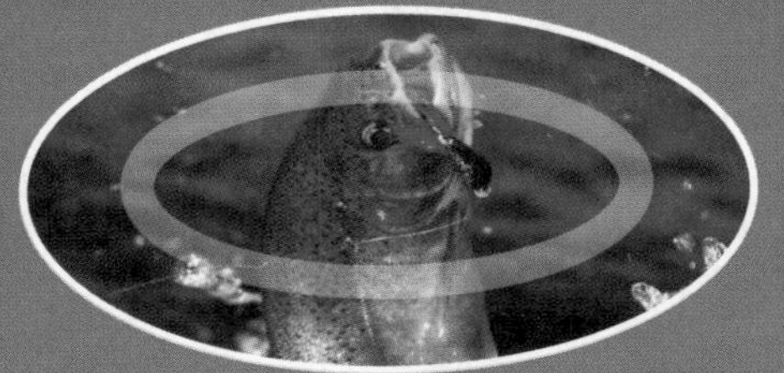

Fish Species

Rainbow Trout

Rainbow trout are native to many streams and lakes in British Columbia. Due to their hardy nature and the fact they are an excellent sportfish, they are stocked throughout the province. Rainbow get their name from the colourful strip they get when spawning in the spring. The mainstay of their diet in many lakes and rivers are small shrimp (scuds), leeches and insects, but they will also eat small baitfish if given the opportunity. During spawning season, they are quite fond of free-floating eggs.

The fish varies in size depending on the waterbody and strain you catch. The Pennask strain are hard fighting acrobats that like to leap high into the air to shake the lure. These fish really like their insects and are part of the reason the interior is one of the world's great fly-fishing destination. Chironomids are popular early in the season, but are replaced by caddisflies, mayflies, damselflies and dragonflies later in the season. In the fall, a water boatman, leech, or attractor pattern can be effective. Also found in the area are the Blackwater strain of rainbow. While not as famous as the Pennask, they are piscivorous, meaning they eat other fish. As a result, they grow big fast. These fish can hit 4.5 kg (10 lbs) or more and what they lack in spirit they make up for in size. The best way to catch these big trout is to use lures that imitate small baitfish. For spincasters, this means a variety of spoons and spinners, while fly anglers usually use patterns like a Muddler minnow.

Trolling is usually the most popular way to catch the fish. Lake trolls, spinners, spoons and plugs have all been known to produce, especially tipped with powerbait or a worm. Even fly anglers have taken to dragging around a leech or nymph pattern in order to cover more water. But on many lakes, a simple hook with bait and bobber can work just as well as any other method.

Sockeye

Sockeye are good eating and are generally easy to catch. They run in schools and can reach 7 kg (15 lbs) in size, but generally are half that size. Sockeye prefer current seams and riffles on downstream sides of gravel bars. During early morning and evening they can be in less than 1.5 m (4 ft) of water, but go deeper in the day. They have diamond-like scales and prominent eyes that make them one of the easiest salmon to identify. Look for them to begin entering the rivers in June, but it is not until late July that the bigger runs arrive. The sockeye fishery lasts until mid-September.

Bottom bouncing is the preferred fishing method. A 9-foot rod with a level wind reel and 15 lb test is all you need. Use light enough weight to bounce every three feet or so. Fish the slots between fast and slow water in no more than a few feet of water, using either fluorescent wool or a size 12 green Spin-N-Glo. In addition to bottom bouncing from shore, anglers can have luck drift fishing by using a float and bait (pink krill or Ghost Shrimp). Fly-fishing for sockeye requires an 8-weight rod with short leaders (5-7 ft) and 10-12 lb tippet on high density sink tip lines. Cast the fly directly across the current allowing it to sink and skip on the bottom. Small size 8 green flies are preferred, although in murky waters you will need bigger flies with a bit of sparkle.

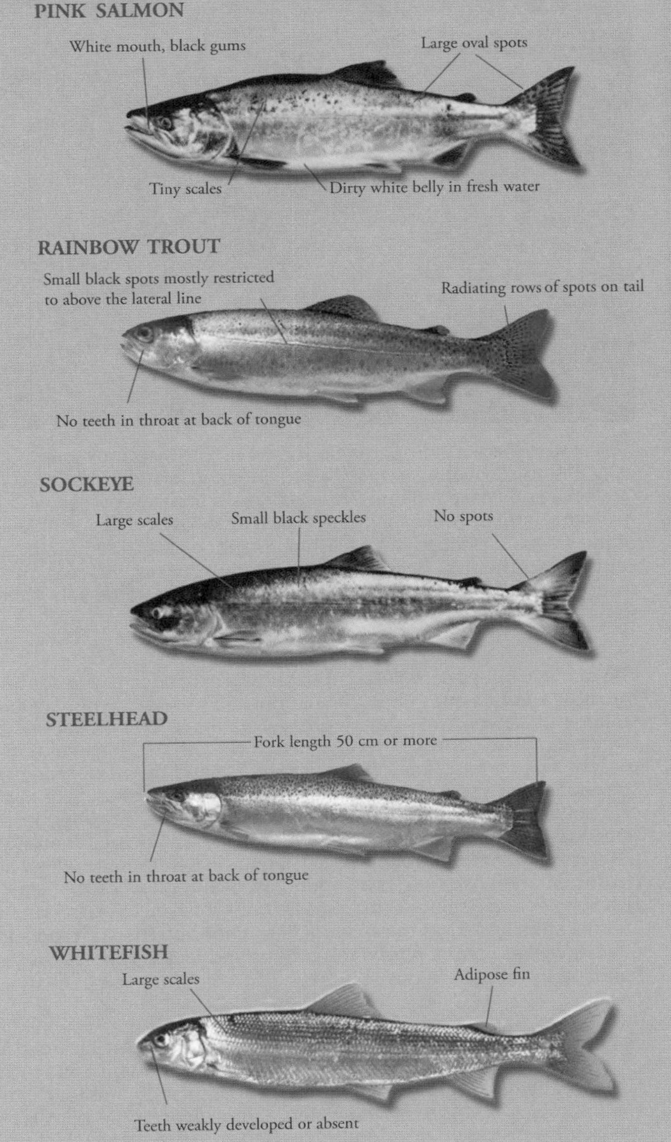

Steelhead

Steelheads are the most prized sportfish in British Columbia and can get as large as 9 kg (20 lbs). They are a sea-run version of rainbow trout known for their acrobatics and fight. However, they are notoriously difficult to catch. The trick is to vary the presentation depending on the season and water conditions. Steelhead like slow presentations so the quicker the water, the bigger the lure. They hold in shallow water close to shore. Fish close to the bottom and cast above holding areas. Drift fishing with a float suspending a ¼" pencil lead weight above a short leader of about 30–50 cm (12–20 in) with 1/0 to #4 hooks is the most common method. However, many anglers bottom bounce. Wool (pink or orange) and a single egg is the most popular attractor. Popular lures include Corkys, Spin-N-Glos, Gooey Bobs and Colorado Spinners.

Fly-fishing for steelhead, especially in the Skeena area, is incredibly popular. Marabou patterns like the Popsicle, small Muddler Minnows or weighted leech patterns are popular. Floating lines and long leaders with a dry fly like a Grease Liner can produce the fish of a lifetime. In deeper pools, work a weighted stonefly or size 10 Glo Bug along the bottom using a sink tip line and short leader.

Steelhead are heavily regulated and regulations are subject to change on short notice.

Whitefish

Whitefish are a silvery fish with large scales. They spawn in the fall and give a good fight even in the winter. They can reach 50 cm (20 in) but average 30 cm (12 in). They are not a popular fish, because they are quite boney and they don't offer the same acrobatics as trout, but they do put up a good fight and are a popular for ice fishing. They feed mainly on insects and will readily strike spinners, spoons or other shiny lures. Fly-fishing can also be effective, especially in the spring during the mayfly hatch.

Message From Brian Chan

Freshwater Fisheries Society of BC

FISHING CHECKLIST

- ☐ Fishing rod and reel
- ☐ Bobbers, swivels, sinkers
- ☐ Lures
- ☐ Hooks
- ☐ Extra line
- ☐ Net
- ☐ Fishing licence
- ☐ Sunscreen
- ☐ Hat
- ☐ Bug spray
- ☐ Lunch or snack
- ☐ Life jacket
- ☐ Sunglasses
- ☐ Camera
- ☐ Extra clothing
- ☐ Nail clippers
- ☐ Pliers
- ☐ Freshwater Fishing Synopsis and Regulations

gofishbc.com

Welcome to the Northern BC edition of the Fishing Mapbook series. Geographically, this book covers over half the province and includes the Cariboo, Skeena, Omineca and Peace regions. This vast area is literally covered with lakes and rivers that anglers could spend several lifetimes exploring and enjoying. Many of the waters described in this Fishing Mapbook are in remote or wilderness settings. Northern BC boasts abundant populations of wild salmon, steelhead, trout and char and anglers can also pursue other game fish such as Arctic Grayling and White Sturgeon.

This guide has been completely updated and expanded to provide anglers with the most accurate information on not only how to get to your favourite lake or stream but also provides details on new waters to explore. Each featured fishing location has information on access, including GPS waypoints, fish species present, tips on best times of the year to fish and the best fishing techniques specific to that waterbody. Contour maps or depth charts are also provided on many of the more popular and productive lakes. Knowledgeable anglers understand the value of knowing the depth of water being fished as water temperature and food availability are key factors in determining where and at what depths different fish species are found. New anglers will also see an expanded Fish Species and Fishing Techniques section which includes information on fish identification and tricks to catching them, choosing the right rod and reel or fly gear, as well as common fishing methods and tackle. There is even proper fish handling techniques in this section.

The Freshwater Fisheries Society of BC has partnered with Backroad Mapbooks on the production of the Fishing Mapbook series as one of our strategic objectives is to inform and educate the public about fish and recreational fishing. Guidebooks are an important tool in achieving this goal. Other Society activities include delivering "Learn to Fish" programs for children and families, developing our "Fishing in the City" program within urban areas and improving access to fishing waters. Our major responsibility is delivery of the provincial fish stocking program and many of the lakes covered in this guide are stocked on a regular basis to ensure a sustainable recreational fishery. Up to date stocking records for all waterbodies stocked in the province and additional information on other society activities is available our website www.gofishbc.com.

This Fishing Mapbook describes a wide range of fishing locations from easily accessible small stocked lakes to popular north coast rivers to more remote lakes and streams to waters that are only accessible by walking or by fly-in access. Detailed information is also provided on a number of world class anadromous river fisheries that should be on every angler's "must fish" list. Northern BC provides the most diverse fishing opportunities within this great province. The vastness of the area provides endless summer vacation opportunities for those traveling great distances to day and weekend trips for those residents fortunate enough to live within the northern regions described. So get the camper, motorhome or tenting gear ready along with this guidebook and Go Fish BC!

Brian Chan
VP Sport Fishing Division
Freshwater Fisheries Society of BC

Quesnel Fishing

If you love fishing you may need to make arrangements for permanent accommodation! There are so many good places to fish here that you'll need a lifetime to discover them all. Our thousands (yes, thousands!) of fishing spots include world famous Dragon Lake, home to record-sized rainbow trout and just a few miles from downtown Quesnel. The fish in this lake are of the Blackwater strain that grow large and are great fighters.

And don't forget the nether reaches of the mysterious Blackwater River in the western mountains, renowned for stunning fly fishing, or Tzenzaiakut Lake south of Quesnel (the name means "fish" in the Carrier language).

There are large runs of Sockeye Salmon in the Quesnel River during the late summer and into the fall. At this time, the big Rainbows and Bull Trout become very aggressive making a great fishing adventure. When the Cariboo River has runs of Chinook Salmon, the fishing becomes really exciting!

Information is available in several different publications, which can be obtained at one of our Visitor Information Centres in Lebourdais Park on Hwy 97, or visit our websites online for information on fishing and living in Quesnel, www.quesnelinfo.com and www.northcariboo.com.

Location: 12 km (7.5 mi) north of 100 Mile House
Elevation: 883 m (2,897 ft)
Surface Area: 119 ha (295 ac)
Maximum Depth: 20 m (65 ft)
Mean Depth: 7 m (23 ft)
Way Point: 51° 44′ 36.1″N, 121° 21′ 41.5″W

108 Mile Lake

Area Indicator

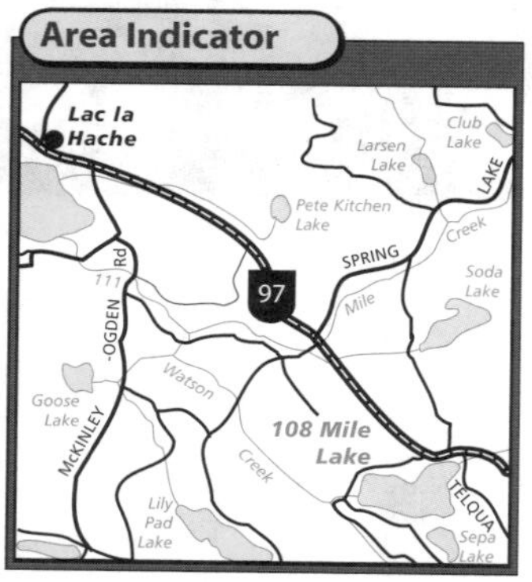

108 Mile Lake			
Fish Stocking Data			
Year	Species	Number	Life Stage
2008	Rainbow Trout	15,000	Yearling
2007	Rainbow Trout	15,000	Yearling
2006	Rainbow Trout	12,000	Yearling

Fishing

Surrounded by the resort community of 108 Mile Ranch, 108 Mile Lake is a moderately productive lake found near just off the Cariboo Highway (Highway 97). The lake is known more for its golf course and Nordic ski centre than fishing.

The lake is connected to nearby Sepa Lake by a channel that was dredged in the late 1980s, allowing water to flow freely between the two lakes. While this has had a dramatic change on the quality of water in Sepa Lake, the fishing has remained pretty stable.

108 Mile Lake has both brook trout and rainbow trout that grow to 1.5 kg (3 lbs) but tend to be in the 20-30 cm (8-12 in) range. The fishing is considered fairly slow as compared to other lakes in the Cariboo due to the heavy fishing pressure.

The lake is infected by redside shiners, suckers and squawfish. These coarse fish compete heavily with the trout for the available food. However, 15,000 Blackwater rainbow are stocked annually to help maintain the fishery and to help control the redside shiners. Blackwater rainbow are a piscivorous strain of rainbow and feed on the smaller course fish. The trout are often found feeding in the shallow shoals and are most active during the day. They are a fast growing, aggressive fish that will usually go after anything that looks like food. In addition to small, non-salmonoid fish like redside shiner, Blackwater will go after dragonfly nymphs, leeches and other larger presentations. Fly anglers can try working one of these patterns, while spincasters will find that a variety of flashy spoons and spinners will work.

Given the depth and elevation of the lake, the fishing is better from May through early June. By the summertime, fishing tails off quite a bit and does not pick up until the fall.

If you are trolling the lake, try at the west and north ends of the lake but note the electric motor only restriction. Fly fishermen should focus around the two sunken islands towards the middle of the lake.

Directions

108 Mile Lake is a resort destination area just north of 100 Mile House. The lake is found just off the Cariboo Highway (Highway 97), about 12 km north of town.

Facilities

The **108 Resort** is a Best Western Hotel situated on the shores of the lake. The resort is considered more of a golf and Nordic ski resort than a fishing camp. For anglers looking for something a little more intimate, there are a number of Bed and Breakfasts within the area.

A popular rest area is found off the highway, while a beach and wharf are found at the east end of the lake. Boat launching is possible at the west end of the lake.

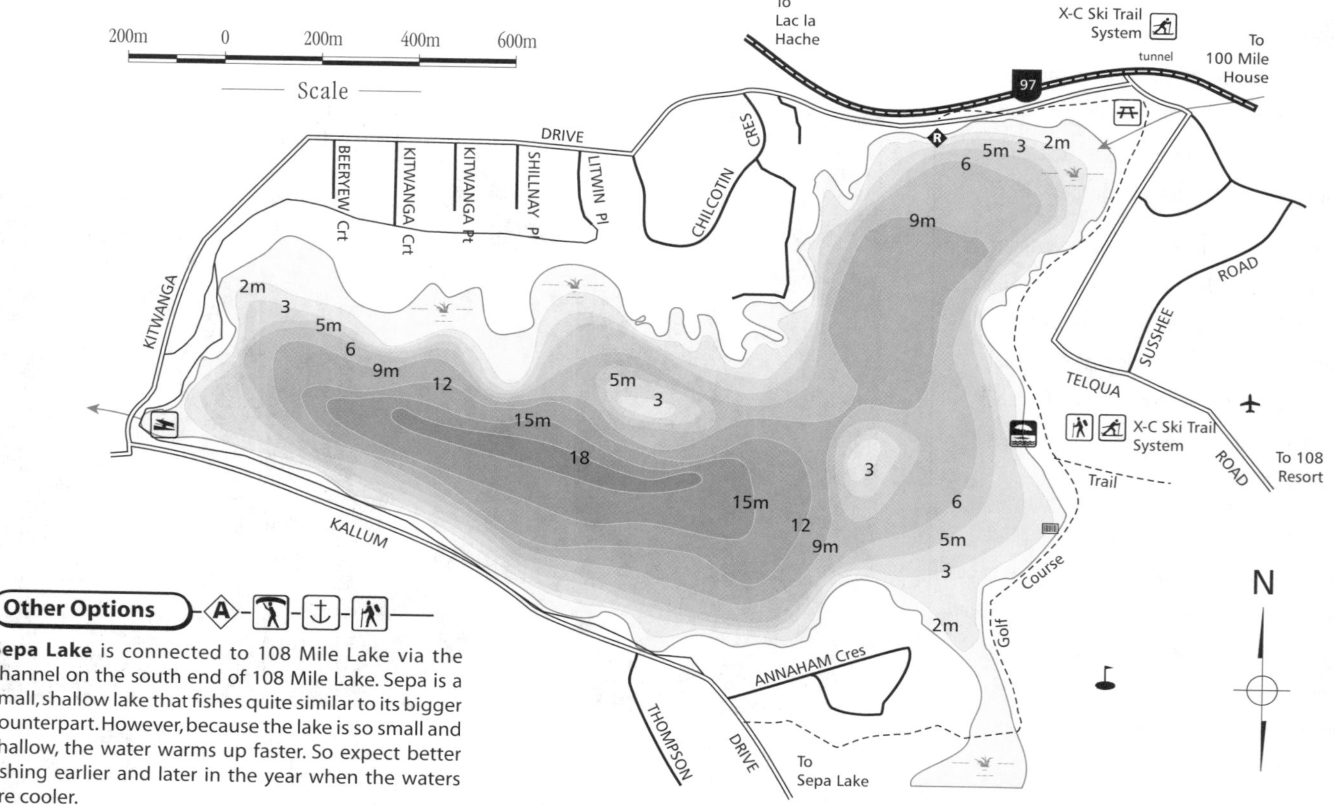

Other Options

Sepa Lake is connected to 108 Mile Lake via the channel on the south end of 108 Mile Lake. Sepa is a small, shallow lake that fishes quite similar to its bigger counterpart. However, because the lake is so small and shallow, the water warms up faster. So expect better fishing earlier and later in the year when the waters are cooler.

Abbott Lake

Location: 48 km (29.8 mi) northeast of Williams Lake
Elevation: 832 m (2,730 ft)
Surface Area: 24 ha (59 ac)
Maximum Depth: 24 m (77 ft)
Mean Depth: 11 m (36 ft)
Waypoint: 52° 19' 30.5" N, 121° 30' 3.7" W

Fishing

Abbott Lake is a small lake that has some feisty trout. Found near the town of Horsefly, the lake has been stocked annually since 1985. More recently, the lake is stocked with 5,000 Pennask All Female Triploid rainbow trout by the Freshwater Fisheries Society of BC. The Pennask strain rainbow are not usually known for their large size, and, truth be told the average catch in the lake is much closer to 1 kg (2 lbs), although every year, there are a few that grow to 3 kg (7 lbs).

However, the lake has very nutrient rich waters, which combined with the abundant lake chub, helps produce fast growing trout. This when combined with the Pennask strains natural fighting ability makes this a fun place to fish. These fish are well known for their fight and frequent leaps high into the air, trying to shake the hook.

Abbott Lake is definitely a better lake to visit during the cooler spring and fall months. The fishery is best in May and again into October. A good portion of the lake is made up of insect holding shoals. When the hatch is on, these shoals are great places to cast a fly. Spincasters can also do well by tossing small spinners such as a Mepps or Panther Martin near the drop off. Vary the depth of each cast until you find where the fish are holding.

Abbott is a perfect lake for a belly boat as it is sheltered and fairly small. The water drops off rapidly from shore except at the outflow at the east end of the lake. Shore fishing is possible if you can cast past the trees and overhanging brush that line the lake. The east side of the lake has floating moss and fishing from shore is difficult there. However, there is a deep hole right off the shore near the southwest end of the lake. The deepest part of the lake is right in the middle. It is at those two deeper locations that you should fish during the summer months, especially if you are trolling.

Despite the stocking program the lake can be quite moody and you are in no way assured of catching a fish here. To help maintain the fishery, there is a single barbless hook restriction as well as a ban on ice fishing and bait fishing. Also, there is an electric motor only restriction at the lake.

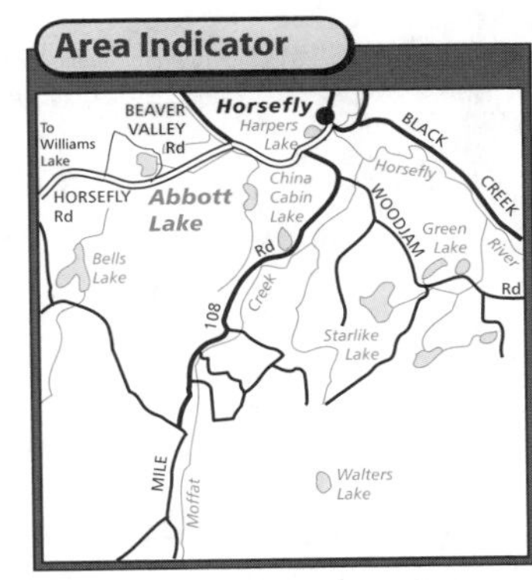

Abbott Lake
Fish Stocking Data

Year	Species	Number	Life Stage
2008	Rainbow Trout	5,000	Fry
2007	Rainbow Trout	5,000	Fry
2006	Rainbow Trout	5,000	Fall Fry

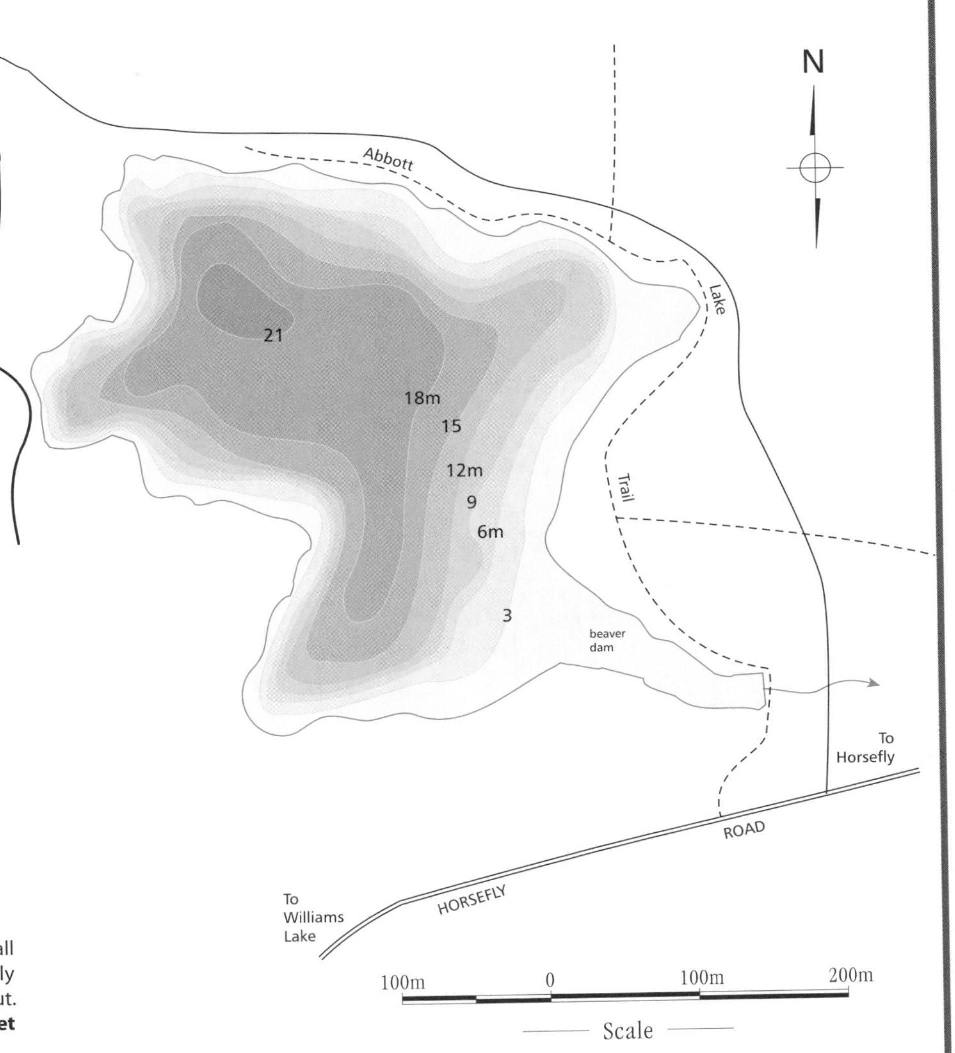

Directions

The lake is reached by driving east from Williams Lake on the Cariboo Highway (Highway 97). At 150 Mile House, the road to Horsefly and Likely heads off to the north. At the first major junction, follow the paved Horsefly Road until you are about 7 km west of the community of Horsefly. You will see a gravel road heading off the main road. Follow that road 200 metres to the parking area and then it is a 400 metre walk to the lake.

Facilities

There are no facilities at the lake. It is possible to launch a small boat or float tube at the lake if you carry in to the lake. You can pitch a tent near the lake.

Other Options

There are several small lakes in the area. Most small lakes, which have feeder streams, offer surprisingly good fishing for hard hitting and fast growing trout. Look for **Bells**, **China Cabin**, **Green**, **Starlike** and **Triplet Lakes** to the south and southeast of Abbott.

Location: 30 km (18 miles) northwest of Alexis Creek
Elevation: 1,039 m (3,408 ft)
Surface Area: 105 ha (259 ac)
Maximum Depth: 25 m (82 ft)
Mean Depth: 5.7 m (19 ft)
Way Point: 52° 16′ 22″ N, 123° 31′ 49″ W

Alexis Lake

Area Indicator

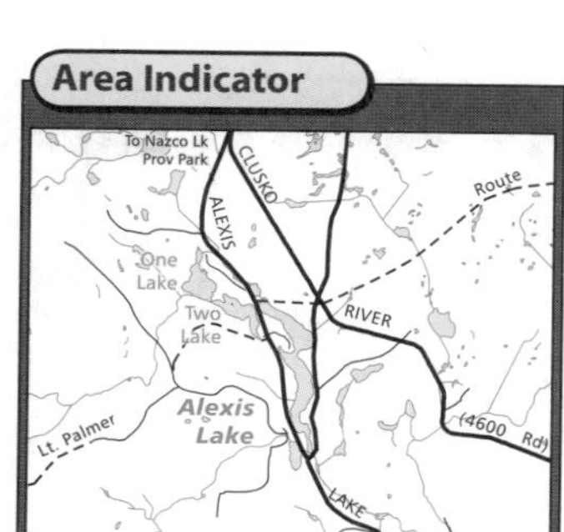

Directions

The lake can be accessed from a variety of roads from the north and south, but the easiest way to the lake is to take Highway 20 from Williams Lake to Alexis Creek. About halfway between the town and Bull Canyon Provincial Park, you will come across Harvey Road heading north, which leads to the Alexis Lake Forest Service Road. Turn right and follow the road to the lake, which is found just past the Tautri Creek turnoff, about 30 km from the highway.

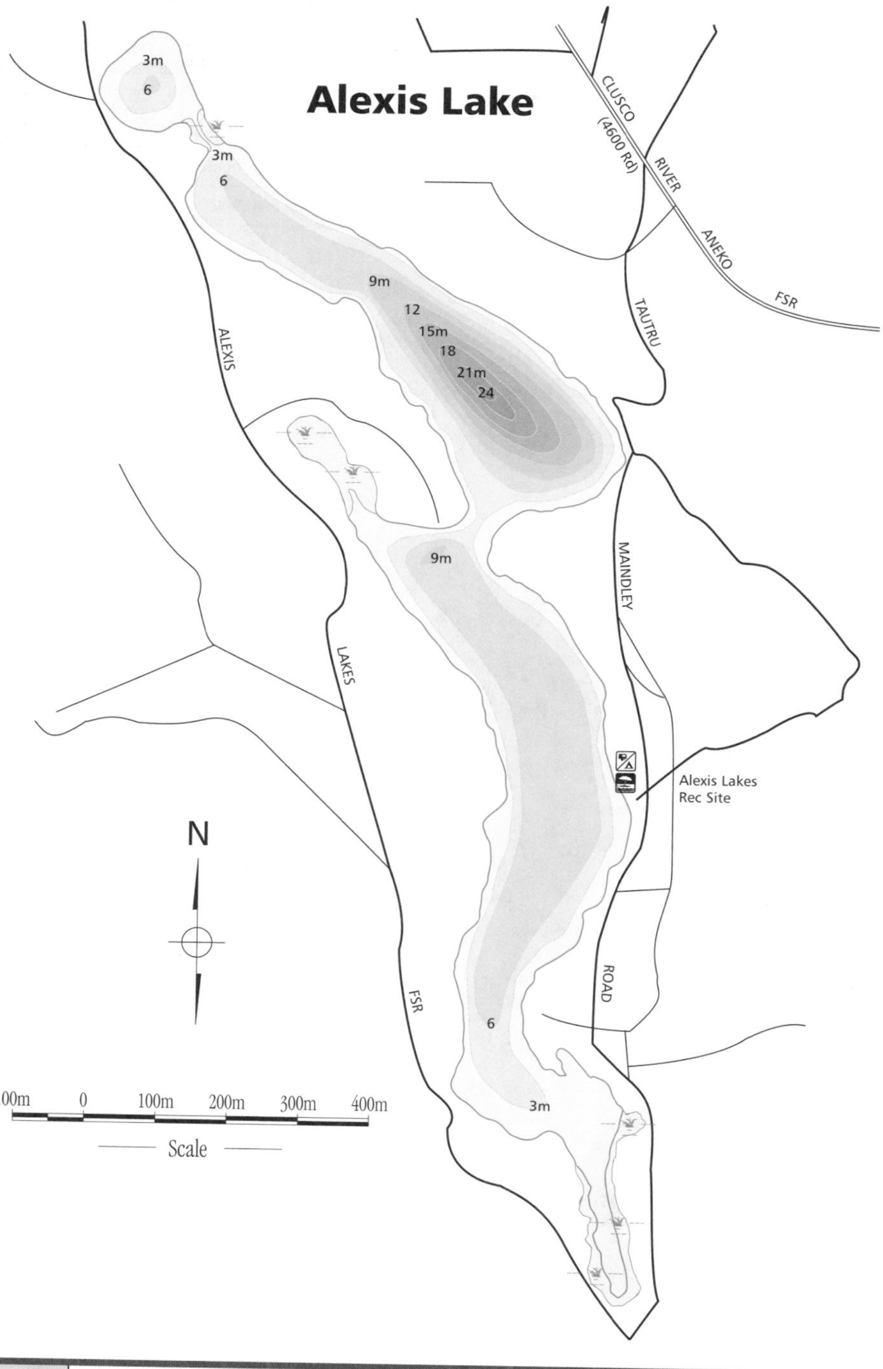

Alexis Lake

CLUSCO (4600 Rd) RIVER ANEKO FSR
TAUTRU
ALEXIS LAKES FSR
MAINDLEY ROAD
Alexis Lakes Rec Site
3m 6 9m 12 15m 18 21m 24
N
100m 0 100m 200m 300m 400m
Scale

Fishing

Alexis Lake is a small lake found just south of Nazko Lake Provincial Park and north of the small town of Alexis Creek. The lake is surrounded by beetle killed pine, the odd green spruce or fir, as well as low deciduous shrubs.

It isn't the prettiest lake around, especially with all the beetle kill, nor does it offer the best fishing around. But it has plenty of small fish that are quite willing to hit most anything you throw at them.

A good-sized fish here is only about 35 cm (14 in), with the average catch being about 30 cm (12 in). It is not a high elevation lake, although it is quite deep and the fishing is fairly consistent throughout the year. This helps makes it a popular summer getaway and there are a number of cottages around the lake, although very few are inhabited year round.

The lake is regulated electric motors only, but most people who fish here will want to fish with a float tube or pontoon boat anyway, as there is no real boat launch. It is possible to wrestle a small boat down to the water at the recreation site and there is a bit of a dam at the south end of the lake where one can get a boat onto the water too, although it is fairly weedy here.

Those weeds at the southwest end of the lake make it difficult to launch a boat, but are prime habitat for insects, which feed the fish in the lake. If you are fishing Alexis Lake, this is probably the most productive area. The lake features the traditional Cariboo/Chilcotin hatches, with early chironomids followed by mayflies, caddis flies and dragon and damselflies. While these hatches are fairly prolific, they are nothing to write home about, either.

Depending on when you are at the lake will determine the best way to fish the lake, especially for fly anglers. If there is no active hatch happening, good searching patterns include a Doc Spratley in red, black or green, a Carey Special, or a leech pattern in black or maroon. In the fall, a water boatman pattern is always a good bet.

The shoreline at the recreation site drops off quickly, meaning that it is possible to fish from the beach, although there aren't many other places to fish from shore.

Facilities

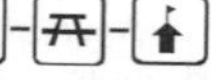

The **Alexis Lakes Recreation Site** has space for maybe five groups. There is a nice beach, but no boat launch. You can get a cartopper down the steep banks and onto the beach or you can choose to launch your boat at the south end of the lake. The lake is a popular swimming hole in summer, as there are not a lot of mosquitoes.

Other Options

Two Lake is located just past Alexis Lake. As the name implies, Two Lake is the second of a pair of small lakes, joined together by a short channel. The lake is well stocked with rainbow that grow to 2.5 kg (5 lbs) and native brook trout to 1 kg (2 lbs). There is a small recreation site on the shore and a cartop boat launch for electric motors only.

Allan Lake

Location: In Dease Lake townsite
Elevation: 791 m (2,595 ft)
Surface Area: 27 ha (66.7 ac)
Maximum Depth: 29.3 m (96 ft)
Mean Depth: 8.2 m (27 ft)
Waypoint: 58° 25′ 48.2″ N, 129° 59′ 59.7″ W

Fishing

Located within the townsite of Dease Lake itself, Allan Lake is a small, but surprisingly deep lake that doesn't see a lot of pressure, despite the fact that it is located a few feet away from the highest populated area for hundreds of kilometres.

That speaks more to the number of people who live in this neck of the woods and should not be interpreted as any sort of commentary on the quality of fishing here. Indeed, there are less than 500 people in Dease Lake.

Allan Lake is stocked every three years or so with up to 10,000 brook trout. There are not many lakes in the area that hold brook trout or speckled trout as some people call them. Brook trout are one of the prettiest fish there is and while they are not as spirited of fighters as rainbow, they are still tenacious and rarely give up on a fight. The fish here can get up to 2.5 kg (5 lbs).

Brook trout are actually a char and prefers to stay deep, making short strong runs, as opposed to the aerial acrobatics of a rainbow. They are a hardier species and can withstand greater extremes in temperature and lower levels of oxygen that would kill off rainbow trout. This is part of the reason they are stocked in Allan Lake.

Spincasting and trolling small lures such as a Deadly Dick and worm or a small Rapala is the most effective manner to fish the brook trout. Flies are not well received by the brook trout, though casting a large attractor type pattern can sometimes work well. The lake does hold leeches, so working a leech pattern might also be productive.

The lake has many bays and points, so there is plenty of structure where the fish can and will hang out. Shore fishing is tricky, though it can be done. Better to use a float tube or small boat.

While the fishing here is good year round, it is best known as an ice-fishing lake. Brook trout like cold water and are often more active when the ice is on the lake. And, because they don't have to worry about predators from above like eagles, they roam freely about the shallow areas of the lake where the food is.

Ice fishing using bait (worm, corn or maggot) and a hook is rewarding. Deadly Dicks work just as well in winter as in summer. Fishing in water 3 m (10 ft) or less, around structure or overtop weed beds is usually the best place to start. Drill multiple holes at the start of the day so you do not constantly have to break out the auger and scare the fish away. Most people just lie on the ice and watch for fish through the hole. If you haven't seen a fish in 15 minutes, move onto the next hole.

Area Indicator

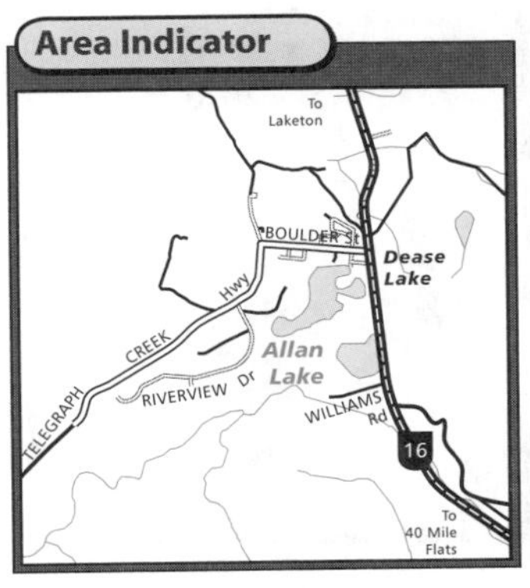

Directions

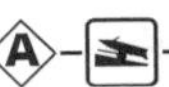

Dease Lake is located about 480 km north of where the Cassiar Highway and the Yellowhead Highway connect. Turn left onto Stikine Street and then left again onto First Avenue, which quickly dead ends in a parking area. From here it is only a few hundred feet to the lake along a rough but two wheel drive accessible trail.

Facilities

Dease Lake is not a large town, but there are lots of facilities. There is a grocery store, a gas station, two motels and a private campground about 10 km north of town, along Dease Lake itself. There are no actual facilities at Allan Lake.

Allan Lake			
Fish Stocking Data			
Year	Species	Number	Life Stage
2007	Brook Trout	7,400	Fingerling
2004	Brook Trout	8,000	Fingerling

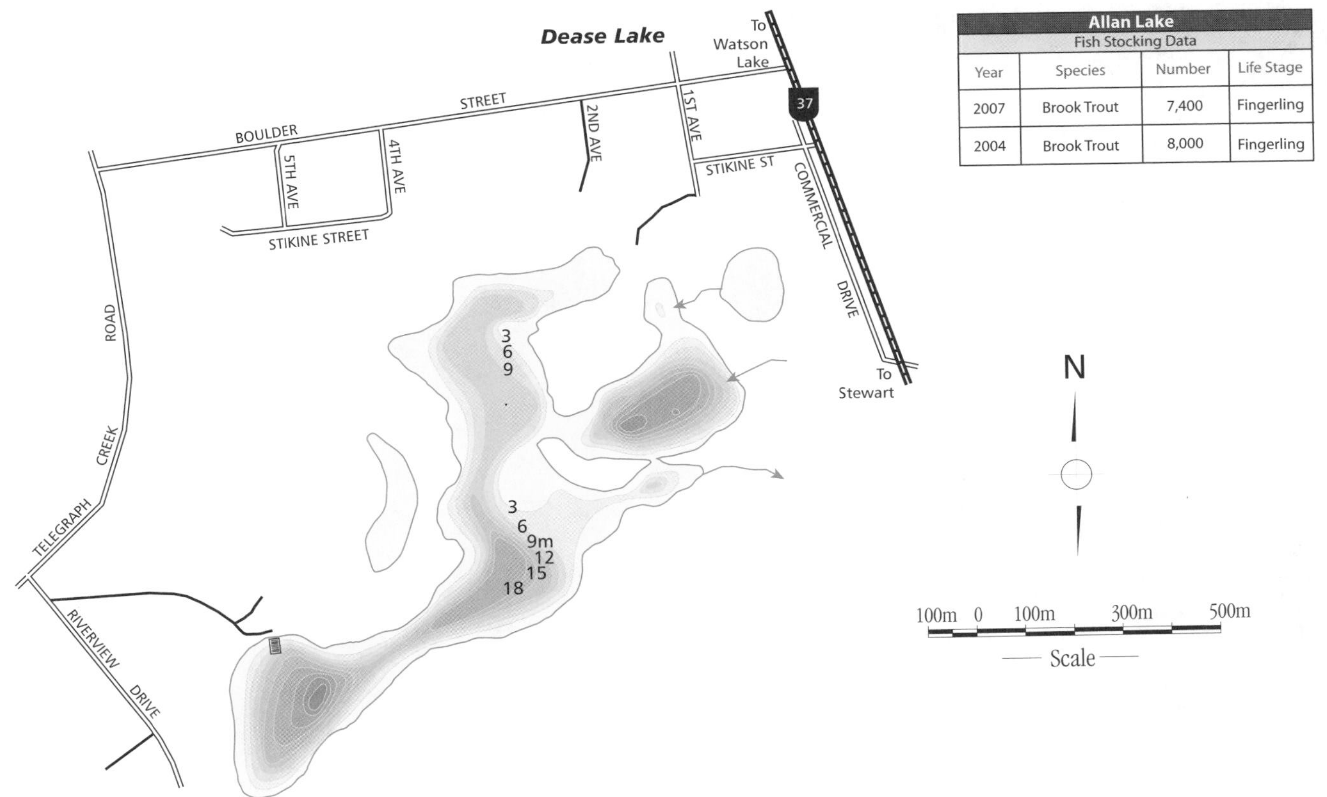

Location: 325 km (200 miles) west of Williams Lake
Elevation: 1,084 m (3,556 ft)
Surface Area: 595 ha (1,471 ac)
Maximum Depth: 4.3 m (14 ft)
Mean Depth: 1.7 m (5.6 ft)
Waypoint: 52° 30' 12" N, 125° 20' 33" W

Anahim Lake

Area Indicator

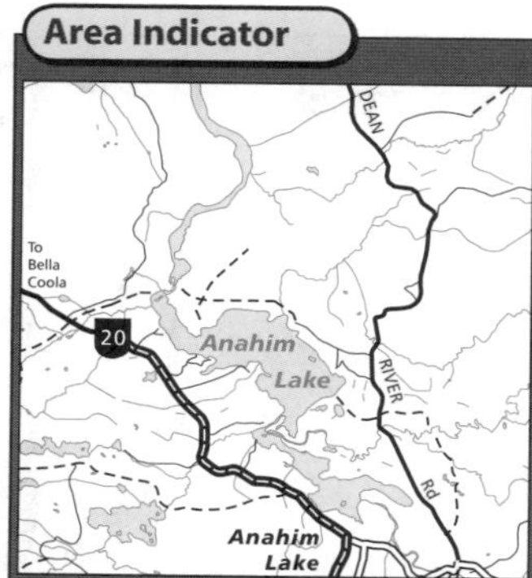

Fishing

Anahim Lake is one of those lakes burned into the collective consciousness of the provinces anglers; not so much for itself, but for the fact that the mighty Dean River flows through the lake. In fact, the lake is not so much a lake as it is a widening of the Dean.

Below the lake, the Dean River is classified waters, while above the lake it is not. Most anglers will work around the mouth of the Dean, even working their way upstream a short ways as there is almost no current up to Corkscrew Creek and the connector to Little Anahim Lake. More importantly, people can canoe down from Little Anahim Lake, from the old recreation site there since there is no public launch on Anahim Lake itself.

The lake holds rainbow trout as well as cuttbows, a cross between rainbow trout and cutthroat trout. There are also a number of course fish species in the lake, too.

Cuttbows are about what you'd expect from a cross between rainbow and cutthroat. A pretty, aggressive but small fish. In fact, finding a fish to 45 cm (18 in) is a very good catch; most come in about 30 cm (12 in) range. But the cutthroat in them makes them hit lures and flies much harder and much more willingly than a rainbow.

As a result, the lake is a popular place to fish with a fly, although trolling a Willow Leaf and Wedding Band, or spincasting a small spoon, spinner or Flatfish certainly will work quite well, too.

The shallow areas have a heavy concentration of lily pads, where the fish love to feed. And the weed cover means the lake has some great hatches, especially the caddis fly hatch at the end of June/beginning of July, when the cuttbows can be taken off the surface with a Tom Thumb, Elk Haired Caddis or other similar pattern. And while the fish are small, they are usually quite willing to attack a slightly larger presentation.

In the fall, the lake is best fished with a water boatman, a leech, or an attractor pattern. The lake also has a good population of freshwater shrimp, or scuds.

The fish in the lake are infested with gill lice, which do not affect their catchability or edibility. However, in an effort to shake the lice, the fish will leap out of the water. While it doesn't mean they're actively feeding, it does make them fairly easy to spot at a distance.

The best place to fish is usually around the inflow or outflow of the Dean, although in summer, the fish usually head for the deeper areas of the lake.

Directions

Anahim Lake is found at the western edge of the Chilcotin Plateau, at the start of the Coast Mountains. The lake drains west to the Pacific, via the Dean River. The town of Anahim Lake is found at the south end of Little Anahim Lake and is about 325 km (200 miles) west of Williams Lake along Highway 20.

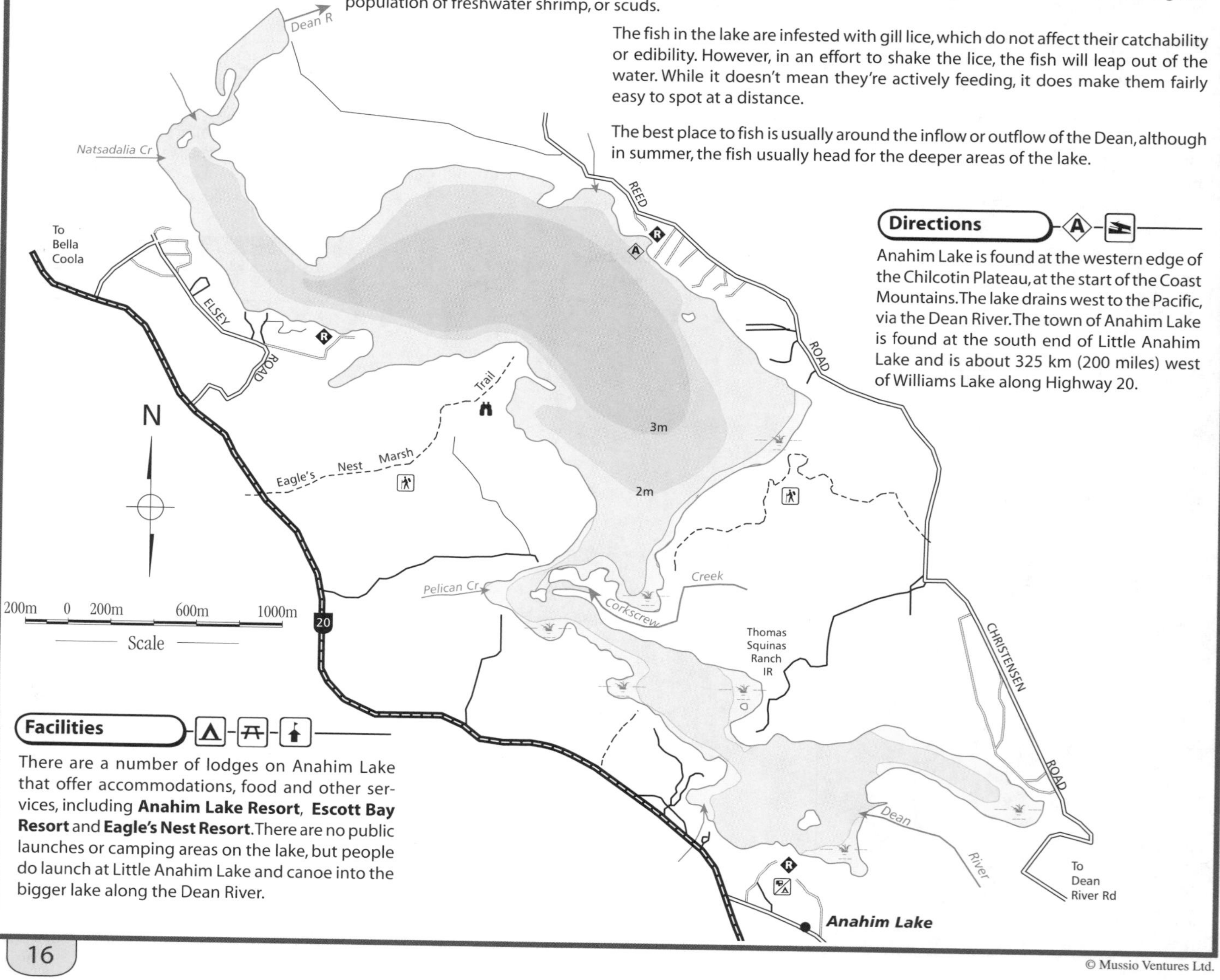

Dean R
Natsadalia Cr
To Bella Coola
REED
ELSEY ROAD
ROAD
Trail
N
Eagle's Nest Marsh
3m
2m
Creek
Pelican Cr
Corkscrew
200m 0 200m 600m 1000m
Scale
20
Thomas Squinas Ranch IR
CHRISTENSEN
ROAD
Dean
River
To Dean River Rd
Anahim Lake

Facilities

There are a number of lodges on Anahim Lake that offer accommodations, food and other services, including **Anahim Lake Resort**, **Escott Bay Resort** and **Eagle's Nest Resort**. There are no public launches or camping areas on the lake, but people do launch at Little Anahim Lake and canoe into the bigger lake along the Dean River.

Augier Lake

Location: 30 km (18.6 miles) north of Burns Lake
Elevation: 893 m (2,930 ft)
Surface Area: 852 ha (2,104 ac)
Maximum Depth: 60 m (198 ft)
Mean Depth: 27.4 m (90 ft)
Geographic: 54° 25′ 8″ N, 125° 35′ 12″ W

Fishing

This medium sized lake is found north of Burns Lake near the much larger Babine Lake. It is one of the most popular of the handful of good fishing lakes found in the area.

Augier Lake is extremely popular with the locals. It isn't too far away from Burns Lake and can be driven to in about half an hour. But it is off the main highway and offers a wilderness experience. There is a beautiful beach here, so when the fish aren't biting, it's a great lake to just hang out at for a few hours.

On busy summer weekends, the recreation site on the shores of the lake can be packed, usually with locals. Despite the fact that the only way to the lake is via half an hour of gravel roads, the boat launch is paved. This adds to the popularity of the site.

The lake is known for its lake trout fishing. Lake trout (or lake char, as they are more accurately called) are a big fish that like to hang out in cold water. As a result, they are usually found down near the bottom of the lake, especially in summer. The lure of choice is a Flatfish sized T50, though every once in a while, you may see someone jigging for lake trout using a big spoon, but that is highly uncommon. Trolling is either done using a downrigger or on a long line. The darker colour Flatfish seem to be the most consistent producers, especially the black with silver flecks, though anything with a bit of green or yellow on the underbelly seems to work, too.

The fishing here is quite consistent throughout the season for lake trout and rainbow trout, the other main sportfish in the lake.

Rainbow trout are generally taken by trolling, though we have heard reports of people fly-fishing off the beach. However, we have not actually heard reports of anyone actually catching anything by doing so. Better to get out onto the lake and fish around the obvious drop offs and incoming streams. The usual trolling gear for rainbow trout works here, specifically a Wedding Band, sometimes dressed with a worm. Other typical trolling gear (Ford Fender, Willow Leaf) are often pressed into services, while small Flatfish patterns are often used trolling, too.

Like most of the lakes in the area, a terrestrial pattern is becoming the hot ticket item. More specifically, the food of choice for the rainbow are some of those tasty pine beetles.

Directions

Augier is located approximately 40 km north of the town of Burns Lake, between Pinkut and Babine lakes. To get to the lake, simply head through Burns Lake to the west end of town on the Yellowhead Highway. Here you will find the Babine Lake Road. Turn north off the highway and follow the road past Pinkut Lake. At 28.4 km, turn east (right) off the road to Babine Lake onto a well marked, good gravel road leading to the recreation site at the north end of Augier.

Facilities

At the north end of the lake is the **Augier Lake Recreation Site.** This eight unit campsite features a popular beach as well as a paved boat launch. The site is quite popular and is often full on late spring and summer weekends.

Location: 170 km (105 mi) south of Whitehorse
Surface Area: 58,900 ha (145,545 ac)
Elevation: 668 m (2,191 ft)
Way Point: 59° 23' 53" N, 133° 36' 37" W

Atlin Lake (Upper)

Fishing

Atlin Lake is about as remote a lake as you can get to by vehicle in BC. To get there, you actually have to leave British Columbia, and drive into the Yukon and then back into the province. It is over 1,200 km (745 miles) from Terrace and over 1,400 km (869 miles) from Dawson Creek. The nearest major city is Whitehorse in the Yukon, which is only 170 km (105 miles) from the town of Atlin. This gives you a sense of just how far north the lake really is.

It is not a lake that you would go to for an evening of fishing, unless, of course, you live in Atlin. If you are planning on going to Atlin Lake, expect to invest some serious time.

Those who do make the effort will not be disappointed. The lake is a spectacular destination. On a perfect summer's evening, the lake is mirror smooth, with snowy mountains (some standing more than 2,000 metres/6,560 feet) plunging straight into west side of the lake. At the south end of the lake is Atlin Provincial Park and Recreation where the spectacular Llewellyn Glacier creeps down towards the lake.

While most anglers don't fish simply to catch fish, scenic values alone aren't enough to get people to travel at least 1,000 km (and more likely at least twice that) just to fish a lake. Fortunately, Atlin Lake is much more than one of the prettiest lakes in the province. It is also one of the best lake trout fisheries in the province and possibly the country.

Atlin Lake is BC's largest natural lake. In fact, it is so big that it spills over into the Yukon. The lake holds lots of lake trout to about 2 kg (4 lbs). More importantly, the lake has produced trophy fish to 20 kg (40 lbs). It is not only a spectacular place to fish, but is also offers some spectacular fishing. And because it is so remote, it is a rare weekend indeed when there are more than, say, half a dozen boats out on the lake. Take a second to think about that: biggest lake in BC, and half a dozen groups fishing it. How much more perfect can you ask for?

In the summer (or extended spring, as locals call it) the lake rarely gets very warm, usually staying below 12°C (55°F). This makes the lake perfect habitat for the cold loving lake trout.

In many lakes, the trout will come into the shallower waters to feed in winter and spring, but that isn't the case with Atlin. Instead, the fish rarely come above 20 metres (60 feet), though don't blame them; they're just following their food source, which is primarily lake cisco.

There are two ways to fish for lake trout: trolling and jigging. Of the two, trolling is by far the most common. Because most people who fish the lake are fishing with a guide, the most common way of trolling is using a downrigger, although a leadcore line troll is sometimes used.

The downrigger is used to get the lures down to where the lake trout hold, which, as mentioned is usually down around 20 metres (60 feet), though can get as deep as 35 metres (110 feet) or so. However, they aren't usually found swimming in the middle of the lake. Rather, look for lakers around structure like drop offs, underwater rock piles and the like. Your lure should be down just off the bottom of the lake, where the lake trout are.

The lake trout seem to fish best in the early morning, before, say, 9:00, and seem to take to lures best on calm, clear days, as well as later in the evening. Because the lake is so far north, the summer days last forever and it is not unusual to be out fishing until 11:00 pm or midnight even.

The cool waters are also great for the lake's Arctic grayling, which are commonly found around the lake's many feeder creeks. They can be caught on Panther Martins, Mepps and a variety of surface and subsurface flies. People have reported catching grayling here on a Royal Coachman or a Black Gnat before the fly even hits the water. Try working around Telegraph, Indian, Glacier, Base Camp or Hitchcock Creeks. Arctic Grayling are small but scrappy, and can be a lot of fun to fish.

The lake also holds whitefish. While these boney fish are not the most popular catch in the lake, they, too can be fun to fish for. They can usually be caught by fishing in a similar manner as for grayling.

Having some form of boat will help on the lake. Even a float tube or canoe will help anglers get along the shoreline to points and creeks mostly inaccessible from the road. Of course, on such a big lake wind is something to worry about and light or small watercraft should be used with caution. Even a canoe is something that shouldn't be taken too far from shelter. It is a lake where bigger boats are advisable, especially since the best lake trout fishing happens near the western shore.

Since most people aren't willing to haul their boat all the way to Atlin, most people hire a guide. Guides are definitely recommended on such a big lake as they often know the best place to find the sometimes hard-to-catch lake trout.

While it is possible to ice fish on the lake, most people avoid it. Not because of the fishing, which can be great, but most do not bother heading out in the winter when the thermometer reaches a balmy -40°C or colder.

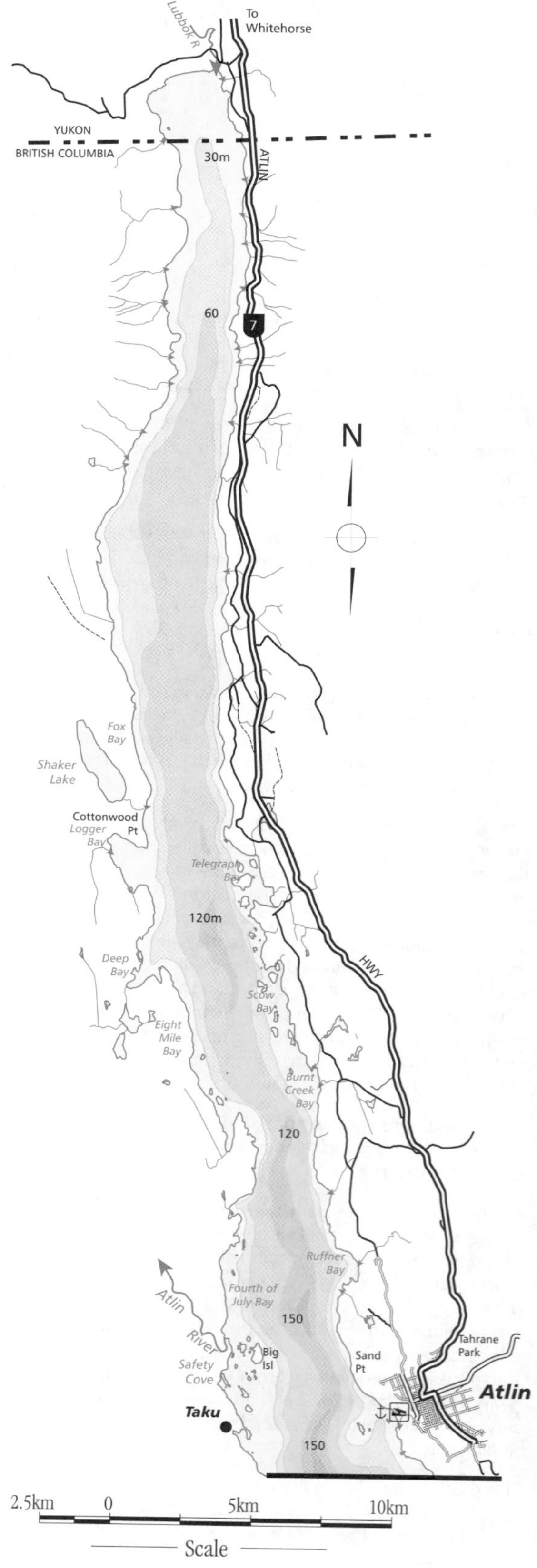

Atlin Lake (Lower)

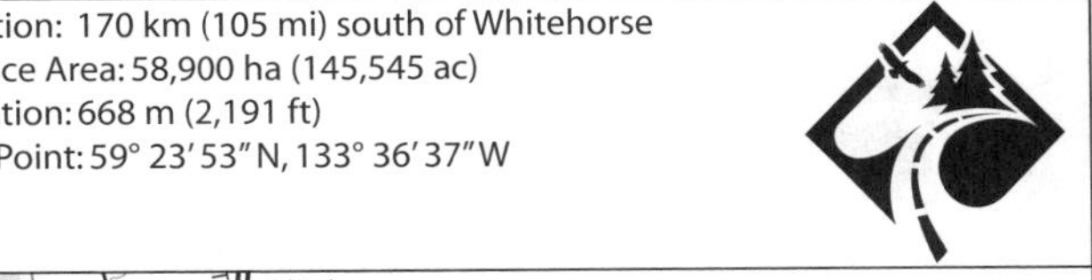

Location: 170 km (105 mi) south of Whitehorse
Surface Area: 58,900 ha (145,545 ac)
Elevation: 668 m (2,191 ft)
Way Point: 59° 23′ 53″ N, 133° 36′ 37″ W

Directions

To get to Atlin, take the Alaska Highway from Dawson Creek 1,323 km (822 miles) north to the Atlin Highway (Highway 7). Turn south and continue along for another 93 km (57 miles) to the townsite. There are two boat launches in town. Many people fly in to Whitehorse in the Yukon and drive south from there.

Facilities

There are recreation sites and random campsites up and down the lake. Some of the main sites are The **Grotto, Palmer Lake** and **Warm Bay Recreation Sites.** These sites are rarely full, mostly because there are so many great B&Bs, cottages, cabins and hotels to stay at. A few options include: **Moore's House Bed and Breakfast, Brewery Bay Chalet, Glacier Views Cabin** (12 km south of town), **Indian Creek Lodge** (30 km north of Atlin), **Minto View Cabins** (34 km north of town), **Sweet Ezzz Bed and Breakfast,** the **Nolan House** and **Quilt and Comforts Bed and Breakfast**. For folks who have gone through the trouble of hauling a boat all the way to the lake, there are a pair of boat launches in town as well as a launch and hot springs at Warm Bay.

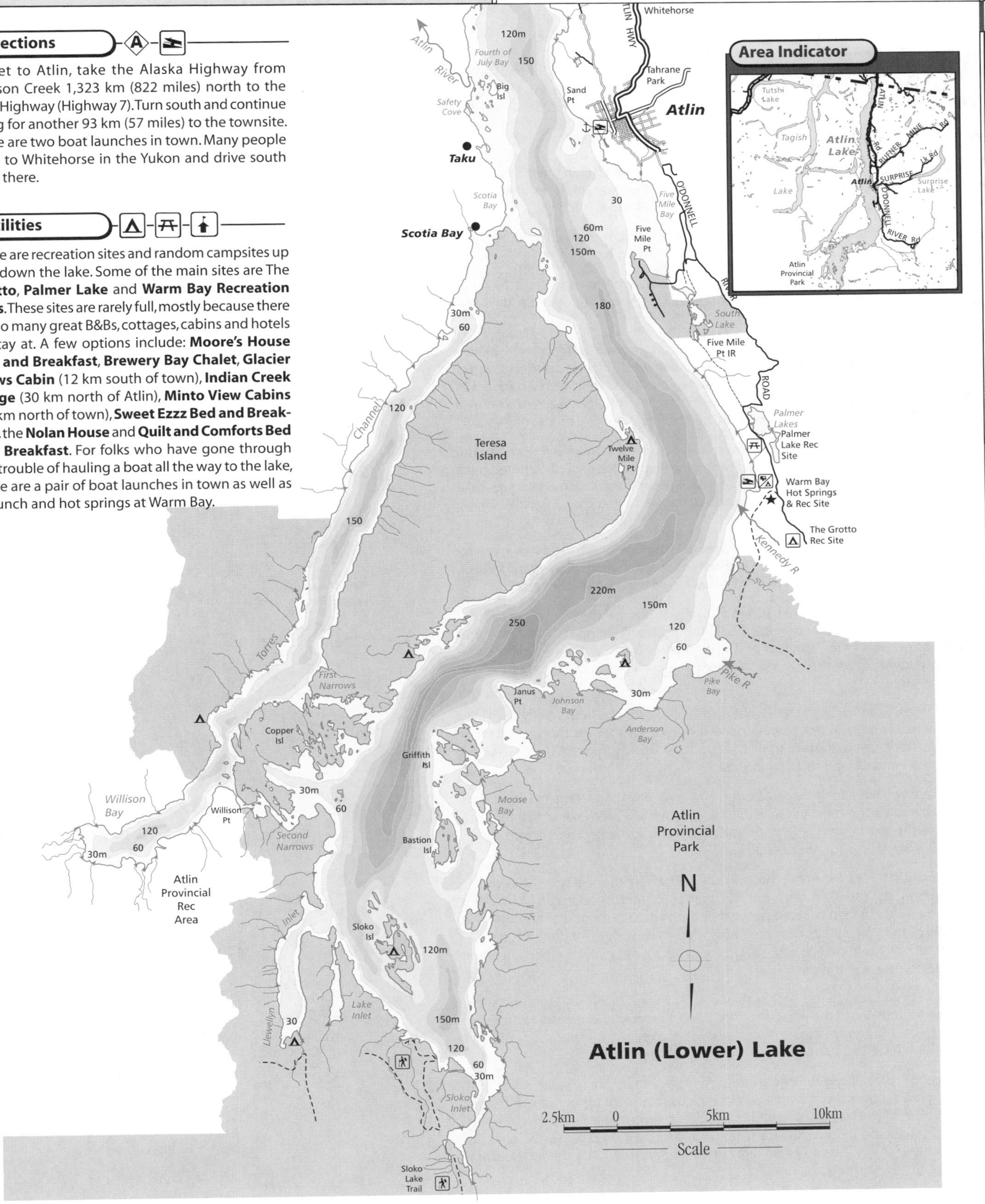

Area Indicator

Atlin (Lower) Lake

2.5km 0 5km 10km
Scale

Location: 40 km (25 mi) north of Burns Lake
Surface Area: 47,900 ha (118,363 ac)
Elevation: 711 m (2,333 ft)
Way Point: 54° 44′ 59″ N, 125° 59′ 59″ W

Babine Lake (Upper)

Fishing

Babine Lake is one of the biggest lakes in British Columbia. While it is not the largest by volume or surface area, it is the longest, stretching 177 kilometres (110 miles) from one end to the other, a fact that locals are proud to point out. (Some will also try and tell you it's the biggest; it's not. Atlin Lake, on the boundary between BC and the Yukon is.)

Locals will also tell you that the lake produces the largest fish in the province, too, with rainbow to 5.5 kg (12 lbs). Again, no, that honour probably goes to Kootenay Lake, with their Gerrard Strain rainbow that get up to 10 kg (22 lbs).

While it might not qualify as the biggest, it is pretty big. And while it may not have the biggest fish in the province, they're still pretty darn big.

The trouble with most big lakes is that they are difficult to fish successfully. Yes, there's lots of fish, but there is also a lot of space for them to hang out and finding the fish can take a long, long time.

That is not the case with Babine, at least, not at certain times. Every year the Babine system is home to a huge return of sockeye salmon, which creates a perfect storm of fishing. In the spring–from about April to early June–sockeye smolts start to gather in large schools around the mouths of creeks that flow into the lake. Rainbow trout also gather around the mouths of these creeks, freely feeding on the tiny fish.

As the trout begin their journey towards the ocean, the rainbows follow into the river. Although we've written about the Babine River too, it should be noted once again that the stretch of water between Babine Lake and nearby Nilkitkwa Lake offers such good rainbow trout fishing that it has earned the nickname "Rainbow Alley".

While this stretch of river is famous, the fishing in the lake just above the river can be pretty spectacular, too. Gear anglers can work a variety of small spinners and spoons, while fly anglers should stick to streamer patterns that imitate the smolts.

However, the fishing here isn't all imitating the sockeye. From late spring to early fall, the lake has some spectacular dry fly-fishing, thanks in no small part to huge hatches of caddis flies, mayflies and two varieties of stoneflies including some large Goldens. When the fish start to rise for these insects, the dry fly-fishing is unbelievable.

Of course, that's just fishing for rainbow trout. The lake also holds cutthroat, Dolly Varden, kokanee, lake trout, whitefish and burbot. Of that lot, the second most popular fish here are the lake trout. Lake trout are usually found in the deep water in summer and can get to 16 kg (35 lbs).

There are two ways to fish for lake trout: trolling and jigging. Of the two, trolling is by far the most common. Because most people who fish the lake are fishing with a guide, the most common way of trolling is using a downrigger, though a long leadcore line troll is sometimes used as well.

The downrigger is used to get the lures down to where the lake trout hold, which, as mentioned is usually down around 20 metres (60 feet), though can get as deep as 35 metres (110 feet) or so. However, they aren't usually found swimming in the middle of the lake. Rather, they are found around structure like drop offs, underwater rock piles and the like. Your lure should be down just off the bottom of the lake, where the lake trout are.

The lake trout seem to fish best in the early morning, before, say, 9:00, and seem to take to lures best on calm, clear days, as well as later in the evening. Because the lake is so far north, the summer days last forever and it is not unusual to be out fishing until 10:00 pm.

Few people actually jig for lake trout in the lake, but it can be quite successful. Jigging is a simple pursuit where you lower a usually baited spoon down to near the bottom of the lake (usually within a couple metres/a few feet), then raise the rod up and let the spoon settle. It will flutter and flip as it does, usually causing the lake trout to strike. This can prove difficult for anglers to actually detect the strike, as the fish bite as the lure is settling.

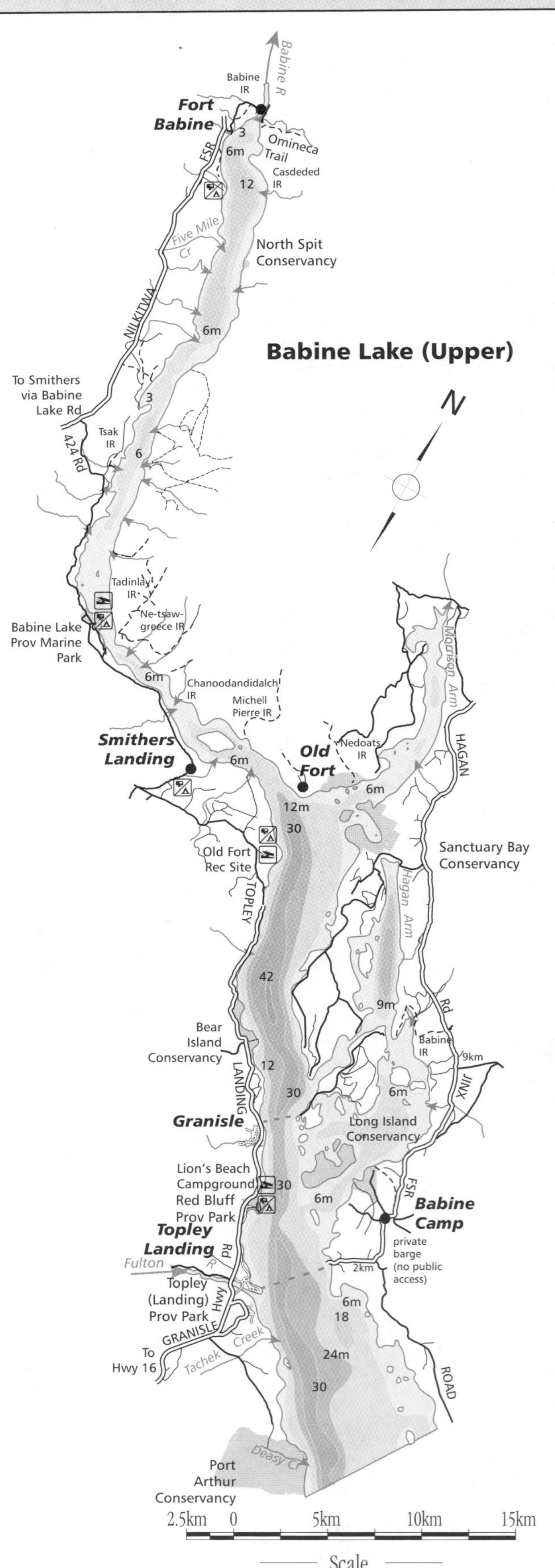

Babine Lake (Lower)

Location: 40 km (25 mi) north of Burns Lake
Surface Area: 47,900 ha (118,363 ac)
Elevation: 711 m (2,333 ft)
Way Point: 54° 44′ 59″ N, 125° 59′ 59″ W

Directions

Babine Lake is located northeast of Smithers and 40 kilometres north of Burns Lake. While there are a variety of backroads that will take you to the lake, the easiest way to get there is along the Granisle/Central Babine Lake Highway. Head west along the Yellowhead Highway from Burns Lake for 50 km to the Granisle Highway (Highway 118) turnoff. Turn right (north) onto the road and follow it north to the lake where a couple provincial parks and a Lion's Campground can be found.

Alternate access points include the Babine Lake Road that starts near the town of Burns Lake and the Babine Lake/Smithers Landing Road that starts south of Smithers. Getting to Rainbow Alley requires following the Babine Lake Road south of Smithers and turning north on the Nilkitwa Forest Service Road at the 53 km mark. It is another 44 km or so to Fort Babine and the start of the popular 'Fishing Alley'. The Northern BC Backroad Mapbook highlights these and many other access points to the big lake.

Facilities

Being such a big lake, there is no shortage of facilities in and around the area. On top of several resorts, there are private campgrounds as well as informal campgrounds. Visitors will also find five provincial parks located on the lake.

Babine Lake Marine (Pendleton Bay) Provincial Park is the most popular. There are twenty sites here, as well as a boat launch. Heading north from here, the next site is **Topley Landing Provincial Park**, which is a day-use park with a large beach. Nearby **Red Bluff Provincial Park** has 27 campsites and a rustic boat launch. On the northern arm, the **Babine Lake Marine (Smithers Landing) Provincial Park** is home to eight rustic campsites and a rough gravel launch. Finally, **Rainbow Alley Provincial Park** is found at the north end of the lake; while this park protects the stretch of river between Babine and Nilkitkwa Lakes, it is a popular place for anglers in the area.

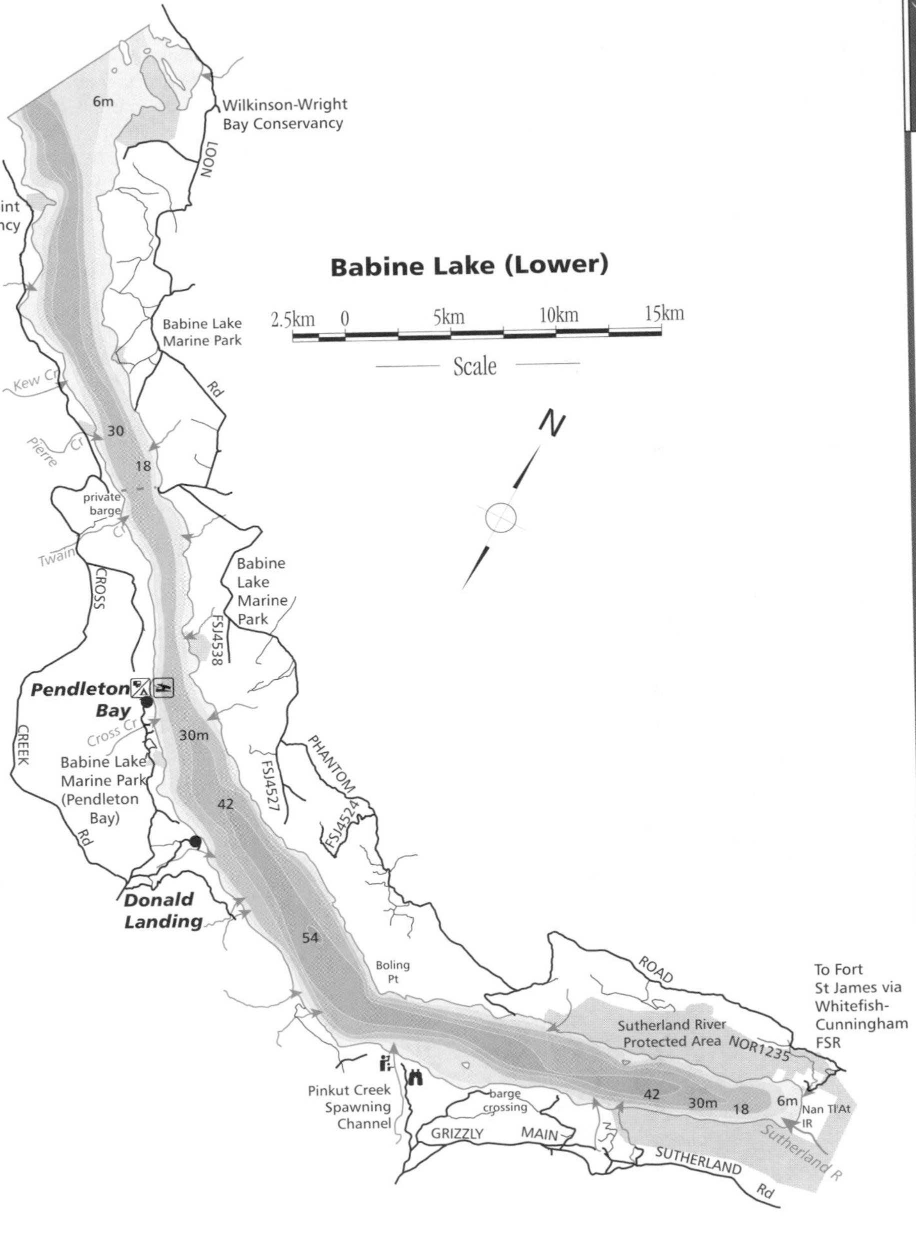

Area Indicator

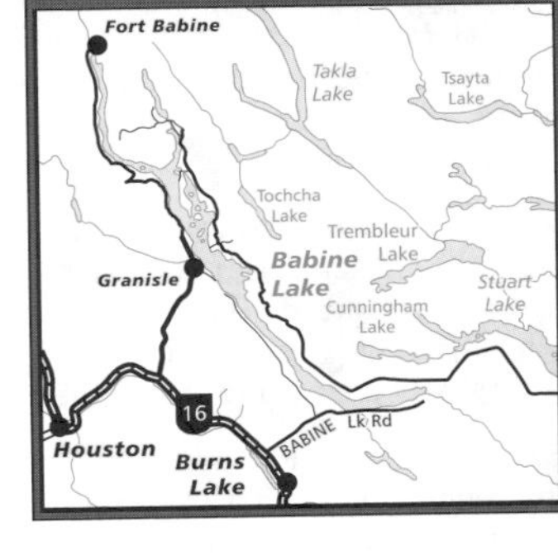

Babine Lake (Lower)

2.5km 0 5km 10km 15km
Scale

Location: 75 km (46.5 mi) northeast of Smithers
Stream Length: 101 km (63 mi)
Geographic: 55° 40′ 59″ N, 127° 41′ 59″ W

Babine River

Fishing

The Babine River is one of the province's epic fishing destinations: great fishing, great scenery and an almost untouched river valley. The river boasts one of the strongest returns of steelhead including some of the biggest steelhead you will ever have the good fortune of landing. Anglers will also find the province's largest run of sockeye salmon and some truly amazing rainbow trout fishing.

It is a tough call to say which fishery is the most popular, but if you are able to land one of this river's 15 kg (30 lb) steelhead, you will probably join the legions of people who say that this is truly the greatest steelhead river in the world. But first you have to catch one. These are steelhead, after all and known not just for their leaping, acrobatic runs, but for their unwillingness to take lures. They run from September to mid-October.

On top of big runs of sockeye, which are open to fishing in August, there are also Chinook from mid-June to the end of December and Coho from late July to the end of September. However, it is the results of the spawned out salmon that attract more of the angler's attention. Rotting fish feed the plants and insects, which in turn feed the river's native rainbow trout. Also when the salmon fry begin their downstream migration, trout go crazy feeding on them. A streamer pattern that imitates a smolt will be extremely productive in the early part of June.

The rainbow are also quite willing to rise to dry flies. One of the most prolific hatches on the river is the stonefly hatch in mid-to-late June. When the hatch is on, the trout aren't particular about your presentation and will take to most any stonefly imitations. Popular choices include an Elk Hair Caddis or a local fly called the Babine Special. The best place to fish is between Babine Lake and Nilkitkwa Lake, the so-called Rainbow Alley. A dry line is necessary for the stonefly hatch, but when the fish aren't rising, a sink-tip is needed for stonefly nymphs and streamers.

While the fishing here is truly spectacular, all is not well; too many people pulling out their limits mean that there are fewer big fish here. While the river is not catch and release, each fish kept means fewer fish reproducing, meaning fewer fish. Help care for the river and release most, if not all, the fish you catch.

Directions

The Babine is a wilderness river and is not easy to get onto. From Smithers, take Eckman/Smithers Landing Road, which becomes the Babine Lake Road. At km 53, watch for the Nilkitwa Forest Service Road heading north. Follow this road to the north end of Babine Lake, a distance of about 58 km.

Facilities

There are a few wilderness lodges on the river including the **Silver Hilton Lodge** and **Babine Norlakes Lodge**. Rainbow Alley is protected by **Rainbow Alley Provincial Park** (no camping), while much of the rest of the river is in the **Babine River Corridor Provincial Park**. Visitors will find 10 campsites in a rustic campground, 4 km west of the park entrance. Be wary of Grizzly bears!

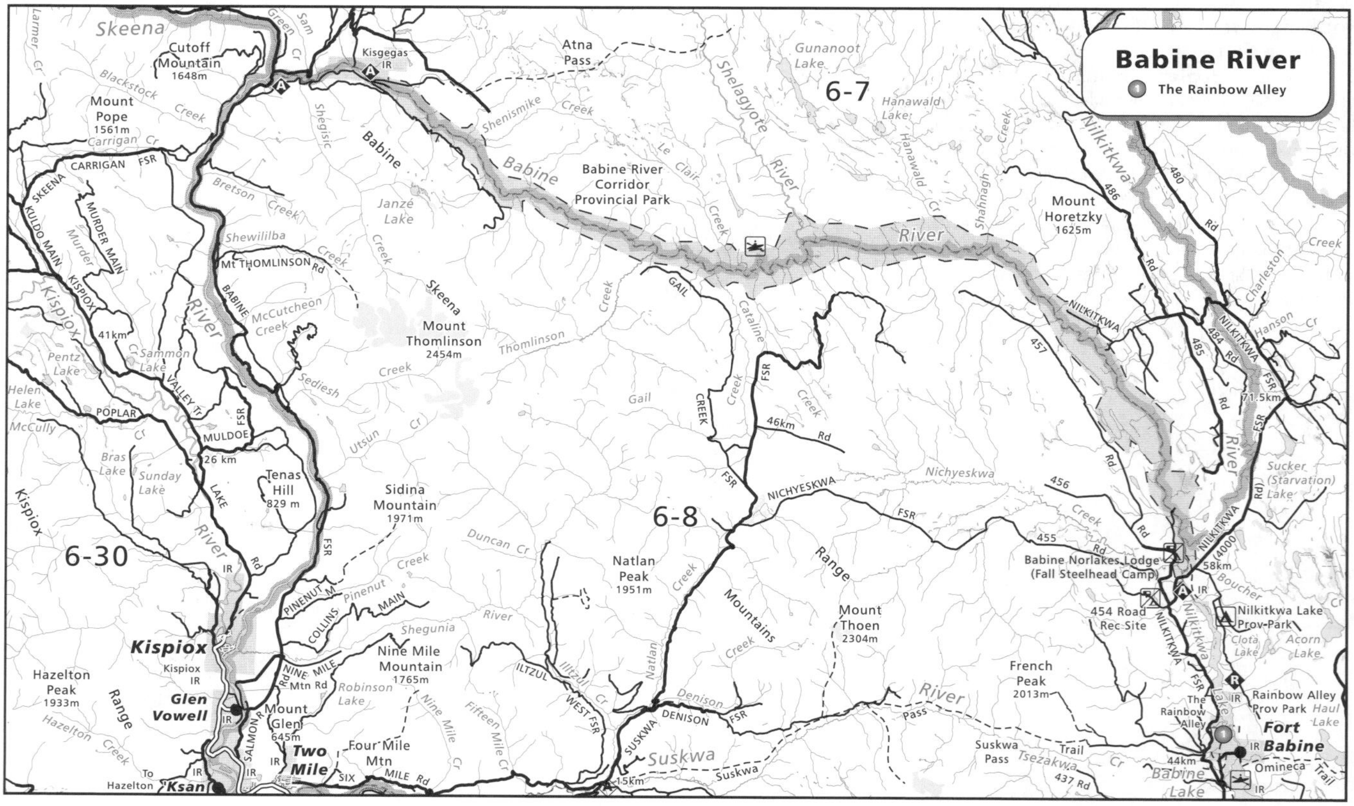

Bella Coola & Atnarko Rivers

Location: East of Bella Coola
Bella Coola River: Stream Length: 63 km (39 mi)
Way Point: 52° 22′ 59″ N, 126° 45′ 0″ W

Atnarko River: Stream Length: 69 km (43 mi)
Way Point: 52° 22′ 0″ N, 126° 6′ 0″ W

Fishing

There are very few rivers that flow from the east side of the Coast Mountains to the west. The Dean is one. The Atnarko and the Bella Coola, which the Atnarko turns into, is another. The river system offers some spectacular fishing for salmon, cutthroat and Dolly Varden.

The Bella Coola drains into the North Benetick Arm, through the towering Coast Mountains. While most mid-coast rivers are fly-in or boat-in only, the Bella Coola is road accessible for most of its length.

This is a river storied in history. Alexander Mackenzie came this way in 1793 and though a trip to fish this river is no longer the epic journey it once was, it is still not something undertaken lightly. The nearest major settlement, Williams Lake, is nearly 400 km (250 miles) away.

The weather here, like most of the coast, is wet and rainy. If the river is blown out, there aren't really any other options for fishing in the area.

The river holds runs of all species of salmon, as well as steelhead and sea-run cutthroat trout. The river also holds Dolly Varden and rainbow trout.

While spring isn't noted as a great time to fish for salmon, it is a great time for cutthroat and dollies, which feed on the emerging fry. Fishing a pattern that imitates a fry can land you some surprisingly large fish.

Spring Chinook return from May to July, pink run every second year in July and August, sockeye return in July and August and Coho return in September and October. There are also runs of chum from mid-July to mid-August, a late summer run and a small run in November. The biggest returns are pink and chum.

While there are several great places to access the river system, a popular way to fish the river is by boat. The river can be drifted using a raft, pontoon boat or similar craft, usually starting above Tweedsmuir Lodge on the Atnarko and down to Thorsen Creek. Note that the last few kilometers of the river are on the Bella Coola Indian Reserve and the First Nation here does not allow access to (or from) the river through their land. There are, however, private campgrounds in this area that allow for good bar fishing.

The steelheads return from March through May, but the river is closed to steelhead fishing to protect the stocks.

Directions

Highway 20 parallels the Atnarko and Bella Coola rivers for a distance of about 70 km. There are a number of access points to the rivers through Tweedsmuir Provincial Park and into the Bella Coola Valley, of which the most famous and easiest accessed is the Fisheries Pool in Tweedsmuir Park. Simply follow the signs to the Fisheries Pool Campground.

Facilities

The Atnarko River flows through **Tweedsmuir Provincial Park.** There are two campgrounds, one at McCall Flats, where you will find 28 sites and one at Fisheries Pool, where there are 14 campsites. Be wary of Grizzlies here!

There is also a lodge on the river in the park. Outside of the park, the Bella Coola River flows through a number of communities, the largest of which is Bella Coola where you will find lodging, camping and a variety of services.

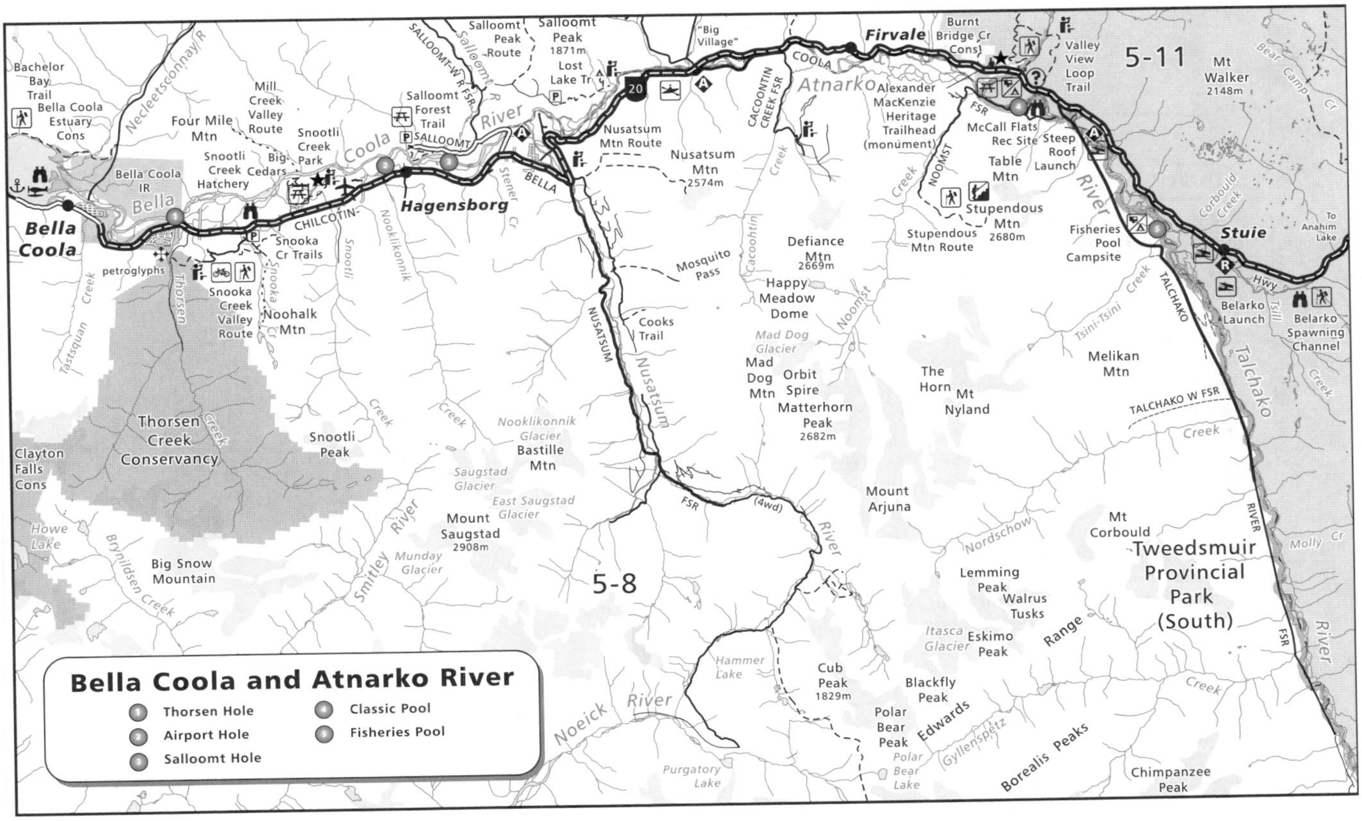

Bella Coola and Atnarko River

1 Thorsen Hole
2 Airport Hole
3 Salloomt Hole
4 Classic Pool
5 Fisheries Pool

Location: 30 km (18.6 mi) southeast of Quesnel

Benson & Robertson Lakes

Benson Lake

Elevation: 964 m (3,162 ft)
Surface Area: 65 ha (160.6 ac)
Maximum Depth: 18 m (59 ft)
Mean Depth: 8.6 m (28 ft)
Way Point: 52° 54′20.4″N, 122° 4′39.2″W

Robertson Lake

Elevation: 969 m (3,179 ft)
Surface Area: 61 ha (150.7 ac)
Maximum Depth: 24 m (79 ft)
Mean Depth: 10 m (33 ft)
Way Point: 52° 53′46.2″N, 122° 3′32.1″W

Area Indicator

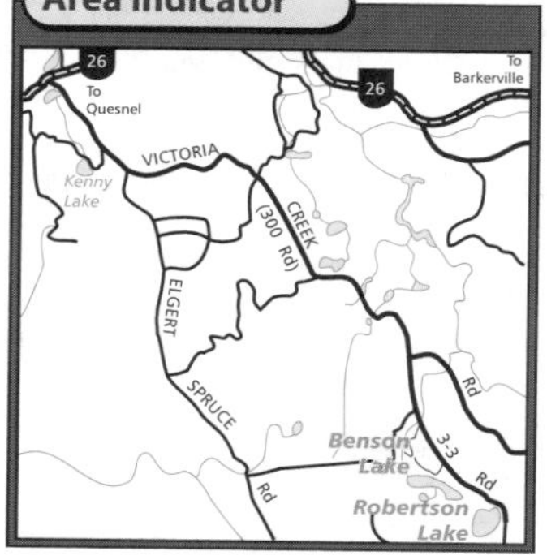

Fishing

Benson and Robertson are a pair of trout lakes found southeast of Quesnel. The ice is off by mid-May and the fishing starts to get good for rainbow trout, beginning in late May or early June.

Because neither lake is very large or deep and rest relatively low in elevation, both lakes suffer from the summer doldrums. Fishing is good in spring and fall, but in the summer, the rainbow start to become torpid and listless; even if you were to manage to snag one, chances are it wouldn't put up much of a fight.

Benson Lake has extensive shoal areas meaning that the insect rearing potential is very good. Unfortunately, the squawfish, suckers and redside shiners all compete for the available food in the lake. The lake is the shallowest near the west end of the lake. The water drops off quick enough from shore along most of the shoreline allowing for decent casting potential. Trolling is best near the east end of the lake. You should try trolling along the fringe area at that location with a small lake troll or spinner. Also try working around the mouth of the stream that flows into the lake from the south.

Robertson Lake also has an extensive shoal area, although not to the same extent as Benson. Still, the shoals provide lots of insects and the fly anglers flock to these lakes. The most common hatches are chironomids, which rise slowly through the water column after hatching. Working a slow hand twist retrieve near the bottom can be deadly.

Similar to Benson, Robertson does offer shore casting possibilities. Of course, hauling in a canoe or pontoon boat is a much better way to fish. Being on the water allows you to cast towards shore and retrieve past the drop-off.

Robertson Lake also holds burbot. Burbot love the cold water and are rarely caught in summer. However, in winter they can be quite easy to catch. While they are incredibly ugly fish, they are also quite tasty. They are best caught on a hook baited with some smelly meat, like chicken liver.

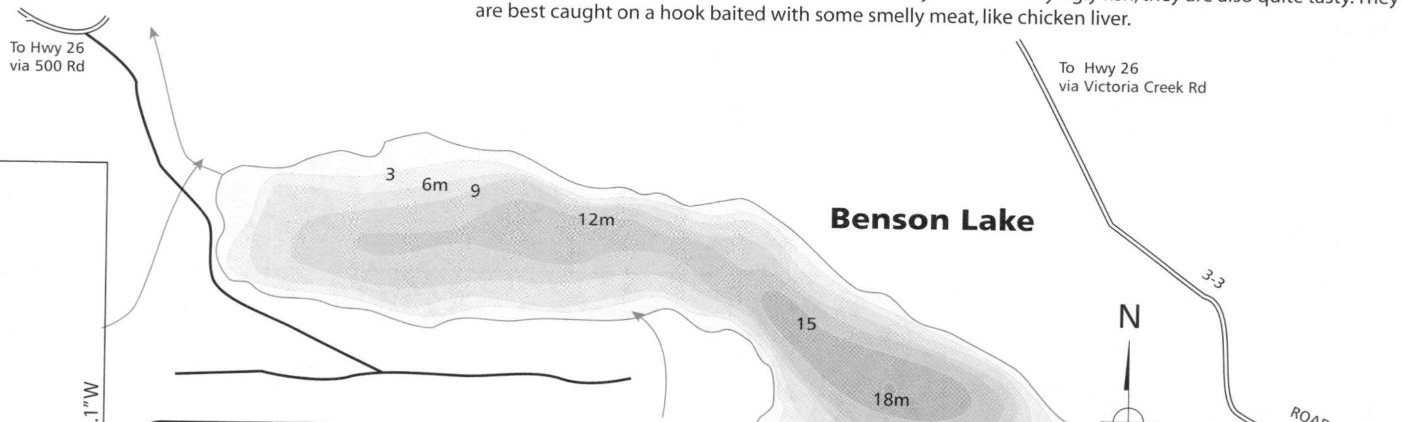

Directions

These two lakes are located southeast of Quesnel and are close to the Cottonwood Valley.

From Quesnel, travel east on the Barkerville Highway (Highway 26). At Fifteen and Sixteen Mile Lakes, before you reach the community of Cottonwood, the Victoria Creek Road (300 Road) leads southeast. Take that road and then at around the 4 km mark, hang a left continuing on the 300 Road. At around the 19 km mark, turn right on the 3-3 Road. Another right along the 3-3 Road after 4 km will lead to the Benson, while Robertson is found off a side road/trail on the 3-3 about 6 km after this last junction.

Due to the confusing nature of roads, a copy of the *Backroad Mapbook for the Cariboo Chilcotin Coast* and a GPS are highly recommended. A 4wd vehicle is also recommended since the roads can be rough in places.

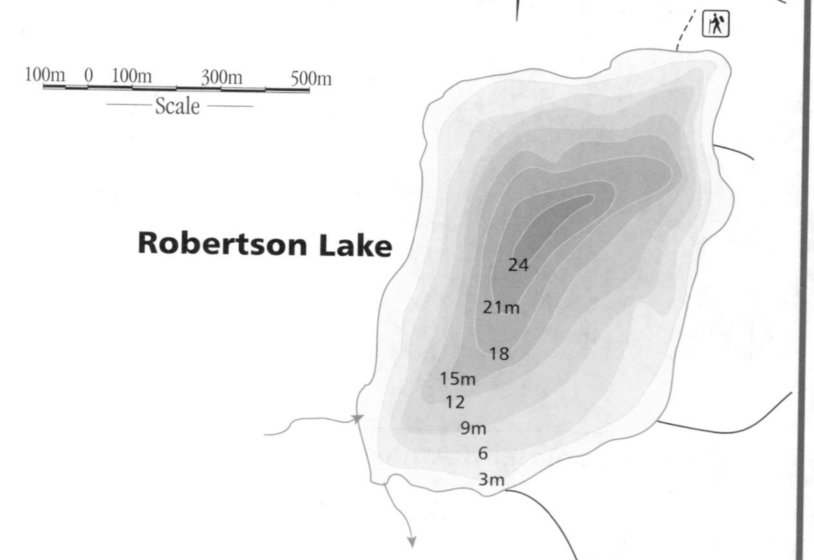

Facilities

Neither lake has any developed facilities. It is possible to hand launch a small boat at either lake and there are places where you can pull off the road and camp.

Big Bar Lake

Location: 25 km (15.5 mi) northwest of Clinton
Elevation: 1,082 m (3,550 ft)
Surface Area: 229 ha (565 ac)
Maximum Depth: 21 m (70 ft)
Mean Depth: 8.5 m (28 ft)
Way Point: 51° 18' 34" N, 121° 47' 41" W

Fishing

Big Bar Lake is found at the heart of Big Bar Lake Provincial Park. The lake is surrounded by a lodgepole pine and spruce forest, which provides a beautiful, semi-open setting for a great family holiday of fishing, biking and hiking. The clear, green water harbours gorgeous, chrome trout eager to take your offerings.

Spincasting, trolling or fly-fishing will yield hard-fighting Kamloops rainbow that average 1 kg (2 lbs), although fish to 2 kg (4.5 lbs) are not uncommon. In 2006, the lake was stocked with 14,000 Pennask All Female Triploid rainbow trout. These rainbow are not the fastest growing strain of rainbow trout, nor are they the largest. However, they are perhaps the hardest fighting of all the strains of rainbow and will frequently jump in an attempt to shake the hook. The Kamloops area is famous for its rainbow trout fishing lakes and most of them are stocked with this strain.

The best fishing is done in the spring and fall. The water warms during the summer and the cool water trout tend to hide in the depths of the lake. Even if you managed to hook one in the summer, they will often not put up the same fight.

The lake has some good hatches, starting with chironomids in early spring, followed by mayfly and caddisfly. Fly fishers do well fishing shoal areas with chironomid patterns, mayfly nymphs or sedge patterns. During the late summer and fall, when the hatches aren't happening, trolling a maroon leech can be quite productive. Another way to catch large trout in the fall is by fishing water boatman patterns on either a sinking or sink-tip line and using quick strip retrieves. A Tom Thumb or Mikaluk Sedge on the surface also works well.

Spincasters can use a variety of lures and trolling a small spinner or spoon can be effective. However, just as effective can be still fishing using a bobber and worm or Powerbait. The most popular lures include Wonder Spoons or Little Hildebrandt in nickel and gold, Willow Leaf lake trolls with a Wedding Band or worm, Mepps spinners and F-4 or F-5 Flatfish in black, green or silver.

While it is possible to cast from shore, it is much more productive to get out onto the water. Anglers should not the 10 kilometre speed restriction in place.

Area Indicator

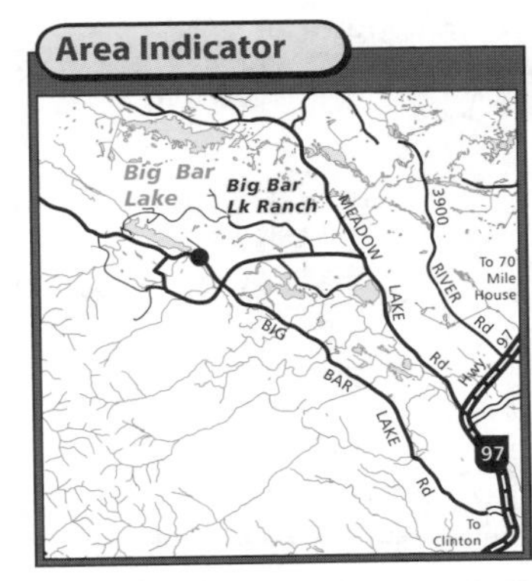

Big Bar Lake Fish Stocking Data			
Year	Species	Number	Life Stage
2008	Rainbow Trout	5,000	Yearling
2007	Rainbow Trout	14,000	Yearling
2006	Rainbow Trout	14,000	Yearling

Directions

From the town of Clinton, follow Highway 97 north for about 10 km and turn west at the top of the hill on the Big Bar Lake Road. If you hit the highway rest area you have gone too far. Continue down this good gravel road for another 32 km to the park entrance. If coming south on Highway 97, turn right on Big Bar Lake road approximately 58 km south of 100 Mile House.

Facilities

Opening on May 15, **Big Bar Provincial Park** provides 27 lakeshore campsites plus 20 sites in the upper campground. All facilities, including toilets and water, are provided along with a trailered boat launch and a developed beach with a roped off swimming area. A 4 km (2.4 mile) hiking trail loops around a wetland at the outlet of the lake, where wildlife can often be seen.

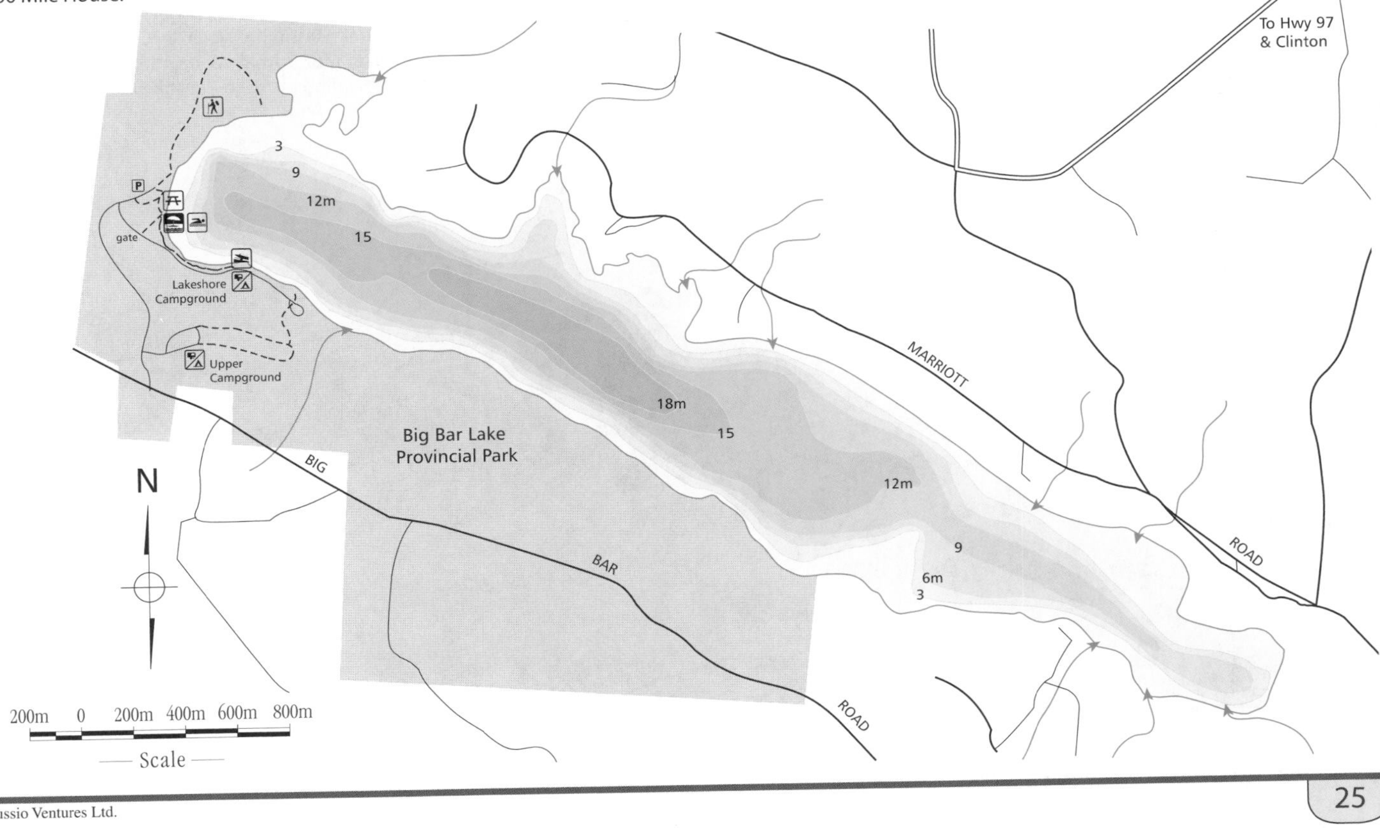

To Hwy 97 & Clinton

Big Bar Lake Provincial Park

Lakeshore Campground

Upper Campground

gate

Marriott Road

Big Bar Road

Scale: 200m 0 200m 400m 600m 800m

Location: 10 km (6 mi) west of 100 Mile House
Elevation: 1,030 m (3,379 ft)
Surface Area: 112 ha (275 ac)
Maximum Depth: 9.1 m (29 ft)
Mean Depth: 3.8 m (12 ft)
Way Point: 51° 39′ 56″N, 121° 26′ 49″W

Big Lake (100 Mile House Area)

Area Indicator

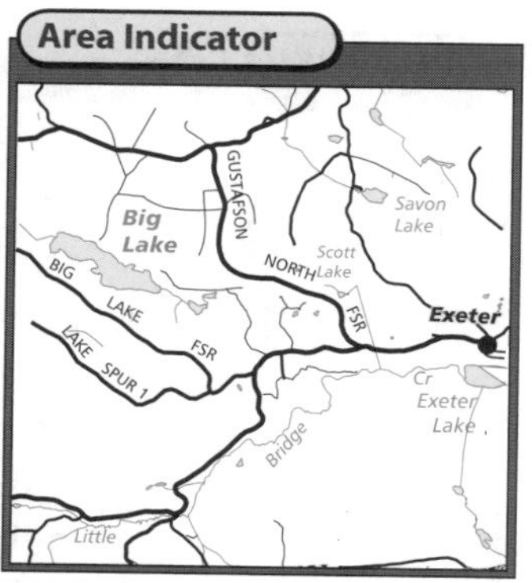

Big Lake (100 Mile House Area) Fish Stocking Data			
Year	Species	Number	Life Stage
2008	Rainbow Trout	5,000	Yearling
2007	Rainbow Trout	5,000	Yearling
2006	Rainbow Trout	5,000	Yearling

Fishing

There are three Big Lakes in the Cariboo district, two of which are written up in this book. This one is found west of 100 Mile House and despite its name, it is anything but big. Sure there are smaller lakes in the area, but with a surface area of just over 100 hectares, it is at best a mid-sized lake.

The lake is blessed with some great fishing and as a result of heavy pressure here in the past, has some strict regulations in place. Currently there is a two trout daily limit, a single barbless hook restriction and a winter closure, from November 1 to April 30.

The lake holds rainbow, brook and lake trout to 3 kg (6.5 lbs) as well as kokanee. Of these, only lake trout has not been stocked in the past, although rainbow trout are the only species currently being stocked in the lake by the Freshwater Fisheries Society of BC.

Fishing techniques for rainbow trout and for kokanee are remarkably similar. While young kokanee eat zooplankton, once they hit a certain size, they start feeding on chironomids, dragonfly and damselfly nymphs and even small leeches. If you go fishing for rainbow, you will find you will catch some kokanee and if you fish for kokanee, expect to catch some rainbow. There are some differences between the two, although. One of the biggest differences is that kokanee are much more sensitive to the temperature of water and prefer to spend their time in a narrow band of cooler water. Like rainbow, they do dart into shallower (or deeper) water to feed. Kokanee are also a schooling fish, while rainbow are much more random. If you find one kokanee, chances are you have found a bunch.

Kokanee are known for their soft mouths and whether trolling, spincasting or fly-fishing, it is advisable to attach some form of shock absorber, to prevent the hook from tearing through the soft flesh. Kokanee are strong, determined fighters and often do damage to themselves when trying to escape.

Brook trout are slightly more aggressive than rainbow trout and can be taken on a Deadly Dick tipped with a worm. Similar to rainbow, they also take to a Panther Martin, Mepps, or Krocodile spoon as well as a lake troll, Wedding Band or Apex Trout Killer tipped with worms or Powerbait.

Lake trout are slow growing fish and we advise releasing most of the fish you catch here. They are best caught on a deep troll using a large spoon or Flatfish.

Facilities

There are no facilities at Big Lake, although the road down to the lake is rarely travelled save by anglers and it is possible to just camp on the shores of the lake. Folks looking for more upscale accommodations should head back to 100 Mile House.

Directions

Big Lake is found about 10 km west of 100 Mile House. From the south, drive through 100 Mile House to the very last light on the north side of town, just past the mall. If you start heading up the hill, you've gone too far. This is Exter Road. Turn left (west) onto Exter and drive for about 5.5 km. Turn right (west again) onto the Big Lake Forest Service Road and watch for a small road, little more than a cart track, heading north to Big Lake after about 4 km.

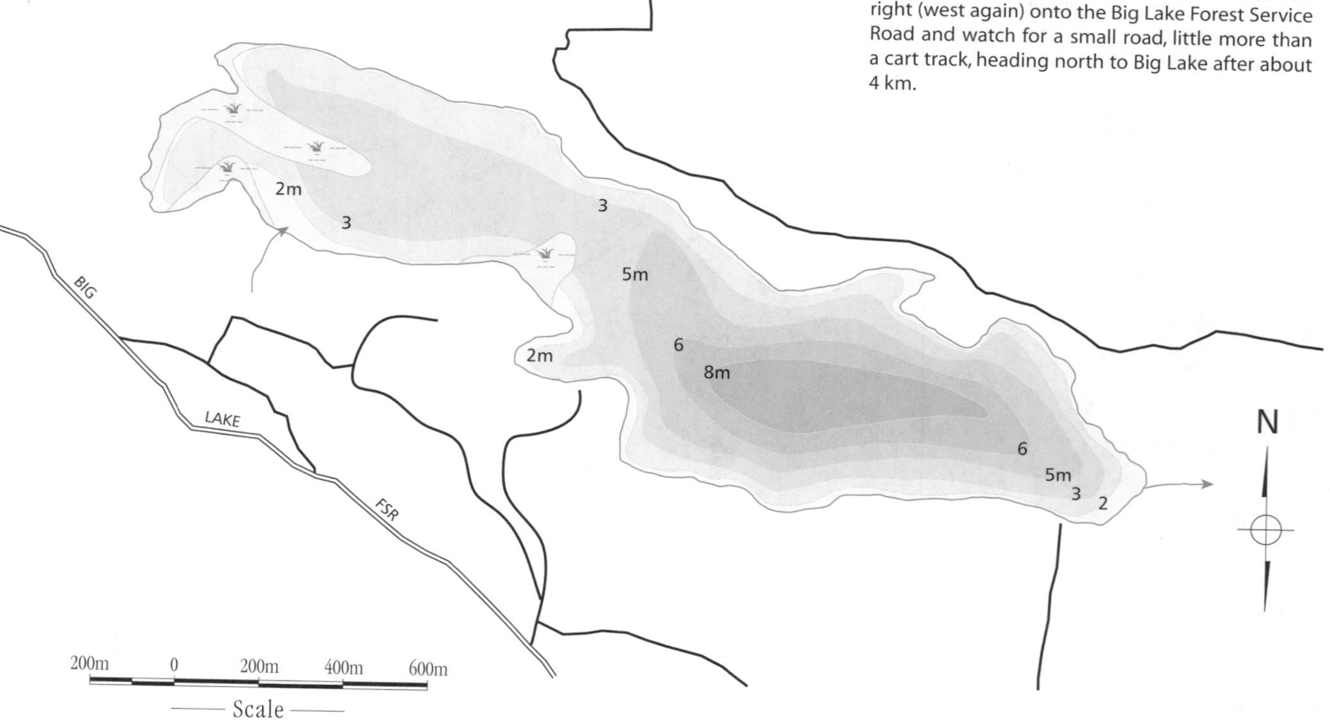

Big Lake (Williams Lake Area)

Location: 50 km (31 mi) east of Williams Lake
Elevation: 821 m (2,693 ft)
Surface Area: 578 ha (1,428 ac)
Maximum Depth: 41 m (45 ft)
Mean Depth: 13.4 m (44 ft)
Way Point: 52° 23' 4" N, 121° 50' 27" W

Fishing

Big Lake has almost all the fish species you can imagine. There are rainbow, steelhead, kokanee, brook trout, burbot and lake trout to choose from. The lake also has its fair share of course fish (squawfish, suckers, chub and redside shiners). The rainbow tend to be in the 0.5–1 kg (1–2 lb) class but there are reports of fish going as high as 5 kg (12 lbs). The kokanee are usually under a pound and the lake trout can grow to 14 kg (30 lbs).

The lake is best suited for trolling particularly in the late spring (late May to early June) and early fall (mid September to mid October). However, spincasters and fly anglers can also have good success. Big Lake has expansive shallows at the northeast end of the lake. There is also a pair of inviting sunken islands nearby, which is a good place to try some fly-fishing. The lake is easily trolled towards the southwest end of the lake, as the lake is over 180 m (400 ft) deep in that location. The water drops off rapidly enough from the shore that shore casting is possible.

Big Lake is set in a partially forested area. There are some cottages and other buildings on the south side of the lake, while the northern shores of the lake are cleared ranch and residential land. There are a couple places to access the lake from the north.

The lake has produced some lake trout to 15 kg (30 lbs), although these slow growing fish should be released once you've taken a photo. Lake trout are best fished with a big spoon or big Flatfish. While the use of single barbless isn't required on the lake, it is always a good idea to use them when you're planning on releasing the fish, as it causes much less harm to the fish.

Lake trout are usually found in the deeper sections of the lake, places where the water is more than 15 m (60 feet) deep. To get down that deep, you will need to let out a lot of line, use a downrigger, or try jigging for the lakers. The first two options are the most popular.

Directions

Big Lake is a popular recreation lake to the east of Williams Lake. Visitors not only fish the lake but also use it for swimming and water sports. From Williams Lake, head south on the Cariboo Highway (Highway 97) to 150 Mile House and follow the paved Likely Road heading north for about 35 km. The first larger lake on the Likely Road is Big Lake. If you reach the community of Big Lake Ranch you have gone too far.

Facilities

There is a campground with a boat launch at the north side of the lake. There is also a boat launch on the south side of the lake. There are no resorts on the lake but a gas station and general store are found on the Likely Road at Big Lake Ranch.

Other Options

Marguerite Lake is located nearby to Big Lake on a rough 2wd road called the Marguerite Lake Road. The lake contains rainbow that grow to 1 kg (2 lbs) and are taken on a fly, by trolling or by spincasting. The lake is best fished in the early spring or later in the fall as the summer doldrums occur at this lake. The lake offers rustic camping and a cartop boat launch.

Area Indicator

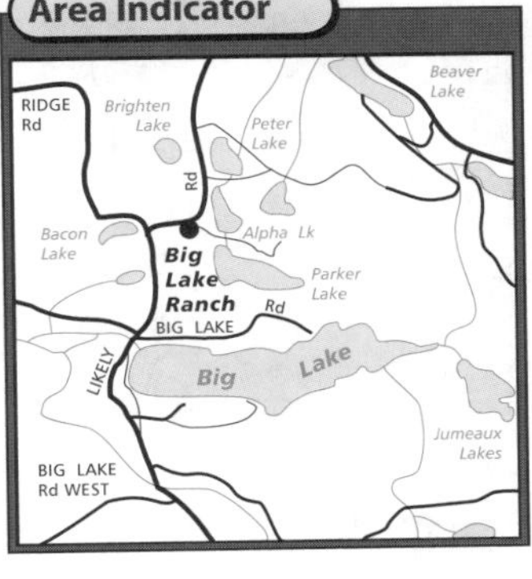

Big Lake (Williams Lake Area)
Fish Stocking Data

Year	Species	Number	Life Stage
2008	Kokanee	60,000	Fry
2005	Kokanee	60,000	Fingerling
2004	Kokanee	60,701	Fingerling

Location: 250 km (155 mi) east of Williams Lake
Elevation: 1,019 m (3,343 ft)
Surface Area: 141 ha (347 ac)
Maximum Depth: 15 m (49 ft)
Mean Depth: 8.5 m (28 ft)
Way Point: 52° 0' 36.2" N, 125° 5' 49.5" W

Big Stick Lake

Area Indicator

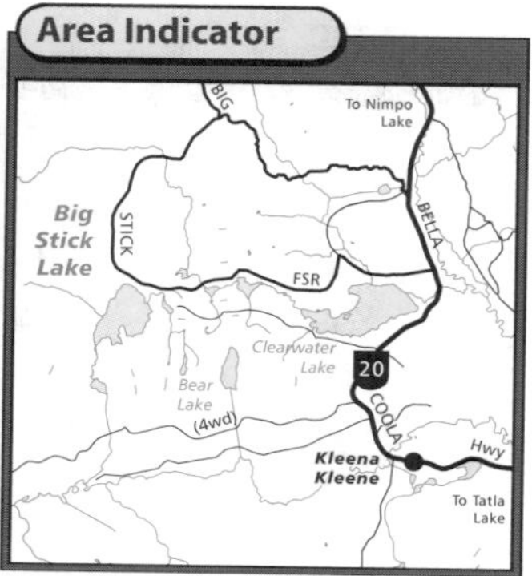

Directions

To get to the lake, take Highway 20 from Williams Lake to Kleena Kleene, a distance of 242 km (150 miles). Beyond Kleena Kleene, the road loops around so it is travelling north, past Clearwater Lake. The next five roads past the lake will bring you, with varying degrees of difficulty, to Big Stick Lake. The best turnoff is the first, about 16 km past Kleena Kleene. This road goes past the north end of Clearwater and then starts to loop north. Watch for the Big Stick Forest Service Road leaving this road to your left. The road into the recreation site is rough and difficult to navigate.

Facilities

The **Big Stick Lake Recreation Site** rests at the north end of the lake offering space for three groups and a sandy beach. There is no boat launch, but it is possible to get a cartopper out onto the lake. Trailers and big vehicles should not be brought to the lake, as there is no place to turn around.

Fishing

Big Stick Lake sits in a pretty bowl near the base of Mount Nogwon. The lake is found at the very edge of the Chilcotin Plateau, between the low rolling hills of the plateau and the start of the Coast Mountains. It is considered one of the richest places in the Chilcotin for wildlife. There are moose, deer, birds and bear.

Ah yes. Bear. There are both grizzly and black bear here and the area is thick with them. There have been a number of anglers chased off the lake by possessive grizzlies. In fact, one angler was out in his float tube on the lake, when he heard a splash and looked up to see a grizzly bear, entering the water. He kicked out of the bear's path, but was shocked when the bear changed direction to follow the angler. Every time he changed path, the bear adjusted to follow suit. Needless to say, our intrepid angler kicked hard for the shore and made it into his truck just as the bear made land.

These are exceptional stories, true and there have been no reports of anyone ever being injured by a bear here. Still, it is something to keep in mind when fishing the lake. Having pepper spray along, even when out on the water, might be a good idea.

For just over a decade in the 1980s and early 1990s, Big Stick Lake was stocked with Blackwater rainbow to the tune of 5,000 every couple of years. The stocking has stopped, but the fast growing trout remain and catches over 2 kg (4.5 lbs) are not out of the question.

The small, compact lake is shallow near the recreation site and deepest on the far (southwest) side of the lake. Most people who fish here troll in a tube or pontoon boat or small cartopper. Fly anglers can troll Doc Spratleys, Carey Specials or any other favourite searching pattern, while gearheads can work a variety of small spoons, spinners or a Flatfish.

Towards the south end of the lake is an underwater island, located between two of the deepest holes in the lake. This is a prime holding area for fish. As well, there is a creek that comes into the lake on the west side, which can also be productive.

The lake is tough to fish from shore, but if you're willing to wade a bit from the beach at the recreation site, it is possible to fish from here.

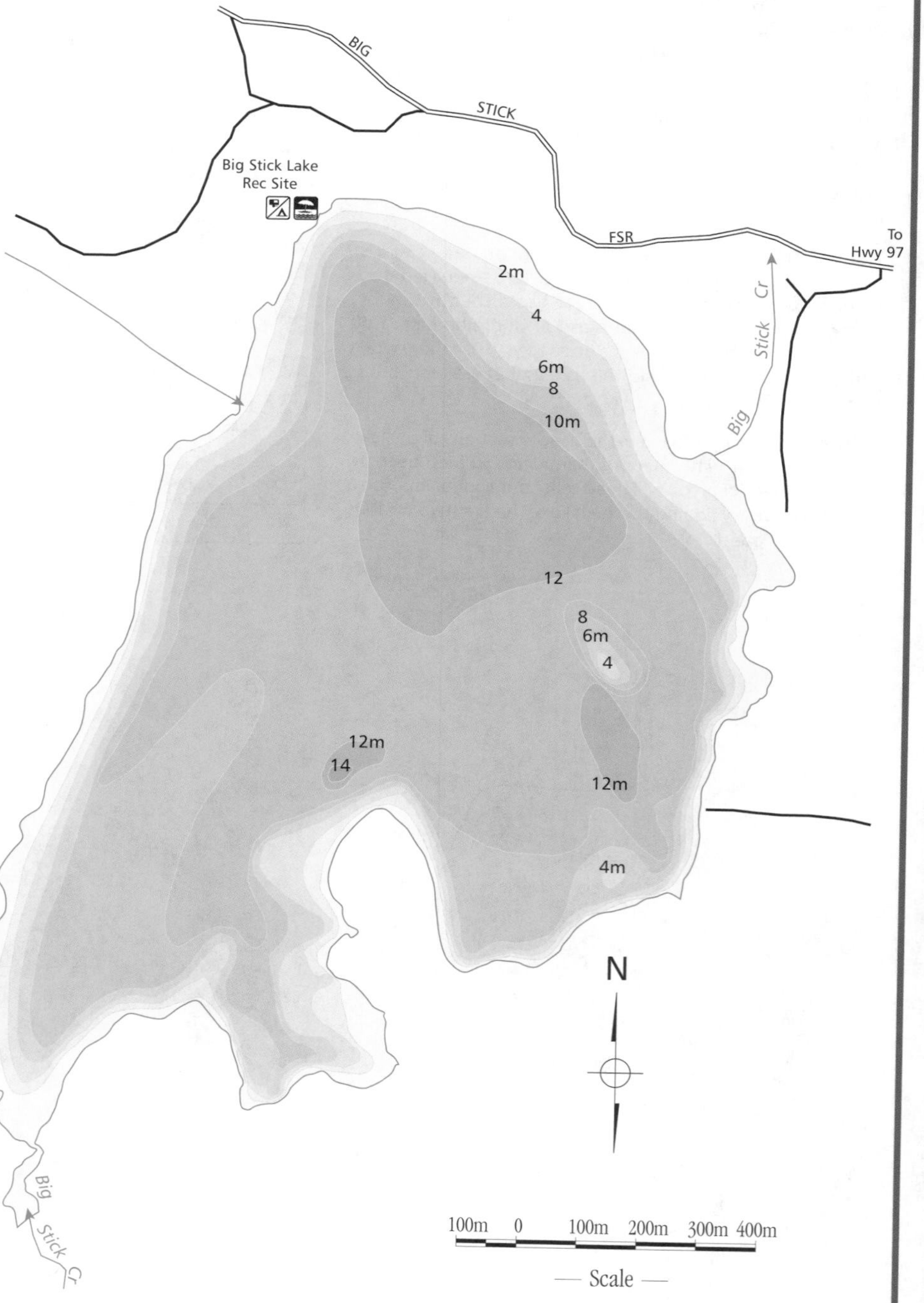

Big Stick Lake Rec Site
Big Stick FSR
To Hwy 97
Big Stick Cr
2m 4 6m 8 10m 12 8 6m 4 12m 14 12m 4m
N
100m 0 100m 200m 300m 400m
— Scale —

Bishop (Brown) Lake

Location: 50 km (31 mi) east of Williams Lake
Elevation: 1,137 m (3,730 ft)
Surface Area: 232 ha (573 ac)
Maximum Depth: 15 m (49 ft)
Mean Depth: 7.4 m (24 ft)
Geographic: 52° 35′ 53″ N, 123° 30′ 39″ W

Fishing

Bishop Lake is a mid-sized lake found north of Nazko Lake Provincial Park, although accessing it from the south is difficult and involves a hike/bushwhack down to the lake. It is much easier to access the lake from the north, coming down from the town of Nazko along the Honolulu Forest Service Road.

Twenty years ago, Bishop Lake was a relatively unknown lake that gave up trout to 4 kg (8 lbs) surprisingly willingly. Once that fact was discovered, though, anglers began to head to the lake in ever increasing numbers. And because the lake wasn't regulated as a trophy fishing lake, many people kept what they caught and the quality of fishing soon plummeted.

However, a two trout restriction was put on the lake and the lake was closed to ice fishing. As a result, pressure has eased and the lake has recovered nicely over the last decade. While you won't be catching fish to the same size and in the same numbers as you might have twenty years ago, there is still a chance that you will find one up to 3 kg (6 lbs).

The lake has tannin stained water with a muddy, sandy bottom. The mud is a perfect home for chironomids and the lake features some amazing chironomid fishing. Some patterns that wok here are a size 12–16 black and brown with silver, gold or red ribbing or a Chironomid Bomber size 10–12 in gray and black.

Chironomids are the first insects to hatch in the season and are often the last ones to stop hatching, making them a great pattern to fish most of the year around. In the early spring, they can be found hatching in shallower water, but as the water warms up, the hatches usually start deeper.

Rainbow trout feed on chironomids close to the bottom of the lake. The traditional method of fishing these tiny insects is to cast out and let the pattern sink down to the bottom of the lake and then slowly retrieve the line using a slow hand twist. This causes the pattern to move horizontally through the water, which is opposite the way chironomids usually move and retrieving too fast will cause the fish to get suspicious. A slow retrieve allows you to work a larger area, while avoiding raising the rainbow's suspicion

Chironomids rise slowly up in the water column and the biggest mistake made by anglers is to retrieve too fast. The best way to fish them is to

Quite quickly although, word got out and within a matter of years, the lake was mostly fished out.

In addition to chironomids, the lake has good numbers of leeches. If there is no active hatch happening, fishing a leech pattern is usually a good fallback. You could do worse than trying a Blood Bugger Leech Pattern in a size 8–14. Dragonfly nymphs are also productive.

Directions

To get to the lake, you must first get to Nazko. The easiest way to get to the small settlement is to take the paved Nazko Road from Quesnel. At the T-junction, turn left onto the Honolulu Road. The road changes into the Nazko Falls Road at the Nazko River Bridge. Take this road for about 8 km (5 miles) to the Brown Creek Forest Service Road. Turn right and drive for 5 km (3 miles) and take the second left down to the lake.

Facilities

There is a random campsite on the lake, but nothing developed. It is possible to hand launch a boat at the lake.

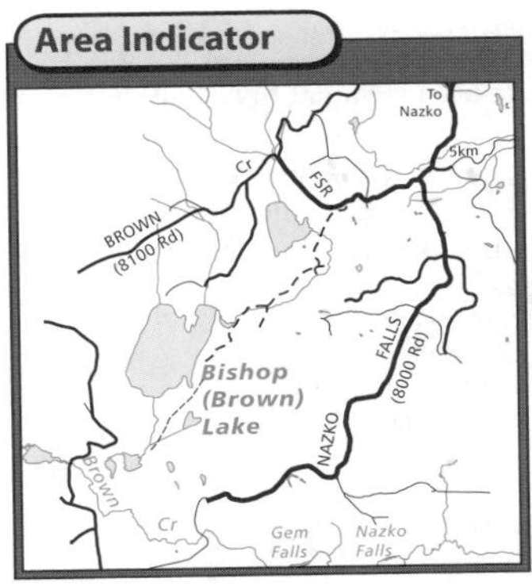

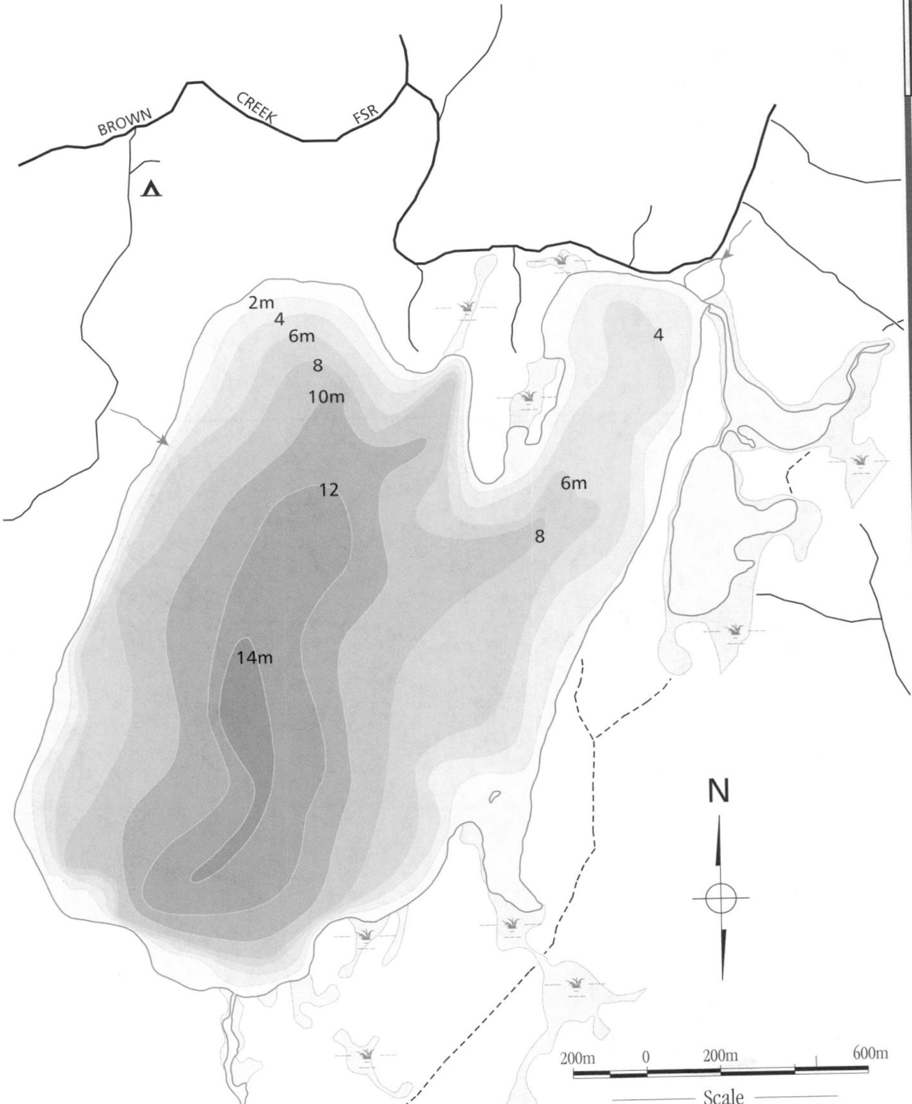

BROWN CREEK FSR
2m
4
6m
8
10m
12
14m
4
6m
8
N
200m 0 200m 600m
Scale

Location: 60 km (37 mi) northwest of Quesnel
Geographic: 53° 19′ 00″ N, 122° 52′ 00″ W

Blackwater (West Road) River

Fishing

The Blackwater or West Road River starts high in the Ilgachuz Mountains and flows east to empty into the Fraser River near Quesnel. The water is tannin stained and is a deep brown, almost black where the water is deep. The Alexander Mackenzie Grease Trail Follows the north side of the river for much of its length, providing good access up and down the river. If you're on foot.

The river is open to angling from June 15 to October 31 and maintained as an artificial fly only river. Although the river is a popular floating river, gas engines are banned.

The river holds plenty of small, feisty rainbow. While there are some salmon runs that make it into the river, the Blackwater is closed to salmon fishing.

In summer, as the water warms up, there are several large hatches of caddis, mayflies, stoneflies, chironomids and dragonflies. The hatches are unpredictable and the well-prepared angler comes with a box full of wet and dry flies.

Of course, dry fly-fishing is the most popular and an Elk Hair Caddis, small Adams, Wulffs and/or Goddards are the most popular flies to use. Stonefly nymphs, Gold Ribbed Hare's Ear Nymphs and a handful of other attractor patterns will be a boon when the fish aren't rising.

For those looking for a truly epic experience, it is possible to fly in to the lakes in the upper reaches of the river and canoe downstream, taking out at either Nazko Bridge or the Blackwater Crossing. This float and fish trip will take about two weeks to do, depending on how much fishing versus how much paddling you do. There are a trio of waterfalls and a couple stretches of rapids, but for the most part, the river is an easy float for anglers.

Facilities

Most of the Blackwater River is inaccessible except by trail, rough 4wd road, or by boat. There is a recreation site at the Nazko Bridge with space for a handful of tenting groups and a larger site at Blackwater Crossing, where you will find space for ten groups, which are large enough for RVs. There are also a few fly-in resorts and camps in the upper reaches of the river.

Directions

Motorized access to the Blackwater is limited. There are rough 4wd tracks along parts of the river, but your best options are by boat or on foot. There is a pair of bridges in the Nazko Valley and most people access the river here. People looking to access the upper part of the river can haul a canoe along a 5 km portage trail from Kuyakuz Lake, though most people take a float plane to one of the lakes in the upper valley and canoe downstream.

To get to the Nazko Bridge, take the Nazko Road (Highway 59) west from Quesnel past the village of Nazko. Continue north on the gravel road to a forestry recreation site at the Nazko/Blackwater River junction. The road parallels the river north from here to the Batnuni Road. Turning right here will bring you over a second bridge over the river. Turning north on the Blackwater Road (about 25 km later) will bring you past the small settlement of Blackwater to the third bridge over the Blackwater. The Blackwater Road is also accessible from Quesnel in the south and Prince George in the north.

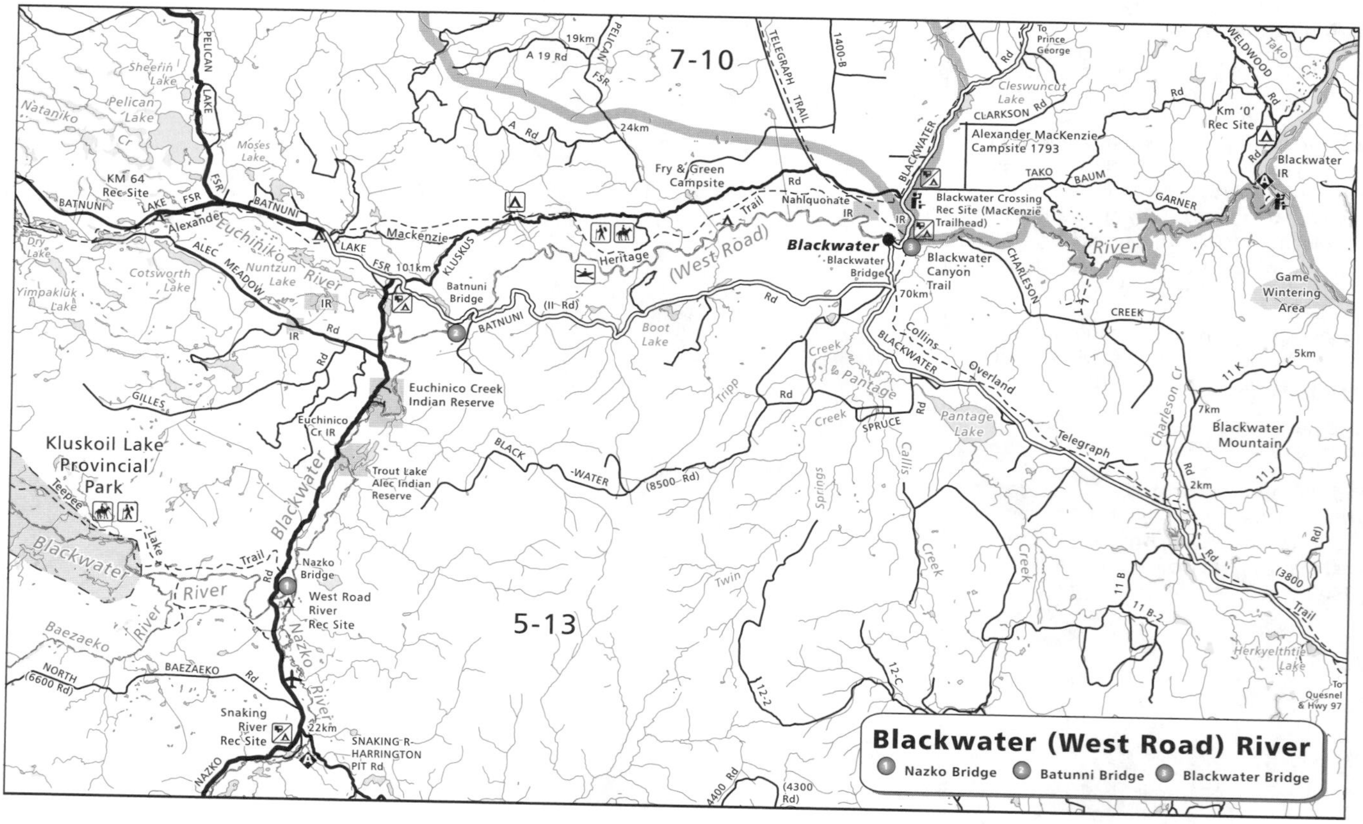

Blackwater (West Road) River

1 Nazko Bridge 2 Batunni Bridge 3 Blackwater Bridge

Blue Lake

Location: 34 km north of Williams Lake
Elevation: 797 m (2,615 ft)
Surface Area: 34 ha (84.5 ac)
Mean Depth: 10.1 m (33 ft)
Max Depth: 22 m (72.2 ft)
Way Point: 122° 14′ 00″ Lon - W 52° 20′ 50″ Lat - N

Fishing

Blue Lake is a crystal clear lake north of Williams Lake. There is a large island in the middle of the lake, and much of the best fishing happens around here. There is a large shoal off the north end of the island, and steep drop-offs, especially on the north side of the island. The lake is best known for its stocked rainbow, but also has a rather large population of kokanee which take willingly to a Wedding Band or Flatfish on the troll.

The rainbow can get to 2–3.5 kg (5–8 lbs) range but usually are under 0.5 kg (1 lb) in size. Despite the intense stocking program (10,000+ fish annually), the trout are notoriously hard to catch. However, there are a number of strategies that can improve your chances.

The lake is one of a very few lakes in the Cariboo with hellgrammites, which are the larval stage of the dobsonfly. The stocked rainbow feed on these ravenously. Anglers who fish down near the bottom with something that resembles a hellgrammite will usually have good success.

Just after ice off fly anglers will also have good success working a micro leech with a bit of red on it around either side of the island. The shoal at the north end as well as the hole to the northwest of the island are also good areas to try. Further into the year, the standard halfback fly patterns are quite successful around the eastern shore of the island. There is a sizeable population of damsel and dragon flies in late May at the south end of the lake, while dry fly patterns can be used off the island shoal successfully.

Starting in 2007 and again in 2008 the lake was stocked with 1,000 Gerrard All Female Triploid rainbows. Gerrard trout are known for being one of the largest trout sub-species, and the all female triploids tend to grow even faster. Gerrard rainbow are also piscivorous, meaning they like to eat small fish, so anglers targeting these fish should work patterns that resemble minnows. Fly anglers will work streamers or Muddler Minnows, while spincasters can work a variety of spoons and spinners.

The lake has an electric motor only restriction.

Facilities

Blue Lake is a popular day retreat for residents of Williams Lake as there is a nice beach that can be used for a fee. The **Blue Lake Holiday Campground** has 30 shaded camping sites, hot showers, a picnic area, a snack bar and boat rentals. Launching a small boat at the lake is possible. There are also two recreation sites at the lake: **North** and **West Blue Lake Recreation Sites**. The west site is a day use site, while the north site has space for about three campers.

Blue Lake
Fish Stocking Data

Year	Species	Number	Life Stage
2008	Rainbow Trout	11,000	Catchable/ Yearling
2007	Rainbow Trout	10,000	Yearling
2006	Rainbow Trout	11,000	Catchable/ Yearling

Directions

Blue Lake is found 34 km (21 miles) north of Williams Lake, east of Soda Creek. Take the Blue Lake Road east off Highway 97 heading east and within a kilometer, the lake will be found just off the road.

The turn-off from Highway 97 is well signed so you shouldn't miss the access road. A car can reach the lake.

Other Options

McLeese Lake is situated to the north of Blue Lake on the Cariboo Highway. Try trolling this lake for the rainbow reaching 1 kg (average 30–35 cm) or for small kokanee. The lake has full facilities and is stocked with rainbow each year.

Area Indicator

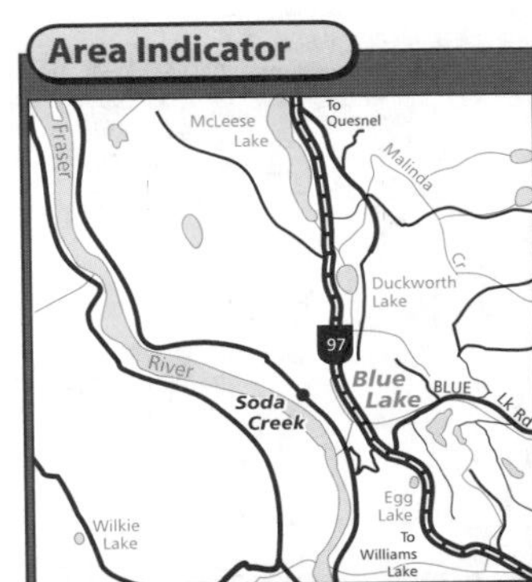

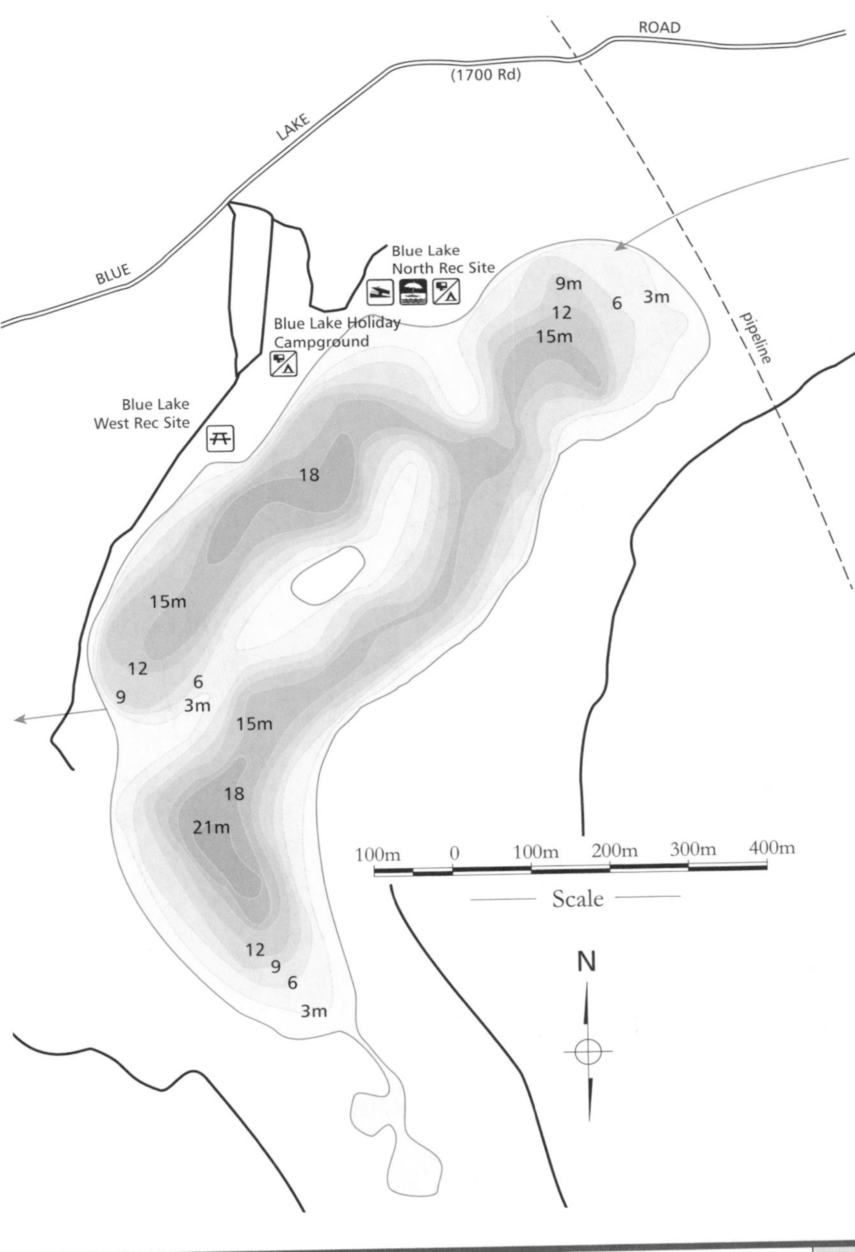

Location: 10 km (6.2 mi) southwest of Likely
Elevation: 984 m (3,228 ft)
Surface Area: 268 ha (662 ac)
Maximum Depth: 17.7 m (58 ft)
Mean Depth: 7.5 m (24.6 ft)
Way Point: 52° 32′ 26″ N, 121° 39′ 11″ W

Bootjack Lake

Area Indicator

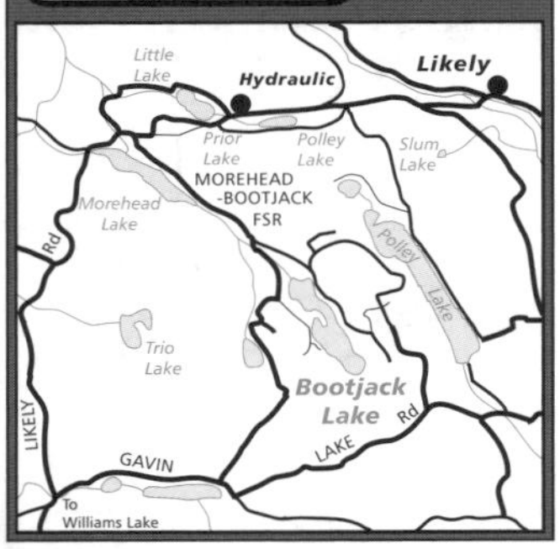

Fishing

Bootjack Lake is nestled in the rolling hills of the Cariboo, well off the beaten path. The lake does not receive a lot of fishing pressure, but those who come here once have a tendency to return again and again.

The lake is partially sheltered from the wind by the surrounding forest. It holds a self-sustaining population of rainbow trout that can get up to 1 kg (2 lbs) or 30 cm (12 in).

The fish are small but hungry and there are plenty of them. Too many, in fact, which is why the catch limit has been raised to eight fish a day. While the action can be fast and furious, the fact is the fish don't get very big because there is too much competition for food. If the population thins out, the average size of catch here will go up. Or at least, that's the theory.

Because the trout aren't particular, choosing the right gear is easy. As long as the gear is small enough, chances are it will attract some attention from the local residents.

Trolling worms or a Wedding Band behind a flashy Willow Leaf around the edges, or over the deeper water in the middle of the lake, is a great way to get these fish to the boat. For lighter tackle, troll a #70 Hot Shot, F-4 or F-5 Flatfish, Kwikfish in green or yellow, or an Apex spoon in gold. Casting or trolling flies, such as the 52 Buick, black leech, or green Carey Special, will also elicit strikes. Use a watercraft when fishing here, as trolling is the most successful way to fish the lake. Try trolling around the drop off at the northwest bay or the southeast bay. At those two locations the water drops off rapidly from shore allowing for shore casting if you do not have a boat.

The lake is not a high elevation lake and the long, hot Cariboo summers can impact the quality of the fishing. While the fishing is great in spring and early summer, expect slower fishing through late July and August. However, the lake is deep enough that the fish won't get too lethargic and dawn and dusk periods can create a frenzy of action.

Bootjack Lake also provides great winter sport through the ice. Locating the fish is the key to success. Try drilling a series of holes starting close to shore and working out to help find the right holding depth. Fish a piece of shrimp or worm on an orange or yellow teardrop jig, or yellow or green marabou ice fly jig.

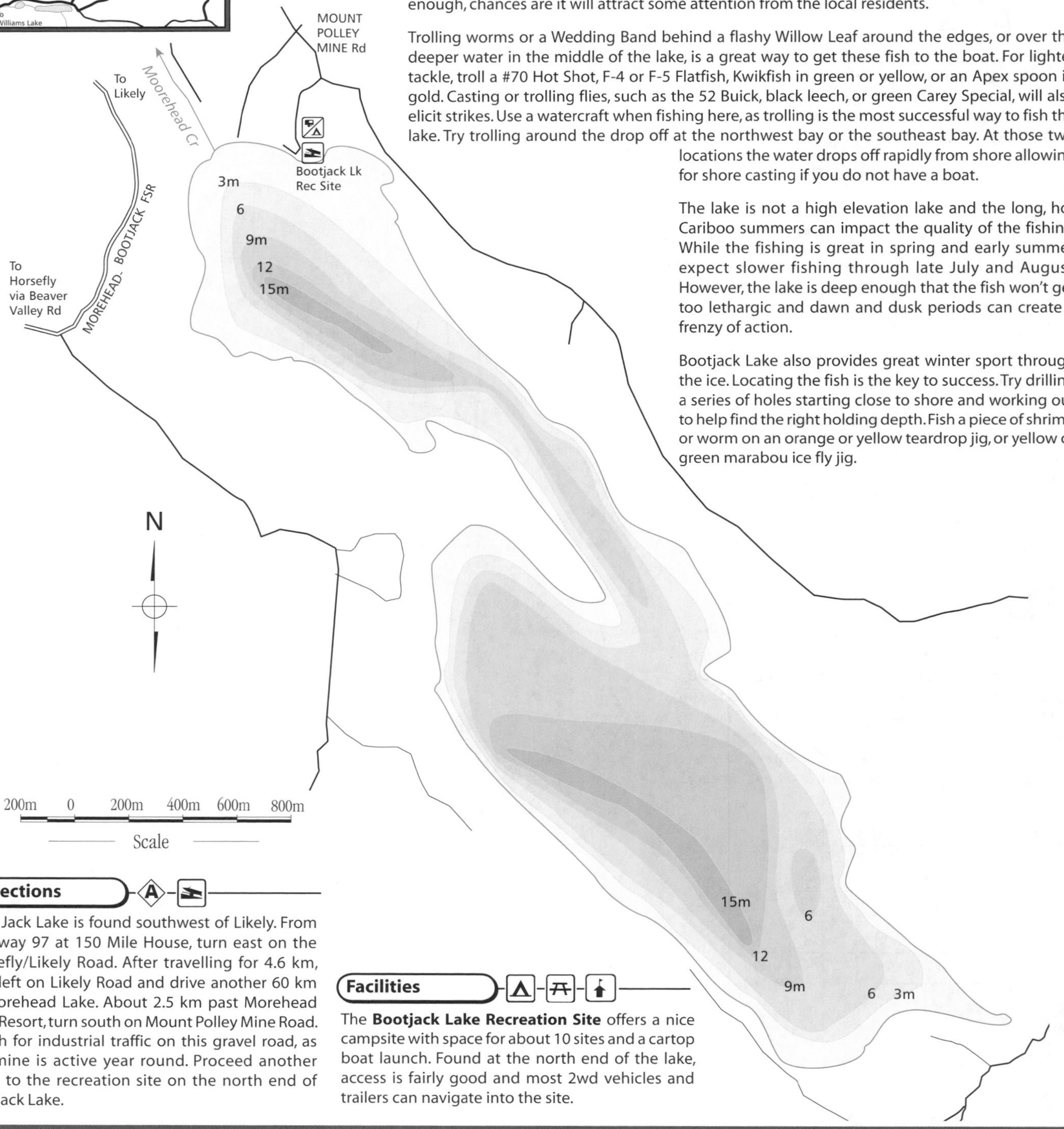

Directions

Boot Jack Lake is found southwest of Likely. From Highway 97 at 150 Mile House, turn east on the Horsefly/Likely Road. After travelling for 4.6 km, turn left on Likely Road and drive another 60 km to Morehead Lake. About 2.5 km past Morehead Lake Resort, turn south on Mount Polley Mine Road. Watch for industrial traffic on this gravel road, as the mine is active year round. Proceed another 9 km to the recreation site on the north end of Bootjack Lake.

Facilities

The **Bootjack Lake Recreation Site** offers a nice campsite with space for about 10 sites and a cartop boat launch. Found at the north end of the lake, access is fairly good and most 2wd vehicles and trailers can navigate into the site.

Bosk (Boss) Lake

Location: 90 km (56 mi) east of Williams Lake
Elevation: 1,000 m (3,280 ft)
Surface Area: 506.7 ha (1,252 ac)
Maximum Depth: 49 m (160.8 ft)
Mean Depth: 19.4 m (63.6 ft)
Geographic: 52° 10′ 12″ N, 120° 47′ 57″ W

Fishing

Bosk Lake is also known as Boss Lake. It is connected to Cruiser Lake by a short channel to the north and is quite large. Anglers will find a good population of sportfish which include rainbow, lake trout, mountain whitefish, burbot and kokanee. There are also a number of course species such as redside shiners, suckers and squawfish. Most of the fishing attention is focused on the rainbow, which are in the 35–45 cm (14–18 in) class. The odd trout grows to a larger size 2.5 kg (5.5 lb) size.

Bosk Lake is, like many of the lakes in this region, a mid-elevation lake and is usually ice free by end of April or early May. The lake is quite deep, which means that the fishing isn't as subject to the summer doldrums as shallower lakes. Still, the fishing is at its best in late May to early July and then in September until late October.

The lake has extensive shoals totaling 126 hectares in size. The island in the northeast bay is a good place to focus your fly-fishing activities, especially if you cast into the shallows. Also, it is a good option to work the fringe area around the island in the middle of the lake using a well-presented fly.

The lake features the typical area insect hatches, but nothing to write home about. Fly-anglers will do well to keep an eye on the lake for what is currently hatching, but there is no single hatch that you must take the week off work to be at.

Given the depth of the lake, it is possible to troll around most of the lake except at the northeast bay. For the rainbow trout, the typical list of gear (lake trolls or a Mepps, Panther Martin, Gibbs spinner) will work well on the troll.

Lake trout are found in limited numbers but can offer a big fish experience. They can be taken on a long line using a big spoon or some large body bait, like a T50 Flatfish. Lake trout are slow growing and prone to over fishing. If you are not planning on keeping the fish you catch (and we recommend you don't), use a single barbless hook. Even if you are planning on keeping your catch, you should still use single barbless.

Area Indicator

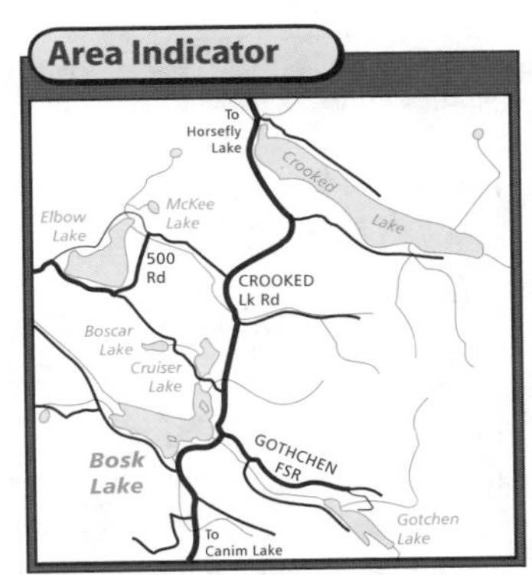

Directions

To reach Bosk Lake involves a long drive from Highway 97 but the access is good. From Williams Lake, take Highway 97 east to 150 Mile House. At that small town, you will see the paved road heading north towards Horsefly and Likely. Rather than continuing north at the first major junction, hang a right on the Horsefly Road and drive on the pavement all the way to the small town of Horsefly. Just before entering town, cross the bridge over the Horsefly River and continue onto the Black Creek Road. That logging road is a well-maintained road so a car can travel along it without much trouble.

Continue past Black Creek and the airport and then take the first right onto the McKinley Lake Road (500 Road). The first lake on the McKinley Lake Road is McKinley Lake followed by Elbow, Cruiser and finally Bosk Lake.

Facilities

The **Bosk Lake Recreation Site** is on the eastern shores of the lake next to the McKinley Lake Road. There are 10 camping pads at the lake together with a sandy beach and a cartop boat launch.

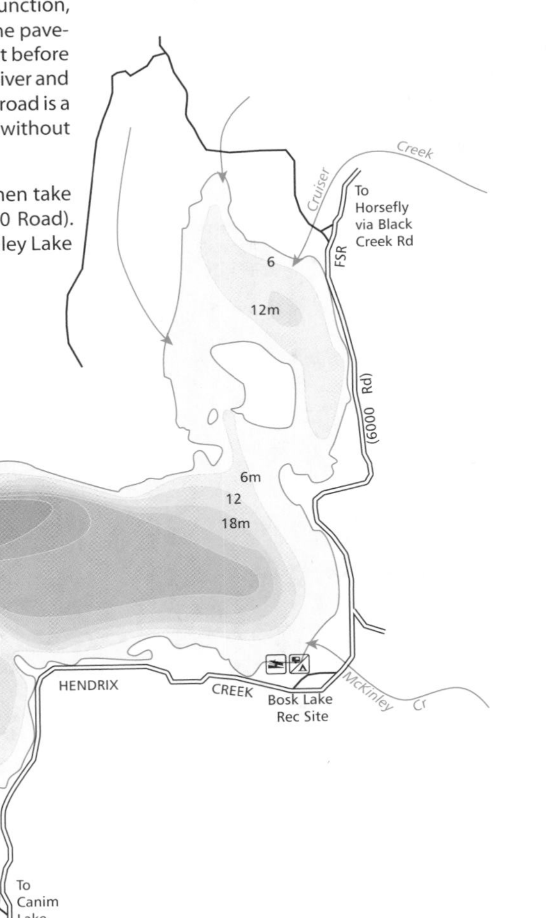

Location: 10 km (6.2 mi) northwest of Quesnel
Elevation: 686 m (2,250 ft)
Surface Area: 29 ha (72 ac)
Maximum Depth: 7.3 m (24 ft)
Mean Depth: 4 m (4 ft)
Way Point: 53° 2′ 8″ N, 122° 37′ 36″ W

Bouchie (Six Mile) Lake

Area Indicator

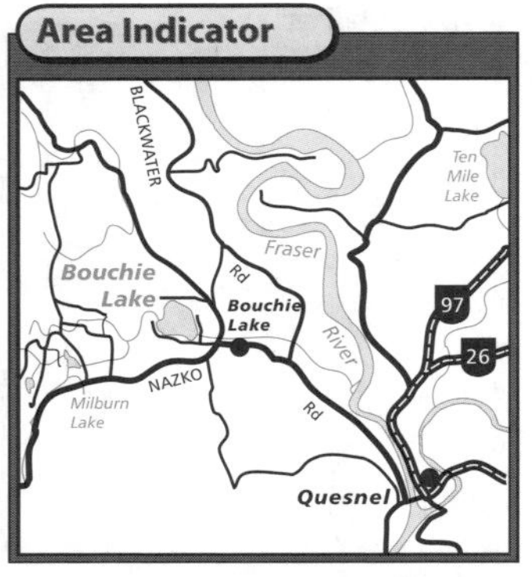

Bouchie Lake			
Fish Stocking Data			
Year	Species	Number	Life Stage
2008	Rainbow Trout	20,000	Yearling
2007	Rainbow Trout	20,000	Yearling
2006	Rainbow Trout	20,000	Yearling

Fishing

Bouchie Lake is also known as Six Mile Lake. It is found to the west of Quesnel and is one of the better early season fisheries in the area. Despite an issue with winterkill during cold winters, the lake is known to produce rainbow to 2 kg (4 lbs).

About 20,000 rainbow trout are stocked each year in the lake by the Freshwater Fisheries Society of BC to ensure that the fishing remains good. It is a catch-and-keep lake, as the shallow lake is prone to winterkill. The mid-sized lake is a relatively low elevation lake and becomes ice-free earlier than many of the other lakes in the region.

The shallow nature of the lake makes it difficult to troll with a lake troll or deep line. Therefore, most fishermen troll flies or light gear or spincast the lake. The shallowness also means that it is also one of the first lakes in the area to suffer from the summer doldrums. Don't expect to fish here any time between July and mid-September with any sort of luck. And even if you were to manage to hook a fish, they are generally sluggish and provide little fight.

The lake is like a giant saucer as the water drops off rapidly from the shoreline and then there is an expansive flat area in the middle of the lake. Try fly-fishing or spincasting the drop off area around the shoreline, as the fish tend to congregate in the fringe area.

One of the best times to fish the lake is right after the ice comes off the lake. At this time, the water is still cold and only the fringes of the lake start to warm. Life begins here, on the fringes of the lake. There are even some small insect hatches once the floor of the lake gets warm enough and the surface of the water contains the most oxygenated water, meaning the fish stay close to the surface. The fish are usually bolder, although they still can easily be spooked. This is a perfect time to practice your sight fishing, targeting individual fish along the shore using a small spoon, spinner or fly.

Fly anglers will not find great hatches here so an attractor pattern like a Doc Spratley or Carey Special. Nymph patterns can also work well throughout most of the year.

Directions

From the south, the Cariboo Highway (Highway 97) becomes Legion Drive in Quesnel, then the Moffat Approach. The highway takes a sharp right, but the road continues on over the Fraser River. The first road on the far side of the river is North Fraser Drive. Turn right and follow the road until it becomes Blackwater Road, which takes you out of town along the western shores of the Fraser River. Where the Blackwater Road takes a sharp right and the road continues on as the Nazko Road, turn right, and then left a few hundred metres along onto Bonny Road. Again, it is only a matter of a few hundred metres before Norwood Road turns off Bonny. Follow this road west to Bouchie Lake. There are a few other roads on the east side of the lake that residents use to access their property.

Facilities

There are a number of full time residences on the shores of the lake but no public facilities. The city of Quesnel is nearby and offers full services including tackle shops, motels and hotels.

Boulder Lake

Location: 40 km (25 mi) south of Chetwynd
Elevation: 1,247 m (4,091 ft)
Surface Area: 15 ha (37 ac)
Maximum Depth: 17 m (54 ft)
Mean Depth: 5.6 m (18 ft)
Way Point: 55° 20′ 14″ N, 121° 38′ 47″ W

Fishing

Boulder Lake is a small, hidden lake found about halfway between Chetwynd and Tumbler Ridge in the Kwoen Hills. Every year, 1,500 rainbow trout are deposited in the lake. While that doesn't sound like a lot, the lake isn't very big and not a lot of people are willing to make the trip out to the lake.

Part of that has to do with the difficulty in getting to the lake. It takes about an hour to drive to the lake from the nearest community. Folks who don't have a 4wd vehicle will want to walk the last 500 metres down to the lake for fear of not making it back up the steep hill. Even if you are able to get down to the Boulder Lake sign, you will still have to hike in a few hundred metres to the lake through a fairly thick stand of bush. While carrying a canoe or small boat is possible, it isn't easy to navigate through the forest. Instead, most people who fish here fish from shore, or more typically, from a float tube. The forest ends right at the edge of the lake and launching a float tube is a little awkward, but not impossible. There is a trail to the east side of the lake, where the forest opens up and shore fishing is possible.

The rainbow stocked here are all-female triploid Pennask rainbow. That means they do not reproduce, but put all their energy into getting nice and fat. Pennask rainbow are the most commonly stocked trout in BC and for good reason. While they are one of the smaller strains of trout, they are also one of the most acrobatic, hard fighting fish you will find. Fished on light gear, they can be as challenging as any fish. The best time to fish here is at dusk.

The launch, such as it is, is found at the southeast end of the lake. While there is a hole right off the launch, the best fishing comes at the northwest end of the lake where you will find a steep transition to the deepest hole in the lake, as well as the outflow of Boulder Creek. There are some weedy areas at both ends of the lake that can also be productive at certain times.

One of the best ways to fish the lake is simply to still fish with a bobber and bait using a worm, powerbait, maggots or roe.

Please note that powerboats are not allowed.

Directions

Boulder Lake is about an hour's drive from Chetwynd, the nearest community. To get to the lake, take Highway 29 south towards Tumbler Ridge. As you are climbing the hill out of the Martin Creek valley, watch for the Dome Petroleum Road to your right. (It is the second main road past the Sukunka River Forest Road turnoff.) There are a couple roads that fall off this main road; just stick to the road most travelled, staying right at the fork in the road and you should be fine.

The road ends at a gated gas well site south of Boulder Lake, where a gas pipeline/road allotment heads north down the hill, almost directly behind you. While it is possible to get a 2wd vehicle to this point, the hill is quite steep and getting back up can be a challenge, especially in wet weather.

It's only about 500 m (1,600 ft) down the hill from the gate to a Forest Service sign pointing the way to the lake. From here it is a short trek though the forest to the lake.

Facilities

While this is technically a forest service site, there is little more than a sign and a trail. The nearest formal camping is at Gwillim Lake, south of the turnoff to this lake on Highway 29.

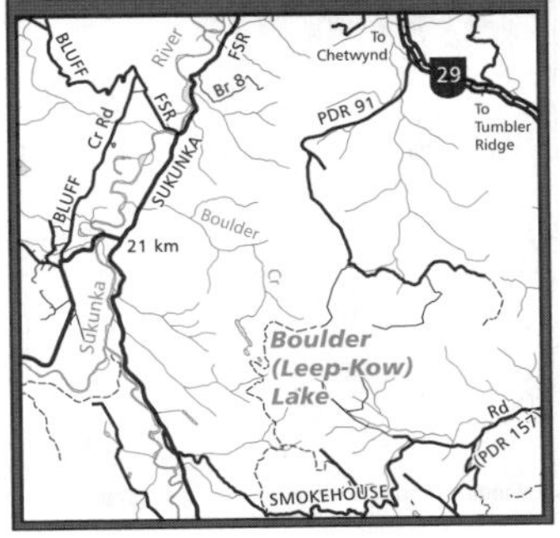

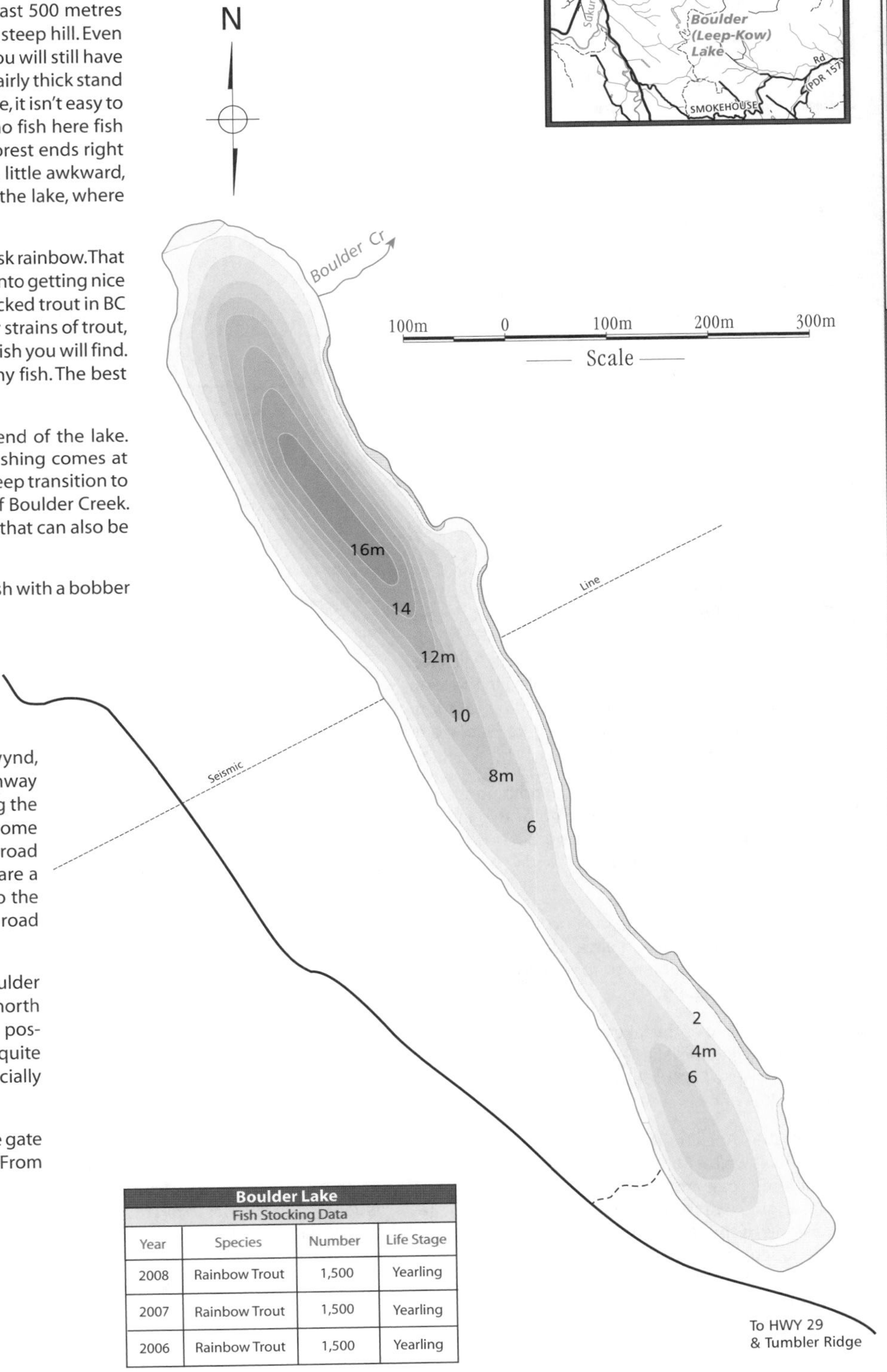

Boulder Lake
Fish Stocking Data

Year	Species	Number	Life Stage
2008	Rainbow Trout	1,500	Yearling
2007	Rainbow Trout	1,500	Yearling
2006	Rainbow Trout	1,500	Yearling

To HWY 29 & Tumbler Ridge

Location: 44 km (27 mi) east of 100 Mile House
Elevation: 1,099 m (3,605 ft)
Surface Area: 603 ha (1,489 ac)
Maximum Depth: 44 m (143 ft)
Mean Depth: 19 m (62 ft)
Way Point: 51° 41′ 23″ N, 120° 41′ 42″ W

Bowers Lake

Area Indicator

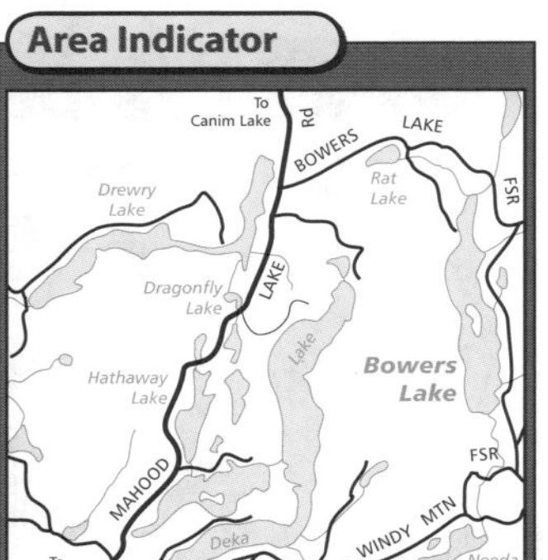

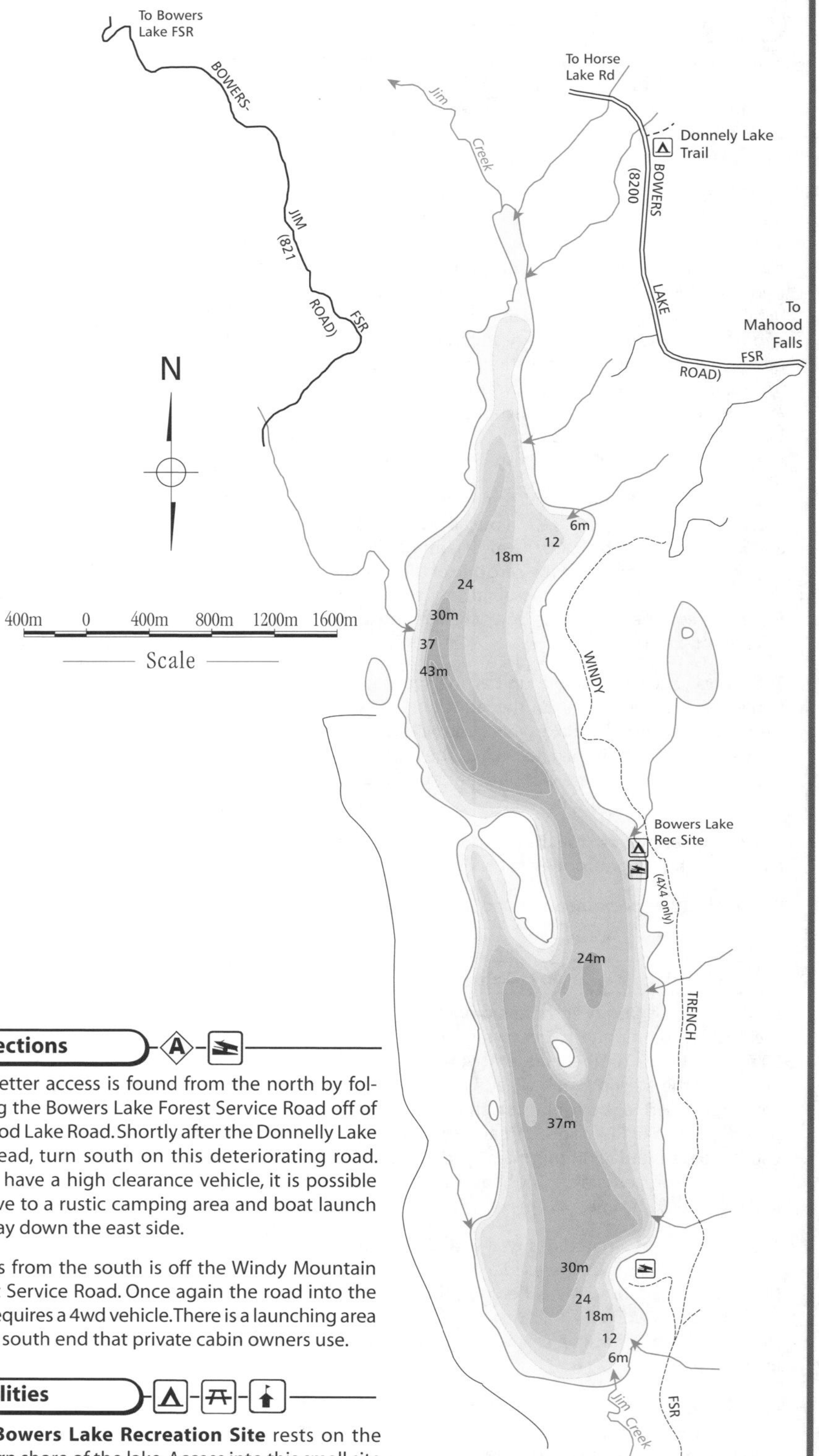

Fishing

Bowers Lake is found to the northeast of Hathaway, Deka and Sulphurous Lakes. Although there are a few cabins at the south and eastern end, access in to the lake can be difficult and is weather dependant.

It is slightly higher in elevation than other lakes in the region and the fishing begins a bit later in the year. The lake is usually ice-free by late May and fishing is usually good from early June until fall.

Despite its fairly large, at 603 hectares, the lake is well suited for fly fishermen and spincasters. The northern end of the lake is a good place to focus as is the fringe area nearby to the two islands in the middle of the lake. Also try working the drop off area.

Fly anglers can work a variety of traditional flies that perform well in the area. Things like Spratleys and Careys and Wooly Buggers will work, but then again, most anything that looks remotely like food usually will have some success. The trout are overpopulated in the lake, which means that they are always searching for food. The rainbow are plentiful but small. A 1 kg (2 lb) trout is considered a great catch in Bowers.

There are some hatches on the lake, but nothing special. You should always have a Tom Thumb or two in your tackle box just in case the fish are rising, but don't come to this lake looking for dry fly-fishing and you won't be disappointed.

It is not a lake to visit if you are looking for trophy trout, but the small trout are caught steadily and it is a great lake for taking new anglers or for people looking to practice their fly-casting.

While fly anglers love the lake, it is also well suited for trolling. Try circling the lake just off the drop off. You can use a lake troll or a Flatfish, but be forewarned, the lake can get quite windy.

For spincasters, Apex Trout Killer, Kamlooper and Krocodile spoons as well as Mepps, Panther Martin, Vibrax and Gibbs spinners cast around the drop off can be deadly. Vertical jigging with spoons or jigs using scented bait, such as one of the Berkley Powerbaits, will also work well. Heck, people have had good success using a simple bobber and worm; the fish here are hungry and fairly indiscriminate.

To Bowers Lake FSR
BOWERS-JIM (821 ROAD) FSR
To Horse Lake Rd
Donnely Lake Trail
BOWERS (8200) LAKE ROAD) FSR
To Mahood Falls
Jim Creek
N
400m 0 400m 800m 1200m 1600m
Scale
6m 12 18m 24 30m 37 43m
WINDY
Bowers Lake Rec Site
(4X4 only)
TRENCH
24m 37m 30m 24 18m 12 6m
FSR

Directions

The better access is found from the north by following the Bowers Lake Forest Service Road off of Mahood Lake Road. Shortly after the Donnelly Lake Trailhead, turn south on this deteriorating road. If you have a high clearance vehicle, it is possible to drive to a rustic camping area and boat launch halfway down the east side.

Access from the south is off the Windy Mountain Forest Service Road. Once again the road into the lake requires a 4wd vehicle. There is a launching area at the south end that private cabin owners use.

Facilities

The **Bowers Lake Recreation Site** rests on the eastern shore of the lake. Access into this small site is very rough and best from the north. If you have a high clearance 4wd vehicle you can lug in a cartopper. There is also a boat launch at the south end of the lake that is used by the cabin owners.

Bowron Lake

Location: 120 km (74.5 mi) east of Quesnel
Elevation: 915 m (3,002 ft)
Surface Area: 1,011.8 ha (2,500 ac)
Maximum Depth: 63.4 m (208 ft)
Mean Depth: 16.2 m (53 ft)
Waypoint: 53° 13' 34" N, 121° 21' 13" W

Fishing

The eleven lakes that make up the Bowron Lake Canoe Route offer a variety of fishing opportunities. Bowron Lake is the best known and easiest accessed of the bunch. The lake was first stocked with rainbow in 1949 and last stocked in 1950. But twice was enough and ever since then, the big lake has offered a decent fishery for trout.

The lake is iced over until late April-early May. As soon as the ice is off, the lake can offer some great fishing, but most people wait until after the lake water turns over. By mid-May, the fishing picks up and is steady throughout the summer months to the fall. This is because the lake is very deep and the water temperature does not rise significantly in the summer. However, in July and August the fish are usually much deeper than in the spring and the summer and a fishfinder would be an asset.

Bowron Lake is best suited for trolling. Indeed, the canoeists on their final leg of the 116 km (72 mile) canoe trip usually drag a line across the lake. But canoeists aren't the only one trolling the lake, as there is a boat launch at the north end of the lake that allows powerboats onto the lake.

Trolling a Willow Leaf and a Flatfish or a small lure with red or pink works. Flies that should be tried are Carey Special, Tom Thumb, a black Wooly Buggers and a dragonfly nymph. Spincasters and fly fishers can work the north end of the lake at the inflow of the Bowron River.

There are ten other lakes in the circuit. Of them all, Isaac and Indianpoint Lakes are probably the best of the lakes. Both lakes offer rainbow, kokanee, lake trout and dollies. Trolling a lure or bait is the preferred method of catching the fish. Hunter Lake, which involves a short hike from the south end of Sandy Lake, is a good fly-fishing lake. All the lakes on the canoe route have a powerboat restriction except Bowron Lake. The fishing is generally the best in June and September.

Area Indicator

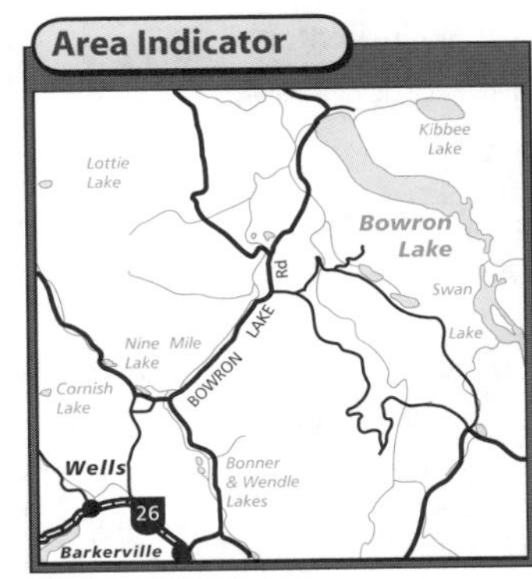

Directions

Bowron Lake is home to the Bowron Lake Provincial Park and the world famous canoe route. The lake is accessed by travelling on the Barkerville Highway (Highway 26) east from Quesnel past the town of Wells. Watch for the signs pointing the way to the Bowron Lake Provincial Park and then turn north on the Bowron Lake Road (2600 Road). This mainhaul logging road is a well maintained, two lane gravel road suited for most vehicles. It will bring you to the lake and park information site.

Facilities

The **Bowron Lake Provincial Park** surrounds the lake chain. At the north end of Bowron lake is a provincial campground with 50 vehicle/tent units and a boat launch. There are also some boat access only camping sites at the south end of the lake and scattered around the entire lake chain. If canoeing, allow about a week to complete the loop.

The **Bowron Lake Lodge and Resort** and **Beckers Lodge** offer accommodation on the lake. Both facilities are canoe outfitters that offer cabins, camping, a restaurant and of course canoe rentals.

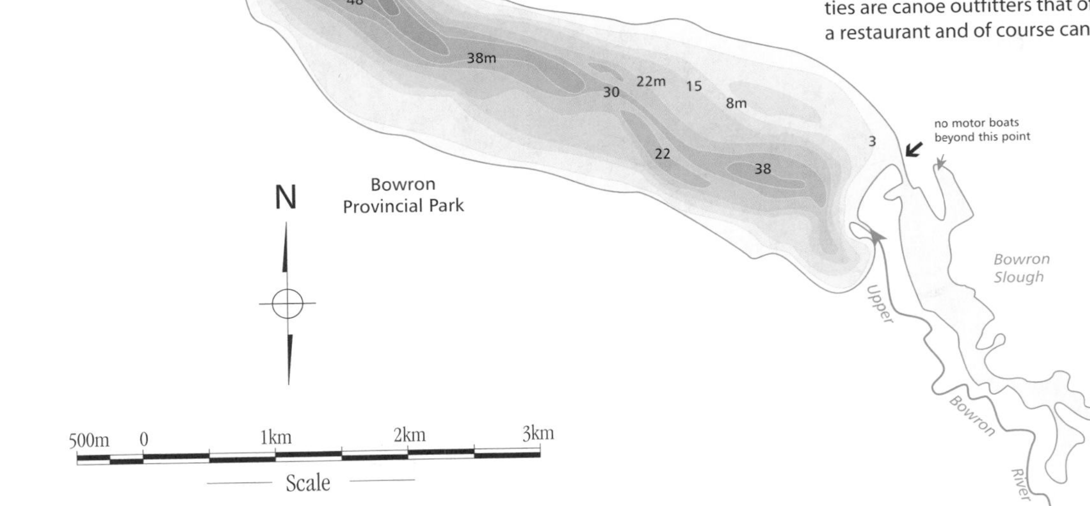

Bridge Lake

Location: 40 km (25 mi) southeast of 100 Mile House
Elevation: 1,136 m (3,727 ft)
Surface Area: 1,376 ha (3,400 ac)
Maximum Depth: 47 m (154 ft)
Mean Depth: 17 m (56 ft)
Way Point: 51° 30′ 27″ N, 120° 43′ 53″ W

Area Indicator

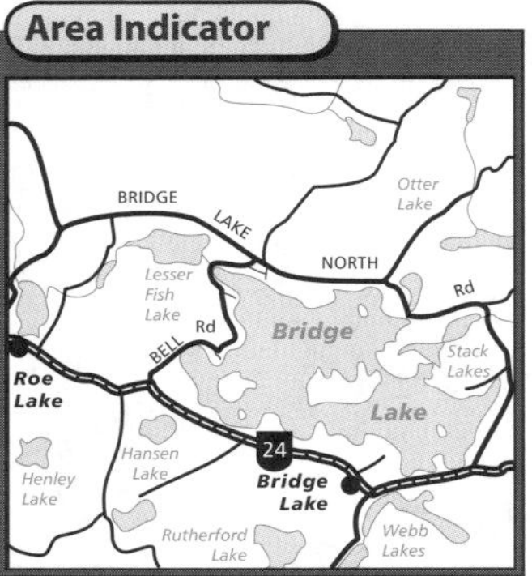

Bridge Lake Fish Stocking Data			
Year	Species	Number	Life Stage
2008	Rainbow Trout	16,315	Yearling
2008	Kokanee	130,000	Fry
2007	Rainbow Trout	13,072	Yearling
2007	Kokanee	130,000	Fry
2006	Rainbow Trout	10,000	Yearling
2006	Kokanee	130,209	Fingerling

Fishing

Bridge Lake is a very popular fishing retreat found right next to the Fishing Highway (Highway 24) west of Little Fort. Bridge Lake is unique in the Cariboo, as it contains arctic char. There are also lake trout, kokanee, rainbow and burbot in the lake together with a number of course fish (squawfish and suckers).

The lake is stocked with kokanee annually and these landlocked sockeye are a favourite with people who fish here. The lake is also stocked with rainbow trout.

Most kokanee are small, but it isn't uncommon to catch one to 1.5 kg (3 lbs). A big catch can exceed 2.5 kg (5 lbs). With such impressive sizes and decent numbers, it is no wonder the kokanee are becoming the main focus of anglers at the lake.

The best way to catch the kokanee is to troll a lake troll (Willow Leaf and Wedding Band with bait) in 6–15 metres (20-50 feet) of water. Hot spots include just east of the large island in the southwestern bay or nearby to the Bridge Creek outflow. Kokanee are very sensitive to water temperature and inhabit a very narrow band of water, depending on what time of year it is. The trick is to vary the speed and depth of your troll to find where they are holding.

Fly fishermen do best using a #10 hook fly tied with bright pink wool with and a tinsel body. Trolling a small red Doc Spratley or Woolly Bugger slowly behind your boat within a few feet of the surface can also work.

The stocked rainbow can grow to 2.5 kg (6 lbs). The best fishing is in the early spring or just before ice-over in the fall. During both times, the fish go on a feeding binge. The summer is a fairly slow time to fish with the best time of day being just around dusk when the fish come to the surface to feed. At this time, dry flies like the Tom Thumb can be a lot of fun.

Bridge Lake has numerous islands and bays. For fly fishermen, there is a very good spring chironomid hatch that offers a great time to catch some rainbow if the hatch is timed right. In particular, there are two islands in the lake around which there are extensive shoals. These areas are ideal for casting a damselfly, dragonfly nymph or mayfly in the spring as the rainbow cruise the shallow water in search of food.

The lake is subject to strong winds. However, because of the numerous bays and islands, it is possible to find a sheltered area to fish.

Directions

Bridge Lake is a very popular fishing retreat found right next to the Fishing Highway (Highway 24) west of Little Fort. There is good access around most of the lake as the gravel Bridge Lake North Road follows the northern shoreline of the lake.

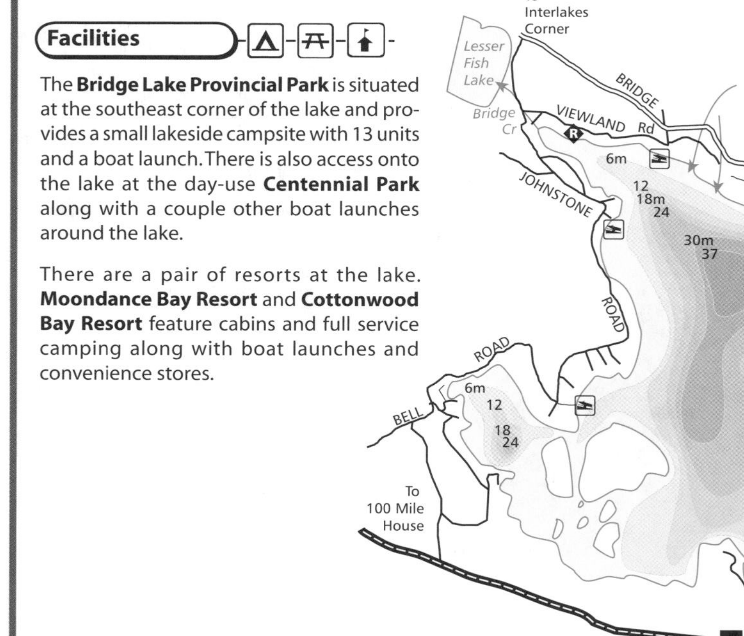

Facilities

The **Bridge Lake Provincial Park** is situated at the southeast corner of the lake and provides a small lakeside campsite with 13 units and a boat launch. There is also access onto the lake at the day-use **Centennial Park** along with a couple other boat launches around the lake.

There are a pair of resorts at the lake. **Moondance Bay Resort** and **Cottonwood Bay Resort** feature cabins and full service camping along with boat launches and convenience stores.

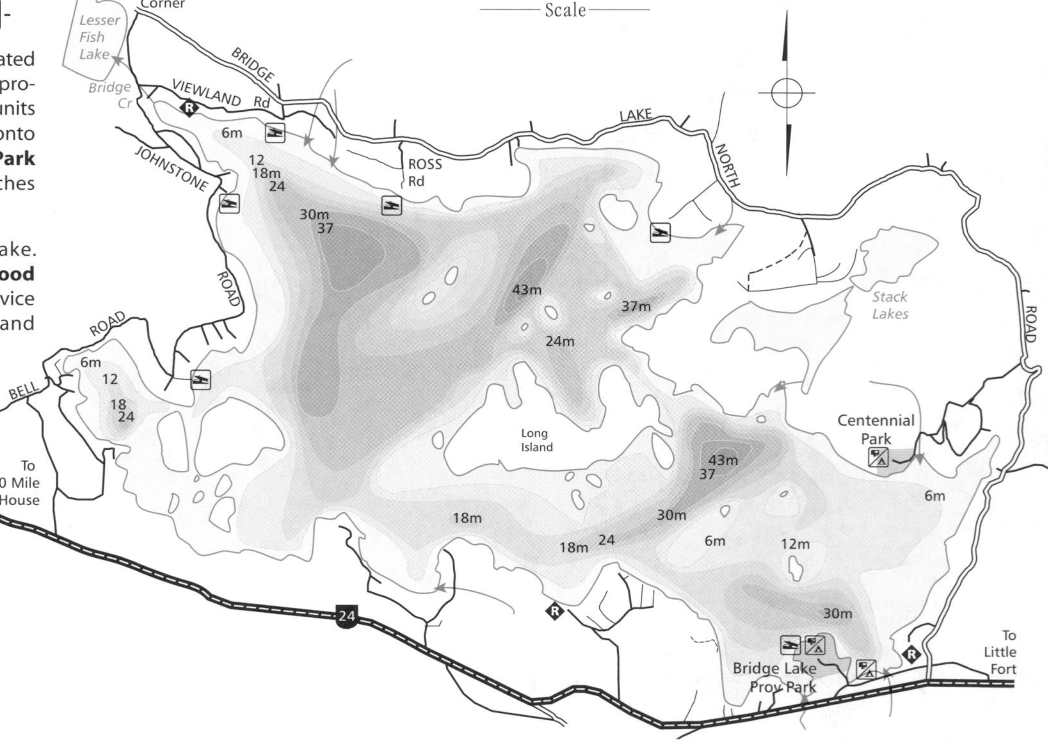

Bulkley River

Location: Flows through Smithers
Stream Length: 259 km (161 mi)
Geographic: 55° 14′ 59″ N, 127° 40′ 0″ W

Fishing

A Skeena River tributary, the Bulkley itself features wide, broad pools that favour spey casting. The river tends to produce smaller fish than other tributaries of the Skeena, but features some of the largest returns of any river. While the returns on rivers down south numbers in the hundreds or even in the dozens, returns on the Bulkley still number in the tens of thousands.

Steelhead usually enter the system starting in mid-August, but the fishing doesn't start to heat up until September. By October, the run is in full swing. The average catch here can be as small as 2.5 kg (5 lbs) some years, but the easy access and the fact the steelhead love coming to the surface makes this a great river to fish.

Angler's fish skating surface flies here (Elk and Deer Hair Caddis) and get as many hits as people fishing a sinking tip line and orange and black Woolly Buggers. The river system features great hatches of caddis, stoneflies and mayflies. Steelhead smolts in the Morice River will frequently stay in the river an extra year, dining on aquatic insects and conditioning them to rise to these insects, something that remains with the fish when they return to the rivers. Locals call these fish players and taking a steelhead on a dry fly is one of the greatest experiences a river angler could ask for.

But it is not a fly-fishing only river and spincasters often have much better catch rates than fly anglers, especially those with a dry fly.

In addition to the steelhead, the river has plenty of resident rainbow trout and Dolly Varden. These fish feast on steelhead eggs and it isn't unusual to catch plenty of these fish while fishing for steelhead (using eggs or egg imitations). These fish also feast on returning smolts in the spring. Fish a streamer pattern or something that resembles a minnow.

There is also a good run of Chinook in July.

Although there is good road access in places, a boat is always helpful. From Houston to Telkwa, the river can be easily navigated in most any small boat. Below Telkwa, a heavier boat like a jetboat is needed. There are two bridges between Houston and Telkwa, creating three nearly equal sections, each of which can be drifted in a day. However, anglers looking for steelhead upstream of Houston will be sorely disappointed.

Directions

From the confluence of the Bulkley to the outflow of Morice Lake is 130 km (80 miles) by road. There are plenty of places to access the river, both from the Yellowhead Highway and logging roads in the valley. Highway 16 is rarely more than a few kilometers from the river between Houston and Burns Lake.

Facilities

The Bulkley flows through Smithers, where you will find all services, plenty of hotels and a number of campgrounds to stay at. The river also flows through a number of other towns, including Houston. For those who prefer, there are a number of full service fishing lodges along the river as well as a number of local guiding services.

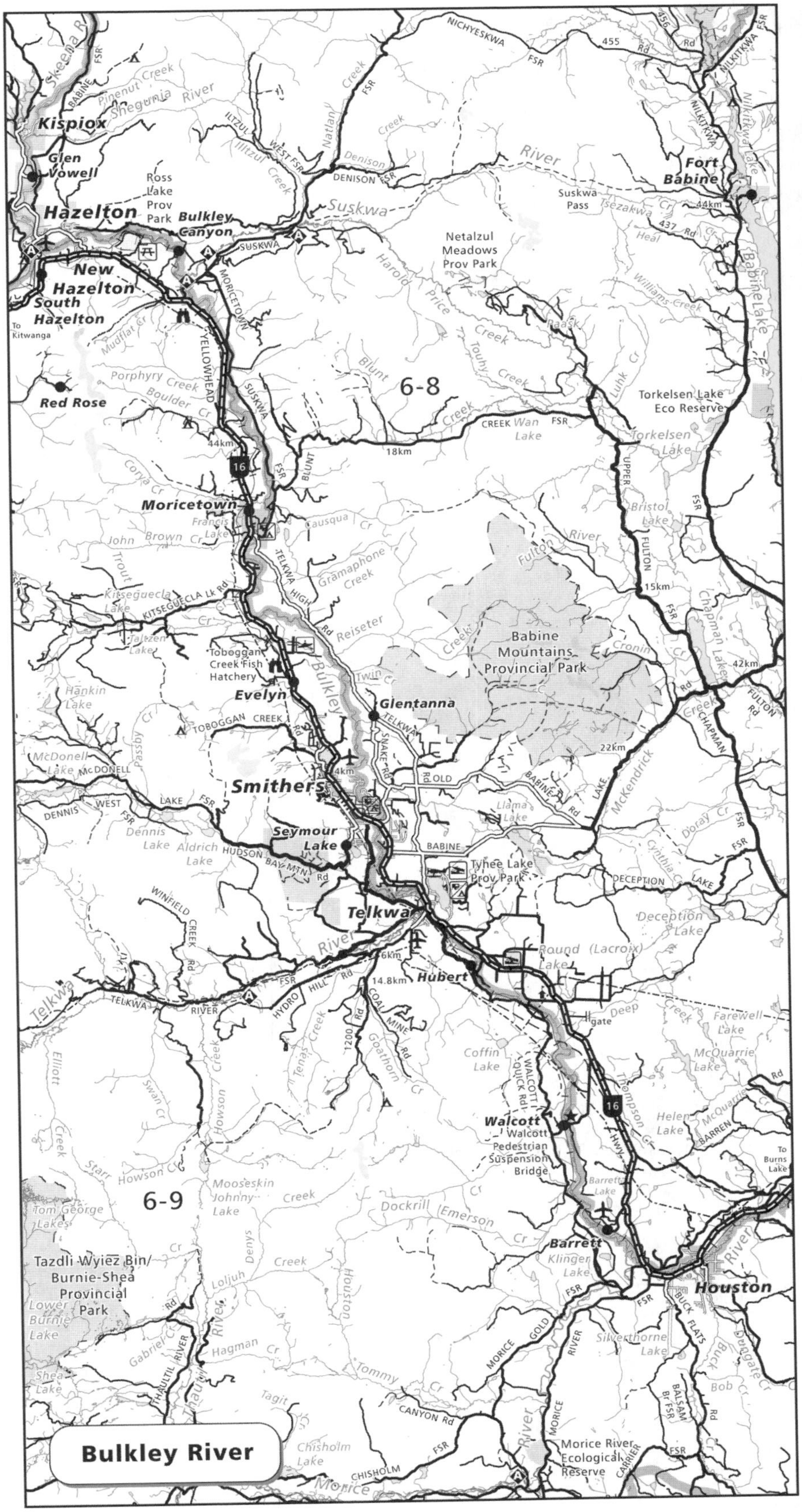

Bulkley River

Location: 35 km (21.7 mi) northeast of 100 Mile House
Elevation: 768 m (2,519 ft)
Surface Area: 5,611 ha (13,866 ac)
Maximum Depth: 209 m (684 ft)
Mean Depth: 85.4 m (280 ft)
Waypoint: 51° 51′ 54″ N, 120° 44′ 39″ W

Canim Lake

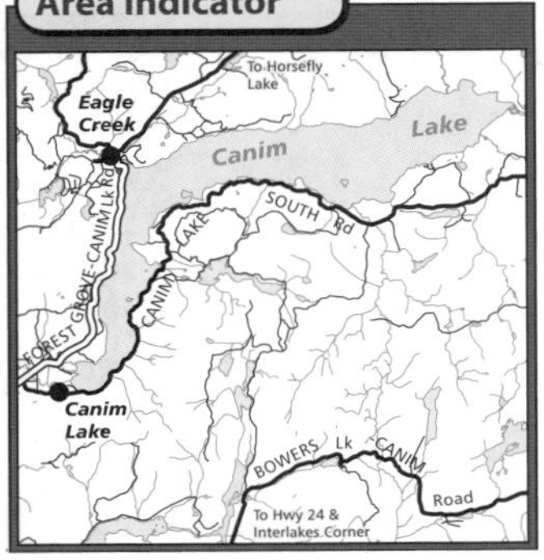

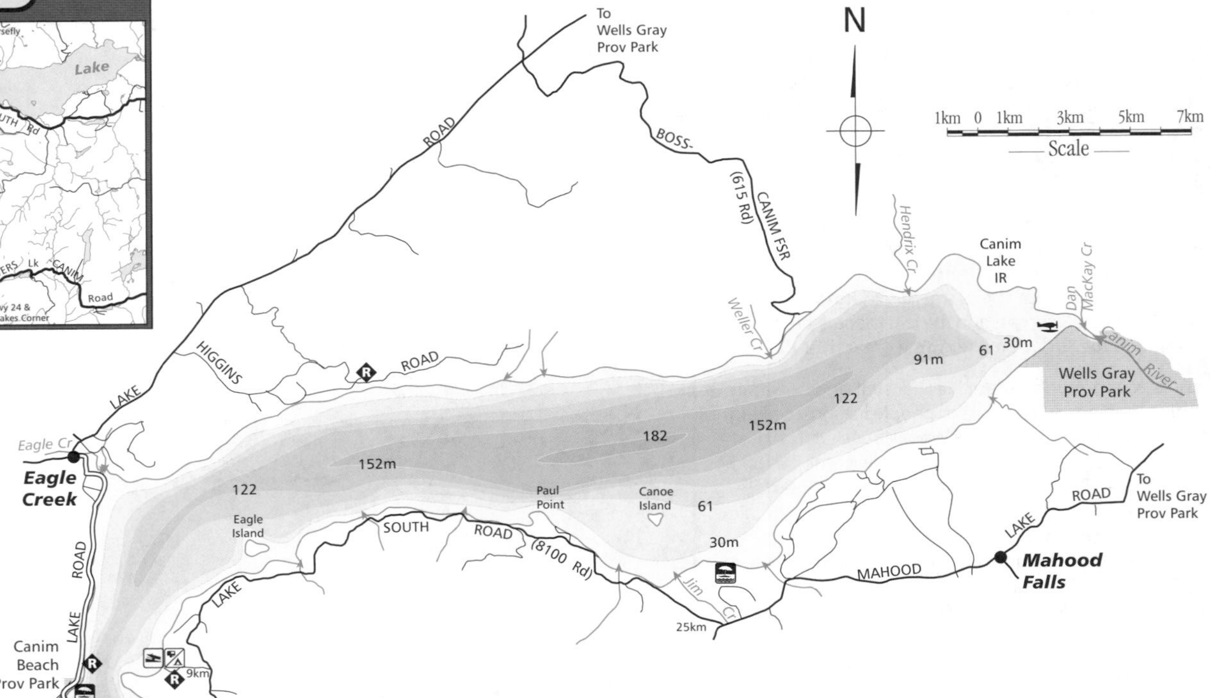

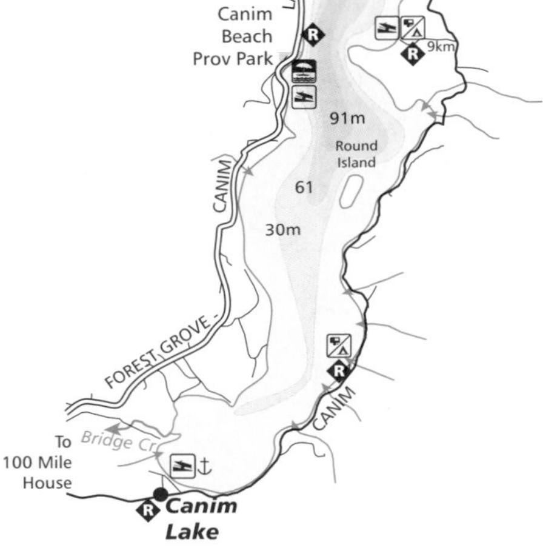

Fishing

Set in the rolling forests of the Cariboo, Canim Lake offers some great fishing. There is plenty of wildlife in the area around the lake and spotting eagles, moose, deer or bear is a common occurrence. The lake, found north of 100 Mile House, holds rainbow trout, lake trout, burbot, kokanee and whitefish.

Of those, the most popular species is the rainbow trout, followed by lake trout and kokanee. Kokanee and rainbow trout have both been stocked in the lake in the past, but both species have established a self-sustaining population here.

The fishing starts at ice out, which occurs around the first of May. The rainbow trout cruise into the shallows looking for insects and other aquatic life attracted to the first warm rays of the sun. Early spring offers a great opportunity to sight cast for these cruising fish.

As the lake warms, the spring insect hatches begin. While the rainbow trout aren't as willing to risk moving into shallow waters, the quality of the fishing increases. The first hatch of the season are chironomids, which last most of the season and can be a good pattern for fly anglers to try when nothing else seems to be working.

Chironomids are followed by mayflies. These insects can offer some good topwater fishing, although mayfly nymph patterns seem to do better earlier in the hatch. Mayflies are closely followed by caddis flies, then dragon and damselflies.

In fall, the best pattern is a water boatman or a small water beetle. Leeches are present in the lake year round, as are dragon and damselfly nymphs.

Gear anglers can catch the rainbow using a variety of small spinners and spoons, or by trolling a Willow Leaf and Wedding Band.

The lake is also home to some very large lake trout. Lake trout are best caught on big plugs and spoons and can get to 15 kg (30 lbs). While the lake is not regulated as catch and release for lake trout, it is best to release most, if not all, the lake trout you catch. These are big, but slow growing fish and the more people who retain their catches means the fewer big lake trout that will be caught.

Lake trout are usually found in the deepest parts of the lake and are best taken on a leadcore line troll or with the use of a downrigger. Some people jig a big spoon, but not many.

People on the lake in small boats should always keep an eye on the weather, as the wind can pick up on the 37 km (23 mile) lake, creating dangerous conditions.

Directions

Head north on Highway 97 from 100 Mile House. As you make your way up the hill, you will reach a stop light well outside of town. This is the Forest Grove–Canim Lake Road. Turn right and follow the road to Canim Lake. There are resort signs directing the way.

Facilities

There is a boat launch at **Canim Beach Provincial Park**, but no overnight camping. However, there are a number of resorts on Canim Lake, which offer cabins, camping and boat launch facilities. **Canim Lake Resort** and **Ponderosa Resort** are two alternatives.

Cariboo Lake

Location: 20 km (12.5 mi) northeast of Likely
Elevation: 813 m (2,667 ft)
Surface Area: 1,109 ha (2,740 ac)
Mean Depth: 18 m (59 ft)
Max Depth: 46 m (151 ft)
Way Point: 52° 46′ 30″ N, 121° 20′ 50″ W

Fishing

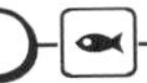

Cariboo Lake is a large, sprawling lake that has a wide variety of fish species including kokanee, lake trout, mountain whitefish, bull trout and Dolly Varden, burbot and rainbow trout. The rainbow average about 0.75 kg (1.5 lbs), the lake char grow to 5.5 kg (12 lbs) and the dollies can grow to 2.5 kg (5 lbs). There are also Chinook and Coho salmon that enter the lake in the fall. If that is not enough, there are even course fish such as sculpin, which is a rarity for lakes in this region, as well as redside shiners and chub.

In another life the lake would be considered two separate lakes, as near the south end, the long, narrow lake is nearly cut in half by a large peninsula jutting out into the lake. As it is, this creates a narrow, shallow channel. There are steep drop offs on both sides of this channel and some of the best fishing happens here.

Cariboo Lake is a deep trolling lake with most of the fishermen trolling off the drop off in the early summer or early fall. The lake is not well suited for spincasters or fly fishermen. If you want to try some casting then work the inflow and outflow areas of the lake, especially during the salmon spawn in the fall. At this time, eggs wash down the creeks and back into the lake and the fish congregate around these areas to feed..

Rainbow trout are best caught on a Wedding Band, usually trolled behind a Willow Leaf or Ford Fender. This is also the most common way to catch kokanee. The big difference is kokanee are suckers for anything that is coloured pink. They are also usually best fished with a rubber snubber attached to the line to protect the fish's soft mouth.

The lake trout can be caught using a T50 Flatfish or a large spoon. Dark colours and silvers and blues seem to work best. No matter how you fish for lake trout, it is best to fish them with a single barbless hook, which makes them easier to catch and release. Lake trout are slow growing and it takes them many years to get to a good size. Lake trout are becoming more popular with anglers and as a result are prone to being over fished.

Directions

Cariboo Lake is situated north of Quesnel Lake and northeast of Likely. From Likely, a gravel road continues a short distance east along the shores of Quesnel Lake and then head north on the Keithley Creek Road for about 24 km. That road will bring you to the small community of Keithley Creek found on the western shores of Cariboo Lake.

If you wish to reach the southern shoreline, simply take the Cariboo Lake Road to the right just before you reach Keithley Creek.

Facilities

The **Cariboo River Provincial Park** encompasses the northeast end of the lake along with the headwaters of the Cariboo River all the way to Kimball Lake. There are no developed facilities in the park. The **Ladies Creek Recreation Site** is found on the southeastern side of the lake and offers half a dozen camping pads together with a pebble beach and an opportunity to launch a small boat.

Area Indicator

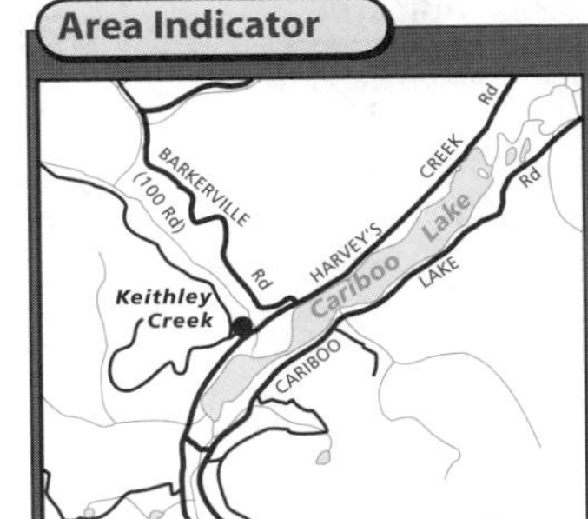

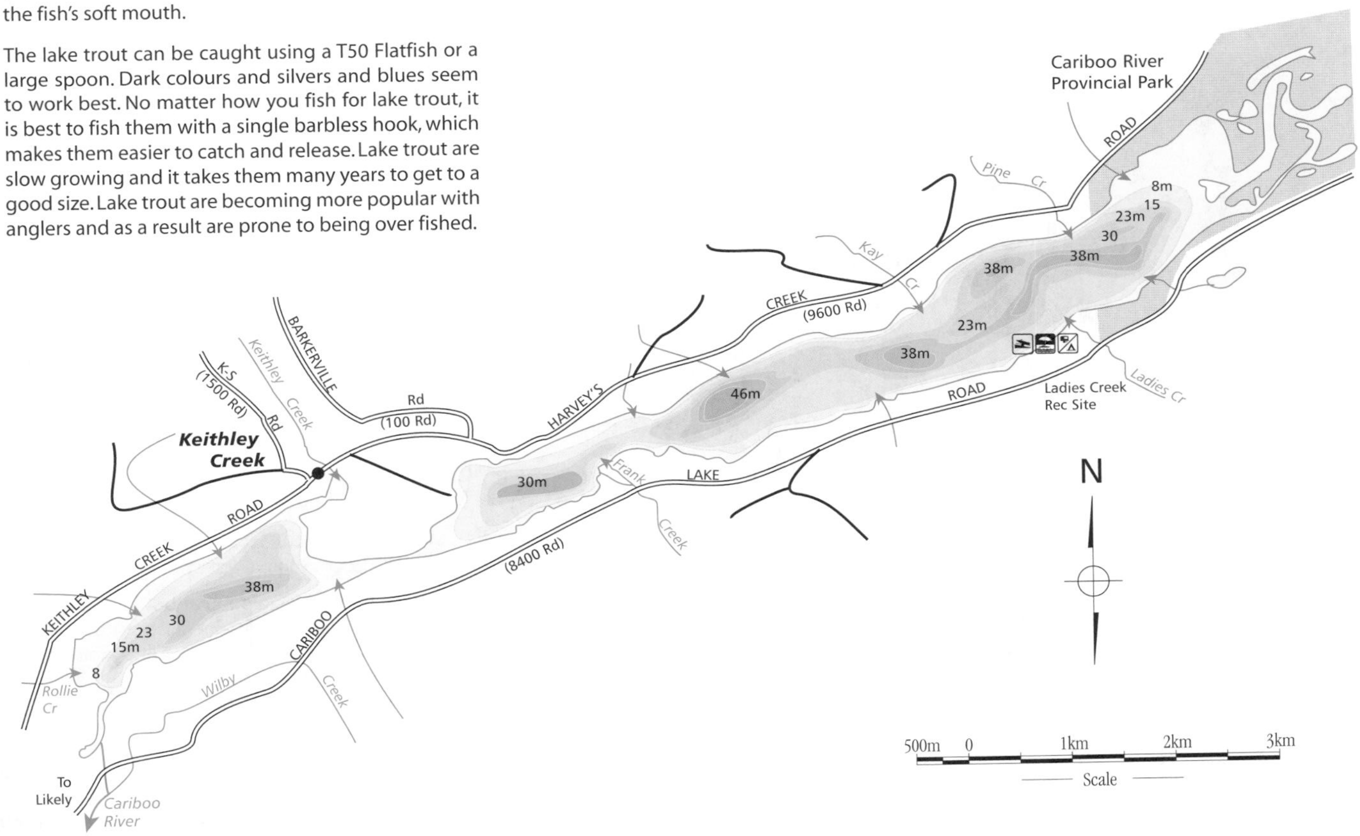

Location: 100 km (62 mi) northwest of Prince George
Elevation: 848 m (2,782 ft)
Surface Area: 5,676 ha (14,025 ac)
Maximum Depth: 2 782m (9,127 ft)
Mean Depth: 17 m (54 ft)
Way Point: 54° 45′ 59″ N, 123° 20′ 7″ W

Carp Lake

Area Indicator

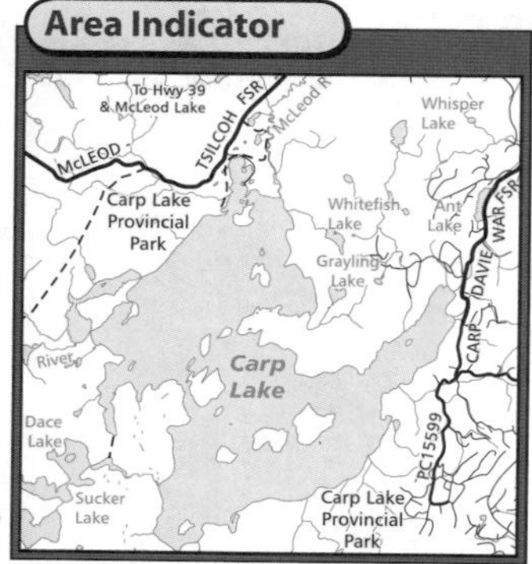

Fishing

Carp Lake is considered one of the best fishing lakes in the Central Interior. It was first noted for its prime fishing potential nearly two centuries ago, by explorer Simon Fraser and these days anglers come from near and far to try their luck with a fly or spinner for the lake's succulent rainbow trout.

The weather here is typical of the northern interior of BC. Summers are short and relatively cool. As a result, fishing here is still a viable activity in July and August. Of course, the fishing is best in spring and again in fall for trout that average 34 cm (14 in). The trout are not huge, but there are plenty of them, making this a great place to bring the kids. However every once in a while, someone will pull a trout out of here to 3 kg (6 lbs).

Unlike many of the other popular fishing lakes in the north, Carp Lake is not stocked and depends solely on natural reproduction. As a result, catch and release is encouraged.

The southern shore of the lake is forested, but has smooth boulder beaches with sandy deltas. The northern shoreline has sandy beaches with belts of sand extending up to 300 metres (1,000 ft) offshore.

The lake is not huge, but it is not small either and is best fished from a small boat or pontoon boat. While belly boats might work close to shore and in the still of a morning or evening, the wind can pick up, which plays merry havoc with light craft. The lake is large enough to troll and for the most part, that's how people fish the lake.

The most common gear is a lake or gang troll, which combines a Willow Leaf, small spinner and worm. Fly anglers can drag around a variety of attractor patterns like Woolly Buggers or Carey Specials.

There other notable sport fish here is burbot. Also known as ling cod, these creatures hang close to the bottom and are usually caught by accident or during winter through the ice. Burbot love the cold water and are not as affected by the lower oxygen levels as rainbow.

Directions

From Prince George head north on Highway 97 for approximately 145 km to McLeod Lake. Watch for the signed turnoff to Carp Lake heading left (west). Following the Carp-Tsilcoh Forest Road for about 28 km will bring you to Carp Lake Provincial Park and the launch site. The road into the park can be rough, but passable by 2wd vehicles except in wet weather.

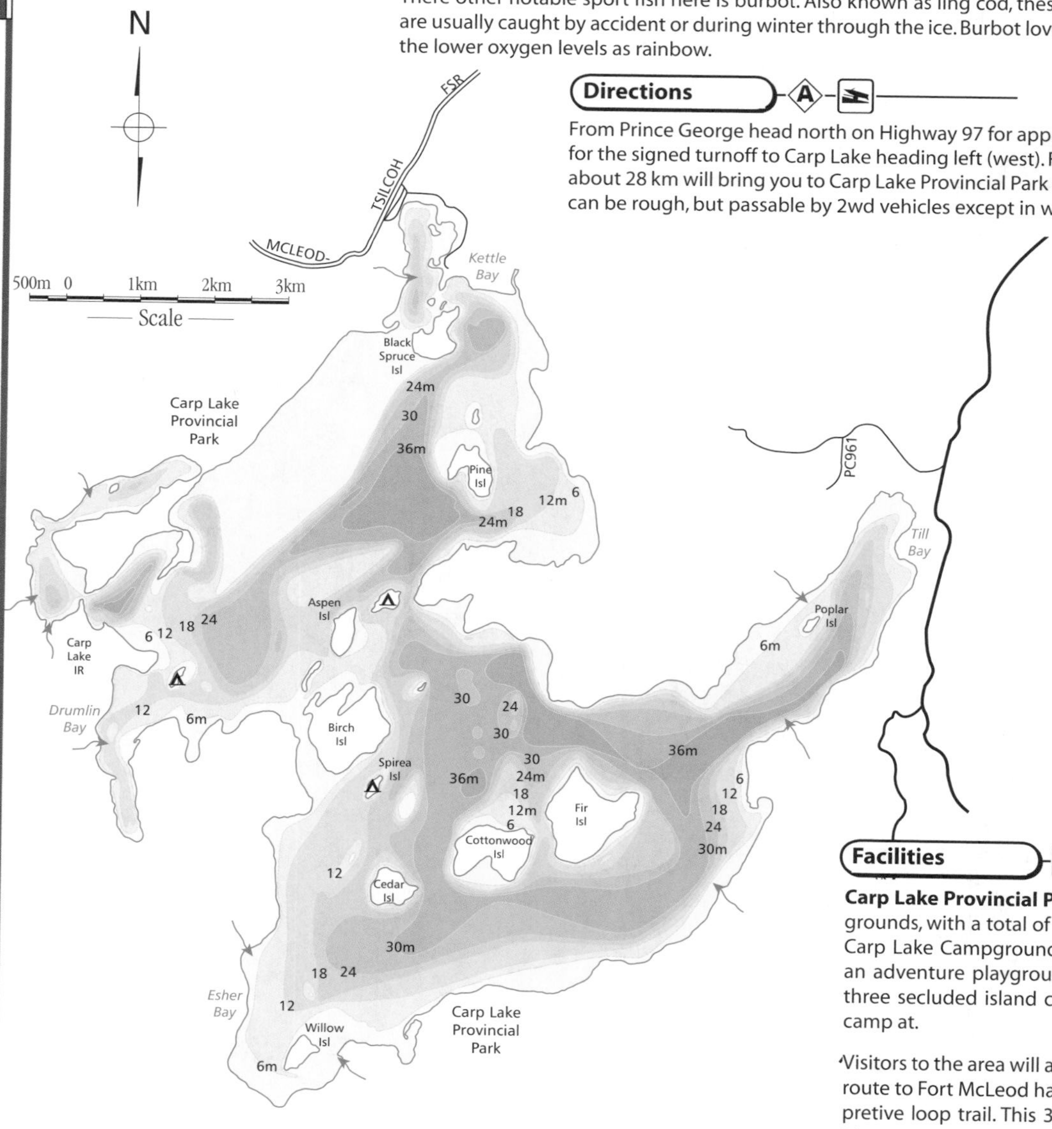

Facilities

Carp Lake Provincial Park has two popular, but rarely full campgrounds, with a total of 102 fully maintained campsites. The main Carp Lake Campground has a picnic shelter, horseshoe pits and an adventure playground to keep the kids busy. There are also three secluded island campsites that boaters and canoeists can camp at.

Visitors to the area will also find portions of the original aboriginal route to Fort McLeod have been developed into an exciting interpretive loop trail. This 3 km hike provides access to the McLeod River, a popular fly-fishing river.

Chapman Lake

Location: 36 km (22.3 mi) east of Smithers
Elevation: 787 m (2,581 ft)
Surface Area: 668 ha (1,650 ac)
Maximum Depth: 32.6 m (106.3 ft)
Mean Depth: 13 m (42.7 ft)
Waypoint: 54° 55' 39" N, 126° 40' 14" W

Fishing

Chapman Lake is a medium sized lake, though dwarfed by nearby Babine Lake. The lake is found northeast of Smithers and features good fishing for rainbow and cutthroat trout and lake trout. It also holds lake whitefish and burbot, though these are rarely fished for.

Cutthroat trout are much more aggressive feeders than rainbow trout and are piscivorous, meaning they eat smaller fish. Fly anglers should work gold or silver bodied Muddler Minnows or some other streamer pattern on a sinking line with a short leader.

Spincasting Kitimat lures, Panther Martin spinners or trolling Willow Leafs/Ford Fenders can also be effective, especially when tipped with a worm. For kids a worm and bobber can often do the trick using light test and a small hook. Cast around the drop off areas as the cutthroat tend to cruise near shore areas in search of baitfish. During cooler weather, fly anglers will need to use searching patterns such as black broadhead leeches or Woolly Buggers.

Rainbow trout, on the other hand, are much more willing to feed on insects and invertebrates and are much more willing to fall for a nymph or leech pattern. Which is not to say that cutthroat don't eat these foods (cutthroat eat anything) or that rainbow don't eat small fish. They do, especially the larger trout. However, rainbow are usually taken on the troll, similar to how you would catch a cutthroat.

The lake trout are usually caught on a deep-water troll, using a downrigger to get the gear right down to the bottom of the lake where these big fish usually hang out. They can be frustratingly hard to catch, but are the biggest fish you will find in the lake.

Both burbot and lake trout are easier to catch in the winter, but the lake is closed from December 1 to April 30. In the winter lake trout usually come up to the shallows to feed and for the first few weeks after ice off can still be found in shallower water, before the surface temperature warms up and drives them to the deep. You may have good luck fishing for lake trout just after the lake opens in spring. The lake trout can get up to 4 kg (8 lbs) here. Burbot can sometimes be taken by deep trolling a smelly bait, like chicken liver near the very bottom of the lake.

Facilities

On the southwest side of the lake is the medium sized **Chapman Lake Recreation Site**. The open, grassy site is big enough for RVs and is found just a short ways from the Babine Lake Road intersection. It is possible to hand launch a boat here. There is also a small resort that offers a trio of cabins for rent at the lake. Contact **Aspen Bay Cabins** for more information.

Directions

Just southeast of Smithers, watch for signs to Babine Lake and Tukii Lodge. This is the Babine Lake Road/ Eckman Road/Smithers Landing Road, depending on where you are on the road. At km 37, the Upper Fulton Forest Service Road (3000 Rd) crosses the road. Turn left (north) here, which brings you to the Chapman Lake Recreation Site.

Area Indicator

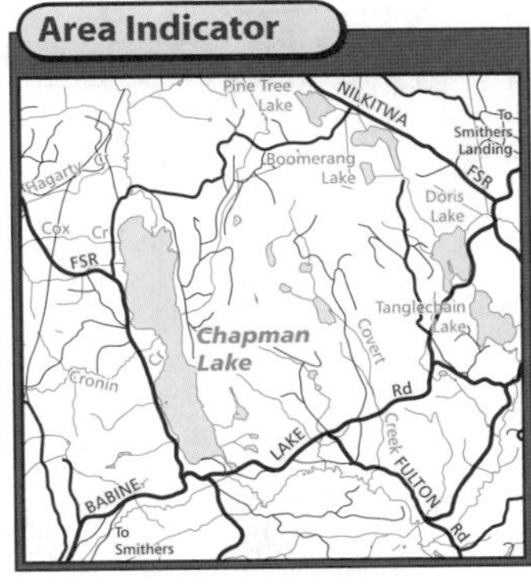

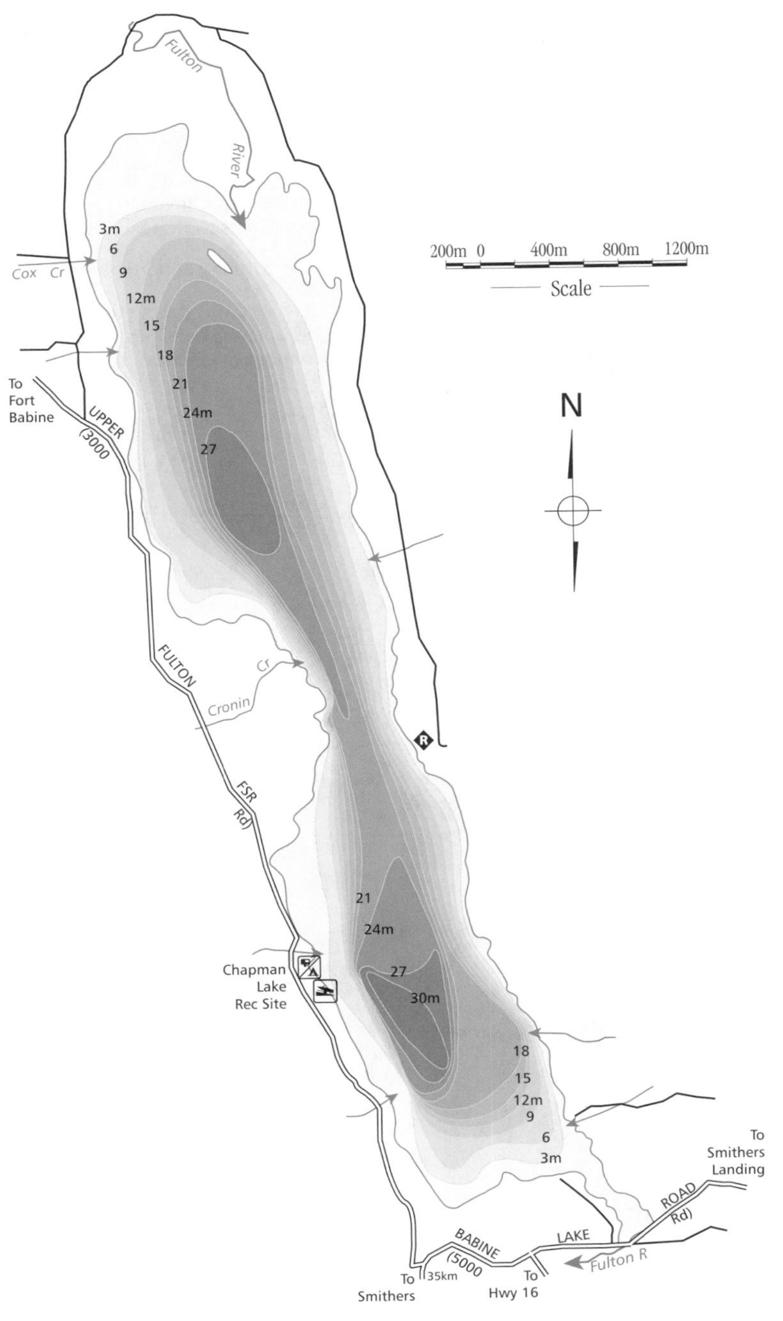

Location: 11 km (6.8 mi) north of Fort St. John
Elevation: 694 m (2,276 ft)
Surface Area: 1,787 ha (4,415 ac)
Maximum Depth: 15 m (49 ft)
Mean Depth: 6.4 m (20 ft)
Way Point: 56° 20′ 0″ N, 120° 59′ 16″ W

Charlie Lake

Area Indicator

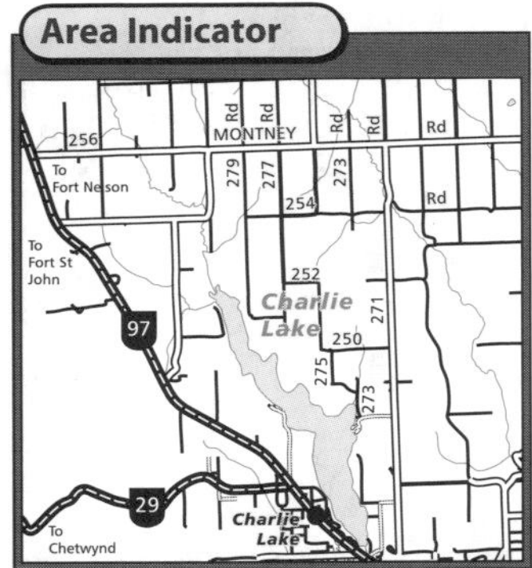

Fishing

Charlie Lake is the most popular lake in the Fort St. John area. Anglers flock here, yes, but so do swimmers, campers, boaters and other recreators. The lake has been popular for many years. In fact, archeologists have found signs of human activity dating back 11,000 years in this area, one of the oldest recorded signs of human activity in North America.

The lake holds the traditional warm water species including northern pike, burbot, walleye and perch. In the 30s and 40s, rainbow trout were stocked here. While there have been a few rumours of people still catching rainbow here, this is not a trout destination. There are rumours of past attempts at stocking the lake with largemouth bass, which proved futile.

If you're a walleye angler, there's no better place in the province to fish than Charlie Lake. The catch rates are high and sizes ranges from 30–45 cm (12–18 in). There are three basic techniques to fish for walleye. One option is a rubber jig baited with a night crawler. These are cast and retrieved near the bottom or fished vertically over the side of the boat. Jigs are the most productive way to fish when water temperatures are colder because walleye are sluggish and you can fish jigs slowly. When the water warms and walleye become more active, use a spinner and crawler harness (a coloured spinner blade tipped with bait) tied behind a bottom-bounce sinker. Another preferred method is to use crankbaits (plastic or wood minnow-shaped lures) by either casting and retrieving them, or trolling. Walleye cruise in shallow water to feed during low light periods, so in the evening and in the early morning try fishing around shore.

Northern pike prefer shallow, weedy bays and shoals in spring and early summer. There are plenty of pike here that average 40–60 cm (16–24 in), but some can get up to 100 cm (40 in) and get up to 9 kg (20 lbs). They are aggressive feeders and will chase almost anything that moves and people have had success trolling or spincasting using spoons, plugs, spinners, crankbaits, topwater lures, spinnerbaits and buzz baits.

There is limited shore fishing opportunities, but kids can still have a good day fishing off the shore for perch.

Charlie Lake also offers a very productive ice fishery for all species. There are a number of popular ice fishing spots within walking distance of shoreline access points. During the winter months a variety of lures work well including jigs topped with worms or maggots.

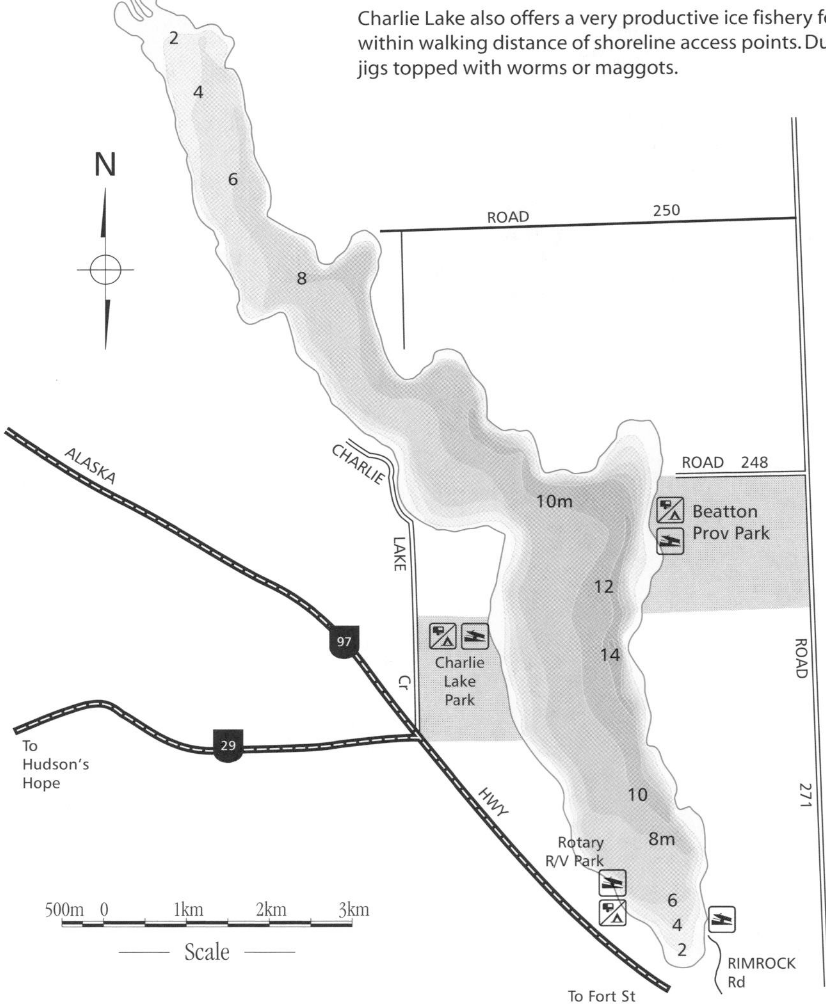

Directions

Charlie Lake is found 11 km north of Fort St. John at the junction of the Alaska Highway and Highway 29. Charlie Lake Provincial Park is found just off the highway, while Beatton is on the eastern side of the park, off the 244 Road.

Facilities

Charlie Lake and **Beatton Provincial Parks** are both open year round and have boat launches, camping facilities and a variety of other amenities. Of the two, Beatton is the prettier, as it is located across the lake from the highway. Alternatively, there is camping and a boat launch at the **Rotary RV Park**. A fourth boat launch is found on the west shore, across from the Mile 54 turn-off.

Charlie Lake
Fish Stocking Data

Year	Species	Number	Life Stage
2008	Brook Trout	20,000	Fingerling
2008	Rainbow Trout	12,000	Yearling
2007	Brook Trout	20,000	Fingerling
2007	Rainbow Trout	10,000	Yearling
2006	Brook Trout	20,000	Yearling
2006	Rainbow Trout	10,000	Yearling

Charlotte Lake

Location: 300 km (180 mi) west of Williams Lake
Elevation: 1,174 m (3,852 ft)
Surface Area: 6,596 ha (16,300 ac)
Maximum Depth: 101 m (331 ft)
Mean Depth: 40.6 m (133 ft)
Way Point: 52° 11′ 53″ N, 125° 19′ 18″ W

Fishing

Charlotte Lake is found at the westernmost edge of the Chilcotin Plateau, tucked up against the Charlotte Alplands Protected Area and the towering Coast Mountains. The lake is crystal clear and offers excellent fishing for rainbow trout. Water from the lake drains west, via the Atnarko River through some of the most remote terrain Tweedsmuir Park has to offer.

The shoreline of the lake features numerous sand and gravel beaches, which are bounded by a thick pine forest. The glacial run-off keeps the water cold and clean, perfect for the rainbow trout.

The big lake–the biggest in the area–is reasonably remote and difficult to get to, especially in wet weather. As a result, the lake sees little pressure and offers some great fishing for trophy sized rainbow trout. The fish in the lake average 1 kg (2 lbs) and every year, there are a few fish caught much bigger than that.

There is one big island and a few smaller islands that dot the lake These islands are magnets for the trout, who hold around the drop offs. There are also many submerged islands hidden beneath the surface as well as plenty of rocky shoals where the rainbow will hold.

The lake is a big lake and as a result is most commonly trolled. Working a lake troll and Wedding Band is the most common method of fishing the lake, but Apex Trout Killers, Kamloopers and Krocodile spoons are often pressed into service. Some people will spincast around the islands and sunken islands using Mepps, Panther Martin, Vibrax and Gibbs spinners. When casting, count to five seconds before retrieving, then to ten, then to 15, until you hit bottom. Once you hit bottom, back off a few seconds. Rainbow are most frequently found near the bottom and retrieving too fast often results in no fish.

Vertical jigging with spoons of jigs and Berkley Powerbait will also work.

Area Indicator

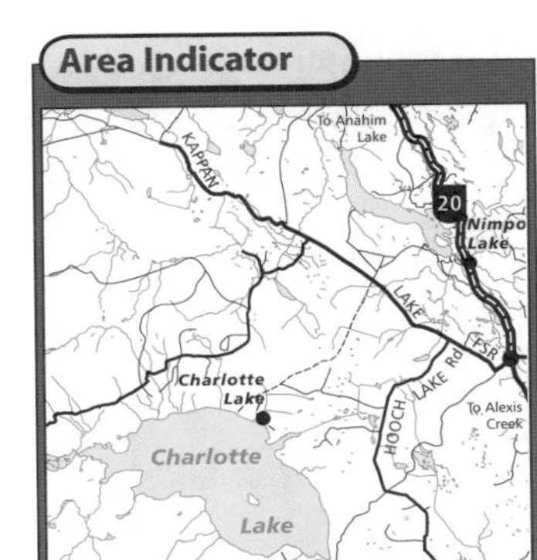

Directions

Charlotte Lake is found south of Highway 20, about 300 km (180 miles) west of Williams Lake. Distance alone is enough to keep most casual anglers out, although the promise of trophy sized rainbow is enough to attract a few hardcore fishers. To get to the lake, turn off Highway 20 about 66 km west of Tatla Lake, before you reach Nimpo Lake. There are signs for the Charlotte Lake Resort pointing the way south along the Charlotte Lake Road. Follow the road for about 18 km (10 miles) to the lake.

Facilities

The **Charlotte Lake Recreation Site** is a small forestry site at the south end of the lake, where campers can stay and launch a boat. Note it is quite shallow here as you can wade out about 100 metres and only be up to your waist. There are also a few resorts on the lake including **Frank and Imee's Cottage on the Lake,** the **Charlotte Lake Resort** and **Atnarko Retreat.**

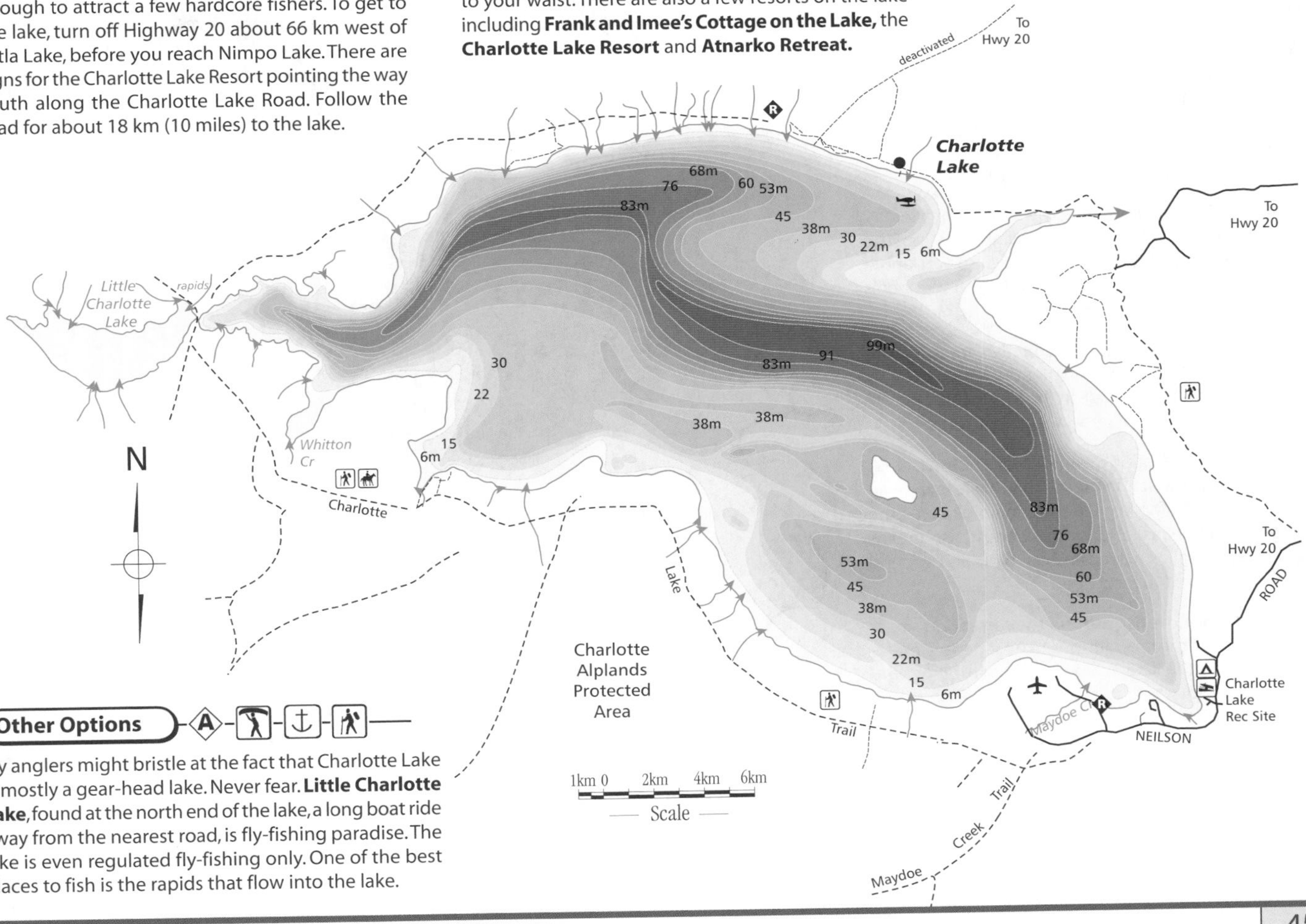

Other Options

Fly anglers might bristle at the fact that Charlotte Lake is mostly a gear-head lake. Never fear. **Little Charlotte Lake**, found at the north end of the lake, a long boat ride away from the nearest road, is fly-fishing paradise. The lake is even regulated fly-fishing only. One of the best places to fish is the rapids that flow into the lake.

Location: 140 km (87 mi) southwest of Williams Lake
Elevation: 1,493 m (4,898 ft)
Surface Area: 460.91 ha (1,138 ac)
Maximum Depth: 51.2 m (168 ft)
Mean Depth: 17.2 m (56 ft)
Way Point: 51° 34′ 18″ N, 123° 53′ 21″ W

Chaunigan Lake

Area Indicator

To Tsuniah Lake
Elkin Lake
Chaunigan Lake
ELKIN -TASEKO FSR
Vedan Lake
Mainguy Lake
To Tasko Lk Rd
NEMAIAH VALLEY Rd

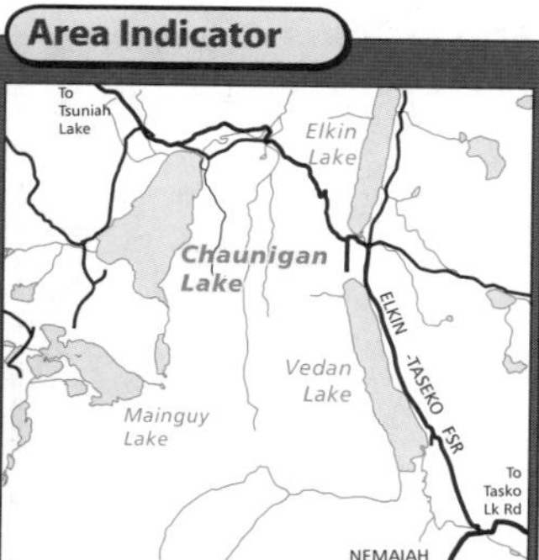

Directions

From Williams Lake, it is about 85 km to the turnoff at Hanceville along Highway 20. Turn south and follow the road signs to Chaunigan Lake Lodge. It is 72 km to the Nemiah Valley Road (mostly along the Taseko Lake Forest Service Road), before the Elkin-Taseko Road branches north. You'll drive between Vedan Lake and Elkin Lake and proceed up the hill to Chaunigan Lake Lodge. This last leg is about 7 km long.

The road to the lake is rough and narrow and while it is not necessary to have a four-wheel drive vehicle when it is nice, it is not the sort of place you'd want to bring a car. Trailers are probably not the best idea, as there isn't much room to turn around. Most people who bring a trailer stay at Vedan Lake, at the bottom of the hill and then drive up to fish Chaunigan.

Facilities

Chaunigan Lake Lodge is a first class resort on the north end of the lake where you can rent a cabin, stay at the lodge or launch your boat. Also in the area is the **Chaunigan Lake Recreation Site**. The site has space for about six groups and a place where you can launch a small boat.

Fishing

Chaunigan Lake is a beautiful lake set in the transition between the low, rolling hills of the Chilcotin Plateau and the high mountains of the Coast Mountains. The views from the lake are spectacular, with towering mountains rising in the south and west.

The lake is a high mountain lake and is subject to the weather that entails. The south end of the lake is much more sheltered and while there can be whitecaps and dangerous waves at the north end, the fishing can be good at the south.

The lake holds good numbers of rainbow trout that average around 1 kg (2 lbs), but can get up to 3 kg (6 lbs). Most people who fish the lake troll the lake, dragging around a Doc Spratley or Carey Special, or your typical gadget bag of gear: Wedding Bands with or without a worm, Flatfish and small spoons and spinners.

However, while trolling is usually the order of the day, people can have good luck stopping and casting. The lake holds plenty of gammarus shrimp, so working a scud pattern slowly across the drop offs, over the shoals and near the weeds can work too.

The lake has plenty of highly productive areas, including rather large shoal areas and plenty of weed growth. Other patterns that work well on the lake include Pheasant Tail Nymphs, Hare's Ears and leech patterns.

While the higher elevation means the lake doesn't ice off until later in the year, it also means that, while low elevation lakes are suffering from the summer doldrums, the fishing can still be fast and furious here. It also means the fish don't usually go deep and can typically be found less than 5 metres (16 feet) deep.

It is possible to shore fish around the recreation site at the north end of the lake, although most people prefer to get out onto the lake in a boat. A float tube or pontoon boat will work, as long as you stick to the north end of the lake and be well aware of the weather.

However, the best fishing happens around the weedbeds and the outflow at the south end of the lake.

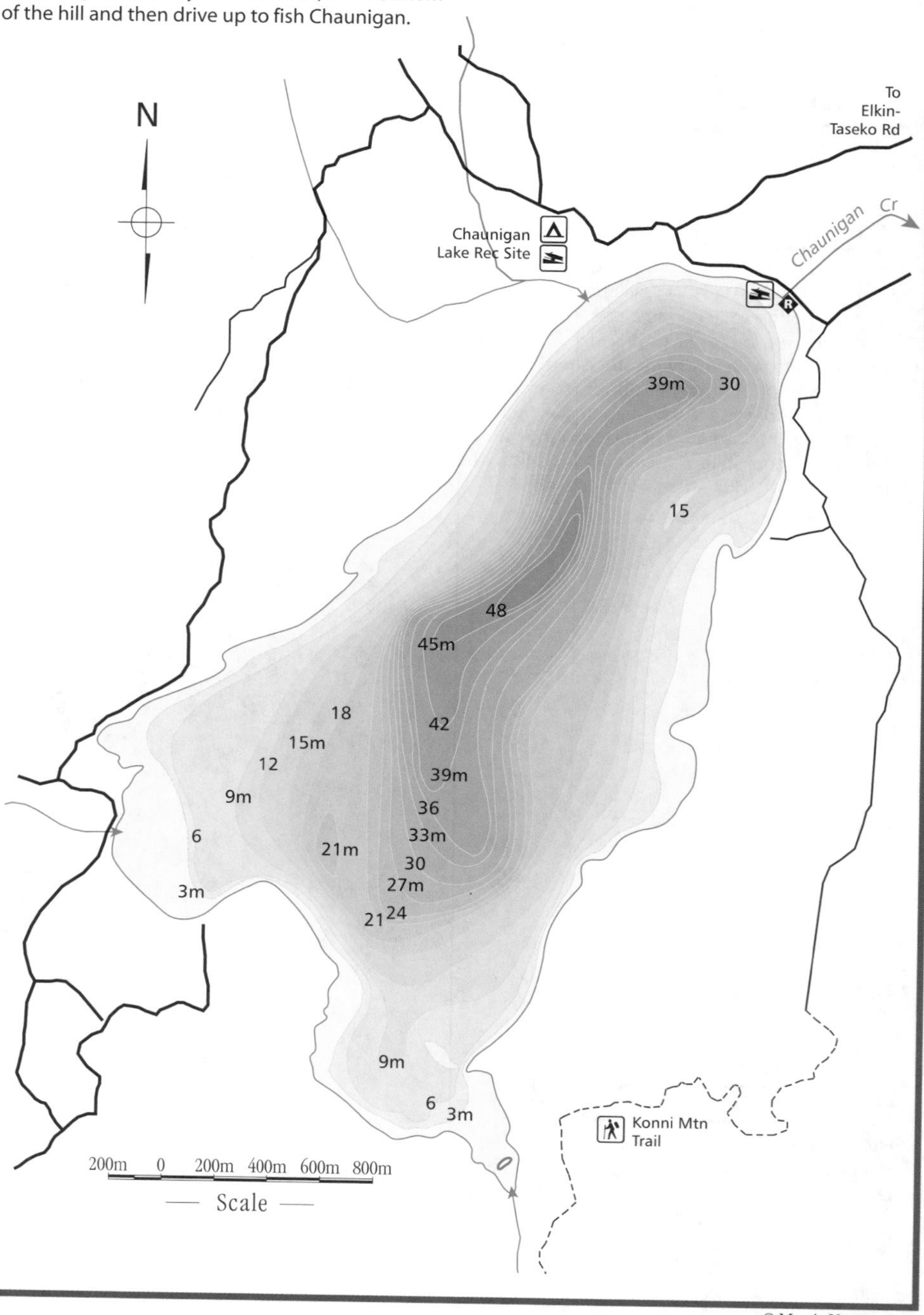

N
To Elkin-Taseko Rd
Chaunigan Lake Rec Site
Chaunigan Cr
39m
30
15
48
45m
18
42
15m
12
39m
9m
36
6
33m
21m
30
27m
3m
21
24
9m
6
3m
Konni Mtn Trail
200m 0 200m 400m 600m 800m
Scale

Chief Gray Lake

Location: 69 km (42.8 mi) southwest of Vanderhoof
Elevation: 926 m (3,037 ft)
Surface Area: 27 ha (66 ac)
Maximum Depth: 15 m (51 ft)
Mean Depth: 8.2 m (27 ft)
Way Point: 53° 35′ 26.0″ N, 124° 46′ 20.5″ W

Fishing

Chief Gray Lake has a reputation of offering trophy fish in a picture perfect setting. It earned its nickname "Bitch Lake" for being one of the more difficult lakes in the area to get to.

The fishing here is similar to nearby Hobson Lake in that it produces large rainbow. Trout up to 5 kg (11 lbs) are not uncommon, while the average range is still a good sized 2 kg (4 lbs). The lake is stocked with all-female triploid rainbow trout that are known to grow big.

Most anglers use float tubes or pontoon boats, although there are a few locations to fish from shore. Whether cast or trolled, the majority of Chief Gray's fishers are fly-rod enthusiasts.

The chironomid hatch usually begins in May and can remain profuse through June. Trout eagerly feed on these tiny pupas as they rise to the surface of the lake. June brings mayfly hatches followed by the caddisfly (sedge) hatch in late June or early July. May through early July produces a wealth of opportunities for nymph and dry-fly-fishing on Chief Gray. When you see evidence of an insect hatch, use a dry fly that imitates the insect as closely as possible. The best time is usually on calm evenings during a hatch. While young rainbow will come to the surface earlier, the bigger, trophy trout tend to wait until the sun is no longer shining on the lake. Tom Thumbs and Adams are common dry fly choices. When nymph fishing, use fly patterns that imitate the juvenile, underwater stages of these same insects.

In non-hatch periods, shrimp and leeches are perennial favourites. Other excellent flies are big dragon and damselfly nymphs, Muddler Minnows and dark streamer patterns on a full-sink line, including the eye raising named "Prostitute", available at nearby Finger Lake Resort. Remember, big fish need to eat more and eating bigger insects or small fish takes less time and energy.

The big rainbow of this lake can also be caught on spinning tackle and trolling such lures as silver or gold Flatfish, brass or silver Dick Nites and Panther Martins. Try trolling these lures in water between 4–6 meters (13–20 feet) deep as that is where a lot of natural food items are found.

Chief Gray is a catch and release lake. Only single barbless hooks are permitted and bait is banned. It is also closed during the winter months.

Facilities

There are no facilities at the lake, but there is a recreation site at Hobson Lake at the start of the hike.

Directions

The lake is found at the end of a 3 km unmaintained trail that starts near Hobson Lake. From Vanderhoof, drive south on the Kenney Dam Road and/or the Kluskus Forest Road. Both roads meet up at either end of the Kluskus-Natalkuz Forest Service or 500 Road. Once on the 500 Road, the unmarked turnoff to Hobson Lake is near the 9 km marker on the north side of the road. The access road is about 3 km (1.8 miles) long and can be difficult to navigate in wet weather. The trailhead is found near the creek on the north side of the lake. In the spring, the trail can be quite muddy, or even snowbound.

Area Indicator

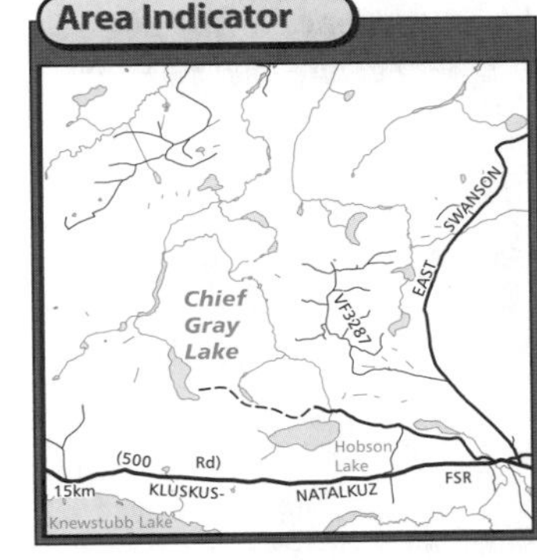

Chief Gray Lake			
Fish Stocking Data			
Year	Species	Number	Life Stage
2007	Rainbow Trout	1,658	Fry
2005	Rainbow Trout	1,700	Fall Fry

10m
12
14m
12
10m
8 6m 4 2m

N

100m 0 100m 200m 300m
Scale

Location: 160 km (100 miles) southwest of Williams Lake
Elevation: 1175 m (3,854 ft)
Surface Area: 16,900 ha (41,760 ac)
Maximum Depth: 366 m (1,200 ft)
Mean Depth: 137 m (449 ft)
Way Point: 51° 21′ 43″ N, 124° 8′ 3″ W

Chilko Lake

Area Indicator

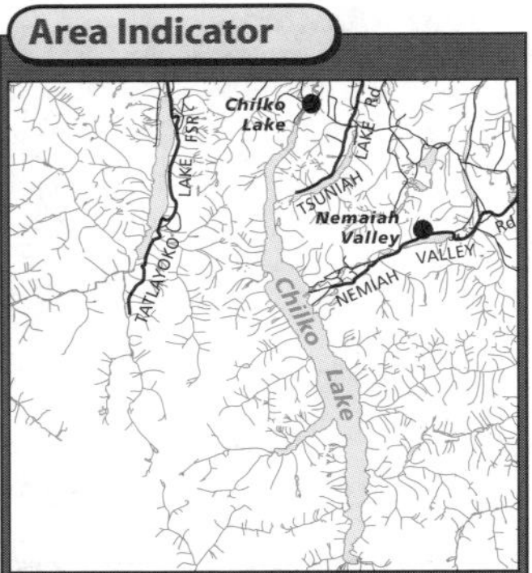

Fishing

Stretching 65 km (40 miles) back into the wild Coast Mountains, Chilko lakes covers 180 km², making it the second-largest lake in the Coast Mountains after Harrison Lake. It is the largest lake in the province above 1,000 metres (3,280 feet) and one of the largest lakes by volume, owing in no small part to the depth of the lake, which is an astonishing 366 metre (1,200 feet).

Because of its sheer size and high elevation, the lake can be unpredictable. Winds can blow down the valley, churning the water to whitecaps in a matter of minutes. Storms and squalls can race through the area. And the shoreline is mostly rocky, often cliff-lined, making finding shelter from the wind difficult.

BC's third largest Chinook and sockeye salmon runs enter the lake from Chilko River in August and continue through to October. The salmon pass through the lake and then into a wide variety of streams, creeks and rivers that flow into the lake.

The salmon spawn in the rivers, but it is a messy process and many of the eggs laid float down the streams and back into the lake, where the lake's resident rainbow trout, bull trout and Dolly Varden wait expectantly for the coming feast.

This is trophy territory, with rainbow trout getting to 10 kg (22 lbs) and dollies getting to 11 kg (24 lbs). These are exceptional catches, to be sure, with the average size catch being closer to 1–2 kg (2¬–4 lbs).

During the fall spawn, the fish will usually go for anything that looks like a salmon egg that is fished around the mouth of a creek or river. Fly casters can work an egg sucking leech or other egg pattern, while spincasters can work single eggs or gooey bobs to attract a strike.

In the spring, the salmon smolts begin working their way down the river and this is the time to work a small minnow pattern, Flatfish, or hook baited with a minnow. The best fishing still happens around the mouth of creeks, but you can find the smolts most anywhere around the edge of the lake, making their way towards the Chilko River and ultimately, the ocean.

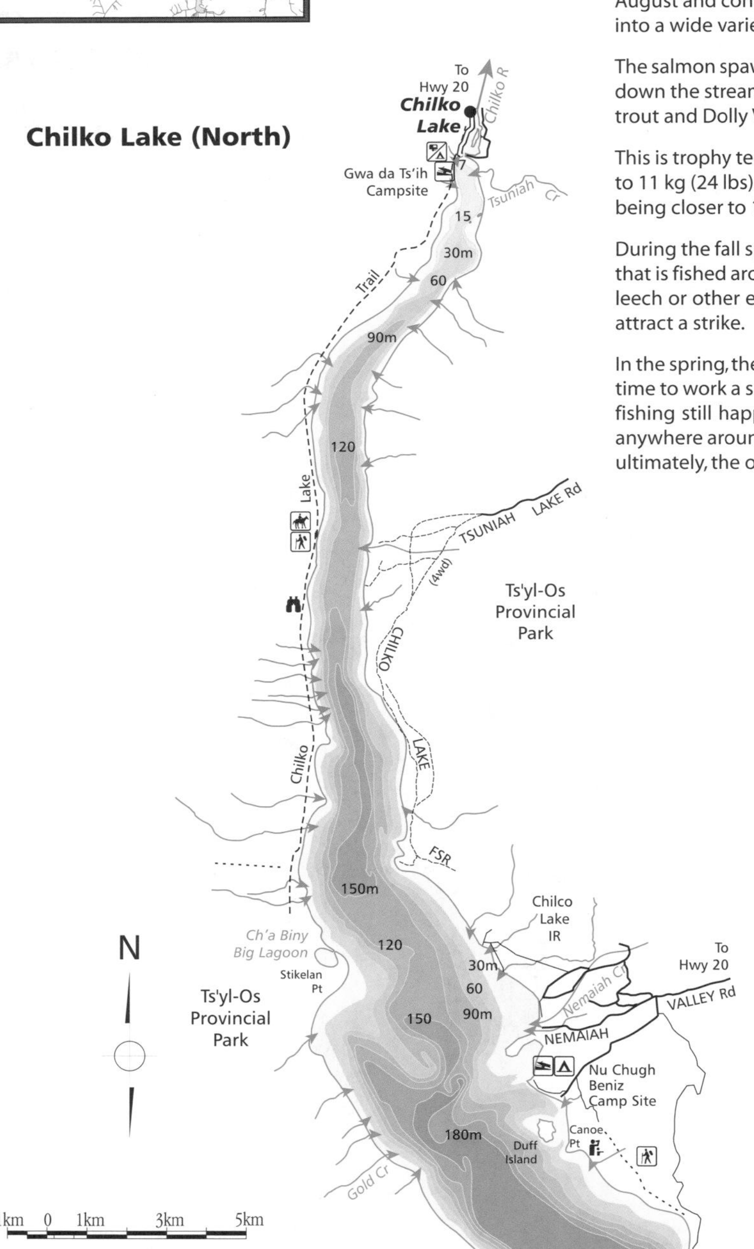

Directions

Chilko Lake is about 160 km (100 miles) southwest of Williams Lake as the crow flies, longer by road. Take Highway 20 past the Bull Canyon Provincial Park and watch for Young Road, which turns into Chilko Newton Forest Service Road. This is one of a number of roads that lead to Chilko Lake. Stay on the main road to the Chilko Airstrip Road and then turn left. This will take you to the old Forest Service campsite at the north end of the lake. The road can be driven in a 2wd vehicle, depending on weather conditions, but a high clearance truck would be better. The roads to the eastern shores of the lake from Hanceville are much rougher.

Facilities

There are two small, rustic campgrounds on the lake: **Gwa Da Ts'ih** at the north end and **Nu Chugh Beniz** at the east end. There is a boat launch at the both campsites, although the one at the north end is much better. Visitors can also stay at **Chilko Lake Lodge** at the north end.

Chilko River

Location: 100 km (62 mi) west of Williams Lake
Stream Length: 89.02 km (55 mi)
Geographic: 52° 06′ 00″ N, 123° 27′ 00″ W

Fishing

The Chilko River flows through the heart of the Chilcotin Plateau. It is a beautiful wild river, offering magnificent scenery and some excellent fishing.

The upper Chilko is one of the best rivers in BC, if not North America, for trophy-sized rainbow trout. They are big, strong, colourful and provide a great fight when caught. In addition to rainbow trout, you will find bull trout, Dolly Varden, whitefish, steelhead, sockeye, Chinook and Coho. The river is closed to salmon fishing for all but Chinook most years. The rainbow and dollies occasionally get up to 4.5 kg (10 lbs).

The upper river is regulated as a catch and release, fly-fishing only stretch of water. There is some great fishing right near the outflow from Chilko Lake. The river cuts though a gap and then fans into a wide bay. Trout are constantly cruising this area looking for food and are quite willing to rise to a dry fly.

The Chilko has great insect hatches, especially stoneflies. Some of these are so big, you will need a #4 hook to imitate them. Golden stoneflies are most common, but there are black, grey and brown hatches as well. There are also plenty of Lime Sally stoneflies. On warm summer evenings, expect lots of caddis hatches, while mayflies are quite prevalent but often ignored in favour of the other hatches. A large Deer Hair Caddis is the most common fly used. Even when there is no hatch, trout will often rise to a well-presented caddis or Lime Sally pattern.

In addition, the river features returns of Chinook and sockeye. The rainbow go wild for salmon eggs during the spawn and for fry during the hatch. Of course, you will have to rely on fly imitations. Fly anglers can use an Egg Sucking Leech during the spawn and a streamer pattern during the hatch. Stonefly nymph patterns also work, but are harder to present properly. Other patterns to try are Woolly Buggers and Shaggy Dragons.

Because the river is so big, it is nearly impossible to wade. And because the forest comes right to the edge of the river, fishing from the banks is difficult. It is best fished from a boat. Guides use jetboats to run the swift river, powering upstream, and then drifting down. Smaller boats with 10 HP engines can usually navigate the upper section down to Canoe Crossing Reach. Below, the river is best left to rafters and jet boaters.

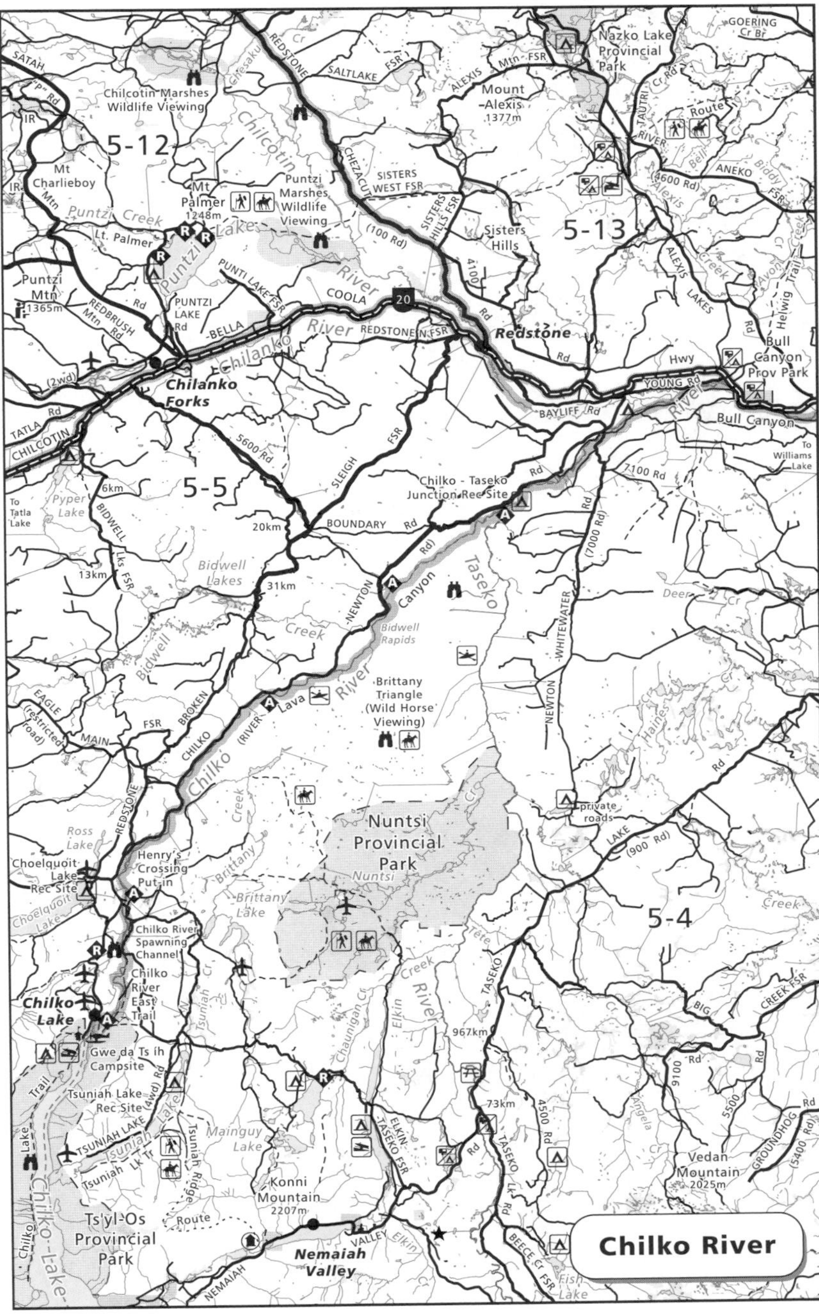

Directions

The Chilko River is accessed from a variety of logging roads. The main road is the Chilko-Newton Forest Service Road, which parallels the river, usually within a few kilometers, up to Chilko Lake. The road is accessed off Young Road, which in turn is off Highway 20, just west of Bull Canyon.

Facilities

There are a couple of campsites scattered along the river, from **Bull Canyon Provincial Park**, near the confluence with the Chilcotin River, up to **Tsy'los Provincial Park**, at the other end. The **Chilko-Taseko Junction Recreation Site** is another camping alternative above the river. There are also a number of lodges offering accommodations and guided trips in the area.

Location: 32 km (20 mi) south of Williams Lake
Elevation: 871 m (2,857 ft)
Max Depth: 19.5 m (64 ft)
Mean Depth: 9 m (29 ft)
Way Point: 51° 54′ 52″ N, 121° 57′ 25″W

Chimney Lake

Area Indicator

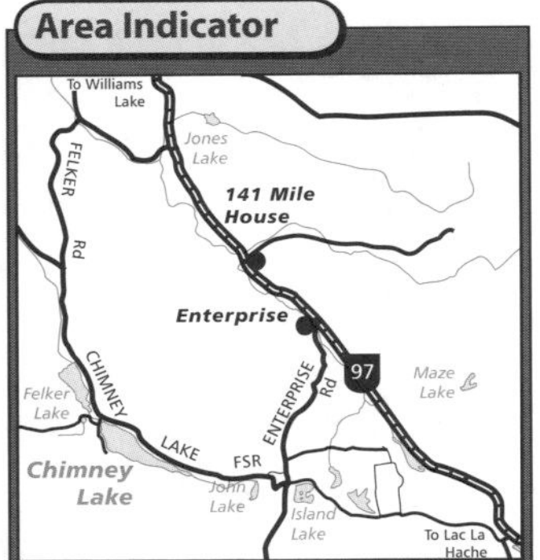

Chimney Lake			
Fish Stocking Data			
Year	Species	Number	Life Stage
2008	Rainbow Trout	50,000	Yearling
2008	Kokanee	60,000	Fry
2007	Rainbow Trout	49,720	Yearling
2006	Rainbow Trout	38,000	Yearling

Fishing

Chimney Lake is found close enough to the city of Williams Lake to be a popular getaway for residents. In the heat of the summer, the lake is much more popular with swimmers and water skiers, but in spring and fall, the fishing here can be great.

The lake is stocked with about 50,000 fish every year. Most of these fish are Blackwater strain in order to help keep the population down on the course fish (suckers, chub and redside shiners) that also inhabit the lake. Blackwaters are piscivorous and because they have plenty of food to dine on, they can grow to be a fair size. They generally fall in the 25–45 cm (10–18 in) category, but it isn't unusual to catch fish bigger than this.

The lake is best fished in the early spring and late fall. One of the most productive methods of fishing the rainbow is to troll a lake troll such as a Ford Fender or Willow Leaf in silver or gold trailing with a Wedding Band and worm. Hotshots in size 70 or F-4 or F-5 Flatfish in green or black are also consistent producers. The most productive area of the lake is between the campsite at the north end of the lake and the island. Also, trolling the northwest end of the lake in the deeper water is a good idea.

In terms of casting, the southeast end of the lake at the edge of the shallows is a good area as is the western shoreline. Shore casters should try at the northwest end where the water drops off rapidly from the shore.

Fly-fishers do well with a black Doc Spratley in sizes 6 to 10 or a black leech trolled on a sinking line. Chironomid fishing is good in the spring and water boatman patterns provoke savage strikes in the fall.

During the heat of summer, when water skiing is more popular than fishing, the trout flee to deeper parts of the lake. At this time, it is best to troll deep or during early dawn or late dusk periods.

Due to the good access, Chimney Lake also offers a good early season ice fishery. As soon as the ice is safe, in December or January, the rainbow can be caught roaming the shallows on shrimp, krill or worms on a hook or jig.

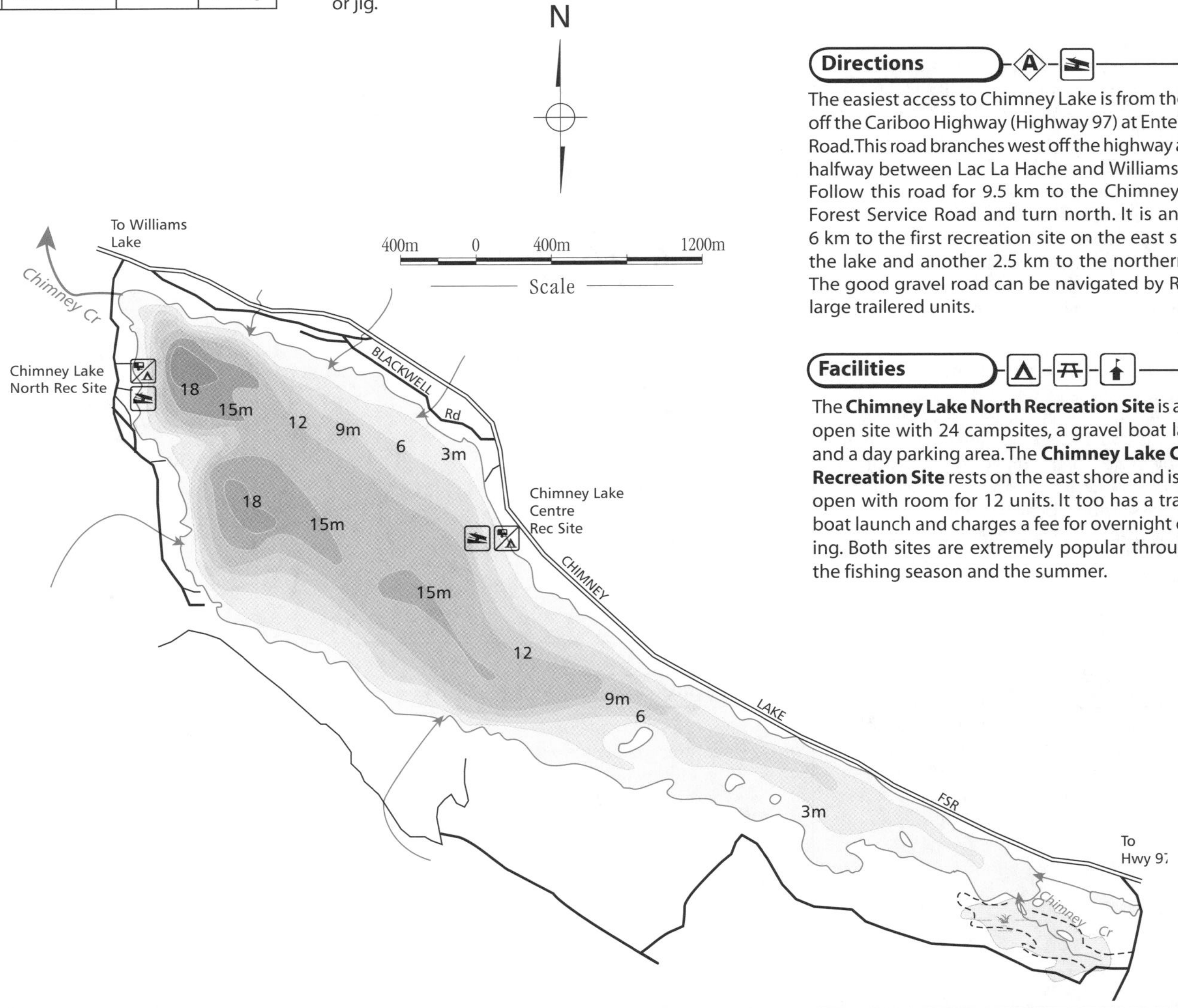

N

To Williams Lake

400m 0 400m 1200m

Scale

Chimney Cr

Chimney Lake North Rec Site

BLACKWELL Rd

18 15m 12 9m 6 3m

18 15m

Chimney Lake Centre Rec Site

CHIMNEY LAKE FSR

15m 12 9m 6 3m

To Hwy 97

Chimney Cr

Directions

The easiest access to Chimney Lake is from the east off the Cariboo Highway (Highway 97) at Enterprise Road. This road branches west off the highway about halfway between Lac La Hache and Williams Lake. Follow this road for 9.5 km to the Chimney Lake Forest Service Road and turn north. It is another 6 km to the first recreation site on the east side of the lake and another 2.5 km to the northern site. The good gravel road can be navigated by RV's or large trailered units.

Facilities

The **Chimney Lake North Recreation Site** is a large, open site with 24 campsites, a gravel boat launch and a day parking area. The **Chimney Lake Centre Recreation Site** rests on the east shore and is semi-open with room for 12 units. It too has a trailered boat launch and charges a fee for overnight camping. Both sites are extremely popular throughout the fishing season and the summer.

Chunamun (Chinaman) Lake

Location: 85 km (53 mi) west of Fort St John
Elevation: 908m (2,978 ft)
Surface Area: 42.7 ha (105 ac)
Maximum Depth: 6m (19.7 ft)
Mean Depth: 2.7m (8.9 ft)
Way Point: 56° 10′ 31.9″ N, 122° 10′ 10.5″ W

Fishing

Chunamun Lake was once known as Chinaman Lake, but the name was recently changed. We mention this just to avoid any confusion if people are thinking that we misspelled the name of the lake, or that this lake sounds suspiciously like a lake they fished a while back but had a different name.

The lake is found off Brule Prairie Road, just past Hudson's Hope. Getting to the lake is the first obstacle to overcome. There is a rough road to the lake, but most people chose to walk the lake three kilometers, as there are a couple of mudholes that will swallow most vehicles. ATV access is also popular.

No matter which name you prefer, the lake holds stocked rainbow trout. While the fish average about 35 cm (14 in) or so, there are a few monsters lurking here. Pulling out a 3.5 kg (7 lb) rainbow, while not a daily occurrence, does happen occasionally.

Part of that has to do with the fact that most fish caught here are usually released and given the chance to grow. This is not due to any sort of regulations, but merely because the shallow lake produces muddy tasting fish.

The deepest hole in the lake is about 6 metres (18 feet) deep and the fish retreat here in the heat of summer. While some people do fish here in summer, the fish are sluggish and provide little fight. In spring and fall, however, the fishing can be fast and furious and catching 30 or more fish in a day is possible.

While it is possible to troll the lake, it isn't the most preferred method. Instead, try spincasting or fly-fishing, especially around the beaver dam area. Gear anglers will find that working a spinner like a Panther Martin or Mepps will work well.

Fly anglers will find a few hatches on the lake, including caddis or mayflies, but there is little dry fly action to speak of. Instead, working a Muddler Minnow, a Woolly Bugger, a bead head nymph or other emerger pattern will get the best results.

The lake is found at the base of Butler Ridge and is in prime grizzly bear habitat. While bear are always a cause for concern fishing in the north, there seem to be more here than you would usually find.

Be sure to review the regulations as the lake is closed to ice fishing. Also, there is a bait ban and a single barbless hook restriction.

Facilities

There are no formal facilities at the lake, although there is space enough to camp on its shores.

Directions

Chunamun Lake is found north of Hudson's Hope at the base of Butler Ridge. To get to the lake, head west on Canyon Drive for 7 km (4.4 miles). Turn right on Beryl Prairie Road and head straight north. At about 13 km (7.9 miles), Beryl Prairie Road takes a sharp left, while Haagsman Street continues straight. Head left on Beryl Prairie Road, which swings back north again. Turn left 3.5 km (2.2 miles) after the road turns back north. There are two roads that head west within 200 metres (600 ft) of each other. Take the second road. This road leads through the last stretch of farmland and then turns left again to enter the forest. This last stretch of road to the lake is extremely rough. Most people quad or hike into the lake.

Area Indicator

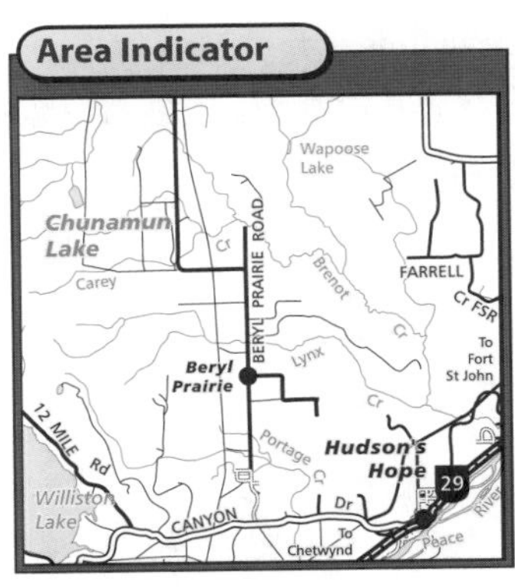

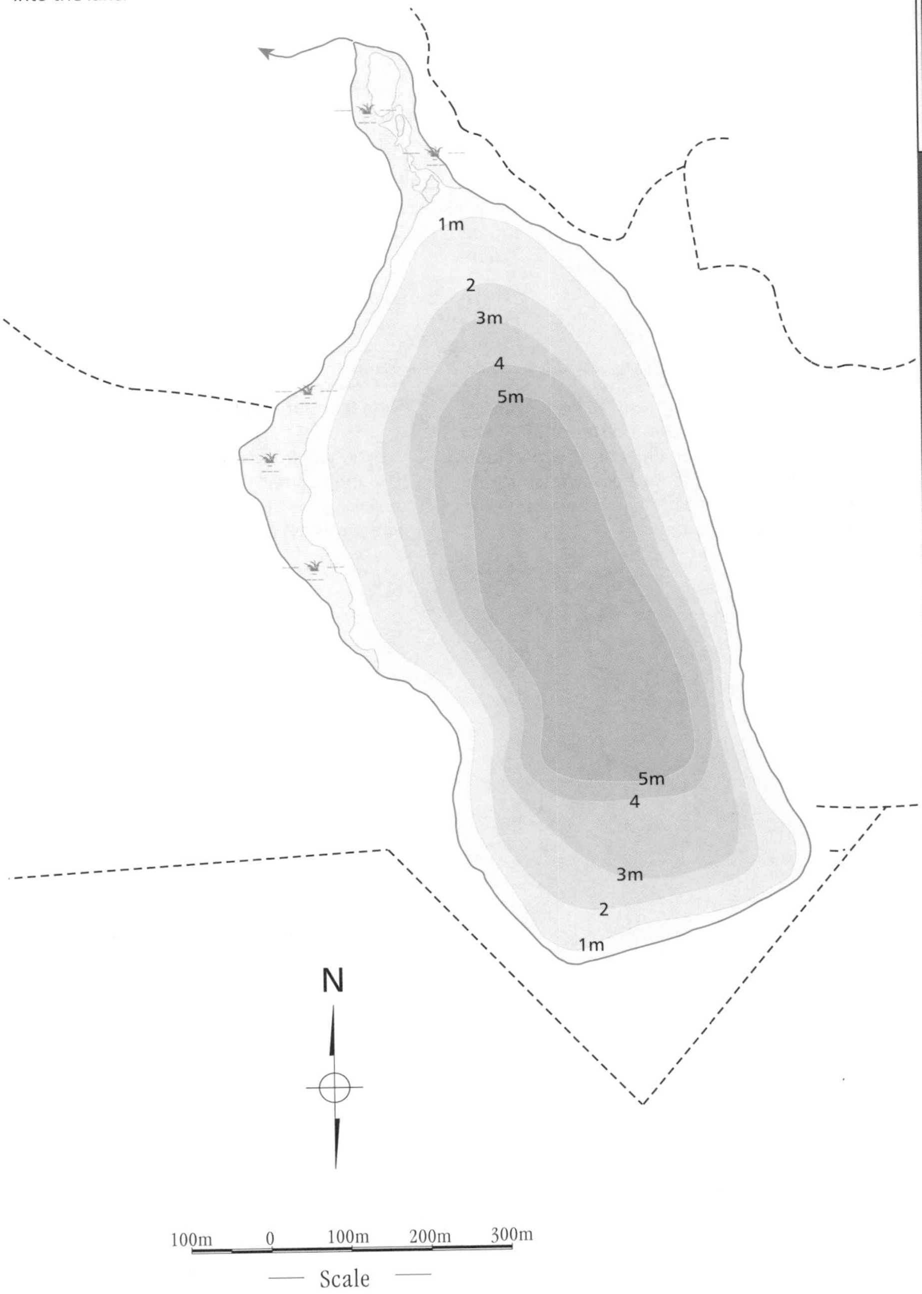

1m
2
3m
4
5m
5m
4
3m
2
1m
N
100m 0 100m 200m 300m
Scale

Location: 245 km (152 miles) west of Williams Lake
Elevation: 956 m (3,136 ft)
Surface Area: 215 ha (530 ac)
Maximum Depth: 5 m (16 ft)
Mean Depth: 2.3 m (7.5 ft)
Way Point: 52° 0′ 41.4″ N, 125° 0′ 30.2″ W

Clearwater Lake

Area Indicator

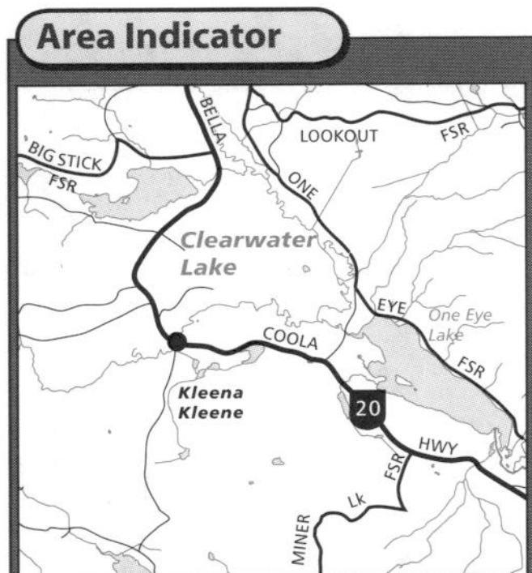

Fishing

Highway 20 is a narrow band that runs across the Chilcotin, a 10 metre (32 foot) wide ribbon of asphalt that crosses the 60,000 square kilometre plateau. As you might imagine, it misses more land than it covers as it makes its way from Williams Lake to Tweedsmuir Provincial Park, which marks the western edge of the Chilcotin Plateau.

So it is always a bit of a shock when the road passes by a lake. Even more so when that lake offers great fishing.

Clearwater Lake does not abut the highway, hidden from view by a few hundred metres of trees and bush. But the lake is one of the easiest lakes to get to in the Chilcotin, if you measure difficulty of access by the amount of gravel that passes under your tires.

The lake is populated with rainbow trout, as well as with a variety of course fish, including redside shiner. The course fish don't out compete the rainbow for food, but the trout don't get as large as one might expect. Still, the fish can be caught to 2 kg (4 lbs), although the average is about half that.

The lake is weedy and shallow, which means that it isn't the best trolling lake. It can be trolled in the middle, as long as you pick your lanes and pull your line in every few minutes to check for weeds.

Although a big trout here is only 2 kg (4 lbs), the lake is best fished with a slightly heavier test of lines. Not because the fish are strong fighters, although they are, but because the rainbow are not acrobats. They do not, when hooked, explode from the water in a wild attempt to shake the hook. Instead, they dive for the bottom of the lake, winding their way around the weeds. It is very easy to snap a line in this situation and sometimes the fish will get so tangled that they can't break free. A heavier line will allow you to manhandle the fish a bit more, keeping it from diving into the weeds and breaking your line.

Because of all the weeds, the lake features some great insect hatches, making it a perfect place for fly-fishers. As with most lakes in the area, you can use Doc Spratleys, Carey Specials, leeches, dragon and damselfly nymphs as searching patterns. Top water patterns will work at times, too, especially around mid-June. Try working a Tom Thumb or Adams.

The lake is one of the first to be ice free in April. On the other hand, it is also one of the first to start suffering the effects of the summer doldrums.

Directions

To get to the lake, take Highway 20 west from Williams Lake to Kleena Kleene, a distance of 242 km (150 miles). Beyond Kleena Kleene, the road loops around so it is travelling northeast. Watch for the turnoff to the south side of the lake just a few kilometres past Kleena Kleene.

Facilities

The **Clearwater Lake Recreation Site** rests on the south side of the lake. It is a small site, with space for maybe two groups and a boat launch. It is possible to launch a small trailered boat…possible. Also on the lake is the **Clearwater Lake Lodge and Resort** where cabins can be rented.

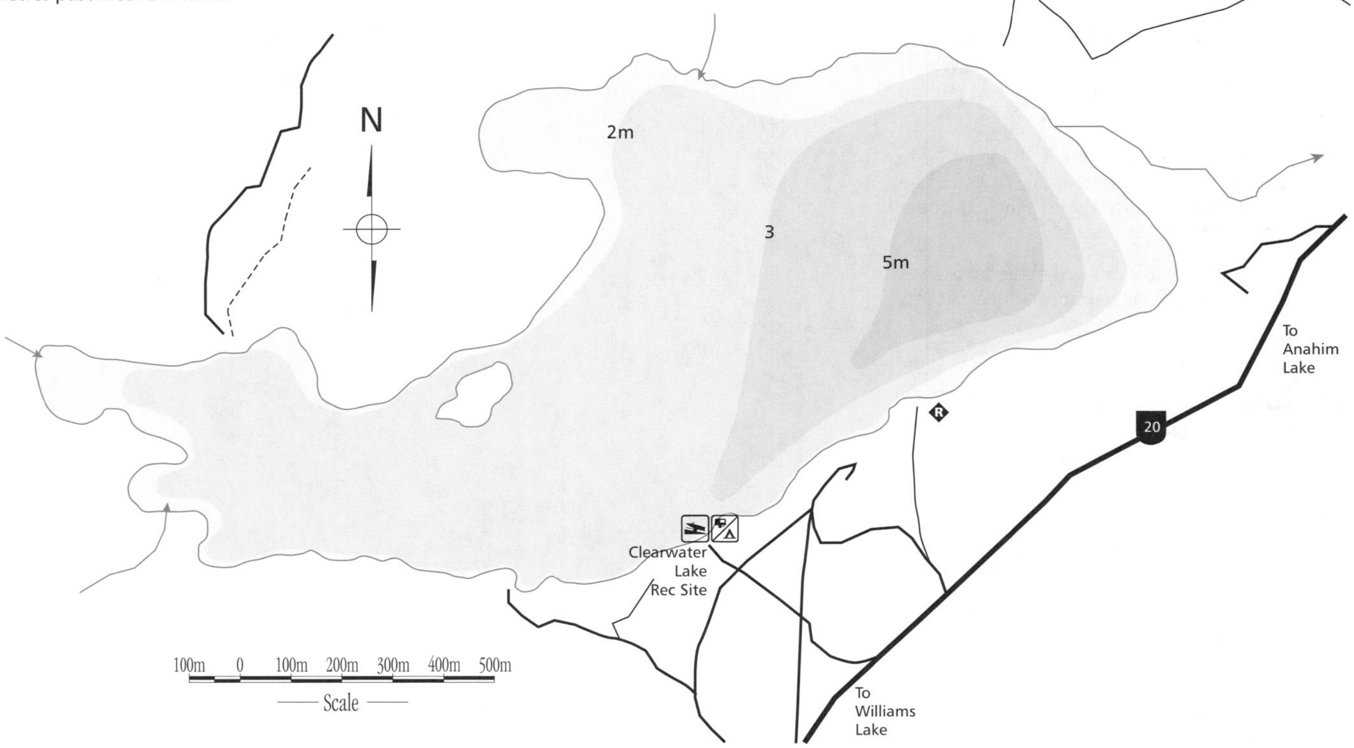

N
2m
3
5m
To Anahim Lake
20
Clearwater Lake Rec Site
To Williams Lake
100m 0 100m 200m 300m 400m 500m
Scale

Cobb Lake

Location: 65 km (40 mi) west of Prince George
Elevation: 771 m (2,529 ft)
Surface Area: 210 ha (518 ac)
Maximum Depth: 10 m (32 ft)
Mean Depth: 5.9 m (19 ft)
Way Point: 53° 57' 15" N, 123° 32' 3" W

Fishing

Cobb Lake is found almost exactly halfway between Prince George and Vanderhoof. Because it can be easily driven to from either direction, the lake sees heavier pressure than many other lakes in the area.

To help offset the fishing pressure, the Freshwater Fisheries Society of BC stocks the lake annually with 20,000 brook and 10,000 rainbow trout. In addition to the stocked brook trout, there is some natural recruitment from breeding pairs. In 2006, the stocking pattern for rainbow was changed to the Blackwater strain trout from Dragon Lake. These piscivorous fish feed on small, course fish in the lake and often grow bigger than other species of rainbow.

In the spring, the fishing is really good for feisty rainbow that are cherished by local anglers for the fight they put up. The small lake is a good fly-fishing lake. Try using chironomid patterns or bead head nymphs for the rainbow; leeches and attractor patterns like a Carey Special also work wonders. Gear trollers can try the usual Willow Leaf and Wedding Band tipped with a worm. The lake is a very good lake to fish from a float tube or small boat. It is found in a bit of a depression in a thick forest and the wind rarely kicks up enough to create problems for light craft.

The fishing tends to slow down during summer, although the water never gets really warm. Instead, the fish tend to hide out in the deep water in July and August. Rainbow can be taken on a troll sometimes, but are not as spunky as they are in the spring.

For brook trout, Mepps Aglia, Blue Fox Vibrax or Rooster Tail spinners can take these aggressive feeders. Also try a Wedding Band or a small Rapala. You have to fish deep to find the brook trout, but they can be very aggressive, even in spring. There are steep drop offs along the northern and especially the southern shore.

In the fall, the brook trout begin to spawn and become even more aggressive and fishing for brookies, which can get up to 2.5 kg (5 lbs) is at its best. You will find them close to shore, especially right around the recreation site. Try using a leech or micro leech pattern.

The good fishing for brook trout continues right into winter as soon as the ice is hard enough to walk on. Ice fishers use shrimp, krill, salmon eggs and worms. These baits can be fished on a plain hook, or a glow hook and jig combination. The key to success is locating the fish; while brook trout are usually found deeper in the ice-free season, they will be found in between 1–3 metres (3–10 feet) of water when the ice is on. Even in winter, though, expect to see other anglers here as ice fishing is extremely popular on the lake.

Area Indicator

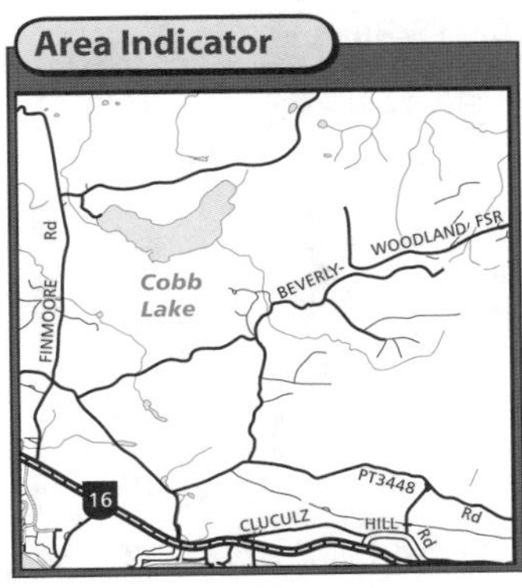

Directions

Cobb Lake is an easy lake to find. To get there, travel about 65 km west of Prince George on Highway 16. Watch for Finmoore Road heading north from the highway opposite Clucuiz Lake. This road leads to a recreation site on the west side of the lake.

Facilities

The **Cobb Lake Recreation Site** is a small site that offers space for a handful of groups here. Launching a cartop boat is possible.

Cobb Lake
Fish Stocking Data

Year	Species	Number	Life Stage
2008	Brook Trout	20,000	Fingerling
2008	Rainbow Trout	12,000	Yearling
2007	Brook Trout	20,000	Fingerling
2007	Rainbow Trout	10,000	Yearling

Location: 24 km (15 mi) east of Burns Lake
Elevation: 885m (2,903ft)
Surface Area: 30.5 ha (75.3 ac)
Maximum Depth: 10.4m (34 ft)
Mean Depth: 3.9m (12.8 ft)
Way Point: 54° 11′ 11.1″ N, 125° 25′ 44.8″

Co-op Lake

Area Indicator

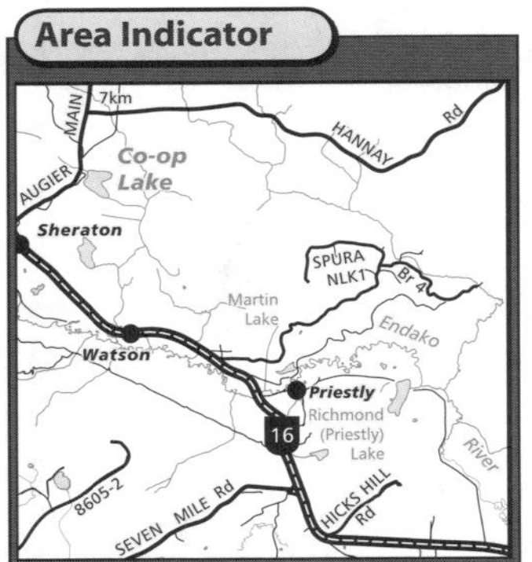

Co-op Lake			
Fish Stocking Data			
Year	Species	Number	Life Stage
2008	Brook Trout	9,987	Fingerling
2007	Brook Trout	10,000	Fingerling
2006	Brook Trout	10,000	Fingerling

Fishing

Since Co-op Lake began to be stocked (more than 40 years ago now), the lake has been one of the most popular fishing spots in the Burns Lake area. It supports a year round fishery for brook trout–through the ice from late November to early April and by boat from spring to fall.

The lake is annually stocked with 10,000 all-female sterile eastern brook trout by the Freshwater Fisheries Society of BC. These fish have been known to get up to 3.6 kg (8 lbs) in Co-op, although the lake is better known for producing lots of smaller fish, making it a great lake for the kids. The large plantings of willing brook trout, easy access and a chance to catch a trophy fish that tastes great make for a winning combination.

You will need a boat or watercraft of some description to fish this lake, as the shoreline is thickly bordered by marshland and willows. The launch/campsite is on the marshy west end of the lake, where the water is less than 4 m (13 ft) deep. To the south lies the deeper part of the lake and it is here you will want to concentrate your fishing in the late spring and summer when the fish seek cooler water.

Brook trout prefer clean, cold water and cannot tolerate the higher temperatures that rainbow can. They are opportunistic feeders and eat a wide variety of organisms from insects to small fish. Brookies often feed in travelling schools so sometimes the action can be frantic; at other times the angler is left wondering "where did they all go?" Brookies also like structure, so if the weather is cool, particularly during the winter ice-fishing season, look for them around downed trees, weed beds, points and drop offs. Angling is best in the spring and early summer when their flesh is still firm and they are most active and again in winter through the ice.

Brook trout are attracted to small lures such as the Panther Martin, Mepps, Vibrax, Kamlooper and Krocodile and will respond to a lake troll, Wedding Band or Apex Trout Killer tipped with worms, leeches, insects or Powerbait. The Mini Fat Rap from Rapala can be very deadly.

Even though brook trout will take a dry fly, subsurface flies generally work better. A dragonfly or damselfly nymph or a black leech pattern trolled or retrieved near the lake bottom often brings success. The Werner Shrimp pattern is another good fly to try, along with muddlers, Woolly Buggers and Clouser minnows. A slow retrieve seems to be the most effective.

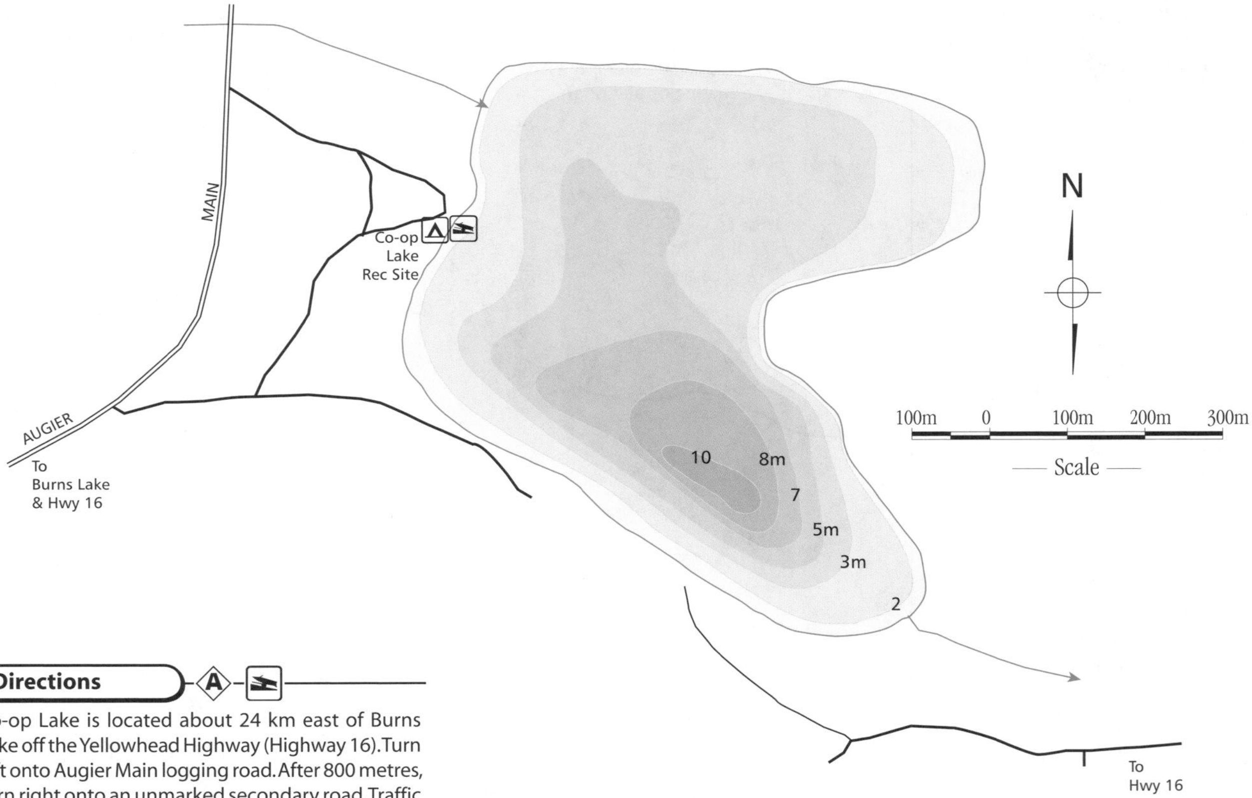

MAIN
Co-op Lake Rec Site
AUGIER
To Burns Lake & Hwy 16
10
8m
7
5m
3m
2
N
100m 0 100m 200m 300m
Scale
To Hwy 16

Directions

Co-op Lake is located about 24 km east of Burns Lake off the Yellowhead Highway (Highway 16). Turn left onto Augier Main logging road. After 800 metres, turn right onto an unmarked secondary road. Traffic on this road is radio controlled (frequency 158.97). Drive 100 metres down this secondary road to the Co-op Lake sign and follow the next road for another 300 metres or so. The road access is generally quite good allowing most vehicles to access the lake.

Facilities

The **Co-op Lake Recreation Site** has space for about five units. Found on the west end of the lake, there is also a boat launch available.

Copper (Zymoetz) River

Location: 20 km (12.4 mi) east of Terrace
Lenght: 130 km (80 mi)
Geographic: 54°34′ 00″N, 127°56′ 00″W

Fishing

The Zymoetz or Copper River is a Skeena River tributary that flows into the Skeena near Terrace. Like most rivers that flow into the Skeena, it offers spectacular steelhead fishing. The river produces steelhead in the 5–10 kg (10–20 lb) range, but bigger fish are caught annually.

As the westernmost tributary, it is the first river to have steelhead in August. Because the steelhead enter the river so early in the season, they are much more aggressive. They are quite willing to attack skating or waking flies or a greased-line presentation with a small wet fly. For dry flies, the steelhead really love big stoneflies and people have caught fish up to 12 kg (25 lbs) with a well-presented stonefly imitation.

Stretching about 130 km, the lower river can be followed for about 40 km by road. The river has muddy, copper-coloured banks (hence the nickname) and often has dirty water when it rains. If the river is running muddy, you can try upstream to find cleaner water, but you may not succeed before running out of road. Past the end of the road, the river runs through steep walled canyons with lots of rapids. Hiking upstream is difficult and dangerous.

While the lower section of the river is road accessible, the road sees little traffic and the surrounding mountains give the appearance of remoteness. However, the river is considered one of the world's best steelhead streams and can see a lot of angling pressure during the peak runs in September and October.

The river can be fished on the fly, using wet or dry flies, or it can be fished using spoons and spinners. While the early season steelhead are willing to take to dry flies on the surface, when the water gets cooler, they become less aggressive. Usually, the dry fly season runs from August 1 through September, but it depends on the temperature of the water. You need to get your lure or fly down to the bottom of the stream.

Fly anglers can use a nymphing technique with a floating line and heavily weighted fly. Watch for places where steelhead can hold: behind a boulder or fallen tree or at the top of a rapid. Work the transition zone where fast and slow currents meet. Also be alert for steelhead in the shallow water near the banks, especially when the water is dirty. Many anglers have spooked trophy-sized steelhead by nearly stepping on them.

The river is classified as a Class I or Class II river, depending on where you are fishing and there are closures along various stretches of river. Check the regulations before heading out.

Facilities

There are no facilities along the river, but there's lots of random camping spots. Or you can stay in nearby Terrace, where you will find accommodations, campgrounds and restaurants. In town, there are a number of outfitters who provide guided trips on the river, including helicopter trips to the upper river.

Directions

Just east of Terrace on Highway 16/37, the Cooper River Forest Service Road heads east. This road parallels the river for about 40 km with decent access points at about the 15 and 30 km mark. Watch out for logging trucks.

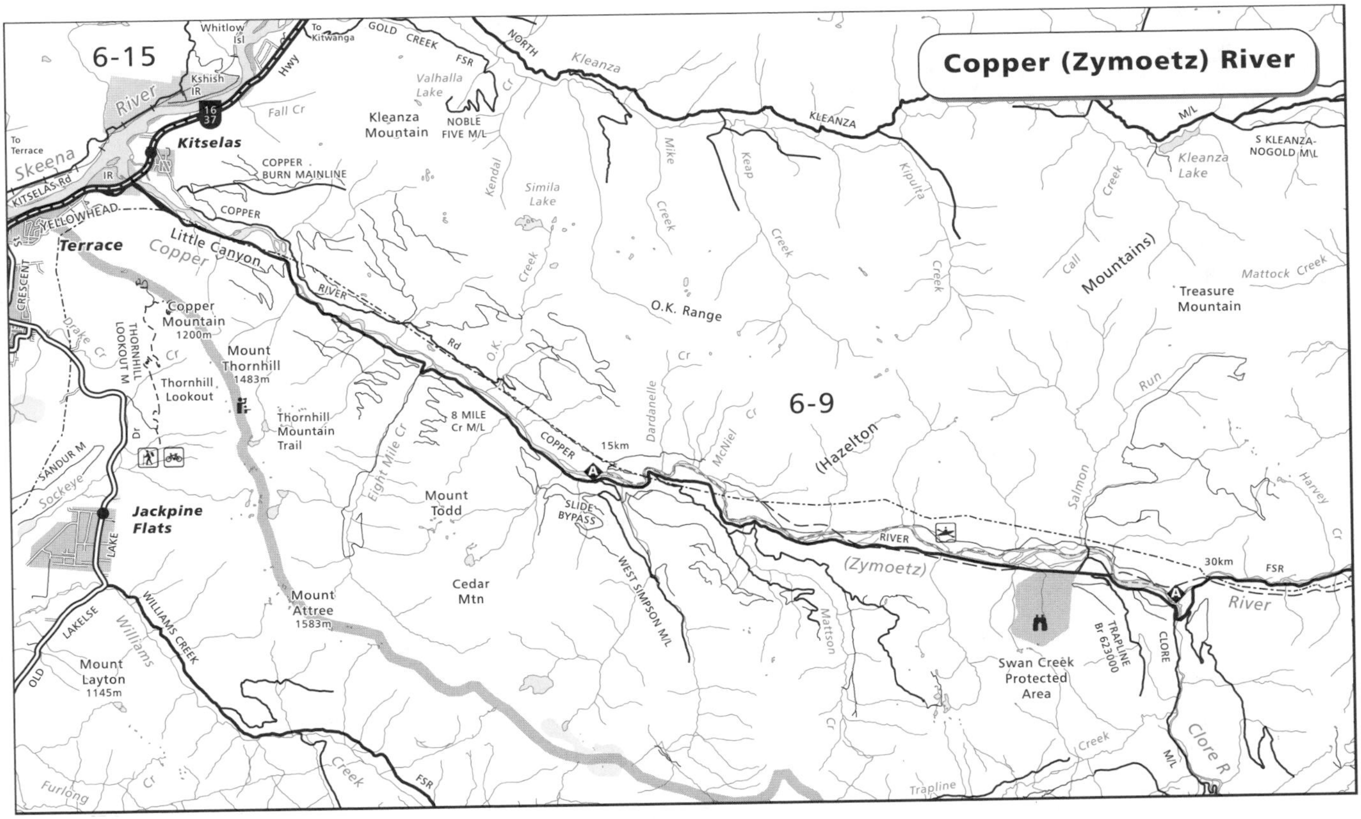

Copper (Zymoetz) River

Location: 100 km (62 mi) east of Williams Lake
Elevation: 935 m (3,067 ft)
Surface Area: 1,092 ha (2,697 ac)
Mean Depth: 35.1 m (115 ft)
Maximum Depth: 83.8 m (274 ft)
Way Point: 52° 16′ 9″ N, 120° 43′ 6″ W

Crooked Lake

Area Indicator

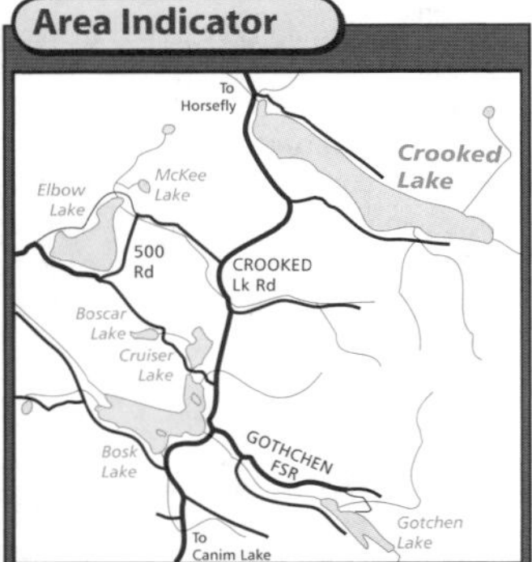

Fishing

Crooked Lake is a fair sized lake that stretches nearly 10 km into the mountains near Wells Gray Provincial Park. This is a scenic area with snow capped mountains rising on either side of the broad valley. As a result, it is a popular destination, not just for anglers, but for hikers, mountain bikers and in the winter, snowmobilers.

Fishing is fairly good from late May to September for the rather abundant rainbow trout. There are also a few course fish that help allow the trout to grow to over 3 kg (6.5 lbs). Of course these are rare catches and fish in the 20–30 cm (10–14 in) range are much more common. They are readily caught by fly-fishing, trolling or spincasting.

The lake is very deep so it is easily trolled. A small Flatfish can work quite well, although most people stick with a traditional lake troll or Willow Leaf and Wedding Band set-up.

The lake features the usual Cariboo Hatches, but not in any large numbers. Fly anglers will do better working the inflow of the Upper McKuskey Creek at the east end of the lake or at the outflow at the west end of the lake. Fish congregate around these areas waiting for food to wash down the creek or to get funneled into the creek. What gets washed into the lake, although, is different from day to day, so keep a close eye out. Terrestrial patterns, like grasshoppers or small black flies that look like pine beetles can be extremely productive, especially around the inflow. If that's not working, try any number of searching patterns like a Doc Spratley or a Wooly Bugger.

Spincasters can also try working these areas with a small spoon or spinner, although they may have better luck anchoring off the drop off and casting into the shallows, retrieving across the drop off. The shoreline is fairly open and the lake drops off quite rapidly allowing for decent shore casting options if you do not have a boat.

Directions

To reach Crooked Lake involves a long drive from the Cariboo Highway (Highway 97) but the access is generally good. From the highway, follow the paved Horsefly Road all the way to the small town of Horsefly. Just before entering the town, cross the bridge over the Horsefly River and begin the drive on the Black Creek Road. That logging road is a well-maintained road so a car can travel along it without much trouble.

Continue past Black Creek and the airport and past the turn-off to the McKinley Lake Road (500 Road). The next major road heading right off the Black Creek Road is the Crooked Lake Road (6700 Road). That road leads to the northwestern end of the lake.

Facilities

Featuring a couple resorts and a couple recreation sites, there is no shortage of places to stay around the lake. Those looking for cabins or RV friendly camping and boat launches can check out **Crooked Lake Resort** or **Lonesome Loon Resort**. The **Crooked Lake North** and **South Recreation Sites** lie in open areas pretty well opposite to each other on closer to the western shoreline. The southern site offers a few camping pads together with a sandy beach, while the northern site sports 20 sites and a boat launch.

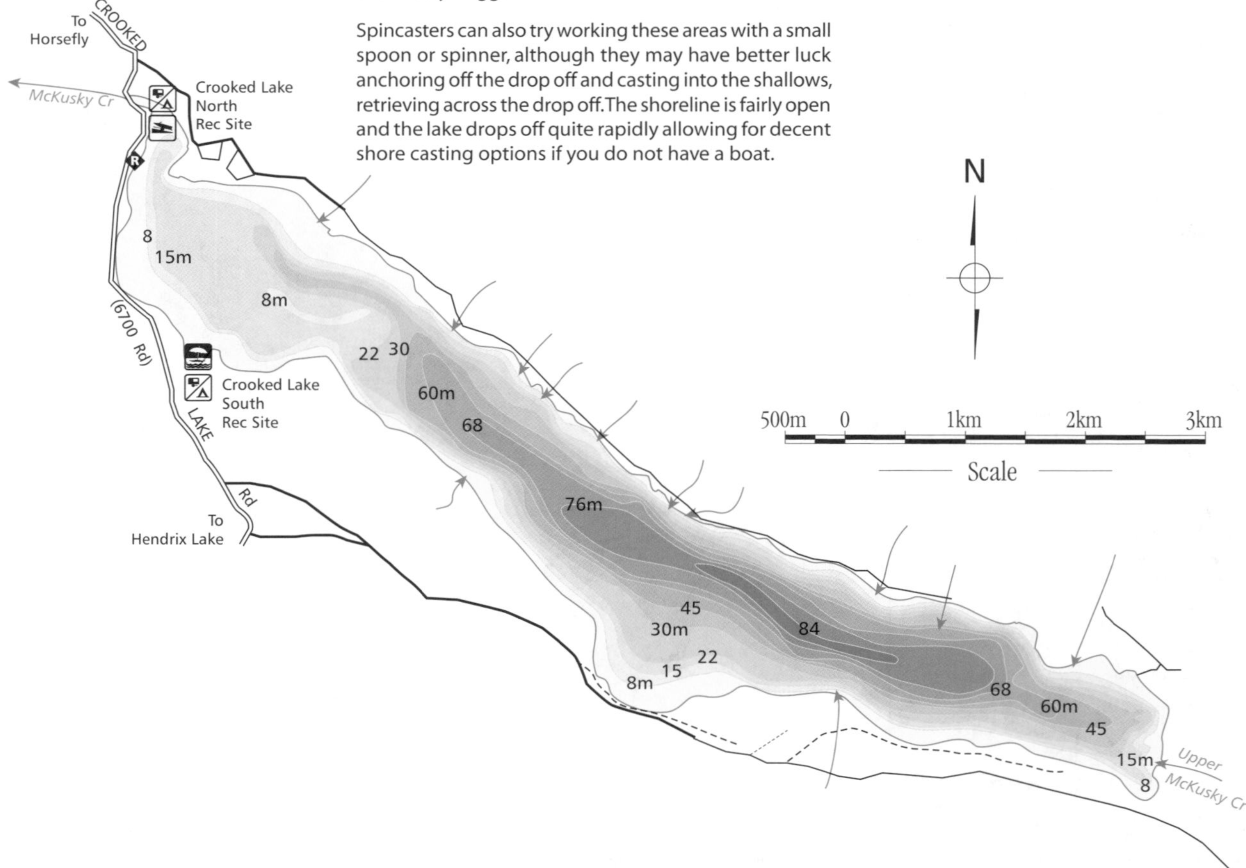

Crooked River

Location: 110 km (68 mi) north of Prince George
Stream Length: 69 km (43 mi)
Geographic: 54°49′ 59″ N, 122° 52′ 59″ W

Fishing

North of Prince George, Highway 97 crosses the Salmon River and then up and over into the Crooked River drainage. The mostly lazy river starts at Summit Lake and flows north, through a number of lakes, including McLeod Lake, where it joins forces with the Pack River to flow into Tudyah Lake and then the Williston Reservoir.

The river is best known for its rainbow trout, which usually top out at about 50 cm (20 in) but it also holds plenty of bull trout to 5 kg (10 lbs). Whitefish are another popular catch, but there are also plenty of squawfish.

A popular way to fish the river is to throw small spinners and spoons at the fish using ultra light gear, but fly anglers love the river, too. There are a number of good hatches in the river, including mayflies, caddis and the odd stonefly hatch.

Some of the best dry fly-fishing comes using terrestrial patterns: ants, spiders, stimulators and small black beetles that resemble the ever-present pine beetle. A three-weight rod is preferred. The slow moving sections of the river hold squawfish, which are quite willing to take whatever you are offering. If you want to avoid catching these course fish, work the slightly faster moving sections of waters where you can see visible riffles on the surface.

Two popular access points are at the 200 Road Bridge and the 100 Road Bridge. At the latter, it is possible to catch up to a hundred whitefish or more in a single evening. To really experience the river, though, it is best fished from a canoe or a pontoon boat. Despite the fact that the highway is so close, the thick bush gives the area a wilderness feel and makes it difficult to bushwhack to when more than a few hundred metres from a road.

Wildlife is plentiful. Be careful of moose in the spring and fall as well as bear year round. There are both black and grizzly bear here and if you spend any amount of time fishing the river, chances are you will encounter both.

There are plenty of feeder creeks which offer as good, if not better, fishing than the main channel itself. One unique spot on the river is Livingstone Spring. Accessed from Crooked River Provincial Park, this area of the river remains ice free during the winter and offers great rainbow trout fishing year round. A lot of anglers, coming to fish Square Lake, will come here for a few hours, too.

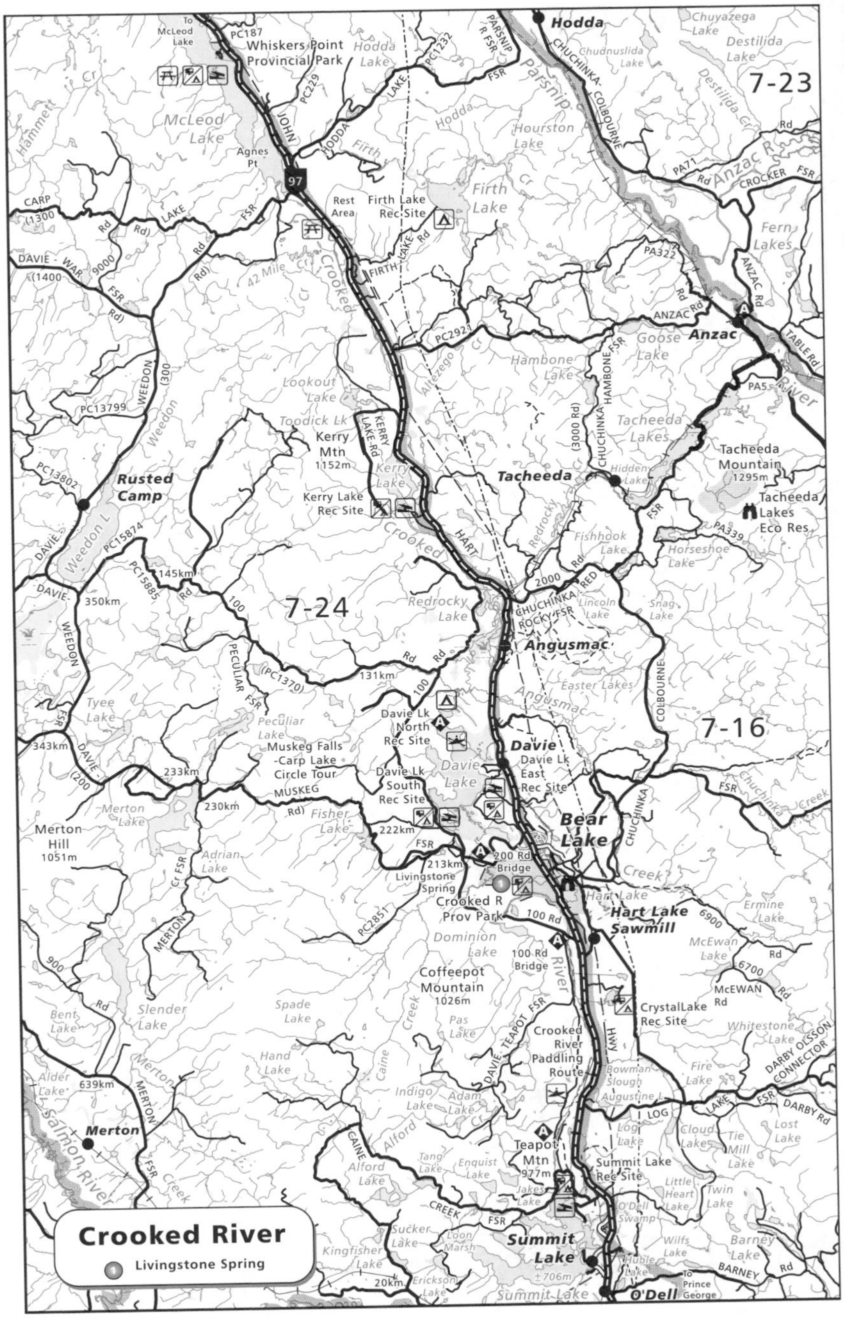

Crooked River

Livingstone Spring

Directions

The Crooked River parallels Highway 97 north of Prince George from Summit Lake to McLeod Lake. There are plenty of places where the river is accessible from the highway, but there are also a number of logging roads that fall off the highway and cross the river, providing great access. Two of the best are the 100 Road Bridge and the 200 Road Bridge.

Facilities

There are a number of recreation sites and parks along the river, including **Summit Lake Recreation Site, Crooked River Provincial Park** and **Crooked River Canyon Recreation Site.** There are also sites on Davie Lake and Kerry Lake, which the river flows through and at Whiskers Point Park on McLeod Lake, where the river terminates.

Cuisson Lake

Location: 42 km (26 mi) northwest of Williams Lake
Elevation: 866 m (2,841 ft)
Surface Area: 164.3 ha (406 ac)
Max Depth: 11.6 m (38 ft)
Mean Depth: 4 m (13 ft)
Way Point: 52° 29' 7" N, 122° 18' 41" W

Area Indicator

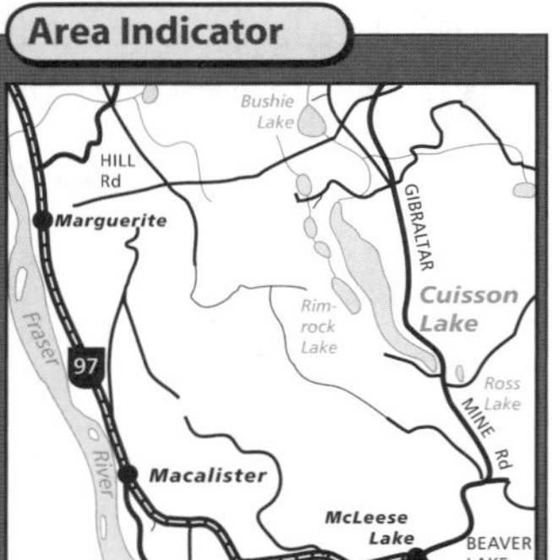

Directions

Cuisson Lake is found on the hills above the Fraser River to the east of the Marguerite. To reach the lake, head to the north end of McLeese Lake on the Cariboo Highway (Highway 97) and then turn north on the Gibraltar Mine Road. The road is well signed and passes right next to Cuisson Lake.

Fishing

At McLeese Lake, the Cariboo Highway takes a sharp left hand turn (heading north), then right again along the Fraser River. This change or direction means the highway doesn't pass along the shores of Cuisson Lake, which lies about 5 km north of McLeese.

But it does mean that Cuisson Lake is a relatively low elevation lake offering its best fishing in the early spring and again in the fall. Bolstered by a fairly aggressive stocking campaign by the Freshwater Fisheries Society of BC (between 2000 and 20,000 rainbow are stocked each year), the lake offers a very good trout fishery. There are also some minnows and suckers found in the lake.

The rainbow–in this case the fish eating Blackwater strain–dine on the minnows that are found in the lake. This diet of fish means the Blackwater trout can get up to 2 kg (4 lbs), although the average is less than half that.

Cuisson Lake is a shallow lake, with a maximum depth around 12 metres (38 feet). As a result, trolling can be difficult unless you use a shallow troll. The lake is long and narrow, with a number of points and small islands that are great place for the fish to hold around.

The north end of the lake is quite shallow and can be very unproductive save in early spring or late fall. Spincasters and fly fisherman should work the deep hole south of the islands or around the fringe areas of the lake. Shore casting is difficult given that the deeper water is out of casting range. Apex Trout Killer, Kamlooper and Krocodile spoons as well as Mepps, Panther Martin, Vibrax and Gibbs spinners work well, as does vertical jigging with spoons or jigs using scented bait, such as one of the Berkley Powerbaits.

Because the lake is stocked with piscivorous trout, fly anglers might want to mix it up a little. If you're not experiencing good luck with the usual Cariboo area patterns (Doc Spratleys, Carey Specials, etc), it might be worthwhile to tie on a streamer or minnow imitation.

Facilities

The **Cuisson Lake Recreation Site** is on the southern most bay of the lake. There are picnic tables at the site together with a cartop boat launch. The site has been used by rowdy partiers in the past, who have destroyed the outhouses continually. While such behavior seems to have settled down, know that the site can be a madhouse at times. Alternatively, there is a rustic resort on the lake to stay at.

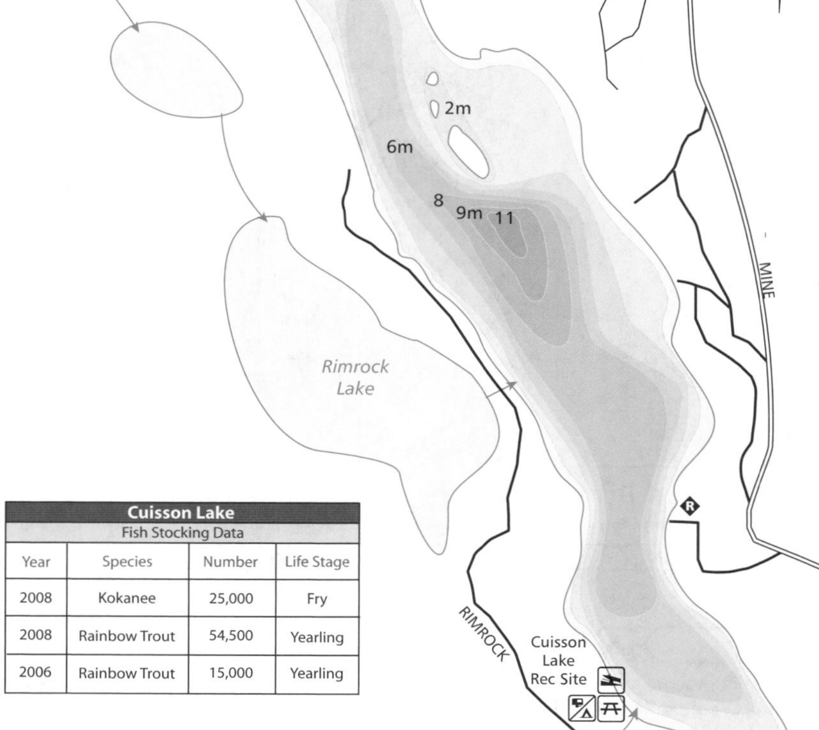

Cuisson Lake			
Fish Stocking Data			
Year	Species	Number	Life Stage
2008	Kokanee	25,000	Fry
2008	Rainbow Trout	54,500	Yearling
2006	Rainbow Trout	15,000	Yearling

Other Options

Bushy and **Souran Lakes** are situated to the north of Cuisson Lake on a secondary road off the Gibraltar Mine Road. The lakes offer a good fishery for rainbow with spincasting and fly-fishing being the preferred methods of fishing. A recreation site is situated at the south end of Bushy Lake.

Dahl Lake

Location: 40 km (24.8 mi) southwest of Prince George
Elevation: 832 m (2,729 ft)
Surface Area: 242 ha (597 ac)
Maximum Depth: 24 m (77 ft)
Mean Depth: 4.5 m (14 ft)
Way Point: 53° 46′ 33″ N, 123° 17′ 54″ W

Fishing

Dahl Lake is a wilderness lake found southwest of Prince George. It is a pretty lake found at the heart of Dahl Lake Provincial Park.

The lake holds a number of course fish species, but amidst them all are three game fish species: rainbow trout, burbot and mountain whitefish.

The lake has a number of points, bays and small islands, meaning there is lots of structure for the fish to hold around. Maybe a little too much structure, as there are not a lot of fish, nor is there any one place that seems to attract more fish than anywhere else.

That said, for many the thrill of fishing is in the chase as much as in the catch. And because the lake does not see heavy fishing pressure, the stocks here remain good.

The lake is closed to motors of any kind, so anyone wishing to troll the lake is going to have to do it by paddling. That's not necessarily a bad thing. The lunge and drift motion set up by paddling is more random, which is usually more enticing to the fish. Taking a hard stroke every once in a while can often encourage fish that are trailing a hook to strike, as the sudden burst of speed makes it look like the fish's food source is trying to get away.

A lake troll is popular, but a small spoon will also work. Try using a spoon with a chrome colour in it, either solid or mixed with blue or green. Gear anglers will also find that rainbow trout like spinners like a Panther Martin or Mepps.

As is typical of most northern lakes, there are few hatches on the lake. The biggest of which are caddis and mayflies. There is little dry fly action to speak of. Instead, working a Muddler Minnow, a Woolly Bugger, a bead head nymph or other emerger pattern will get the best results. However, on a late spring evening, you might luck out and find the fish rising.

Ice fishing is quite popular on the lake. While the rainbow trout fishing slows down through the winter, there is some great fishing for burbot. Burbot love the cold water and are not as affected by the lower oxygen levels. Burbot are an ugly fish. As a result, they aren't a popular species among the catch and release crowd. However, those in the know realize that burbot are one of the tastiest freshwater fish around. Burbot are the only freshwater species of cod (and are also known to many anglers by their other name: ling cod).

Area Indicator

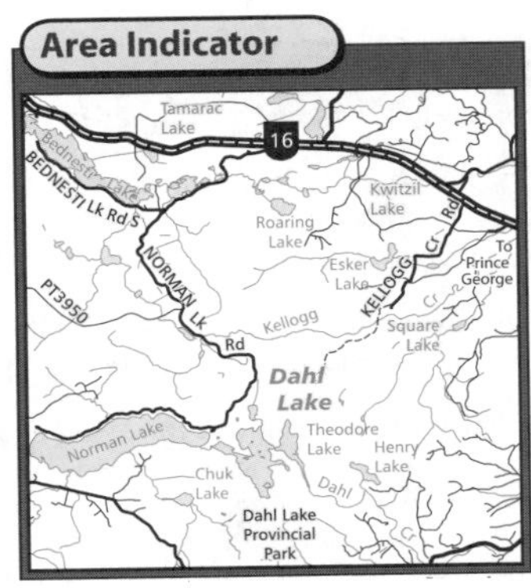

Directions

To get to Dahl Lake, travel west from Prince George on Highway 16 for 42 km to Normal Lake Road. Turn south on this gravel road and drive for 17 km to Dahl Lake Provincial Park. The parking area is on Norman Lake, but Dahl Lake is connected to this bigger lake by a short creek. Launch a canoe or small cartopper at the beach on the east end of Norman Lake and paddle south along the shore to the creek. From here it is only about 200 metre (600 feet) to Dahl Lake.

Facilities

Dahl Lake Provincial Park surrounds Dahl and Theodore Lake and protects the east end of Norman Lake. It is a day-use park with rustic picnic facilities, a sandy beach, short walking trail and great canoeing and wildlife viewing opportunities.

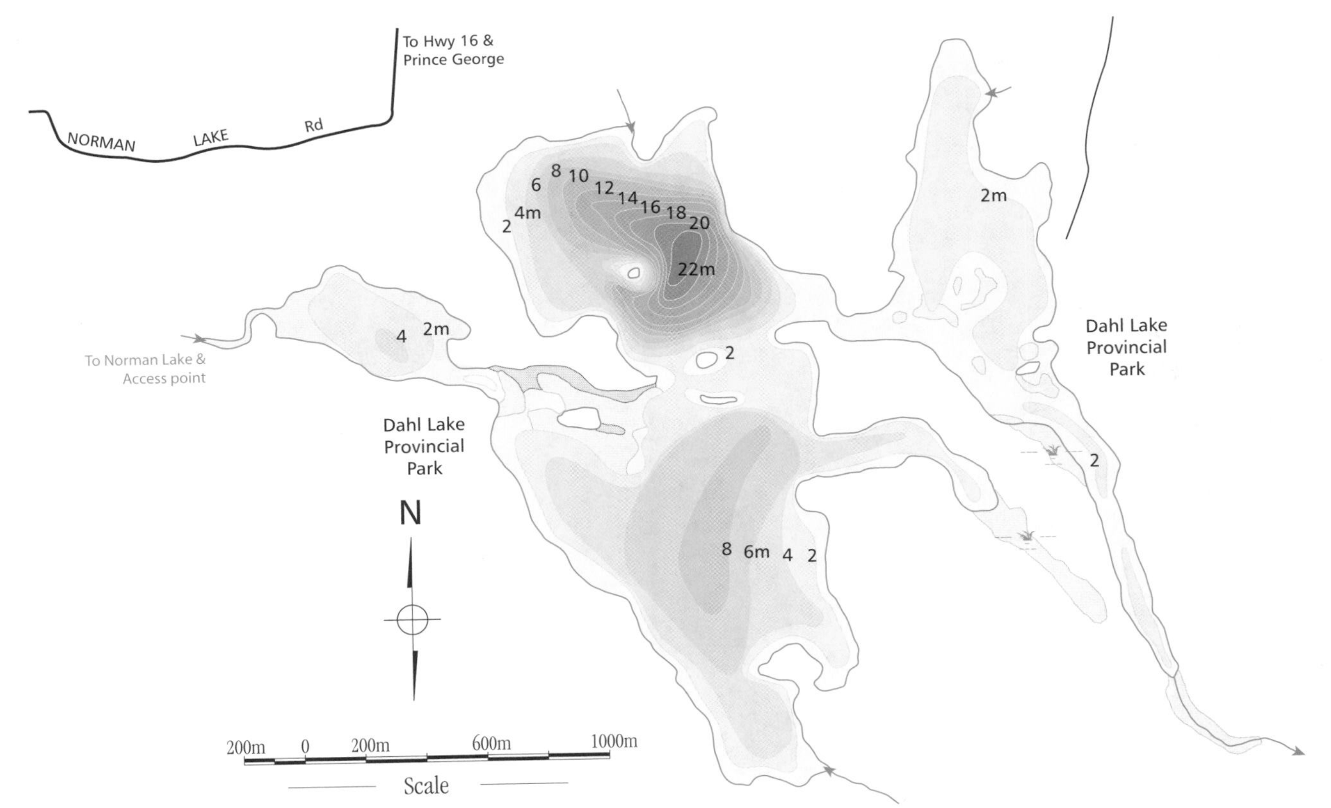

Location: 50 km (31 mi) north of Bella Coola
Stream Length: 253 km (157 mi)
Geographic: 52° 47′ 59″ N, 126° 58′ 00″ W

Dean River - Lower

Fishing

This is it. When people talk great fishing rivers, the Dean is usually somewhere near the top of that list. And people who put the river below the top spot are usually folks who haven't fished here.

The river has a few sea-run cutthroat, as well as large runs of Chinook and Coho. The Chinook run starts in June and continues through mid-July and it mostly passes without notice, as does the Coho run in August and September. Below the canyon, people have caught Chinook to 20 kg (50 lbs). But when the steelhead show up, all angling attention turns to these silver bullets.

Dean River steelhead are noted for their strength and fight. There are a couple reasons proposed for this. The first is that there is a fairly major canyon near the mouth of the river and only the strongest fish make it up into the Dean. As a result, the fish that do make it through are extremely strong.

Another reason for the Dean steelhead's amazing strength is that these fish head up river quickly. Steelhead can be caught within hours of leaving the ocean. And of course, steelhead are always more active and aggressive in warmer water and they willingly take to a dry fly. Elk or Deer Hair Caddis and stonefly imitations can work wonders.

There are two runs of steelhead on the Dean. First is a late spring run bound for the Takia River about 72 km (45 miles) from the ocean. The second run enters the Dean a few weeks later. This is the main run of steelhead that spawns in the Dean itself.

The best time to fish the lower section of the Dean (from the river's mouth the lower canyon, a distance of about 3 km/1.8 mi) is from mid-July to mid-September, while the fishing gets going about two weeks later and ends two weeks earlier on the upper section of the Lower Dean (basically up to Crag Creek). The best sections to drift are from Kalone Creek down to the lower canyon.

This is not really a place for DIYers. The river is difficult to access (fly-in or boat-in access only) and getting above the first section is nearly impossible. The first 8 km (5 miles) of the Dean are accessed via a gravel road, though how you get a vehicle here is another issue entirely; most people rely on guides from the area lodges to drive them upstream, as well as to provide jetboat transportation to the upper sections of the river.

As you float down the river, you can chose to camp of stay at one of the resorts near the mouth of the river. We recommend the later due to Grizzly bear concerns.

On top of great fishing, the scenery is spectacular. The river passes through untouched Coastal Mountain Scenery with peaks more than 2 kilometres tall rising in all directions.

Directions

The lower Dean River is only accessible by boat or air. As a result, most people who come here do so with one of the lodges on the lower reaches of the river.

Facilities

There is random camping along the river, as well as several lodges near the mouth of the river. The **Lower Dean River Lodge** and the **Dean River Lodge** are certainly worth checking out if you want to explore the river.

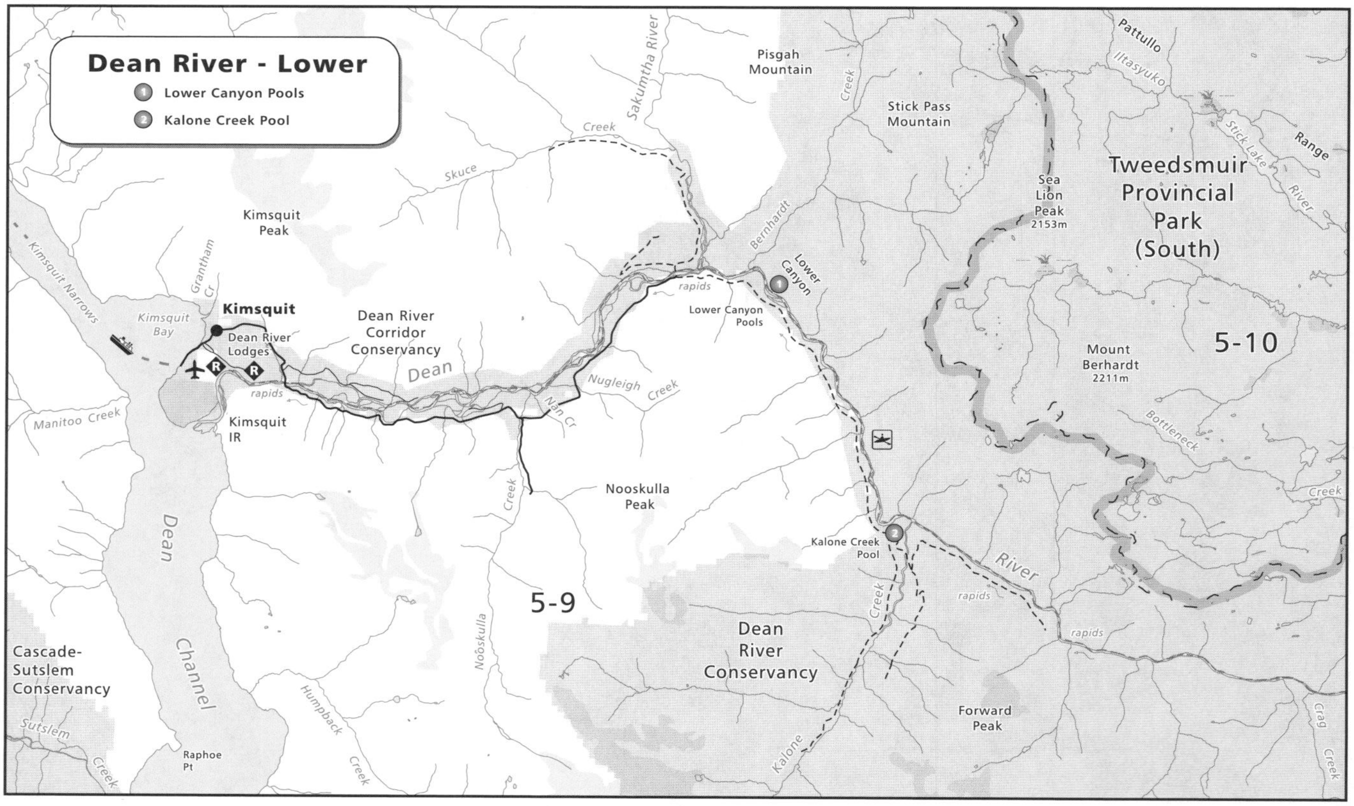

Dean River - Lower
1 Lower Canyon Pools
2 Kalone Creek Pool

Dean River - Upper

Location: 50 km (31 mi) north of Bella Coola
Stream Length: 253 km (157 mi)
Geographic: 52° 47′ 59″ N, 126° 58′ 00″ W

Fishing

Although the Dean River is best known for steelhead fishing in its lower portion, the Upper Dean River offers excellent fishing, too.

The Dean River flows out of Nimpo Lake, starting out as little more than a small stream, meandering northwest through the interior high-altitude forest and grasslands and into Anahim Lake. As it flows out of Anahim, then through Abuntlet and Lessard Lake, it becomes larger and larger and is accessible by boat.

The Upper Dean River ends at a 20 metre (60 foot) high waterfall near the junction with the Iltasyuko River, about midway through Tweedsmuir Provincial Park. The water is rich in dissolved minerals and the nutrient-rich water produces larger quantities of insects, which in turn feed the trout populations. However, the Chilcotin Plateau features long, extremely cold winters and relatively short but hot summers. The growing season is short and trout, although plentiful, grow slowly.

The river is best fished early in the year, when the water levels are high. From opening day (June 15) to mid-July the dry fly-fishing is amazing. The fishing tails off over the heart of summer.

The river holds plenty of small, feisty rainbow and rainbow-cutthroat crosses called cuttbows. In summer, as the water warms up, there are several large hatches of caddis, mayflies, stoneflies, chironomids and dragonflies. The hatches are unpredictable and the well-prepared angler comes with a box full of wet and dry flies. Of course, dry fly-fishing is the most popular and an Elk Hair Caddis, small Adams, Wulffs and/or Goddards are the most popular flies to use. Stonefly nymphs, Gold Ribbed Hare's Ear Nymphs and a handful of other attractor patterns will be a boon when the fish aren't rising.

The Dean is one of the most regulated rivers in the province and has a variety of different regulations based on where you are fishing. Always check the regulations before you head out. For the upper Dean, the most important regulation to note is that the river is fly-fishing only using a single barbless hook from Anahim Lake to the Iltasyuko River from June 15 to September 30.

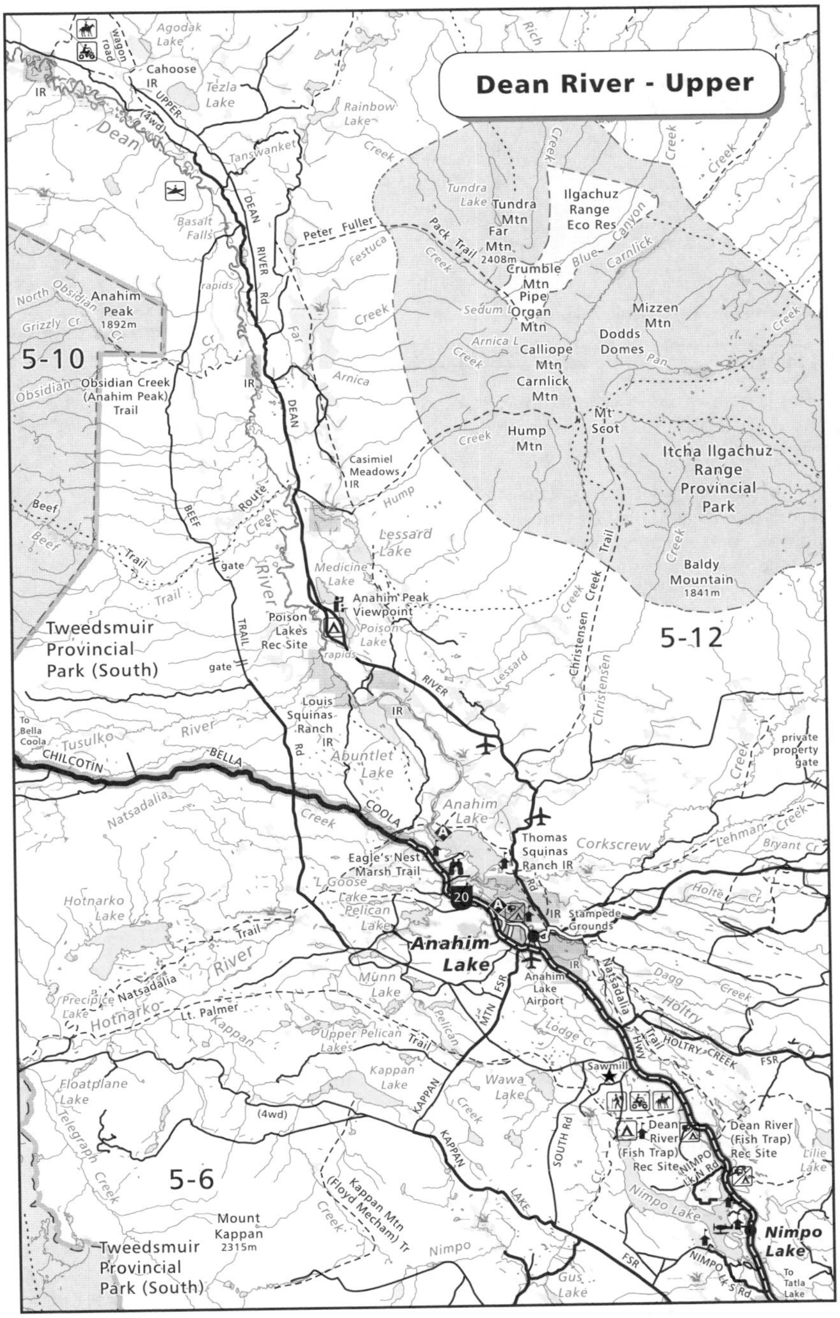

Directions

The Dean River is accessed from Anahim Lake, which is found along Highway 20, 316 km (198 miles) west of Williams Lake. The Upper Dean River Road follows the Dean downstream from Anahim Lake. To get to the road, turn north onto McInroy Road, then right on Christensen Road. Watch for the Upper Dean River Road to your left. This road gets progressively rougher until it peters out near the Tweedsmuir Park boundary. From here, there is a rough wagon road that follow the river to the Alexander Mackenzie Heritage Trail a few kilometers within the park boundaries.

Facilities

The Nimpo Lake/Anahim Lake area has a number of resorts. Nimpo Lake is the float plane capital of BC and from here you can fly into a wide variety of lakes in the area. There are bed and breakfasts as well, but no hotels as such. The **Poison Lake Recreation Site** is found along the Upper Dean River Road. There is space for six groups at the site.

Location: 32 km (20 mi) east of 100 Mile House
Elevation: 1,111 m (3,645 ft)
Surface Area: 1,154 ha (2,851.6 ac)
Maximum Depth: 101 m (331 ft)
Mean Depth: 21.6 m (71 ft)
Way Point: 51° 38′ 59″ N, 120° 47′ 5″ W

Deka Lake

Area Indicator

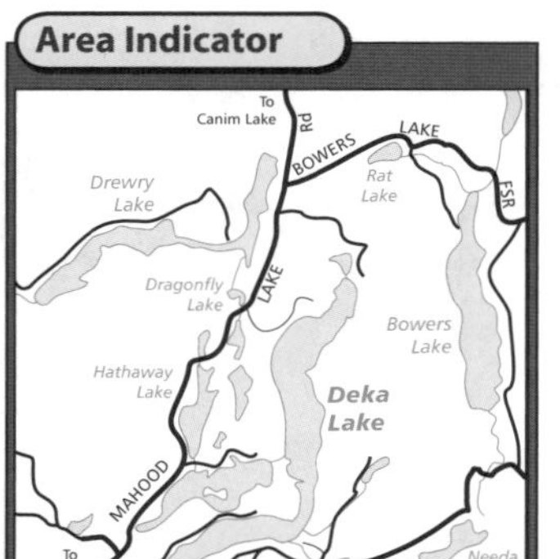

Directions

Deka Lake is found nearby to a series of good fishing lakes (Sulphurous Lake, Drewry Lake, Bowers Lake, Needa Lake and English Lake) and about 35 minutes east of 100 Mile House. The 16 km long lake is best reached by traveling along the Fishing Highway (Highway 24). At Interlakes Corner, the Mahood Lake Road heads north from the highway. Pass by the Judson Road/Horse Lake Road intersection and look for the signed Womack Road on the right. That road heads east to the southern shore of Deka Lake and beyond.

Fishing

This large lake has stocked rainbow, stocked kokanee, burbot and wild lake trout. There are also course fish such as redside shiners, squawfish, chub and suckers.

Deka Lake is considered a good trolling lake given its depths. (At its deepest, the lake is more than 100 m/330 ft deep). There are two distinct bodies with a shallow channel separating the western section from the northern section. Trollers should note where the deeper holes are, while spincasters and fly anglers should try the deeper water off the channel, as the fish tend to congregate in that location. Also be wary that wind can play havoc with small boats.

By far the most popular fishing is trolling for kokanee. A lake troll trolled along the drop offs works the best for the kokanee, which tend to be small but can be found in the 1.5 kg (3 lb) range. A recent increase in stocking levels (over 100,000 each year) should result in even better fishing in years to come.

Kokanee are known for their soft mouths and whether trolling, spincasting or fly-fishing, it is advisable to attach some form of shock absorber, to prevent the hook from tearing through the soft flesh. Kokanee are strong, determined fighters and often do damage to themselves when trying to escape. They will also take to a variety of flies. Once they hit a certain size, they start feeding on chironomids, dragonfly and damsel fly nymphs and other invertebrate. In fact, their feeding patterns are remarkably like rainbow trout and you will find that you will catch a mixture of both.

Kokanee are sensitive to the temperature of water and prefer to spend their time in a narrow band of water, although they will dart into shallower (or deeper) water to feed.

The rainbow are typically in the 0.5 kg (1 lb) range but can grow to 7 kg (15 lbs). They are caught by trolling a lake troll or by casting a variety of flies or lures.

The lake trout grow to 14 kg (30 lbs) and are caught on a deep troll using a spoon or larger lure such as an Apex or a large Flatfish. Try working a blue and silver lure or a black Flatfish with silver flakes. Lake trout are a slow growing fish and quite susceptible to over fishing, so we recommend you release most, if not all the lake trout you catch.

Facilities

There is public access and a boat launch to the lake. Those looking to overnight in the area can stay at **Deka Lake Resort**. The resort offers waterfront log cabins as well as RV and tenting sites along with a general store and boat rentals.

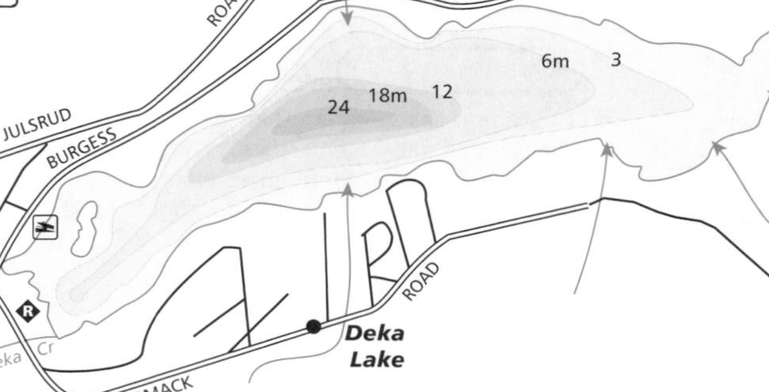

Deka Lake Fish Stocking Data			
Year	Species	Number	Life Stage
2008	Brook Trout	15,280	Yearling
2008	Rainbow Trout	20,000	Fry
2007	Brook Trout	60,000	Yearling
2007	Kokanee	100,000	Fry
2006	Rainbow Trout	60,000	Yearling
2006	Kokanee	100,900	Fingerling

Dewar Lake

Location: 20 km (12.5 mi) east of Williams Lake
Elevation: 987 m (3,238 ft)
Surface Area: 41.3 ha (102 ac)
Maximum Depth: 10 m (32.8 ft)
Mean Depth: 4 m (13 ft)
Way Point: 52° 11′46.3″N, 121° 51′58.5″W

Fishing

Dewar Lake produces large rainbow. The big fish are partly a result of the Blackwater and Fraser Valley triploid strain of trout that are stocked here. They also grow big because of the abundance of aquatic growth that make the lake rich in nutrients and teeming with insects and shrimp.

As a result, the lake is very popular with residents of Williams Lake. The ice-free periods of spring and fall are the most productive times to visit. During summer, the shallow water gets quite warm and fishing is usually quite slow then.

At only 10 metres (33 feet) in depth, the lake is better suited to spincasting and fly-fishing. However, shore casting is difficult as the near shore water is rather shallow. It is best to work the fringe area of the deeper water from a float tube or small boat for best success. The deeper part of the lake is at the south end away from the rec recreation site so it is best to paddle to the south end. Be careful not to make too much noise when paddling around as you may spook the fish.

Fly anglers can do well trying to match the hatch. Most of the hatches common to the Cariboo are found in this lake. Use a floating line and long leader or sink-tip line with chironomids, damselflies, caddisflies or dragonflies when these insects are emerging. One of the favourite times to fish is in mid to late June, when the damselflies start to emerge on the reeds. If you can get your presentation in close hold on. Shrimp and leech patterns work well, too.

Trollers are successful with a size 70 Hot Shot or F-3 to F-5 Flatfish in green or black. Trolling a black or maroon leech in size 6 or 8 3X long will also produce fish.

With relatively easy access, ice fishing is also popular here. However, anglers should note that a lake aeration project maintains the oxygen levels to sustain fish but the thin ice can be dangerous for ice fishermen. Thin ice areas are signed and cordoned off.

Ice fishers do well with a Hildebrandt spoon, removing the hook and replacing it with a 12-inch leader and size 8 or 10 pink, chartreuse or black and blue jig hook, baited with a pink or white maggot, worm or shrimp. Another proven method is to jig a yellow, lime green or purple and black marabou ice fly. Keep trying different lures and techniques until one works!

Directions

Dewar Lake is easily reached along the paved Horsefly Road, although the last bit of road into the recreation site can be muddy in wet weather. From 150 Mile House, turn east from the Cariboo Highway (Highway 97) and head north on the Likely Road. Stay right at the Horsefly Road junction at 4.5 km and continue another 8 km. Look for the Spokin Lake Forest Service Road leading right. Follow this road 300 metres to the recreation site.

Facilities

The **Dewar Lake Recreation Site** is situated on the northern shore of the lake. The small site has four picnic tables, pit toilets and a cartop boat launch.

Area Indicator

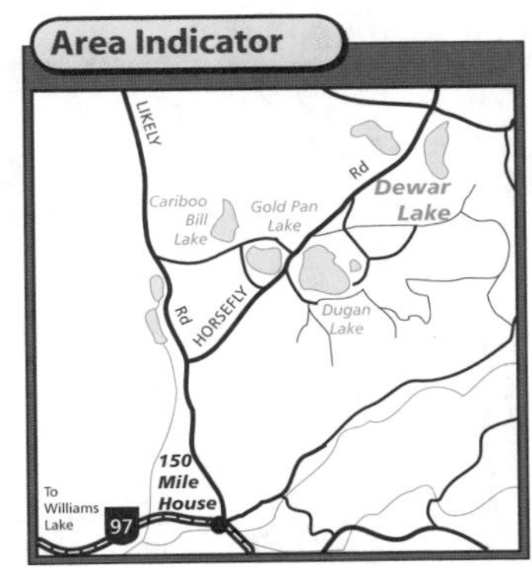

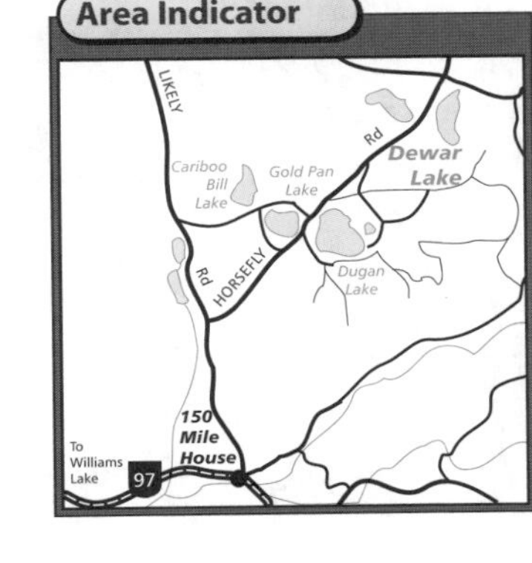

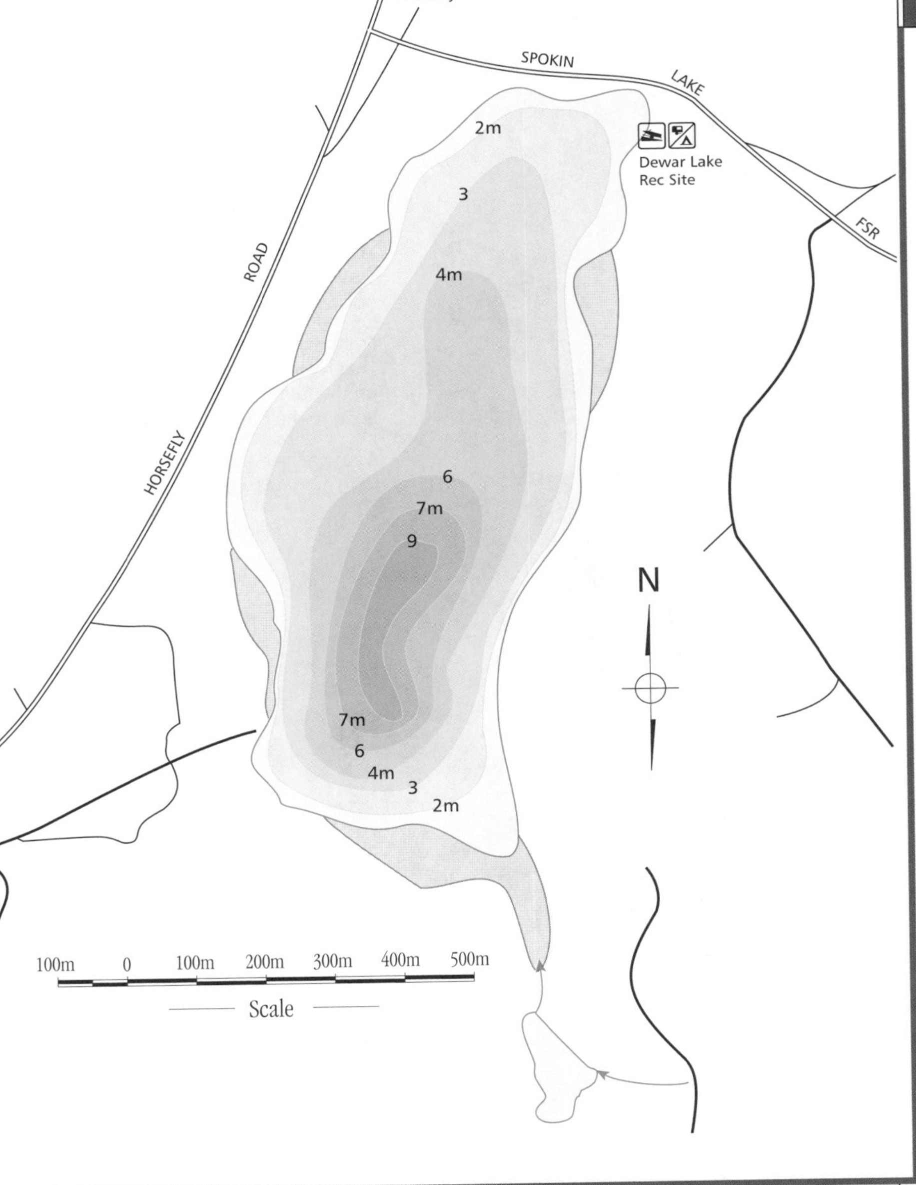

Dewar Lake Fish Stocking Data			
Year	Species	Number	Life Stage
2008	Rainbow Trout	1,000	Spring Catchable
2008	Rainbow Trout	10,000	Yearling
2007	Rainbow Trout	331	Spring Catchable
2007	Rainbow Trout	5,000	Yearling
2006	Rainbow Trout	5,000	Yearling
2006	Rainbow Trout	1,000	Catchable

Location: 45 km (30 mi) northeast of 100 Mile House
Elevation: 1,164 m (3,819 ft)
Surface Area: 113 ha (279 ac)
Maximum Depth: 35.5 m (116 ft)
Mean Depth: 11 m (36 ft)
Way Point: 51° 45′ 14″ N, 120° 40′ 26″ W

Donnely Lake

Area Indicator

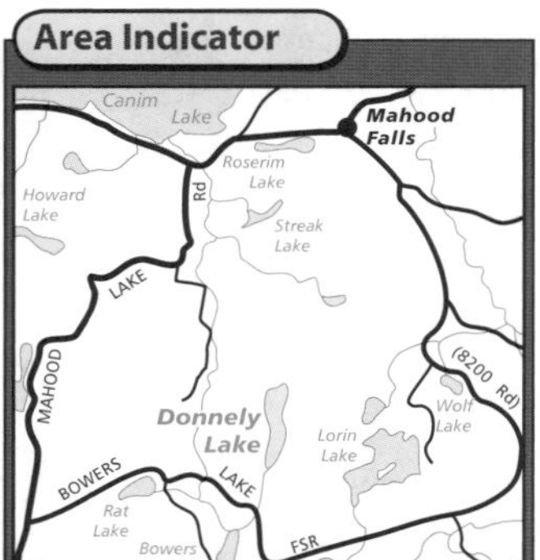

Fishing

Donnely Lake is a hike-in lake situated to the north of Bowers Lake. The hike in isn't long–about 2 km one way, but that is enough to keep most anglers from making the trip.

The lake has a good population of rainbow as the lake is stocked annually with 5,000 to 7,500 rainbow trout.

The hike and the shallow depth (over 10 metres/35 feet) of the lake discourage trollers from doing their rounds. The lake is shallow in the middle so if you are trolling, stick to the north and south ends of the lake around the deeper holes.

While it is possible to fish from shore, a float tube will help anglers get to the best spots.

Spincasters and fly anglers should cast around the fringe of the two deeper holes. A lure such as a Deadly Dick, Black Knepps or Blue Fox is the best choice for spincasters.

Fly anglers should try a chironomid imitation in the early spring. Chironomids come in many sizes and colours, so it's best to have a wide selection. Some fly fishers have entire boxes dedicated to chironomids and bloodworms, the larval stage of a chironomid.

Chironomids can hatch in a wide depth range, but most emergences happen between 2 and 8 metres (6–20 feet). The earliest emergences usually happen in shallow water and then move out deeper as the water temperature rises. By late spring, the emergences are in the 8–10 metres (20–30 feet) depth range and takes are often very gentle. A strike indicator will help detect these fish.

Later in the year, a shrimp or leech pattern work well. Some prefer to use classic searching patters such as the Doc Spratley or Carey Special.

No powerboats are allowed on the lake, although considering the hike it, that isn't much of a worry. ice fishing is not allowed. Also, there is a bait ban and a single barbless hook restriction.

Directions

The lake is accessed two ways. From the Fishing Highway (Highway 24), travel to Interlakes Corner and head north on the Mahood Lake Road. At the 8,010 km mark, look for the Bowers Lake Forest Service Road heading east. Follow that road for another 9 km to the well-signed trailhead on the north side of the road. The hike is about 2 km one-way.

From Highway 97, head north from 100 Mile House and take the Canim Lake Road leading northeast. That road will take you all the way to Canim Lake. Once at the lake, drive south around Canim Lake on the Canim Lake South Road (8100 Road). At the 25 km mark, turn south on the Mahood Lake Road to the Bower Lake Forest Service Road and follow the directions noted above.

A car can certainly reach the trailhead but remember you will be driving on several kilometers of logging roads.

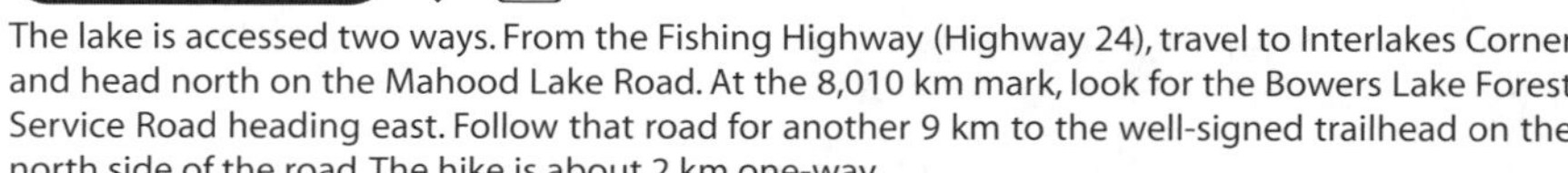

Facilities

There are no developed facilities at the lake, although it is possible to camp or hand launch near the south shore. Other, user maintained, campsites are also scattered along the lakeshore.

Other Options

Rat Lake is found west of Donnely Lake on the Bowers Lake Forest Service Road. The weedy lake requires a boat or float tube to get to the deeper areas. Casting towards shore near the outflow can produce the odd small trout.

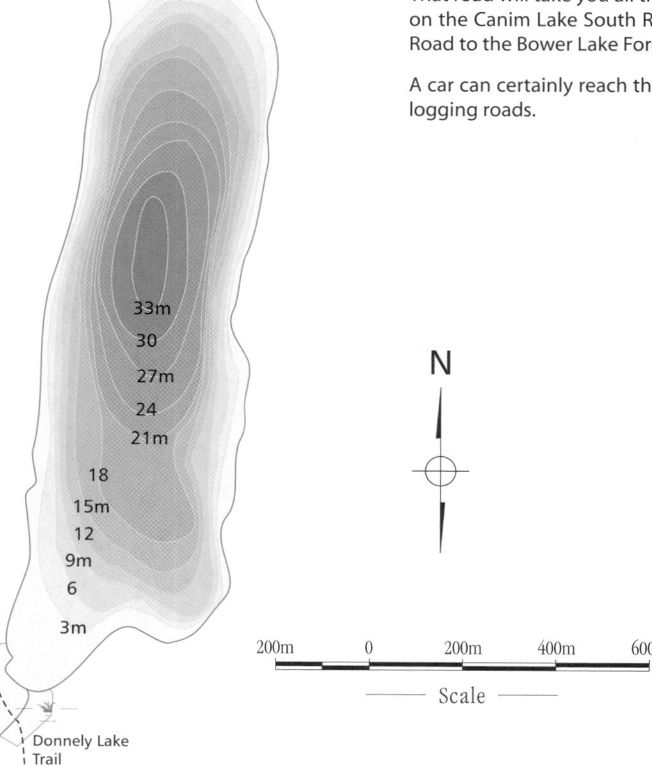

Donnely Lake Fish Stocking Data			
Year	Species	Number	Life Stage
2008	Rainbow Trout	5,000	Fry
2007	Rainbow Trout	5,000	Fry
2006	Rainbow Trout	5,000	Fall Fry

Doreen Lake

Location: 80 km (50 mi) northeast of Williams Lake
Elevation: 1,097 m (3,599 ft)
Surface Area: 19 ha (47 ac)
Maximum Depth: 11 m (36 ft)
Mean Depth: 6 m (19 ft)
Way Point: 52° 17′ 44.5″ N, 120° 57′ 13.3″ W

Fishing

Doreen Lake is reported to have good numbers of rainbow trout that once reached 2 kg (4 lbs). Unfortunately, the beaver dam let go and now the fish are quite small averaging 25 cm (10 in). However, the lake receives little fishing pressure so the lake is a good choice if you want a secluded lake that produces plenty of small fish.

If you are able to get into the area, the lake offers an early season fishery beginning in early May. The season extends to November with the summertime being the slowest time.

The lake is well suited to trolling as it is fairly deep and many prefer the classic lake troll (a Willow Leaf and Wedding Band), while small Flatfish or traditional trout lures always seem to produce. Trollers should circle the drop off area around the lake working the shallows during cooler periods and focus on the deep hole towards the middle of the lake in the summer. Follow the contours so you can see bottom on one side of the boat only. As you make the gentle turns the inside lure/fly drops and the outside lure/fly speeds up. This way you can vary the depths you are trolling. Also try shutting off the motor to allow your offering to drop a few feet, then kick it into gear again. This method can be used with trolls and lures, as well as flies.

The majority of a trout's diet consists of nymphs, including chironomids, caddis, mayflies, leeches, dragons, damsels, scuds and water boatman. Artificial flies imitate these insects best and can be fished with light spinning gear as well as fly gear. A little weight will get the fly to the right depth and a strike indicator with a fly can effectively work the surface.

Spincasters and fly fishermen can work the near shore area for good success. Shore casters are able to cast out far enough so that there is a good chance of catching a fish.

Use as light a line as possible to do the job. A 4–6 lb test line is plenty strong. Casting and retrieving lures such as; Mepps, Panther Martin and Krocodiles is also a proven method when using spinning or spincasting gear.

Directions

To reach Doreen Lake involves a long drive from Highway 97 or Horsefly. You will also need a 4wd vehicle and maybe even an ATV to access the lake.

Just before entering the town of Horsefly, cross the bridge over the Horsefly River and begin the drive on the Black Creek Road. That logging road is a well-maintained road so a car can travel along it without much trouble. Continue past Black Creek and the airport and then look for the turn-off to the McKinley Lake Road (500 Road) at the 126 km mark. At the west end of McKinley Lake a rough road leads north then east towards Doreen Lake. This last stretch may not be drivable.

The old access from the Black Creek Road is no longer passable. The bridge over the Horsefly River is out.

Facilities

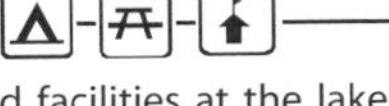

There are no developed facilities at the lake. It is possible to launch a small boat at the lake and to camp at roadside.

Area Indicator

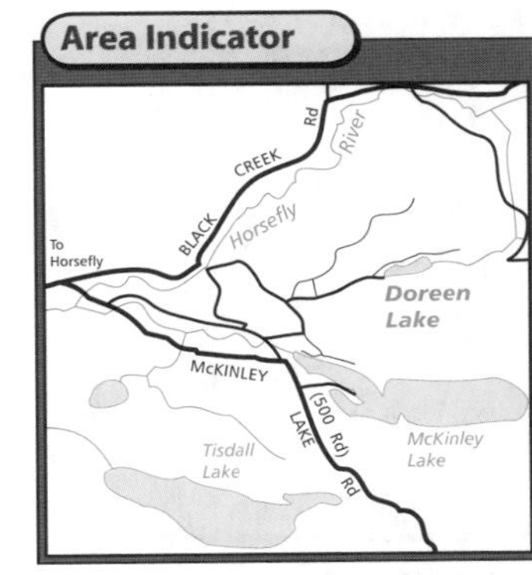

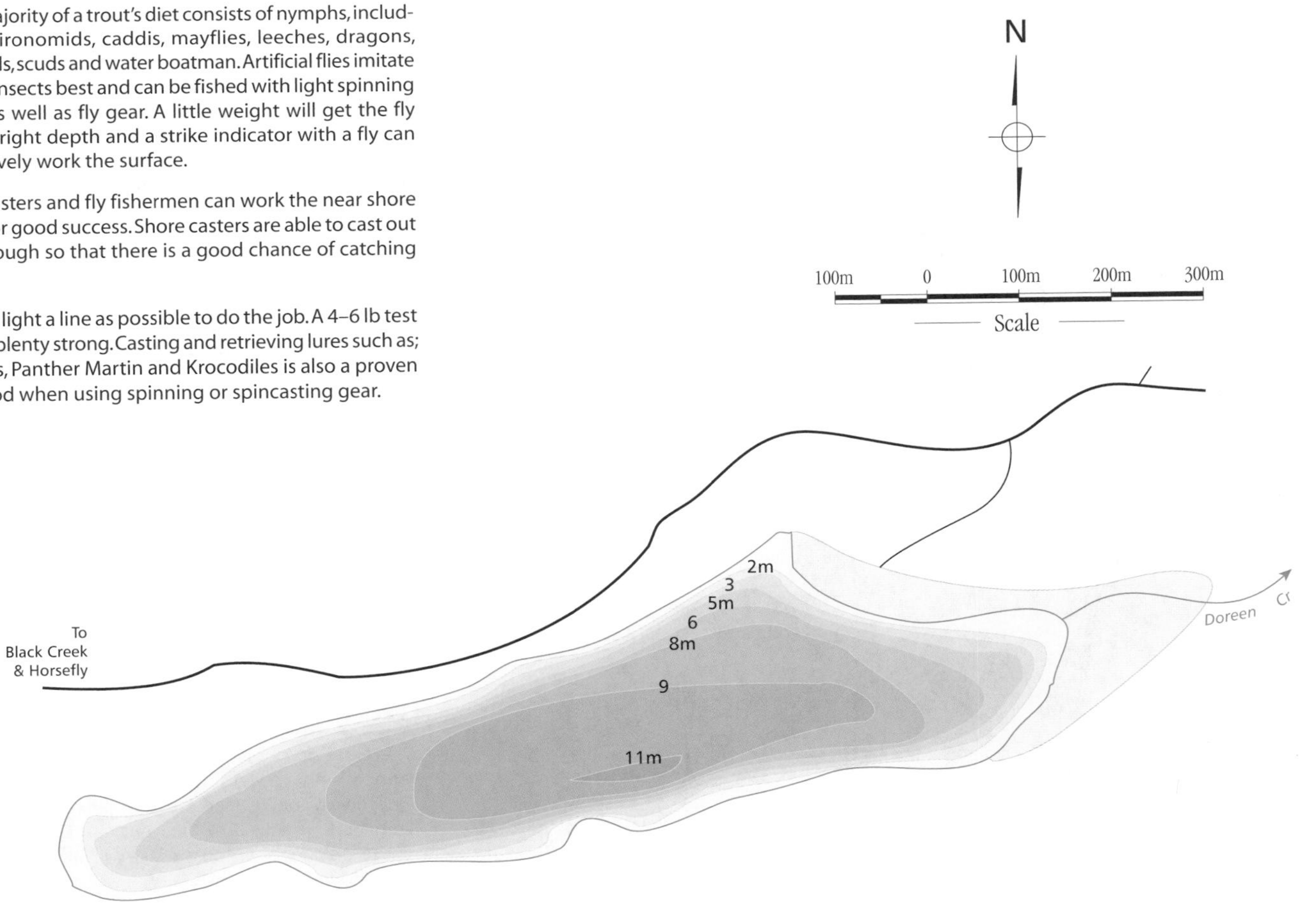

N

100m 0 100m 200m 300m
Scale

2m
3
5m
6
8m
9
11m
To Black Creek & Horsefly
Doreen Cr

Location: 5 km (3 mi) southeast of Quesnel
Elevation: 598 m (1,962 ft)
Surface Area: 225 ha (556 ac)
Maximum Depth: 8 m (26 ft)
Mean Depth: 7 m (23 ft)
Way Point: 52° 56′ 56″ N, 122° 25′ 27″ W

Dragon Lake

Area Indicator

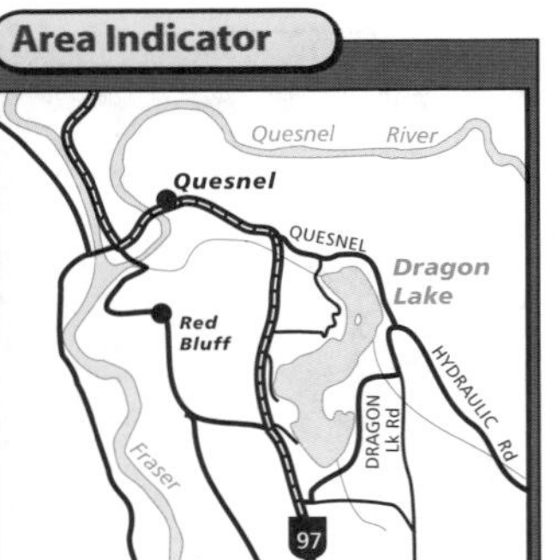

Year	Species	Number	Life Stage
2008	Rainbow Trout	25,079	Yearling
2007	Rainbow Trout	25,307	Yearling
2006	Rainbow Trout	20,019	Fry
2006	Rainbow Trout	25,107	Yearling

Dragon Lake Fish Stocking Data

SALES
ROAD E
LAKE
6
5m
3
2m
DRAGON
To Williams Lake
N
400m 0 400m 800m 1200m
Scale

Directions

Dragon Lake is a popular lake found about 5 km south of Quesnel. The lake is lined by private residences, but there is public boat launch at the north end of the lake off Quesnel Hydraulic Road. This site is found about 3 km from Highway 97.

Fishing

While the Cariboo region produces many fine trout lake, Dragon Lake is one of the finest. It is treasured by the locals and is known across North America as one of the finest early season trout fishing lakes there is.

Dragon Lake is one of three native rainbow trout sources in BC for egg collections. Between four and five million eggs (15 per cent of the provincial total) are collected annually for stocking. It is a nutrient rich lake lined with weedbeds ideal for insect rearing. There is a good population of scuds (freshwater shrimp) that help fatten up the trout. Although the lake is rather moody, if you can catch a fish, it is almost certain to be a big one, often up to 4.5 kg (10 lbs).

The lake is one of the first lakes to ice off in the early spring. It is at that time (April/May) that the lake is very popular with fly fishermen who work the weedbeds in hope of a big brook trout or rainbow. It is not uncommon to get a rainbow in the 1.5 kg (3 lb) class on a wet fly at that time. A small boat will be helpful, but the wind can play merry havoc with a tube.

Over the summer months, fishing is slow since the lake is shallow and the water warms up significantly. Also, the fish become very muddy tasting and so catch and release is highly recommended. By the fall (September/October), the lake becomes productive again. In fact, the chances are better at this time of year to catch a big trout.

Fly anglers often concentrate on fishing near the reeds that surround the shoreline and shoals on the west side of the lake that lie near the golf course and permanent residences. Flies are a seasonal preference, with chironomids, mayflies, and micro leeches in various colours and sizes working well in the spring. Leeches, dragonflies and woolly buggers produce until ice-up in the fall. Try bigger attractor type flies to attract those aggressive spawning brookies in the fall. Scud or shrimp patterns can also be effective year round.

Trollers do well in the deeper water in the middle of the lake. Trollers have found that using a Willow Leaf or Bolo lake troll with a Wedding Band and worm works just fine. Use an F-4 or F-5 Flatfish, or Hot Shot in orange, green or black, to get some large fish in your net. Spincasters should try silver and gold Mepps, Panther Martin or Blue Fox spinners or spoons fished near the reeds. Don't overlook the ever popular bobber and worm.

Dragon Lake is also a popular ice fishing destination. Ice fishers use maggots, roe or shrimp on a 3/8-ounce jig in water up to 4 metres (12 ft) deep.

Facilities

There are no public campsites but a trailered boat launch, with a toilet and day parking, is located on Quesnel Hydraulic Road. Small watercraft can also be launched off Lakeview Crescent and Crystal Street. Those looking to stay on the lake will find a resort and bed and breakfast.

Drewry Lake

Location: 30 km (18.6 mi) east of 100 Mile House
Elevation: 1,058 m (3,471 ft)
Surface Area: 565 ha (1,397 ac)
Maximum Depth: 39 m (128 ft)
Mean Depth: 13 m (42.7 ft)
Way Point: 51° 42′ 47″ N, 120° 51′ 16″ W

Fishing

Drewry Lake is a deceivingly big lake surrounded by a thick Douglas-fir forest. The lake is found north of the Fishing Highway or east of 100 Mile House. It is a long, clear lake with a slightly greenish tinge to the water.

Drewry Lake is a highish elevation lake and fishing begins in late May and remains active until early July. The lake, despite being quite deep, does not offer much in the way of a summer fishery, as fishing can be very slow at that time. By the fall, the good fishing returns again.

The lake has good numbers of wild rainbow growing to 2 kg (4 lbs) that tend to be a lot smaller (in the 20–30 cm or 8–12 in range). The lake also has a few course fish (suckers, redside shiners and squawfish).

Trolling is the main fishing method at the lake as the water is fairly deep. The better trolling is towards the western arm where the water is deeper. The eastern arm can also be trolled but the shallow channel between the lakes cannot. Wind can play havoc on smaller boats.

The lake has thick aquatic vegetation, including lily pads, reeds and submerged vegetation. All this plant growth means that there are a lot of insects and invertebrate, which in turn means that there's a lot of food for the fish. Trolling around the weeds can be a mixed proposition, as the weeds tend to foul hooks fairly easy. Instead, these areas are best left for spincasters or better yet, fly anglers. A popular area to fish is the fringe area leading to the shallow channel between the western and eastern arms. Working around the islands in the western arm is also effective. Fly anglers should note what is hatching, looking for chironomids early in the year followed by mayflies, caddis flies and dragon and damselflies.

Directions

The better access is to travel along Highway 24 to Interlakes Corner and then head north on the Horse Lake and Mahood Lake Roads. The later is paved until Burgess Road where it turns into a good logging road that all vehicles can travel. Drewry Lake is found about 10 km up the road.

From 100 Mile House, head north a few kilometers from 100 Mile House on the Cariboo Highway (Highway 97) and turn onto the Canim Lake Road. At Buffalo Creek, turn east on the Buffalo Creek Road and follow that road to Buffalo Lake. Hang a left on the Drewry Lake Forest Service Road to access the west end of the lake. In wet weather, this road can get rather muddy so a truck is highly recommended.

Facilities

The **Drewry Lake East Recreation Site** is a large site on the eastern shore that can be accessed by larger units. Launching a small boat is certainly possible. The **Drewry Lake West Recreation Site** also offers a nice recreation site with several camping sites. Launching a boat at the site involves a short carry.

Other Options

Buffalo Lake is found off the Buffalo Creek Road en route to the western shore of Drewry. The shallow lake offers an excellent fly-fishing alternative in the early spring and fall. Casting around the near shore area off Buffalo Creek can be deadly. It is possible to launch a small boat at the lake.

Area Indicator

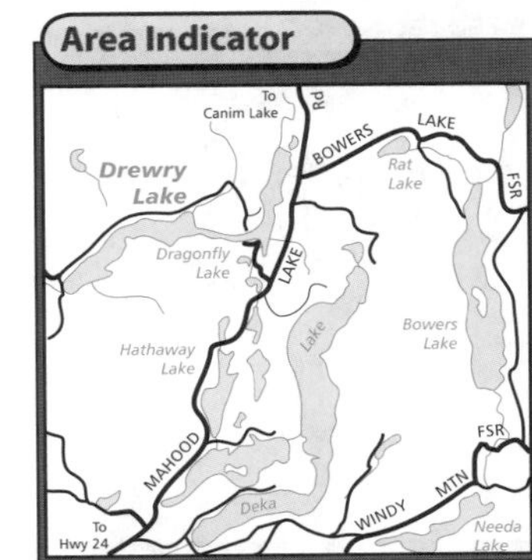

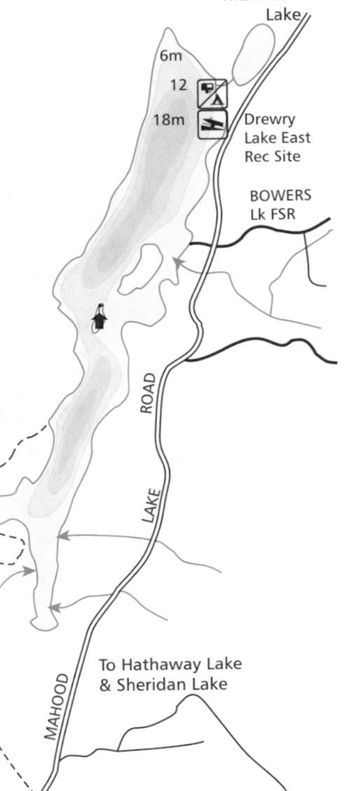

Location: 30 km (18.6 mi) north of Smithers
Elevation: 571m (1,873 ft)
Surface Area: 9.9 ha (24.5 ac)
Maximum Depth: 9.8 m (32 ft)
Mean Depth: 4.1m (14 ft)
Way Point: 55° 1′ 5.7″ N, 127° 17′ 29.9″ W

Duckbill Lake

Area Indicator

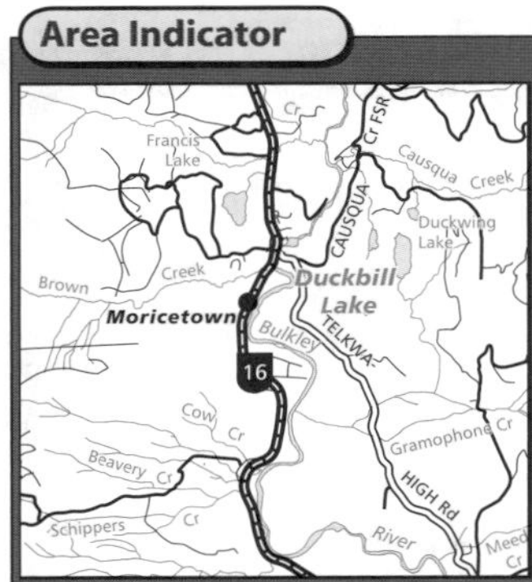

Directions

Although close to the highway, Duckbill is not an easy lake to access. In fact an ATV (or walking) is needed for the last stretch of road. To find the lake, turn off the Yellowhead Highway at Moricetown, north of Smithers, onto the Telkwa High Road. Drive for 0.5 km and then turn left onto the 2000 (also known as Causqua) Forest Service Road. Travel for about 4 km and then turn right onto a rough, unmaintained road. A 4wd vehicle is recommended for the first couple kilometres, but after that you will either need an ATV or be prepared to walk. Continue onto the fork in the road and turn right. It is another 400 metres down this road to another fork. Turn right to Duckbill Lake or left to Duckwing Lake.

Duckbill Lake			
Fish Stocking Data			
Year	Species	Number	Life Stage
2007	Rainbow Trout	1,000	Fingerling
2005	Rainbow Trout	1,000	Yearling

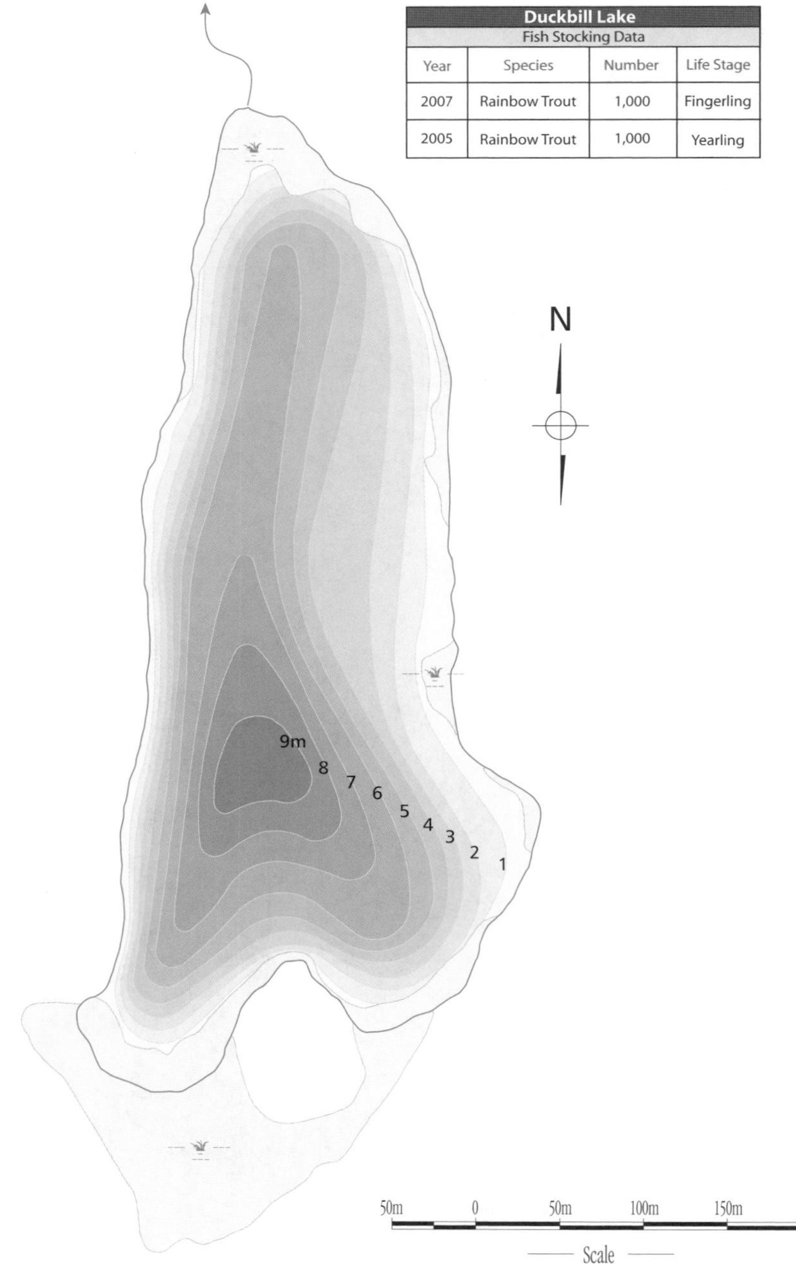

Fishing

Duckbill Lake is a sheltered, quiet little beauty, about a quarter the size of its big sister, Duckwing Lake. Its small size allows anglers to easily cover the surface with a canoe, pontoon boat or float tube. The clear waters also hold some very nice rainbow trout up to 60 cm (24 in) in length.

Duckbill is stocked every second year with 1,000 yearling rainbow by the Freshwater Fisheries Society of BC. Fly-fishing is the most common way to fish the lake, but your spinning gear stands an equally good chance of a strike. A torpedo bobber with a fly can effectively work the surface for those with spinning gear. Trying adding a little weight if you are fishing deeper. A Mepps, Panther Martin, Vibrax or Gibbs spinner cast out working different depths around the drop off are other promising options. Vertical jigging with spoons or jigs using flavoured bait, such as one of the Berkley Powerbaits, will also work well.

Fly anglers should note what is hatching, remembering that trout tend to be very particular when a hatch is on. They prefer the exact colour and size, which can be the most frustrating part of the learning curve when fly-fishing. It can also be the most rewarding.

Chironomids are the most prolific early insect hatch on Duckbill. Chironomids (also known as midges) look like a mosquito but thankfully don't have the biting parts. They can be from 2–25 mm (barely visible to slightly less than an in) in length and are mainly brown, green, black or red. The larvae live and hide in burrows in the mud-water interface, becoming available to the trout when they pupate and slowly rise to the surface.

Early summer caddisfly hatches can really turn the fish on. The newly emerged caddis adults run across the surface of the lake before flying away. Trout know this and attack caddis with ferocity.

Dragonflies are the full-meal deal for a trout. They can be huge. Damselflies look like smaller, slimmer, more delicate dragons. Trout will feed exclusively on either of these when the hatch is on.

Mayflies are numerous on Duckbill, available year round and taken both as nymphs and adults. There are many varieties and colours in this species. Also available year round are scuds or freshwater shrimp. They are usually grey, green, brown, tan, olive or cream in colour.

There is some ice fishing on Duckbill but the overgrown road and snow load on the branches can make for a challenging trip. Jigs tipped with bait fished close to the steep shoreline are the best bet.

Facilities

There are no facilities available on the lake, although people do camp at a private site in Moricetown. Smithers, to the south, has full services.

Duckwing Lake

Location: 30 km (18.6 mi) north of Smithers
Elevation: 547 m (1,794 ft)
Surface Area: 46 ha (114 ac)
Maximum Depth: 35 m (115 ft)
Mean Depth: 14 m (47 ft)
Way Point: 55° 0′ 53.2″ N, 127° 16′ 45.3″ W

Fishing

Anglers in search of solitude and large rainbow trout should set their sights on the quality waters of Duckwing Lake. The lake is managed as a quality fishery. The largest fish captured in a recent assessment was 61 cm (24 in) and the average size was 41 cm (16 in). Some local anglers tell tales of even larger fish.

The Freshwater Fisheries Society of BC stocks Duckwing every alternate year with 2,000 yearling rainbow trout. From the parking area, a five-minute walk takes you to the shore. The launch area often contains floating trees that you will have to work around. The lake is most often fished with pontoon or belly boats as not many anglers want to pack a boat, motor, gas and gear to the lake.

The centre of the lake is quite deep and the best method of fishing is the "count down" tactic. Whether using lures or flies, cast from along the shore outwards and count as you wait before retrieving. Increase your waiting time after each cast by five seconds until you encounter the bottom. Now cut back a couple of seconds and your next cast will be following the slope upwards. Experiment, until you find the depth the trout prefer.

Big fish don't get big or old by biting the first offering; so catching these larger fish can be difficult. You will need to try different lures, flies, depths and retrieves to be successful. Catching big fish is akin to feeding children. It is much easier to please them with what they want, not what you want to give them.

Chironomids are the fly of choice in the first part of the season. Always keep an eye open for chironomids swimming to the surface and try to match the size and colour with one in your fly box.

Trout are opportunistic feeders and can seldom resist a leech, damsel or dragon pattern. Make sure you include a few good shrimp, caddis and mayfly patterns. From June on, you will need some dry flies. For those with spinning or spincasting gear, you are good to go with small lures such as the Panther Martin, Mepps, Vibrax, Kamlooper and Krocodile.

The overgrown road and snow load discourages access for ice fishing, but there are some nice fish to be caught during the winter. Jigs tipped with Powerbait, worms, maggots or krill/shrimp are the best choice.

Facilities

There are no facilities available on the lake, although people do camp at a private site in Moricetown. Smithers, to the south, has full services.

Duckwing Lake			
Fish Stocking Data			
Year	Species	Number	Life Stage
2007	Rainbow Trout	2,000	Yearling
2005	Rainbow Trout	2,000	Yearling

Directions

Although close to the highway, Duckwing is not an easy lake to access. In fact an ATV (or walking) is needed for the last stretch of road. To find the lake, turn off the Yellowhead Highway at Moricetown, north of Smithers, onto the Telkwa High Road. Drive for 0.5 km and then turn left onto the 2000 (also known as Causqua) Forest Service Road. Travel for about 4 km and then turn right onto a rough, unmaintained road. A 4wd vehicle is recommended for the first couple kilometres, but after that you will either need an ATV or be prepared to walk. Continue onto the fork in the road and turn right. It is another 400 metres down this road to another fork. Turn right to Duckbill Lake or left to Duckwing Lake.

Area Indicator

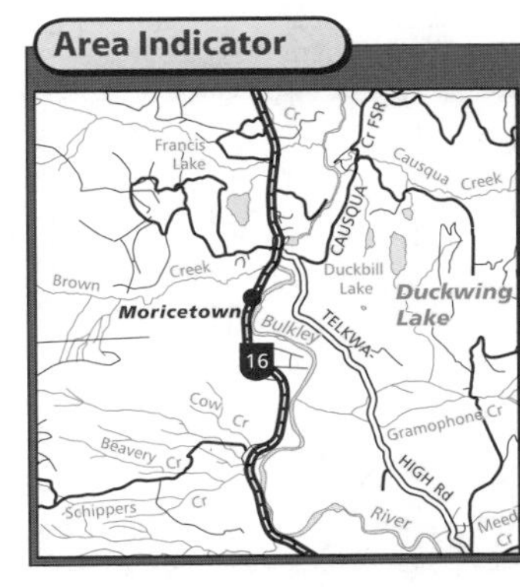

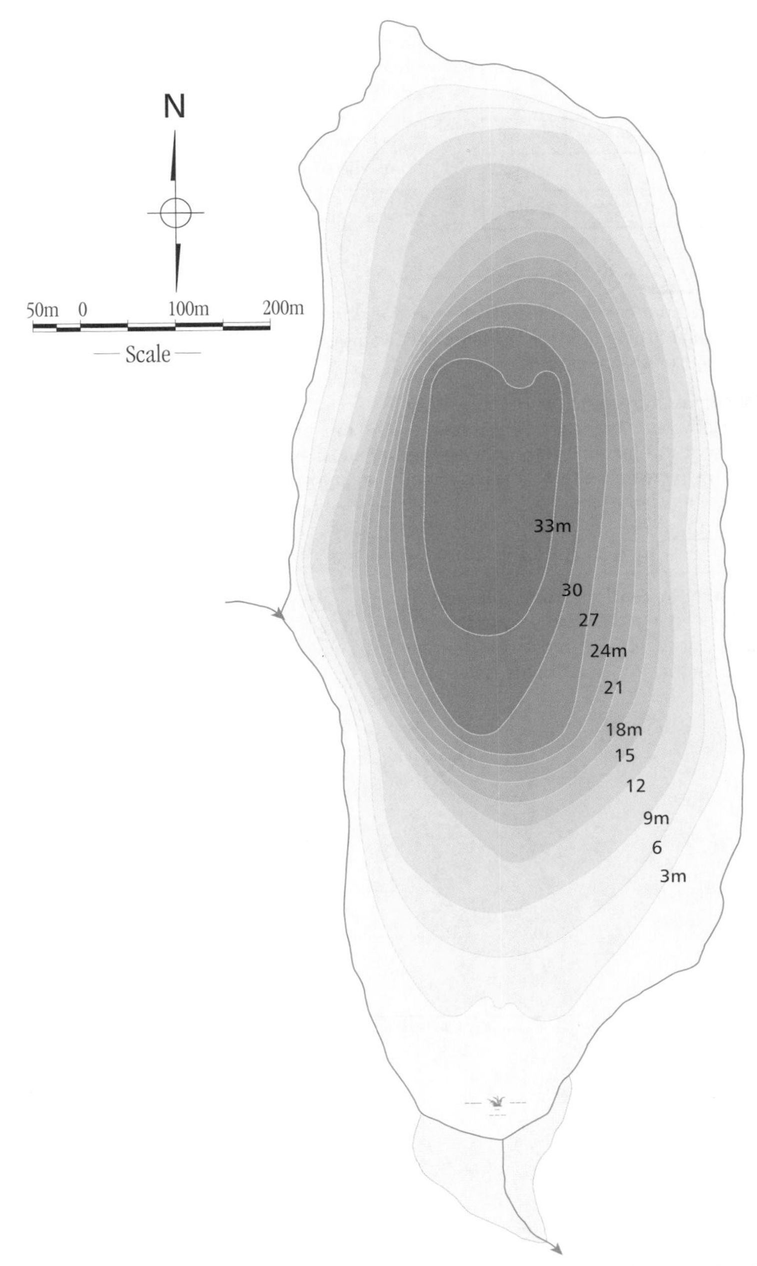

Location: 15 km (9.3 mi) east of Williams Lake
Elevation: 922 m (3,095 ft)
Surface Area: 96.3 ha (238 ac)
Maximum Depth: 14 m (46 ft)
Mean Depth: 6.4 m (21 ft)
Geographic: 52° 10′ 11.8″ N, 121° 54′ 14.3″ W

Dugan Lake

Area Indicator

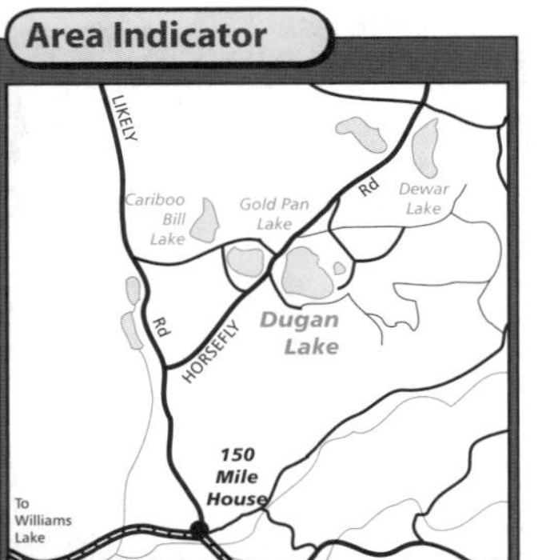

Dugan Lake			
Fish Stocking Data			
Year	Species	Number	Life Stage
2008	Brook Trout	15,280	Yearling
2008	Rainbow Trout	20,000	Yearling
2007	Brook Trout	14,900	Yearling
2007	Rainbow Trout	20,000	Yearling
2006	Brook Trout	13,994	Yearling
2006	Rainbow Trout	20,000	Yearling

Fishing

Dugan Lake is a highly productive lake with an intensive stocking program. In fact, 70,000 brook trout and 5,000 rainbow trout are stocked each year at the lake by the Freshwater Fisheries Society of BC. The lake also has a few brown trout, which are not very common in Central BC.

The brook trout are the main focus of the lake with the fish reaching 1-2 kg (2-4 lbs) in size but averaging 33-40 cm (13-16 in) in size. Brook trout fishing is good in the spring and fall or through the ice in winter.

In the ice-off season, the best way to catch brookies is to cast an attractor type fly or a lure tipped with a worm towards the weedbeds that line the lake. Since the lake is fairly deep, it is possible to troll the lake without too many hang-ups. For shore casters, there are several areas where the grassy meadows reach the shoreline. At those locations, casting is fairly easy. Other areas are limited due to the heavy vegetation in and around the lake.

By far the most popular fishing is trolling for kokanee. A lake troll trolled along the drop offs works the best for the kokanee, which tend to be small but can be found in the 1.5 kg (3 lb) range. A recent increase in stocking levels (over 100,000 each year) should result in even better fishing in years to come.

However, Dugan Lake is best known for its ice fishing and as soon as the ice is thick enough to support their body weight, anglers head out onto the lake. Both brown trout and brook trout are more active in the winter than rainbow.

Brook trout like hanging around structure, especially in winter and the fishing is usually best around underwater points, jumbles of rocks and other places that the trout can hang around. As there is no danger from above and as the most oxygenated layer of water is closest to the ice, brook trout are usually found in less than 3 metres (10 feet) of water. Put the two together (shallow water and underwater structure) and you will find most of the fish close to shore, sometimes in as little as 1 metre (3 feet) of water. The best way to fish is by drilling a series of holes. The sound of the ice auger can scare fish away, so best get it over with in one go. After things have settled, use a jigging spoon, a baited hook or a combination of the two and fish just a few feet off the bottom of the lake, occasionally lifting the hook and letting it fall back down.

Directions

Dugan Lake is located east of Williams Lake on the Horsefly Road. It is a popular fishing hole for residents of Williams Lake, especially during ice fishing season.

From 150 Mile House, turn east from Highway 97 onto the Likely Road. The Horsefly Road branches off this road at 4.5 km and about 2.5 km past this junction turn right on the Dugan Lake Road to reach the recreation site. Access is good allowing most vehicles to easily reach the lake.

Facilities

The **Dugan Lake Recreation Site** is a large, popular site located in a meadow next to the lake. The site is accessible to most vehicles including RVs. Launching small boats is certainly possible.

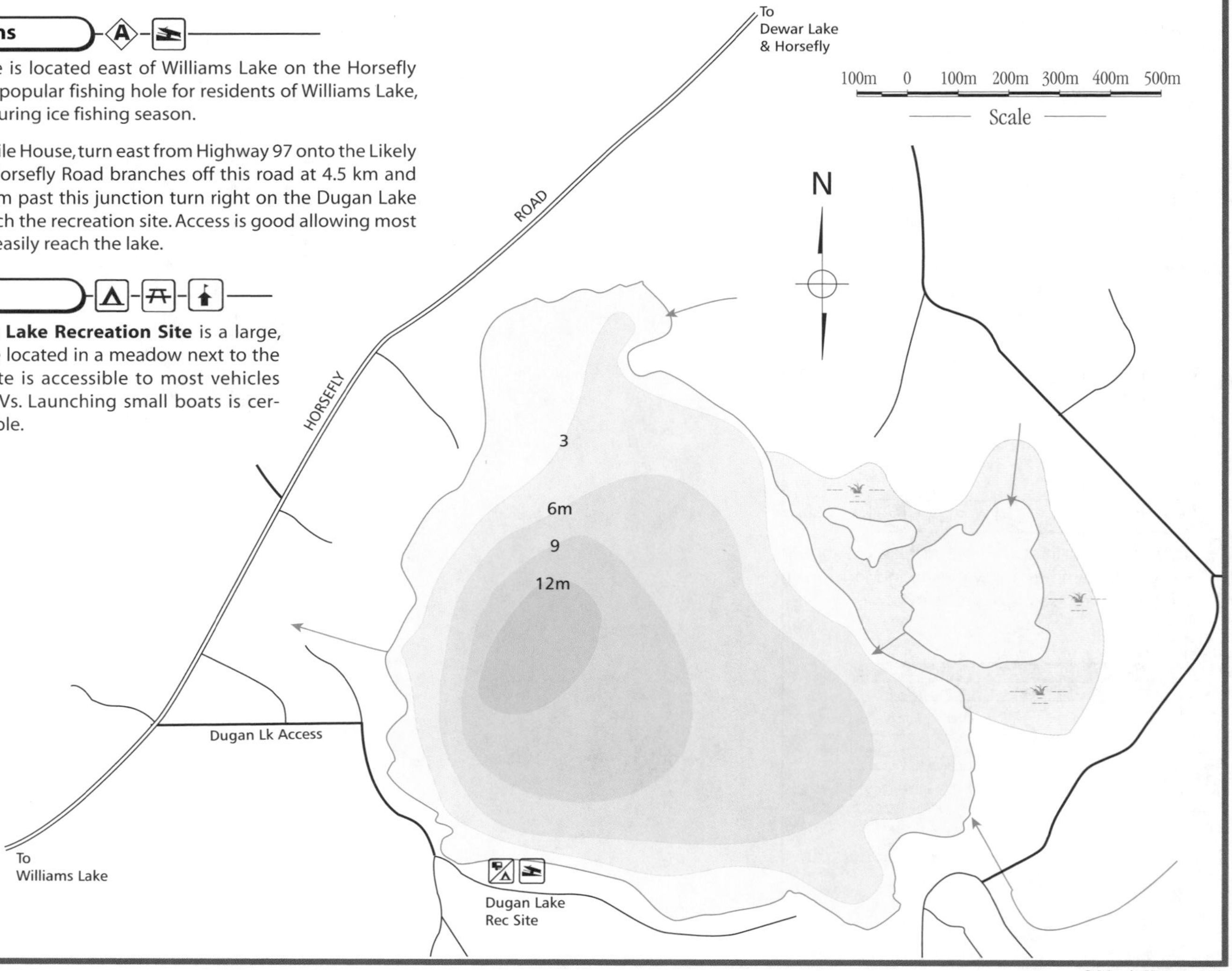

To Dewar Lake & Horsefly
100m 0 100m 200m 300m 400m 500m
Scale
N
Horsefly Road
3
6m
9
12m
Dugan Lk Access
To Williams Lake
Dugan Lake Rec Site

Dunalter (Irrigation) Lake

Location: 15 km (10 mi) west of Houston
Elevation: 796m (2,611 ft)
Surface Area: 23 ha (56 ac)
Maximum Depth: 18 m (59 ft)
Mean Depth: 5.5 m (18 ft)
Way Point: 54° 28′ 15″ N, 126° 45′ 20″ W

Fishing

Widely known as Irrigation Lake, Dunalter Lake is the perfect place to introduce novice anglers of any age to the rewards of lake fishing. The District of Houston acquired the 44 acres of Crown land surrounding the lake to develop a public park. It is now a well-used recreation playground for many activities including fishing.

Dunalter's popularity as a year round fishing lake began in the mid-1980s following a successful rehabilitation. The non-sportfish were removed, freshwater shrimp were brought in and the lake was initially stocked with rainbow trout, followed in subsequent years by cutthroat trout. The Freshwater Fisheries Society of BC continues to release 3,000 yearling cutthroat into Dunalter each year. In a recent biological assessment, the largest cutthroat captured at Dunalter was 42 cm (17 in); the average size was 31 cm (12 in).

The dock/launching area is a good spot to fish from shore. Shore anglers can expect some action with little more than a No. 4 hook tipped with cocktail shrimp or a worm and a small to medium split shot about 2 m (6 ft) above the hook. Weed beds prevent shore fishing around the rest of the lake, so most anglers use cartop boats, canoes, pontoon or belly boats. Small spoons such as Triple Teasers, Dick Nites and needlefish in silver, silver/red head, chartreuse or prism are proven producers. Since these spoons are very light, use a small to medium split shot about 2 m (6 ft) above the lure.

Flies are also effective and can be trolled with fly or spinning gear. If you are using spinning gear just add a little weight as described above. Great fly patterns for the cutthroat include the '52 Buick, damsel and dragonfly imitations, Muddler Minnows and a beadhead micro leech in black and red. And don't feel left out if you only have a spinning rod. Purchase a couple of torpedo bobbers and attach a leader about the same length as the rod to the fly. The torpedo bobber gives you the weight to cast a good distance. It is a very effective tactic when the fish are close to the surface.

Dunalter also enjoys an active winter fishery. Most ice anglers drill their holes fairly close to shore in 1.5–3 metres (5–10 ft) of water. Berkley Powerbaits, maggots or worms–either by themselves or on a small jigging spoon–are tough to beat. Winter is also a good time to introduce novice anglers to fishing since ice fishing techniques are easy to master.

Facilities

Home to a municipal park, visitors will find a host of facilities. The day use area hosts a dock, swimming beach, day-use picnic area and change rooms. People can hand launch small boats here too, but please note the electric motor only restriction. For added adventure, there are two hiking/cross-country ski trails, a 1.5 km loop on the west side of the lake and a 2 km trail on the east.

Directions

Dunalter Lake is located 15 km west of Houston, off the Yellowhead Highway (Highway 16). Look for a blue picnic table sign and a blue Irrigation Lake sign. Turn west and drive for 0.3 km on a good gravel road.

Area Indicator

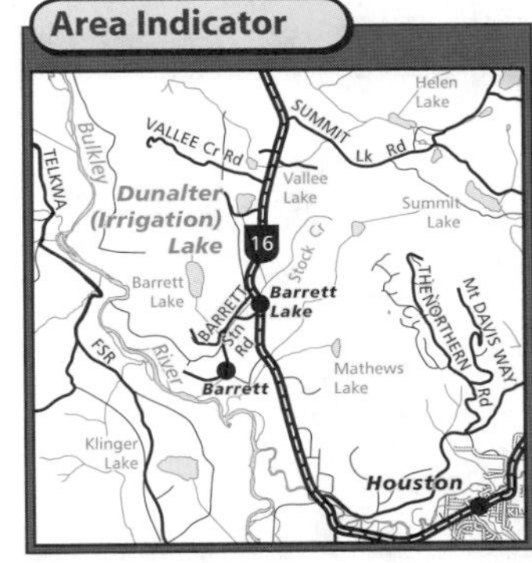

Dunalter Lake Fish Stocking Data			
Year	Species	Number	Life Stage
2008	Cutthroat Trout	3,000	Yearling
2007	Cutthroat Trout	3,000	Yearling
2006	Cutthroat Trout	3,000	Yearling

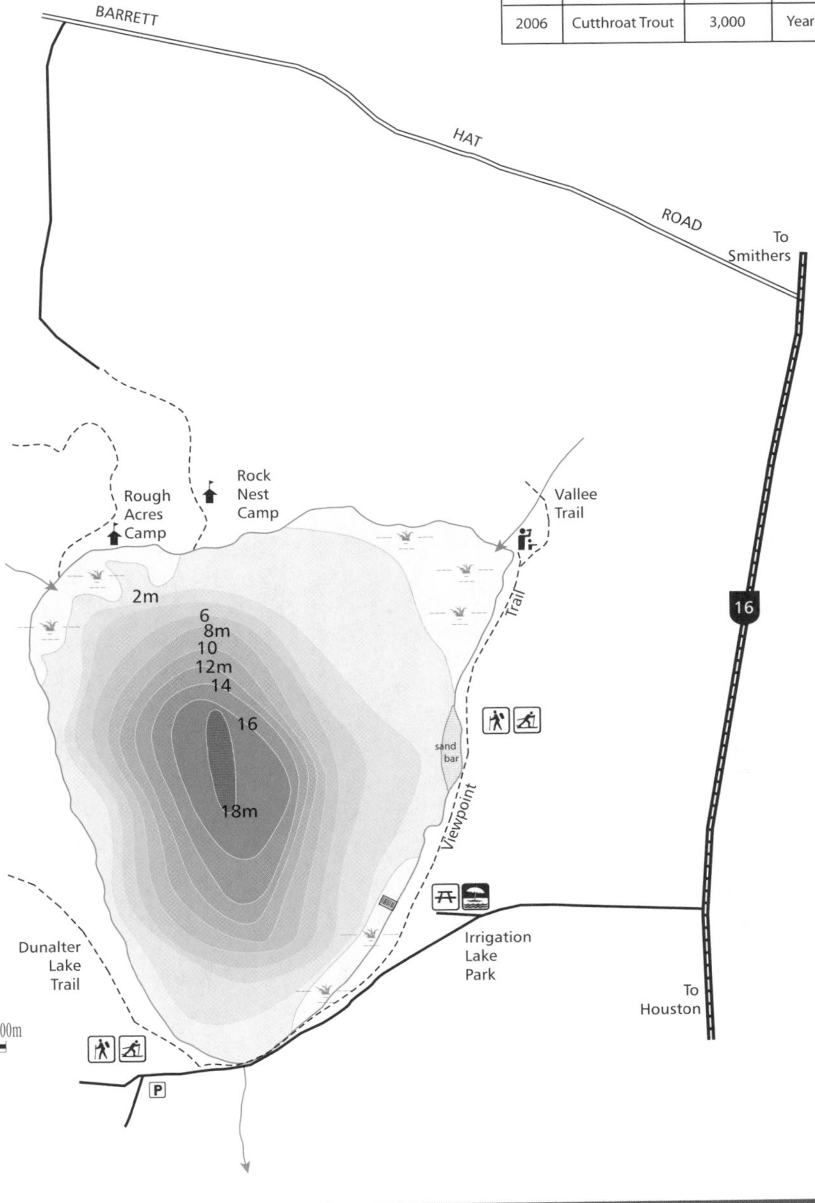

BARRETT HAT ROAD
To Smithers
16
Rough Acres Camp
Rock Nest Camp
Vallee Trail
2m
6
8m
10
12m
14
16
18m
sand bar
Viewpoint Trail
Irrigation Lake Park
Dunalter Lake Trail
To Houston
P
N 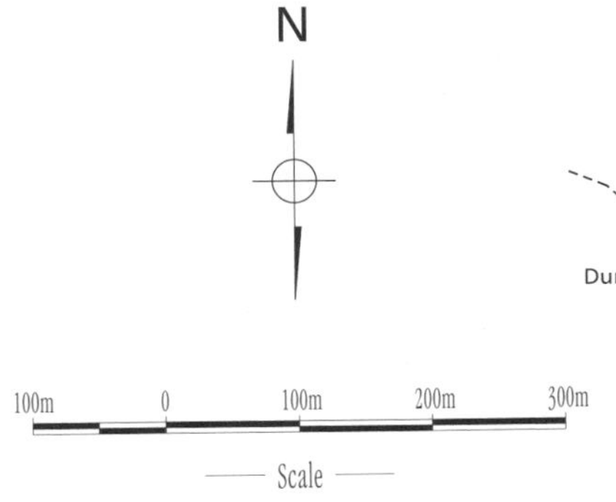
100m 0 100m 200m 300m
Scale

Eagle (Murphy) Lake

Location: 56 km (35 mi) east of Williams Lake
Elevation: 867 m (2,844 ft)
Surface Area: 1,065 ha (2,632 ac)
Maximum Depth: 23 m (75 ft)
Mean Depth: 12 m (39 ft)
Way Point: 52° 2′ 32″ N, 121° 14′ 2″ W

Area Indicator

Fishing

Eagle Lake is sometimes referred to as Murphy Lake. It is a mid-sized lake found tucked in the hills to the east of Williams Lake. Fishing is pretty steady throughout the open water season for rainbow to 2 kg (5 lbs).

Since Eagle Lake is quite deep, it can be trolled easily. There is one deep hole at the northwest end of the lake and one at the southeast end. Working these locations with a lake troll, Flatfish or other popular trout lures can be rewarding.

For spincasters and fly fishermen, the inflow creek (Eagle Creek) or outflow creek are good areas to try. Also, there are a couple sunken islands towards the middle of the lake to test. Spinners like Mepps, Panther Martin, Vibrax and Gibbs or spoons like an Apex Trout Killer, Kamlooper and Krocodile all work well. The best way to spincast is to anchor your boat just off the drop off, cast into the shallow, then count to ten before you begin your retrieve. If the lure didn't hit bottom, add an extra five seconds to each cast before you retrieve. Once you have found bottom, subtract a couple seconds from the total time and cast again. You are trying to retrieve just above bottom, not drag the lure along the bottom.

Vertical jigging with spoons or jigs using scented bait, such as one of the Berkley Powerbaits, will also work well. Others prefer to simply cast a worm and bobber. Make sure the distance between the bobber and the hook is sufficient to dangle the hook a few in to a few feet above bottom. One of the most common mistakes anglers make is to set the bait too high, above where the trout will notice it.

Fly anglers can work a mixture of traditional Cariboo flies, like Spratleys and Careys. Chironomids are always good in spring and scud patterns and leech patterns can work well later on. Nymph patterns are also a good standby pattern.

Facilities

A boat launch is situated towards the northwest end of the lake. There is no camping on the lake, but cabins may be rented if you inquire locally.

Directions

There are a few possible access routes off of Highway 97. However, the access is long and dusty and can be rough, especially in wet weather. Private land can affect access into the lake. A copy of the Backroad Mapbook for the *Cariboo Chilcotin Coast BC* is a definite asset when looking for the lake.

From the south, near the town of Lac la Hache, look for Timothy Lake Road (1500 Rd) branching north. Follow this road for about 8 km and then make a left on the Komori Road (3200 Rd). Continue north past Rail Lake and Sprout Lake. Eventually, the road turns into the Eagle Creek Road. Turn right at the second major junction and you should pass Two Mile Lake en route to the northwest end of Eagle Lake and the launch site.

Access is also possible near Williams Lake at 150 Mile House. Just south of the gas station complex, look for Pigeon Road branching east. Follow this road a short distance to the McIntosh-Moffat Lakes Forest Service Road (2300 Rd). This road continues east, eventually linking to the Knife Creek Road, which links to the Eagle Creek/Komori Road junction described above.

Earle Lake

Location: 15 km (9.3 mi) east of 100 Mile House
Elevation: 1,083 m (3,553 ft)
Surface Area: 57 ha (141 ac)
Maximum Depth: 12 m (39 ft)
Mean Depth: 4 m (13 ft)
Way Point: 51° 37′ 38.8″ N, 121° 5′ 40.2″ W

Fishing

In an effort to increase the fish size yet maintain the fishery, the Freshwater Fisheries Society of BC has recently reduced the number of fish being stocked here. The lake is now stocked annually with 4,000 to 6,000 of the hard fighting Pennask strain of rainbow. These fish are famous for their powerful runs when hooked and their aerial displays as they try and shake the hook.

With these changes, anglers should expect the average fish size to be bigger than 30 cm (12 in) in the near future. The small lake is high enough in elevation to delay the fishing season until the later part of May. Fishing remains productive until the early part of July. The summer is not a good time to fish the lake as the fish are inactive and can taste muddy. By the fall, the fishing picks up again until just before ice-over in the early part of November.

The lake is well suited for a belly boat or canoe. Cast a fly or lure tipped with a worm towards the shallows. Casting from shore is difficult as vegetation and marshy areas surround the lake. Also the lake is not very deep and quite weedy, so trolling is limited unless you want to drag a surface fly or lure. The deepest part of the lake is right in the middle of the lake so you should try trolling there to reduce hang-ups.

The weeds and marshy areas do provide a great habitat for aquatic insects and invertebrates, making this a great place for fly anglers. The lake features the typical area hatches, starting with chironomids in late May, followed by mayflies, caddisflies and dragon and damselflies. While dry fly-fishing is the most exciting way to fish the lake, it is not always the most productive; fishing a mayfly or damselfly nymph usually elicits better results. Other common patterns include a Doc Spratley or a Carey Special. If you happen to hit the lake when the fish are rising, make sure to have a handful of dry flies, including a bunch of Tom Thumbs or Adams, to throw at the lake. More recently flies that resemble the pine beetle can be a lot of fun too.

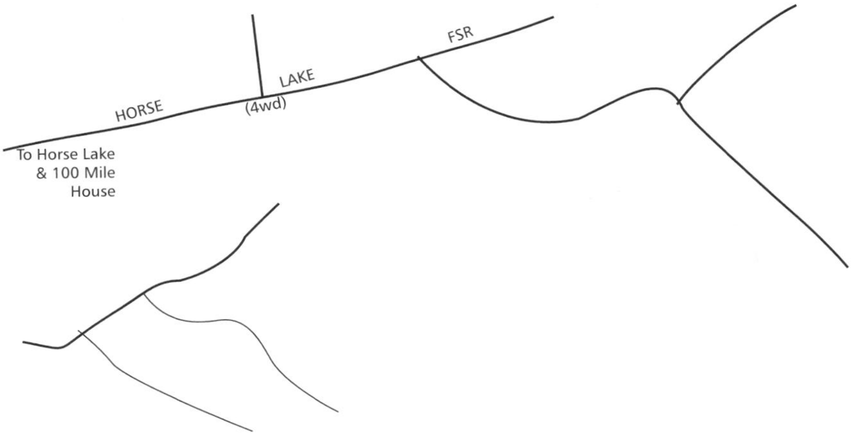

Facilities

There are no developed facilities at the lake, but some people do camp at a small clearing on the north end. Launching a small boat requires a short pack.

Other Options

Fiset Lake is a hidden, tiny lake found north of Earle Lake. There are rumors of good trout fishing in the spring and fall.

Earle Lake			
Fish Stocking Data			
Year	Species	Number	Life Stage
2008	Rainbow Trout	6,000	Fry
2007	Rainbow Trout	6,000	Fry
2006	Rainbow Trout	6,003	Fall Fry

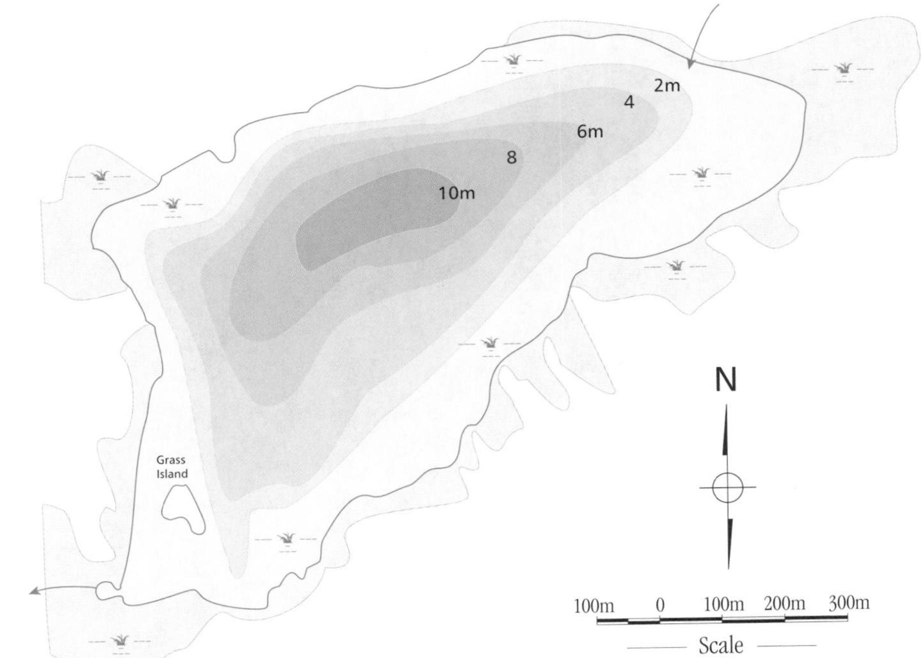

Directions

Travel east from 100 Mile House on the paved Horse Lake Road. At 9 km keep straight on the Horse Lake Road North Road (where the main road turns south), which turns to gravel. Continue another 7.5 km and look for a small, rough road to the right that leads to a parking area about 200 metres down. Another track leads left from here for about a kilometre to a small clearing that some people use to camp at. The lake is a short walk from either area.

If you miss the small side road, the Horse Lake Road North Road leads to a private ranch. Please do not trespass.

Area Indicator

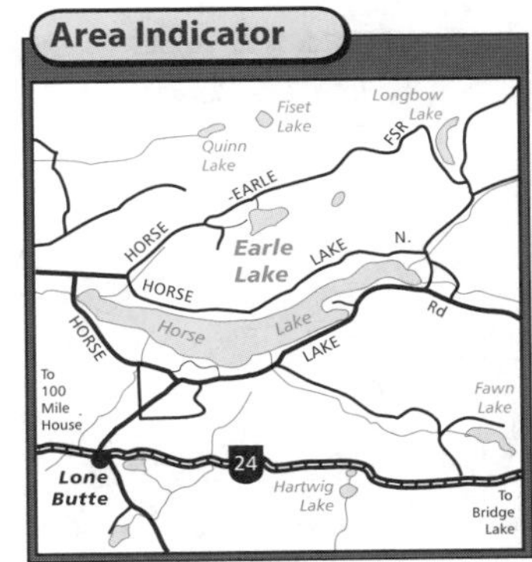

HORSE LAKE FSR (4wd)
To Horse Lake & 100 Mile House

2m
4
6m
8
10m
Grass Island
N
100m 0 100m 200m 300m
Scale

Location: 9 km (5.5 mi) southwest of 100 Mile House
Elevation: 1,195 m (3,920 ft)
Surface Area: 91 ha (225 ac)
Maximum Depth: 14.3 m (47 ft)
Mean Depth: 2.9 m (9.5 ft)
Way Point: 51° 35′ 58″ N, 121° 24′ 13″ W

Edmund Lake

Area Indicator

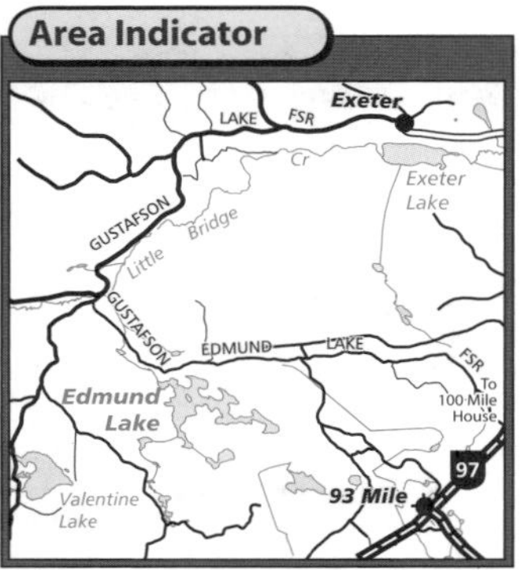

Edmund Lake			
Fish Stocking Data			
Year	Species	Number	Life Stage
2008	Rainbow Trout	3,000	Yearling
2007	Rainbow Trout	3,000	Yearling
2006	Rainbow Trout	3,000	Yearling

Fishing

Edmund Lake is a sprawling lake with many arms, bays, islands and peninsulas found southwest of 100 Mile House. Every year, between 1,500 and 3,000 All Female Triploid rainbow trout are stocked in the lake. All Female Triploid trout do not reproduce and so tend to grow bigger than other trout. In fact, 4 kg (9 lb) fish have been reported out of Edmund.

With the many bays, points and other structure, Edmund is a near-perfect fishing lake. The eastern reaches of the lake are quite shallow, rarely reaching more than 2 metres (6 feet) deep. While trout will cruise this area shortly after ice off, for the most part, you will find few fish in this area. This leaves the western part of the lake. There is a bay on the northern shores of the lake with a deep hole and a fairly steep drop off that is worth trying, but the best place on the lake to fish is near the island in the middle of the western half of the lake. The water drops off from the island into the deepest hole on the lake and depending on what time of year it is, fish will be found at varying depths along this drop off.

Trollers can work a circular pattern, trolling along the western side of the island to near the northern short of the lake and return along the western shore of the lake. Common lures include a Wedding Band and Willow Leaf troll, a Flatfish, or a small spoon. Try trolling in an 'S' Pattern, which causes the lures to move in a more random pattern. Many trollers insist on using oars, as this gives them more control over the motion of the lure. Pausing a moment allows the lure to sink and, when next you pull on the oars, the lure leaps forward like it is trying to escape. This often triggers a strike from fish that have been following the lure for a while.

Spincasting and fly-fishing both work on the lake. Again, the best places to work are in the bays in the northwest of the lake, as well as around the island. The lake features hatches as are typical to the Cariboo. The shallow areas in the east provide a lot of food for the fish, but do get warm and so the fish are unwilling to head into the area.

While ice fishing is not that popular on the lake, Edmund Lake is found along the newly developed Gold Rush Snowmobile Trail. Anglers who are snowmobilers (and vice versa) can test their luck as soon as the ice is safe.

Directions

To get to the lake, head west of 100 Mile House on Exter Road. The first section of this road is paved, but soon turns into a good gravel road now called the Gustafsen Lake Forest Service Road. Follow these roads for about 12 km to the 1108 km marking and look for the Gustafsen-Edmund Lake Forest Service Road heading southeast. Follow this smaller road for a couple kilometres to a turnoff to Edmund Lake. If you hit the power lines, you've gone too far, although a road follows the power lines down to the lake, too.

Facilities

There are no facilities on Edmund Lake, but there is nothing stopping you from camping near the lake. Be sure to avoid private property in the area though. Full services, including motels, restaurants and informative fishing retailers can be found in nearby 100 Mile House.

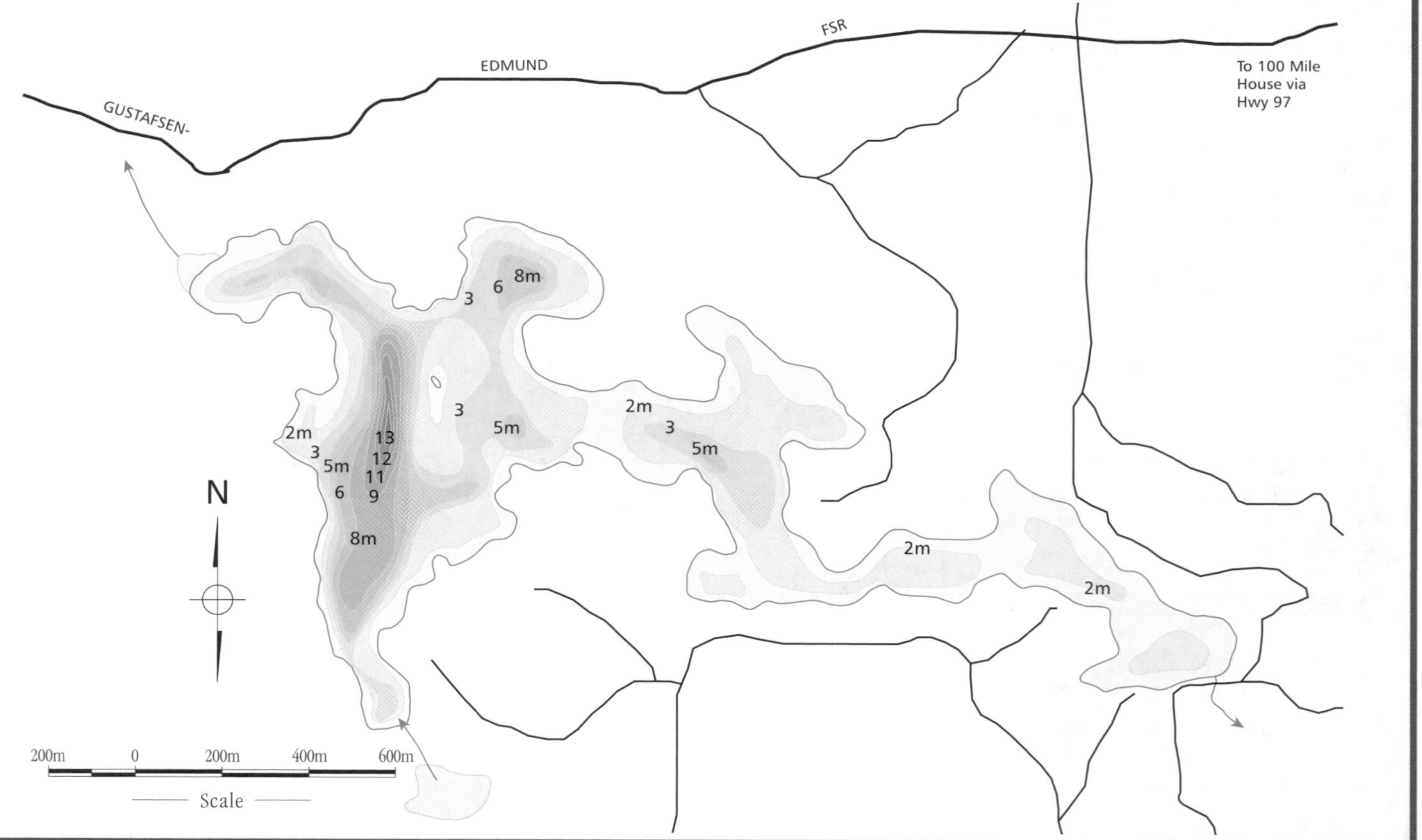

GUSTAFSEN- EDMUND FSR
To 100 Mile House via Hwy 97
N
200m 0 200m 400m 600m
Scale

Eena Lake

Location: 28 km (17.4 mi) northwest of Prince George
Elevation: 762 m (2,500 ft)
Surface Area: 54 ha (134 ac)
Maximum Depth: 23 m (75 ft)
Mean Depth: 5.5 m (18 ft)
Way Point: 54° 3′ 3″ N, 123° 1′ 18″ W

Fishing

Eena Lake is a popular four season fishing lake, known for its natural beauty and fast fishing. The lake is easy to get to and is a great place for young anglers to start fishing, because the fish are more than willing to chase after most any lure you throw at them.

Stocked annually with 5,000 rainbow trout by the Freshwater Fisheries Society of BC, these fish grow quickly in the food-rich waters of the lake. During the open water season, the lake can be fished from a float tube, from a small boat or from several good access points around the edge of the lake. When the water freezes, you can fish basically anywhere around the lake, but the best fishing comes around the weed beds at the south end of the lake.

The lake has two deep basins–a 14 metre (46 foot) hole at the north end of the lake and a 23 metre (75 foot) hole at the south–which are prime locations in the summer when the fish head for the cooler, deeper water. But on cool summer evenings and in the spring and fall, there are large patches of shoal area around the lake and around the tear-shaped islands between the basins that become the hotspots. Trolling these areas works great as does spincasting or fly-fishing.

A popular fly pattern is a Doc Spratley, especially in green, red or black. These work best trolled slowly on a sink tip or slow-sink lined. Also worth trying are a variety of leech, micro-leech and nymph patterns.

The lake is a highly productive lake and there are hatches that happen nearly all through the ice-free season. There's a good chance that there will be a hatch on no matter when you show up. Of course, the spring is always the most productive time, but look for shucks floating on the surface, swarms of tiny insects hovering over the water and the telltale rings set off from a rising fish. Your only challenge will be to figure out what is hatching: chironomids, mayflies, caddisflies, damselflies or dragonflies. If you can't tell what is hatching, you can always use a Tom Thumb, which does a good job of imitating most anything.

Spincasters can try working Panther Martins, Roostertails and black and silver or frog Flatfish. Willow Leafs with a Wedding Band or small spinner and worm are also popular.

During the ice fishing season, try bobbing with shrimp meat, an ice fly, or live maggots. The lake is stocked with rainbow trout, which tend to slow down towards the end of winter, when oxygen levels in the water drop. Because of this, it is much more fun to fish early in the season, rather than late.

Area Indicator

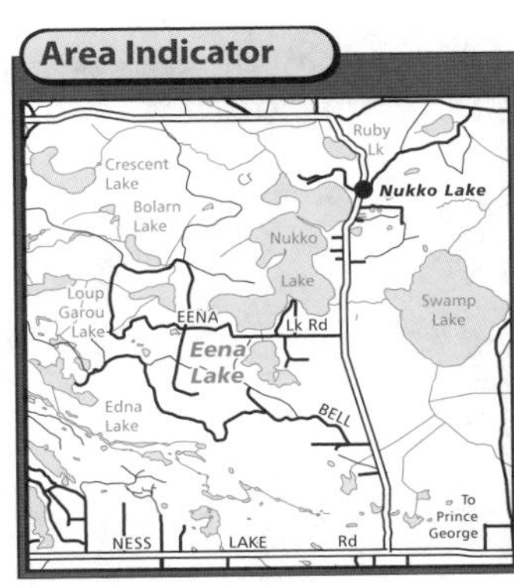

Directions

Eena Lake is found northwest of Prince George via a series of backroads. Take Highway 97 north for about 15 km to Chief Lake Road. Turn left and follow this road for 12 km to a fork in the road. Head right on Nukko Lake Road and 5 km later, watch for Eena Lake Road. Follow Eena Lake Road for 1.2 km to Wood Road. Turn left onto Woods, then right onto Quinn Road. Quinn Road ends at the boat launch.

Facilities

There is a gravel boat launch on the northeast side of the lake. Note that this is an electric motor only lake.

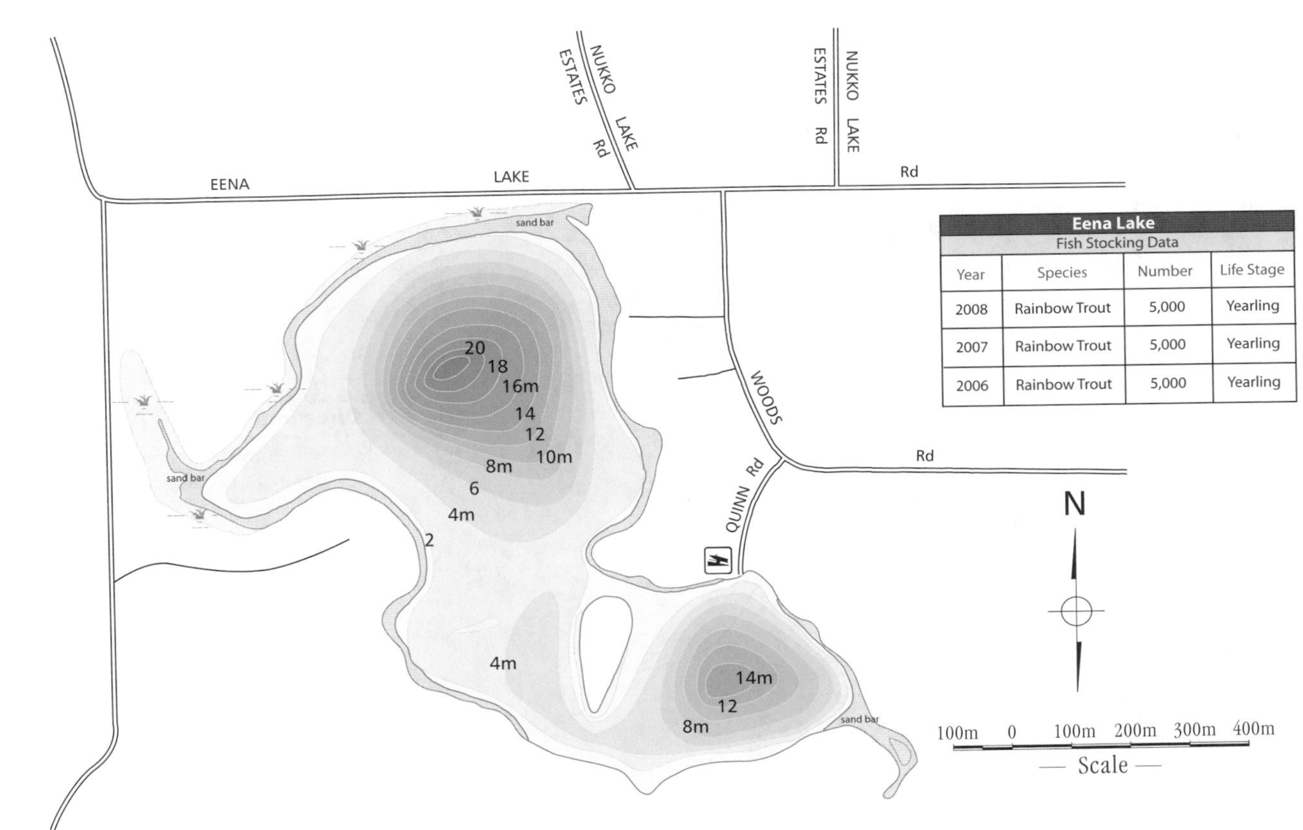

Eena Lake			
Fish Stocking Data			
Year	Species	Number	Life Stage
2008	Rainbow Trout	5,000	Yearling
2007	Rainbow Trout	5,000	Yearling
2006	Rainbow Trout	5,000	Yearling

Location: 90 km (56 mi) east of Williams Lake
Elevation: 913 m (2,995 ft)
Surface Area: 325 ha (804 ac)
Maximum Depth: 126 m (413 ft)
Mean Depth: 45 m (147 ft)
Way Point: 52° 13′ 50″ N, 120° 49′ 47″ W

Elbow Lake

Area Indicator

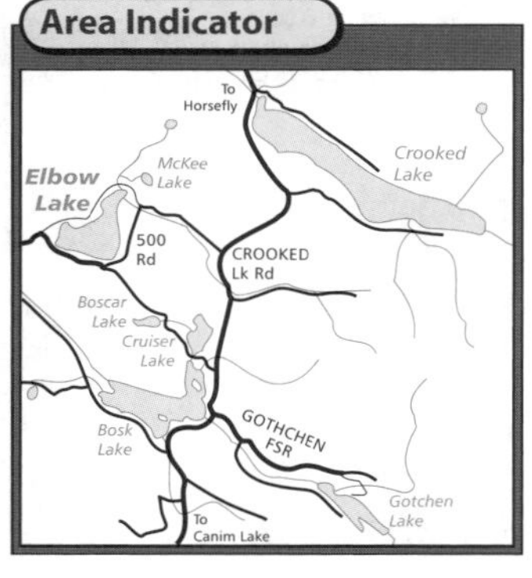

Fishing

Elbow Lake is a medium sized lake found in the popular fishing area located in the Horsefly/Likely area east of the Cariboo Highway and west of Wells Gray Park. There are a handful of other, equally popular lakes set nearby.

The lake is a mid elevation lake, which means that the fishery begins in the early part of May. The lake is very deep (over 125 metres or 410 feet) so the water does not warm significantly in the summer months. As a result, the lake can be fished for its wild rainbow trout throughout the ice-free season with reasonable success.

While it is not as large as nearby Crooked Lake, Elbow Lake is a trolling lake. The fish are spread out and are hard to catch so trolling allows you to cover some much-needed ground.

The deepest part of the lake is towards the west end, off the Elbow Lake Recreation Site. Troll around the main body of the lake, following the edge of the drop off. If you can see the bottom on one side of the boat, you are in the optimal place to troll. As you work your way along the drop off, slowly, make gentle turns. This causes the flies or lures to speed up and slow down, which is much more enticing to the fish than something that moves at a steady speed in one direction. You can even try stopping for a second or two to let the lure sink, then gun the engine. This sudden movement often triggers a strike, as the fish interpret it as the lure trying to escape.

Spincasters can try casting a lure tipped with a worm or a fly towards the drop off. The water level drops rapidly from shore allowing for shore casting.

If fly-fishing, it is best to work search patterns deep. A little weight on the line will help get the fly to the right depth quickly. Suspending it beneath a strike indicator allows you to slowly drift the fly across the drop off. If you aren't having any luck, try fishing closer to the bottom or try retrieving slower. Chironomids, especially, aren't the fastest insect in the sea and a retrieve that is too fast is a dead giveaway that the fly is not a real insect.

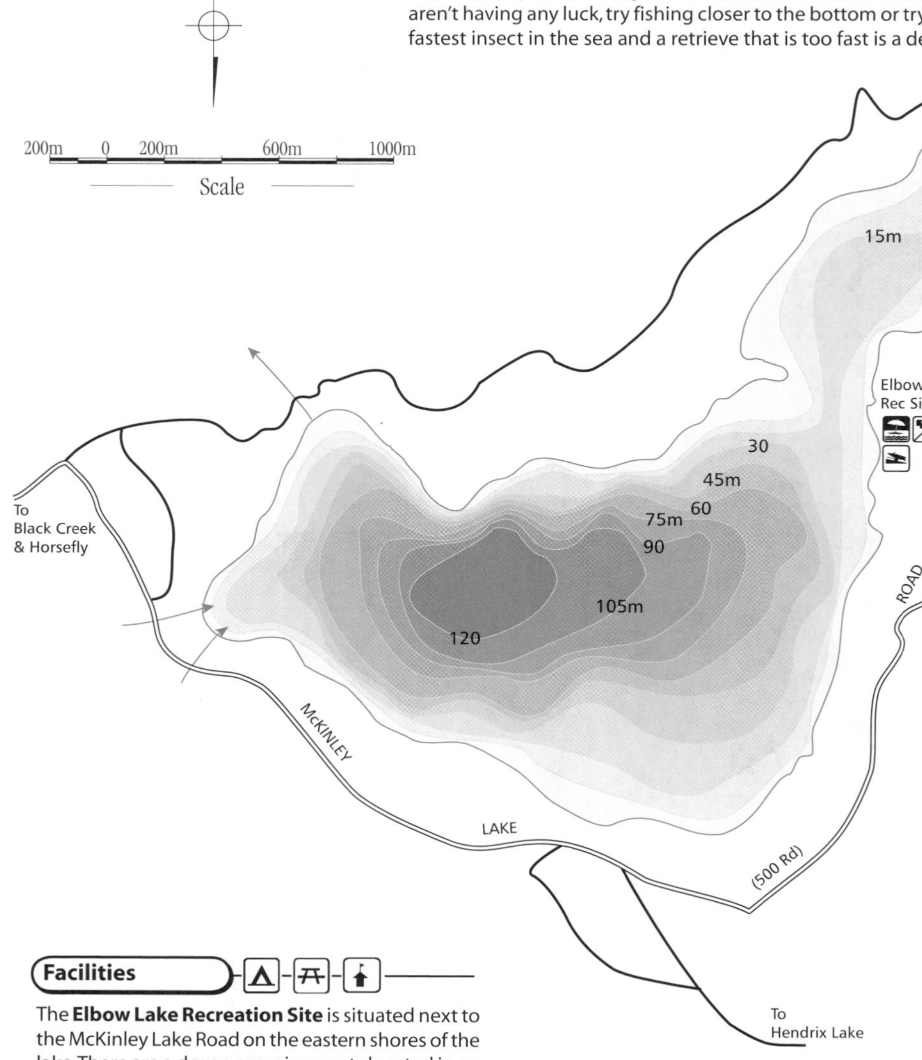

Directions

To reach Elbow Lake involves a long drive from Highway 97. If you are coming from Williams Lake, take Highway 97 east to 150 Mile House and look for the Likely Road branching north. At 4.5 km, turn right on the Horsefly Road and drive on the pavement all the way to the small town of Horsefly. Just before entering town, cross the bridge over the Horsefly River and begin the drive on the Black Creek Road.

Continue past Black Creek and the airstrip and then take the first right onto the McKinley Lake Road (500 Road). Elbow Lake is the second lake you will come to as you drive down the McKinley Lake Road. The complete trip is made on a good all-season gravel road.

Facilities

The **Elbow Lake Recreation Site** is situated next to the McKinley Lake Road on the eastern shores of the lake. There are a dozen camping spots located in an opening next to the lake. There is also a beach and a boat launching area at the recreation site.

Elk (Island) Lake

Location: 38 km (23.5 mi) north of Williams Lake
Elevation: 835 m (2,739 ft)
Surface Area: 58 ha (144 ac)
Maximum Depth: 20.4 m (67 ft)
Mean Depth: 5.6 m (18 ft)
Way Point: 52° 28′ 17″ N, 122° 3′ 28″ W

Fishing

Elk Lake is a scenic little lake with numerous small islands. As a result, the lake is often called Island Lake. No matter the name, it is well suited for the float tube crowd.

The lake does not see a lot of pressure, although, like its neighbour Jackson or Jack's Hole Lake, it offers very good fishing for rainbow. Elk Lake is regulated as an artificial fly only lake, which probably explains why it is not fished as hard as one might expect.

If you are planning a trip to the lake, the late spring to early summer (late May to June) or later into fall are the best times to fish the lake. This is because the trout become highly inactive during the turnover period that extends up to 3 weeks after ice-off. Also, the water warms in the summer months as the lake is not very deep.

The numerous sunken islands, huge shoals and extensive weedbeds provide for some good insect rearing. Although there are redside shiners that compete with the rainbow for the available aquatic insects, the trout do grow rapidly here. In fact, the rainbow average 38–45 cm (15–18 in) in size with some fish reaching 3 kg (6 lbs). This is a surprising fact considering that each year, 10,000 rainbow trout are stocked in the lake.

The deepest part of the lake is at the north end with the rest of the lake being a large weed covered shoal. Thus, the northern end is the best place to cast or better troll a wet fly.

Trolling is not the only way to catch a fish here, though. Anglers will have plenty of luck anchoring off the drop offs and casting a variety of insect or attractor patterns and retrieving across the drop off. Fly anglers should note what is hatching, remembering that trout tend to be very particular when a hatch is on. They prefer the exact colour and size, which can be the most frustrating part of the learning curve when fly-fishing. It can also be the most rewarding.

Anglers should also note that no gas motors are allowed on the lake, there is a bait ban and you must use a single barbless artificial fly.

Area Indicator

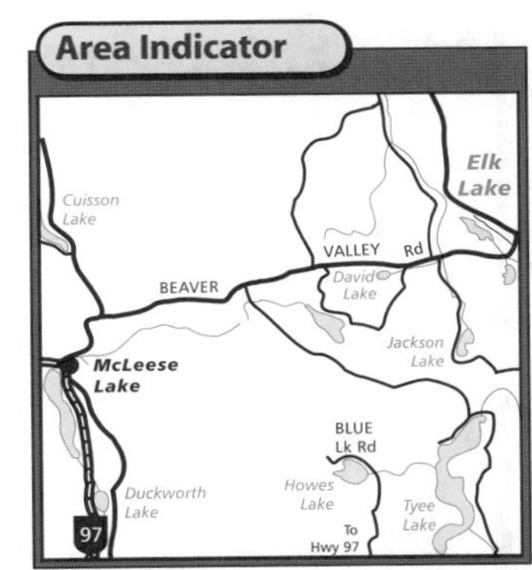

Elk (Island) Lake			
Fish Stocking Data			
Year	Species	Number	Life Stage
2008	Rainbow Trout	10,000	Yearling
2007	Rainbow Trout	10,000	Yearling
2006	Rainbow Trout	10,000	Yearling

Facilities

The **Elk Lake Recreation Site** is found near the southeast end of the lake. The recreation site is in a grassy meadow surrounded by aspen tree with four camping spots set off from the shoreline. There is a small dock to moor your boat and a cartop boat launch is available if you do not mind the short carry.

Directions

There are two main access routes into the lake. From the north end of McLeese Lake on Highway 97, the Beaver Valley Road leads to the east. The road can be rough in places and leads to the lake and recreation site.

The second route is to take the Likely Road from 150 Mile House and just past the Big Lake Ranch, head north on Ridge Road. That road intersects with the Beaver Valley Road. Continue west and just the junction with Beedy Road, there is a short access road leading north to Elk Lake. The lake is less than a kilometer from the main road.

Other Options

Whitestone Lake is connected to Elk Lake via a small steam. As a result the smaller lake does hold a few smaller trout that migrate in during the spring run off. The hidden lake can winterkill so do not expect any trophy class trout here.

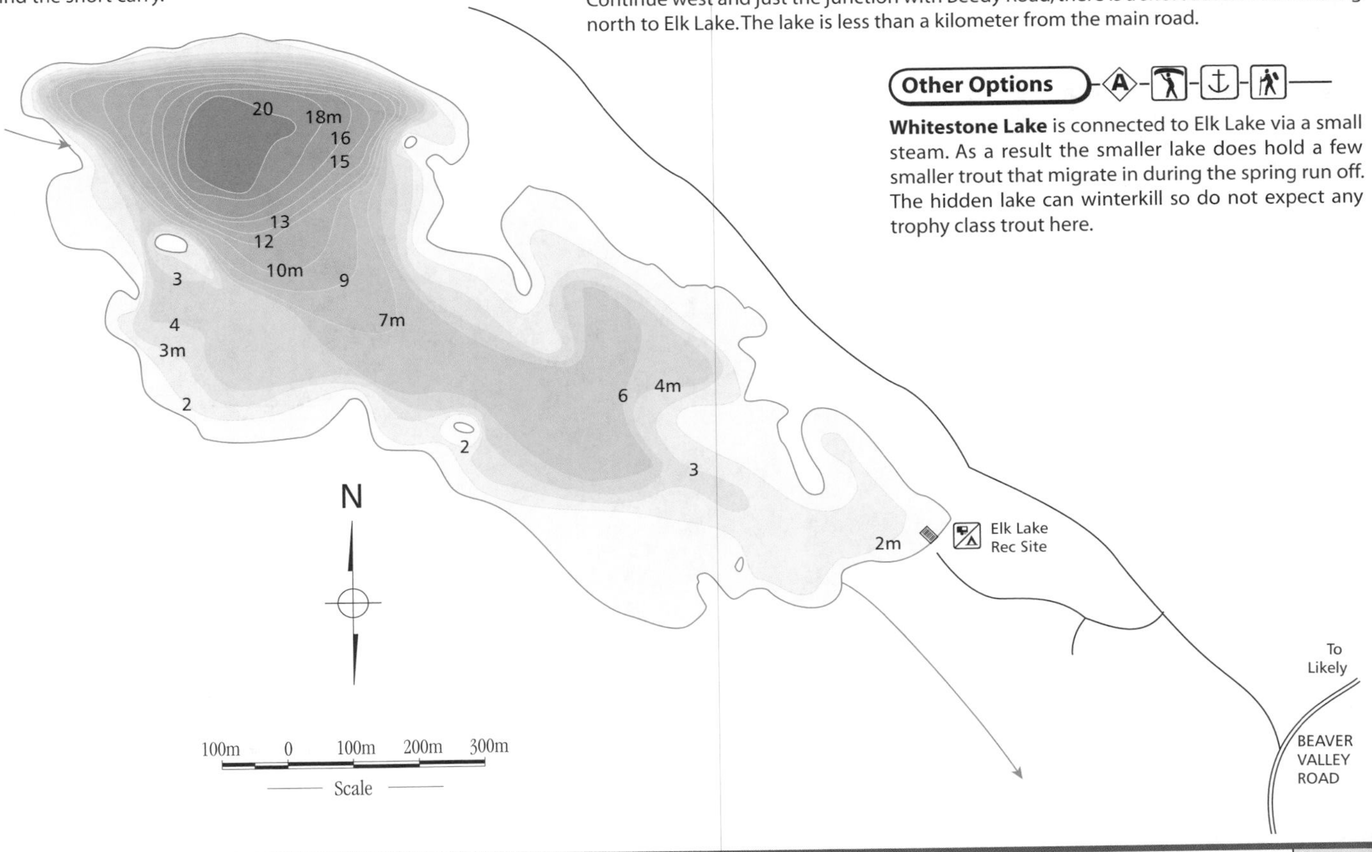

Location: 45 km (28 mi) east of 100 Mile House
Elevation: 1,166 m (3,825 ft)
Surface Area: 189 ha (467 ac)
Maximum Depth: 26 m (85 ft)
Mean Depth: 10.5 m (34 ft)
Way Point: 51° 35′ 13″ N, 120° 38′ 36″ W

English Lake

Area Indicator

Fishing

English Lake is situated to the northeast of Bridge Lake. Finding the lake is an adventure unto itself. although it isn't that far off Highway 24 as the crow flies, the roads are at best washboard and at worst a rutted mess. A four wheel drive vehicle is recommended.

Once you've found the lake, the fishing is usually quite good during the ice-free season. Due to its elevation, English Lake does not become fishable until mid to late May. The lake is relatively deep and added to its relatively high elevation, the lake can withstand the summer doldrums to a better extent than lower elevation lakes and fishing remains active throughout the ice-free season.

While the fishing can be fast and fun, don't expect to find trophy trout here. Instead, expect good numbers of hungry rainbow that are not usually too fussy about what they eat. Try casting near the drop offs or around the sunken islands. Also, the near shore area around the large island in the middle of the lake is a good area to focus. Shore casters are able to get to the deeper water from the area nearby to the Meridian Lake Road.

The lake is easily trolled so long as you stay out a little ways from shore and avoid running aground on the sunken islands. Of course, these underwater islands are great holding place for the fish, so trolling near them, or better yet, anchoring off the islands and spincasting or fly casting around the edges of the islands can produce some nice trout. Trollers can use a Wedding Band tipped with a worm, while spincasters will find that Apex Trout Killers, Kamlooper and Krocodile spoons or Mepps, Panther Martin and Gibbs spinners work well.

Fly anglers will find that a Doc Spratley, a beadhead micro leech, a '52 Buick or a marabou damselfly nymph are good bets. While matching the hatch is often the most effective way of fishing, these slightly bigger flies present an appealing opportunity to the fish, as one damselfly nymph is the equivalent of a whole bunch of chironomids.

There are occasional surface fishing opportunities and having a Tom Thumb or two, as well as other top water patterns, is always a good idea. Some options include an Elk Hair Caddis and terrestrial patterns like pine beetles. More likely, though, the trout will be feeding down near the bottom.

Directions

From the east end of Bridge Lake off the Fishing Highway (Highway 24) take the Bridge Lake North Road to Judson Road. Leave that road on the signed Windy Mountain Forest Service Road (1900 Rd) and look for the Judson Creek Branch Road. Continue past the headwaters of Judson Creek and follow the rough road heading northeast to the west end of the Lake.

Alternatively, one can access the southeast end of the lake off the Wavey Lake (2000 Road) and the Meridian Lake (207 Road) Forest Service Roads.

Facilities

There are no developed facilities at the lake. It is possible to pitch a tent at the roadside and then launch a small boat.

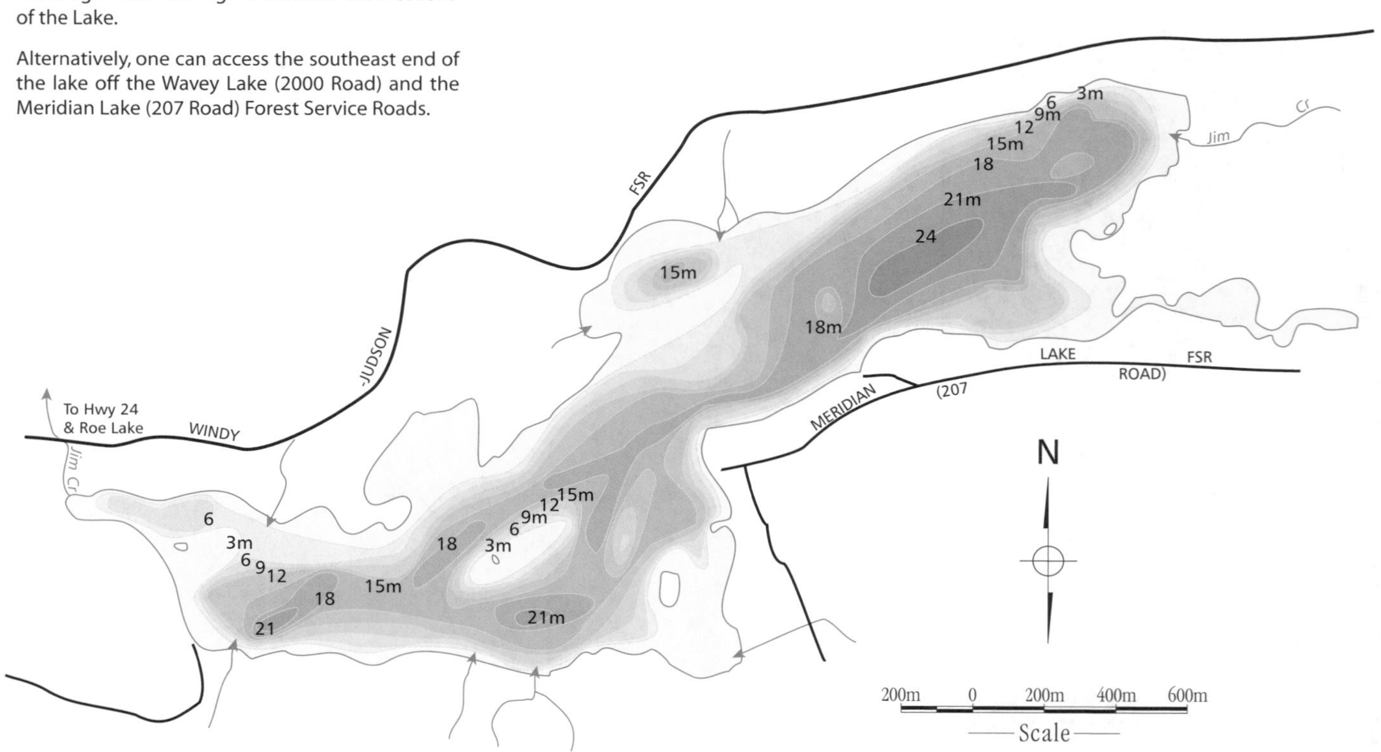

Faulkner Lake

Location: 50 km (31 mi) east of 100 Mile House
Elevation: 1,216 m (3,989 ft)
Surface Area: 22 ha (54 ac)
Maximum Depth: 20 m (65 ft)
Mean Depth: 7 m (23 ft)
Way Point: 51° 32′ 6.6″ N, 120° 36′ 19.4″ W

Fishing

Faulkner Lake is a tiny lake found northeast of Bridge Lake along Highway 24, the so-called Fishing Highway. The lake is stocked with 1,000 Pennask strain rainbow trout each year. The Freshwater Fisheries Society of BC has recently changed the trout stockings to All Female Triploid and reduced the number of fish stocked here in an attempt to improve the size of the catches here.

The lake is high enough in elevation to delay it from opening up until early to mid-May. The fishing remains pretty steady through the ice-free season, although the lake is not extremely deep and the water warms up in summer, causing the fishing to slow down at this time.

The lake's bottom is fairly featureless, featuring a gradual, bowl-shaped drop off. Finding where the fish are will take a bit of work and a fish finder would be quite effective. Because there are not many places where the fish will congregate, trolling the lake will help anglers cover the most ground possible.

The southern shores of the lake are marshy and weedy and offer some good hatches. Fly anglers can try working this area during the early part of the season, especially near the small island near the mid-point of the lake. The lake features the typical Cariboo area hatches, although starting a few weeks later than other lakes, due to the higher elevation. Because the lake is a shallow, high elevation lake, expect plenty of overlapping hatches. This can seem like a great thing, but if the fish are being fussy and only targeting one food source, it can sometimes be a pain trying to figure out what the fish are eating that day at that time.

Spincasters and fly fishermen can also do well casting into the tiny hole in the bay east of the wharf, near the shallows or around the drop off. The deepest part of the lake is right in the middle. Trollers will do well with a lake troll like a Willow Leaf, a small spoon, or a Flatfish. Since the drop off is well out from the shoreline, casting from shore is difficult.

Directions

Faulkner Lake is situated to the west of Bridge Lake on the Wilson Lake Road. This deteriorating road is narrow and muddy and usually requires a 4wd vehicle.

From the east end of Bridge Lake off the Fishing Highway (Highway 24), take the Bridge Lake North Road. Leave that road on the signed Wilson Lake Road. Past Wilson Lake turn left on the old road and make your way northeast.

The road does not go through to Wavey Lake.

Facilities

There is a small lakeshore camping area and old dock on the northern shore of the lake. This lovely meadow makes a nice secluded place to camp. A small boat can be launched at that location.

Other Options

Around Bridge Lake and on the Wilson Lake Road are numerous small fishing lakes. Each of the lakes offers good fishing for rainbow. A few larger fish are pulled from these lakes every year. Fishing from a float tube or small boat is recommended.

Area Indicator

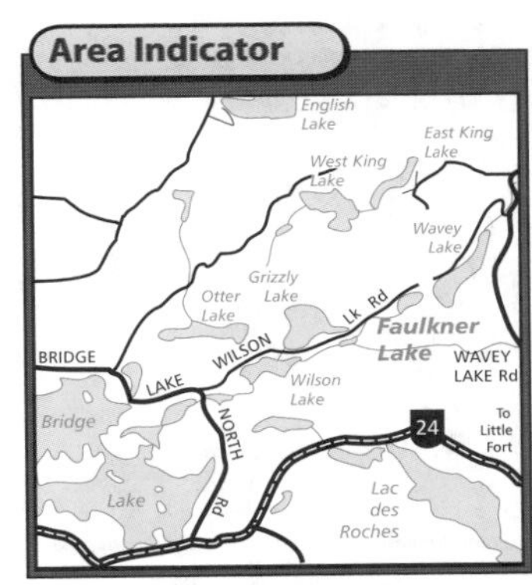

Faulkner Lake			
Fish Stocking Data			
Year	Species	Number	Life Stage
2008	Rainbow Trout	1,000	Fry
2007	Rainbow Trout	1,000	Fry
2006	Rainbow Trout	1,000	Fall Fry

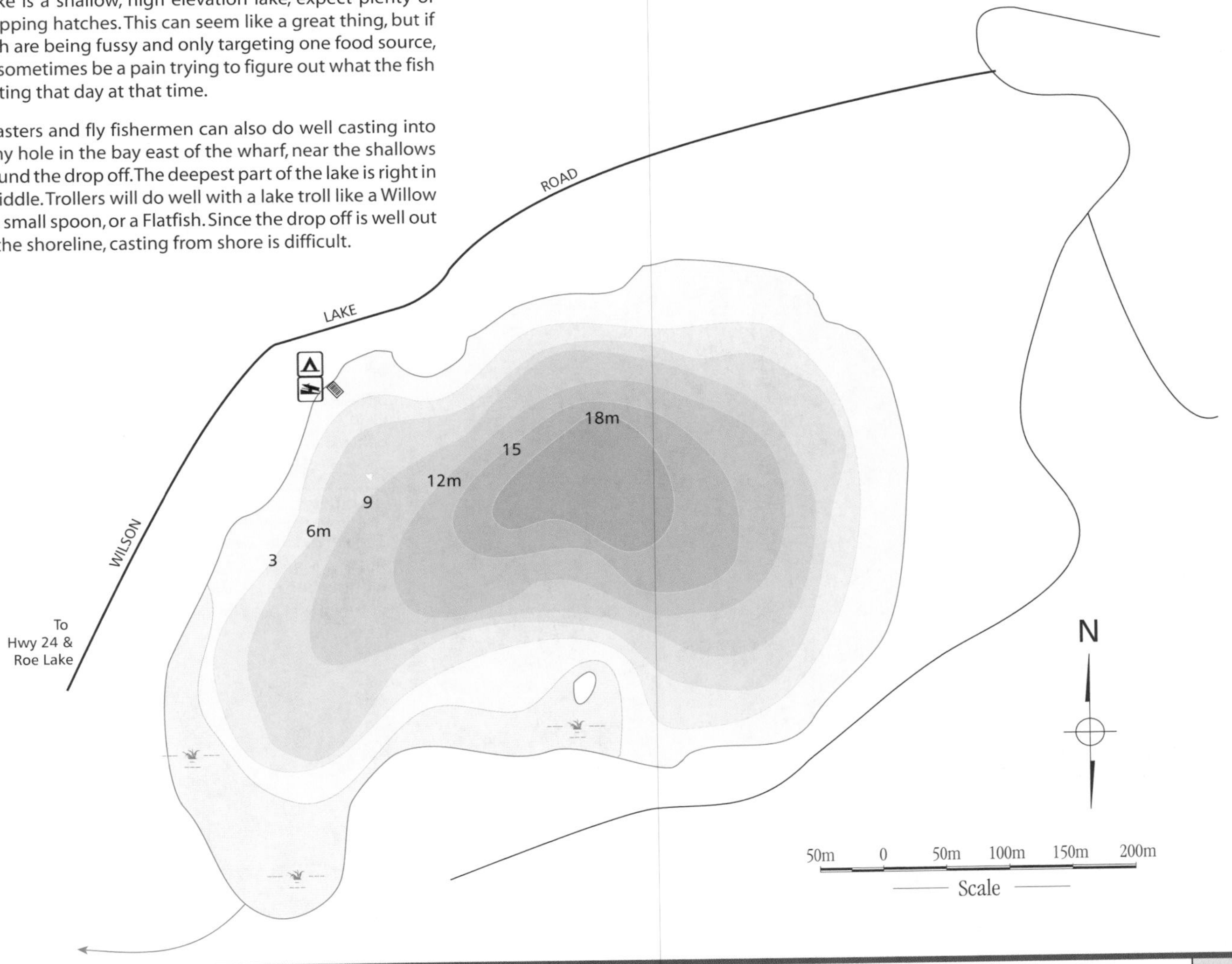

Location: 25 km (15.5 mi) east of 100 Mile House
Elevation: 1,102 m (3,615 ft)
Surface Area: 32 ha (80 ac)
Maximum Depth: 8.8 m (29 ft)
Mean Depth: 4.8 m (16 ft)
Geographic: 51° 33' 6.7" N, 120° 58' 49.6" W

Fawn Lake

Area Indicator

Fishing

Fawn Lake is a highly productive lake that regularly yields rainbow in the 2-3 kg (5-6 lb) category. There are also rumors of much larger fish exceeding 5 kg (10 lbs). The rainbow grow to large size partly due to the abundance of the lake chub they love to feast on.

Despite the potential for a good-sized rainbow, the lake does not receive as much pressure as the nearby lakes such as Watch and Hammer Lakes to the south. Still the Freshwater Fisheries Society of BC stocks the lake 15,000 rainbow each year to ensure a healthy trout population. The fish average a healthy 1 kg (2 lbs) and are often caught much bigger here.

The small, clear lake has a deep hole just off the boat launch, but much of the lake is fairly shallow. The lake is surrounded by a fairly dense forest that shelters it from the south and west winds that can force anglers off larger lakes.

For fly fishermen, the spring chironomid hatch is very good. Ice-off usually occurs around the end of April and the chironomids usually are in full swing by mid May. Other hatches continue throughout the spring and into the summer ensuring decent fishing during the entire ice-free season.

Spincasters and fly fishermen can do very well casting towards the weedbeds right off the shoreline nearby to the boat launch and the Fawn Lake Resort. There are shoals at both ends of the lakes, too, which will attract the attention of fly anglers as well. The best flies to use are a chironomid or bead head pheasant tail nymph in May or June and a green Carey in August or September. Spincasters do well with a gold Mepps, Panther Martin or Blue Fox Vibrax spinner.

However, it is best to fish this lake from the water, either in a small boat or tube. The lake is not easily trolled due to its shallow depth. There is a fairly deep hole just off the boat dock and trollers can work this relatively small area. Heading elsewhere in the lake is just asking to foul the hook on the many weeds and water plants. Trollers use a gold Hildebrandt spoon or F-4 or F-5 Flatfish in blue or orange, or leeches in black or red on either a monofilament line, or a sinking fly line with a longer leader.

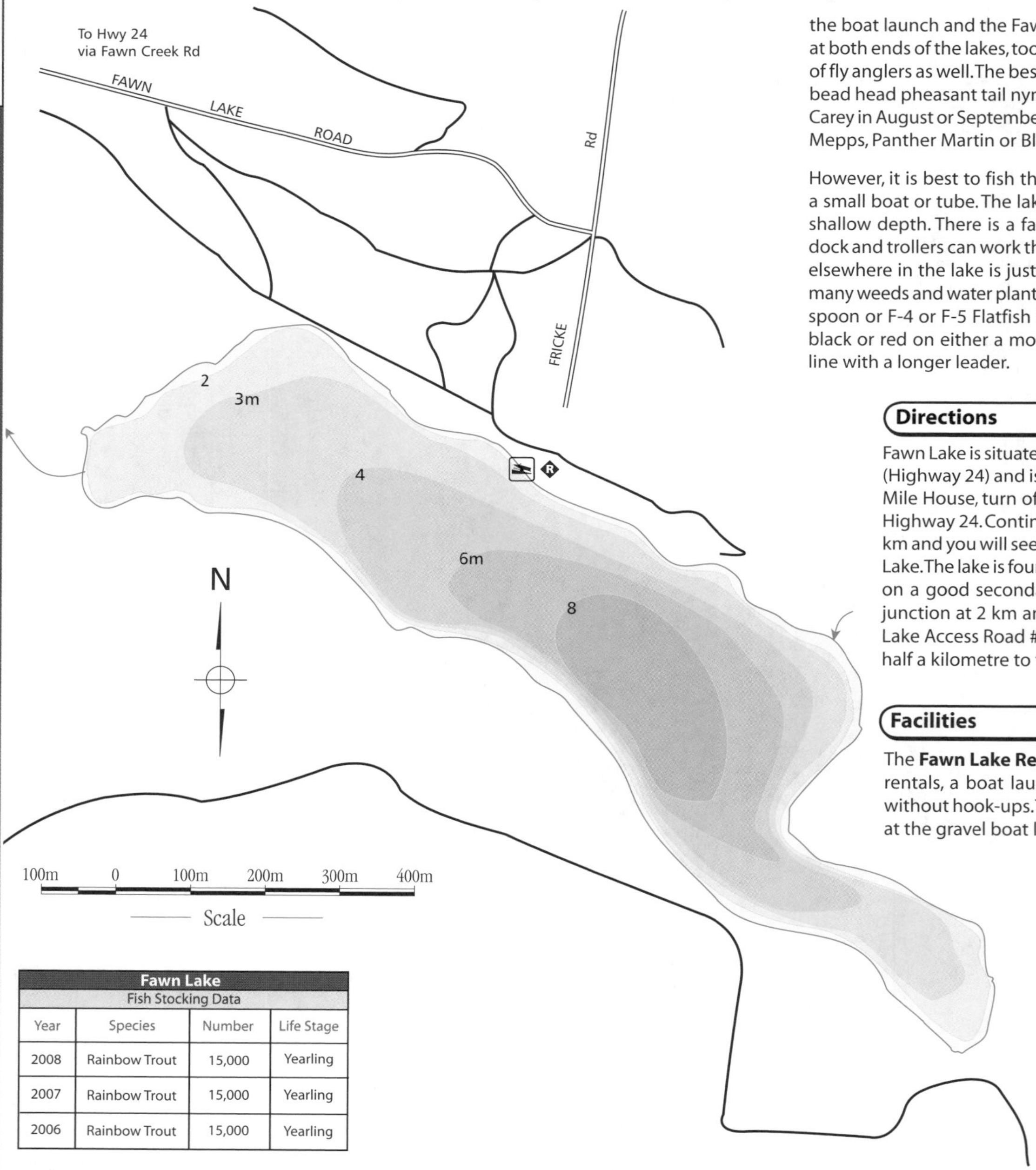

To Hwy 24
via Fawn Creek Rd

FAWN LAKE ROAD

FRICKE Rd

2
3m
4
6m
8

N

100m 0 100m 200m 300m 400m
Scale

Directions

Fawn Lake is situated nearby to the Fishing Highway (Highway 24) and is a popular fishing hole. From 93 Mile House, turn off Highway 97 and head east on Highway 24. Continue past Lone Butte for about 14 km and you will see a sign pointing the way to Fawn Lake. The lake is found about 4 km from the highway on a good secondary road. Stay right at the road junction at 2 km and then right again at the Fawn Lake Access Road #1 after another 2 km. It is about half a kilometre to the launch on this last road.

Facilities

The **Fawn Lake Resort** offers lakeside cabins, boat rentals, a boat launch and camping sites with or without hook-ups. There is public access to the lake at the gravel boat launch adjacent to the resort.

Fawn Lake Fish Stocking Data			
Year	Species	Number	Life Stage
2008	Rainbow Trout	15,000	Yearling
2007	Rainbow Trout	15,000	Yearling
2006	Rainbow Trout	15,000	Yearling

Felker Lake

Location: 22 km (13.6 mi) south of Williams Lake
Elevation: 860 m (2,822 ft)
Surface Area: 227 ha (561 ac)
Maximum Depth: 11 m (36 ft)
Mean Depth: 5.1 m (17 ft)
Way Point: 51° 56′ 55″ N, 122° 0′ 3″ W

Fishing 

Felker Lake is part of the Chimney Valley chain of lakes. It is a popular destination for residents of Williams Lake.

This lake offers burbot and rainbow trout and is one of the earlier lakes in the Cariboo to open up in the spring. There are also some non-game fish like suckers, chub and red side shiners.

To maintain the fishery, 30,000 rainbow trout are stocked in the lake each year by the Freshwater Fisheries Society of BC. The lake is quite shallow so it is considered a better casting than trolling lake. The deepest part of the lake is at the north end so if you want to troll, stick around that area.

Fly fishers and spincasters should work the near shore area particularly near the north end of the lake where the most prominent drop off exists. Shore casting from that location is possible as well.

The lake has some weedy, grassy areas where insects and other aquatic life spawn. These areas are prime feeding areas for the rainbow trout, especially early in spring, before the water gets too warm. As the bottom of the lake warms, hatches happen in deeper water and the fish don't come as far into the shallow.

Area Indicator

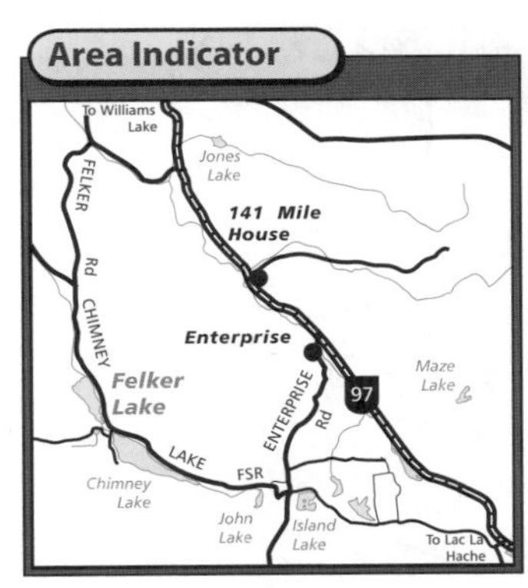

Burbot fishing is not extremely popular on the lake, although some people do fish for them in winter through the ice. Even in winter, burbot are usually found quite deep. While this fish is quite ugly, it is also one of the best tasting fish you can catch in freshwater, sometimes called "the poor man's lobster."

You can fish for rainbow through the ice as well, but note that rainbow are much more sensitive to cold and declining oxygen levels, so are best fished in the earlier part of the year, when the lake has just frozen. By the end of the winter, the rainbow trout are usually quite sluggish, providing little fight and their flesh is soft, providing poor eating. Try baiting a hook or jig with shrimp, krill or worms. You can use a bobber on your line to detect the strike, but because rainbow are usually caught in less than 3 metres (10 feet) of water, another popular method is to lay on the ice and peer down through the hole.

Directions

From Williams Lake, follow Highway 20 towards Bella Coola. When you have passed the turn-off to the golf course, hang a left on the Dog Creek Road. This paved road will wind its way through a residential area. Almost at the bottom of the first major hill on the Dog Creek Road heading south, you will see the turn-off to the Chimney Lake Road. This good gravel road will bring you along the shores of Brunson Lake followed by Felker Lake.

If you are coming from the south, the easiest access is off Highway 97 at Enterprise Road. Follow this road for 9.5 km to the Chimney Lake Forest Service Road and turn north. It is another 10 or so km to the recreation site on the east side of the lake.

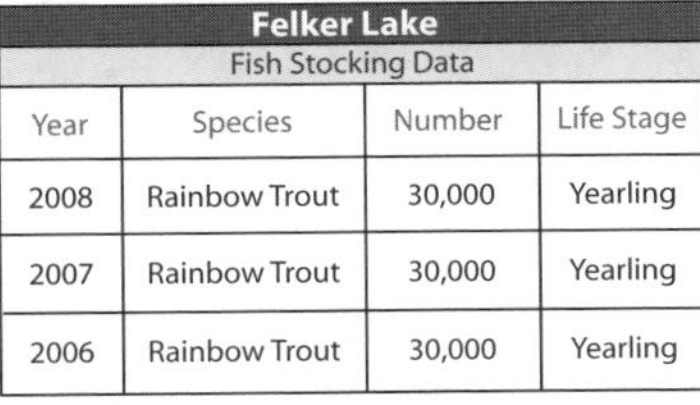

Felker Lake Fish Stocking Data			
Year	Species	Number	Life Stage
2008	Rainbow Trout	30,000	Yearling
2007	Rainbow Trout	30,000	Yearling
2006	Rainbow Trout	30,000	Yearling

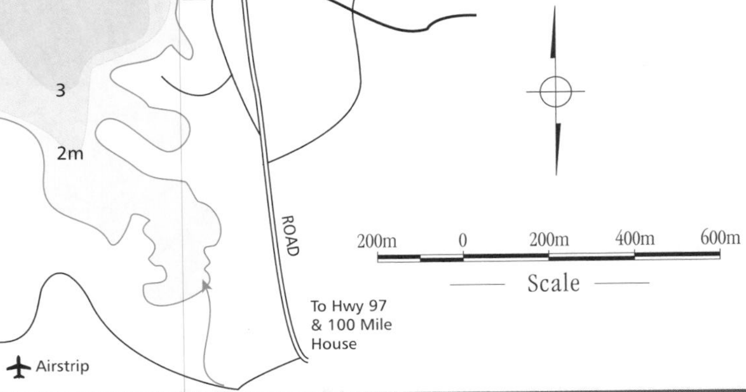

Facilities

The **Felker Lake Recreation Site** rests on the eastern shore of the lake next to the Chimney Lake Road. The recreation site is set in an opening and has eleven camping spots as well as a cartop boat launch. It is an enhanced recreation site, which means there is a host and a fee to camp here.

Location: 53 km (33 mi) southwest of Vanderhoof
Elevation: 957 m (3,140 ft)
Surface Area: 877.3 ha (2,168 ac)
Maximum Depth: 11.9 m (39 ft)
Mean Depth: 7.3 m (24 ft)
Way Point: 53° 34′ 8″ N, 124° 18′ 8″ W

Finger Lake

Area Indicator

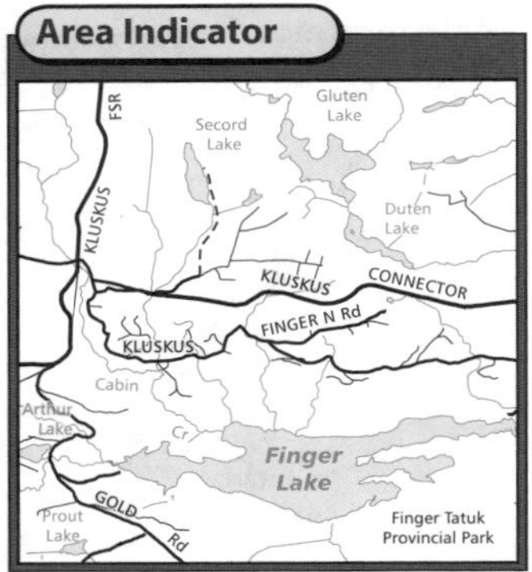

Fishing

Located southwest of Vanderhoof, Finger Lake is the epicenter for a bunch of great fishing lakes. It makes a weekend getaway from Prince George, as it is just a little far away to go after work

Finger Lake is 9 km (5.6 miles) long and about 18 metres (60 feet) deep. There are four islands that stretch down the centre of the lake, so there's always a drop off nearby. As a result, fishing can be quite productive through the open water season for wild rainbow trout that can get up to 2.5 kg (5 lbs). Trout in the 1 kg (2 lb) range are much more frequently caught.

Trolling small spinners with or without a Willow Leaf can be very productive. Most people who bring fly gear here use a sink tip or a full sink tip to drag around dragon fly nymphs, Doc Spratleys or a leech pattern. Fly anglers will usually want to concentrate their efforts on the weedy bays. These are also prime areas to look for moose.

While most standard trout lures and colours will work on most days, a chartreuse and black bead Hornet has become a local favourite. It has even gained the nickname "suicide hornet" because it is just so effective at winding up in a fish's mouth.

In addition to the rainbow trout, the lake also holds plenty of kokanee. These landlocked salmon are known for their unwillingness to take lures, but with a bit of planning, a bit of luck and a lot of skill you can usually manage to hook one. A lake troll with Wedding Band tipped with bait is your best bet. Be sure to troll these slow in an erratic pattern to vary the depth and presentation of the lure. Kokanee are soft mouthed, so lures such as the Gibbs Kokanee Katcher lake troll, which incorporate a "snubber" in the troll, will increase the chance of landing one.

If Finger Lake had a thumb, Eagle Bay on the northern side of the lake would be its thumb. This long, narrow bay offers shelter on days when strong winds blow in from the west. It is also a great place to fish.

There are a number of other hot spots around the lake, including the Narrows just south of the first and second islands, and at the mouth of Finger Creek. The fishing is also reported to be pretty darn good just off the dock at the resort. This fact also makes is a great family fishing destination as kids especially love to cast from docks.

Directions

From Vanderhoof, head south on Nechako Avenue, which turns into the Kenny Dam Road. Reset your odometer here and follow the resort signs. Continue on the Kenny Dam Road past Tachick Lake where the Kluskus Forest Service Road branches south at 26.4 km mark (there is a sign pointing towards Finger Lake Resort here). Follow this road to the 59 km marker and the Gold Road/Kluskus-Lavoie Forest Service Road. From here it is another 4 km to the entrance of the resort.

Facilities

The only way onto the lake is through **Finger Lake Resort**. Many anglers stay here, even if they're heading for a nearby lake, like Hobson of Chief Gray. There is a $10 day use fee and a $10 boat launch fee for anglers not staying at the resort. It is also possible to rent a boat from the resort.

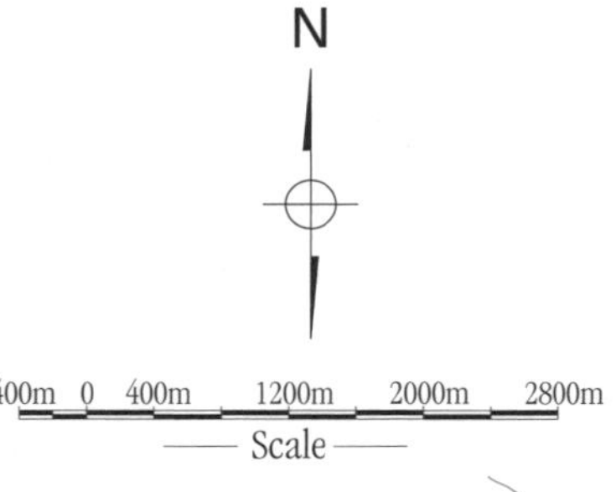

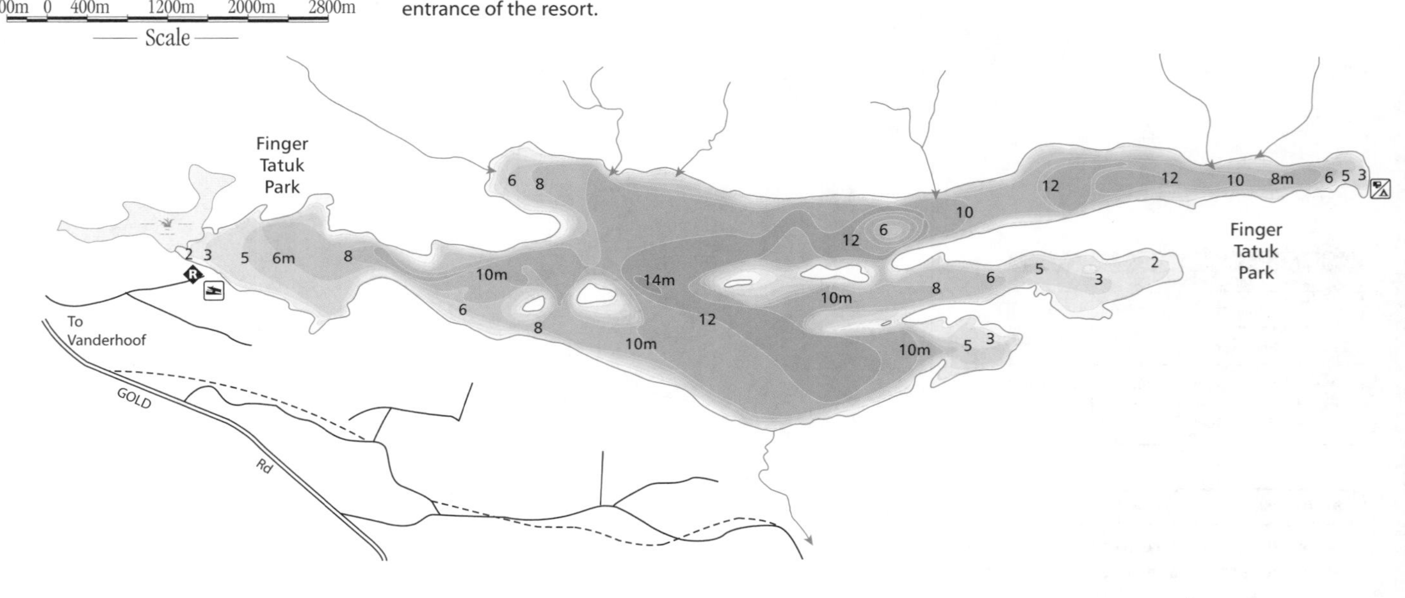

Fir Lake

Location: 56 km (34.7 mi) west of Williams Lake
Elevation: 1,196 m (3,924 ft)
Surface Area: 87 ha (211 ac)
Max Depth: 6.5 m (21 ft)
Mean Depth: 3.1 m (10 ft)
Way Point: 52° 15′ 34″ N, 122° 50′ 38″ W

Fishing

Situated in a shallow bowl surrounded by spruce and pine trees, Fir Lake is located quite close to Williams Lake. The insect-rich water features rocky points and shallow bays that make great feeding areas for rainbow trout that cruise into the clear, shallow water. Chironomids, dragonflies, damselflies, mayflies and a healthy population of shrimp provide an abundance of food.

The lake is stocked with 20,000 Pennask rainbow trout, 5,000 of which are All Female Triploid. Pennask rainbow are the trout that made Kamloops famous and while they are not as big as some strains, they are aggressive fighters that love to jump to try and shake the hook. However, the triploids don't reproduce and pour all their energy into getting nice and big.

The lake is not very deep, making it a bit difficult to troll. However, fly anglers and spincasters love the lake. Like most lakes in this region, fishing Fir is best done from a watercraft.

The lake is crystal clear and it is easy to spot the trout along the marl shoals. The trouble with that is the fish can see you, too and are easily spooked. Casting directly to the fish is a sure way to send them running but by watching the fish move, you can sometimes drop a lure or a fly far enough in front of them so it sinks down to the right depth before they get there.

In May, June and again in the fall, Fir Lake can produce rainbow up to 3 kg (6.5 lbs), but fish average less than half of that. Fish shrimp patterns over aquatic weed patches or cast black or green leeches towards the rocky points. Suspend a size 12 black, maroon or chrome chironomid pattern below a strike indicator along the shoreline, where cruising fish generate heart-stopping action for anglers.

In late June, use a Tom Thumb or Mikaluk Sedge during the sedge hatch to produce more top water action. A size 6 or 8 Knouff Lake Special or '52 Buick fished deeper can imitate a rising pupae.

Trollers find success in deeper sections of the lake when using pink, green or black F-4 or F-5 Flatfish or Hot Shots. A small Willow Leaf with a Wedding Band or worm will also

be effective. Spin fishers can cast from a boat, either toward the shore or deeper water, using a Rooster Tail in olive or maroon, a Blue Fox Vibrax in silver or gold, or a Len Thompson #8 yellow and black spoon.

Area Indicator

Directions

From Williams Lake, turn onto Highway 20 and travel west towards Bella Coola for about 30 km to Meldrum Creek Road. Turn right and head north for 40 km to the Rosita-Meldrum Forest Service Road intersection. Turn west and continue 36 km on the main road and about 100 metres past the 165 km marker, turn south onto the 100 G or Rosita-Fir Forest Road. Continue for about 6.5 km on this road and turn east for the final jog to the recreation site.

Although most vehicles, including RVs and trailers, can make it here, it is not the easiest lake to find. A GPS and a copy of the Cariboo Chilcotin Coast Backroad Mapbook would certainly help track your way in.

Facilities

The **Fir Lake Recreation Site sits** at the north end of the lake. There are nine sites here, five with tables and a rustic boat launch suitable for small trailered boats.

Fir Lake Fish Stocking Data			
Year	Species	Number	Life Stage
2008	Rainbow Trout	20,000	Fry
2007	Rainbow Trout	20,000	Fry
2006	Rainbow Trout	20,000	Fall Fry

N
ROSITA
FIR
FSR
Fir Lake
Rec Site
1m
2
3m
4
5m
6
100m 0 100m 200m 300m 400m
Scale

Location: 20 km (12.4 mi) north of Williams Lake
Elevation: 932 m (3,057 ft)
Surface Area: 98 ha (242 ac)
Max Depth: 16 m (53 ft)
Mean Depth: 4.9 m (16 ft)
Way Point: 52° 17' 40.7" N, 122° 2' 15.5" W

Forest Lake

Area Indicator

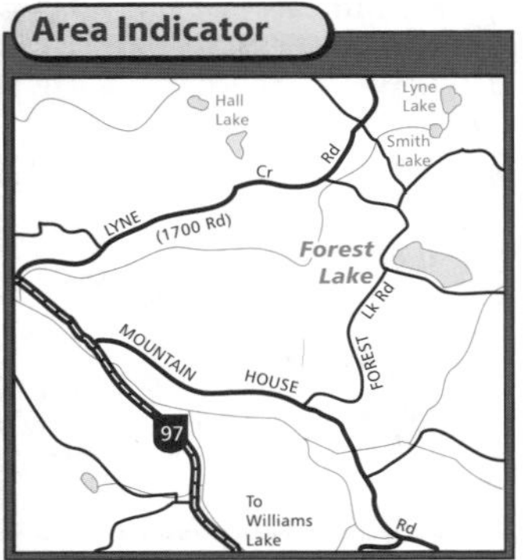

Forest Lake			
Fish Stocking Data			
Year	Species	Number	Life Stage
2008	Rainbow Trout	20,000	Fry
2007	Rainbow Trout	20,000	Fry
2006	Rainbow Trout	20,000	Fall Fry

Fishing

Managed as a trophy lake for feisty Pennask rainbow trout, Forest Lake is supplemented each year by an aggressive stocking program since the fish are unable to spawn naturally at the lake. Some of the rainbow in the lake can be over 8 kg (18 lbs) but these trophies are very hard to catch.

Even if you don't hook into one of these monsters, the lake is famous for producing plenty of fish in the 2 kg (4 lb) range. As a result, the lake is quite popular with fly-fishers out of Williams Lake. The lake is designated artificial fly only.

The lake is best fished in the spring. Ice-out can occur in April and it fishes well through May and early June. In the early season, try a black or green chironomid pattern in size 12 or 14 in shallow water (2–6 metres/6–12 feet deep). A black, green, or yellow Doc Spratley, or large black or dark green gold beadhead leech trolled with a sinking line also works well. There is a good caddisfly hatch towards the second week of June. Try using a brown colour imitation fished just before dusk. You could also consider using a Tom Thumb or brown sedge pupae to take fish.

During the mayfly hatch in June, try a gold beadhead pheasant tail nymph in size 10 or 12. Other typical Cariboo lake flies such as dragonfly and damselfly nymphs, chironomids and shrimp patterns can produce. Trolling a leech pattern can also work.

The lake is not very good in the summer as the lake water warms and the fish are inactive. Also, the fish are muddy tasting so catch and release at that time of year is well advised. Fall brings another surge of feeding as the water cools. The water boatman flights on a sunny September day really get the fish feeding. Casting to the rises with a Tom Thumb or water boatman pattern may fool the fish into thinking a boatman has just landed or is about to take off. Make sure there is plenty of backing on the reel as these fish can even spool seasoned anglers.

The lake has two deep holes; one at the east end near the campsite and one near the middle. These holes are known to be the resting place of the big trophy fish. Shallows full of water lilies cover the rest of the lake. The reeds out in front of the campground are a particularly good spot to try. However, shore casting is difficult as there are shallow areas near the road and campground limiting the ability to cast out to the deeper water.

In addition to the artificial fly designation, there is a limit of one fish per day over 50 cm (20 in), a 10 hp motor restriction and a fishing closure from November 1 to March 31.

Directions

The lake is accessed by heading north from Williams Lake on Highway 97 for about 25 km. Look for the Lyne Creek Road (1700 Rd) and head east for about 8 km then take a right on the Forest Lake Road. Keep right at the next intersection and the lake should appear about a kilometre later. The access is fairly good and people often bring in larger trailers or cars to the lake.

Facilities

There **Forest Lake Recreation Site** is found in an opening on the northern shores of the lake. There are nine RV suitable campsites and a rustic boat launch.

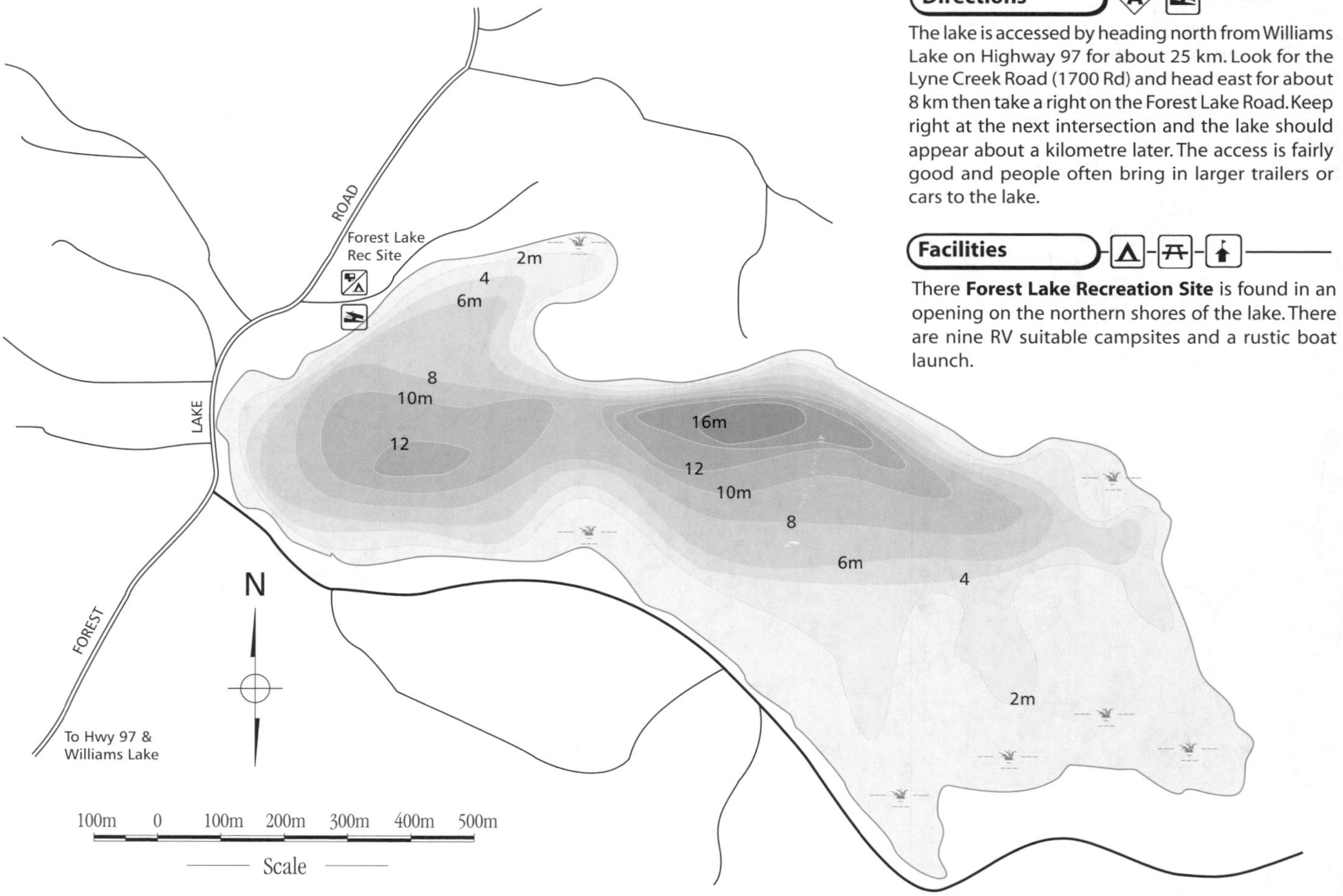

Fraser Lake

Location: 60 km (36 mi) west of Vanderhoof
Elevation: 676 m (2,500 ft)
Surface Area: 5,463 ha (13,500 ac)
Maximum Depth: 31 m (100 ft)
Mean Depth: 13 m (43 ft)
Way Point: 54° 4′ 56″ N, 124° 45′ 1″ W

Fishing

West of Vanderhoof along the Yellowhead Highway, the town of Fraser Lake sits at the west end of the lake that gave the town its name. The lake, while tiny in comparison to nearby Francois Lake, is still a good sized lake, stretching 20 km (12 miles) alongside the Yellowhead.

Known as the White Swan Capital of the world, birdwatching is the big draw. However, the lake is also home to a wide variety of wildlife, while the area is an outdoors paradise, with hiking, camping, canoeing, rafting, swimming and of course, fishing being popular pursuits.

Ah yes, the fishing. Fraser Lake is an outstanding fly-fishing lake. While gear casters will find plenty to love about this lake, the lake is known for its great fly-fishing and when the hatches are on, the fishing can be unbelievable.

The lake is a part of the Nechako River system, which in turn is the third largest tributary of the Fraser River. In the summer, there are large returns of sockeye up the river and into the lake. Following the sockeye up the river and into the lake are some big rainbow and Dolly Varden. Fly anglers can often find these big fish lurking around the mouths of streams and rivers that flow into the lake, waiting for sockeye eggs to float downstream. Fishing a pattern that resembles a floating egg, or in the case of gear anglers, fishing a single egg as bait can provide fast action when the salmon spawn is on.

When the salmon aren't spawning, the mouths of the rivers and streams can still be great places to fish, as a variety of insects and other food sources get washed down into the lake. Trollers and gear casters can also work just off the cliffs that plunge straight into the lake in many locations. The trout gather up against the cliffs and can be quite easy to catch. They can also get quite big, too, up to 7 kg (15 lbs) on occasion. Everything from a Willow Leaf and Wedding Band to Flatfish or Apex can work. Fly anglers trolling the lake should use big leeches and other attractor patterns.

The biggest fish you will find here are lake trout or lake char as they are more accurately called. Lakers can get up to 9 kg (20 lbs) here. In the summer, they are usually found in the deepest areas of the lake and can be caught on a deep troll using a downrigger, or less commonly, on a deep jig. Trollers use a variety of big plugs, like a Flatfish. As always, they are more readily caught in the spring when they are closer to the surface.

Area Indicator

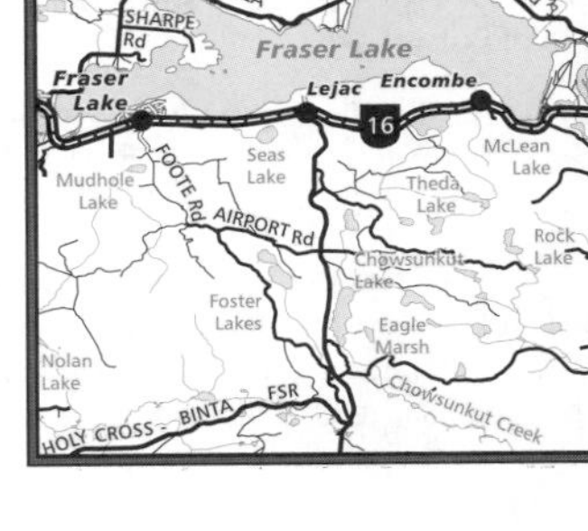

Directions

Fraser Lake is found alongside the Yellowhead Highway (Highway 16) east of the village of Fraser Lake, about 60 km (36 miles) west of Vanderhoof.

Facilities

The village of Fraser Lake has a number of hotels and restaurants. There is also camping at **Peterson's Beach Recreation Site** on the north shore of the lake and at **Beaumont Provincial Park** at the southeast end of the lake. There are boat launches at both sites and a third in town.

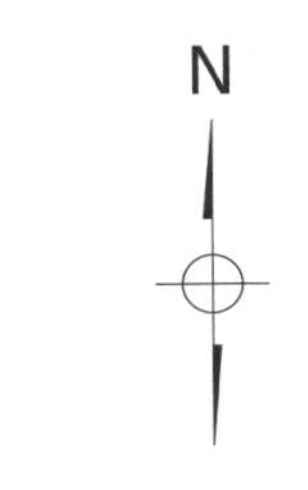

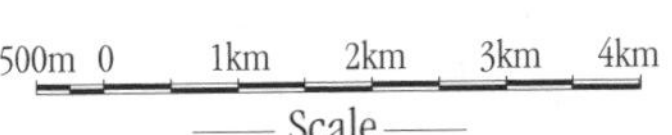

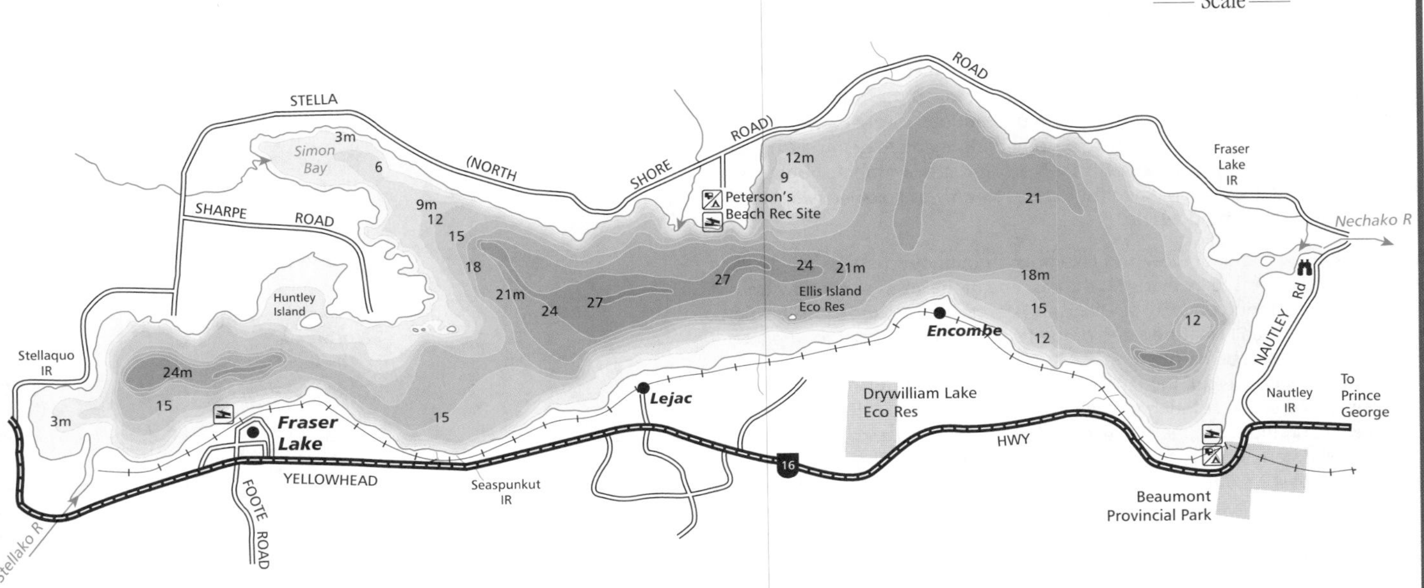

Location: 25 km (15.5 mi) south of Burns Lake
Elevation: 858 m (2,815 ft)
Surface Area: 25,779 ha (63,675 ac)
Max Depth: 244 m (802 ft)
Mean Depth: 86 m (284 ft)
Way Point: 54°2′ 00″ N, 125°49′ 00″W

Francois Lake

Fishing

Francois Lake is the second longest natural lake in the province, stretching 110 kilometres (66 miles) from tip to tail. It is a beautiful lake and is extremely popular for anglers, boaters and other recreators. The lake is found 25 kilometres south of Burns Lake.

The Nadina River flows into the lake's west end, while the world-famous Stelako river–a 10 km (6 mile) long river that features some excellent fly-fishing for rainbow trout to 2.5 kg (5 lbs) flows out of the east end.

Big lakes like Francois Lake are often unproductive lakes. It isn't that they don't hold fish. There are hundreds of thousands of fish in the lake. It's just that because the lake is so big, it's often tough to find the fish. However, that is not the case with Francois. The lake offers some spectacular fishing, especially towards the east end of the lake where the Stelako flows out of it. It is said that you have to try really hard, or have no clue how to fish to come away without catching at least something.

The big lake holds a number of game species, including Dolly Varden, kokanee, whitefish and burbot, but the usual catch is rainbow trout and lake trout (char). Rainbows can get to 2.5 kg (5 lbs), while lake trout are found over 15 kg (30 lbs), though only rarely.

Francois is cold and deep, with some points reaching as much as 300 m (1,000 feet) deep. It is possible to fish the lake from the shore, though there is just so much shoreline that a boat is usually much preferred. However, if you are fishing from shore, the best places to try are areas around feeder creeks, especially if there is a point near the creek that will extend your casting range.

The fishing towards the west end of the lake is better for certain species–Dolly Varden and kokanee–than it is at the west end.

Kokanee are usually caught on the troll, using a Willow Leaf and Wedding Band, often tipped by a worm, maggot or Powerbait. They are not the most aggressive fish, and will often follow your lure curiously for a long time before deciding to strike or deciding that it just isn't worth it.

To encourage strikes, you need to make your presentation more appealing. First, you need to troll slowly. Troll too fast and the kokanee will simply look at each other. "You hear anything strange?" The optimal speed is just fast enough to make the lake troll do its thing. The fluttering, flashing motion that attracts the fish's attention, as well as creating an audible noise in the water that also draws the fish's attention.

If the lure simply moves in a straight line the fish will often get bored of it, decide it isn't food after all, and swim off. By slowly turning in an S curve back and forth along the drop-off, the lure will speed up, and then slow down. Giving the lure a little tug will cause the lure to dart forward, then stop and slowly start to sink until the tension is back on the line, and the lure darts forward again. This can be what finally triggers a strike from the cautious kokanee, as the sudden darts give the lure the appearance of something trying to get away. The only other thing to note for kokanee is their soft mouths; a rubber snubber is an important addition, even when fishing for rainbow, as kokanee will often hit the same lures as rainbows do.

While you will find rainbow and lake trout throughout the lake, the average sized catch seems to be bigger at the east end of the lake. For rainbow trout, it is as easy as picking a bluff or an island and start fishing around those locations. These areas usually feature steep drop offs where the rainbow congregate in the cooler waters below the surface. John's Island–a small volcanic island about 15 km (9 miles) west of the ferry landing near the south side of the lake–is a popular place to fish. Indeed, it was once the communal fishing grounds for three First Nations around the lake. Trolling a Wedding Band with or without bait is the standard way to fish the lake, while lake trolls like a Ford Fender or Willow Leaf is are often used in conjunction with the Wedding Band as well as with other lures such as a Kamlooper or Krocodile spoon. Use the same trolling technique described above for kokanee, as the two species tend to have similar feeding habits.

Continued >>

François Lake (West)

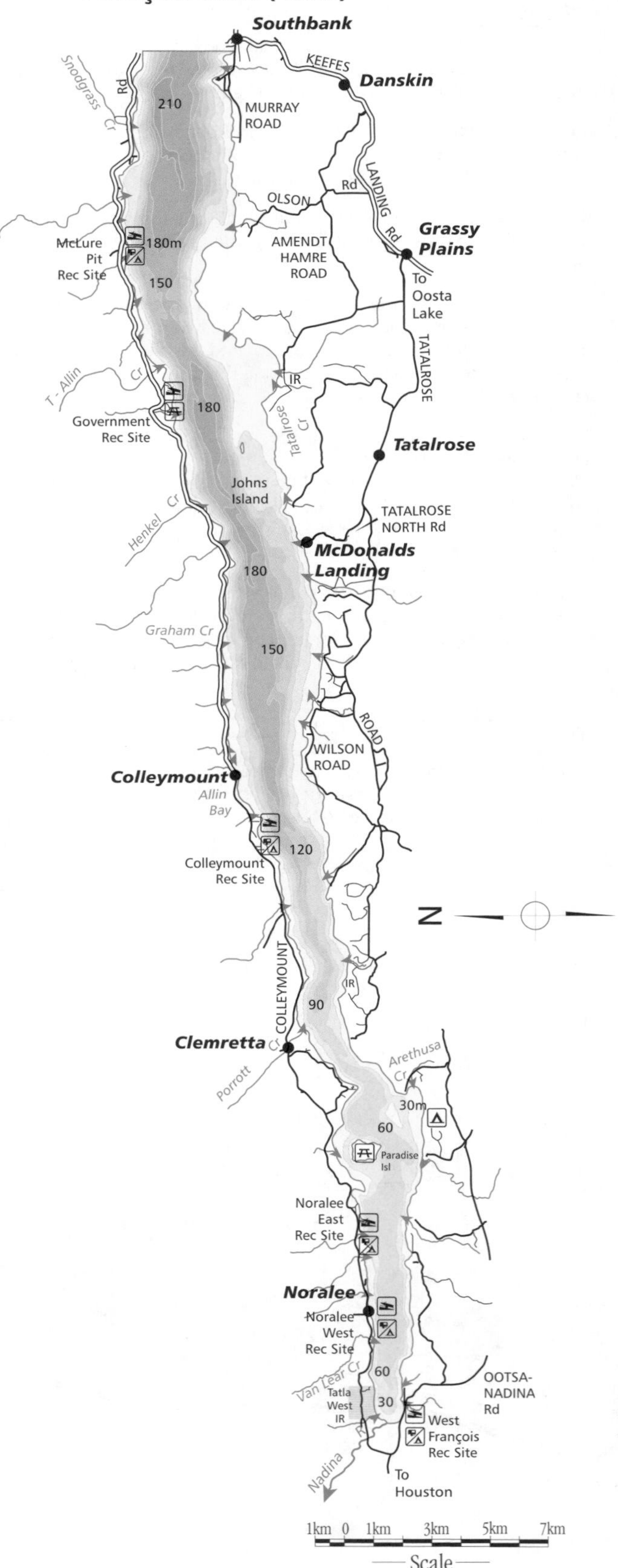

Francois Lake

Location: 25 km (15.5 mi) south of Burns Lake
Elevation: 858 m (2,815 ft)
Surface Area: 25,779 ha (63,675 ac)
Max Depth: 244 m (802 ft)
Mean Depth: 86 m (284 ft)
Way Point: 54°2′ 00″ N, 125°49′ 00″ W

Fishing 

Continued

Large spoons and plugs are used for the big lakers. A local favourite is the T50 Flatfish, usually in blues and silvers, though dark colours are gaining in popularity, especially black with silver flakes. Leadcore line trolling or using a downrigger are the two most common methods of fishing for lake trout, though some people will jig. The lake trout are usually found down around the 20–35 metre (65–110 feet) mark especially in summer, although in the spring they are usually in the shallow waters, feeding on bait fish.

Directions 

There are a number of ways to get to the lake. The easiest is to head to Burns Lake and watch for the turn-off onto Highway 35 just east of town. This 23 km (14 mile) road takes you to the Francois Lake Ferry. From here, the Colleymount Road continues west to access a series of recreation sites. Some prefer to take the ferry to the south shore and access the lake at Indian Bay off Uncha Lake Road.

The eastern end of the lake is accessed off the Francois Lake Road, which branches south from the Yellowhead, just west of Fraser Lake townsite.

Facilities  

There are several bed and breakfasts and private campsites around the lake. Visitors will also find an impressive series of forest recreation sites. At the west end of the lake are the **Noralee** and **West Francois Lake Recreation Sites**. The central part of the lake is home to **Colleymount**, **Government Point** and **McClure Point Recreation Sites**, while the **Indian Bay Recreation Site** lies on the southern shore. These sites all vary in size and development but do offer boat launches.

Much of the east end of the lake is protected by provincial parks, but there is little camping, save at the former Black Point Recreation Site, now in **Francois Lake Provincial Park.** There is however, a boat launch at this end of the lake off the Francois Lake Road.

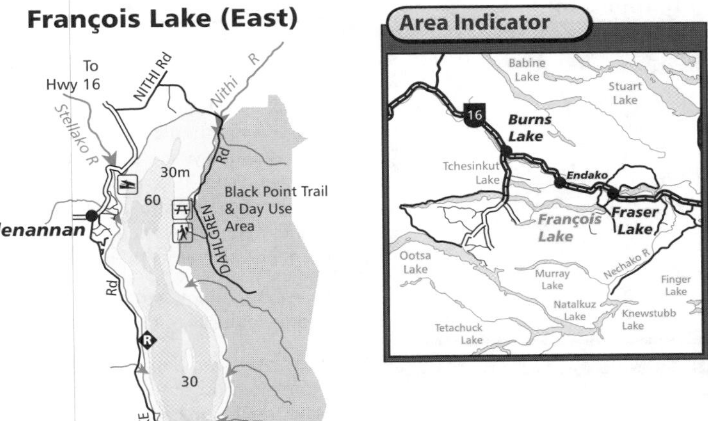

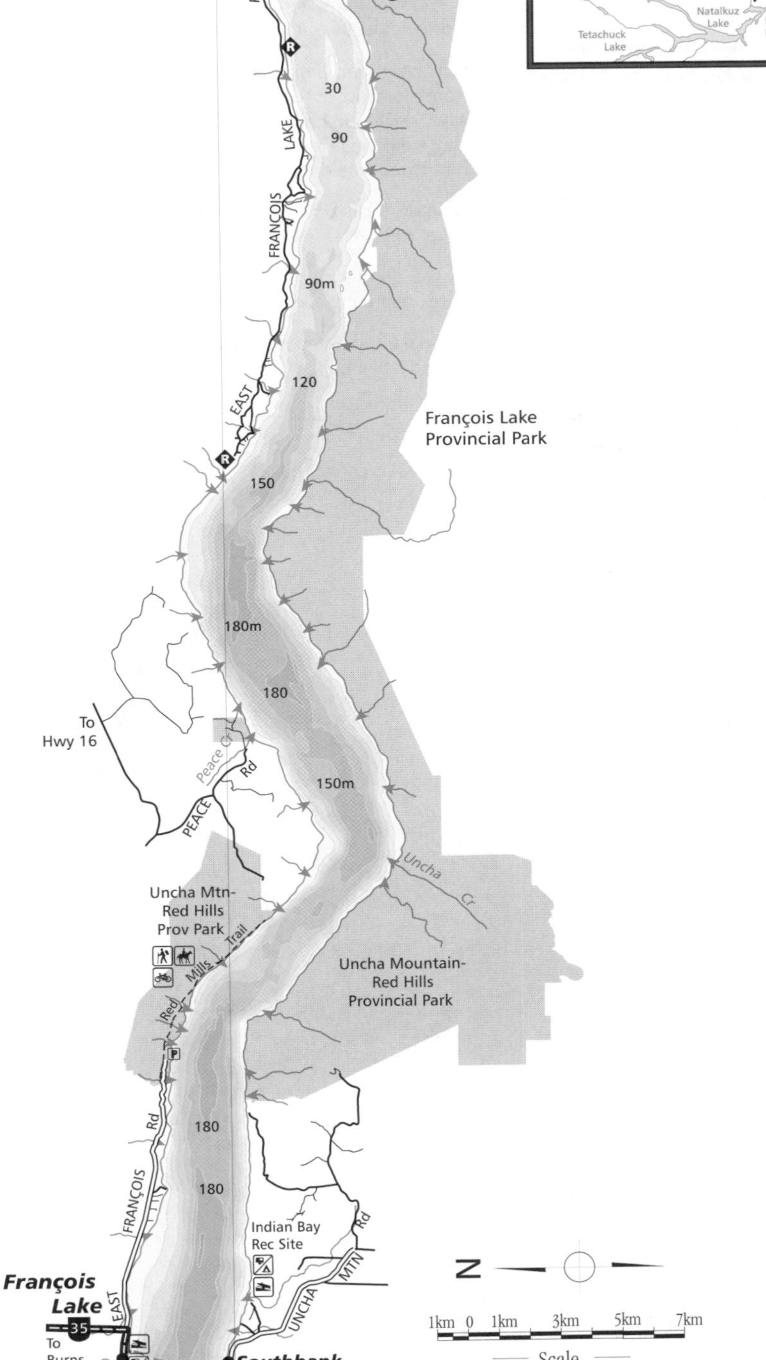

Location: 38 km (23.6 mi) east of 100 Mile House
Elevation: 1,141 m (3,743 ft)
Surface Area: 57 ha (141 ac)
Maximum Depth: 29 m (95 ft)
Mean Depth: 12 m (39 ft)
Way Point: 51° 35' 34.7" N, 120° 45' 49.4" W

French Lake

Area Indicator

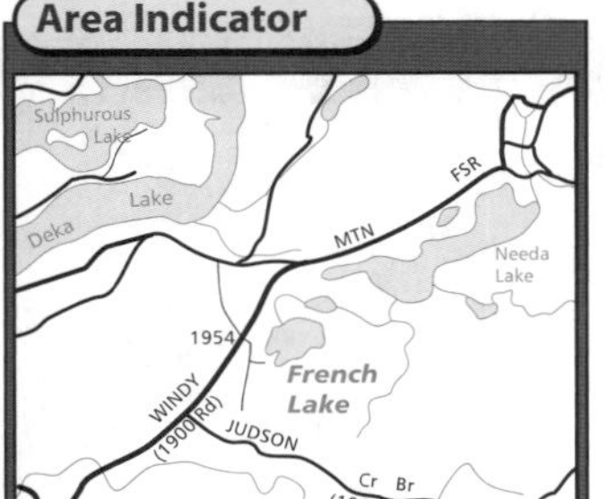

French Lake Fish Stocking Data			
Year	Species	Number	Life Stage
2008	Rainbow Trout	3,000	Yearling
2007	Rainbow Trout	3,000	Yearling
2006	Rainbow Trout	3,000	Yearling

Fishing

French lake is a hidden lake situated north of Bridge Lake. It can be fished beginning in mid to late May and provides pretty good fishing for small rainbow into late June and again in the fall.

The lake is not very big, but is quite deep and is a popular lake for trolling. The lake is the deepest in the middle; this is where you should focus your efforts in the summer months when the fish retreat to the deeper water. During the rest of the year, troll along the prominent drop off, slowly turning back and forth so that the lure or fly slows down and speeds up and travels in a more random pattern; this is far more intriguing to the trout than a lure that simply travels in a straight line at a constant speed. Slowing down (maybe even stopping for a second or two) and speeding up will also help imbue your offering with a sense of something living. And a sudden acceleration can trigger a strike, as it appears the lure or fly is trying to escape.

Even in summer, the trout will be found where water and land meet; they will rarely be found just swimming in the middle of the lake. A fish finder will be quite helpful in determining the location and depth of the fish.

Spincasters and fly fishermen should anchor 20–50 metres (60–150 feet) off shore and cast back towards the shoreline. Most of the popular Cariboo flies work at this lake beginning with the ever popular chironomids in May. During non hatch periods, searching patters such as Woolly Buggers, Carey Specials and a variety of nymphs work well. The lake does offer some dry fly-fishing with mosquito, beetle and other insect imitations working at the appropriate times.

Spincasters can do well with a Panther Martin, Krocodile or Black Knepps tipped with a worm. Trollers often work a lake troll or Flatfish just off the drop off.

There is an island at the northwest end of the lake and an almost-island at the northwest end of the lake. Both these are great places to try fishing, as they create structure for the fish to hold around.

The lake is regulated by a single barbless hook requirement, no ice fishing, a powerboat restriction (less than 10 hp) and a bait ban.

Directions

To access the lake, follow Highway 24 to the Bridge Lake North Road near Roe Lake–a distance of about 37 km from Highway 97. Follow this road north for about 2 km and continue straight on Judson Road. Follow that road for 3.5 km and then take the first major logging road to the right, which is called the Windy Mountain Forest Service Road (1900 Road). Travel this road to the 1954 km marker where you will find a small, rough road leading down to the lake on your right (east).

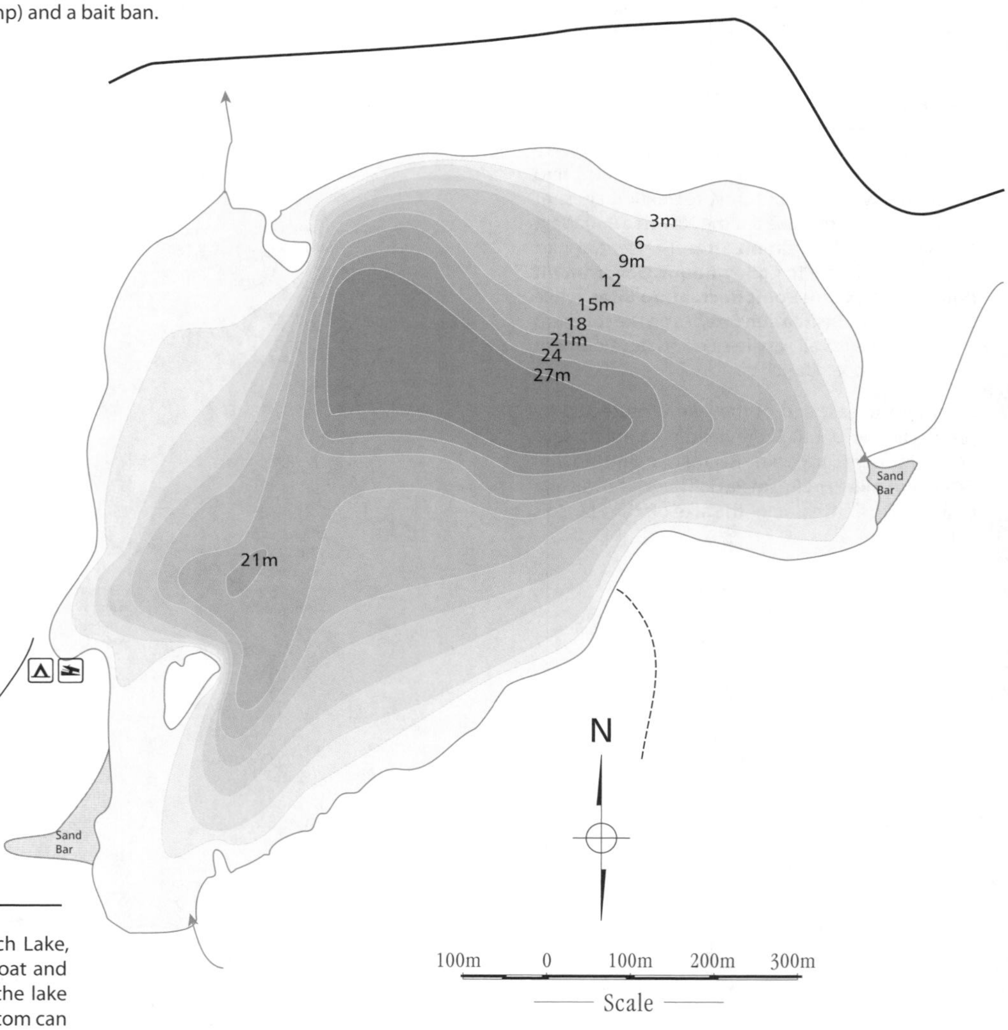

3m
6
9m
12
15m
18
21m
24
27m
Sand Bar
21m
To Windy Mtn FSR
Sand Bar
N
100m 0 100m 200m 300m
Scale

Facilities

There are no developed facilities at French Lake, however it is possible to launch a small boat and pitch a tent at the lake. Early in the year, the lake can be busy and turning around at the bottom can be a challenge.

Gavin Lake

Location: 48 km (30 mi) northeast of Williams Lake
Elevation: 966 m (3,169 ft)
Surface Area: 95 ha (235 ac)
Maximum Depth: 25 m (82 ft)
Mean Depth: 9.6 m (31.5 ft)
Way Point: 52° 29' 20.2" N, 121° 43' 53.5" W

Fishing

Gavin Lake is the main lake in the UBC Alex Fraser Research Forest northeast of Williams Lake. It is located along the northern boundary of the research forest and is easily reached by car some 6.4 km off the paved Likely Road.

As part of the Research Forest, the lake is better known for its Forest Education Centre, where students from Districts 27 and 28 come to learn about their natural environment.

However, anglers know Gavin Lake as a lake where the fishing is steady for small trout.

Because the fishing is so steady, the lake is a great place to take children or people who have never fished before. The fish are fairly indiscriminate and will take most anything you throw at them.

One of the best ways to fish the lake, especially for new anglers, is using a bobber and a worm. The only trick to this is to have enough space between the bobber and the hook so the worm is within about 1 metre (3 feet) of the bottom of the lake, the closer to the drop off the better. While it is possible to fish from shore, it is better to get out onto the water and fish from a small boat or a float tube.

Gavin Lake was stocked way back in 1962 with 110,000 rainbow and since then, the trout have been able to reproduce naturally, establishing a self-sustaining population. Although the trout are usually small, rainbow up to 35 cm (16 in) or 1 kg (2 lbs) are possible.

The lake is best in late May to early July and again in October. However, the lake is fairly deep and the lake water does not warm as much as the shallower nearby lakes allowing for decent fishing throughout the summer months.

The lake, given its depth, is well suited for trolling. Spincasters or bait fishermen can cast from shore as the water drops off rapidly. Spincasters and fly fishermen in a boat should work the near shore areas around the lake or the inflow and outflow creek areas.

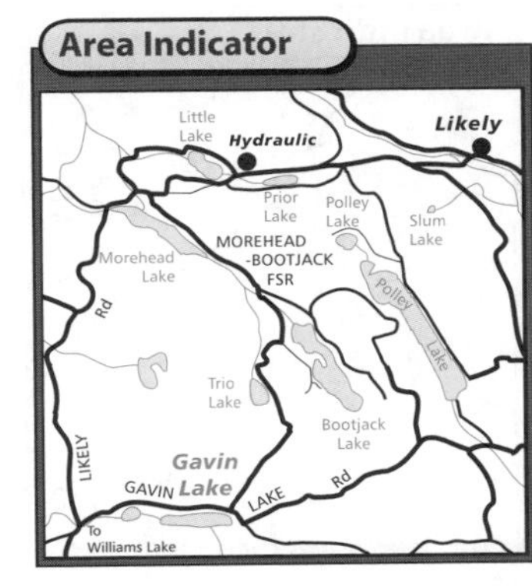

Directions

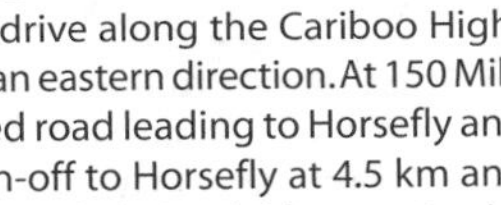

From Williams Lake, drive along the Cariboo Highway (Highway 97) in an eastern direction. At 150 Mile House, take the paved road leading to Horsefly and Likely. Avoid the turn-off to Horsefly at 4.5 km and continue on the paved, Likely Road. After passing by the Big Lake Ranch and the turn-off to the Beaver Valley Road, you will see a sign pointing the direction to the Gavin Lake Forestry Centre. It is another 6.4 km to the center on a well maintained gravel road. In total, it is about 72 km from Williams Lake.

Facilities

The **Gavin Lake Forestry Centre** is an all season forestry camp run by the BC Forestry Association. The centre focuses on forestry education for youths and includes interpretive trail system to explore. At the east end of the lake is the Gavin Lake Recreation Site with eight lakeshore camping spots and a boat launch.

Other Options

Within the research forest are a series of lakes including **Dorsey, Prouton** and **Cloate Lakes**. Each of these lakes offers small rainbow and is well suited for a belly boat and a fly rod.

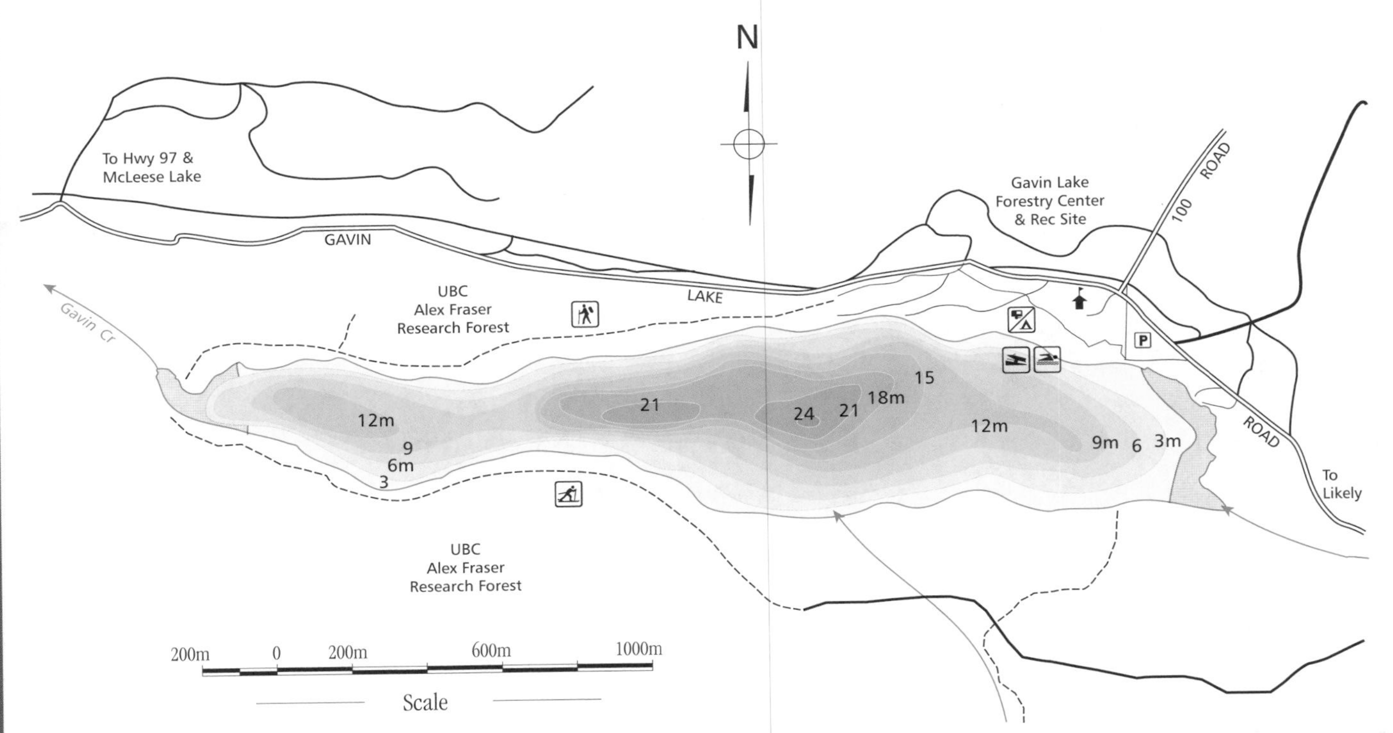

Location: 37 km (23 mi) west of Fort St. James
Elevation: 965 m (3,166 ft)
Surface Area: 666 ha (1,646 ac)
Maximum Depth: 23.7 m (77 ft)
Mean Depth: 7.9 m (25 ft)
Way Point: 54° 30' 5" N, 124° 48' 10" W

Grassham Lake

Area Indicator

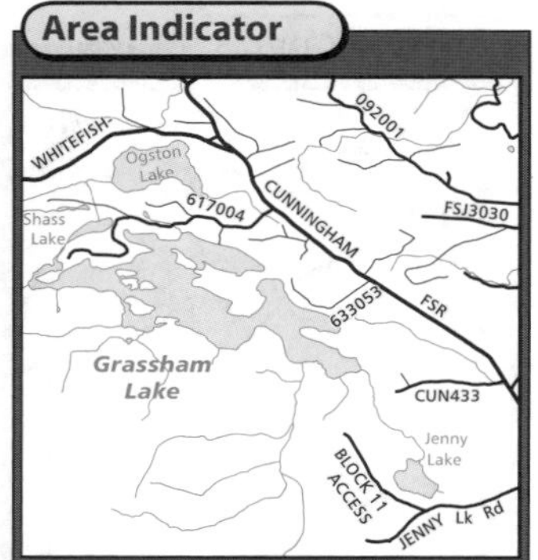

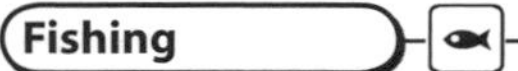

Fishing

Grassham Lake is mid sized lake found south of Stuart Lake and west of Fort St. James.

The lake is full of small, easy to catch rainbow trout that really like taking to the fly. A good sized catch here is 35 cm (14 in), but expect more action with the smaller ones.

Because the fish don't get very big, a lot of people give this place a miss, especially because the access into the lake is fairly rough. This helps keep the fishing steady and the crowds down.

Unlike a lot of northern lakes, Grassham Lake is an excellent dry fly lake from May to October. Catching 30 or more trout in a day is a frequent occurrence. There are lots of caddis hatches and chironomids and more importantly, the fish really like coming to the surface. Traditional interior dry flies work here: Elk Hair Caddis, interior nymph patterns, Tom Thumbs, even a mosquito pattern or two.

There is no one place that attracts the rainbow more than others. Instead, you will find them scattered around the lake, usually within casting distance of the drop offs. Because of this, you don't have to go far to get good results. In fact, fishing off the shore from the recreation site is as productive as anything. The shore here is open enough to fly cast, but many people will fish with spoons, spinners, or even a worm and bobber. If the recreation site is busy (though it is rarely busy), or you just want to get out onto the lake, there's lots of shoreline to cover and plenty of small bays that you can anchor in. There is nothing better than spending a few hours casting (and catching) in a quiet bay.

There isn't a boat launch on the lake, but launching a cartopper is easy enough. Trolling the lake with a Willow Leaf or with a streamer or leech pattern works well, too.

If you are trolling, or getting out onto the lake with a boat, note that the water is a lot shallower around points and many people have trashed their motors by running over the rocks. There is also a pile of rocks towards the west end of the lake that many people have run aground on, too.

Directions

Grassham Lake is fairly easy to locate along the Cunningham Forest Service Road. However, the road can be rough and a four-wheel drive vehicle is recommended, especially when the road is wet. From Highway 27 and Fort St. James, the easiest access to the Cunningham is along the Sowchea Road, which leads west from town. This road leads to the Lind Lake Pit Road, which branches south and turns into the Cunningham Forest Service Road. It should take about an hour to drive the rough road to the lake. If you hit the junction with the Whitefish-Cunningham Road, you are about 5 km (3 miles) too far.

Facilities

The **Grassham Lake Recreation Site** is a small, rustic forest service site with space for about five groups. It is possible to hand launch a boat here or at the informal launch site at the west end of the lake. Alternatively, **Omineca Guide and Outfitters** have a lodge on Grassham Lake. They mostly do guiding and full-service trips rather than renting boats and selling bait.

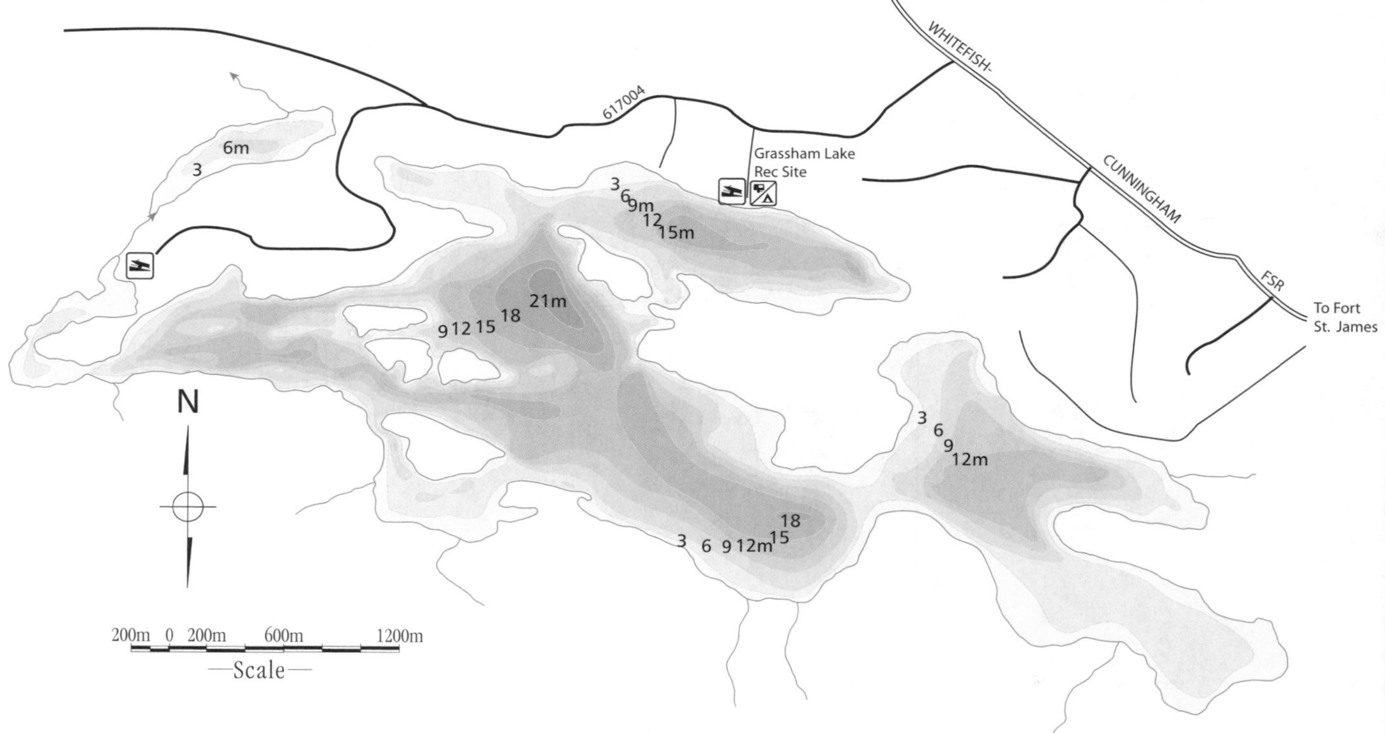

Green Lake

Location: 25 km (15.5 mi) south of 100 Mile House
Elevation: 1,074 m (3,523 ft)
Surface Area: 2,760 ha (6,820 ac)
Maximum Depth: 36 m (118 ft)
Mean Depth: 10 m (33 ft)
Way Point: 51° 24′32″N, 121° 13′9″W

Fishing

Green Lake gets its name from the brilliant emerald colour of the lake. This is caused by a combination of the high alkalinity and algae blooms in the lake. While the original Fur Brigade Trail ran along the shores of Green Lake, later roads and trails, including the Cariboo Wagon Road, which is now Highway 97, run further west.

This is fortunate for all the folks who head up to fish Green Lake. The lake does not have an inlet or outlet stream of any note and could quite easily become polluted, but the lack of access and good planning has kept the lake healthy.

Despite its popularity, the lake is not a great fishing lake, at least when compared to other lakes in the region. The big lake holds rainbow trout, kokanee, lake chub and redside shiner. The rainbow trout can get to 30–35 cm (12–14 in), while the kokanee are rarely found bigger than 30 cm (12 in) and usually much less.

The lake has very little aquatic vegetation, featuring instead a gravel bottom and gravel beaches. There are 18 public access points and three campground along the lake, so it can get quite busy; if you're looking to find a place to call your own, the east end is usually has the least boat traffic.

The lake is usually free of ice and ready to fish by mid-May. The fishing is at its best in the early part of the spring and towards September. However, you can still catch fish in the summer months.

The large, deep lake is better trolled. There's lots of area to cover and few spots that are consistent produces. The kokanee take well to lake trolls (a Willow Leaf and Wedding Band and worm) trolled slowly in 6–12 metres (20–40 feet) of water. The better spots to try are around the 30 metres (100 feet) depth in the middle of the lake or around the 24 metre (80 foot) hole near the west end of the lake. Troll in a slow S-pattern, which gives the lure a much more random pattern. Don't be afraid to pull on the rod just a bit, too, causing the lure to speed up and slow down. Often times, kokanee will follow a lure for a long way, by pulling on the rod (or speeding up a bit) you may trigger the chase instincts, as it appears your lure is trying to make a run for it.

Spincasters and fly fishermen will not find this lake too appealing. However, there are many bays and islands where you can find shelter from the prevailing winds and some nice drop offs. There are also a few shoals to discover.

Area Indicator

Directions

Green Lake is a popular recreation lake found 15 km northeast of 70 Mile House. Known for its emerald green, warm water and sandy beaches, the access to the lake is well signed. There are several possible routes in. From the Cariboo Highway both the Eighty Three Mile Road and the North Bonaparte Road lead to the lake. From Highway 24, follow Watch Lake Road south.

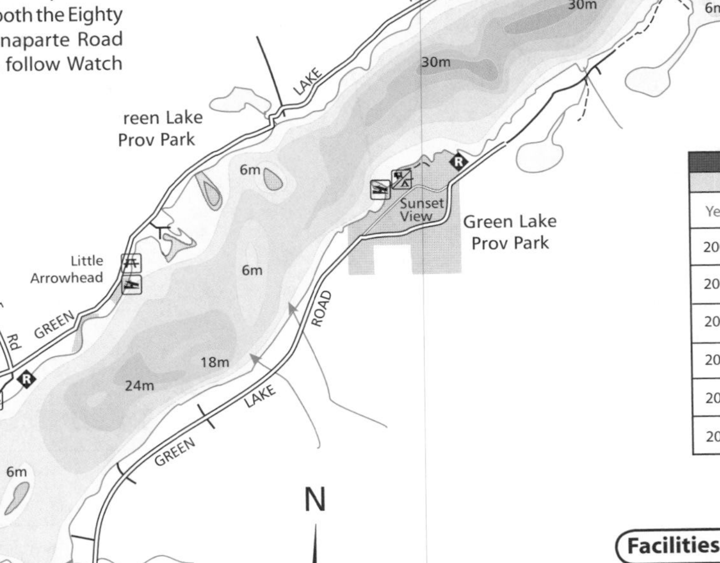

Green Lake Fish Stocking Data			
Year	Species	Number	Life Stage
2008	Rainbow Trout	155,776	Fry
2008	Rainbow Trout	98,594	Yearling
2008	Kokanee	127,670	Fry
2006	Kokanee	36,739	Fingerling
2005	Rainbow Trout	64,998	Yearling
2005	Kokanee	146,805	Fingerling

Facilities

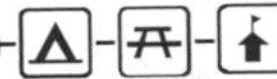

Within the **Green Lake Provincial Park,** there are three campgrounds. Emerald Bay is arguably the nicest and has 51 sites, Sunset View has 54 sites and Arrowhead has 16 sites. Sunset View also offers a boat launch. There are two day use areas in the park as well: Blue Spring and Little Arrowhead.

For a little more luxury, there are several resorts at the lake including the **Green Lake Lodge, Little Horse Lodge** and the **Poplar Beach Resort**.

Location: 38 km (23.6 mi) northeast of 100 Mile House
Elevation: 901 m (2,956 ft)
Surface Area: 29 ha (72 ac)
Maximum Depth: 25 m (82 ft)
Mean Depth: 9.0 m (30 ft)
Way Point: 51° 50′ 29″ N, 120° 53′ 12″ W

Greenlee Lake

Area Indicator

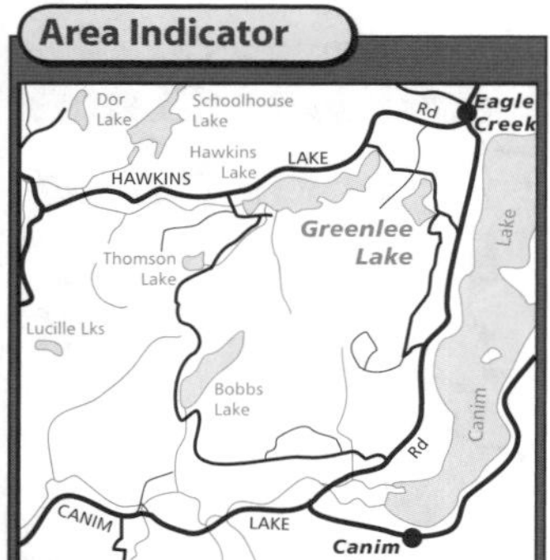

Directions

To reach the lake, drive northeast on the Canim Lake Road, which begins on Highway 97 just north of 100 Mile House. Continue to the western shores of Canim Lake and past the tiny Canim Beach Provincial Park. A steep access road leads west from a point north of the provincial park. A truck is definitely needed to reach the lake, as the access is steep and difficult to navigate in wet weather.

Fishing

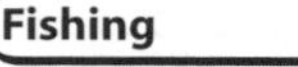

Greenlee Lake is located within a kilometer of the western shores of Canim Lake and is a productive fly-fishing lake with rainbow that can grow to 2.5 kg (5 lbs). The lake is stocked annually with 3,500 rainbow trout to ensure the lake continues to be very good for fishing.

Despite this, the lake receives very little fishing pressure except from locals. This is due to a couple factors, including the fact that it a very small lake, surrounded by dozens of other great fishing lakes and easy to overlook. Also, the road into the lake is steep and difficult to travel with a two-wheel drive vehicle. Given the choice, most people will go to another one of the great fishing lakes that define this area. Those willing to make the trip will find that the fish do get big, but are not the easiest fish to catch.

Greenlee Lake is located high enough and is deep enough to offer a steady fishery that runs from May to October. The lake has lake chub and redside shiners, which compete for aquatic insects with the smaller rainbow but become a food source for the larger rainbow.

Since the lake is quite deep, it is well suited for trolling. The deeper parts of the lake are near the southern end. It is best to troll around the center towards the drop offs. A fish finder will help locate the fish, especially in the summer, when the fish often hold a little deeper. Trolling in a random pattern–sometimes slowing down, sometimes speeding up and changing directions fairly frequently–keeps the fish interested in your offering, whether trolling a fly or a lure and usually encourages more strikes than simply travelling in a straight line.

For fly fishermen or spincasters, a sunken island at the north end of the lake is a good area to try casting. Also, work the deep hole at the eastern bay. Spincasters can try casting a torpedo bobber with a fly to effectively work the surface or try adding a little weight if you are fishing deeper. A Mepps, Panther Martin, Vibrax or Gibbs spinner cast out using the count down method to work different depths around the drop off are other promising options. Vertical jigging with spoons or jigs using flavoured bait, such as one of the Berkley Powerbaits, will also work well.

There is an electric motor only restriction at the lake.

Greenlee Lake Rec Site

To Canim Lake

Greenlee Lake Fish Stocking Data			
Year	Species	Number	Life Stage
2008	Rainbow Trout	3,500	Yearling
2007	Rainbow Trout	3,500	Yearling
2006	Rainbow Trout	4,400	Yearling

Facilities

The **Greenlee Lake Recreation Site** is situated in a heavily treed area on the eastern shores of the lake. At the recreation site, you will find space for a couple campsites along with a rustic launch to hand launch small boats.

Greeny (Greene) Lake

Location: 23 km (14 mi) north of 100 Mile House
Elevation: 941 m (3,087 ft)
Surface Area: 75 ha (186 ac)
Maximum Depth: 14 m (46 ft)
Mean Depth: 4.5 m (15 ft)
Way Point: 51° 51′ 6.0″ N, 121° 20′ 53.4″ W

Fishing

Greeny Lake is a small, shallow lake found near Mount Timothy, east of Lac La Hache. The lake is usually free of ice by mid-May. After that, the lake offers good fishing throughout the ice-free season except after a heat wave.

Greeny Lake is nestled in rolling hills and surrounded by a mixed coniferous and deciduous forest, which provides shelter from prevailing winds. A few permanent residences and a nursery sit on the shore.

The lake is stocked with rainbow trout that average 20–30 cm (8–12 in), although every once in a while, someone will pull out a fish in the 1 kg (2 lb) range. About 20,000 rainbow are stocked in the lake each year to ensure that the fishery is maintained. These are Blackwater strain, which feed on the redside shiners that inhabit the lake.

Spincasters take rainbow by working the shoals and drop offs near the islands in the middle of the lake. Anglers are successful with a variety of spinners including the Mepps Black Fury and Aglia. Casting a #8 Len Thompson silver or green spoon can also be productive. Spincasters and fly fishermen can do well casting off the deeper holes south of the island or east of the island.

Even though the extensive shoals on the west and east ends of the lake make this a perfect fly-fishing lake, trollers are successful in the deep water in the centre of

the lake, east of the two islands. Shore casting is difficult and a small boat or tube is nearly a necessity. If you do use a boat, note that there is a 10 hp restriction on engines.

Trollers get action on silver Willow Leaf lake trolls and a Wedding Band with worms, a F-4 or 5 Flatfish, or by trailing a green Apex spoon. Trolling a green Doc Spratley, Carey Special or green sized 70 Hot Shot on a sinking fly line or leadcore line and long leaders will capture the attention of the big ones.

Fly fishers should cast silver or gold-bodied minnow patterns along the drop offs. Fish the chironomid, mayfly or caddis hatches in the spring and early summer.

In the winter, nearby Timothy Mountain sports a good ski hill, so don't overlook the opportunity to mix skiing with ice fishing. Worms, maggots and shrimp on a small jig or

a yellow marabou jig will take fish when they are hitting.

Area Indicator

Greeny Lake
Fish Stocking Data

Year	Species	Number	Life Stage
2008	Rainbow Trout	20,000	Yearling
2007	Rainbow Trout	20,000	Yearling
2006	Rainbow Trout	20,000	Yearling

Facilities

The **Greeny Lake Recreation Site** is situated on the northern shores of the lake right next to the Timothy Lake Road. The easy access ensures the site is often full on weekends. It has 16 camping spots, some of which are in a treed setting and others in a grassy meadow. A boat launch is available for cartoppers or small trailered boats.

Directions

Greeny Lake is found to the east of Lac La Hache. To access the lake, drive to the town of Lac la Hache on the Cariboo Highway (Highway 97) and take the paved Timothy Lake Road (1500 Road) heading northeast. At 6.8 km turn right and drive another 4 km to the recreation site.

Location: 32 km (20 miles) southwest of 100 Mile House
Elevation: 1,079 m (3,540 ft)
Surface Area: 142 ha (351 ac)
Maximum Depth: 14 m (46 ft)
Mean Depth: 5.0 m (16 ft)
Way Point: 51° 32′ 21″ N, 121° 43′ 22″ W

Gustafsen Lake

Area Indicator

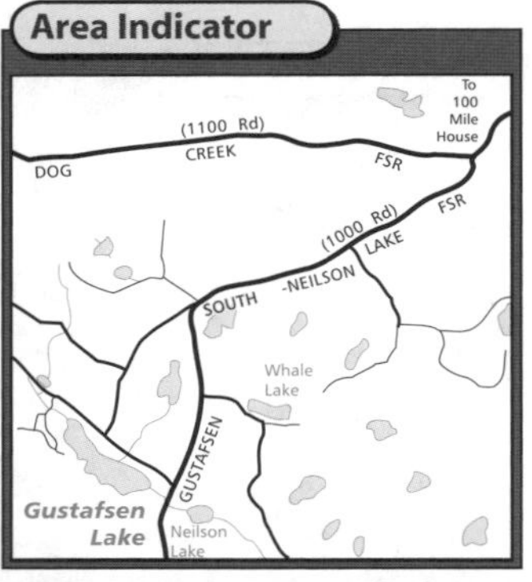

Gustafsen Lake			
Fish Stocking Data			
Year	Species	Number	Life Stage
2005	Rainbow Trout	10,000	Fry
2004	Rainbow Trout	10,000	Fall Fry

Fishing

Gustafsen Lake is best remembered as the site of a standoff in 1995 between the Secwepemc First Nations and the RCMP, resulting in one of the largest police operations in Canadian history and one of the most dramatic moments in BC History.

For a few years before the conflict, anglers were routinely warned away from the lake as the native sun dance approached.

Today, there is little here to remind visitors of the conflict and that what does remain is on private land. Instead, the small, unassuming lake, situated southwest of 100 Mile House offers good fishing in the spring and fall for previously stocked trout. Up until 2005, the lake was stocked with 10,000 Blackwater strain rainbow, which have since established a self-sustaining breeding population at the lake.

Gustafsen Lake offers a good fishery for rainbow beginning in the late spring. Fishing during the summer months is better than other lakes in the area but it is still slow. The early fall is a better time to fish. The rainbow grow to 1.5 kg (3 lbs) or 40-50 cm (16-20 in). They average smaller than that and are caught by spincasting, trolling or fly-fishing. Using a long thin leader is a good idea as the water is fairly clear.

The lake, given its depth, is hard to troll. The west end of the lake is quite shallow and offers limited fishing opportunities. Spincasters and fly anglers should work the drop off area near the middle of the lake. Shore casters can do well particularly along the southern shoreline.

Trollers can use the traditional Wedding Band with Willow Leaf, spoon or Flatfish, while spincasters can work a variety of lures, from an Apex Trout Killer to a Vibrax or Gibbs spinner. Fly anglers will find the usual assortment of hatches at the lake, although the best fishing happens below the surface, with a chironomid, a nymph, or some sort of searching pattern like a Carey Special.

No ice fishing is allowed at the lake.

Directions

The access to the lake is through private property. The current owners are kind enough to allow public access but that may change without notice. Please show respect.

To reach the lake, head west on the paved Exeter Road at the northern end of 100 Mile House. That road turns into the Gustafsen Lake Forest Service Road (1100 Rd), which leads pass the Moose Valley Provincial Park. At the next major junction, continue south on the Gustafsen-South Neilson Lake Road (1000 Rd). The lake is about 16 km south of the junction and accessed by a small side road.

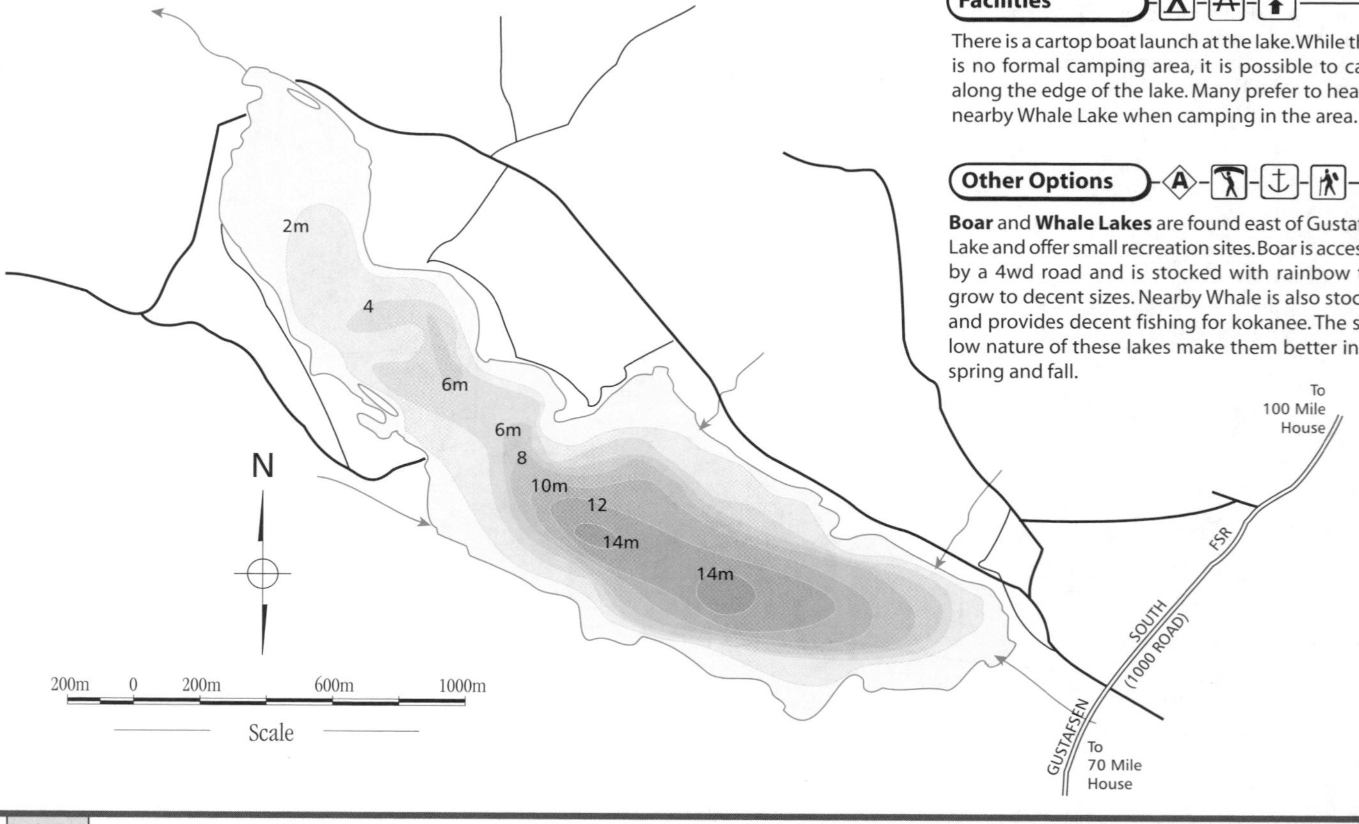

Facilities

There is a cartop boat launch at the lake. While there is no formal camping area, it is possible to camp along the edge of the lake. Many prefer to head to nearby Whale Lake when camping in the area.

Other Options

Boar and **Whale Lakes** are found east of Gustafsen Lake and offer small recreation sites. Boar is accessed by a 4wd road and is stocked with rainbow that grow to decent sizes. Nearby Whale is also stocked and provides decent fishing for kokanee. The shallow nature of these lakes make them better in the spring and fall.

To 100 Mile House
FSR
SOUTH (1000 ROAD)
GUSTAFSEN
To 70 Mile House
N
2m
4
6m
6m
8
10m
12
14m
14m
200m 0 200m 600m 1000m
Scale

Gwillim Lake

Location: 50 km (30 miles) south of Chetwynd
Elevation: 787 m (2,582 ft)
Surface Area: 1,121 ha (2,769 ac)
Maximum Depth: 48 m (157 ft)
Mean Depth: 31 m (101 ft)
Way Point: 55° 21' 20" N, 121° 18' 56" W

Fishing

Gwillim Lake can be a cold, heartless lake, unwilling to offer up any of the species that swim the lake. These include Arctic grayling, bull trout, burbot whitefish and lake trout.

When we say that Gwillim Lake is cold, we weren't just referring to its mood. The lake rarely gets above 8°C in the heart of the lake. While the shallows do warm up enough that brave campers have been known to go for a swim, it is still quite cold.

The lake is best known for being stubborn, but once you figure out the lake's secret, you should have fairly good results. One of the biggest secrets is that there isn't a lot of fish in the lake and there's plenty of natural food, meaning that coercing a fish to take what you're offering can be frustrating at best.

The lake is best known for its lake trout fishing. While there are plenty of stories of 18 kg (40 lb) lakers being pulled out of the lake, the average size is closer to 3 kg (6 lbs). The best lake trout fishing happens towards the east end of the lake. The lake narrows substantially near its mid point and fishing near either shore in about 18–30 metres (60–100 feet) of water can be quite productive. Fishing along the drop off near the pair of inflow creeks on the south side of the lake or directly opposite can be productive. But here's the thing. If you find fish in one spot, chances are, the other spots will be completely dead. If you find where the lake trout are, don't go looking elsewhere.

At the very far end of the lake, where the Gwillim River flows out of the lake, is some good fishing for whitefish and pike. The pike in the lake can get huge. The story is told of someone diving in the lake starting to swim over a sunken log, only to have it swim away from him. In that story, the fish was close to 2 metres (6 feet) long, but nobody has pulled anything that size out of the lake and provided proof. Local anglers will tell you that the pike don't seem to like traditional pike spoons or lures. What they won't tell you is what actually works for pike on the lake, especially as the lake is regulated single barbless, no bait.

West of the boat launch is a small creek that flows into the lake. The best rainbow trout fishing is had here, while the very west end of the lake offers great fishing for grayling.

Surrounded by Gwillim Lake Provincial Park, the lake is 11 km (6.6 miles) long and 1.5 km (1 mile) wide. The lake lies east and west and can get very windy very fast.

Area Indicator

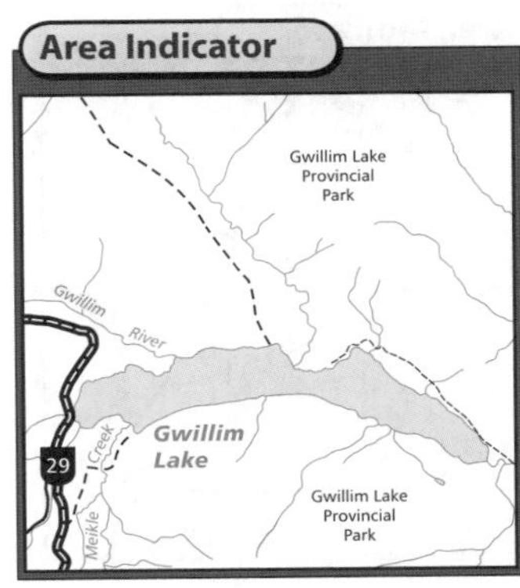

Directions

Gwillim Lake marks almost exactly the halfway point between Tumbler Ridge and Chetwynd, approximately 50 km from either town along Highway 29. Keep an eye out for the BC Parks signs as you make your way south from Chetwynd. The lake is visible from the highway.

Facilities

Gwillim Lake Provincial Park provides good access to the lake. There is a concrete boat launch that is suitable for larger boats as well as a small pier next to the launch. There are even canoe rentals available. The park also offers 49 campsites and a series of trails.

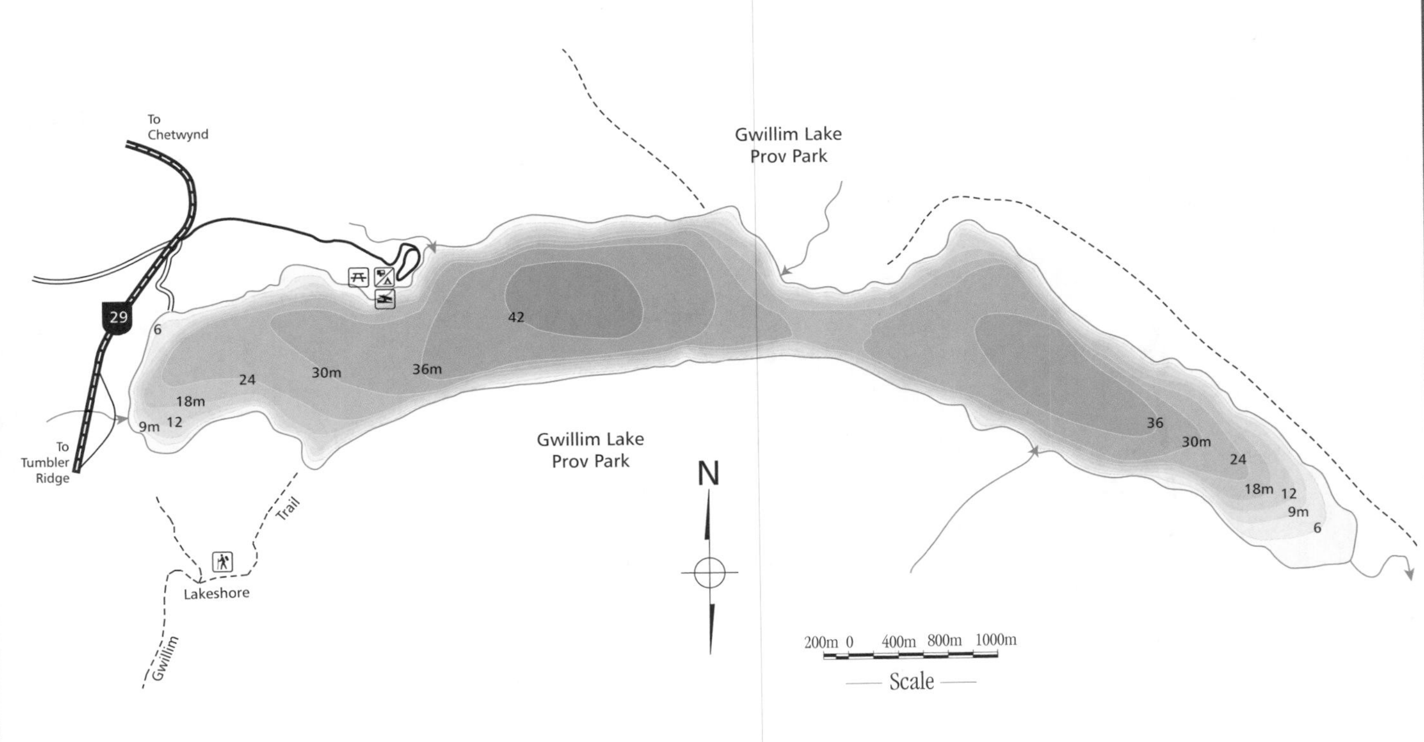

Location: 69 km (43 mi) northeast of Prince George
Elevation: 715 m (2,345 ft)
Surface Area: 56 ha (138 ac)
Maximum Depth: 8.7 m (29 ft)
Mean Depth: 5.0 m (16 ft)
Way Point: 54° 28′ 7.2″ N, 122° 39′ 13.0″ W

Hart Lake

Area Indicator

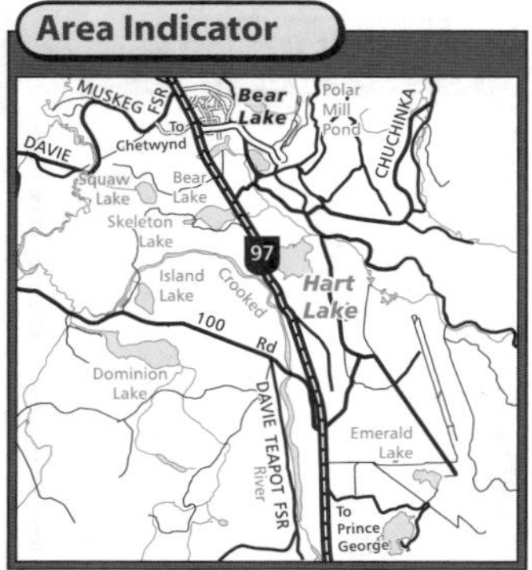

Fishing

Hart Lake is a popular fishing lake found in Crooked River Provincial Park north of Prince George. The park itself is one of the largest and most popular in the area, meaning the lake can see its fair share of anglers.

The lake is managed as a trophy rainbow trout lake, but all is not well in the lake. A weir was installed to prevent non-game fish from entering the lake, but lately, the lake is being overrun with course fish, including sucker, redside shiner and prickly sculpin. As a result, in 2004, there was a change in stocking at the lake. The former trout being stocked in the lake (diploid Dragons) were spawn bound making them long but not very big. Now the lake is being stocked with Blackwater trout. Half of the fish stocked are all-female triploid that don't reproduce, so they pour all their energy into getting big. And, because they are piscivourous, they like to eat the small coarse fish in the lake, especially the redside shiner.

Results of this change in stocking patterns have not fully played out and people are still reporting that they're pulling out rather large suckers in the last few years. If the trout can not take over on there own, there are rumours that they might chemically treat the lake to kill off the course fish. If this is the case, the fishery may suffer for a year or two.

Regardless, Hart Lake has abundant feed so the trout grow quickly. There are many shoals in this lake for the angler to explore. The fishing can be quite good all season, although it does slow down when the weather gets too hot, usually in August.

Popular fly patterns include scuds and leeches, which can work well at any time of the year, damselfly nymphs from mid-June to mid-August, dragonfly nymphs from early May to the end of September, chironomids from early May to mid-July and again in late September, caddisflies from mid-June to the end of August and mayflies from late spring through to fall.

For spincasters and trollers, gold and silver Dick Nites and black and silver or frog Flatfish work quite well. Don't fish too deep, though; the productive zones for food are found in less than 8 metres (28 feet) of water. The lake is best fished from a small boat or float tube, but anglers will have to carry their watercraft a short distance from the highway.

Be sure to check the current Freshwater Fishing Regulations before you go. Hart Lake has several unique regulations including a single barbless hook, bait ban, and electric motors only restrictions. It is also closed to fishing from November 1 to April 30.

Directions

Hart Lake is found in Crooked River Provincial Park, which is 77 km north of Prince George or just south of Bear Lake on Highway 97. The lake is visible from the highway and there is a parking lot just off the highway. It is a short (100 metre/300 foot) walk from the parking lot to the lake, where it is possible to launch a cartop boat or a float tube.

Facilities

Despite resting in **Crooked River Provincial Park,** there is little more than an area to hand launch small boats. The park does have a large campground on Bear Lake, about 1.6 km (1 mile) away.

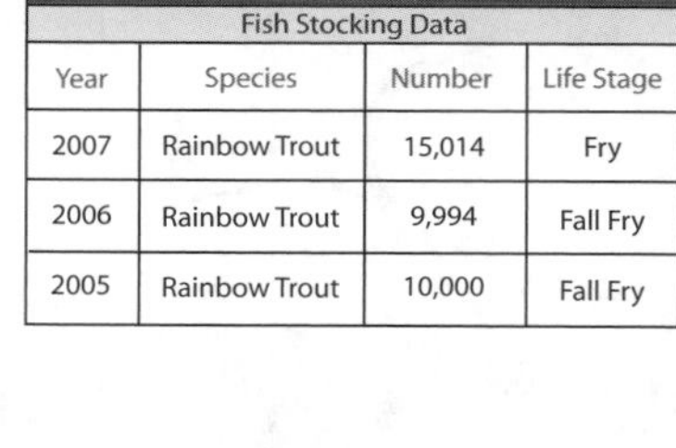

Hart Lake Fish Stocking Data			
Year	Species	Number	Life Stage
2007	Rainbow Trout	15,014	Fry
2006	Rainbow Trout	9,994	Fall Fry
2005	Rainbow Trout	10,000	Fall Fry

Crooked River Prov Park
ALASKA
P
97
HWY
9m
8
6m 5 4m 3 2m 1
Crooked River Prov Park

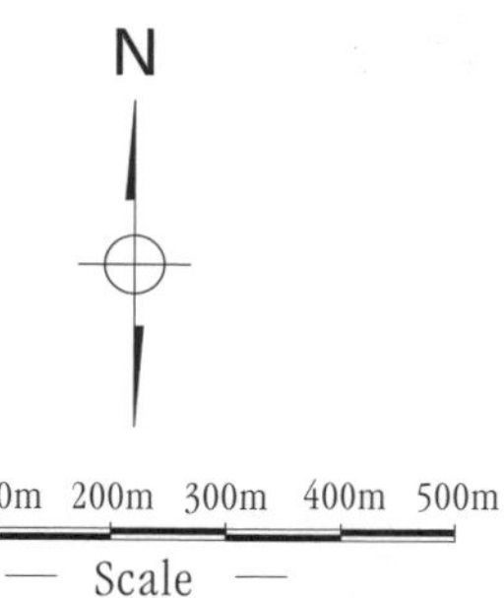

Hathaway Lake

Location: 33 km (20.5 mi) east of 100 Mile House
Elevation: 1,120 m (3,674 ft)
Surface Area: 152 ha (375 ac)
Maximum Depth: 45 m (147 ft)
Mean Depth: 20 m (65 ft)
Way Point: 51° 39' 28" N, 120° 50' 6" W

Fishing

Hathaway Lake is the prettiest lake in the Cariboo, or so claim the folks who own property on the shores of the lake. The lake is 5 km (3 miles) long from tip to tail and just over half a kilometre wide at its widest point.

The lake is best known for its rainbow trout fishing and is stocked to the tune of 10,000 rainbow each year. The rainbow can get up to 2.5 kg (5 lbs), but average only about half of that. In addition to the rainbow trout, the lake has good numbers of lake trout, which average about 3.5 kg (8 lbs).

The elevation, plus the depth of the lake means that the lake is fishable throughout the ice-off season, although the fishing is better in spring and fall. Because the lake is so long and narrow, it is a perfect lake for trolling. The drop off is located between 50–100 metres (150–300 feet) off shore on average. Because the insect growth is most pronounced in places where the sun can penetrate, you can usually troll by sight, although a depth finder won't hurt, especially if you pass over fish that aren't biting on the first go around. Keep the drop off generally under the boat, so that you can see the lighter colour of the shallow water on one side and the dark, deeper water on the other. As you troll, make 'S' curves back and forth over the drop off. This causes the lures to speed up and slow down, making them more tantalizing for the trout. A sudden burst of speed (not much, mind you, just a little burst) after a moments pause can often trigger a strike as the rainbow think the lure is making a run for it.

The lake is also well suited for fly-fishing and spincasting. The far side of the lake across from the public boat launch is a sunken island where the fishing can be good if you work the drop off area.

Lake trout are a cold-water species. While they can be found in the shallows just after ice off, they quickly move into the deep, cold waters of the lake. The best way to find them is using a deep troll, either with a long line or with a downrigger. A depth finder is very important when fishing for lake trout, as these fish are usually found within a few metres of the bottom of the lake. Being able to adjust the depth of a downrigger to keep the lure in the right depth will increase your odds. Lake trout often congregate around small underwater structures–slight bumps and ridges that provide structure.

Facilities

There is a picnic site and a boat launch along the western shore of the lake. There are a pair of resorts found at the south end of the lake. Contact the **Hathaway Lake Resort** or **Moosehaven Resort** for more details on what they have to offer.

Directions

Hathaway Lake is found nearby to a series of good fishing lakes (Sulphurous, Drewry, Bowers, Deka, Needa and English Lakes). Hathaway is best reached by traveling along the Fishing Highway (Highway 24). At Interlakes Corner, the Horse Lake Road heads north from the highway. Continue straight on the Mahood Lake Road when you come to the Judson Road-Horse Lake Road intersection. You will first come to Sulphurous Lake followed by Hathaway Lake.

Area Indicator

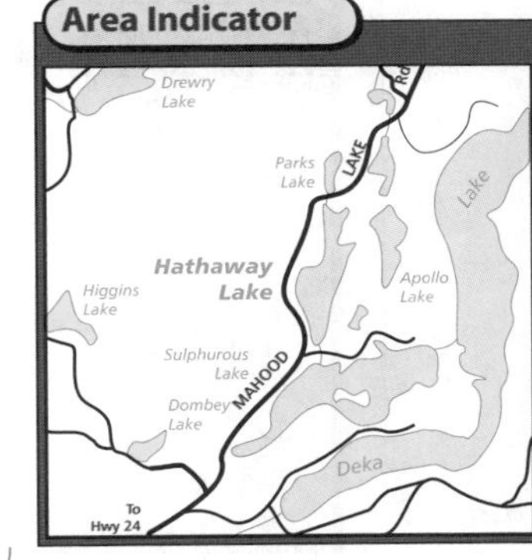

Hathaway Lake			
Fish Stocking Data			
Year	Species	Number	Life Stage
2008	Rainbow Trout	9,999	Yearling
2007	Rainbow Trout	10,000	Yearling
2006	Rainbow Trout	10,000	Yearling

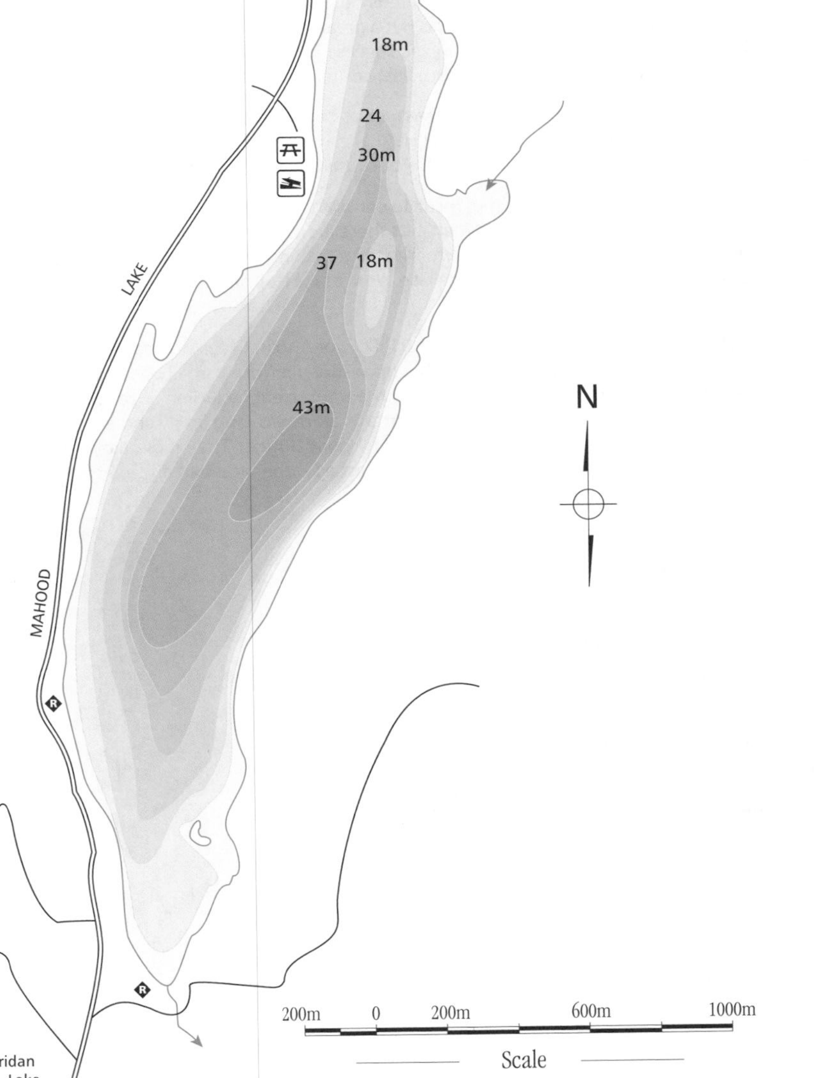

Location: 50 km (31 mi) northeast of Quesnel

Hay & Lodi Lakes

Lodi Lake

Elevation: 947 m (3,107 ft)
Surface Area: 169 ha (418 ac)
Maximum Depth: 13.4 m (44 ft)
Mean Depth: 7 m (23 ft)
Way Point: 53° 22' 45" N, 122° 4' 47" W

Hay Lake

Elevation: 948 m (3,110 ft)
Surface Area: 47 ha (116 ac)
Maximum Depth: 6.4 m (21 ft)
Mean Depth: 4 m (13 ft)
Way Point: 53° 21' 23.2" N, 122° 4' 59.4" W

Area Indicator

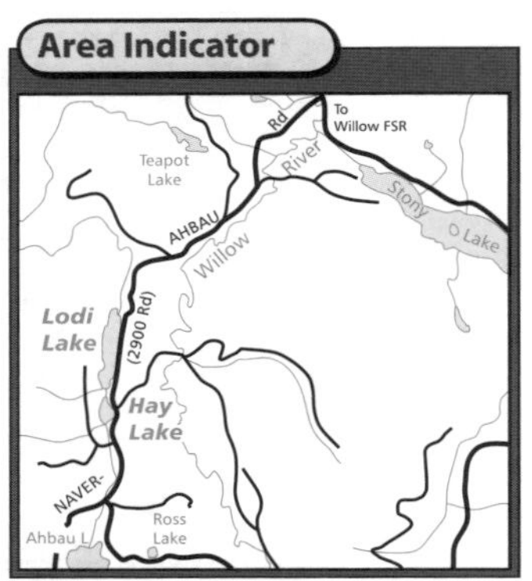

Directions

There are a few different access roads leading into the area. Perhaps the easiest of the bunch is the Naver-Ahbau Road (700 Rd), which leads east from Highway 97 near Dunkley. This small community lies between Quesnel and Hixon. Follow the Naver-Ahbau Road east avoiding all branch roads until the road eventually skirts the eastern shoreline of Hay and then Lodi Lake.

Despite the distance of backroad travel, most vehicles should be able to navigate their way into the lakes.

Fishing

Hay and Lodi Lakes are a pair of lakes situated to the northeast of Quesnel. A shallow channel separates the lakes with Hay Lake to the south and Lodi Lake to the north. The lakes are mid-elevation lakes and are usually ice free by the end of April. Turnover usually happens early in May and both lakes are fishable by mid May and see the best action in June to the first week of July. After that, the lakes warm up and fishing is very slow. By early October, the fishing picks up and stays fairly good until ice over.

Of the two, Hay Lake is smaller and shallower. The lake contains plenty of rainbow trout but also has a lot of course fish (suckers, redside shiners and pike minnow). The lake is only not very deep, meaning that it is not a great lake for trolling, although people do pull around a shallow troll, with mixed success. Better is to cast around the fringe of the deepest hole, found in the northwest corner of the lake.

Lodi Lake also contains small rainbow, as well as course fish like suckers and redside shiners. It is nearly four times the size of Hay Lake and about twice as deep. The larger size means that there are more fish here, because there is more space for them.

The south end of the lake is much shallower than the north end of the lake. This makes trolling the south end difficult, but there aren't going to many fish hanging out in this area anyway. Instead, look for the trout to hang just off a pair of prominent points along the western shore of the lake. Work a lake troll or small spinner or spoon around these areas.

Another great place to fish is around the inflow of Ahbau Creek. You can troll here, but it's better to spincast or fly-fish, either from shore or from a small boat. The creek washes nutrients into the lake and food for the trout to eat, including terrestrials like grasshoppers and pine beetles. If these patterns aren't working for fly anglers, tie on a searching pattern like a Carey Special or a Woolly Bugger. The inflow, along with the points noted above, are perfect place to cast a bobber and bait and wait for the gentle bob indicating a strike.

Facilities

There is a rustic campsite at the south end of Hay Lake. A small boat can be hand launched at either lake. Those looking for more formal camping in the area can continue north to either Teapot or Stony Lakes.

Other Options

Teapot Lake is accessed by a rough road and is a decent trout fishery in its own right. **Stony Lake**, on the other hand, is a much bigger lake and is best trolled for its kokanee, lake trout, bull trout and rainbow trout.

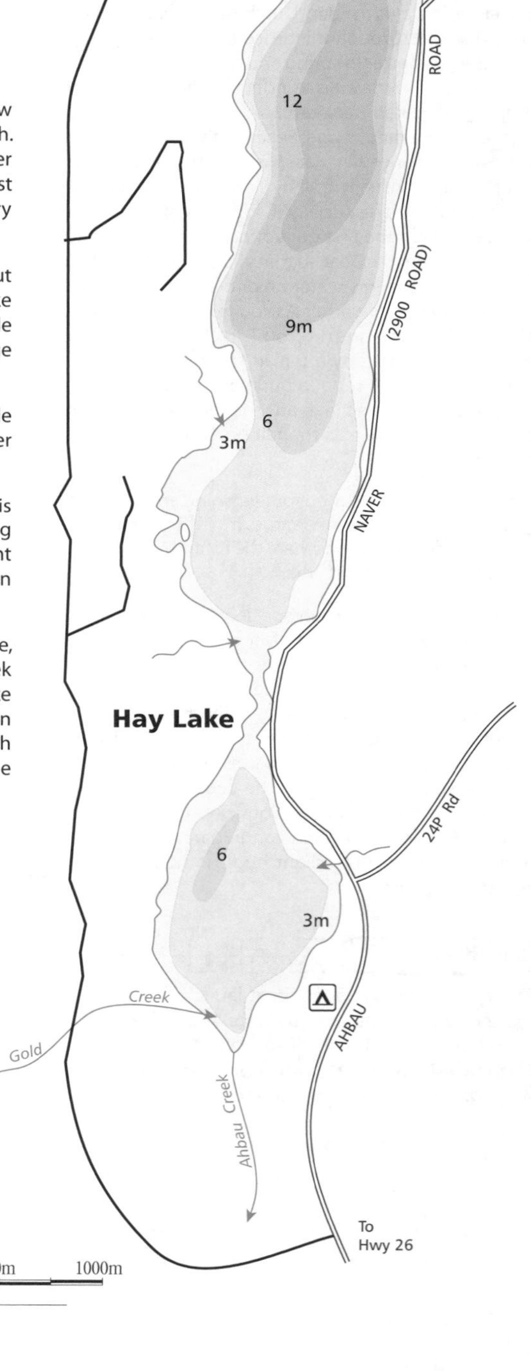

Helena Lake

Location: 28 km (17.4 mi) northwest of 100 Mile House
Elevation: 955 m (3,133 ft)
Surface Area: 238 ha (587 ac)
Maximum Depth: 13 m (41 ft)
Mean Depth: 3.4 m (11 ft)
Way Point: 51° 47′ 20.6″ N, 121° 38′ 30.1″ W

Fishing

Helena Lake is situated to the southwest of Lac la Hache in the heart of the Cariboo. It is a notoriously moody lake with rainbow that average 1 kg (2 lbs) but can grow over 5 kg (10 lbs). The spotty fishing is a surprise given that the lake is stocked with 30,000 rainbow trout annually.

If you are able to catch a fish, chances are it will be a good size one. This is because the fish grow rapidly given the abundance of shrimp and aquatic insects. Also, the larger fish prey on the lake chub allowing for even faster growth.

The lake is at 960 m (3,149 ft) in elevation and is 238 ha in size. Most of the western part of the lake is shallow (less than 4m or 10 feet) and not well suited for fishing. The deeper part of the lake, near the recreation site, is where anglers should concentrate.

Given the depth of the lake, it is best suited for spincasting or fly-fishing. In particular, fly anglers are most successful using a wet fly (nymphs) on a sinking line. Trollers should stick around the deeper waters and try near the surface to avoid weeds and hang-ups.

After ice over in November, the lake becomes a good ice fishing destination. The best fishing occurs early in the season, shortly after ice-up. This is because rainbow trout are susceptible to low oxygen levels and, as winter rolls along, the oxygen levels in the lake start to fall.

Directions

Helena Lake is easily accessed off Highway #97 from either the west end or east end of Lac la Hache. Either way, the main access road is good so you can bring a trailer or car into the lake.

From the northwest end of Lac la Hache, take the first left off the highway on the Wright Station Road and cross the San Jose River and the railway tracks near Wright Station. Hang a left after the tracks and then a right about 3 km later. Continue south for around 2 km and then take another right on a small road and the lake should appear within a few kilometers. The road can be difficult to drive during the early spring or in wet weather.

From the east end of Lac la Hache, head south off the highway on the McKinley-Ogden Road. Take a right about a kilometer from the highway and you will be travelling on the Tatton-Canima Forest Service Road. Stay on this road when it swings to the south and you will soon be at the lake.

Area Indicator

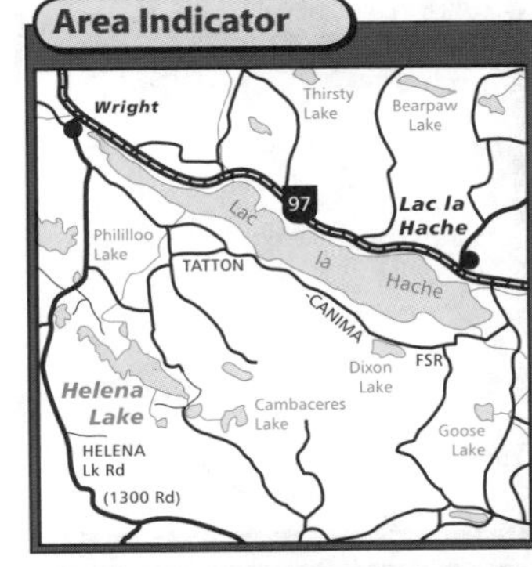

Helena Lake			
Fish Stocking Data			
Year	Species	Number	Life Stage
2008	Rainbow Trout	25,000	Yearling
2007	Rainbow Trout	25,000	Yearling
2006	Rainbow Trout	50,000	Fall Fry

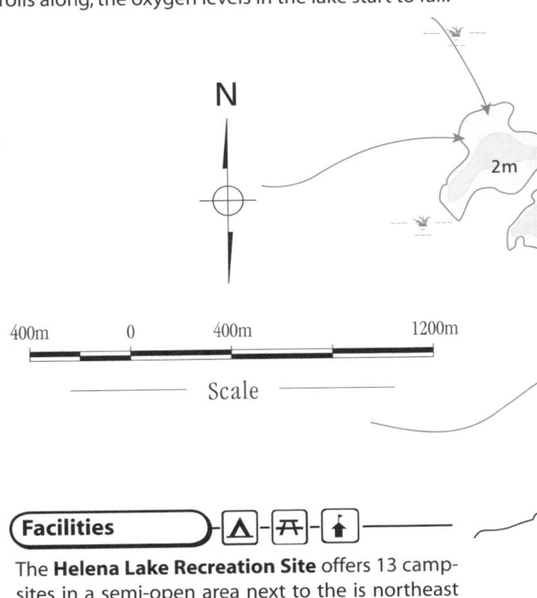

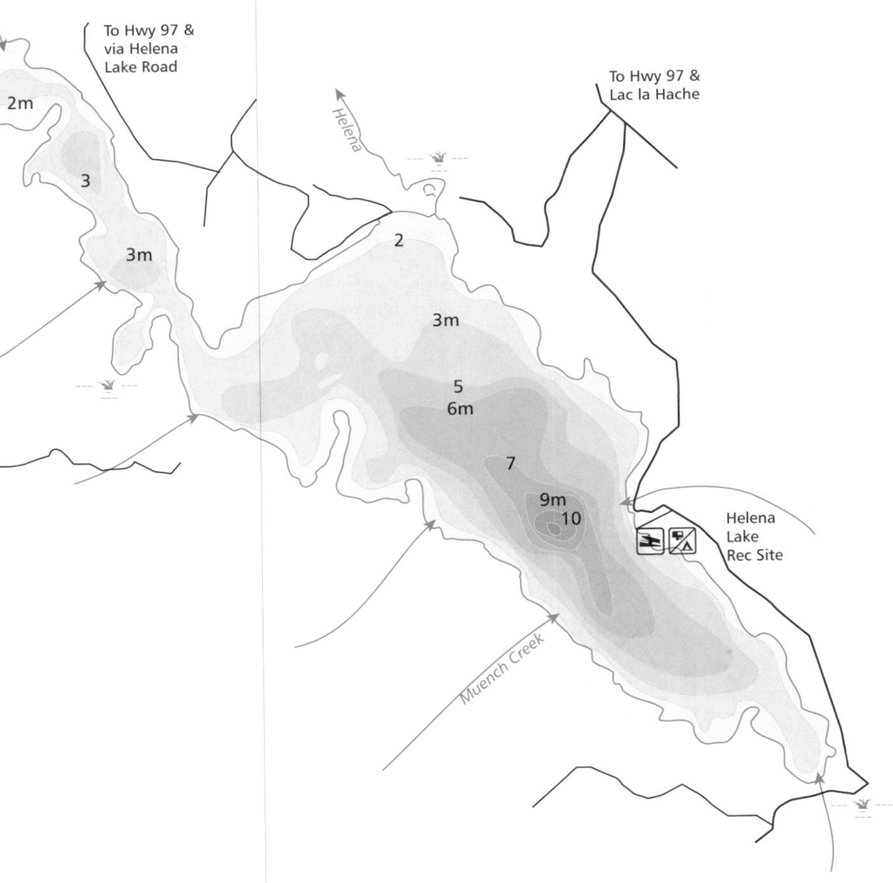

Facilities

The **Helena Lake Recreation Site** offers 13 campsites in a semi-open area next to the is northeast end of the lake. There is a boat launch at the rec site, which can be used by cartoppers or anglers with small boats on trailers.

Other Options

Nearby **Camacho** and **Cambaceres Lakes** are connected to Helena Lake via Helena Creek. Both lakes are quite small making them better suited for a float tube. Trout migrate from the bigger lake to these smaller lakes so fishing can be spotty. Due to the difficult access, Cambaceres Lake rarely sees a lure.

Location: 84 km (52 mi) northeast of Williams Lake
Elevation: 913 m (2,995 ft)
Surface Area: 368 ha (908 ac)
Maximum Depth: 38 m (124 ft)
Mean Depth: 12 m (39 ft)
Way Point: 52° 27′ 38″ N, 121° 0′ 19″ W

Hen Ingram (9 Mile) Lake

Area Indicator

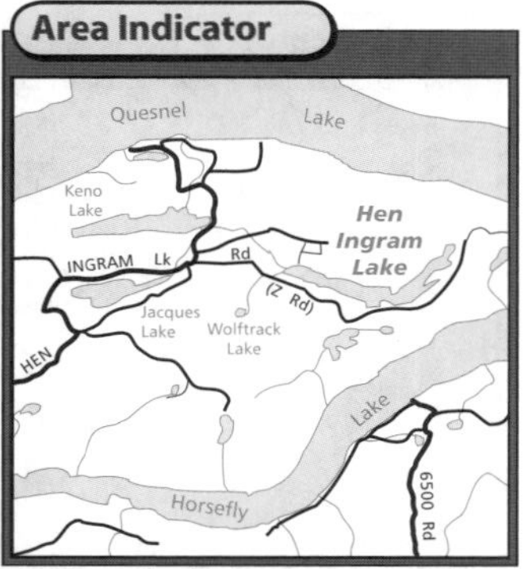

Hen Ingram (9 Mile) Lake Fish Stocking Data			
Year	Species	Number	Life Stage
2008	Rainbow Trout	3,000	Yearling
2007	Rainbow Trout	3,000	Yearling
2006	Rainbow Trout	3,000	Yearling

Fishing

Tucked into the rolling hills between Horsefly and Quesnel Lake, Hen Ingram offers surprisingly good fishing for fish that can get up to 1.5 kg (3 lbs).

Also known as 9 Mile Lake, Hen Ingram Lake also contains redside shiners, which compete for the available food. However, like many stocked lakes in the Cariboo with a redside shiner problem, there was a recent shift by the Freshwater Fisheries Society of BC in stocking practice here. Up until 2001, there were 20,000 rainbow trout stocked in the lake, usually the Dragon strain. As of 2004, though, a smaller amount of Blackwater strain rainbow have been stocked annually in the lake. Blackwaters feed on the redside shiner, reducing the competition and causing the trout to grow up big and fat.

The lake is fairly deep, meaning that it is a good trolling lake. Also, the water drops off rapidly allowing for some shore fishing, although it is much preferred to get out onto the water. Trollers can use a silver Willow Leaf lake troll and a worm, or Wedding Band and worm, along the drop offs on the north and south shorelines or down the centre of the lake. The F-4 or F-5 Flatfish and Hot Shots in green, yellow or black will work well if they're pulled behind a boat. Another favourite is the Apex Trout Killer in rainbow, red with a black dot, or black with silver specks.

Spincasters do well with a Blue Fox Vibrax in silver, a Rooster Tail in green or yellow and #8 Len Thompson spoons in green with black spots. A casting bubble with flies will entice fish that are near the surface.

Trolling black leeches or Knouff Lake Specials on a sinking line, casting dragonfly nymphs in the shallows along the drop offs at either end of the lake, or using Tom Thumbs when the mayflies and caddisflies are emerging will get the fish biting.

The late spring (late May to June) and the fall (October) are the best times to fish. However, the water temperatures do not increase greatly in the summer time allowing for decent fishing through the ice-free season. Although it is a consistent producer throughout the season, the trout do stay deeper during the warmer days of summer.

Directions

To reach the lake, travel to the town of Horsefly and then take the Black Creek Road heading east across the Horsefly River. Where the pavement ends, turn north on the Horsefly Lake Road and continue for another 26.5 or km and keep right at the sign indicating Quesnel Lake Resort. Continue for another 5.7 km and turn right on the Hen Ingram Lake Forest Service Road. It is another 13 km to the recreation site.

Towards the end of the journey, the road gets rougher so a truck may be necessary, especially in wet weather or in the early spring.

Facilities

With decent access most of the year, the **Hen Ingram Lake Recreation Site** is suitable for RV's and trailered units. The well developed site offers eight campsites and a good trailered boat launch at the east end of the lake. There is a separate site at the northwest end of the lake that is much quieter do to the more difficult road access.

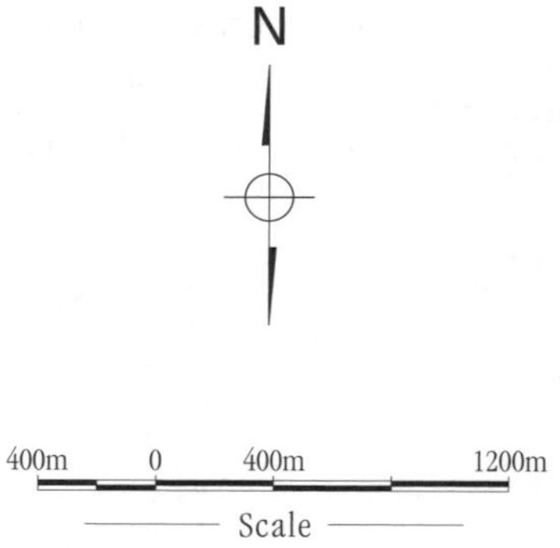

N

400m 0 400m 1200m
Scale

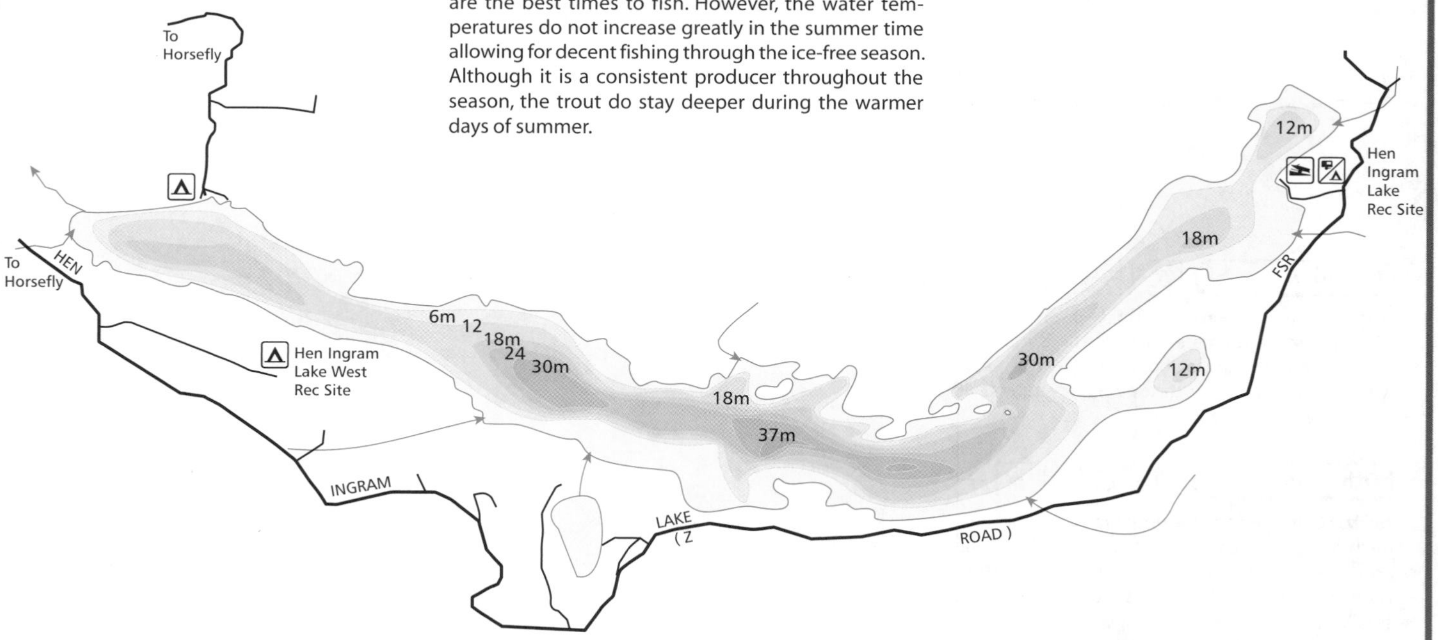

To Horsefly
To Horsefly
HEN
Hen Ingram Lake West Rec Site
INGRAM
LAKE (Z
ROAD)
FSR
Hen Ingram Lake Rec Site
12m
18m
6m 12 18m 24 30m
18m
37m
30m
12m

Higgins Lake

Location: 28 km (17.3 mi) east of 100 Mile House
Elevation: 1,137 m (3,730 ft)
Surface Area: 22 ha (54 ac)
Maximum Depth: 12 m (38 ft)
Mean Depth: 5 m (16 ft)
Way Point: 51° 37' 27.2" N, 120° 53' 34.3" W

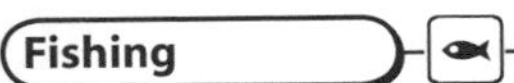

Higgins Lake is a small Interlakes lake tucked to the west of the bigger Sulphurous, Drewry, Bowers and Needa Lakes. It is a great destination for those looking to catch fish. The trout may be small (averaging 25 cm/10 in), but there are lots of them making this a good destination for the beginner or kids.

Each year, there are 7,500 rainbow stocked in Higgins by the Freshwater Fisheries Society of BC to ensure that the fishery is maintained. The lake is much smaller than these other lakes, but is fairly deep for its size, reaching over 12 metres (almost 40 feet). The lake is usually ice free by early May and offers good fishing by late May.

The deepest part of the lake is right in the centre of the lake. Trollers can work around the edge of this deep section with a lake troll, like a Willow Leaf or Ford Fender, often with a Wedding Band and dressed with a worm or Powerbait. Other options for trolling include a small Flatfish or a small spoon.

The south end of the lake has a rapid drop off allowing for shore casting by spincasters and fly anglers. This is also the best spot for casters out on the water, too, because of the prominent drop off. Most any small lure or spinner will work, but nothing beats the worm and hook combination suspended just off bottom.

Rainbow trout have a number of impulses that they need to balance. They need to eat, they need to be comfortable and they need to be safe. As summer progresses, the top layer of water becomes too warm for them, but instead of dropping off in degrees, the water usually stratifies, with a drop of several degrees between two distinct layers of water. The most oxygenated water is usually just below the top layer of water, making this the most comfortable place for the fish to hang out. The fish also need to be close to food and the best feeding areas are in the shallow water. The trout will make furtive dashes into this area to grab some food and then dart back into deeper water. The deeper water also allows the fish an avenue of escape if they feel threatened.

As a result of these impulses, the fish tend to hang out in a very few places around the lake. Places where they can get into and out of the shallow water quickly, places where there is plenty of food and places where there is a quick transition between the deep water and the shallow water.

The lake used to have a problem with winterkill but an aerator installed in the lake has reduced the problem. There is an electric motor only restriction at the lake.

Area Indicator

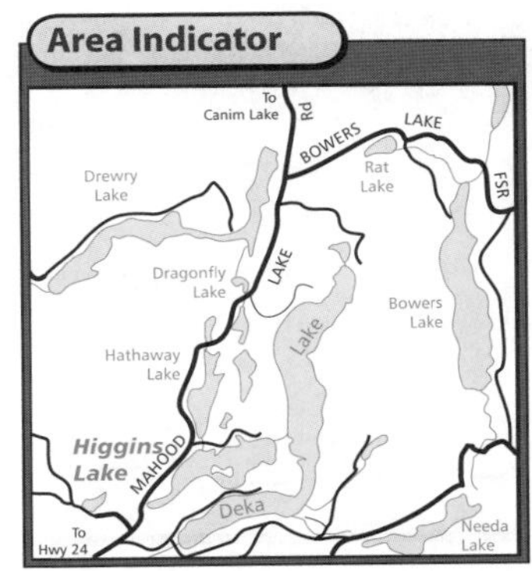

Higgins Lake Fish Stocking Data			
Year	Species	Number	Life Stage
2008	Rainbow Trout	7,500	Fry
2007	Rainbow Trout	7,500	Fry
2006	Rainbow Trout	7,500	Fry

Directions

The lake is best reached by traveling along the Fishing Highway (Highway 24). At Interlakes Corner, the Horse Lake Road (which turns into the Mahood Lake Road) heads north from the highway. Continue past Burgess Road to the signed Higgins Lake Road to the left.

Facilities

There is a cartop boat launch and public access to the lake.

Other Options

Nearby **Sutherland Lake** is connected to Higgins Lake via the feeder stream at the north. Some trout are able to get past the dam and into this smaller lake. Fishing reports in Sutherland Lake are sketchy but the small lake is certainly worth a try.

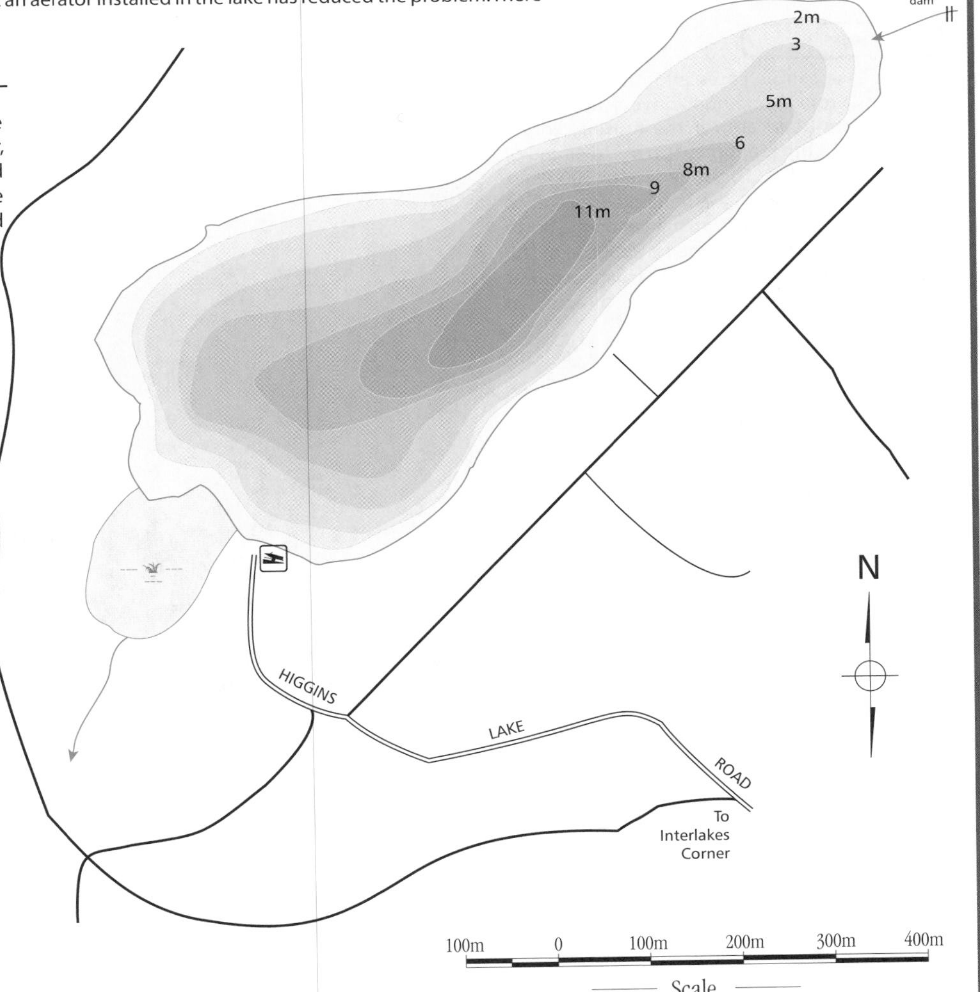

Location: 67 km (41.5 mi) southwest of Vanderhoof
Elevation: 906 m (2,972 ft)
Surface Area: 72 ha (179 ac)
Maximum Depth: 7.0 m (23 ft)
Mean Depth: 3.3 m (11 ft)
Way Point: 53° 34′ 50.0″ N, 124° 43′ 51.9″ W

Hobson Lake

Area Indicator

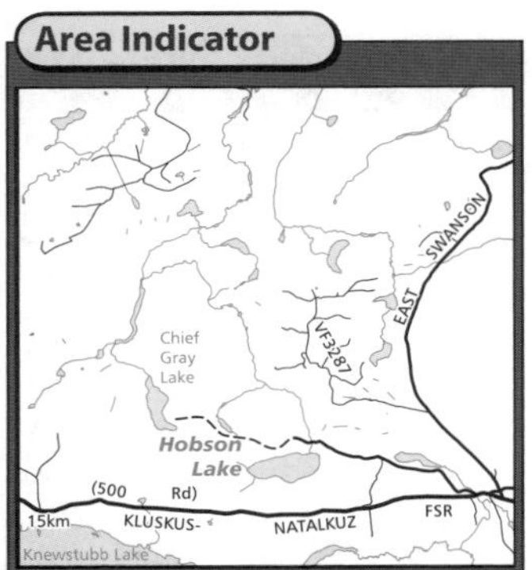

Hobson Lake Fish Stocking Data			
Year	Species	Number	Life Stage
2007	Rainbow Trout	2,500	Fry
2005	Rainbow Trout	2,500	Fall Fry

Fishing

Hobson Lake is a decent sized lake located on the Vanderhoof Plateau, near the headwaters of the Nechako River. It is just north of the much larger Knewstubb Lake.

The lake is named after local author and cattle rancher Rich Hobson and is managed as a catch and release lake for trophy sized rainbow trout. In addition to the single barbless hook restriction, no bait is allowed. This has helped the fish get up to 4 kg (9 lbs), with the average being reported to hover around a chunky 2 kg (4 lbs).

Mountain pine beetle is prevalent in the area and have shown up in the stomachs of some of the lake's trout. Using a terrestrial beetle pattern when there is a flight of pine beetles can be quite productive. Other abundant food sources in Hobson include gammarus shrimp. Fishing a scud pattern can work year round, but are especially effective in the early spring, before the insects start to hatch. Two popular variations are the Werner shrimp and the baggy shrimp.

The lake features a spectacular caddisfly hatch in June and July. Using a Tom Thumb size 8 to 12 can produce some exciting top water action, especially on a calm early summer's evening. Alternatively, there is a good chironomid hatch starting in late April and continuing to early July, then again in September and October. Bloodworm imitations are quite effective during the warmer months.

The lake even has a large number of leeches found near shore. Unlike many of the lakes in the area, these leeches are a dark green colour, so make sure you have the right pattern before heading out. Other popular flies include green, red, brown and black-bodied Doc Spratleys and Carey Specials, Muddler Minnows, green Woolly Buggers, glitter leeches, micro leeches and Anderson's Stonefly Nymph.

Trollers will find that silver Dick Nite spoons, orange and black, silver and black and plain silver Flatfish and Kwikfish and weighted spinners like Roostertails, Mepps, Blue Foxes and Panther Martins all produce well.

While there is no boat launch, the lake is best fished from a small boat rather than a float tube. However, there is a rather shallow, reedy section stretching out about 300 m (900 ft) from shore and kicking through here with a float tube requires a great deal of effort.

Directions

Hobson Lake can be accessed from a variety of directions. From Vanderhoof, drive south on the Kenney Dam Road and/or the Kluskus Forest Service Road. Both roads meet up at either end of the Kluskus-Natalkuz Forest Service or 500 Road. Once on the 500 Road, the unmarked turnoff to Hobson Lake is near the 9 km marker on the north side of the road. The access road is about 3 km (1.8 miles) long and can be difficult to navigate in wet weather. In good weather, the lake can be accessed by a 2wd vehicle.

Facilities

The **Hobson Lake Recreation Site** is a small forestry site with space for two or three groups. There is a spot to launch cartop boats as well as a trail to neighbouring Chief Gray Lake.

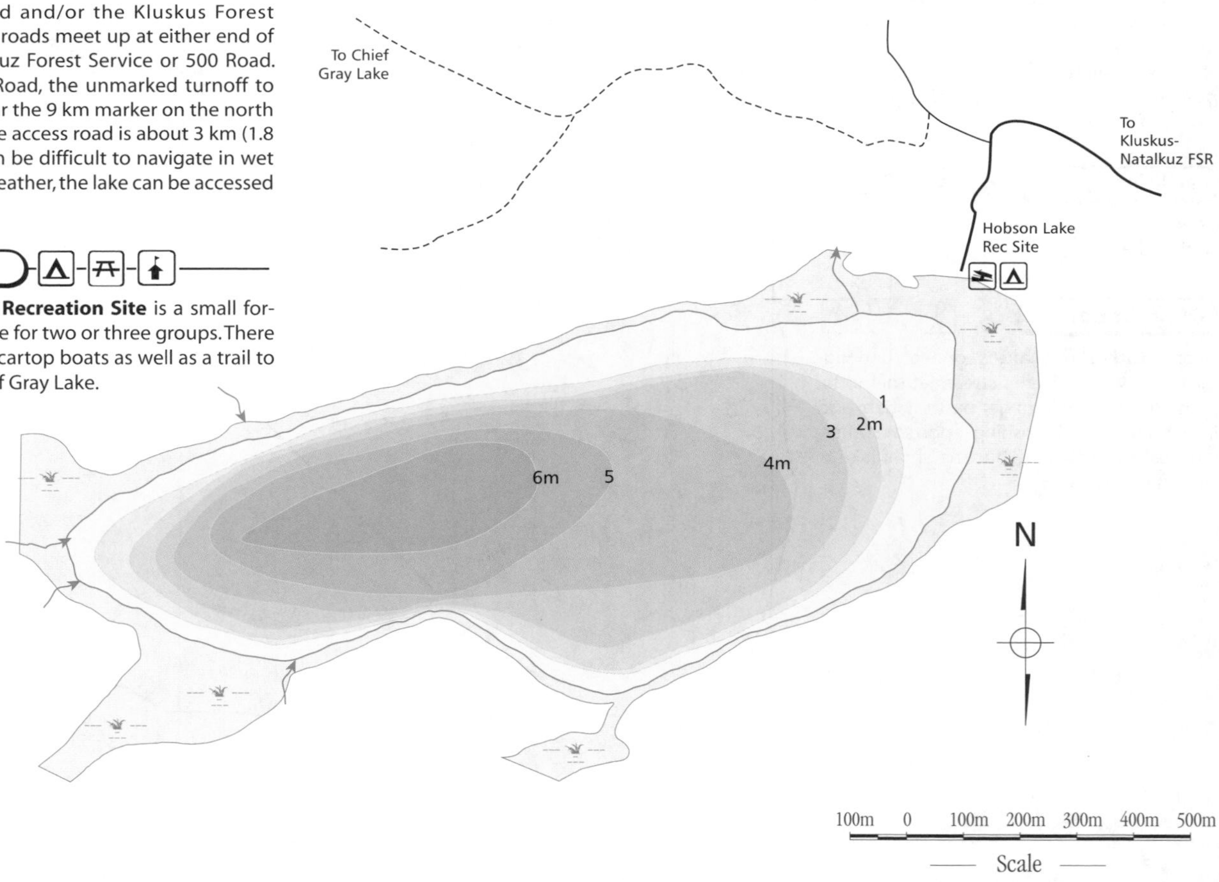

To Chief Gray Lake
To Kluskus-Natalkuz FSR
Hobson Lake Rec Site
1
2m
3
4m
5
6m
N
100m 0 100m 200m 300m 400m 500m
Scale

Horn Lake

Location: 230 km (143 mi) west of Williams Lake
Elevation: 940 m (3,084 ft)
Surface Area: 171 ha (422 ac)
Maximum Depth: 39 m (130 ft)
Mean Depth: 19 m (61 ft)
Way Point: 51° 48′ 3″ N, 124° 42′ 15″ W

Fishing

Scenic Horn Lake is nestled in a valley between the north end of the Niut Mountain Range and Sapeye Mountain, near the headwaters of Mosley Creek. The lake is surrounded by mountains and set in a thick forest of Lodgepole pine and Douglas fir.

It can get windy, but the south end is fairly protected by the dense stand of fir and spruce around the shoreline.

Horn Lake, which is usually ice-free by early May, is deep and fishes well throughout the season for spunky rainbow trout that average 3–4 kg (6–8 lbs). It is stocked annually with around 20,000 rainbow.

Despite the relatively long drive to the lake from Williams Lake, Horn Lake is still quite popular with anglers. Of course, the lake is far enough out of the way to be much less busy on weekdays than on weekends.

At the north end of the lake, where patches of aquatic plants provide an area for insects to thrive, the depth is relatively shallow. The south end has rocky shoals and a small weedbed with drop offs near the steep eastern shore. The western shore is a mixture of gravel shoals interspersed with beds of aquatic plants. There is a sunken island near the centre of the lake that is productive during the caddisfly and mayfly hatches. During that time, at least two species of mayflies emerge: one in late May and a prolific hatch of larger ones, thought to be hexagenia, in late June.

These trout take dry flies or nymphs with equal tenacity. Chironomids, damselflies and dragonflies and shrimp are also staples of the Horn Lake trout diet. Trollers do well with a silver or gold Willow Leaf lake troll or with a Wedding Band and worm or just a worm. Using a Flatfish in green, black or perch scale, or a black or maroon leech on a long leader or sinking line, will also produce fish.

There is limited areas for casting from shore, so fishing is best done from a watercraft. Mepps and Blue Fox or Rooster Tail spinners work well, as do bobbers with a worm or suspended Powerbait when the fish are cruising the shoreline.

In addition to the rainbow trout, the lake is home to a population of bull trout. Bull trout have a voracious appetite and will rarely pass up an easy meal. Anything that looks like a smaller fish (Muddler Minnow flies or other streamer pattern as well as a number of small spoons, spinners or even crankbaits) will usually work for bull trout. However, don't expect to find them in any great numbers here.

Facilities

The **Horn Lake Recreation Site** is one of the bigger and nicest sites in the area. The site is suitable for RVs and larger trailers and has space for 14 units at the south end of the lake. Visitors will find a nice gravel boat launch and a day-use area as well.

Directions

From Williams Lake, follow Highway 20 west across the Chilcotin Plateau for about 215 km. Just as you are about to reach the community of Tatla Lake, turn south on the graveled road where signs indicate Chilko and Tatlayoko Lakes. Travel for 4 km to the top of the hill and turn west on the West Branch Road. Drive another 12.5 km to reach the Horn Lake Recreation Site.

Area Indicator

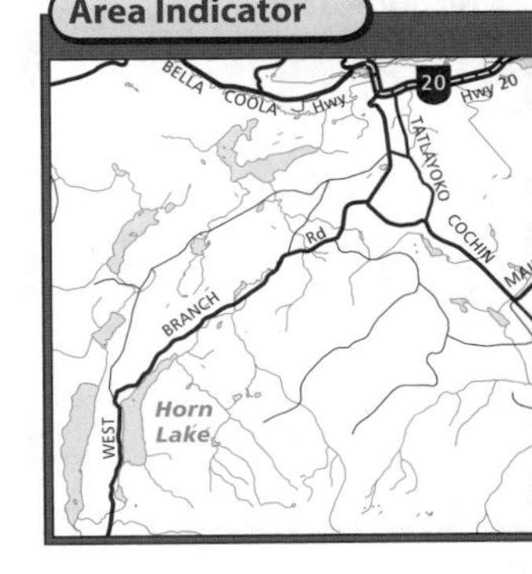

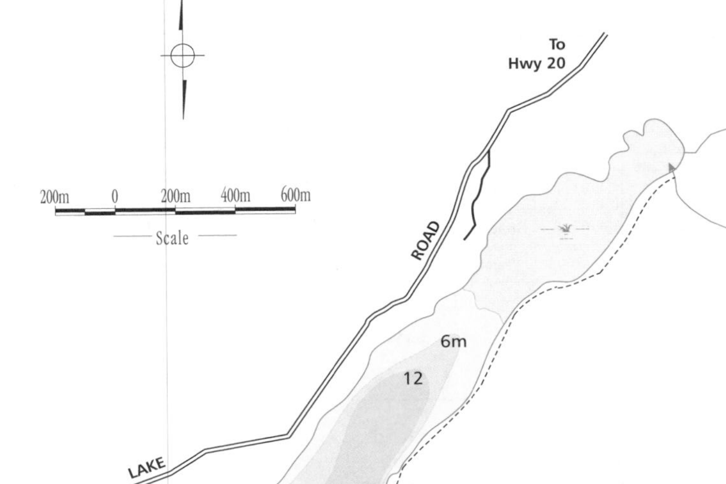

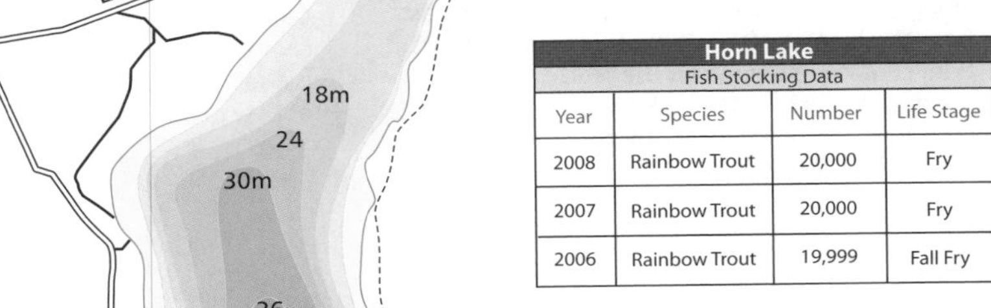

Horn Lake
Fish Stocking Data

Year	Species	Number	Life Stage
2008	Rainbow Trout	20,000	Fry
2007	Rainbow Trout	20,000	Fry
2006	Rainbow Trout	19,999	Fall Fry

Location: 10 km (6.2 mi) southeast of 100 Mile House
Elevation: 992 m (3,254 ft)
Surface Area: 1,160 ha (2,866 ac)
Max Depth: 34 m (113 ft)
Mean Depth: 15 m (50 ft)
Way Point: 51° 35′ 16″ N, 121° 6′ 45″ W

Horse Lake (100 Mile Area)

Area Indicator

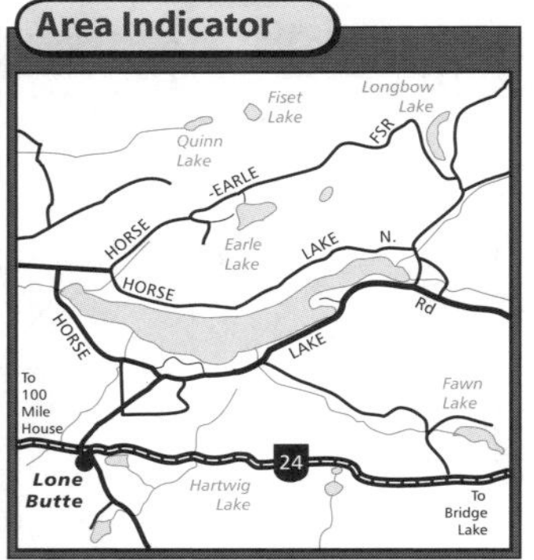

Horse Lake (100 Mile Area) Fish Stocking Data			
Year	Species	Number	Life Stage
2008	Kokanee	120,000	Fry
2008	Rainbow Trout	50,000	Yearling
2007	Kokanee	110,000	Fry
2006	Kokanee	120,000	Fingerling
2006	Rainbow Trout	44,700	Yearling

Fishing

Horse Lake is an 18 km (11mi) long, destination type lake found just southeast of 100 Mile House. It receives heavy fishing pressure because of its easy access and close proximity to 100 Mile House and the Fishing Highway.

The bigger lake offers rainbow, lake trout and kokanee. To ensure that there is a vibrant fishery, each year, 50,000 rainbow and 120,000 kokanee are stocked in the lake. Despite the stocking levels, the fishing can still be hit and miss, depending on when you're at the lake, what gear you use, the position of Venus in relation to Sagittarius and the general attitude of the fish on that particular day.

The kokanee are a popular attraction at the lake, due in no small part to the sheer number of these landlocked salmon. To catch them, try a slow troll using a Willow Leaf, Wedding Band and worm or maggot fished near the surface with up to a 1oz weight. Trolling in a "S" pattern results in better success as the Willow Leaf is gaining and losing speed as the boat rounds the corners. This entices the fish to bite.

Kokanee will also take to a variety of flies. While kokanee grow big by eating zooplankton, once they hit a certain size, they start feeding on chironomids, dragonflies and damselfly nymphs. The even like small leeches.

Kokanee feeding patterns are remarkably like rainbow trout and you will find that you will catch a mixture of both. The biggest difference is that kokanee are much more sensitive to the temperature of water and prefer to spend their time in a narrow band of water, although they will dart into shallower (or deeper) water to feed. Kokanee are known for their soft mouths and whether trolling, spincasting or fly-fishing, it is advisable to attach some form of shock absorber, to prevent the hook from tearing through the soft flesh. Kokanee are strong, determined fighters and often do damage to themselves when trying to escape.

The rainbow average 30-45 cm (12-18 in) but can grow over 2.5 kg (5 lbs). They are best fished by trolling a Flatfish or a lake troll with bait. Fly anglers do well casting a mayfly, damselfly nymph or caddisfly imitation in the spring and summer or a water boatman, leech or dragonfly nymph in the fall.

The lake trout average 1.5 kg (3 lbs) and are best caught using a plug or large minnow imitation. Fish as deep as you can without getting hook-ups.

Directions

Horse Lake is easily found via a series of backroads. The best access is from south of 100 Mile House along the Horse Lake Road. This road leads east from the highway for just over 8 km. At the junction, continue straight on the Horse Lake North Road and shortly after look for Lakeshore Drive leading south. This leads to the public access point and boat launch.

Facilities

The well developed lake is surrounded by many homes and cottages. Visitors can check out the **Cariboo Bonanza Resort**, which offers cabins, camping a boat launch and a whole lot more. There is also a public boat launch on the northeast shore of Lakeshore Drive.

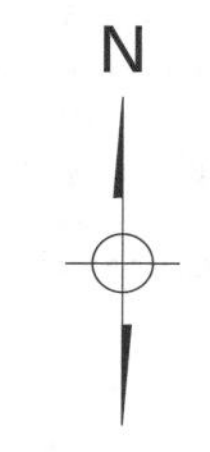

500m 0 1km 2km 3km
Scale

Horsefly River

Location: 55 km (34 mi) northeast of Williams Lake
Stream Lenght: 100 km (60 miles)
Geographic: 52° 19′ 58″ N, 120° 58′ 15″ W

Fishing

The Horsefly River watershed provides some of the best rainbow and bull trout fishing in the region. The river also has runs of sockeye, Chinook and Coho, although it is currently closed to salmon fishing.

So why mention the salmon? Simply this: when the salmon spawn, especially the sockeye (whose runs numbers in the hundreds of thousands), rainbow and bull trout come up the Horsefly to feast on their eggs.

The river is just over 100 km (60 miles) long, originating in the Quesnel Highlands near Wells Gray Park and flowing generally west to the lake. There are sections of nearly flat water mixed with whitewater that flows through steep-walled canyons. A 10 metre (32 foot) waterfall about 55 km upstream effectively prevents upstream migration for fish. It is also the end of the Class II portion of the river. Below the falls, the river is catch and release for trout and char and is an artificial fly only river.

During the sockeye spawn, there are thousands of rainbow in the river, but the trouble is that the sockeye run is dependant on water conditions–flow, temperature, etc. People have travelled to the river from great distances, only to find the water too low and too warm. During these times, the sockeye queue up in Quesnel Lake waiting and the anglers wait, too.

The average rainbow here is about 40 cm (16 in), while bull trout can get up to 5 kg (10 lbs). However, people have caught rainbow to 6 kg (12 lbs) during the sockeye run fishing a simple single egg pattern.

Of course, the sockeye spawn is not the only time you will find trout in the river. There are native rainbow and bull trout present year round and the big Quesnel Lake rainbow move into the river to feed at various times of the year. In spring, when the sockeye fry are moving downstream, the rainbow and bull trout once again come upstream to feed. Try a streamer pattern. And in July, they come upstream to feast on caddisflies and terrestrials that fall into the river. While the fishing is much more modest during these times, it can still be extremely fun fishing a dry fly caddis or grasshopper imitation.

Most of the people who fish this river do so on foot, although drifting the river has become quite popular in recent years. Note that the river can be quite shallow in late summer, when the big fish are in the river.

In August and September when the Chinook return, the spawning channels are a great place to view these amazing fish.

Facilities

The town of Horsefly is located on the Horsefly River offering a few basic supplies, while there are a couple resorts and a number of companies that offer guided trips along the river. Those looking to camp in the area will find a small recreation site at the mouth of the river and another further down river near McKinley Lake.

Directions

From Williams Lake, travel south for about 14 km to the Horsefly-Likely Road. Turn left (north) and follow the Horsefly Road for 45 km to the town of Horsefly. From here you can follow the Mitchell Bay Road downstream and the Black Creek (100 Rd) Road upstream.

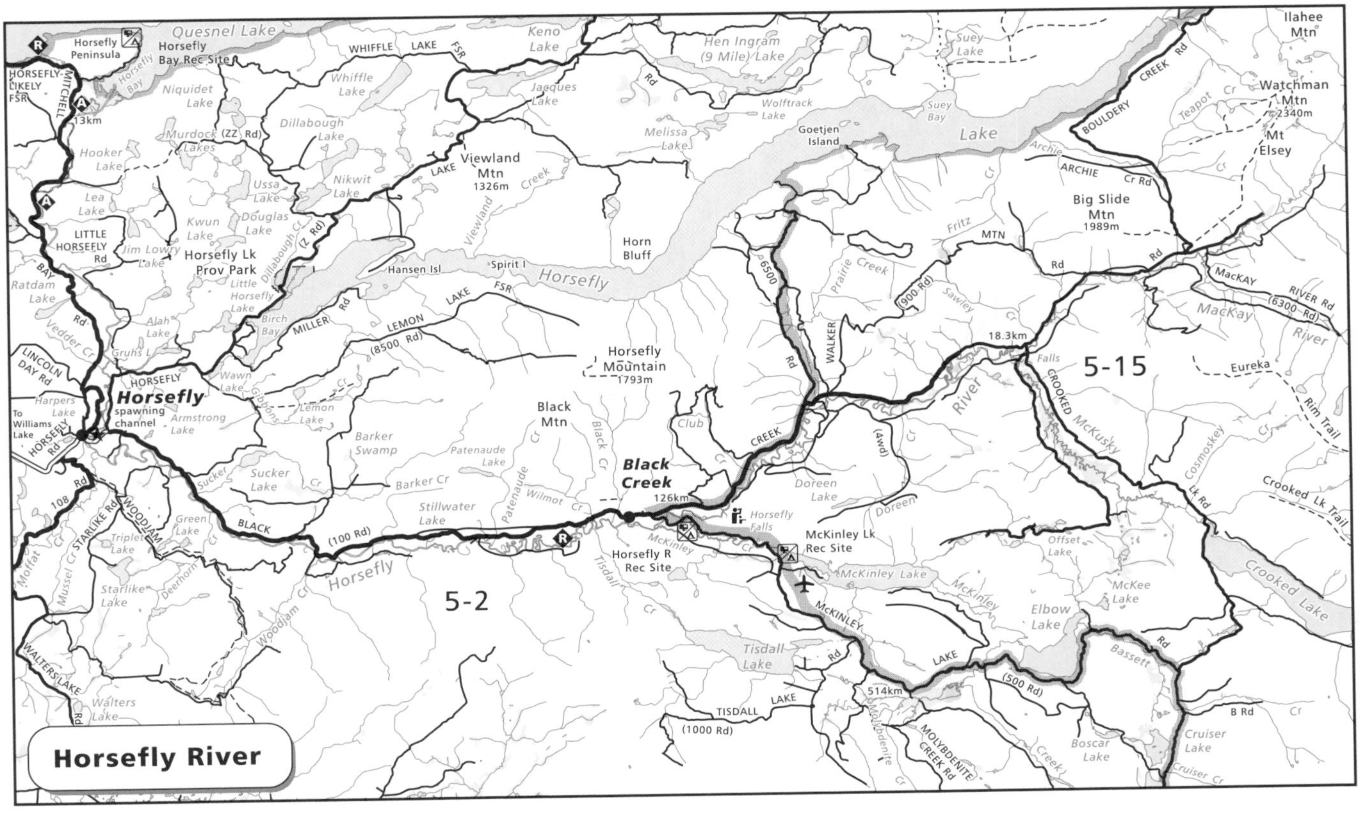

Horsefly River

Location: 50 km (31 mi) northeast of 100 Mile House
Elevation: 943 m (3,094 ft)
Surface Area: 167 ha (413 ac)
Maximum Depth: 36 m (117 ft)
Mean Depth: 9.6 m (32 ft)
Way Point: 51° 35′ 16″ N, 121° 6′ 45″ W

Howard Lake

Area Indicator

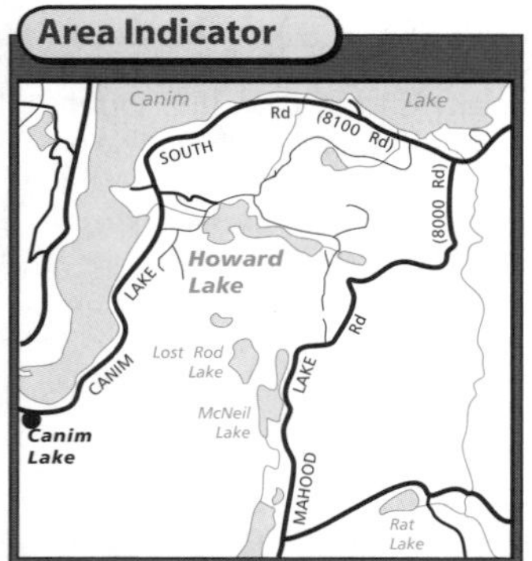

Howard Lake Fish Stocking Data			
Year	Species	Number	Life Stage
2008	Rainbow Trout	20,000	Fry
2007	Rainbow Trout	20,000	Fry
2006	Rainbow Trout	20,000	Fall Fry

Fishing

Howard Lake is a popular fishing hole nearby to 100 Mile House. Despite the heavy fishing pressure, the lake still produces well for rainbow in the 2 kg (4 lb) plus category.

This is mainly due to the heavy stocking program of the Freshwater Fisheries Society of BC. Each year, about 20,000 rainbow are dumped into the lake to help maintain the fishery. Although, the average fish is usually quite small (in the 16-20 cm/6-8 in class), the lake is closed to fishing from December 1 to March 31, which helps let a few of the trout grow a bit bigger.

The lake is a good fly-fishing lake as there are some very nice shoals, drop offs and weedbeds to focus around. These underwater structures are easily seen through the clear water. Best known for its chironomid hatches, anglers flock here in the early spring to take advantage of this great fishery.

Fly fishers concentrate on the shallow areas in the narrows or at the east end of the lake and present black, chromie or green chironomid patterns on floating lines and long leaders or strike indicators to fool fish in clear waters. As the water warms and the fish move to deeper water, fish leech or dragonfly patterns along the drop offs.

There are not many people who troll the lake, but those who do spend most of their time in the deep end at the west or east bay. Use Bolo, Beaver Valley or Willow Leaf lake trolls with a worm, or trail a dragonfly nymph or maroon leech to take fish consistently. For lighter trolling, use flies, a Hot Shot, or Flatfish in back and silver, skunk or silver.

Unless you have a watercraft, spincasters are limited to either casting from shore near the recreation site or on the east end off the old landing found there. Spincasters and fly anglers can work most of the shoreline out from the shoals and weedbeds. Spinners like Mepps Aglia or Black Fury, Blue Fox in silver and gold, or a Strike Zone black and silver fool fish in this lake.

There is a 10 hp maximum restriction for power boats.

Directions

From Highway 97 and Exeter Station Road in 100 Mile House, travel north for 2 km to the top of the hill. Turn right (east) at the stoplight onto the Forest Grove/Canim Lake Road and drive 20 km to the community of Forest Grove. Keep right and follow the Canim Lake Road for another 12 km. Turn right (east) on Canim Lake South (8100) Road and continue down this road for about 14 km. Look for the Howard Lake Road on your right and continue another 3.5 km or so to the lake.

This last road is a bit rough and is quite steep and narrow in places. Be careful when hauling in bigger units or trailers as there are few places to pass by vehicles travelling in the other direction.

Facilities

The **Howard Lake Recreation Site** is a large site in an open meadow that was once a sawmill. There is space for 16 groups or so, with 12 tables and a decent launch for trailered boats on the gravel beach. Although there are a few sites set back in the trees, tenters looking for a little more seclusion occasionally camp at the east end of the lake.

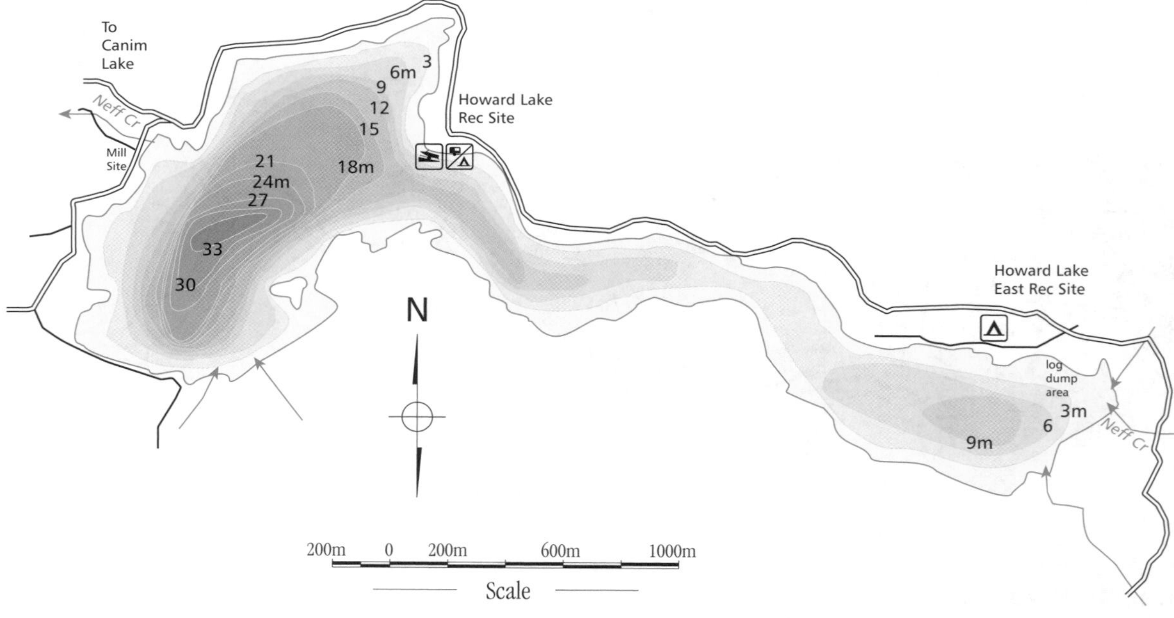

Howes Lake

Location: 28 km (17.4 mi) north of Williams Lake
Elevation: 999 m (3,278 ft)
Surface Area: 65 ha (159 ac)
Maximum Depth: 6.4 m (21 ft)
Mean Depth: 2.4 m (8 ft)
Way Point: 52° 23′ 1.1″ N, 122° 7′ 57.3″ W

Fishing

Howes Lake is found southeast of McLeese Lake off the Blue Lake Road. It is a fairly small lake that holds rainbow trout as well as course fish such as suckers and redside shiner. To help the trout fishery, the rainbow are stocked annually.

These trout are Blackwater strain rainbow, which are piscivorous. This means that they eat other fish, especially the redside shiner. The Freshwater Fisheries Society of BC also added 4,200 All Female Triploid Blackwaters in 2008 to help increase the size of some of the trout in the lake. Although the average catch here is usually less than 0.5 kg (1 lb), it is hoped that the Blackwaters will start producing trout about twice that size.

The lake is fairly high in elevation, which means it is usually ice free by May 1. However, the lake is quite shallow and the waters warm up substantially in the summer. This is definitely a spring or fall destination. The lake is also subject to winterkill during severe winters.

The shallow nature added to the lake's small size means that it isn't really a good trolling lake. Instead, the best way to fish is by spincasting or better yet, fly-fishing. The northwestern bay is very shallow so it is better to stick towards the southwest end of the lake. Working the edge of the deeper water will produce the best results.

Still fishing with a worm and bobber at the lake is a great technique. In order to get the best results, you need to get the hook out near the drop off and you need to get it down to within about a metre (3 feet) of the bottom of the lake. Of course, you can also spincast using spoons like a Kamlooper or a Krocodile, or a spinner like a Mepps or Vibrax.

Fly anglers can work a variety of nymph patterns or attractor patterns like a Doc Spratley when there is no set hatch on the lake. But by paying attention to what is happening on the water, you should be able to match the hatch. Chironomid hatches start in early May and continue through most of the spring and early summer. There is usually a secondary hatch near the end of September. Damselflies emerge mid-June to mid-August; and the caddisfly/sedge hatch takes flight mid-June to the end of August. Leech and halfback nymph patterns are usually successful all year long.

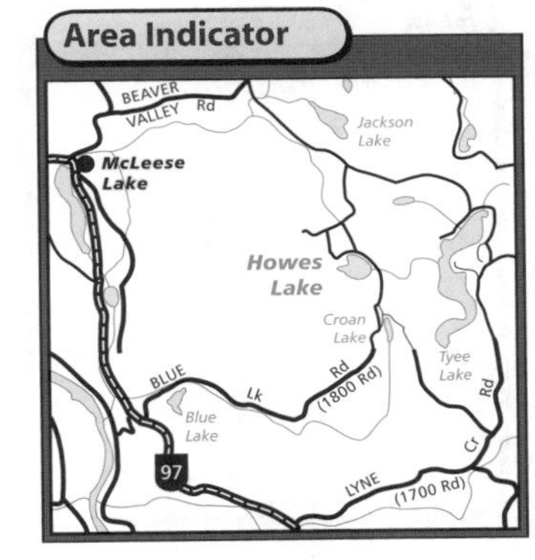

Directions

Howes Lake is northeast of Blue Lake and southeast of McLeese Lake. Heading northwest on Highway 97 from Williams Lake, look for the Blue Lake Resort signs and follow this road east. Soon after Blue Lake, the road deteriorates before turning north. Howes Lake is about 15 km past Blue Lake.

It is also possible to access the lake from the north, off the Beaver Valley and Tyee Lake Roads. If you plan to do this, a copy of the Backroad Mapbook for the *Cariboo Chilcotin Coast* and a GPS are handy tools for navigation. We also recommend having a 4wd vehicle, especially in wet weather.

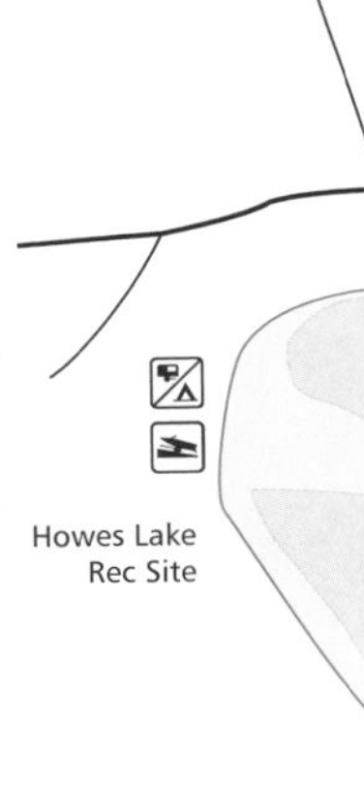

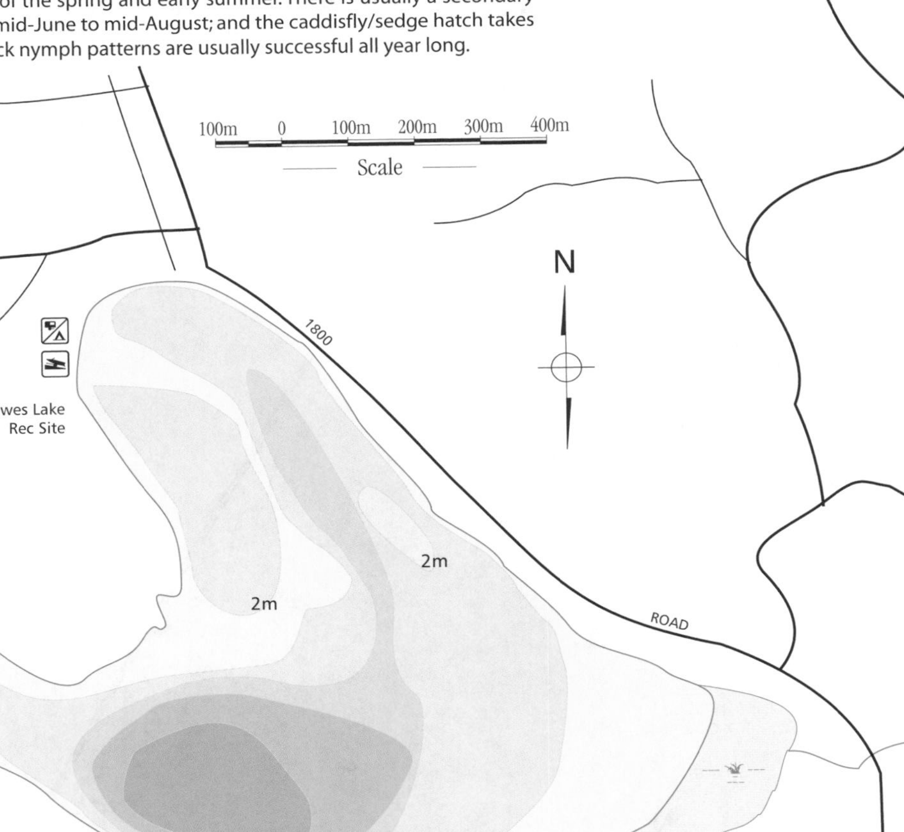

Howes Lake Fish Stocking Data			
Year	Species	Number	Life Stage
2008	Rainbow Trout	4,200	Yearling
2007	Rainbow Trout	3,500	Yearling
2006	Rainbow Trout	3,500	Yearling

Facilities

The **Howes Lake Recreation Site** is found on the north end of the lake. The difficult road access limits visitors, but there are still 12 sites set in the second growth timber next to the lake. It is possible to launch a small boat at the lake.

Location: 24 km (15 mi) north of Quesnel
Elevation: 843 m (2,766 ft)
Surface Area: 5.3 ha (13 ac)
Maximum Depth: 10 m (33 ft)
Mean Depth: 5.5 m (18 ft)
Way Point: 53° 9′ 8.7″ N, 122° 21′ 37.4″ W

Hush Lake

Area Indicator

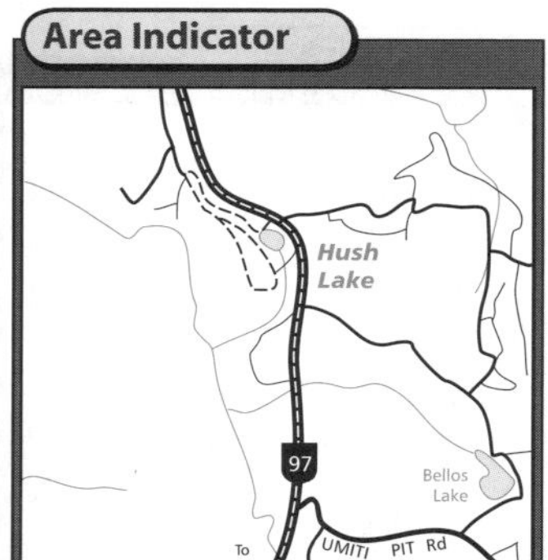

Fishing

Despite its close proximity to the Cariboo Highway, Hush Lake has surprisingly good fly-fishing for brook trout. Although these brookies are generally small, they do reach 1 kg (2 lbs) in size. The eastern brook trout are stocked each year at the lake to help maintain the fishery.

However, it should be noted that some inconsiderate person has transplanted gold fish into the lake. Don't be surprised if you actually catch one as they have actually developed a self-sustaining population.

The scenic little lake is a good early spring or fall fishery. It is too small and shallow to consider fishing in the summer, although many do. Just expect mushy, inspirited fish at that time.

Hush Lake is lined with lily pads, which provide cover for the small trout. Try casting a dragonfly or damselfly nymph pattern towards the lily pads. Although a small boat would be helpful to get past the lily pads, you can cast from shore near the boat launch. If you do have a watercraft, trolling a black or green leech or other attractor type pattern can also be effective. Please note that no powerboats are allowed on the lake.

Brook trout are more aggressive than the rainbow trout and can be caught using a variety of small spoons or spinners cast from the deep water towards the lily pads. For some spincasters, the lure of choice is a Deadly Dick, although other small spinners and spoons can work, too, such as the ever popular Panther Martin.

When a hatch is on, brook trout will rise to a dry fly as willingly as a rainbow. However, they are mostly fished sub-surface. Brook trout take to the fly very gently compared to a rainbow and they have bony mouth, meaning that it can be difficult to detect a strike and it can be difficult to set the hook. Keeping your hooks sharp is important. Brook trout tend to gather into schools more than rainbow; if you manage to find one fish, chances are you will find more brook trout in that area.

Flies like the Muddler Minnow or Woolly Bugger are other patterns to try. A slow retrieve seems to be the most effective.

Surprisingly, the lake is not a popular ice-fishing destination despite holding brook trout and sitting next to the highway. Brook trout are much hardier than rainbow trout and do not suffer the effects of oxygen deprivation as much. As a result, they offer a much better fishery in the winter months.

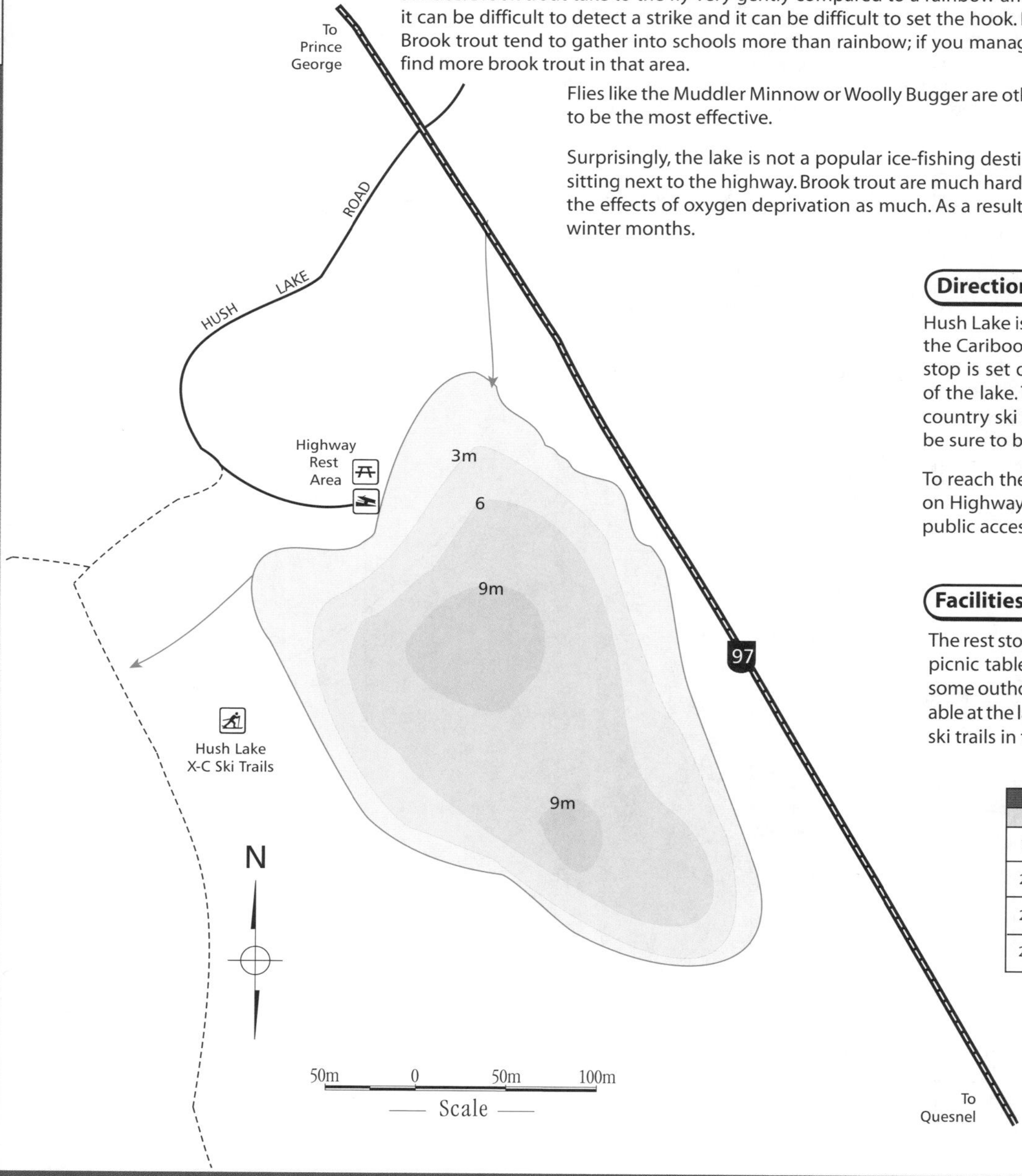

Directions

Hush Lake is found 24 km north of Quesnel next to the Cariboo Highway (Highway 97). A popular rest stop is set on a bench overlooking the north end of the lake. The area also offers a fine set of cross-country ski trails. If you visit the lake in the winter be sure to bring along your skis.

To reach the lake simply head north from Quesnel on Highway 97. Look for the rest stop marking the public access to the lake.

Facilities

The rest stop at the north end of the lake has several picnic tables that overlook the lake together with some outhouses. A good gravel boat launch is available at the lake. In the winter, there are cross-country ski trails in the area.

Hush Lake Fish Stocking Data			
Year	Species	Number	Life Stage
2008	Brook Trout	1,500	Fingerling
2007	Brook Trout	1,500	Fingerling
2006	Brook Trout	1,500	Fingerling

Inga Lake

Location: 73 km (45.3 mi) north of Fort St. John
Elevation: 832 m (2,729 ft)
Surface Area: 57 ha (140 ac)
Maximum Depth: 4.3m (14 ft)
Mean Depth: 2.8m (9.2 ft)
Way Point: 56° 36′ 54″ N, 121° 38′ 23″ W

Fishing

Inga Lake is a stocked lake found about an hour's drive north of Fort St. John off the Alaska Highway. The lake holds plenty of small rainbow trout that willingly take to the fly or lure.

Because of this, the lake is an excellent lake for novice anglers or families with young children. Catch rates are relatively high, which will keep the interest of the young ones. And, because there are several great fishing spots along shore, you don't need a boat. One of the best places is from along the dyke on the south shore, but there are several other spots along the east shore as well.

The rainbow range from 20–40 cm (8–16 in) and spincasting with live bait such as worms and maggots or artificial bait, like powerbait can be fast and furious. Locals recommend using a small lure tipped with a maggot, trolled along the shoal areas or along the drop offs. Fly anglers can try micro leeches and Doc Spratley patterns.

Of course, you don't need to get complicated to catch one of these rainbow trout. A simple bait and bobber setup, with the bait suspended less than 1 metre (3 feet) off the bottom can be just as productive as the most complicated fly-rod set-up. It is also interesting to note that barbs and treble hooks are allowed.

The lake also has a productive ice fishing season. Rainbow trout tend to become sluggish as the winter draws on, so the best time to ice fish is as soon as the ice is thick enough. Jigging artificial and live bait up and down frequently during the early part of winter should attract the fish. Deli shrimp are a popular and productive bait for ice fishing. Anglers should also note that the lake is aerated over the winter to maintain fish stocks. Stay outside of the fenced area.

Inga is a small, man-made lake with no natural inlet. To prevent the trout from becoming spawn-bound, a condition which decreases their capacity to grow to a larger size, an artificial spawning channel was built on the east shore in the late 1970s by the Habitat Conservation Trust Fund. Every year, between 200 and 300 rainbow trout enter the channel from mid-May to mid-June to spawn. The North Peace Rod and Gun maintains the channel and provides funds for local students to visit and observe this natural phenomenon. Public viewing opportunities are also available, or arrangements can be made through the club for a tour.

The lake was once stocked with brook trout, although rumours of brookies being caught here anymore are few and far between. White suckers are also found in the lake.

Directions

Inga Lake is found about 73 km north from Fort St. John on the Alaska Highway. Look for the 170 Road leading southwest. It is about a 3 km drive to the recreation site on a generally good road. As usual, care should be taken during wet weather as the road can get slippery.

Facilities

The **Inga Lake Recreation Site** has space for about 18 groups at the northeast end of the lake. There is also a gravel boat launch suitable for small boats, as well as outhouses here. A 10 hp outboard motor restriction applies on the lake.

Area Indicator

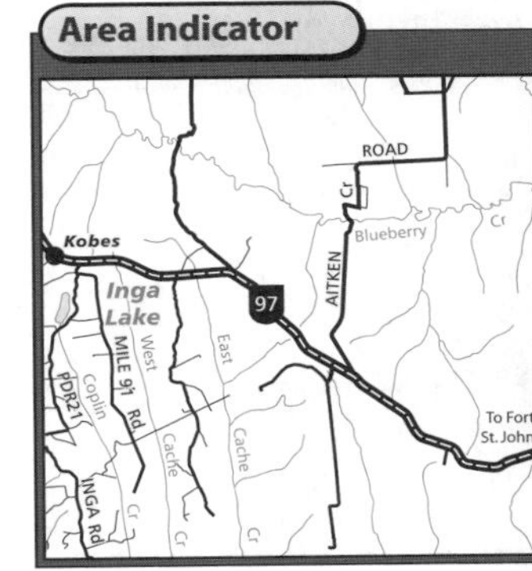

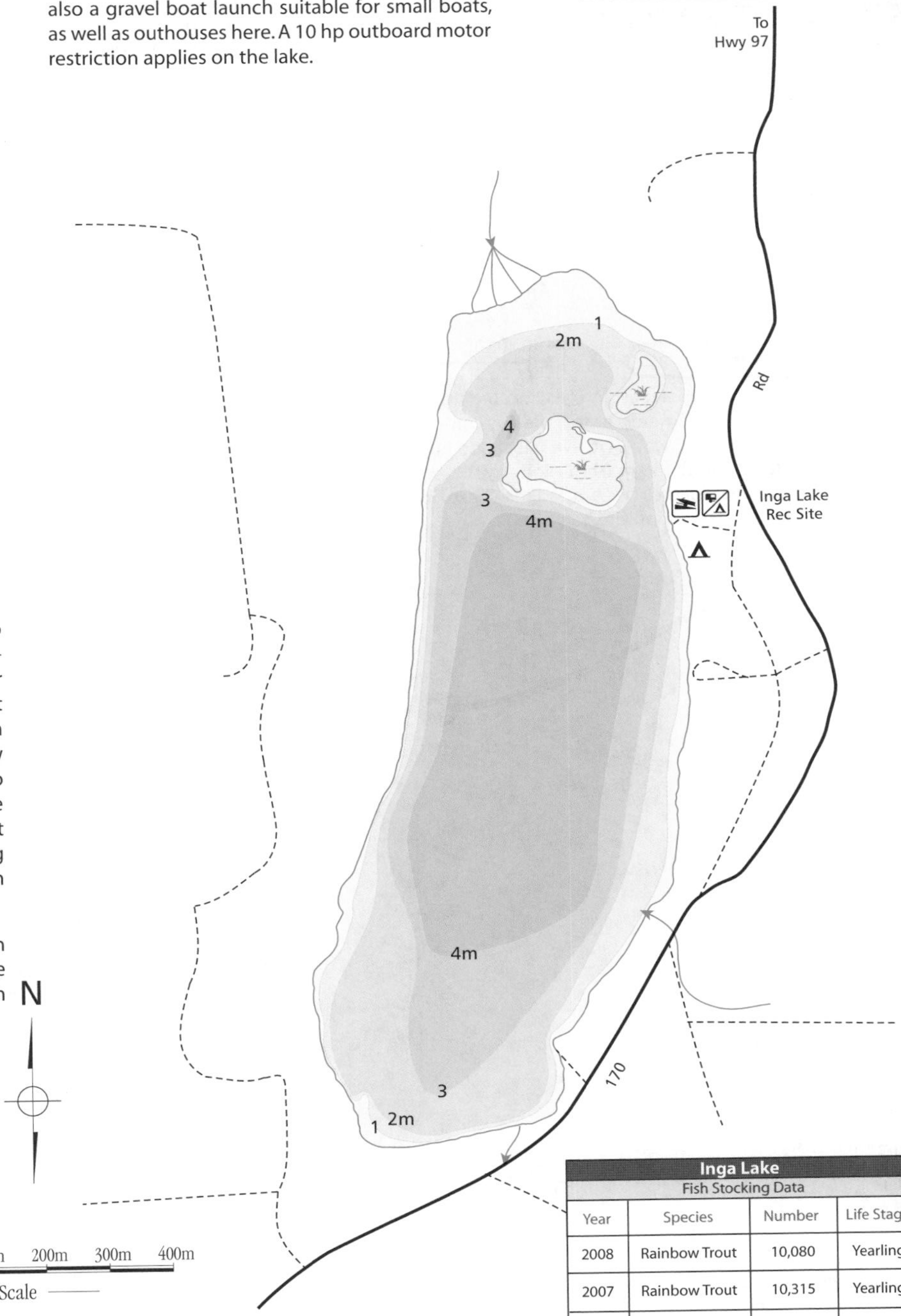

Inga Lake			
Fish Stocking Data			
Year	Species	Number	Life Stage
2008	Rainbow Trout	10,080	Yearling
2007	Rainbow Trout	10,315	Yearling
2006	Rainbow Trout	10,000	Yearling

Irish (Iris) Lake

Location: 14 km (8.7 mi) southeast of 100 Mile House
Elevation: 1,174 m (3,851 ft)
Surface Area: 28 ha (69 ac)
Maximum Depth: 8 m (26 ft)
Mean Depth: 4 m (13 ft)
Way Point: 51° 32' 53.1" N, 121° 10' 11.3" W

Area Indicator

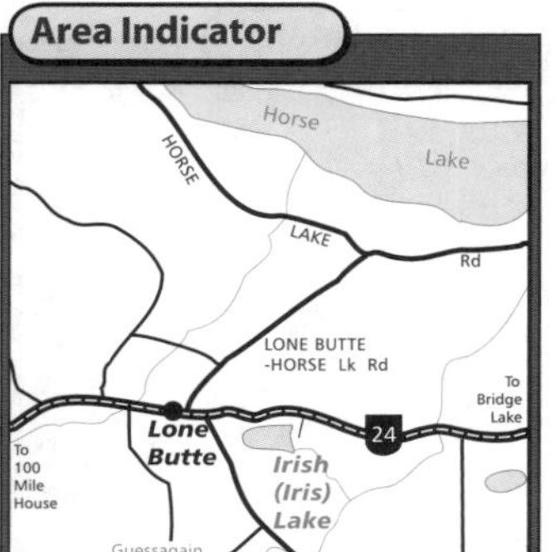

Irish Lake			
Fish Stocking Data			
Year	Species	Number	Life Stage
2008	Rainbow Trout	10,000	Fry
2008	Rainbow Trout	1,000	Spring Catchable
2007	Rainbow Trout	10,000	Fry
2006	Rainbow Trout	10,000	Fall Fry

Fishing

Irish Lake (sometimes called Iris Lake, mostly by people who can't spell) offers an excellent fishery for rainbow in the 35-45 cm (14-18 in) class. The lake receives heavy fishing pressure but the stocking program of 15,000 fish per year helps maintain the fishery.

These fish are usually stocked three times a year and are a mix of strains. Some of the stocked fish are All Female Triploid, which grow faster than diploid trout. In 2008, the lake was also stocked with 1,000 catchable fish.

Irish Lake's popularity is due in no small part to its ease of access. The lake can be seen from Highway 24 and, while it can't be accessed directly from the highway (there is a railway track between the lake and the highway), it is still an easy lake to access.

The lake is found at a slightly higher than average elevation, about 1,170 m (3,840 feet) above sea level. This means that the lake is not ice free as soon as other, lower elevation lakes. While it is often ice free by early May, the lake turns over in mid-May. This means that the fishing doesn't really get started here until lat May or even early June. True, some of the best fishing happens just after ice off, when the trout are ravenous, but many people have shown up at the lake just in time for turnover. This is not a great time to fish and we recommend moving onto one of the many other lakes in the area.

Since the lake is quite shallow and small, the water warms in the summer months meaning the fishing slows down. By October, fishing is good again.

The lake is best suited for fly anglers and spincasters as the lake is simply too shallow to troll without constant hang-ups. The deepest part of the lake is towards the middle with a nice drop off area at both the east and west ends of the lake. Try casting your fly (match the hatch or work a nymph or leech deep), lure or spinner just off the drop off and near the inflow and outflow streams. Sometimes a bit of bait on your spinner is all that is need for spincasters to find success. Be sure to vary your depths of your fly or lure to see where the fish are holding.

An aerator has been installed at the lake to reduce winterkill. This means that the lake cannot be fished in the winter safely as the ice is too thin. There is also an electric motor only restriction at the lake.

Directions

Irish Lake is a popular fishing lake located right next to the Fishing Highway (Highway 24) about two kilometers east of the tiny community of Lone Butte. From 93 Mile House, head east on Highway 24. Drive past Lone Butte and then the junction to the Watch Lake Road, about 14 km from Highway 97. About 2 km past the Watch Lake Road, a much smaller road circles around Irish Lake. Turn right onto this road and then right again to the recreation site.

Facilities

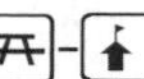

There are a number of private residences around the lake, but the **Irish Lake Recreation Site** is a small day-use recreation site where it is possible to launch a small boat at the lake. The recreation site is on the east side of the lake.

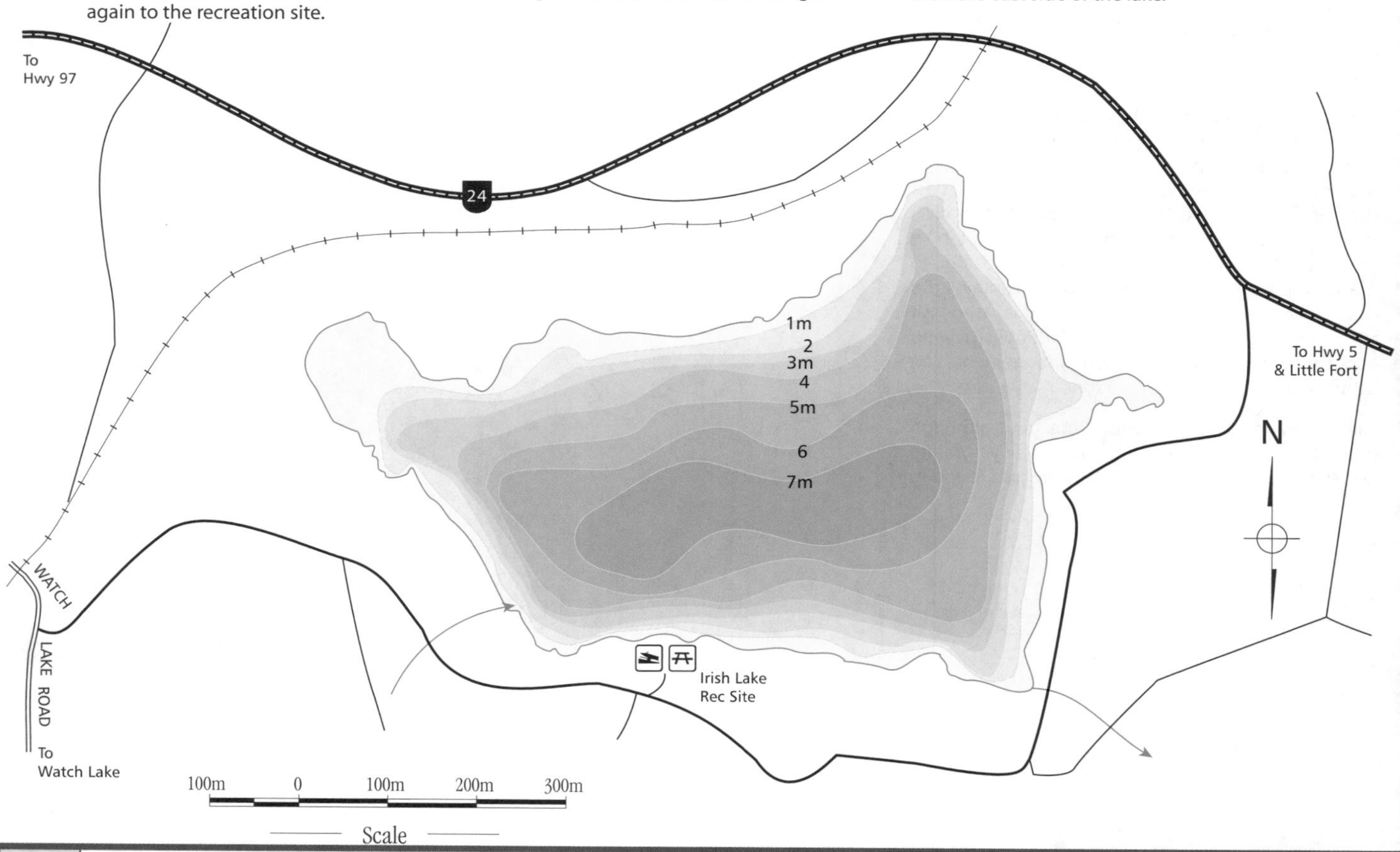

To Hwy 97
24
To Hwy 5 & Little Fort
1m
2
3m
4
5m
6
7m
N
WATCH LAKE ROAD
To Watch Lake
Irish Lake Rec Site
100m 0 100m 200m 300m
Scale

Jackson (Jack's Hole) Lake

Location: 34 km (21 mi) north of Williams Lake
Elevation: 900 m (2,953 ft)
Surface Area: 37 ha (91 ac)
Maximum Depth: 16.5 m (54 ft)
Mean Depth: 6.7 m (22 ft)
Way Point: 52° 25' 48.4" N, 122° 4' 12.0" W

Fishing

Found on a plateau west of the Beaver Valley, this popular lake has a good population of rainbow. It is set in a thick forest and is designated as an artificial fly only lake. There are many different names for this lake including Jack's Hole and Jackson Lake.

The lake is a very good fly-fishing lake containing large numbers of trout in the 0.5 kg (1 lb) range, although some fish reach over 2.5 kg (5 lbs). The lake has crystal clear water allowing you to see the shoals over which you can cast your fly.

However, clear water means the fish can see you to and as a result are easily spooked. Care needs to be taken, not just in how you move through the water, but in how you lay down your line, as an obvious presentation will cause the fish to flee. But there's no greater feeling than hooking a rainbow that you've been sight fishing for.

The fishery is maintained by an intensive stocking program involving 10,000 rainbow a year. Course fish are no longer a problem as the lake was rehabilitated some time ago.

The lake is quite deep so it can be trolled effectively. The best trolling is around the perimeter of the deep holes, one in the middle of the lake and one in the southwestern bay. The lake has prominent drop off meaning that fly anglers should work the shoals nearby to the drop offs.

The lake is quite productive, with significant insect hatches throughout the year. The damselfly emergence at Jackson produces some terrific action near the reed beds in mid-June. In July and August, use smaller caddis dry flies with black, brown or tan bodies and dark or light wings. The fall is very productive during the water boatman mating flights and when the fish return to shallows to feed on shrimp and leech for the winter.

Use a long leader when fishing chironomid and shrimp patterns in the spring to avoid spooking the fish off the shoals by the shadow of the dry fly line. Early season fly casters use small subsurface water boatman imitations, bloodworms, halfbacks and mayflies. Trolling a Doc Spratley, leech or Woolly Bugger pattern along the banks or in deep holes can also be effective.

The best place to cast from shore is at the southwestern bay as the deeper water is within casting distance of shore. Cast a dragonfly nymph, black or green leech, or Woolly Bugger over weedbeds or along the drop offs.

The lake is subject to winterkill despite the aeration program in place. There is also an electric motor only restriction on the lake.

Facilities

The **Jackson's Hole Recreation Site** is found in a grassy opening next to the north end of the lake. There are six sites that are well suited for campers and small RV's, but only half of those have tables and fire rings. A rough boat launch is also available.

Directions

Jackson Lake is found off the Beaver Valley Road north of Williams Lake. This good gravel road leads east from Highway 97. At about 17 km point, look for Jackson Lake Road leading south. This road continues for almost 4 km to the recreation site. Although RV's can access the lake, the road can be rough in wet weather.

Area Indicator

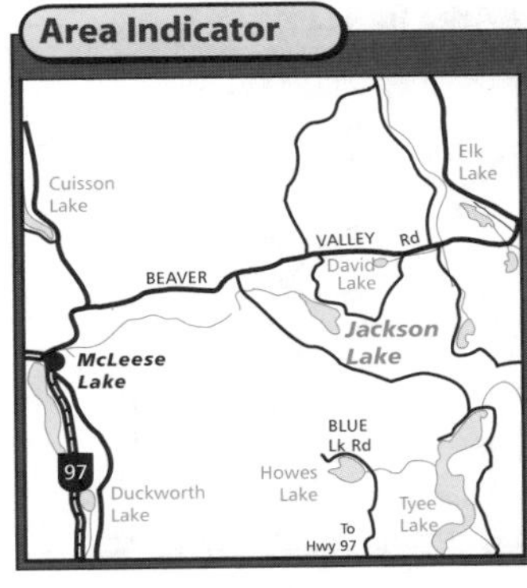

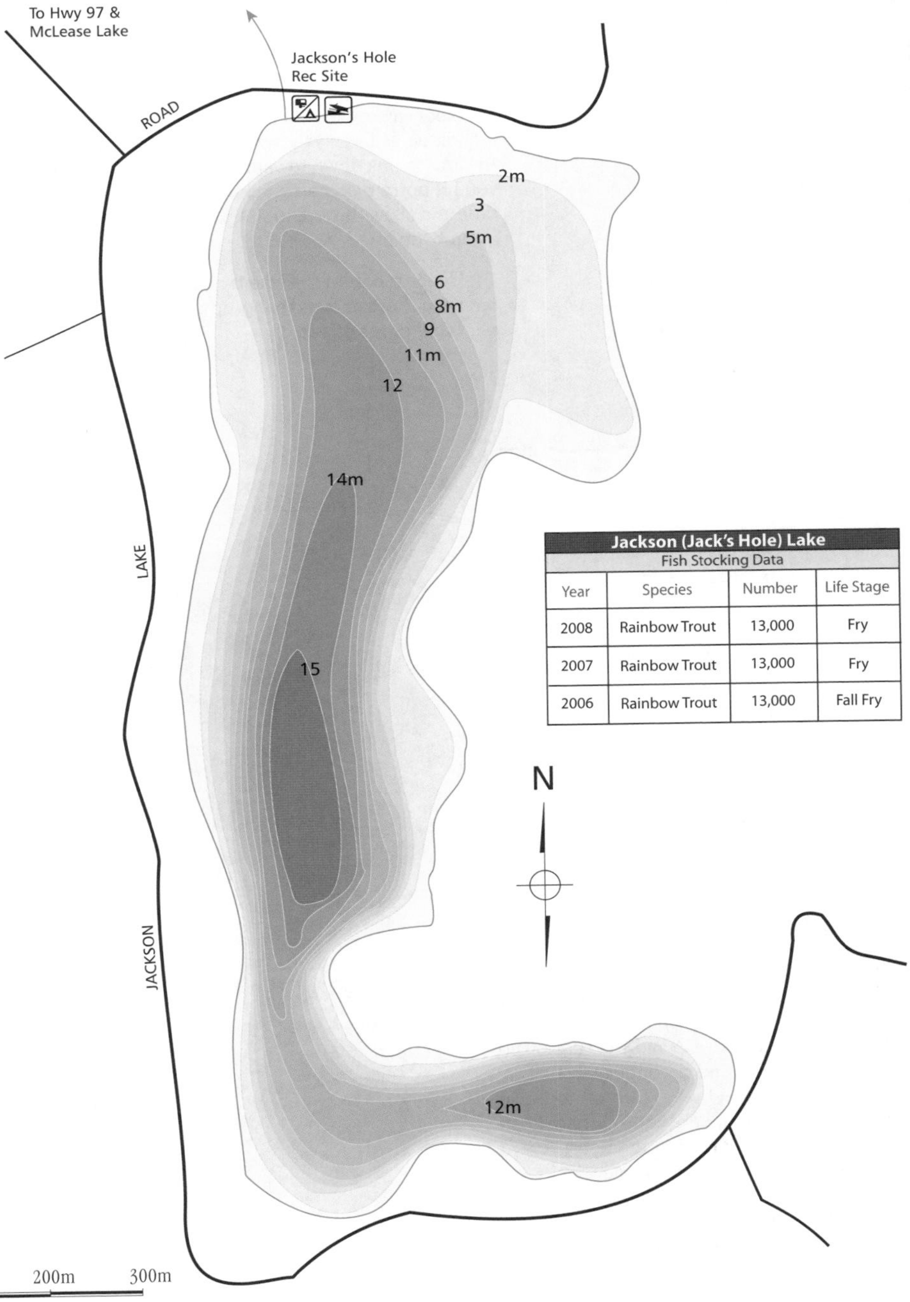

To Hwy 97 & McLease Lake

Jackson's Hole Rec Site

JACKSON LAKE ROAD

2m 3 5m 6 8m 9 11m 12 14m 15 12m

N

Scale: 100m 0 100m 200m 300m

Jackson (Jack's Hole) Lake Fish Stocking Data			
Year	Species	Number	Life Stage
2008	Rainbow Trout	13,000	Fry
2007	Rainbow Trout	13,000	Fry
2006	Rainbow Trout	13,000	Fall Fry

Location: 54 km (33.5 mi) northeast of Williams Lake
Elevation: 1,121 m (3,678 ft)
Surface Area: 91 ha (225 ac)
Maximum Depth: 20 m (66 ft)
Mean Depth: 7 m (23 ft)
Way Point: 52° 32′ 41″ N, 121° 45′ 37″ W

Jacobie Lake

Area Indicator

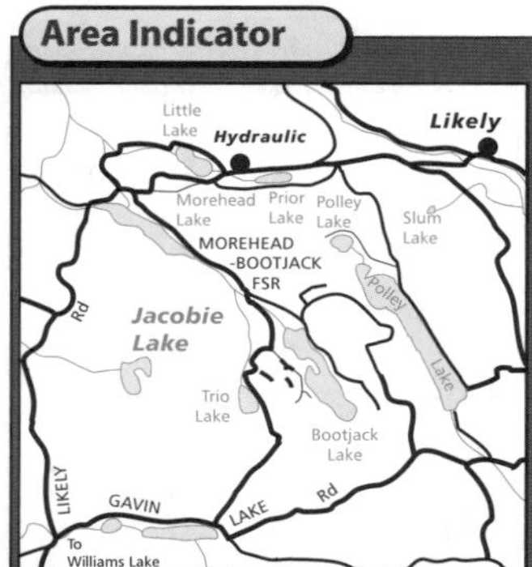

Fishing

Jacobie Lake is found to the north of the UBC Alex Fraser Research Forest. About half of the lake has been logged to the shoreline and is slowly reforesting. The rest of the lake is surrounded by a mixed Douglas-fir, spruce and willow forest.

Sitting a little higher in elevation than many lakes in the Cariboo, Jacobie Lake is clear of ice by mid May. However, the fishing doesn't start to heat up until early summer (June to early July) and again in the fall. The lake is not deep enough nor high enough to escape the summer doldrums completely so don't expect the fishing to be hot in late July and August.

There are plenty of small fish that average in the 25–35 cm (10–14 in) range. Spinners, lures and flies all work. In fact, because the fish are usually so indiscriminate, it is a great place to take the family as an introduction to fishing, as the action is usually fairly steady.

One of the simplest ways of fishing is simply to attach a worm or maggot or Powerbait to a hook, add a bit of a weight to get the hook down and then attach a bobber to the line, with enough space between the hook at the bobber to allow the hook to sink down to within a few feet of the bottom. Then, simply cast the hook and bobber out and wait. This is a great technique for kids, as all they have to do is watch the bobber and if it goes underwater, then pull!

For older kids, or for adults who have never fished but would like to, it is a great lake to practice your spincasting technique, especially the countdown method, where the lure is cast out and left to sink for five seconds. This allows the lure to sink down towards the bottom. With each cast, an extra five seconds is added to the sinking time until you hit bottom or start catching fish. Once you do hit bottom, subtract a few seconds from the total sink down time and allow the lure to sink that far with each cast. Try perennial favourites like a Mepps, Panther Martin, Vibrax or Gibbs spinner.

The deepest part of the lake is near the middle. Try trolling lake trolls or trout lures around the drop off keeping out from shore to avoid hang-ups. Shore anglers can cast from the access road or from the western banks where the water drops off rapidly.

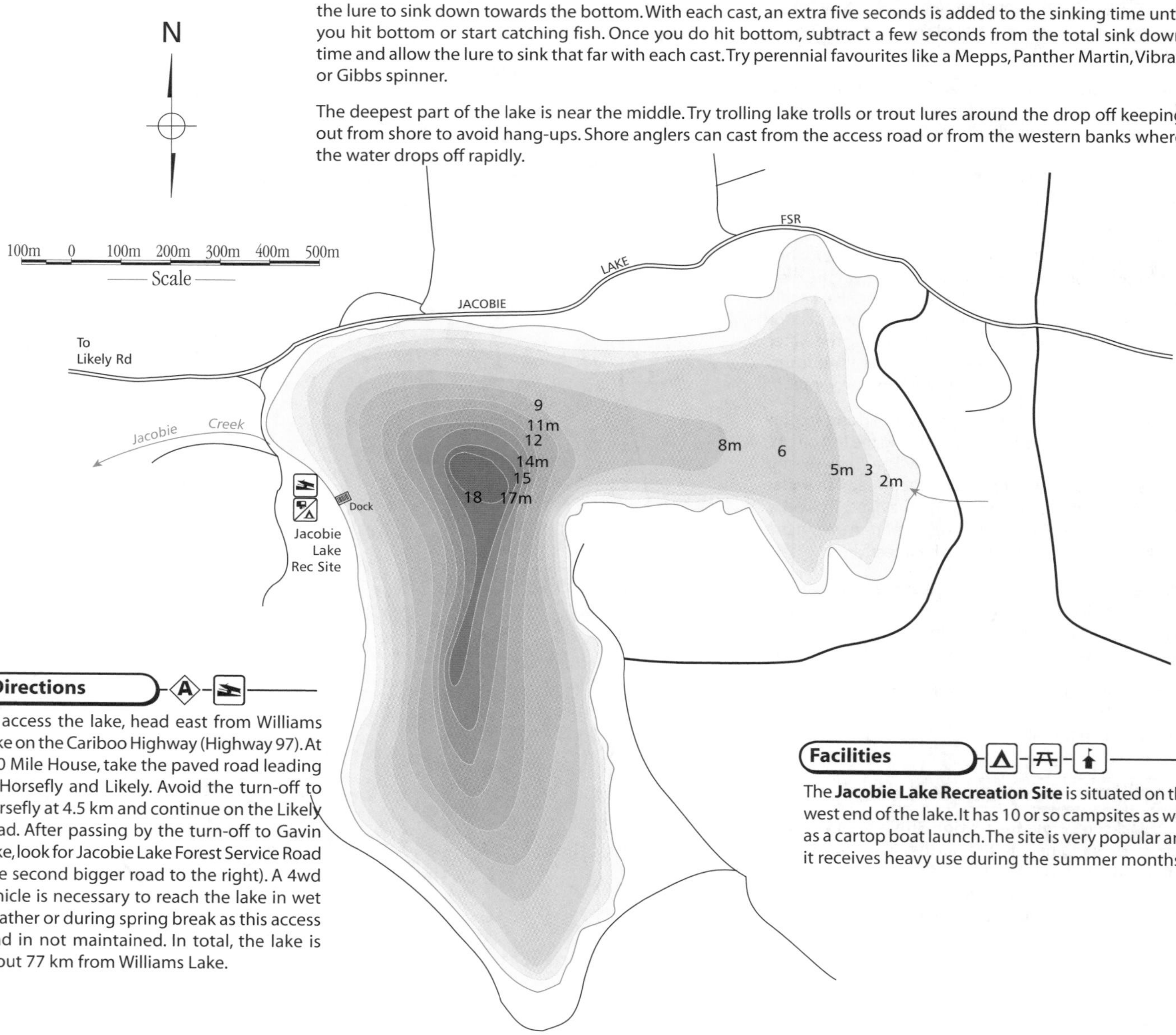

N

100m 0 100m 200m 300m 400m 500m
Scale

JACOBIE LAKE FSR
To Likely Rd
Jacobie Creek
Dock
Jacobie Lake Rec Site
9
11m
12
14m
15
18 17m
8m
6
5m 3 2m

Directions

To access the lake, head east from Williams Lake on the Cariboo Highway (Highway 97). At 150 Mile House, take the paved road leading to Horsefly and Likely. Avoid the turn-off to Horsefly at 4.5 km and continue on the Likely Road. After passing by the turn-off to Gavin Lake, look for Jacobie Lake Forest Service Road (the second bigger road to the right). A 4wd vehicle is necessary to reach the lake in wet weather or during spring break as this access road in not maintained. In total, the lake is about 77 km from Williams Lake.

Facilities

The **Jacobie Lake Recreation Site** is situated on the west end of the lake. It has 10 or so campsites as well as a cartop boat launch. The site is very popular and it receives heavy use during the summer months.

Jacques Lake

Location: 76 km (47 mi) northeast of Williams Lake
Elevation: 890 m (2,920 ft)
Surface Area: 171 ha (424 ac)
Maximum Depth: 37 m (121 ft)
Mean Depth: 10 m (33 ft)
Way Point: 52° 27′ 48″ N, 121° 9′ 2″ W

Fishing

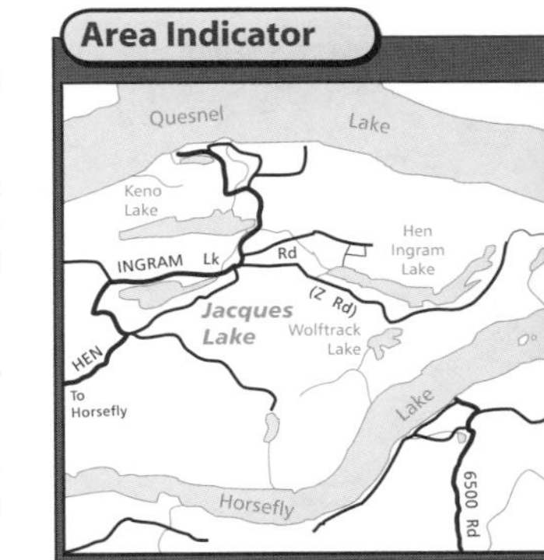

Jacques Lake is found between the much larger Quesnel and Horsefly Lakes. The smaller lake produces good numbers of rainbow trout that can get as big as 2.5 kg (5 lbs) due in part to the nice shoals that dominate the near shore area.

As you're fishing the lake, don't dwell on the fact that the mountain over there is an eroded cinder cone, or that you're sitting next to one of the easternmost volcanoes in BC. The Jacques Lake cone hasn't actually erupted since the Pleistocene era, so there's (probably) nothing to worry about. But pointing it out is the sort of thing that impresses the fishing buddies.

Jacques Lake was stocked with rainbow in the early 1960's and has since established a self-sustaining population. Although good size trout are commonly caught, they generally average under 0.5 kg (1 lb).

The lake is best fished in the early season, with the most popular method of fishing being trolling. The usual list of effective trolling lures works here, too: Willow Leaf, Wedding Band, small Flatfish, small spoon or, for the fly anglers, Woolly Buggers, Carey Specials and Doc Spratleys. Trollers should stick around the middle of the lake off the drop off area.

Summer fishing is slower than the spring but still worth a try. The fish are usually found a little deeper in the summer and a fish finder will prove useful. Fly anglers and spincasters should cast off the sunken island near the middle of the lake. Shore casters should try off the northern shoreline of the main body of the lake as the water drops off most rapidly in that area. Common lures include an Apex Trout Killer or Krocodile spoon or a Mepps, Panther Martin or Gibbs Spinner. A Mini Fat Rap is another great choice. Fly anglers, on the other hand, can work a nymph or leech pattern, or an attractor pattern like a Spratley. The lake has the usual Cariboo hatches, although none that are really prominent. Keep an eye out for signs of hatches occurring and try and match what the fish are currently eating.

Directions

Jacques Lake is found northeast of the town of Horsefly. To reach the lake, travel to the town of Horsefly and then take the Black Creek Road heading east across the Horsefly River. Where the pavement ends, turn north on the Horsefly Lake Road and continue for another 26.5 km and keep right at the sign indicating Quesnel Lake Resort. Continue for another 6 km and turn left and follow this road to eventually meet the recreation site on Jacques Lake. Towards the end of the journey, the road gets rougher so a truck may be necessary, especially in wet weather or in the early spring.

Facilities

At the north end of the lake, the **Jacques Lake Recreation Site** offers 10 lakeside camping spots as well as a boat launch.

Other Options

Jacques Lake is found in an area thick with great fishing lakes. One option is **Whiffle Lake** to the west. This lake has numerous small rainbow making for a good family fishery. There is a cartop boat launch at the lake.

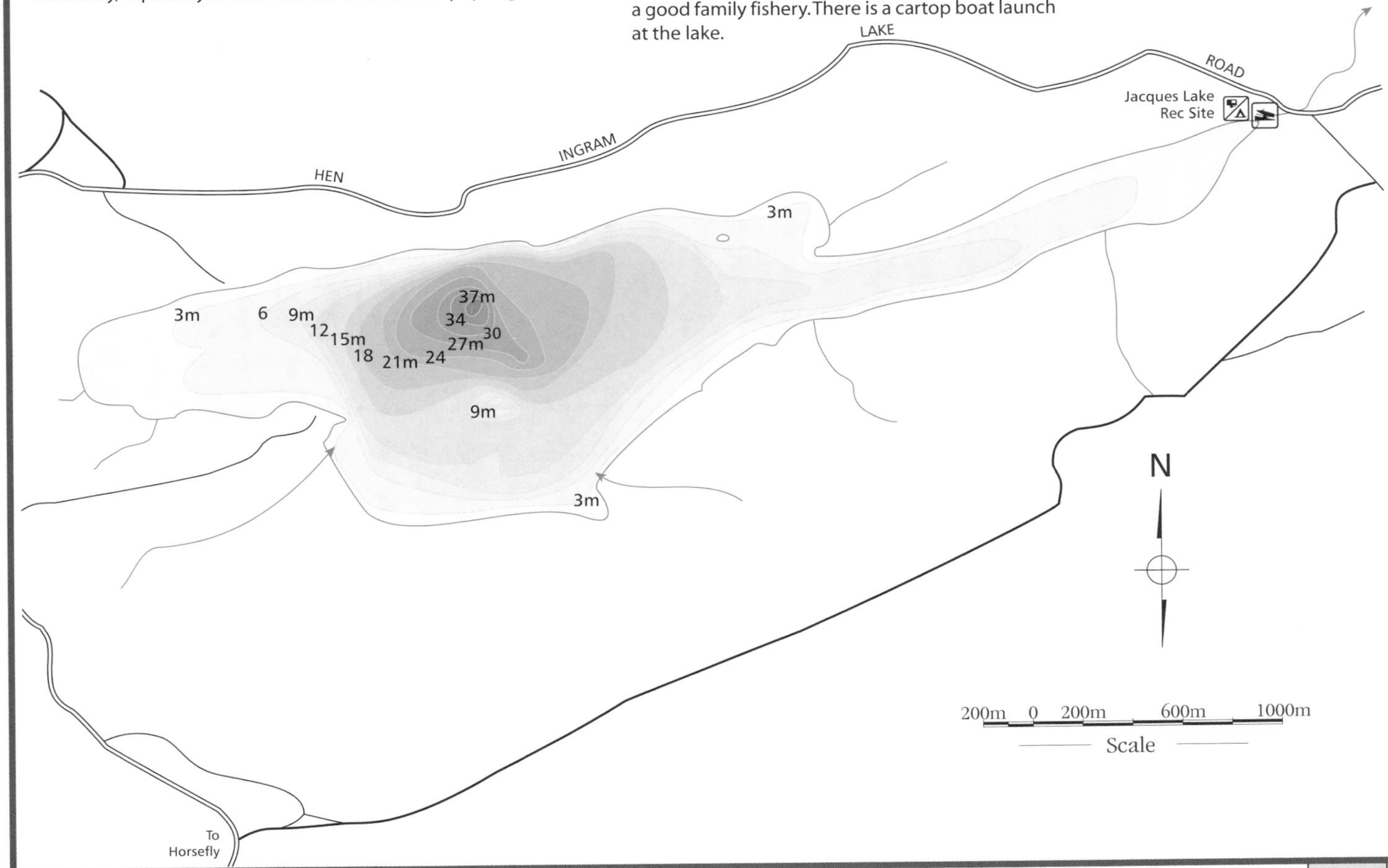

Location: 30 km (18.6 mi) south of 100 Mile House
Elevation: 1,161 m (3,809 ft)
Surface Area: 110 ha (271 ac)
Maximum Depth: 22 m (71 ft)
Mean Depth: 8 m (26 ft)
Way Point: 51° 24′ 2.4″ N, 121° 6′ 59.8″ W

Jim Lake

Area Indicator

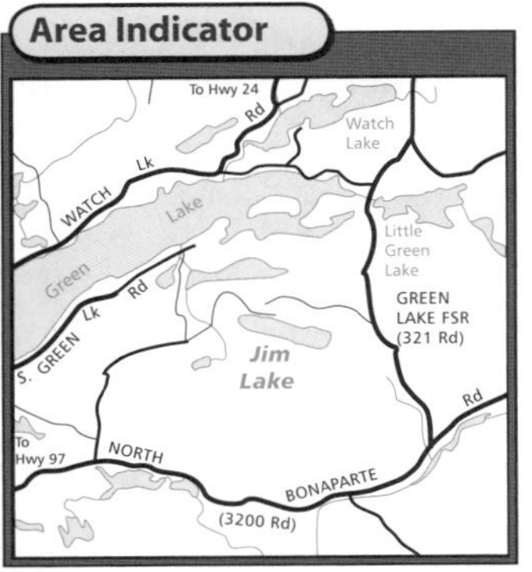

Jim Lake Fish Stocking Data			
Year	Species	Number	Life Stage
2008	Rainbow Trout	10,000	Yearling
2007	Rainbow Trout	10,000	Yearling
2006	Rainbow Trout	10,000	Yearling

Fishing

Jim Lake is a small lake found to the south of Green Lake and Watch Lake. It offers excellent fishing for stocked rainbow trout. The lake is also home to some course fish, such as lake chub and suckers.

Being one of the higher elevation lakes written up in this book, the fishery is often delayed until late May to early June. The best fishing is from mid-June to mid-July. In July and August, the waters do warm, but not significantly and it is still possible to fish the lake. In fact, this is when the lake sees its most action, as people head to higher elevation lakes like Jim when the lower elevation lakes are suffering from the summer doldrums. The fishing picks up again in September and remains good until fall turnover, just before ice over in early November.

The lake is quite deep and is a popular trolling lake. Stick around the northern and southern shores of the lake off the drop off area. A good trick is to troll erratically along the drop off keeping the lighter water representing the shoreline visible on the shore side of the boat. It is also a good idea to vary your speed and occasionally jerk your line to entice any curious trout into striking. Fly anglers can pull around a Carey Special, which is one of the best trolling flies, a Doc Spratley or a Woolly Bugger. Gear anglers can stick with a Willow Leaf or other lake trolls or a small Flatfish.

Spincasters and fly anglers do well working the shallows at the west and east ends of the lake where there you will find the inflow and outflow creeks. The lake features the traditional Cariboo hatches, although because the ice isn't off until later in the season, there is usually overlaps between the hatches, with chironomids, caddis and mayflies all hatching on the same day. Figuring out what the trout are feeding on at what time of day in that particular bay can be a challenge. If you're not having luck with matching the hatch, tie on a searcher pattern like a Spratley or a leech. If the trout are rising to the surface, a Tom Thumb is probably the best all-purpose topwater fly out there.

Directions

From 70 Mile House and Highway 97, head north-east on the Green Lake Road. Keep straight at the first major junction on what is now called the South Green Lake Road. Follow that road past the Sunset View Campground where the next right takes you southeast towards Jim Lake. Turn left (east) at about 2 km and right about 3 km later and you should reach the northwest shore of the lake. In addition to a four wheel drive vehicle, a copy of the Backroad Mapbook for the *Cariboo Chilcotin Coast* and a GPS are recommended accessories to find the lake.

Facilities

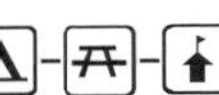

There are no developed facilities at the lake, although there is a trio of private cottages surrounded by Crown land. It is possible to hand launch a small boat at the lake and there's nothing stopping you from setting up camp here, either. However, if you prefer, the lake is less than 10 km from the Sunset View Campground at Green Lake Provincial Park.

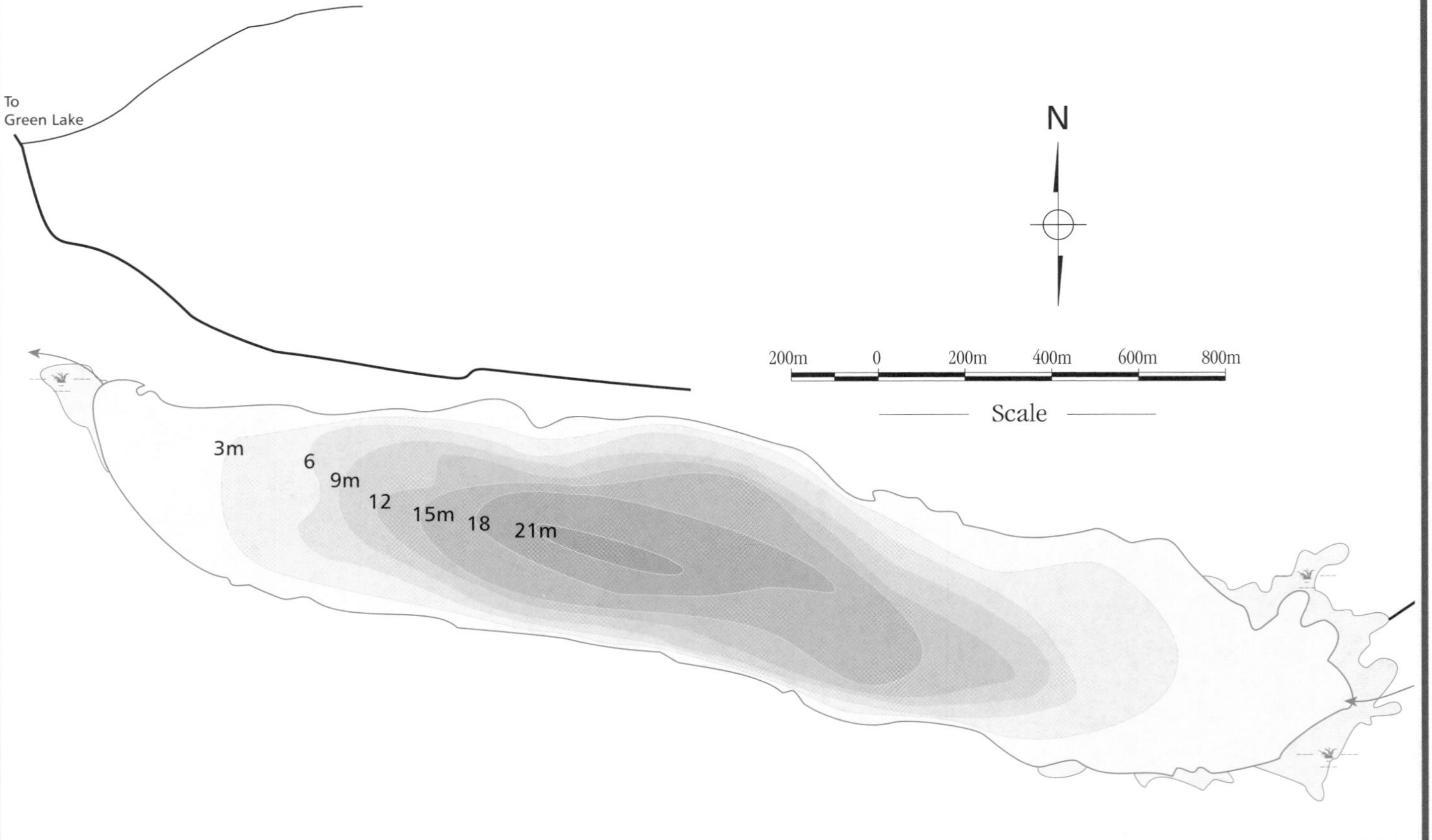

To Green Lake

N

200m 0 200m 400m 600m 800m

Scale

3m 6 9m 12 15m 18 21m

Kathie & Esker Park Lakes

Location: 32 km (20 mi) northwest of Prince George
Elevation: 759m (2,490 ft)
Surface Area: 45 ha (110 ac)
Maximum Depth: 17m (56 ft)
Mean Depth: 7m (23 ft)
Way Point: 54° 4′ 20.7″ N, 123° 10′ 17.9″ W

Fishing

There are five lakes in Eskers Provincial Park, northwest of Prince George that are managed as great family fisheries. Resting amongst the tall, thin Eskers that give the park its name, Kathie Lake is one of the most popular destinations in the park.

Kathie Lake supports good populations of stocked rainbow and wild brook trout and fishing can be fast and furious. The average size fish here is an impressive 38 cm (15 in) for the rainbow, while the average brook trout is about 30 cm (12 in). Although not as big as the rainbow, the wild brook trout are often more aggressive and quite willing to take your offering.

The lake was originally stocked as a put and take lake, but the naturalized population of brook trout have really taken off here. Unfortunate, too, that for some anglers put and take has become take and put, as in take the brookies from here and drop them in other lakes in an attempt to "improve" the fishing there. These small lakes can only support so many fish. As the fish become more plentiful, the average catch becomes smaller and smaller. Although there may be a lot of fish in the smaller lakes around the park, there is rarely anything of decent size.

Kathie Lake is the largest lake in the park, but it is still small enough to be fished from shore in some places. However, many prefer to fish using a canoe or float tube. There is a portage trail for canoeists to access the lake. Bow and Camp Lakes are also accessible from this canoe route.

No matter which lake you choose in the park, concentrate your fishing around the islands and shoal areas. Bright, colourful flies work well for brookies, as do Clouser Minnow or Muddler Minnow flies, which imitate small fish. Many brook trout are also caught on small spoons and spinners, or trolls with a worm attached. For anglers using spinning or spincasting gear, try such lures as Flatfish, Panther Martin or a Dick Nite. Dry-fly-fishing can also be effective for brook trout–and certainly for rainbow when insects such as mayflies or caddisflies are hatching. Elk Hair Caddis and Parachute Adams are two good dry or floating fly patterns to have in your tackle bag.

Some of the best fishing for rainbow and brook trout comes in early winter not long after the ice is on. At this time, the oxygen levels and water temperatures are high enough that fish are still actively feeding. For safety's sake, be sure the ice is at least 15 cm (6 in) before ice fishing. Brook trout are much more active in winter and the fishing for them remains strong throughout the ice-on season. A jig with bait is quite effective.

Area Indicator

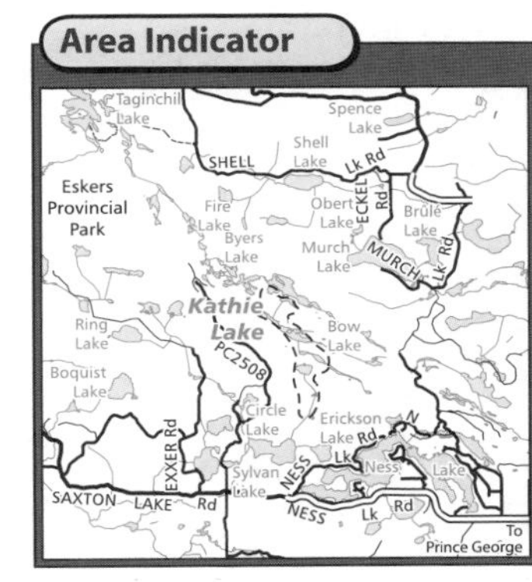

Directions

Eskers Provincial Park is located 32 km northwest of Prince George. Turn west off Highway 97 onto Chief Lake Road. Continue west for 27 km to the west end of Ness Lake and turn north onto Ness Lake Road North. Follow this road for 1 km to the park entrance and the parking area on your right. Access to Kathie Lake is by foot along a developed trail system, or by canoe.

Facilities

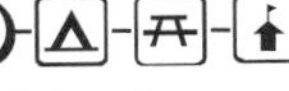

Eskers Provincial Park is a day-use park with no overnight facilities. There are hiking and portage trails leading to Kathie Lake as well as outhouses at the lake.

Kathie Lake Fish Stocking Data			
Year	Species	Number	Life Stage
2008	Rainbow Trout	4,000	Yearling
2007	Rainbow Trout	3,000	Yearling
2006	Rainbow Trout	3,000	Yearling

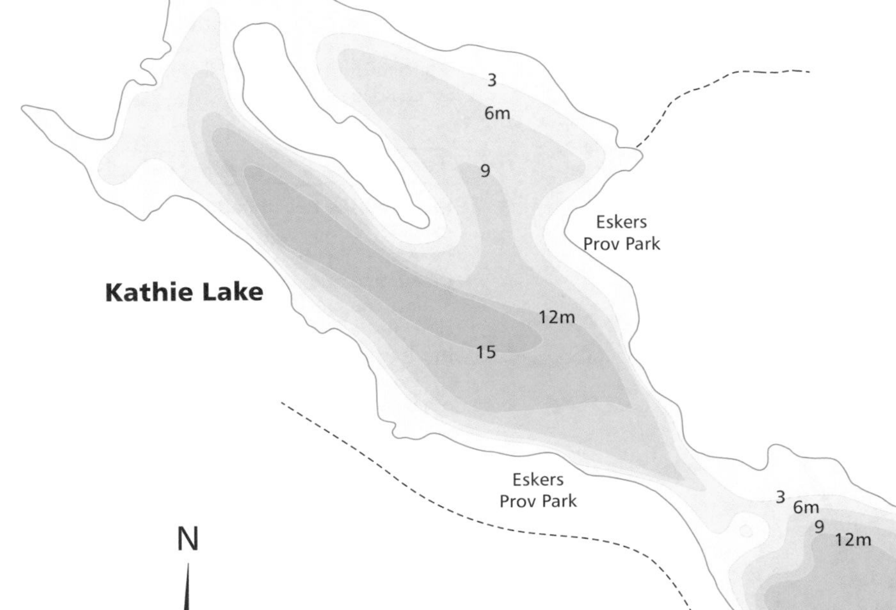

Location: 5 km (3 mi) north of Smithers
Elevation: 510 m (1,673 ft)
Surface Area: 170 ha (420 ac)
Maximum Depth: 9.4 m (30.9 ft)
Mean Depth: 4.6 m (15 ft)
Way Point: 54° 49′ 27.3″ N, 127° 12′ 23.2″ W

Kathlyn Lake

Area Indicator

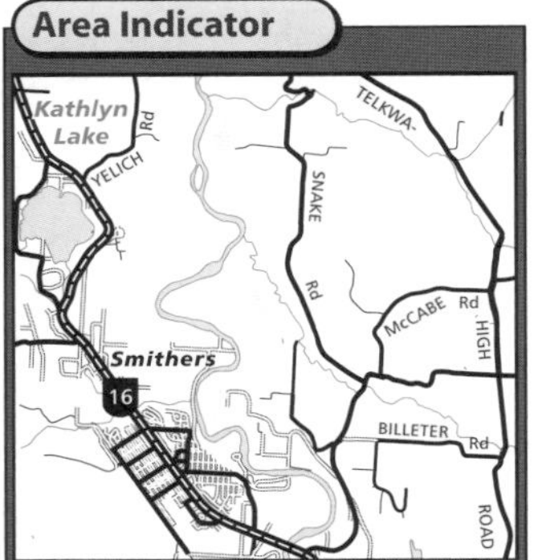

Fishing

Kathlyn Lake is a small lake located just north of Smithers along the Yellowhead Highway. The lake is quite pretty and is a popular destination for locals and visitors alike.

The lake holds a number of small cutthroat trout. Indeed finding a cutthroat as large as 1 kg (2 lbs) would be the catch of the year since the average sized fish is half that. This is despite the fact the fish have now established a self-sustaining population and feed readily on the other course fish in the lake. Although cutthroat are piscivorous and do eat smaller fish like the redside shiner, there is just so much competition in the lake for food so the cutthroat don't grow very big.

And most of the bigger fish get fished out rather quickly. The lake can be extremely busy, especially on summer weekends. While many people come to the lake for the beach, it is also a popular place for anglers and seeing a dozen boats out on the lake on a weekend is fairly common.

Cutthroat prefer colder water and spawn in the spring. At this time try bait fishing using small minnows, casting a small silver lure, or fly-fishing a silver minnow imitation. Gold or silver bodied Muddler Minnow or Wool Head Sculpin are two fly patterns to try. Sinking line with short leaders is preferred to work the steep shorelines of lakes.

In summer, dry flies like the Elk Hair Caddis, Tom Thumb or an ant pattern can create a frenzy of action. However, like most of the lakes around this area, pine beetles have become a staple in the fish's diet. Try fishing a small black beetle pattern. Fishing around the drop offs or near stream mouths along the lake with fast sink line and long leaders is another possibility. During the cooler periods fly anglers will need to use searching patterns such as black broadhead leeches or Woolly Buggers.

Spincasting Kitimat lures and Panther Martin spinners can be effective, but the most common way of fishing the lake is by trolling Willow Leafs/Ford Fenders, even though there is a ban on power boats at the lake.

For kids a worm and bobber can often do the trick using light test and a small hook. Cast around the drop off areas as the cutthroat tend to cruise near shore areas in search of baitfish.

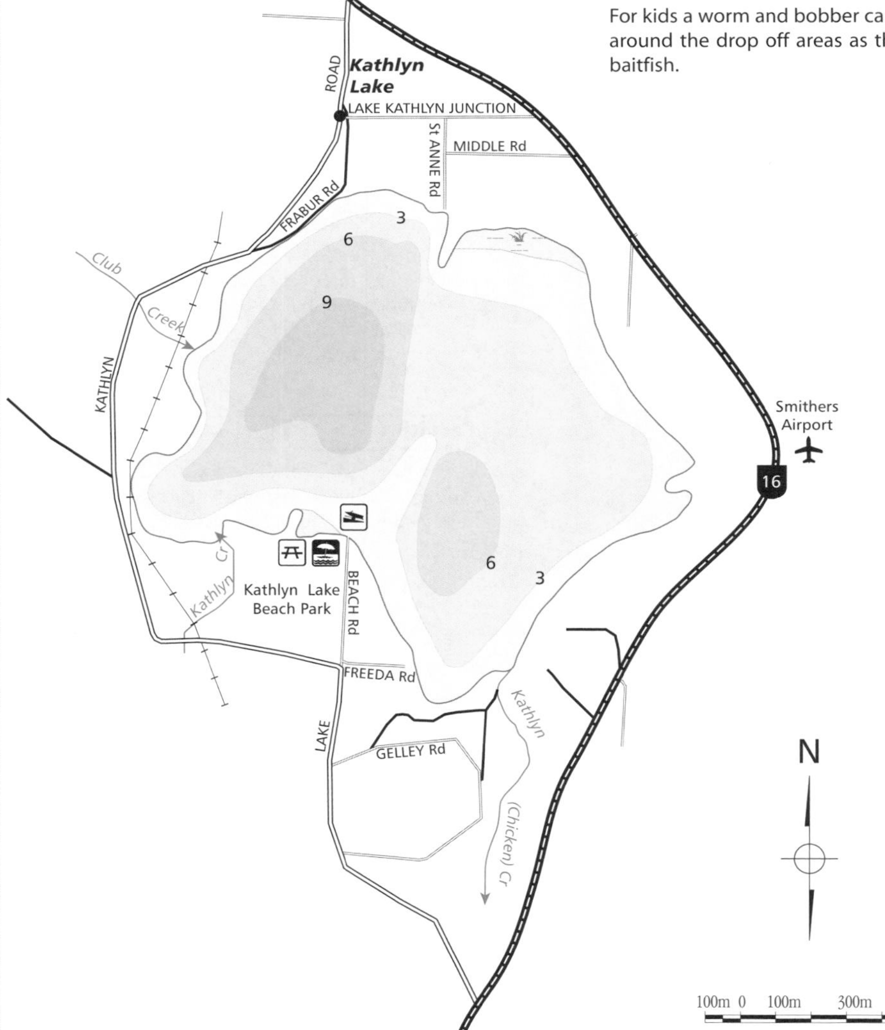

Directions

The lake is located on the outskirts of Smithers. From Smithers, drive northwest on the Yellowhead Highway and turn left on Lake Kathlyn Road. If you miss the first turnoff, don't worry, as you can access the same road from the north. About 1 km along the road from the south, the road makes a sharp right hand turn. Continuing straight brings you onto Beach Road and to the park.

Facilities

Kathlyn Lake Beach Park is a small community park that is situated in a rural neighbourhood near the edge of Smithers. It is extremely popular during the summer months for swimming, canoeing and fishing. The park has a small day use area with a cartop boat launch as well as a small sandy beach that is backed by a large grass field. The there are picnic tables and outhouses as well. Accommodations and other services are available in Smithers.

Keno Lake

Location: 80 km (50 mi) northeast of Williams Lake
Elevation: 817 m (2,680 ft)
Surface Area: 228 ha (563 ac)
Maximum Depth: 31 m (100 ft)
Mean Depth: 11 m (36 ft)
Way Point: 52° 29′ 17″ N, 121° 7′ 47″ W

Fishing

Keno Lake is a mid sized lake located north of Jacques Lake and south of Quesnel Lake. It is a slightly lower elevation lake than some of the other lakes in the area and may be ice-free a day or two earlier than other lakes in the region. While a day or two doesn't seem like much, if you are there that one day, you will be grateful for that extra day. Of course, the lake also turns over a couple days sooner than other lakes in the area, too.

The lake contains rainbow trout as well as some red-side shiners and suckers. Keno Lake was stocked with rainbow in the early 1960's and has since established a self-sustaining population. Today, Keno offers fast fishing for rainbow that average under a pound but can grow to 2 kg (4 lbs) or more. The lake is best fished early in the spring or later in the fall.

The lake is quite deep and is best fished on the troll. There are three distinct holes in the lake that are good areas to focus, especially if you are trolling in the summer. Rather than trolling through the heart of the deepest spots, work along transition zones, especially where there is a steep drop off. Rainbow aren't usually found more than 15 metres (50 feet) down or so since they prefer sitting near the bottom of the lake in the thermocline. A fish finder is useful in locating the fish and the depth they are at.

Most people trolling use a lake troll. There are a variety of different trolls, with different shapes of blades and different lengths of shaft or cable. The shape of the blade determines how fast it will rotate and the sound it produces. A narrow bladed lake troll like a Willow Leaf spin fast and close to the shaft. These types of trolls are best suited for medium to fast trolling. Many people also use a Flatfish or small spoon on the troll. Remember not to troll too fast. In fact, many prefer to row their boat as it gives them more control over the speed of the boat and better action on the lure.

For spincasters and fly anglers, casting off the south shore near the mid-lake island or around the drop off area out from the three deep holes is recommended.

Directions

To reach the lake, travel to the town of Horsefly and then take the Black Creek Road heading east across the Horsefly River. Where the pavement ends, turn north on the Horsefly Lake Road and continue past the Hen Ingram Lake Forest Service Road, following the Quesnel Lake Resort signs. The road to the south side of Quesnel Lake leads right past the eastern shoreline of Keno Lake providing relatively easy access to the recreation site.

Facilities

The **Keno Lake Recreation Site** is a seven unit site set on the eastern shores of the lake. The site receives heavy use during the summer months. Launching small boats at the lake is possible.

Other Options

Klinee Lake is located north of Keno Lake nearby to Quesnel Lake. The fly-fishing only lake receives light fishing pressure so it has good fishing for stocked rainbow to 1 kg (2 lbs). It is best fished off the weedbeds using a long, fine leader as the water is very clear. A small recreation site offers lakeshore camping and a cartop boat launch.

Area Indicator

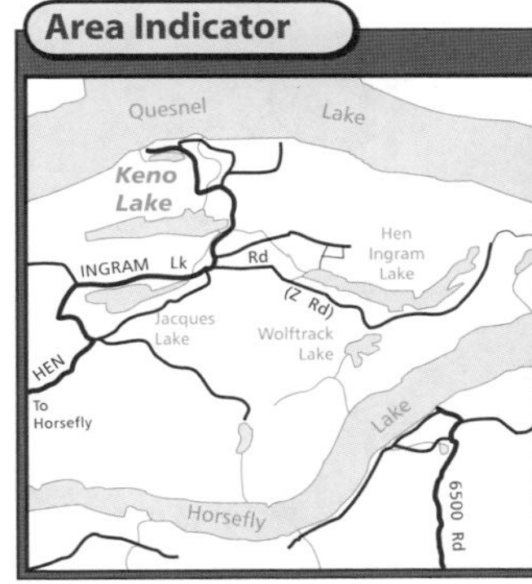

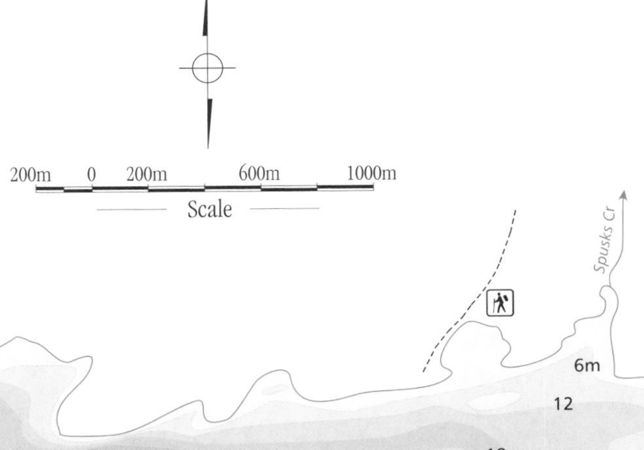

Location: 50 km (31 mi) east of 100 Mile House

Kings Lakes (East & West)

Kings Lake (West)

Elevation: 1,266 m (4,153 ft)
Surface Area: 47 ha (116 ac)
Maximum Depth: 18 m (59 ft)
Mean Depth: 6.4 m (21 ft)
Way Point: 51° 33′29.1″N, 120° 37′38.9″W

Kings Lake (East)

Elevation: 1,267 m (4,157 ft)
Surface Area: 34.7 ha (86 ac)
Maximum Depth: 13 m (42 ft)
Mean Depth: 4.2 m (14 ft)
Way Point: 51° 33′47″N, 120° 36′25″W

Area Indicator

Fishing

This pair of lakes is found northeast of Bridge Lake in an area thick with other great fishing lakes. While the lakes offer good fly fishing for small rainbow trout, there are just so many options in the area that these two lakes don't see heavy pressure.

Part of the low pressure is also due to the difficult access, as a truck is needed to get to the lake. And there are no longer forestry recreation sites on the shores of these lakes so many prefer to fish elsewhere.

Both lakes are slightly higher elevation than most of the lakes in this book and aren't ice free until early May. By the time turnover is done, you probably aren't going to catch many fish until mid to late May. The lakes see the best action in June to the first week of July. After that, fishing slows until the early fall.

Visitors will find good number of rainbow, which are usually small 20–30 cm (8–12 in) but can grow to 1 kg (2 lbs). The lakes are small enough for a belly boat and a fly rod. Try near the inflow creek at the northern end of East King Lake or at the inflow creek at the east end of the West King Lake. The lakes have fair hatches of all the traditional insects: chironomids, caddis, mayflies and dragon and damsel flies. If you are not having any luck matching the hatches, try casting or trolling an attractor pattern. Once you catch a fish, a throat pump will show you what the fish are feeding on. If you do use a throat pump, be careful. Using a pump improperly can kill the fish.

Both lakes are deep enough to troll. If trolling West King Lake, stick to the main body of water towards the east end as the water is deepest in that location. For the East King Lake, troll northeast of the small island nearby to the deeper water. Woolly Buggers and Carey Specials are among the traditional trolling flies.

There is an artificial fly only restriction on the lakes along with a bait ban, ice fishing ban and an engine power restriction (less than 10 hp).

Directions

This pair of lakes is located north of Highway 24 near Bridge Lake. To reach East King Lake, turn north along the Wavey Lake Forest Service Road, which is found about 60 km east of the Highway 24 and Highway 97 junction. Continue north on this deteriorating road past Wavey Lake and turn left (west) at the next prominent junction. If you miss the turn off to the left, the road takes a sharp right had corner and begins heading east past Ripple Lake. Turn around. The road to East King Lake slowly begins to fracture into smaller and smaller roads, which terminate in clearcuts near the eastern shores of the east lake.

West King Lake can be reached off Bridge Lake North Road. Turn onto the Grossett Road and follow this road to where it terminates on the western shores of the lake. Both routes are rough and a truck with good clearance and good tires will be needed to get to the lake.

Facilities

There are several rustic camping sites on East King Lake and one rustic camping site on West King Lake. It is possible to launch a boat on both lakes.

Kispiox River

Location: 15 km (9.3 mi) northeast of New Hazelton
Stream Length: Unavailable
Geographic: 55° 21′ 00″ N, 127° 41′ 59″ W

Fishing

While this river has been fished by the local First Nations from time beyond memory, it was first discovered by the international fishing community in 1954. This is when Field and Stream Magazine reported that not one but two world record steelhead–one 15 kg (33 lbs) and one 16 kg (36 lbs)–had been pulled out of the Kispiox River. Further, six of the ten largest steelhead recorded as part of a fishing contest the magazine was running came from the Kispiox.

Suddenly, everyone wanted to fish the Kispiox and the river quickly became one of the world's best-known steelheading rivers. While the world record sized steelhead has moved on, the river still produces giant steelheads. It is considered the best place to find steelhead that are bigger than 15 kg (30 lbs).

Steelhead most often return to spawn for the first time after two years in the ocean, but the Kispiox River has an abnormally large number of fish that stay in the ocean for three years, meaning they are on average bigger than the average steelhead. And since steelhead, unlike salmon, do not die after spawning, many of the fish here are returning to the river for the second or third time.

The run begins in late August or early September when a few fish (often the largest males) begin returning into the lower river. The peak of the run comes in September and into October. While a boat is not necessary, it can help you travel from place to place. Do not that it is illegal to actually fish from a boat.

Popular patterns include leeches, including the egg sucking leech, Woolly Buggers or a marabou fly. For some reason, these fish are not as willing to rise to a dry fly as other Skeena steelhead.

Recently, the steelhead returns have been dropping. Poor survival rates in the ocean and commercial fishing have knocked the population down. And the river valley has seen extensive logging meaning the water quality is quite poor when it rains in fall.

The Kispiox also reports a good return of Chinook salmon. These large fish return in July, when the river is still running high and dirty. You will need brighter presentations like a Spin-n-Glo to entice strikes at this time.

Directions

The Kispiox Valley Trail is the main road up the Kispiox Valley, although there are a few other logging roads in the area that also offer access. To get to the Kispiox Valley, take the Yellowhead Highway to New Hazelton. Turn north onto Highway 62 to Hazelton. As you are entering Hazelton, the Kispiox Valley Road turns off the road to your right (north). The road crosses the Skeena and then the Kispiox as it heads up the Kispiox Valley, eventually turning into the Kispiox Trail.

Facilities

There are a pair of recreation sites along the river: the **Upper Kispiox Ford Recreation Site** and the **Sweetin River Recreation Site**. There are also a couple recreation sites at lakes near the river, like Elizabeth Lake, Pentz Lake and Little Fish. During prime steelhead season, expect these sites to be packed. There are also a few lodges along the river as well as private campgrounds.

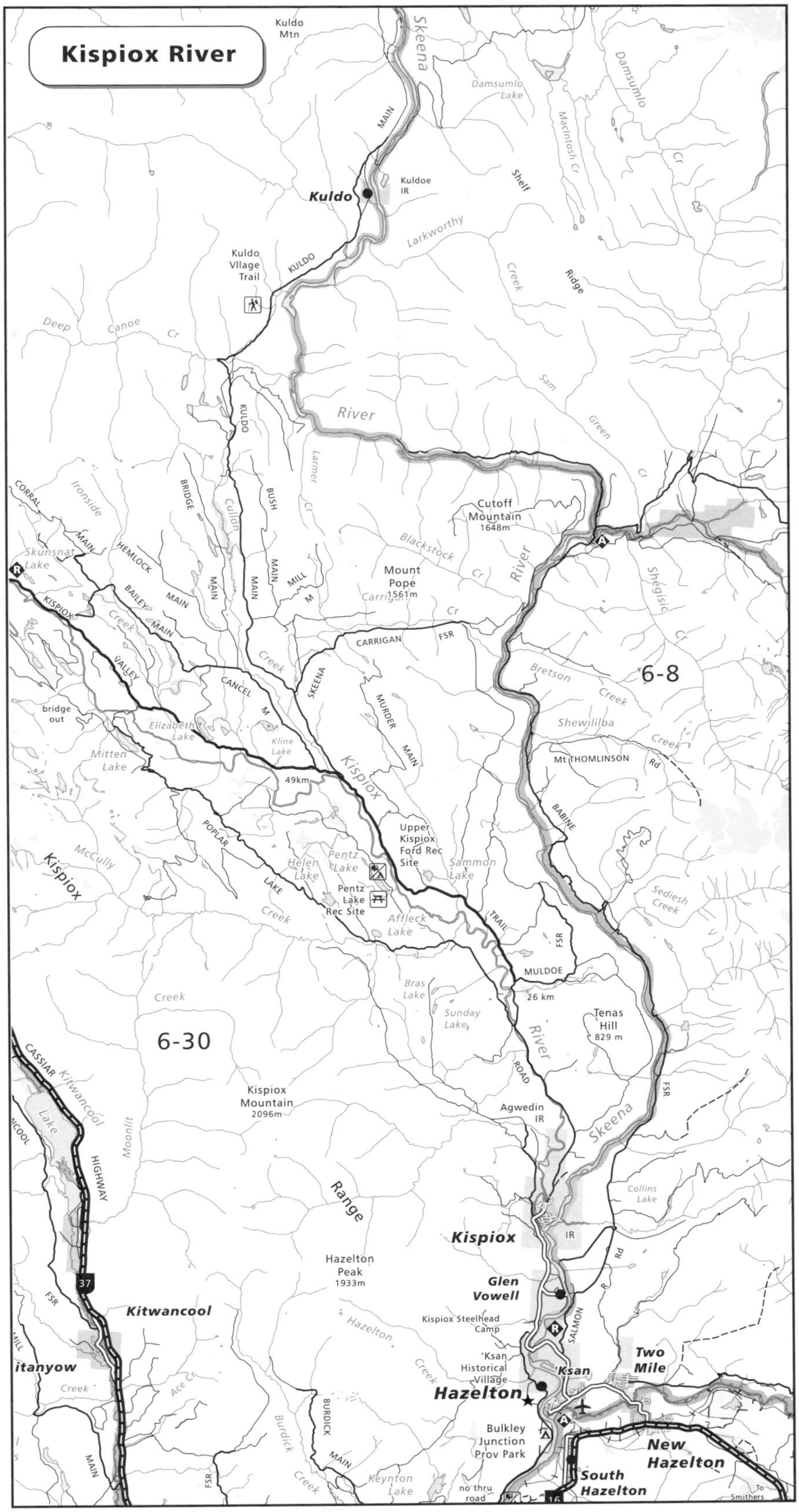

Location: Flows through Kitimat
Stream Length: 97.7 km (61 mi)
Geograhic: 54°07′ 08″ N, 128°10′ 34″ W

Kitimat River

Fishing

The Kitimat River is a medium sized river that empties into the Douglas Channel near the city of Kitimat. The highway follows the Kitimat River Valley for about 25 km before the river heads east into the Coast Mountains. The river is hatchery enhanced and receives higher than average returns of salmon, trout and steelhead due to its close proximity to the ocean.

People have caught steelhead on the river to 12 kg (25 lbs). Unlike the nearby Skeena system, the Kitimat River has a mix of wild and hatchery steelhead, which show up in the river in April and May. You are allowed to catch and keep one hatchery steelhead a day, after which you are required to stop fishing for the remainder of that day.

Steelhead can be caught using a variety of methods including hot shotting or back-trolling. Usually done with the help of a guide, this method requires one person to man the oars while the other(s) fish. Hot shotting traditionally uses a plug such as a Hot Shot, which is let out 15 metres (50 feet) behind a boat. The oarsman works against the current, slowly allowing the boat to drift backwards, while the current causes the lure to dip and dive and weave near the bottom of the river. As the boat drifts backwards, the lure will bump and bounce and weave right in front of the steelhead's nose, causing them to strike. The trick is to drift backwards very slowly, as the longer the lure is in front of the steelhead, the more chance there is of a strike. A metallic colour works well in clear water, while pinks or purples work better when the water is murky.

The Kitimat is also a great fly-fishing river with lots of shallow tailouts. Working egg imitations, Woolly Buggers or other classic attractor patterns can work well for steelhead.

Salmon back up in the ocean during low tide, waiting for the tidal water. When timed properly, waves of fresh fish can be found. Chinook enter the river in mid-May and continue until the end of July when the fishery closes. The best fishing is weather dependent as they wait for water levels to rise before passing through. From shore, bottom bouncing Spin-n-Glos, corkies or gooey bobs can be very productive. Back-trolling with Flatfish, Hot Shots or Kwikfish can be deadly. The record catch here was a 33.5 kg (74 lb) monster.

During this time, chum salmon enter the river, too. Chum are hard fighters, but not a very popular fish to angle for despite their size. They peak at the end of July/early August and love to come to the fly. Flies such as a '52 Buick (a small, green shrimp imitation) or big Marabou flies (green, pink or orange) work well. Beadheads help vary the presentation.

The Coho run is from mid-August to mid-September and there are cutthroat in the river mostly year round, although the river is usually unfishable from October to February.

Directions

From the city of Kitimat, Highway 37 parallels the Kitimat for about 25 km. About 4 km after the river turns sharply to the east, look for the Upper Kitimat Forest Service Road heading east.

Facilities

Closer to the mouth of the river, the city of Kitimat offers a variety of accommodations and other services. Further upstream, the **Upper Kitimat Recreation Site** offers a more rustic experience. It is found about 6 km off Highway 37 and has space for eight campers.

Kitimat River
Fish Stocking Data

Year	Species	Number	Life Stage
2008	Cutthroat Trout (Anadromous)	2,324	Smolt
2008	Chinook	1,500,000	Fry
2008	Chum	5,000,000	Fry
2008	Coho	5,000	Fry
2008	Steelhead	48,277	Smolt
2007	Cutthroat Trout (Anadromous)	13,126	Smolt

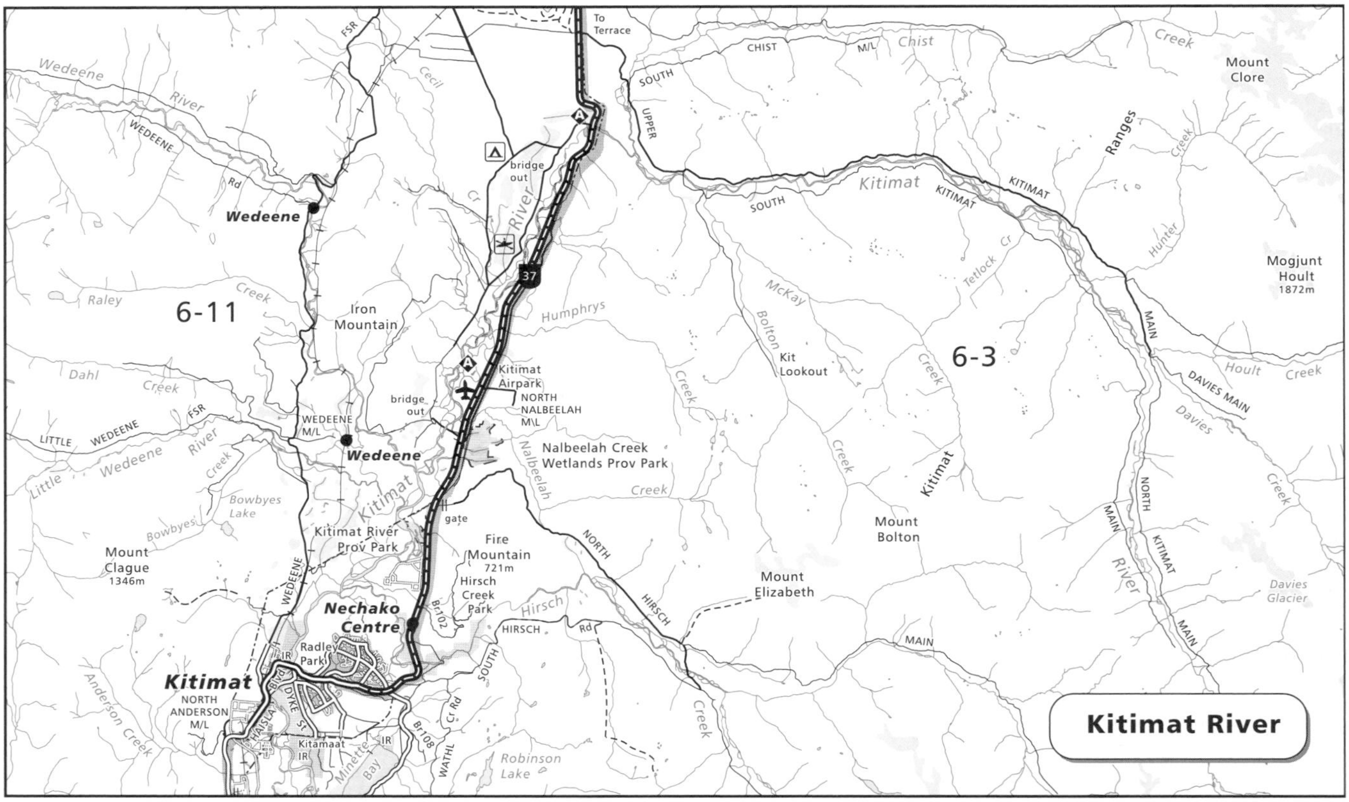

Kitimat River

Kitsumkalum Lake

Location: 26 km (16 mi) north of Terrace
Elevation: 148 m (485 ft)
Surface Area: 1,969 ha (4,867 ac)
Maximum Depth: 140 m (459 ft)
Mean Depth: 77 m (254 ft)
Way Point: 54° 45′ 49″ N, 128° 47′ 5″ W

Fishing

Surrounded by towering, snow-covered peaks, Kitsumkalum offers good fishing for cutthroat trout, Dolly Varden and the odd rainbow or whitefish. The lake is also part of the Kitsumkalum River system and every year thousands of Coho and Chinook salmon pass through the river on the way to the lake's upper tributaries. The lake is open to Chinook and Coho fishing, although not many people actually fish the lake for salmon.

After leaving the ocean, the salmon stop actively feeding. In order to catch them in a river or in a lake, you need to trigger a defensive or annoyed reaction out of the fish. This is much easier in a river, where the fish hold in pools below rapids. The moving water causes lures to flutter and jump and basically irritate the salmon into biting.

In a lake, however, it is much harder to get a lure into the fish's face and cause it to strike. It is not impossible, just more difficult.

The best place to try fishing for salmon is right at the outflow of the Kitsumkalum River and wherever a spawning creek or river flows into the lake. Salmon will often pile up at the mouths of these creeks and rivers, waiting for the water conditions to be right to continue spawning. As the fish don't strike out of hunger, your best approach is to irritate them using big, floppy spoons or large, garish marabou flies.

For the resident cutthroat and Dolly, the best fishing happens during the salmon spawn, where spawning creeks and rivers flow back into the lake. These creeks wash down thousands of salmon eggs into the lake and it is a veritable feeding frenzy. Working a single egg pattern (for fly anglers) or a hook baited with salmon eggs is by far the most productive way of fishing at these times.

Dolly Varden can also be taken on the troll, using a green or orange Flatfish or a Krocodile lure. Trolling plugs or larger lures on a downrigger with a flasher can produce big fish. Also, jigging with a bucktail and flasher in the winter or spring near a large creek mouth can be very successful.

For cutthroat, gold or silver bodied Muddler Minnow or Wool Head Sculpin are two fly patterns to try. Spincasting Kitimat lures, Panther Martin spinners or trolling Willow Leafs/Ford Fenders can also be effective. Cast around the drop off areas as the cutthroat tend to cruise near shore areas in search of baitfish and returning salmon smolts.

Facilities

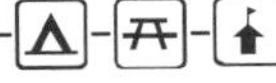

There is a good variety of camping and recreational facilities at the south end of the lake. The **Kitsumkalum Provincial Park** is a small park with a seven site user maintained campground. You can launch a cartop boat and there is a sandy beach, great for swimming. Also in the area are the popular **Hart Farm** and **Redsand Lake Recreation Sites**. Both offer good sized campgrounds, access to the lakes as well as trail systems to enjoy.

Directions

The Yellowhead Highway crosses the Kitsumkalum River 6.5 km from the bridge over the Skeena coming into Terrace from the east. There are roads on either side of the river that lead up to the lake. The Nass Forest Service Road on the west and Kalum Lake Road on the east.

Area Indicator

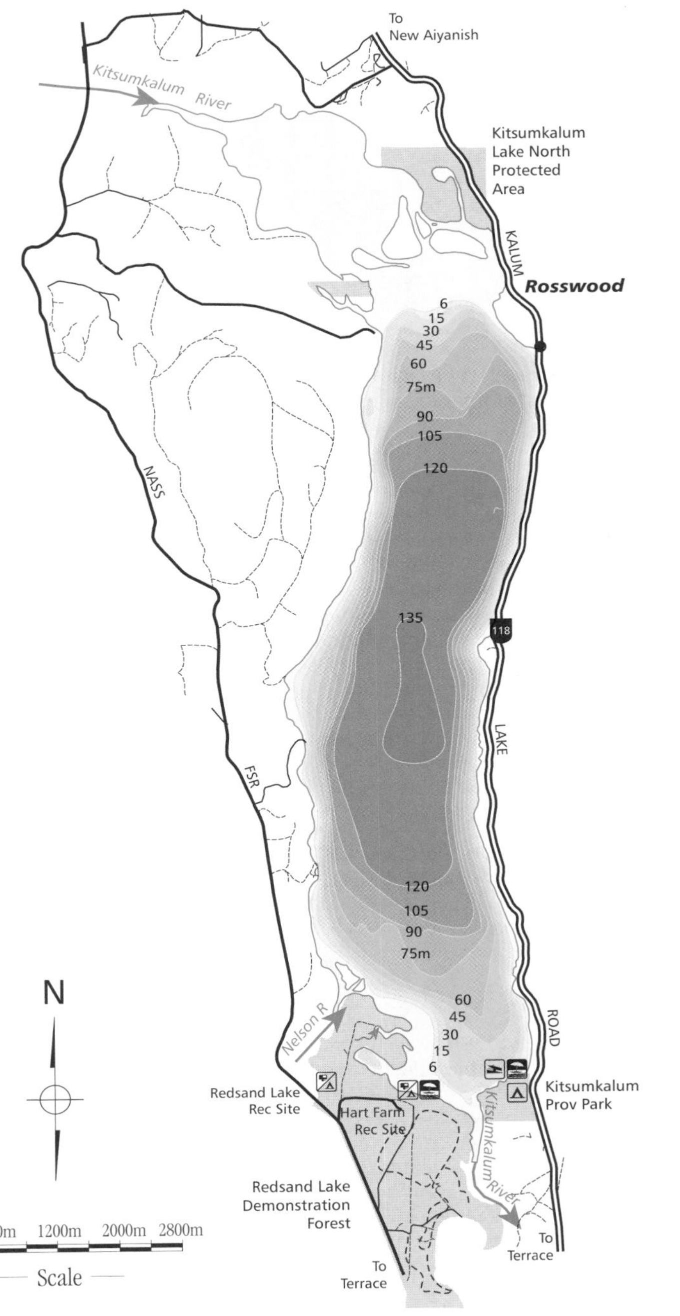

Location: 6.5 km (4 mi) west of Terrace
Stream Length: 94 km (58 mi)
Geographic: 54° 40′ 6″ N, 128° 43′ 35″ W

Kitsumkalum River

Fishing

The Kitsumkalum River is a Skeena River tributary, flowing into the Skeena just a few kilometres west of Terrace.

The Kalum (as it is usually referred to) flows out of the high country west of Kitsumkalum Lake. However this section of river is rarely fished even though it contains good runs of salmon, steelhead and native cutthroat, bull and rainbow trout. The farthest upstream most people fish is at the Nass Forest Service Road Bridge just west of the lake.

Instead, most people fish the lower section of the river from Kitsumkalum Lake to the Skeena. This section is about 25 km (15 miles). The middle stretch (about 8 km) passes through a canyon and should be left to the hardcore whitewater rafters or jet boaters if there is enough water. It is a narrow canyon with steep walls and huge boulders, but fortunately, no large waterfalls that block access to the fish, which power their way up the fast moving water.

This middle section features 27 pools, making it a great place to drift. These start at the put in with the uniquely named "Put-in Pool" and carry on right to the "Last Chance Pool" right above the canyon. Don't miss the take-out. Some of the best holes are the Kenai Run, the Lower 16K and the Horseshoe, but there are more than two dozen others to test your luck in. Unfortunately, the take-outs are located on private property so you would need permission from the landowner if you don't have a jet boat.

The river is unique in that it features four separate runs of steelhead. While other Skeena tributaries may have bigger runs or bigger fish, the Kitsumkalum has steelhead nearly year round. Of course, the best fishing here is for the late spring/fall run steelhead, which can be fished for using a dry fly waked across the surface of the water. When the water is colder, or if you aren't a dry fly angler, stick to more traditional fishing methods. Steelhead like slow presentations so the quicker the water, the bigger the lure. Drift fishing with a float suspending a ¼" pencil lead weight above a short leader of about 30–50 cm (12–20 in) with 1/0 to #4 hooks is the most common method. Popular lures include Corkys, Spin-N-Glos, Gooey Bobs and Colorado Spinners. Hot shotting is also popular.

The river also features good runs of Chinook in May and July. These fish are huge; averaging 15 kg (35 lbs) but getting up to a whopping 38.5 kg (85 lbs). The salmon are best caught by drift fishing.

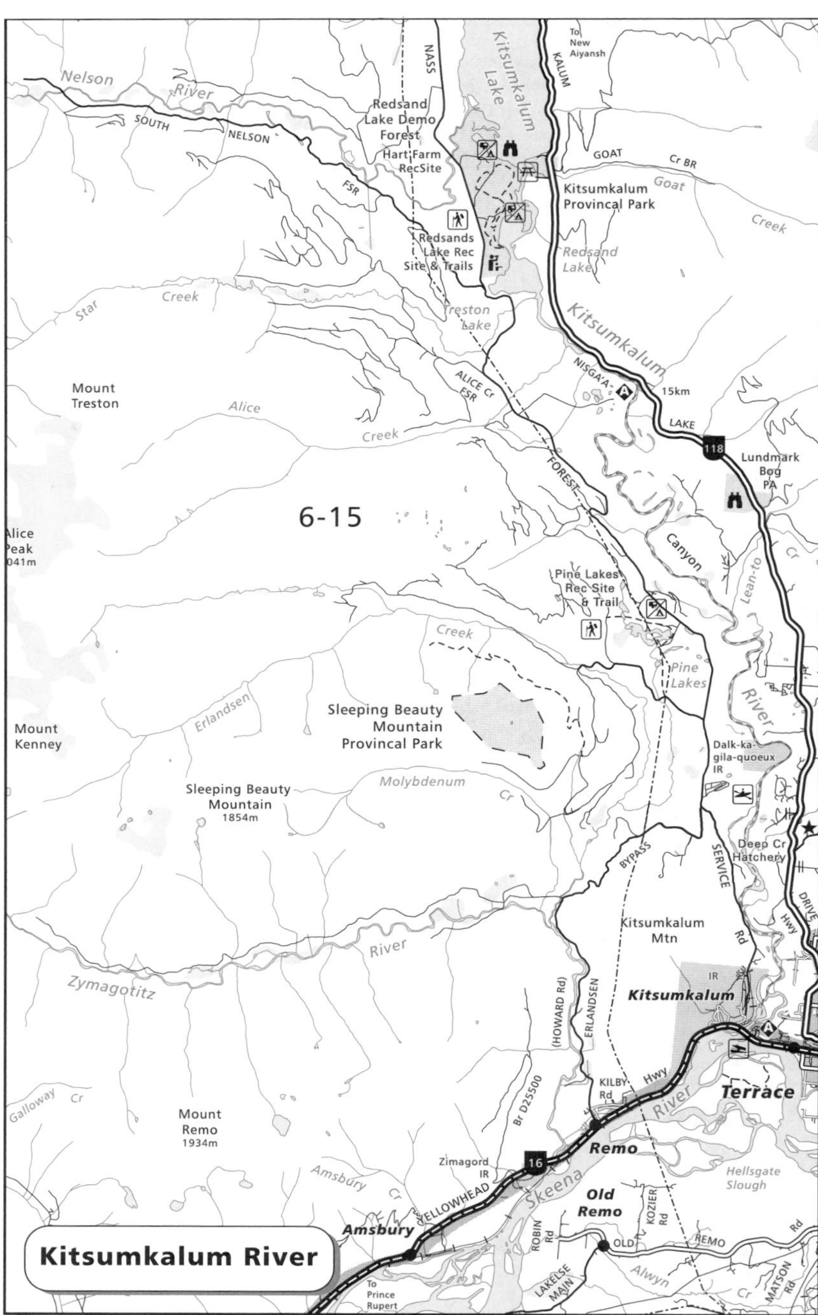

Directions

The Yellowhead Highway (Highway 16) crosses the Kitsumkalum River 6.5 km from the bridge over the Skeena coming onto Terrace from the east. There are roads on either side of the river. The Nass Forest Service Road on the west and Kalum Lake Drive on the east. However, many people jetboat up the river from the Skeena or drift down from Kitsumkalum Lake. Note that there is a rather long section of whitewater that is impassible to most drift boats and jetboats right in the middle of this section.

Facilities

The Kitsumkalum passes by Terrace, where you will find all manner of accommodations and services. If you really want to test the better middle section we recommend arranging a trip with a local guide. Those looking to camp in the area will find several alternatives on the west side off the Nass Forest Service Road. These include the **Pine Lakes, Redsands Lake** and **Hart Farm Recreation Sites.** The later two are further north and quite popular during the Chinook and steelhead seasons.

Lac des Roches

Location: 52 km (32.3 mi) east of 100 Mile House
Elevation: 1,128 m (3,701 ft)
Surface Area: 657 ha (1,622 ac)
Maximum Depth: 44 m (145 ft)
Mean Depth: 17 m (56 ft)
Way Point: 51° 28′ 24″ N, 120° 34′ 15″ W

Fishing

Lac des Roches is a destination type fishery located on the Fishing Highway. The lake is separated into two distinct bays by a narrow channel and has many small islands. It is the largest lake of the Nehalliston Group and is considered by many to be one of, if not the best fishing lakes in an area.

Although it is 9 km long, the lake appeals to both trollers and fly anglers. The Freshwater Fisheries Society of BC has been experimenting in recent time in their stocking program such that there are now several strains of rainbow in the lake including the famous Gerrard Trout, although over the last decade or so, the lake has been stocked with a mix of Blackwater, Pennask and Tunkwa strain fish. The Blackwaters are piscivorous and tend to get bigger faster by eating smaller bait fish like redside shiner, which are found in the lake, while the Pennask are known for their aerial displays and dogged determination when hooked. The rainbow average 1–1.5 kg (2-3 lbs) and have been known to top 4 kg (8 lbs).

For fly anglers, the lake offers a good spring chironomid hatch after ice-off in early May and when there is a spell of warm water. Black, brown, maroon and green are all good colours in sizes #8 to #16. By the end of May, the mayfly hatch is in full swing. Leech patterns will also work. Try a brown and black bunny leech or a Jack Shaw blood leech

The mayfly hatch is considered one of the best in the Cariboo as it extends for three to four weeks into the mid part of June. Pheasant tail nymphs, prince nymphs and small halfbacks work quite well. For sedges, the Tom Thumb, Nations green or grey body sedge and the Mikulak sedge are best. Towards the middle of June, the damselfly hatch is very good.

By summer, the fishing at Lac des Roches slows off significantly despite the fact it is still busy on the water. Try focusing around the deeper water and along the steep drop offs. By fall, the fishing heats up again. A leech pattern (black or burgundy) and a shrimp pattern can be particularly effective. Damsel and dragonfly nymphs, such as halfbacks and Carey Specials, also work well.

When there is no hatch, shrimp are good patterns to use. Back swimmers, water boatman and Wooly Buggers and Wooly Worms in black, brown and maroon are also good all season choices.

Trollers can do well with a lake troll (Willow Leaf and worm), Flatfish or other trout lure worked along the shoreline. Stick just offshore so you can see the shallow water on one side of your boat.

Area Indicator

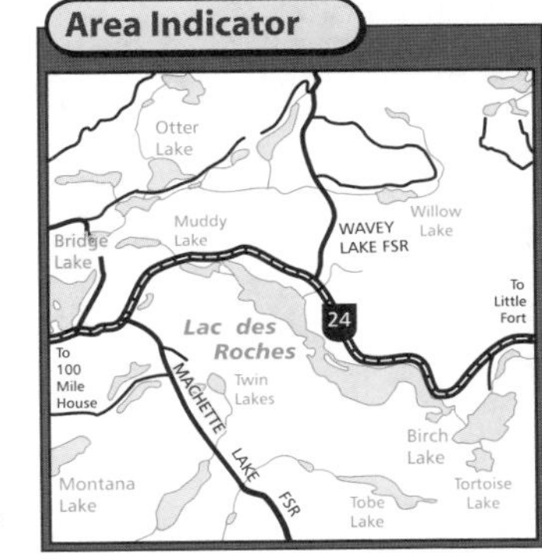

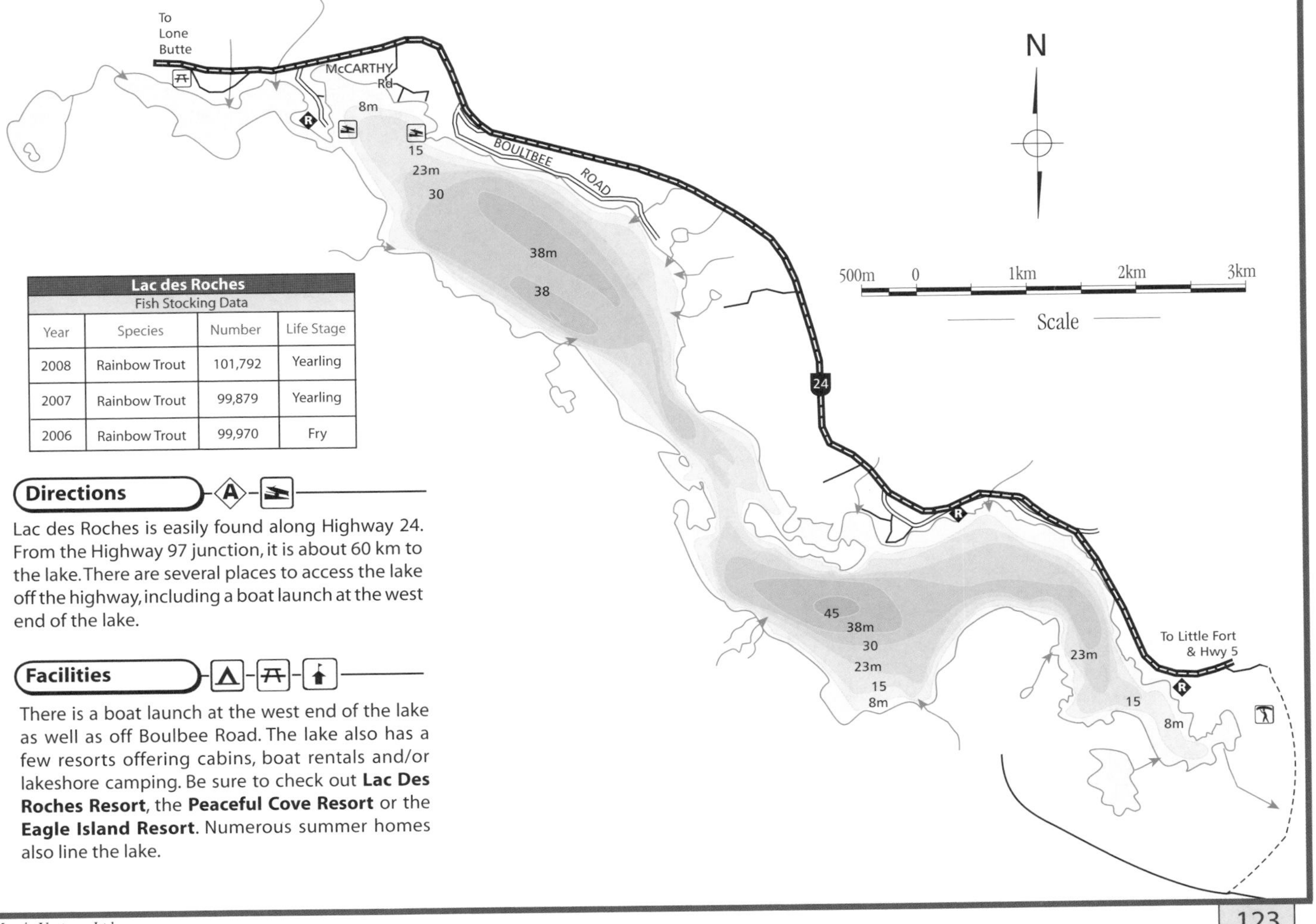

To Lone Butte
McCARTHY RD
BOULTBEE ROAD
8m
15
23m
30
38m
38
N
500m 0 1km 2km 3km
Scale
24
45
38m
30
23m
15
8m
23m
15
8m
To Little Fort & Hwy 5

Lac des Roches Fish Stocking Data			
Year	Species	Number	Life Stage
2008	Rainbow Trout	101,792	Yearling
2007	Rainbow Trout	99,879	Yearling
2006	Rainbow Trout	99,970	Fry

Directions

Lac des Roches is easily found along Highway 24. From the Highway 97 junction, it is about 60 km to the lake. There are several places to access the lake off the highway, including a boat launch at the west end of the lake.

Facilities

There is a boat launch at the west end of the lake as well as off Boulbee Road. The lake also has a few resorts offering cabins, boat rentals and/or lakeshore camping. Be sure to check out **Lac Des Roches Resort**, the **Peaceful Cove Resort** or the **Eagle Island Resort**. Numerous summer homes also line the lake.

Location: 25 km (15.5 mi) northwest of 100 Mile House
Elevation: 809 m (2,654 ft)
Surface Area: 1,807 ha (4,465 ac)
Maximum Depth: 31 m (100 ft)
Mean Depth: 15 m (48 ft)
Way Point: 51° 49′ 32″ N, 121° 33′ 21″ W

Lac la Hache

Area Indicator

Fishing

Lac La Hache is a 20 km (12 mile) long lake found right next to the Cariboo Highway. The lake is lined with private residences on the eastern shoreline while the western shoreline is forest covered. Although rainbow and kokanee are the main sportfish in the lake, there are also burbot, lake trout and mountain whitefish.

The preferred method of fishing here is trolling. Kokanee are the main focus with most anglers using a Willow Leaf, Wedding Band and worm trolled slowly near the surface.

Although usually small, there are several 40 cm (16 in) kokanee caught each year. For added excitement, anglers have taken to spincast or even fly fish for them. While kokanee grow big by eating zooplankton, once they hit a certain size, they start feeding on chironomids, dragonfly and damselfly nymphs. They even like small leeches.

Kokanee feeding patterns are remarkably like rainbow trout and you will find that you will catch a mixture of both. The biggest difference is that kokanee are much more sensitive to the temperature of water and prefer to spend their time in a narrow band of water, although they will dart into shallower (or deeper) water to feed. Kokanee are known for their soft mouths and whether trolling, spincasting or fly-fishing, it is advisable to attach some form of shock absorber, to prevent the hook from tearing through the soft flesh.

The rainbow, which grow to 2 kg (4 lbs), are best caught trolling along the drop off area or off one of the islands. For the bigger lake trout, stick to the deeper water trolling a larger spoon or a black or silver T50 Flatfish. Although they do grow to 14 kg (30 lbs), do note that they are a slow growing species and the more fish that are caught and kept the fewer (big) fish there will be. While the lake is not regulated single barbless, we advocate that you voluntarily use single barbless hooks to help protect these big, beautiful fish.

Ice fishing can be very good, especially for kokanee and burbot. Jigging with bait, the smellier the better for burbot that get to 9 kg (20 lbs), can be quite effective.

Directions

Lac La Hache is easily found next to the Cariboo Highway (Highway 97) northwest of 100 Mile House. The tiny village of Lac La Hache is at the southeast corner of the lake, while resorts and a provincial park are found further along the highway.

Facilities

Being a popular recreational destination, there is no shortage of places to stay at or around the lake. **Lac La Hache Provincial Park** has 83 campsites, a picnic and beach area as well as a boat launch. There are also a host of resorts and other commercial accommodations. These include the **Fir Crest Resort**, the **Lazy 'R' Campsite**, the **Kokanee Bay Motel & Trailer Court** and the **Crystal Springs Resort**. Be sure to contact these establishments for details on there many services. The village of Lac La Hache also has stores and restaurants to check out.

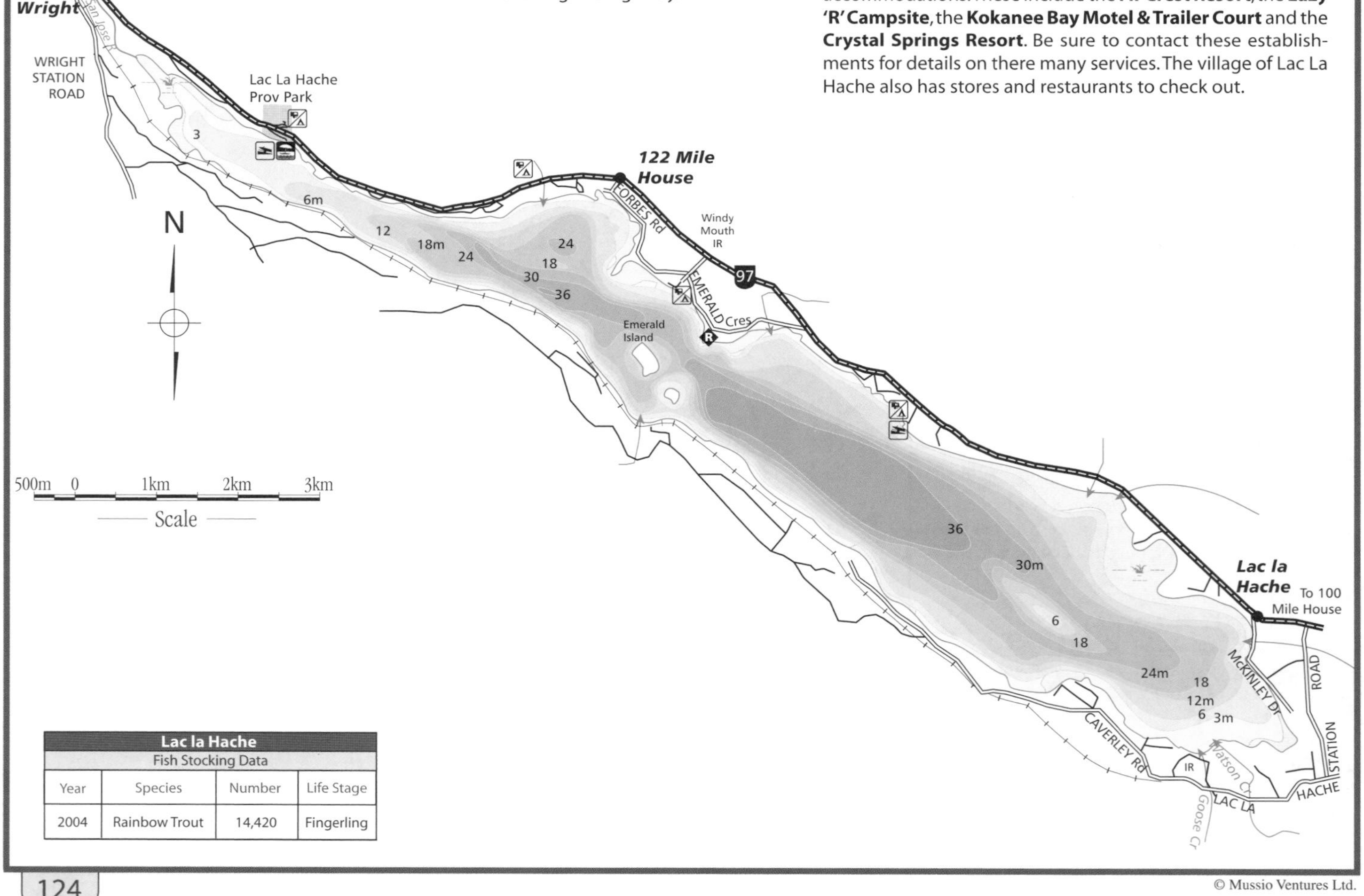

Lac la Hache Fish Stocking Data			
Year	Species	Number	Life Stage
2004	Rainbow Trout	14,420	Fingerling

Lakelse Lake

Location: 18.5 km (11.5 miles) south of Terrace
Elevation: 76 m (249 ft)
Surface Area: 1,460 ha (3,608 ac)
Maximum Depth: 32 m (104 ft)
Mean Depth: 8.5 m (28 ft)
Way Point: 54° 22′ 48″ N, 128° 33′ 37″ W

Fishing

Lakelse Lake is a beautiful lake that is surrounded by mountains to the south of Terrace. It is a popular recreation lake with a nice park and a number of cabins ringing the lake.

The lake is about 8 km (5 miles) long and is fed by several creeks that flow out of the mountains. This causes the lake to be flushed approximately five times a year.

Such a high flushing rate means that the lake doesn't retain a lot of nutrients and the fish here don't grow all that fast. The primary fish species in the lake is cutthroat trout, which aren't exactly known for their fast growth rates. The lake also holds plenty of whitefish.

Much of the fishing in the lake centres around the sockeye return. Not so much for the sockeye themselves (as you are not allowed to fish for salmon in the lake), but for the cutthroat that feed on the sockeye fry and on their eggs. However, the sockeye stocks have dropped over 90% in the last 12 years, meaning that there aren't as many sockeye eggs or sockeye fry and the cutthroat action isn't quite as fast and furious as it once was.

But the fishing is still pretty good for cutthroat that average about 35 cm (14 in). In July and August, the sockeye enter the system and the fishing should be focused on the mouth of feeder creeks into the river, especially Williams Creek. Fishing an egg pattern or a hook baited with a single egg are the methods of choice.

In spring, the fry begin their migration back to the ocean and once again, you will find cutthroat stacking up around river mouths and chasing returning salmon along the edge of drop offs around the lake and down to the Lakelse River.

The south end of the lake is quite marshy, with lots of weeds. Fly anglers should focus their energies down at this end of the lake. Nymphs can produce well, as can dry-fly patterns such as caddisflies and mayflies.

There are a number of weed beds around the lake, including one about 100 metres from the Furlong Bay Campground. It easy enough to get out in a float tube or canoe and work the area around this weedy area.

There are a couple other places easily accessible in the park. One is at the inflow of William's Creek. However, people fishing from shore should note that the moving water tends to liquefy the sandy bottom here, creating an area of quicksand. There is another smaller creek beside the picnic site, which can also be fished from shore and people have had good luck fishing around the boat launch.

But really, this is a lake that is best fished from a boat. One of the best places to fish is Mailbox Point, on the west shore of the lake towards the south end of the lake. Trolling cutthroat lures and spinners or a lake troll tipped with bait can often entice a strike or two.

Directions

Lakelse Lake is just south of Terrace. Follow Highway 37 south from the Yellowhead towards Kitimat for about 18.5 km to the turnoff to the provincial park.

Facilities

There are 158 campsites in the Furlong Bay Campsite in **Lakelse Lake Provincial Park**. There is also a large, paved boat launch on the lake, a beach, showers and a sani-dump.

Area Indicator

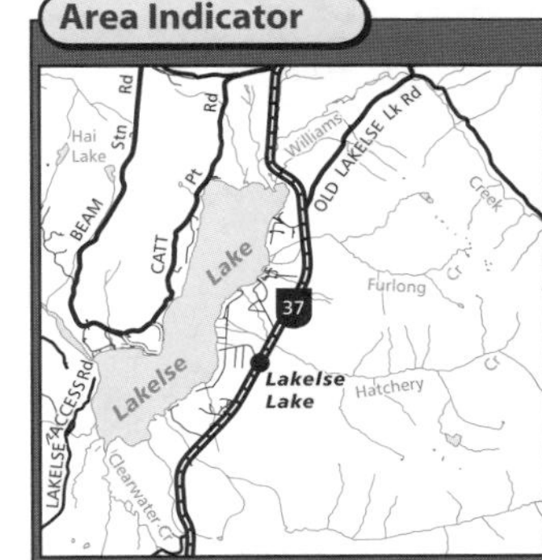

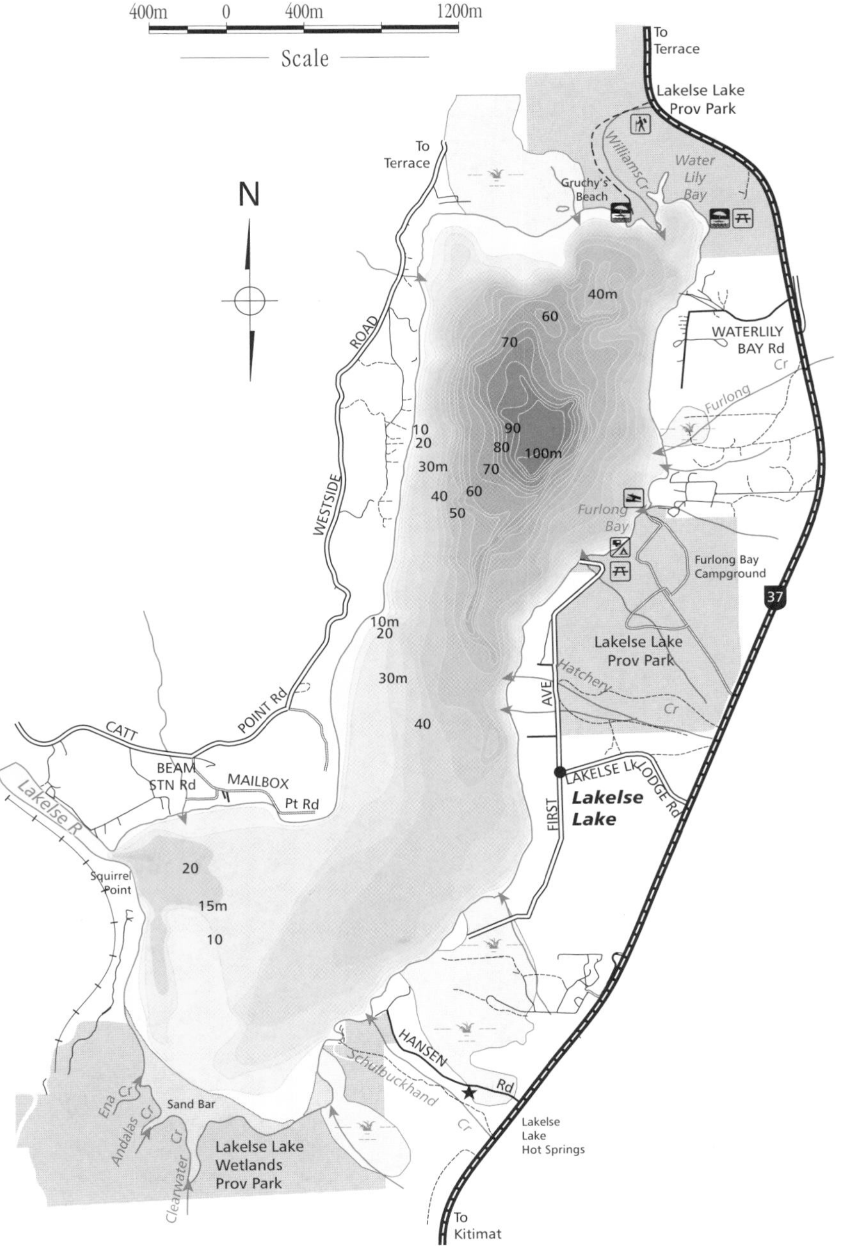

Location: 29 km (18 mi) southeast of 100 Mile House
Elevation: 1,068 m (3,504 ft)
Surface Area: 125 ha (309 ac)
Maximum Depth: 4 m (13 ft)
Mean Depth: 1 m (3.3 ft)
Way Point: 51° 26′ 8″ N, 121° 3′ 20″ W

www.backroadmapbooks.com

Little Green Lake

Area Indicator

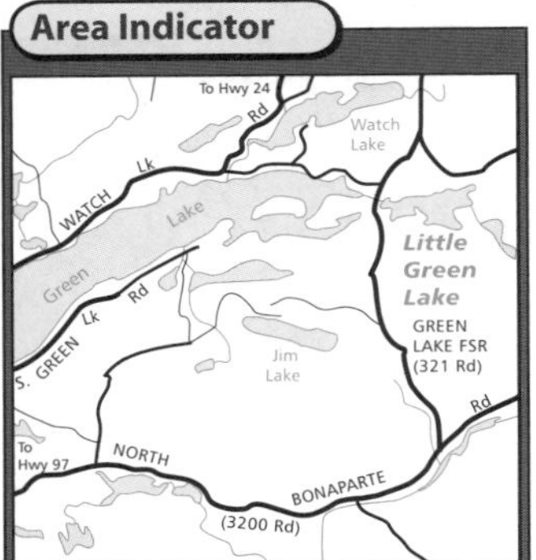

Fishing

Little Green Lake is a small lake just east of Green Lake and southeast of Watch Lake.

This smaller lake contains good numbers of rainbow as the lake is stocked with 2,000 rainbow each year. The lake does not receive the same fishing pressure as nearby Green Lake or Watch Lake so you may want to try this lake to get away from the crowds in the spring or fall.

The lake is best fished in late May to the end of June. During that time, there are some good insect hatches like the chironomid and mayfly hatches. The lake is essentially one big shoal that is ideal for insect rearing. This makes it a great fly-fishing destination. Try at the outflow creek leading to Green Lake as the fish migrate between the two lakes. Another option is to try the hole at the east end of the lake.

A bloodworm or chironomid pattern is usually quite effective and while it isn't as flashy as top water fishing, it is more rewarding, at least so say the true converts, who usually have an entire box full of chironomid patterns. Trout are usually quite particular about their chironomids. If you don't have the right colour and the right size during a hatch, it's possible to get completely skunked. Having a dip net to check the colour and size of the hatch, or a throat pump to check what the fish are eating (assuming you can catch one) is a good idea.

Chironomid fishing is a study in patience. The most popular method is to cast the pattern out on a full sink line with a strike indicator set so that the chironomid is hanging just a few feet off the bottom, usually right next to a drop off or some sort of structure.

Later in spring, you should move to mayflies, caddisflies or dragon and damselfly nymphs. Although there is some great top water fishing using Tom Thumbs or other imitation patterns, you will find the fishing is usually subsurface.

In the summer, the water in the lake is soupy warm and so the fish are not very active. Thus, fishing is very slow at that time of year. The shallow nature of the lake also means winterkill is a real problem. It does not affect the fishing as the lake is stocked and the trout also migrate in, but it does affect the average fish size.

Directions

The lake is accessed from Highway 97 at 70 Mile House. Turn east and follow the 70 Mile/Green Lake Road to the North Green Lake Road. Follow this road along the north shore of the bigger lake. Avoid the temptation to follow the Watch Lake Road and continue east. Eventually the road turns into the Green Lake Forest Service Road (321 Rd), which soon abuts Little Green Lake. Alternatively, from Highway 24, follow Watch Lake Road south to where it meets the North Green Lake Road. Turn left (east) and follow this road until it joins the Green Lake Forest Road.

Facilities

There are no developed facilities at the lake, although it is possible to launch a small boat. However, Little Green Lake is next to Green Lake, where you will find Green Lake Provincial Park and its trio of campsites at Arrowhead, Emerald Bay and Sunset View. There is space for 121 camping groups between the three sites.

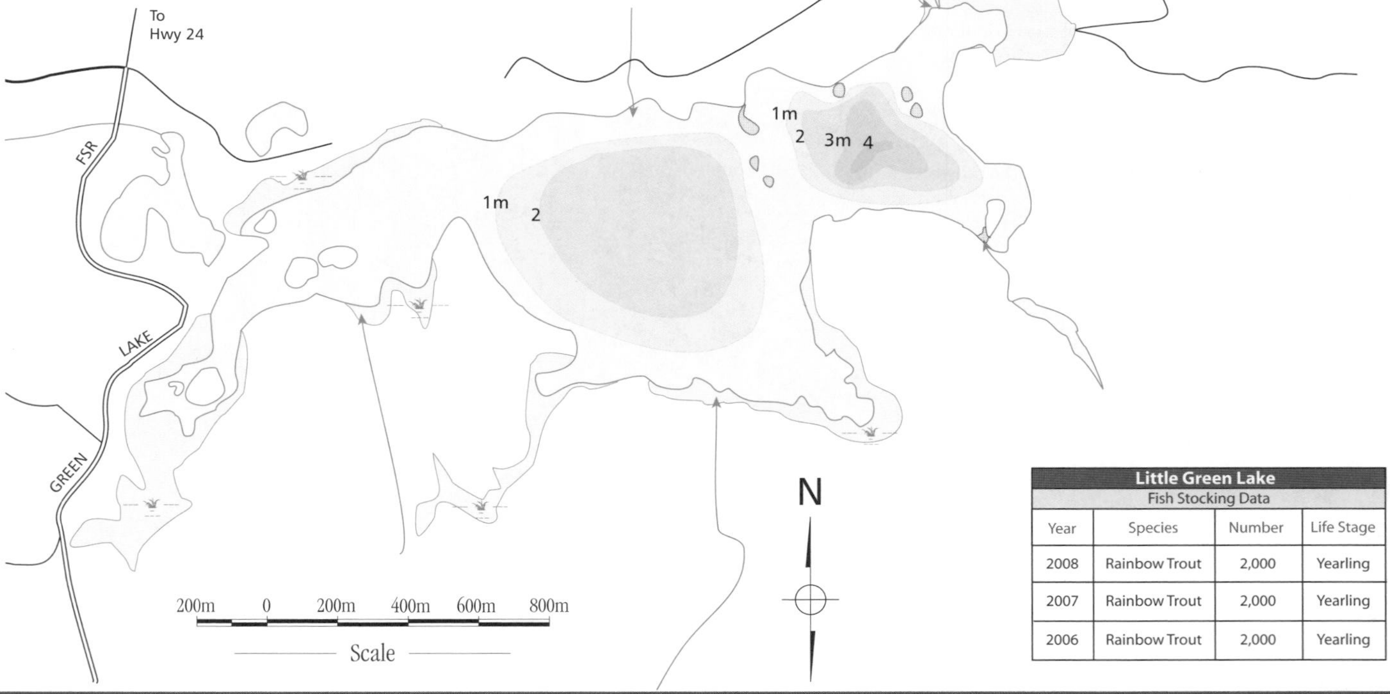

Little Green Lake			
Fish Stocking Data			
Year	Species	Number	Life Stage
2008	Rainbow Trout	2,000	Yearling
2007	Rainbow Trout	2,000	Yearling
2006	Rainbow Trout	2,000	Yearling

Lorin (Airplane) Lake

Location: 48 km (30 mi) northeast of 100 Mile House
Elevation: 1,278 m (4,193 ft)
Surface Area: 277 ha (684.5 ac)
Maximum Depth: 36 m (118 ft)
Mean Depth: 14 m (46 ft)
Way Point: 51° 44′ 35″ N, 120° 37′ 19″ W

Fishing

Lorin Lake is situated to the south of Canim Lake and north of Bridge Lake. The lake was barren until the early 1980s, when the lake was first stocked with 10,000 rainbow trout. Since that time, the lake has been stocked nearly every year. For the last decade or so, the stocking has settled on 15,000 Pennask strain rainbow trout every year. Pennask trout are noted for the hard fighting nature and aerial acrobatics as they leap to shake the hook.

The deep lake is found at a slightly higher elevation than the average lake in this book, thus it opens up a bit later in May. It is also deep enough to maintain a decent fishery throughout the open water season. The lake offers good fishing for rainbow that average between 0.5–1 kg (1.5–2 lbs).

The lake is usually fished on the troll using a Willow Leaf or other lake troll. However, there are several bays and islands providing shelter from the prevailing winds so belly boating and casting a fly or small spinner is possible. The lake has a large, inviting island in the middle where spincasters and fly anglers can do well. The deepest water is north of the island. A few sunken islands also provide nice areas to work.

Fly anglers should work the near shore areas using a damselfly or dragonfly nymph, shrimp pattern or leech pattern. Spincasters will find the usual trout lures, such as a Mepps, Panther Martin or Gibbs spinner, cast out using the count down method to work different depths around the drop off are promising options. Vertical jigging with spoons or jigs using flavoured bait, such as one of the Berkley Powerbaits, will also work well.

The lake is closed to ice fishing.

Facilities

The **Lorin Lake Recreation Site** is found on an opening on the northeast shore of the lake. There is space for about 10 campers and is quite well suited for larger vehicles including RVs and trailers. There is also a boat launch suitable for small trailered boats. It is perhaps not the most scenic of sites, as it is set in an old mill site near an auto wrecker's yard, but it does provide good access to the lake.

Please note that most of the surrounding shoreline of the lake is private property.

Directions

From 100 Mile House, head a short distance north on Highway 97 and turn east on the Canim Lake Road. Follow that road to the southern shores of Canim Lake, where the Canim Lake South Road (8100 Road) continues along the shores of the big lake. This road leads past a few resorts, before reaching the tiny hamlet of Mahood Falls. At that point, head south on the Bowers Lake Forest Service Road (8200 Road). About 9 km down this road, look for the access road leading southwest to Lorin Lake. If you pass tiny Wolf Lake you have gone too far.

The lake is also accessible from the south off the Mahood Lake/Bowers Lake Roads. Regardless of which direction you choose, a copy of the Backroad Mapbook for the *Cariboo Chilcotin Coast* and a GPS is recommended. During wet weather, a 4wd vehicle is also a good idea.

Area Indicator

Lorin (Airplane) Lake			
Fish Stocking Data			
Year	Species	Number	Life Stage
2008	Rainbow Trout	15,000	Fry
2007	Rainbow Trout	15,000	Fry
2006	Rainbow Trout	15,000	Fall Fry

N

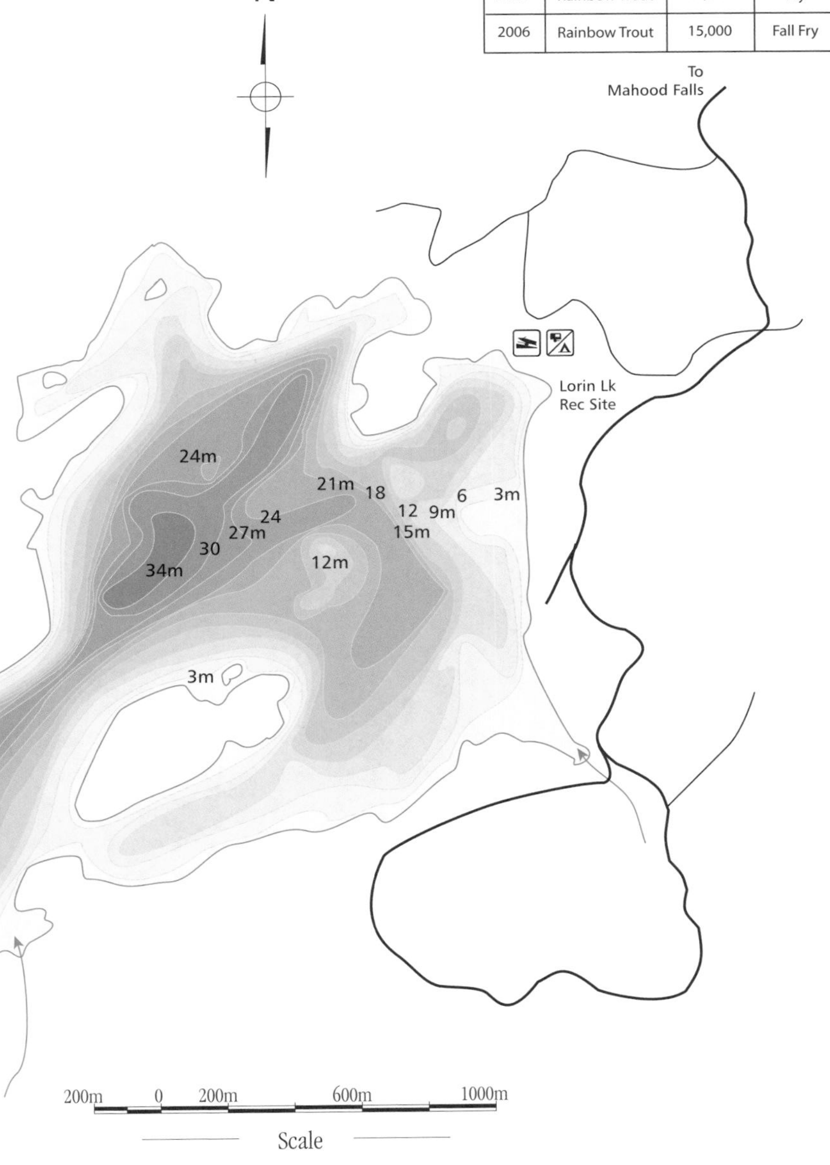

Location: 34 km (21 miles) southeast of Houston
Elevation: 1,291 m (4,235 ft)
Surface Area: 16 ha (40 ac)
Maximum Depth: 9.4 m (31 ft)
Mean Depth: 2.9 m (9.5 ft)
Way Point: 54° 12′ 15.1″ N, 126° 18′ 3.4″ W

Lu Lake

Area Indicator

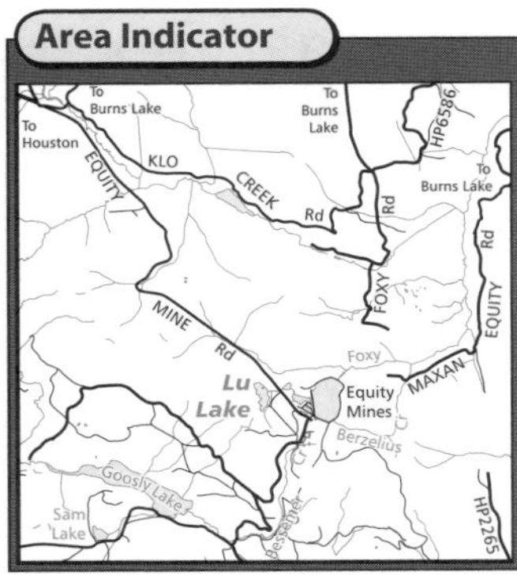

Directions

Lu Lake is located 34 km southeast of Houston on Equity Mines Road. If you reach the mine site you have gone too far.

Lu Lake			
Fish Stocking Data			
Year	Species	Number	Life Stage
2008	Rainbow Trout	2,000	Yearling
2006	Rainbow Trout	2,000	Yearling
2004	Rainbow Trout	2,000	Yearling

Fishing

An easy drive south of Houston on the Equity Mines Road brings you to the productive, rainbow trout filled waters of Lu Lake. A grass border encircles the lake, which is swampy in a few spots, but generally provides good access for those casting lines from the shore.

The launch area is on the northeast side of the lake and directly in front is the deepest part of the lake. The southern half of Lu is quite shallow, less than 3 metres (10 feet) deep. Three tributary creeks empty into the deeper, north half of the lake, bringing cooler waters and feed.

These can often be productive areas. Lu Lake is stocked every second year with 2,000 yearling rainbow trout by the Freshwater Fisheries Society of BC. Brook trout are also present, but in the future only rainbow will be stocked.

Trolling along the drop off is a productive fishing method on the lake. Follow the contours so you can see bottom on one side of the boat only. As you make the gentle turns the inside lure/fly drops and the outside lure/fly speeds up. This way you can vary the depths you are trolling. Also try shutting off the motor to allow your offering to drop to the depths before kicking it into gear again. This method can be used with trolls and lures, as well as flies.

The majority of a trout's diet consists of chironomids, caddis, mayflies, leeches, dragons, damsels, scuds and water boatman. Artificial flies imitate these insects best and can be fished with light spinning gear as well as fly gear. A little weight will get the fly to the right depth and a torpedo bobber with a fly can effectively work the surface. Use as light a line as possible to do the job. A 4 to 6 lb test line is plenty strong.

Check for activity at the mouths of the creeks. Casting and retrieving lures such as; Mepps, Panther Martin and Krocodiles is also a proven method when using spinning or spincasting gear.

Fly-fishers can try the following tips on choosing flies and how to fish them. Dragon and damsel nymphs should be retrieved with a strip strip and pause method. Freshwater shrimp or scuds look spastic in the water, so make your retrieve erratic with strips, pauses and twitches of the rod tip. Mayflies swim to the surface with vigour, so a steady hand- twist retrieve is favoured. Most chironomids are fished with a "heave and leave" or an agonizingly slow hand-twist retrieve. Try to match your retrieve to the insect's natural movement pattern.

Easy access also makes Lu Lake a popular ice-fishing destination. Powerbait, maggots or mealworms, krill or shrimp fished in 1.5–3 metres (5–10 feet) are the most proven method. The mouths of the creeks are always a good place to start as fish are attracted to these areas with higher levels of oxygen. As always, be careful of thin ice around the edges of the lake.

Facilities

There is a launch area on the northeast side of the lake, but no other facilities.

Marmot Lake

Location: 93 km (57.7 mi) west of Quesnel
Elevation: 840 m (2,756 ft)
Surface Area: 54 ha (133 ac)
Maximum Depth: 16 m (52 ft)
Mean Depth: 8.5 m (28 ft)
Way Point: 52° 55′ 25.0″ N, 123° 34′ 0.2″ W

Fishing

Found about an hour west of Quesnel, Marmot Lake is one of those lakes. You know the ones. The ones that you can fish for a weekend and come up with nothing and then, just as you're about to pack it in, a gargantuan trout hits your presentation like a freight train and puts up one of the biggest fight of your life. The average catch is around 1 kg (2 lbs), but it isn't unusual to pull out a 3 kg (6 lb) trout or more.

The lake sits on a large plateau dominated by pine forests interspersed with spruce. The lake is not very big, but has lots of food for the fish. It is high enough for the fishing to remain steady althrough the summer. Just don't get there too early in the spring as the ice may not be off until a little later in the year.

While trolling is a good method for taking these solid trout, fly-fishing is also productive. During the wintertime, Marmot Lake is a popular ice fishing lake for residents. Summertime is the least productive times of year because of the warm water as fish seek the comfort of deeper waters.

Although trolling a Willow Leaf and worm is the most popular method, attaching a Wedding Band will also elicit strikes. Hot Shot and Flatfish in green or black are also consistent on Marmot Lake.

Spincasting is productive, but a watercraft is almost essential to cover the entire lake. Use a Mepps black Aglia, green or maroon Rooster Tail, green, gold or silver Blue Fox Vibrax spinner or green Len Thompson spoon.

In the spring, fly fishers take fish with leeches, dragonflies, Careys or damselflies. Any shade of green usually works. Okay, that's a bit of an overstatement. Olive tends to work well, too. As the water warms, go for Tom Thumb patterns to tempt rising trout. The lake has lots of insects. Unfortunately for the ill prepared, most of them are mosquitoes. Bug juice is good, a mosquito jacket or hat is better.

A favourite bait for ice fishers is krill on a bare hook fished with a bobber to suspend the bait in the feeding zone. Various fluorescent jigs tipped with a piece of worm or shrimp will also get strikes.

Facilities

The Nazko Community Association has developed a campsite just off the road, along the north end of the lake. It has 37 gravel sites that are suitable for RVs and a paved boat launch for trailered boats. There is also a large picnic area, place to swim and a gravel beach that makes it ideal for families or large groups. There is a fee to camp or a launch a boat here.

Other Options

The **Nazko River** is a lazy river that flows north into and out of the lake. The river is best fished after spring run-off in late spring. Wild rainbow, whitefish and the odd bull trout to 5 kg (10 lbs) entice anglers to test their luck.

Directions

From Quesnel, turn west off of Highway 97 on Anderson Drive, cross the Fraser River and immediately turn right on the Bouchie Lake/Nazko Road (Blackwater Road). Drive north until you reach the junction of the Nazko Road (3.5 km) and turn west (left). Follow this paved road for 90 km to Marmot Lake.

Marmot Lake			
Fish Stocking Data			
Year	Species	Number	Life Stage
2008	Rainbow Trout	10,000	Fry
2007	Rainbow Trout	10,000	Fry
2006	Rainbow Trout	10,000	Fall Fry

Area Indicator

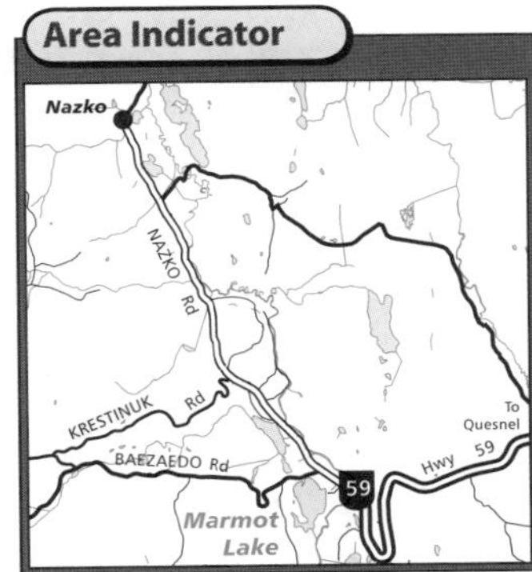

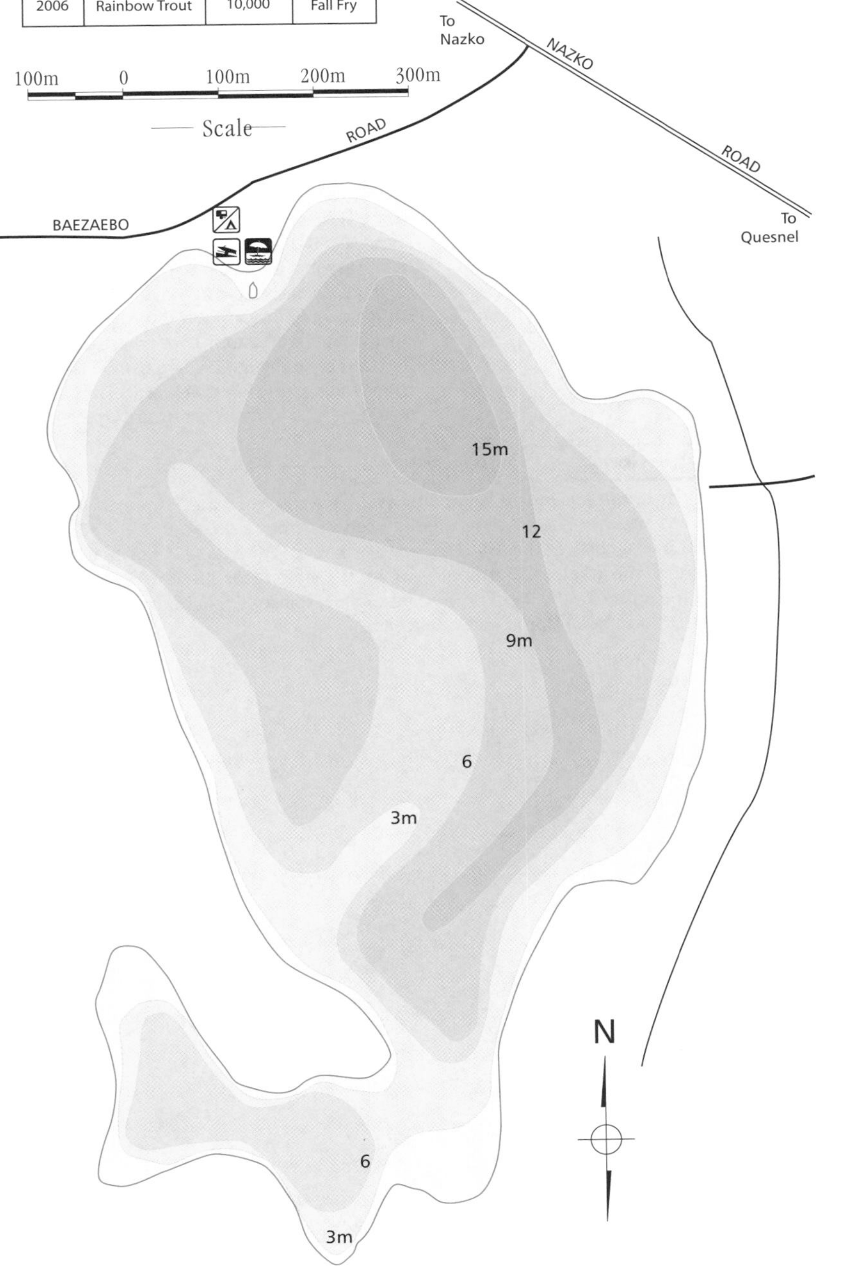

Location: 19 km (11.5 miles) north of Atlin

McDonalds Lake

Upper McDonald Lake

Elevation: 937 m (3,073 ft)
Surface Area: 124.5 ha (307.6 ac)
Maximum Depth: 22.6 m (74 ft)
Mean Depth: 8.1 m (26.5 ft)
Way Point: 59° 43′ 9″ N, 133° 34′ 35″ W

Lower McDonald Lake

Elevation: 932 m (3,058 ft)
Surface Area: 47 ha (116 ac)
Maximum Depth: 8.2 m (27 ft)
Mean Depth: 2.1 m (6.9 ft)
Waypoint: 59° 42′ 11″ N, 133° 36′ 24″ W

Area Indicator

Fishing

There are two lakes that share the name McDonald found 19 km north of town off the Atlin Highway. Lake trout and burbot are the two main species found in the system. The other two species are whitefish and Arctic grayling, which aren't usually found in the body of the lakes, but are present around the inflow and outflow of Fourth of July Creek.

The lower lake is the first lake you will come across, but most people give the lake a pass. Access is difficult, with willows crowding in around the lake. Fishing here is…well, we're not sure, because we couldn't find anyone who actually fished the lake. It should basically hold the same species as Upper McDonald since it is connected to that lake by Fourth of July Creek. However, the smaller lake is also a lot shallower, which means that the lake trout and burbot are more than likely not found in this lake. The odd whitefish and Arctic grayling may however, be found roaming the lake on occasion.

In small lakes like the McDonalds, lake trout do not get as big as they do in larger lakes like nearby Atlin Lake. While you can pull out fish to 20 kg (40 lbs) in the big lake, here you're hard pressed to find them past 4.5 kg (10 lbs). The largest fish we've heard about coming out of here was 6 kg (13 lb) laker. Usually, though, they are in the 1–2 kg (2–4 lb) range.

Lake trout are usually found around the 10–20 m (30–70 foot) mark. Locals prefer to troll for lakers using bigger spoons like a Daredevil or Williams. While body baits like a large Flatfish will work well, they have too many hooks, often snagging the fish multiple times and making it very difficult to catch and release the fish safely.

Arctic grayling are much smaller and finding one to even 0.5 kg (1 lb) is a catch indeed. The average sized catch is about half that. But what they lack in size, they more than make up for in beauty and ferocity. They are hard fighting fish that are best found at the north end of the lake, where Fourth of July Creek flows into the lake. You will want a small boat or a float tube to get there, as fishing from shore is extremely difficult. Grayling can be taken on very small spoons, like a little Panther Martin. They also fish very well on a variety of topwater and subsurface flies.

Directions

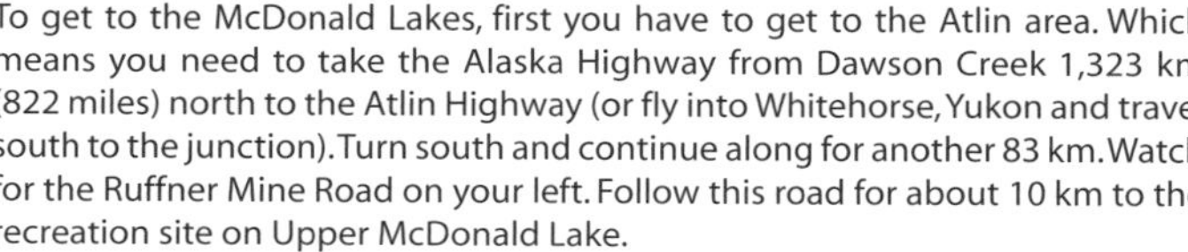

To get to the McDonald Lakes, first you have to get to the Atlin area. Which means you need to take the Alaska Highway from Dawson Creek 1,323 km (822 miles) north to the Atlin Highway (or fly into Whitehorse, Yukon and travel south to the junction). Turn south and continue along for another 83 km. Watch for the Ruffner Mine Road on your left. Follow this road for about 10 km to the recreation site on Upper McDonald Lake.

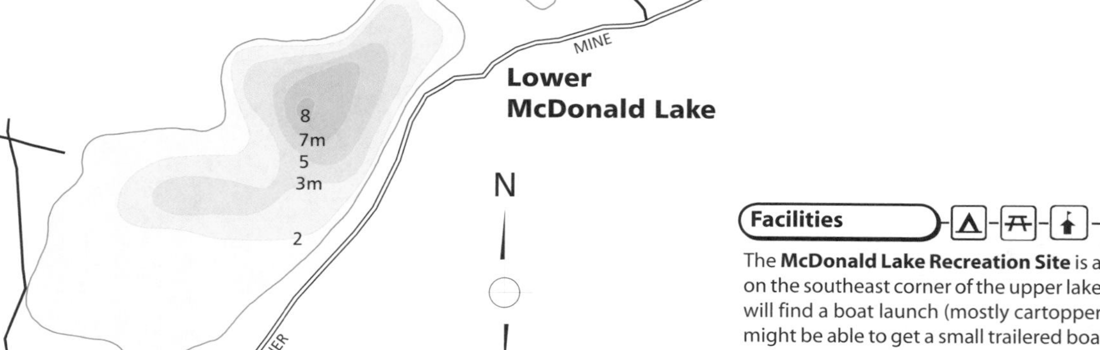

Facilities

The **McDonald Lake Recreation Site** is a small site on the southeast corner of the upper lake. Here you will find a boat launch (mostly cartoppers, but you might be able to get a small trailered boat onto the lake) and space for maybe four camping groups. The site is rarely used, as most visitors to Atlin chose to stay at a hotel or bed and breakfast in town.

McIntyre Lake

Location: 30 km (18.6 mi) southwest of Williams Lake
Elevation: 921 m (3,021 ft)
Surface Area: 17.7 ha (43.7 ac)
Maximum Depth: 5.5 m (18 ft)
Mean Depth: 2.9 m (9.5 ft)
Way Point: 51° 58′ 25.3″ N, 122° 20′ 53.6″

Fishing

McIntyre Lake is a small, shallow, but highly productive lake found on a low plateau just above the Fraser River. Because it is a low elevation lake, it is one of the earlier fishing lakes to become ice-free in mid-April and for the next few months it is an extremely popular trout fishing destination.

The lake is set in a thick forest and there are only a couple of places around the shallow, shoreline that an angler could theoretically cast from. But the shallow waters are weedy and is nearly impossible to cast from shore without fouling your hook. Even if you could get out to the where the fish are, it probably isn't worth the effort except right after ice off, before the weeds start to grow. While there are no motor restrictions on the lake, its small size makes it easier to navigate with oars or an electric motor.

The lake is best suited to fly-fishing, or trolling with a fly or other light tackle (not lake trolls). The lake is stocked, although not heavily, with brook trout and rainbow trout, generally more of the former than the latter. Both species grow fast because of its abundant aquatic vegetation, which is teeming with dragonflies, mayflies, damselflies, caddisflies, scuds and leeches. A quick take is not uncommon when presenting the proper pattern to feeding fish.

McIntyre Lake is a put and take lake, as it has a tendency to both winterkill and even summerkill. Before heading out, check to see if there has been any recent die-offs (or stockings) with a local sporting goods store in Williams Lake.

Locating fish in McIntyre is difficult because the fish are constantly cruising the shallows in search of a meal. When the sun is high or the water is warm, these fish hold up in the deep trough down the centre of the lake. Casting or trolling black leeches,

dragonflies, damselflies or mayflies with a floating or sinking line will take most fish. A green Carey Special is also a popular fly here.

Lures of choice include an F-4 or F-5 Flatfish, size 70 Hotshot in black, frog or perch, or a Mepps Black Fury or silver Aglia.

Ice anglers do well using maggots on a jig for the brook trout. A piece of worm, krill or salmon egg works well for the rainbow. Be sure to visit this lake earlier in the ice fishing season. Not only are the rainbow more active then, but also the shallow nature of the lake means oxygen levels are depleted near the end of the year and the fish are often sluggish.

McIntyre Lake
Fish Stocking Data

Year	Species	Number	Life Stage
2008	Rainbow Trout	1,600	Spring Catchable
2008	Brook Trout	3,000	Fingerling
2007	Rainbow Trout	342	Spring Catchable
2007	Brook Trout	3,000	Fingerling
2006	Rainbow Trout	1,600	Catchable
2006	Brook Trout	3,000	Fingerling

Directions

From Williams Lake, turn onto Highway 20 leading to Bella Coola. Travel southwest for about 32.5 km, crossing the Fraser River and driving to the top of Sheep Creek Hill. Turn north (right) on Meldrum Creek Road and drive for 0.5 km to the first access road to the lake. The recreation site road parallels the Meldrum Creek Road for another half a kilometre.

Facilities

There **McIntyre Lake Recreation Site** runs up the west side of the lake. The site has two openings, at either end of the site, for carrying a cartop or small watercraft to the water. There are two pit toilets, four tables and five fire rings available.

Area Indicator

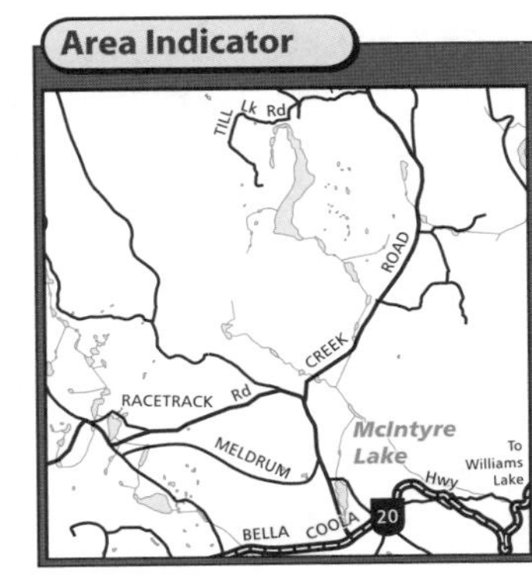

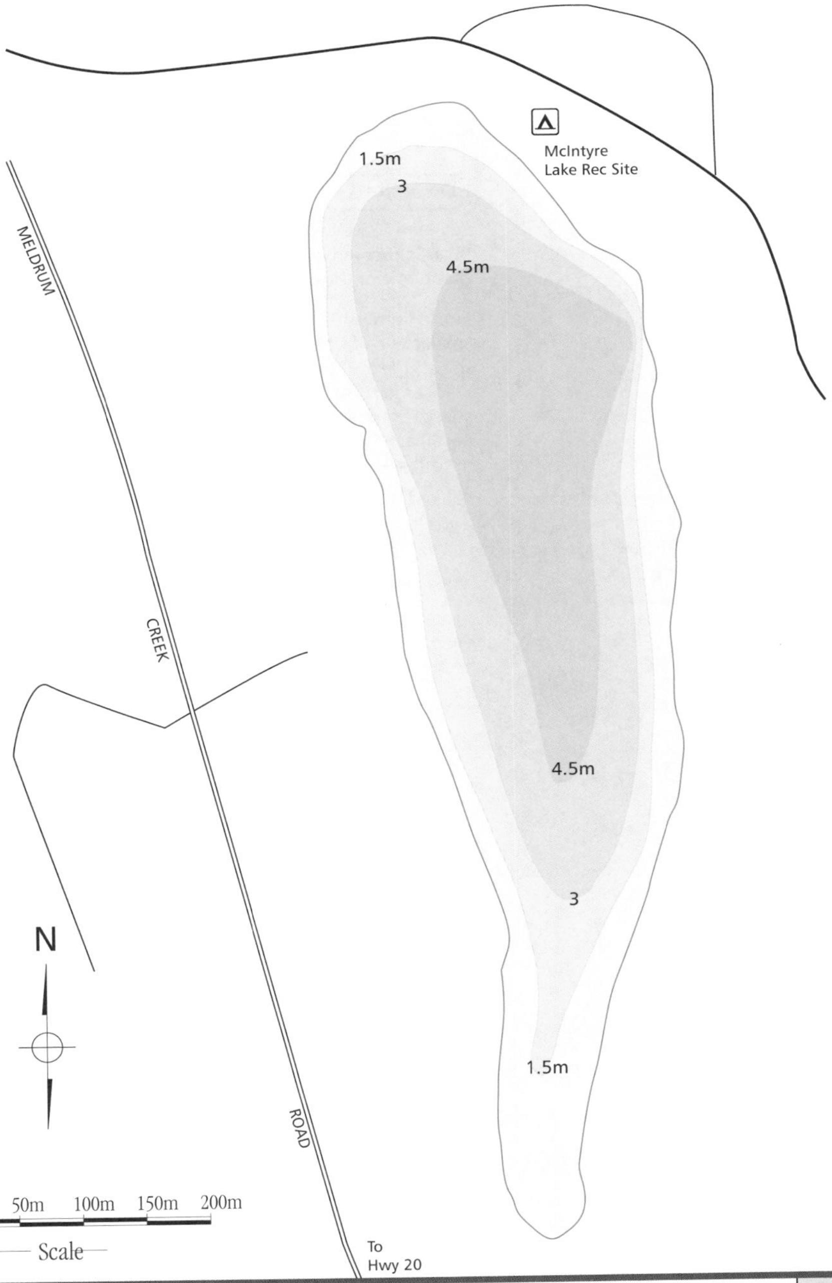

McKinley Lake

Location: 80 km (50 mi) northeast of Williams Lake
Elevation: 865 m (2,838 ft)
Surface Area: 512 ha (1,265 ac)
Maximum Depth: 65 m (213 ft)
Mean Depth: 24 m (79 ft)
Way Point: 52° 16' 1" N, 120° 56' 40" W

Area Indicator

Fishing

McKinley Lake is a good-sized lake found east of Horsefly near the transition from the rolling hills of the central interior to the big mountains of Wells Gray Provincial Park. The lake is quite deep and holds a variety of fish species including burbot, kokanee, lake trout and rainbow trout. There are also a number of course fish species in the lake, while salmon spawn up McKinley Creek and through the lake.

The lake is best known for its lake trout and rainbow trout fishing. The latter can get up to 1.5 kg (3 lbs) and are best caught using a lake troll, or a lure like a Krocodile or Kamlooper.

They can also be caught by spincasting and fly-fishing, although these methods aren't as popular as trolling due to the bigger nature of the lake. The western half of the lake, near the recreation site, is not as deep as the eastern half of the lake. While there is still some good fishing for rainbow trout in the western half of the lake during the early part of the year, there are plenty of feeder streams coming into the lake along the northeastern shores of the lake. When the salmon spawn through the lake in fall, these become trout magnets, as many salmon eggs wash down the creeks and into the lake. At this time, the fish will usually go for anything that looks like a salmon egg. Fly casters can work an egg sucking leech or other egg pattern, while spincasters can work single eggs or gooey bobs to attract a strike.

In the spring, the salmon smolts begin working their way down the creeks and this is the time to work a small minnow pattern, Flatfish, or hook baited with a minnow. The best fishing still happens around the mouth of creeks, but you can find the smolts most anywhere around the edge of the lake.

The lake trout in the lake can get to 4 kg (8 lbs) and are best caught on a deep troll, especially in summer. Many people use a downrigger to get their lure down to where the fish are. Lake trout can be difficult to find, as most fish finders aren't sensitive enough to pick up trout at that depth. However, if you can get your lure to within a few feet of the bottom and troll around structure, you can usually find a laker or two.

Directions

To reach McKinley Lake involves a long drive from Highway 97. It is recommended to pick up a copy of the Backroad Mapbook for the Cariboo to help navigate to the lake.

From Highway 97 follow the Horsefly Road all the way to the small town of Horsefly. Just before entering the town, cross the bridge over the Horsefly River and begin the drive on the Black Creek Road. That logging road is a well maintained road so a car can travel along it without much trouble. Continue past Black Creek and the airport and then take the first right onto the McKinley Lake Road (500 Road). McKinley Lake is about seven kilometers from the junction.

Facilities

McKinley Lake Recreation Site is found at the west end of the lake next to the McKinley Lake Road. The site has six treed camping spots together with a beach and cartop boat launch. The camping spots are big enough for larger trailers and RVs.

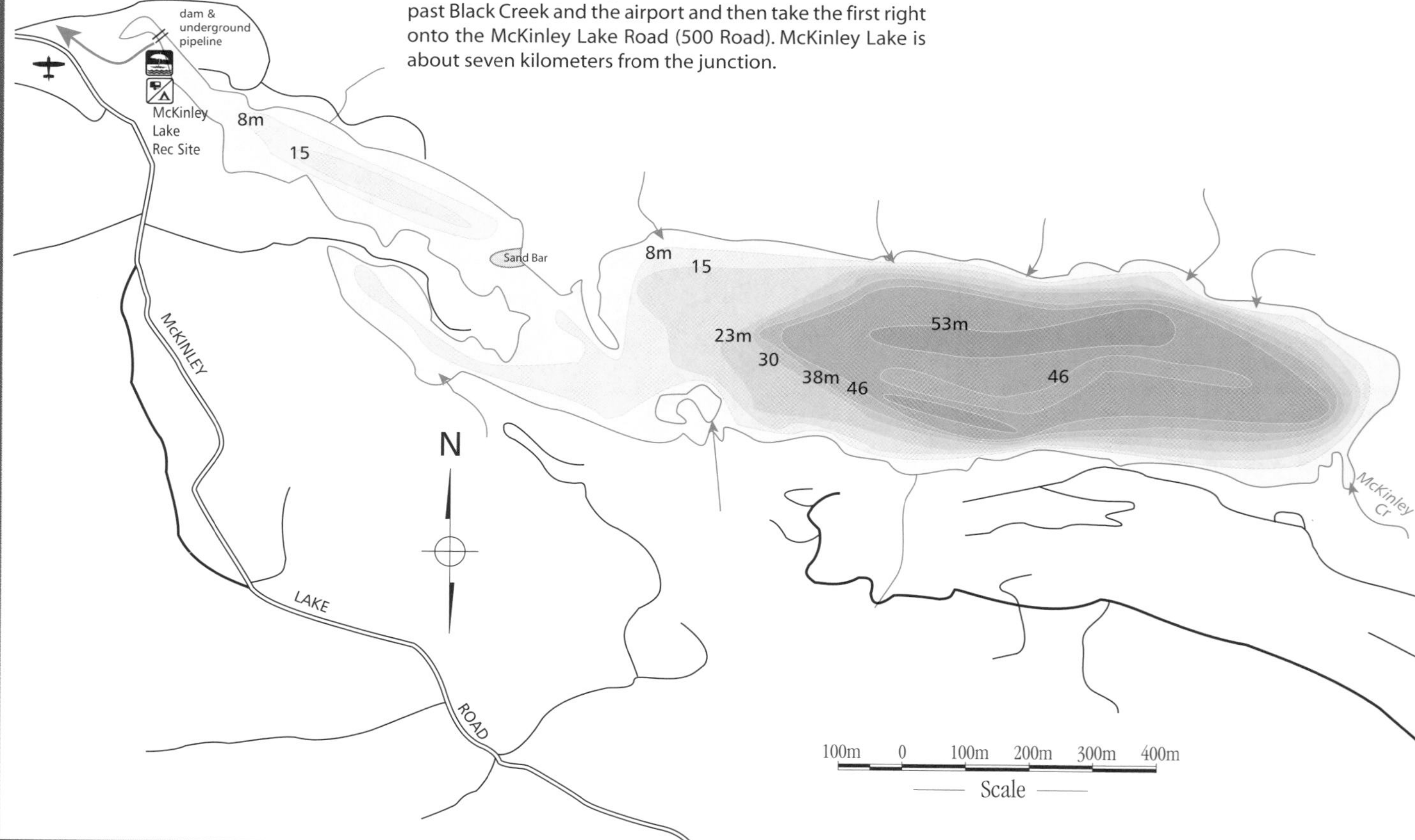

McLeese Lake

Location: 35 km (21.7 mi) northwest of Williams Lake
Elevation: 676 m (2,218 ft)
Surface Area: 341 ha (841 ac)
Maximum Depth: 46 m (152 ft)
Mean Depth: 16.3 m (53.5 ft)
Way Point: 52° 24′ 39″ N, 122° 17′ 58″ W

Fishing

McLeese Lake is a popular stopping spot for travellers along the Cariboo Highway. The lake, found about half an hour northwest of Williams Lake is a perfect spot to stop for a rest on a warm summer's day for travellers on their way to or from Prince George.

The lake is a low elevation lake (for the Cariboo) that offers one of the earliest fisheries in the Cariboo. The low elevation also means that the lake fishing slows down earlier in the summer than other lakes in the Cariboo and does not pick up again until late fall.

The lake receives heavy fishing pressure, especially from the locals.

Visitors will find kokanee, whitefish and rainbow as well as a number of course fish (suckers, squawfish and chub, redside shiners). The rainbow grow to 1 kg (2 lbs), averaging 30-35 cm (12-14 in) in length and the kokanee remain quite small (20-30 cm or 8-12 in). The lake is heavily stocked by the Freshwater Fisheries Society of BC, to the tune of 25,000 rainbow and 30,000 kokanee annually, to help maintain a fast and steady fishery.

Trolling is by far the most popular method of fishing as the lake is easily trolled due to its depth (over 46 metres or 150 feet). Try trolling a Willow Leaf with a Wedding Band or Dick Nite spoon and worm for both rainbow and kokanee. Darker coloured Flatfish work better for the trout. The lake is deepest at the north end and is fairly shallow towards the south end. Therefore, it is easier to troll the north end of the lake without getting hang-ups.

Fly-fishing is also becoming a popular alternative on the lake for the kokanee (as well as the trout). Kokanee grow big by eating zooplankton, however, larger kokanee can be found feeding on chironomids, dragonfly and damselfly nymphs and even small leeches. Their feeding patterns are a lot like rainbow trout and you will find that you will catch a mixture of both by working the shoals and feeder streams. The biggest difference is that kokanee are much more sensitive to the temperature of water and prefer to spend their time in a narrow band of water, although they will dart into shallower (or deeper) water to feed. Kokanee also have soft mouths and whether trolling, spincasting or fly-fishing, it is advisable to attach some form of shock absorber, to prevent the hook from tearing through the soft flesh. Kokanee are strong, determined fighters and often do damage to themselves when trying to escape.

Facilities

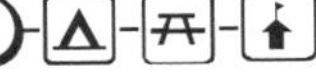

Full facilities are offered at the lake. For day trippers, there is a rest stop at the north end of the lake and anglers with cartoppers or float tubes can access the lake from here. For those looking to stay longer, the **McLeese Lake Resort** and **Oasis Resort** offer everything from cabins and campsites to boat rentals and boat launches. There are also numerous private residences that line the lake.

Directions

McLeese Lake is easily accessed off the Cariboo Highway (Highway 97). It is located 43 km (27 miles) northwest of Williams Lake, near the town that bears the same name as the lake.

McLeese Lake Fish Stocking Data			
Year	Species	Number	Life Stage
2008	Kokanee	15,000	Fry
2007	Kokanee	15,000	Fry
2006	Rainbow Trout	15,000	Yearling

Area Indicator

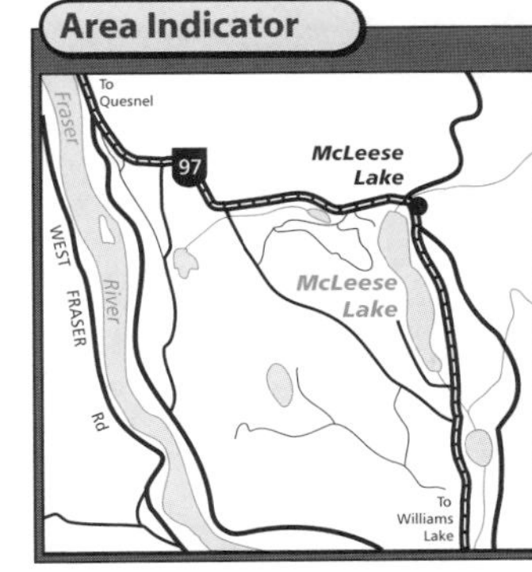

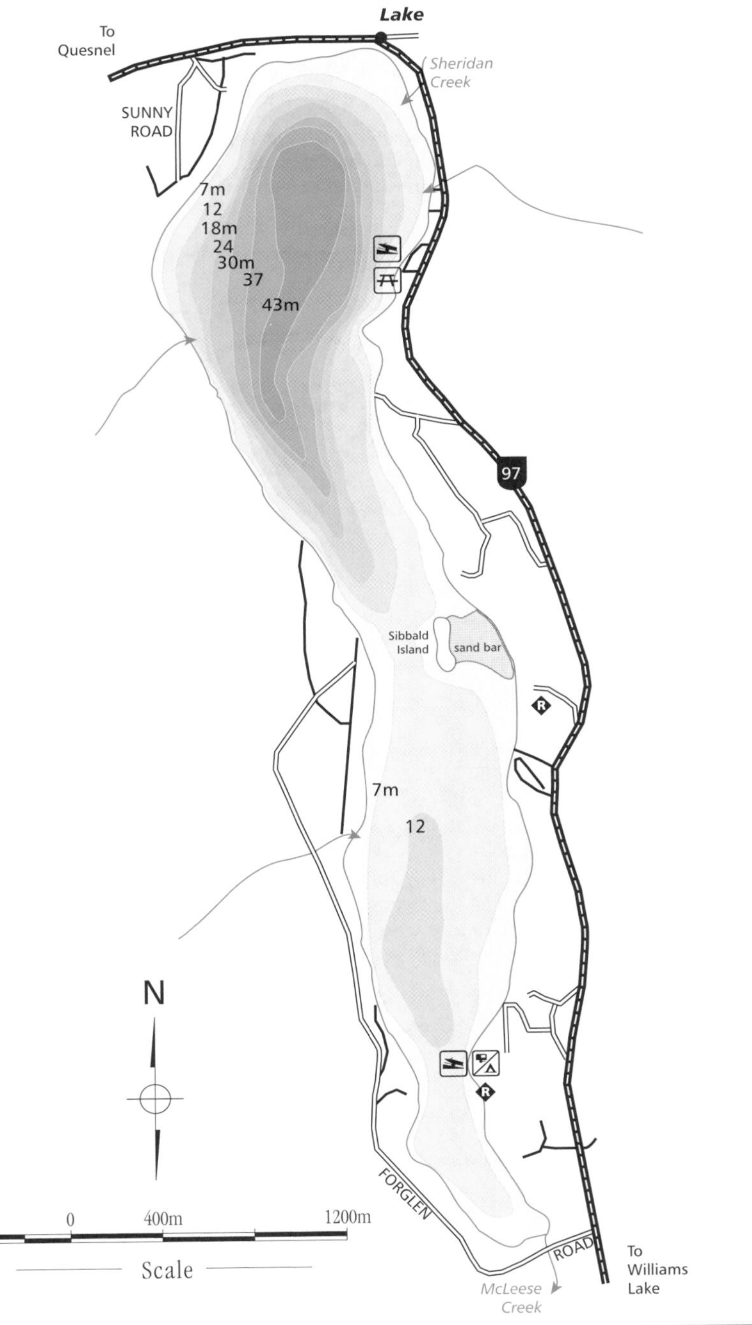

Location: 250 km (155 miles) north of Terrace
Elevation: 246 m (807 ft)
Surface Area: 3,110 ha (7,684 ac)
Mean Depth: 45 m (147.6 ft)
Max Depth: 120 m (394 ft)
Way Point: 56° 3′ 46″ N, 129° 17′ 35″ W

Meziadin Lake

Area Indicator

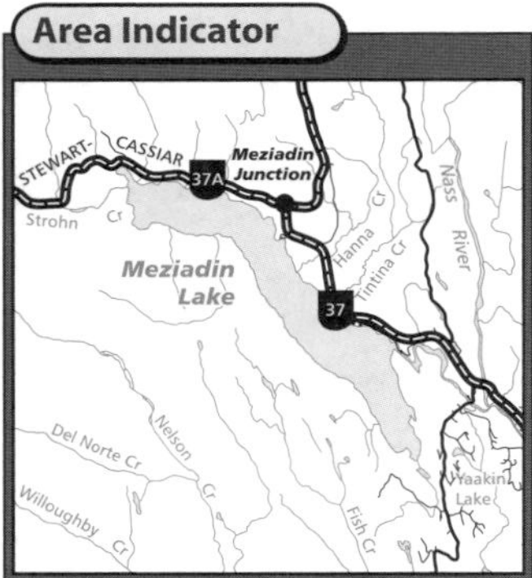

Fishing

Meziadin Lake is a beautiful lake found along the Cassiar Highway, at Meziadin Junction on the way to Stewart. From the lake you can see up to Bear Pass, as well as all the mountains that surround the lake. The lake is fed by water that flows off the Cambria Glacier as well as other snowfields in the area. It is not, as you might have guessed, a popular swimming lake, though it is usually warm enough in summer to go for a quick dip.

The lake is chock full of rainbow trout and Dolly Varden. There are rumours of cutthroat here, too, although none have been caught in any fish inventories taken here.

The lake is a good size and quite long. As a result, the winds can get quite strong and getting out onto the lake in a smaller craft can be a big scary.

In August and September, sockeye spawn up the river and pass through the lake. You can actually fish for sockeye in the lake using a large spoon. While it isn't the most productive fishing, some people have had good success. You may also want to try fishing for Coho during their return (which overlaps the sockeye, but continues on into October). The Coho return is much smaller, though.

The sockeye returns are more notable for how the affect fishing for rainbow and dollies. During this time, free-floating eggs flow down the spawning creeks and into the lake. The rainbow and dollies gather around the mouth of these creeks and feast on the eggs as they float back into the lake. Anglers could do worse than fish around these creeks using either an egg pattern (for fly anglers) or a single egg on a hook (for gear chuckers).

Even when the salmon aren't spawning, fishing around the creek mouths can prove productive. In spring, of course, the smolts begin their long swim to the ocean. Once again, the rainbow and dollies gather eagerly around the creek mouths, but this time they will also follow the smolts as they make their way down to the Meziadin River.

While it is possible to fish off-shore around the park and the boat launch (and people have snagged 2 kg/4 lb dollies here), the best way to fish the lake is with a boat, as it is tough to get to any of the creek mouths along the shore.

Some people do fly fish (using streamer patterns in spring and egg patterns in fall), but most people who fish here either troll or cast small spoons and spinners around the creek mouths.

To Stewart
Strohn Cr
37A
Meziadin Junction
37
To Dease Lake
Hanna Cr
Meziadin Lake Prov Park
Tintina Cr
120
105
90
75
60m
45
30
15
6
Meziadin R
To Terrace
Meziadin Fish Ladder
N
400m 0 400m 1200m 2000m
Scale

Directions

Meziadin Lake is a reasonably large lake found alongside the Cassiar Highway at Meziadin Junction. From Terrace, the lake is about 250 km (155 miles) north. Head northeast on Highway 16 to Hazelton and the Cassiar Highway turnoff. Take the Cassiar north almost to the Meziadin Junction and watch for signs leading to Meziadin Lake Provincial Park.

Facilities

Meziadin Lake Provincial Park has 66 camping units including the option to rent a camping trailer. The fairly popular park also has a gravel boat launch, a day use area and a convenience store on-site. There is another private campsite to the south, as well as the **Mezadin Fish Ladder** at the south end of the lake.

Milburn Lake

Location: 15 km (9.3 mi) west of Quesnel
Elevation: 819 m (2,687 ft)
Surface Area: 34 ha (84 ac)
Maximum Depth: 7.6 m (25 ft)
Mean Depth: 2.6 m (8.5 ft)
Way Point: 53° 1′ 22.0″ N, 122° 40′ 50.2″ W

Fishing

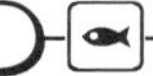

Milburn Lake is a relatively low elevation lake that has both brook trout and rainbow. Resting close to Quesnel, the lake is not as busy as one would think. However, the Freshwater Fisheries Society of BC stocks 10,000 rainbow and 15,000 brook trout every year to ensure a vibrant fishery.

The rainbow tend to be in the 0.5-1 kg (1-2 lb) range where as the brook trout grow to 1 kg (2 lbs). The lake is quite shallow and is not well suited to trolling. Rather, most anglers try casting a fly or small lure from a small boat or float tube. In fact, there are many bays and islands ideal for casting. Try working the two deeper holes in the southern bay.

For the spin caster trying for the brook trout, a Deadly Dick and worm is a popular combination, while anglers looking either species can try a variety of lures, including Apex Trout Killer, Kamlooper and Krocodile spoons and Mepps, Panther Martin, Vibrax and Gibbs spinners. Vertical jigging with spoons or jigs using scented bait, such as one of the Berkley Powerbaits, will also work well.

Springtime is a good time for the fly angler to test a dragonfly nymph pattern or a floating line with a chironomids or mayfly. Another productive time is just prior to the brook trout spawning season in the fall. Casting into the shallow bays produces well using any large attractor fly pattern. This is due to the pre-spawning aggressiveness of the males.

The lake is actually more popular during the ice fishing season. Brook trout are much hardier than rainbow trout and do not suffer from the effects of cold water and oxygen deprivation as much as rainbow. After a few months under the ice, rainbow will become sluggish and their flesh tends to soften, making them less desirable to catch or to eat. Brook trout, in the meantime, remain spry and healthy throughout the winter.

Ice fishing is a much simpler proposition than fishing in summer. While there is a variety of specialized gear, from special rods and lures to custom built ice fishing huts, all you really need is fishing line, a lure, or a hook and bait. Even with a jigging lure, baiting the hook is a good idea as it adds an extra attractor for the trout. Corn, maggots, worms or even marshmallows can be pressed into service.

Directions

Milburn Lake is a small lake located to the west of Quesnel. To reach the lake, cross the Fraser River to West Quesnel. The first road on the far side of the river is North Fraser Drive. Turn right and follow the road until it becomes Blackwater Road, which takes you out of town along the western shores of the Fraser River. When the Blackwater Road takes a sharp right, continue west (left) on the Nazko Road. About five kilometers later, you will see the Rawlings Road heading north. Take that road and within a few hundred meters you will reach Milburn Lake.

Facilities

There is a small, private camping facility at the lake together with a cartop boat launch. Private residences also line the lake, limiting public access.

Milburn Lake Fish Stocking Data			
Year	Species	Number	Life Stage
2008	Brook Trout	15,000	Fingerling
2007	Rainbow Trout	5,000	Yearling
2007	Brook Trout	15,000	Fingerling
2006	Brook Trout	19,000	Fingerling

Area Indicator

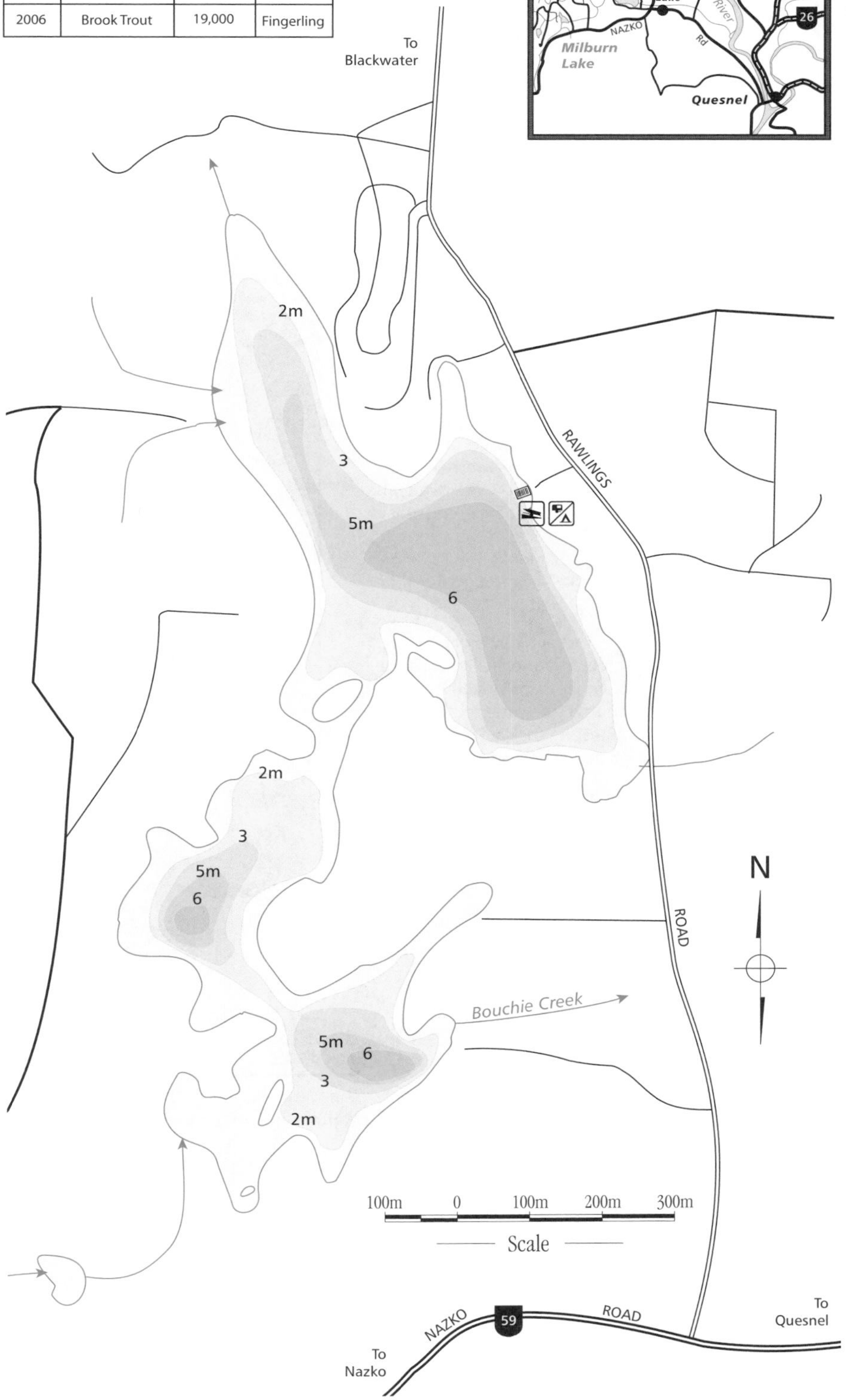

Ten Mile Lake
Blackwater Rd
Fraser River
Bouchie Lake
Bouchie Lake
Nazko Rd
Milburn Lake
Quesnel
97
26

To Blackwater
Rawlings Road
2m
3
5m
6
2m
3
5m
6
5m
6
3
2m
Bouchie Creek
N
100m 0 100m 200m 300m
Scale
To Nazko
Nazko Road
59
To Quesnel

Location: 55 km (34 mi) northeast of Likely
Stream Length: 31 km (19 mi)
Geographic: 52° 50′ 38″ N, 120° 47′ 13″ W

Mitchell River

Fishing

The Mitchell River is a remote river, located in Cariboo Mountain Provincial Park. Most people access this river by jetboat, by plane or by foot. It is a spectacular area, featuring crystal clear water, glacier capped peaks, wildlife, old growth cedar and some amazing catch and release fishing for giant rainbow and bull trout.

There are four separate colour variations of rainbow in this river, which is quite unique. The average rainbow here is about 40 cm (16 in), while bull trout can get up to 5 kg (10 lbs). However, people have caught rainbow to 9 kg (20 lbs) during the sockeye run.

The fishing starts in early July, when salmon fry begin leaving the river, heading for Quesnel Lake. Fishing a minnow imitation like a Muddler Minnow at this time can be quite productive.

There are resident trout in the river and during the summer they feed on caddis and mayflies and terrestrials that fall into the river. Fishing a dry fly like a Deer Hair Caddis, a grasshopper or beetle imitation can be quite exciting at these times. Although these fish are quite small, they can be very aggressive.

Towards the end of August, the real magic happens. Hundreds of thousands of sockeye salmon begin to return to the river. While the river is closed to salmon fishing year round, the big trout from Quesnel Lake–rainbow and bull trout–follow the sockeye upstream. These trout are waiting for any free-floating eggs that get away during the spawn. The trout are voracious at this time and will hit anything that looks like a salmon egg. Fly anglers should use flies like an Egg Sucking Leech or Marabou Egg dead drifted.

The only gotcha is that the sockeye run is dependant on water conditions–flow, temperature, etc. People have travelled here from Vancouver, from the United States... even from Europe, only to find the water too low and too warm. During these times, the sockeye queue up in Quesnel Lake waiting. The anglers have to wait, too.

Once the salmon begin to die off, bits of salmon flesh come lose. Local guides actually use flesh pattern flies, which are surprisingly effective, especially for the bull trout.

The Mitchell River is open from July 1st to September 30th and is managed as a catch and release, fly-fishing river only. Above Cameron Creek, the river is closed to fishing.

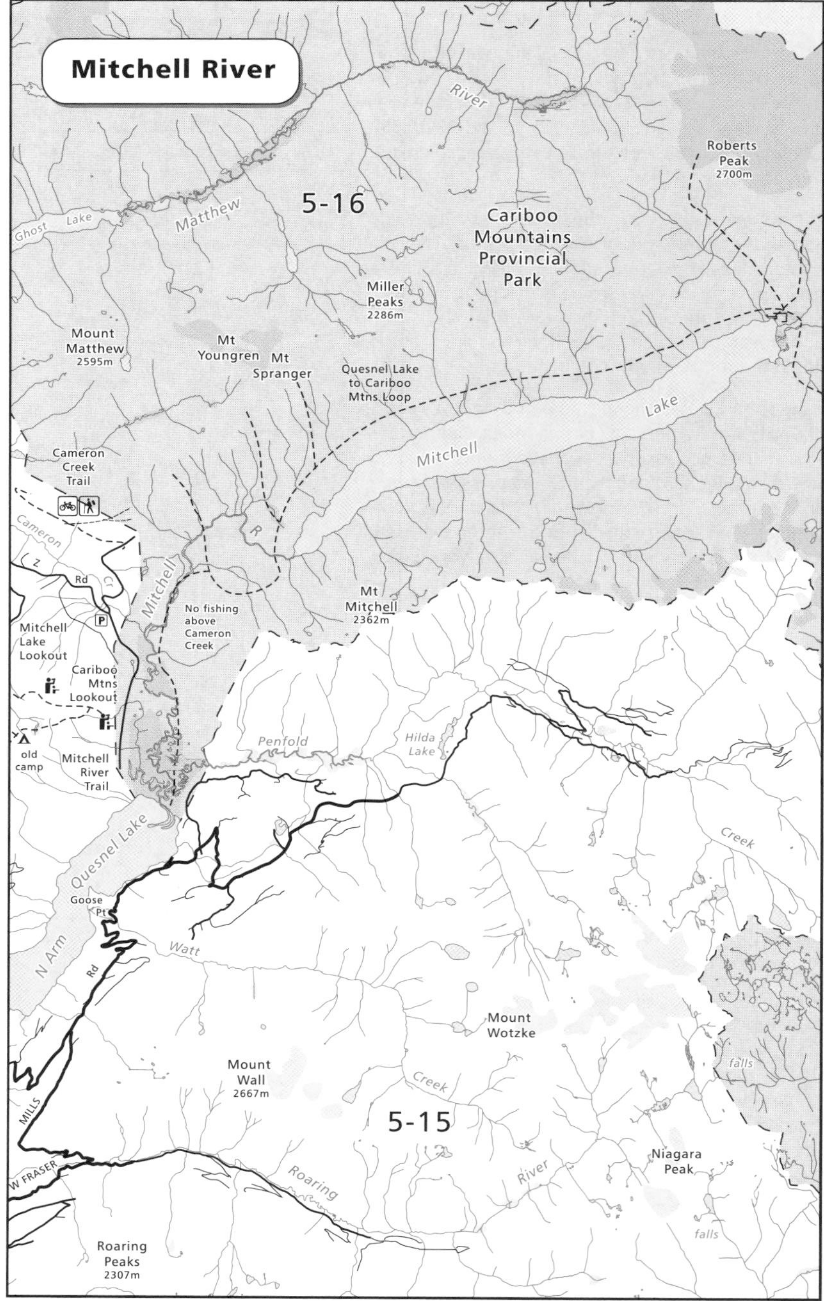

Directions

To get to the Mitchell River, the first thing you have to do is get to Quesnel Lake. There are a couple of places to launch a boat on the big lake including at Cedar Point Provincial Park. To get to the park, drive to Likely along the Likely Road. This well signed and paved road leaves Highway 97 south of Williams Lake. The provincial park is 6 km south of Likely along Cedar Creek Road.

Other launch sites as well as a couple roads that run close to the river are shown in the Backroad Mapbook for the Cariboo Chilcotin Coast.

Facilities

The Mitchell River flows through the **Cariboo Mountain Provincial Park.** That sounds impressive, but it is a wilderness park. There is a rough trail alongside the river, but that's about it. Most people who fish the river either have their own jet boats or depend on local guides to run them up river. Many of the guiding services operate out of nearby lodges and will arrange for accommodations and meals as well.

Other Options

Nearby **Mitchell Lake** is another fly-in alternative that also offers very good fishing for large rainbow and bull trout. Fish in the 5 kg (11 lb) class are not uncommon.

Morchuea Lake

Location: 490 km (304 miles) north of Terrace
Elevation: 908 m (2,978 ft)
Surface Area: 129 ha (318 ac)
Maximum Depth: 7.5 m (25 ft)
Mean Depth: 3.2 m (10.5 ft)
Way Point: 57° 58′ 47.3″ N, 130° 5′ 11.6″ W

Fishing

If Morchuea Lake was within driving distance of Kamloops, it would be managed as a trophy lake. However, the lake is located about a thousand miles (1,400 km) by road from Kamloops and, as a result, the lake remains unprotected.

But it should be a trophy lake and a number of locals have asked the government to make it a trophy lake, but no dice. If you do go to fish Morchuea Lake, we would ask you treat it as one. Use single barbless hooks to make it easier to release the trout you catch and limit your retention of fish to one a day, or none at all.

Of course, you may not have to limit your retention, as it is a self-limiting lake. Meaning there are days when you come here that you may be skunked. Much of that has to do with the fact that the lake sees a lot of fishing pressure and no regulations to protect it. As a result, the fish population has plummeted over the last few years as more and more people fish this lake. And, because the lake does not have good access to spawning ground (as there are beaver dams blocking access to the spawning area), the fish don't breed quickly. Because of all this attention, the lake is being fished out

Indeed, Morchuea is one of the heaviest fished lakes along the Cassiar Highway because it, more than any lake in the region, produces trophy sized trout. If you're lucky, you too can catch a fish to 2 kg (4 lbs) or even a bit bigger. Like all the lakes within the area, the lake holds rainbow trout and nothing else.

Most people who come to the lake troll, even though it is a tiny lake, with only a small area right down the middle that can be trolled. This is especially true later in summer, as the weeds grow in around the edge of the lake. But many people don't know any other way to fish and that's how they fish here, too. While trolling does work, it would be better to park near the edge of a weed bed and spincast a small lure like a Mepps or a Panther Martin.

Even better would be to bring a fly rod. The lake doesn't feature very active hatches and there isn't an awful lot of top water fishing (at least, not that we've heard), but using any of the traditional subsurface attractor patterns (nymphs, Woolly Buggers, Doc Spratleys, etc.) should work well. You can also try fishing a shrimp pattern or a leech pattern. And, with the tremendous amount of weed growth, we're pretty sure that there are going to be at least some hatches on a warm summer's evening, though whether the fish will rise to them or not is another story.

Area Indicator

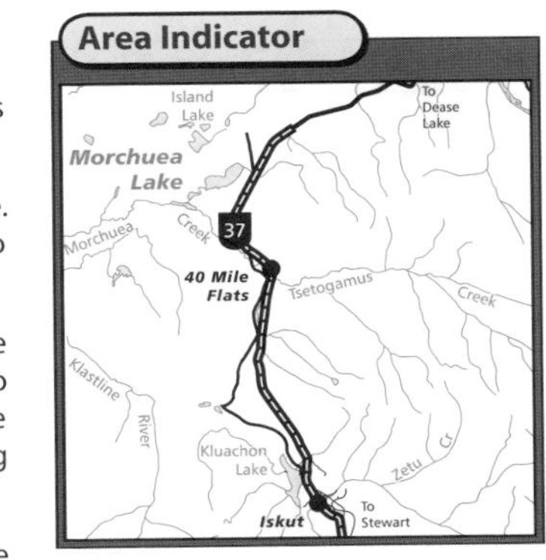

Directions

Morchuea Lake is found along the Cassiar Highway (Highway 37) south of Dease Lake. To get there, head north from Highway 16 at Kitwanga past Tatogga and 40 Mile Flats. If you cross the Stikine River Bridge, you've gone too far. The rough access road to the lake is on the west side of the road. This road is steep and is probably best left to a four-wheel drive vehicle.

Facilities

The **Morchuea Lake Recreation Site** has space for about eight camping groups. There is a boat launch suitable for cartoppers or small trailered boats.

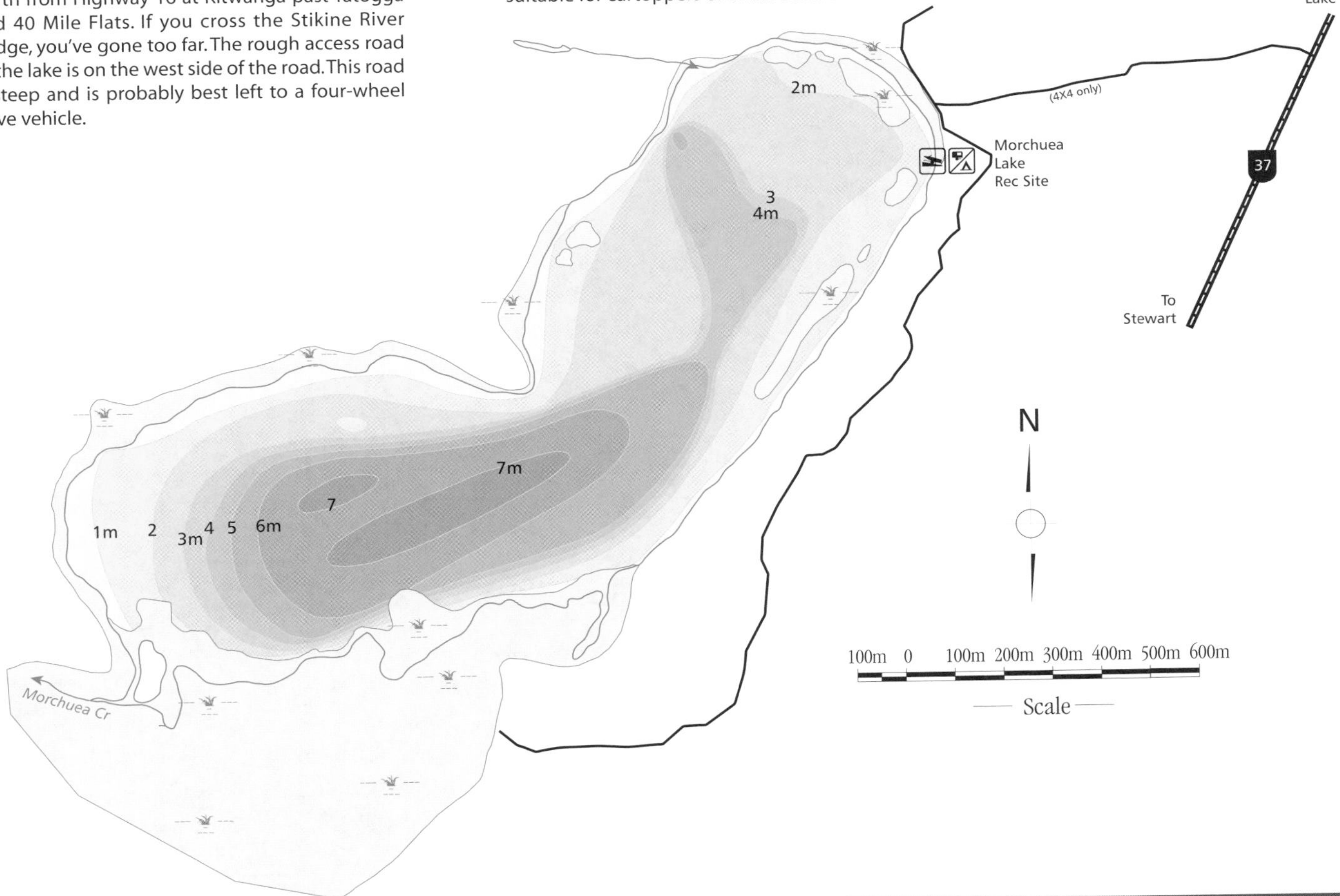

Location: 8 km (5 mi) west of Houston
Stream Length: 80 km (50 mile)
Geographic: 54° 12′ 26″ N, 126° 53′ 51″ W

Morice River

Fishing

The Morice River supplies over 90% of the water to the Bulkley, which is the largest tributary of the Skeena River. As a result, the Morice features some amazing steelhead fishing. The 80 km (50 mile) long river drains Morice Lake and holds resident populations of rainbow trout, cutthroat trout and Dolly Varden but these are rarely fished for. Instead, the river is known for its Chinook, Coho and steelhead runs.

Chinook are in the river from mid-July to late August and are taken on red Spin-N-Glos suspended just off the bottom, Kitimat spoons or white, red or pink wool are also effective. Fly anglers will need heavy gear and fast sinking lines get down into deep holes. Patterns mixing bright and dark colours can be effective. Woolly Buggers, Egg Sucking Leeches or Marabou Eggs dead drifted are equally good.

September and October are the months for Coho and steelhead. The river is not known for producing monster steelhead, like the Kispiox, but it, together with the Bulkley, has the largest return of any steelhead river anywhere in the world.

The Morice is a wild, untamed river that is a bit off the beaten path. While you don't have to fly-in or anything like that, it doesn't attract the same crowds as some of the other rivers. And, because Morice Lake acts as a giant filter for the river, it is still running clean when other rivers look like chocolate milk.

The river is an easy walk and wade river. The fish usually rest just after passing through a rapid, so fishing at the top of a rapid is usually a good place to find steelhead, usually hiding behind a rock or someplace where the current isn't as strong.

For fly anglers, the Egg Sucking Leeches or Marabou flies are good patterns to use. If the water is still warm enough, the steelhead will often come to the surface for a dry fly. The most common way to fish a dry fly is to wake the fly across the water. This means that the fly leaves a small wake, as you would see behind a boat, which the steelhead can see. In fast moving water, a bigger fly needs to be used to create a bigger wake, while in slow moving water a lighter fly will work. This technique works best before the sun is fully up or in shady areas.

Directions

To get to the river, take the Yellowhead Highway (Highway 16) to the town of Houston. Turn south onto the Morice River Forest Service Road, which follows the Morice for nearly its entire length. To access the upper reaches of the river, it does get confusing along a maze of backroads and a copy of the Northern British Columbia Backroad Mapbook will help you get to where you want to go.

Facilities

There are several recreation sites located along the forestry road and offer several locations to fish, or put in a pontoon boat. **Aspen Recreation Site** is the first you will come across offering space for nine campers, while the **Owens Flat A** and **B** sites have space for a dozen campers or so.

Of course, the Morice flows into the Bulkley nearly at Houston. Here you will find food, lodging and river guiding services.

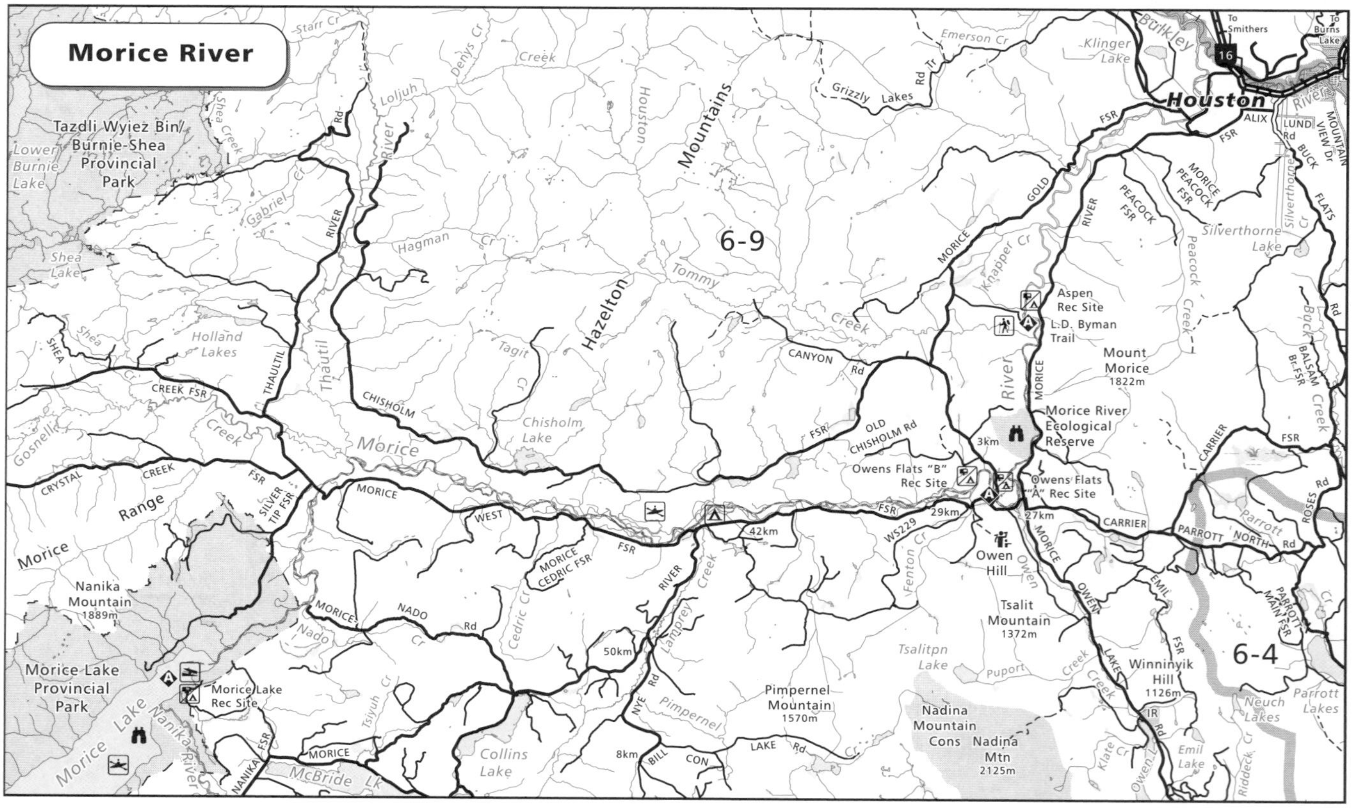

Morice River

Murray River

Location: 75 km (46.5 mi) west of Dawson Creek
Stream Length: 217 km (135 mi)
Geographic: 55°8′00″N, 121°2′00″W

Fishing 

The Murray River originates in the high country of Monkman Provincial Park as a trickle, then a stream and finally, as a full-blown river. The river holds your typical Northeastern BC species: bull trout, Arctic grayling, whitefish, rainbow trout and even some burbot, though few anglers ever report catching these.

Much of this upper section is difficult to access. However, the fishing can be wonderful. A photograph dating back nearly 70 years shows Carl Brooks below the waterfall that now bears his name holding two dozen fish that he caught in less than 18 minutes. While modern day anglers quell at the sight, it speaks volumes to the fishing. However, to get here requires hiking nearly six hours along a fairly good trail before dropping down along a very rough route down to the falls.

The first place the river is really fished is at a hole just downstream of where the Bulley Creek and Murray River Forest Service Road meet. However, most people chose to fish below Kinuseo Falls in the large pool. These falls acts as a rather imposing natural barrier, preventing the migration of fish. Note that it is catch and release for Arctic grayling for 2 km (1.2 miles) below the falls. There are signs.

A flood a few years ago played havoc with the river, destroying habitat and killing fish, but the river seems to have recovered. In 2008, a local angler pulled a 5 kg (11 lb) bull trout from the river, a sure sign that the fishing has recovered.

The river is big and wide and it can be difficult to fish from shore. Bull trout are best caught around deep holes and eddies. They also like hanging around feeder creeks like Flatbed, Monkman and Kinuseo Creeks. Work Mepps spinners and spoons to catch these voracious feeders.

Arctic grayling are the other fish usually targeted by anglers. They can be caught on small spinners. Fly anglers will have good luck using streamers, Egg Sucking Leeches or similar.

Directions 

You can access the lower Murray by jetboat from the Pine River boat launch near Chetwynd. Otherwise, head south on Highway 29 towards Tumbler Ridge. There are several side roads that take you to the river (some walking/bushwhacking required) or you can access the river at the second launch near the Murray River Bridge.

South of Tumbler Ridge, the Murray River Forest Service Road branches southwest towards Monkman Park. There are a pair of bridges, another jetboat launch and a number of places where you can access the river. The road is rough, but two wheel drive accessible.

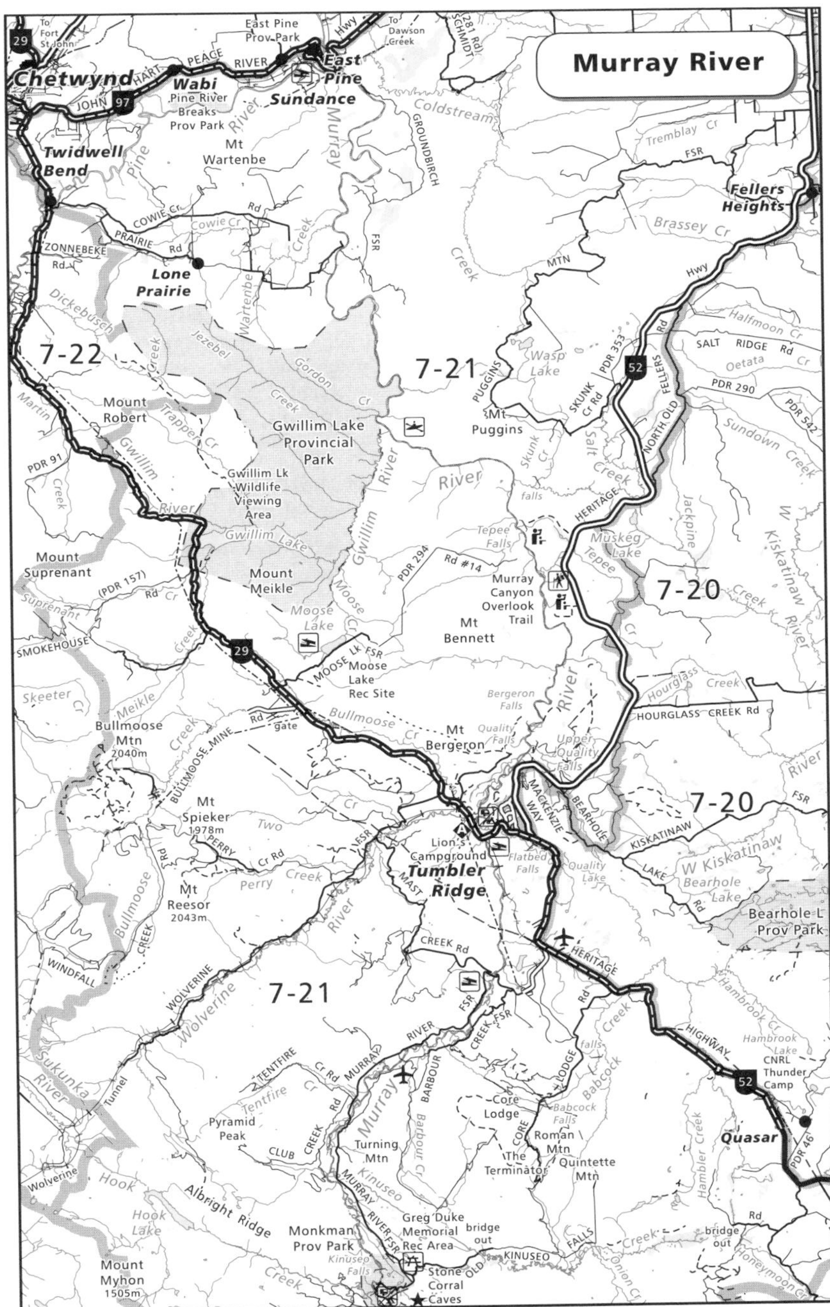

Facilities

The campground at **Monkman Provincial Park** near Kinuseo Falls has been ravaged by pine beetle and partially closed. There are still 20 sites open, but all the dangerous trees (almost all of them) have been logged out. Camping is now free, but it is almost like camping in a woodlot. Alternatively, there is a nice **Lions Campground** on Flatbed Creek, about a kilometre from the Highway 29 boat launch. There are three boat launches, as described above.

Location: Flows past Fort Nelson
Stream Lenght: 257 km (160 mi)
Geographic: 58°16′00″N, 123°39′00″W

Muskwa River

Fishing

The Muskwa River is one of the biggest rivers in Northeastern BC, giving its name to an entire wilderness area larger than Switzerland in the process. Together with the Kechika, this vast area encompasses hundreds of square kilometers of roadless Northern Rockies wilderness.

Where there are no roads, the rivers themselves become liquid highways for jet boaters.

The area is known for having an abundance of large wildlife–moose, deer, wolf, bear, Stone sheep and more–and has earned the nickname "The Serengeti of the North."

The Muskwa and its tributaries like the Tuchodi hold bull trout and Arctic grayling primarily.

Arctic grayling are one of the prettiest fish around, having the smooth, sleek lines of a trout, but with a prominent dorsal fin. The head is olive-green with a mauve iridescence, with dark green and gold eyes. The dorsal fin is black, but with a narrow wine coloured edge and sometimes a blue band beneath and vertical rows of spots that vary in colour from fish to fish. Its body is dark on the top, black or blue-black fading to a silvery gray or blue. In the direct sun, the iridescent scales often show yellow outlines and there are diamond-shaped markings on the sides. A good sized grayling is 35 cm (14 in).

The Muskwa is a northern river. It has long winters and short summers. There is little weed growth in the cold glacier-fed river and few insect hatches. The grayling feed on whatever insects they can find, while the bigger bull trout tend to feed on small grayling.

Grayling spawn in the spring and don't eat for a few weeks before spawning. By late June they are back to feeding and will feed voraciously on whatever they can find. Fly anglers can try working a weighted Hare's Ear Nymph or a surface fly. Because there are so few hatches, it can sometimes be hard to know what to present, but grayling are fairly egalitarian and will usually chase anything you throw at them, as long as it isn't too big.

Spincasters will find grayling will hit tiny spinners. Cleos, Mepps, Blue Foxes and Panther Martins all in size zero work great. It's best to stay with natural dark colors like black, gray, dark green or brown, which are colors native to local insects.

For the bull trout, try working streamer and minnow patterns or lures, as they like to feed on small fish.

Directions

The Muskwa is a rarely visited paradise found southwest of Fort Nelson. The 257 km (160 mile) river is a major tributary of the Fort Nelson River and flows into that river just east of town. There is a boat launch on the Muskwa River, accessed off the Alaska Highway at km 452 (Mile 281). For folks travelling up river or people without access to a jet boat, there is a second launch at km 520 (Mile 321) that will cut hours off your travel time up river. Anglers can cast from here, or put in with a small watercraft and float down to the next launch.

Facilities

In addition to the two boat launches mentioned in the directions, visitors will find random campsites along the river. The city of Fort Nelson offers full services, including food, accommodations and fuel.

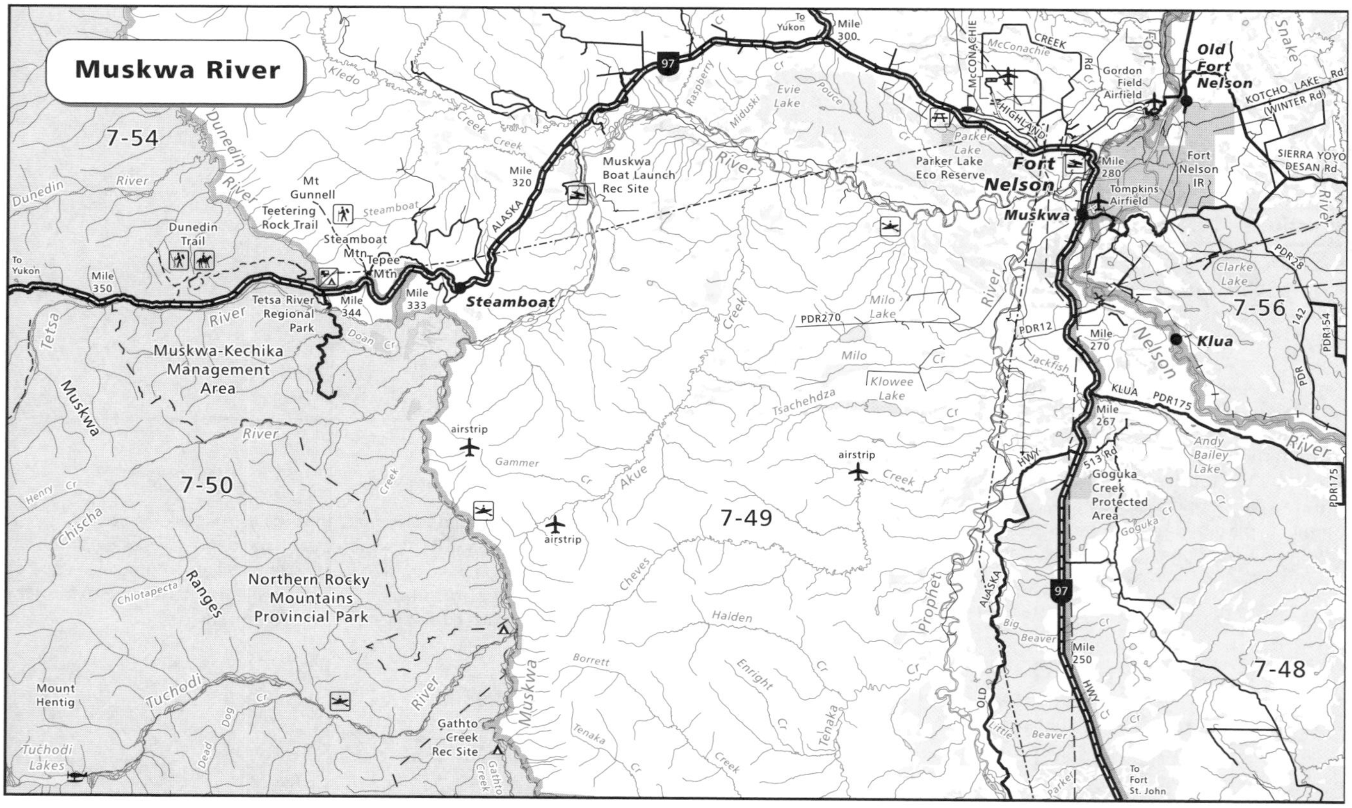

Muskwa River

Nass River

Location: 200 km (120 miles) north of Terrace
Stream Length: 406 km (252 mi)
Geographic: 55° 12′ 23″ N, 129° 9′ 50″ W

Fishing

At its headwaters, the Nass River is a cold, clear river that is fed by a series of small lakes and melting snow. But as it makes its way along it picks up silt and dirt and most of the road accessible stretches of the river usually run a chocolate brown.

The Nass has runs of all five species of salmon and a good run of steelhead. Coho average about 4.5 kg (10 lbs) with 9 kg (20 lb) Coho commonly caught. Chinook average 9-18 kg (20-40 lbs) and are found in fair numbers in excess of 27 kg (60 lbs). The river also produces well for steelhead that average about 4.5 kg (10 lbs) in size. Other salmon species such as sockeye can be a ton of fun from shore with simple fly gear or spinning rods. Resident rainbow, bull trout and sea-run cutthroat are also available, but rarely fished for.

The river is extremely dependant on weather and when it rains, even the upper stretches of the river can blow out. Only for a few weeks in late summer does the river clean up…if you're lucky.

The better fishing is found in the upper river, which is mostly inaccessible except by helicopter. The lower reaches of the river are accessed off of Highway 37 and the road to New Aiyansh. The parts of the river that are accessible by road often require a four wheel drive vehicle to get to and possibly some bushwhacking.

The river is nowhere near as popular as the Skeena River to the south; it is not as big, does not have quite so many fish and it is not as easily to access or fish. Those who do fish it, tend to focus around the mouth of the tributaries–the Tseax, the Meziadin, etc. These feeder streams are usually cleaner flowing than the mainstem of the Nass and fishing can be quite good along the clean seams of the river, where the clean water of the tributaries meets the dirty water of the Nass.

Directions

The Nass River is the next main river valley north of the Skeena. From Terrace to New Aiyansh is about 50 km (30 miles), but the rough logging roads between the two will take at least an hour, possibly two to drive.

More likely, drivers will take Cassiar Highway (Highway 37) north to the Nass. The Cassiar leaves the Yellowhead at Kitwanga and it is about 200 km (120 miles) from Terrace to where the road meets up with the Nass River. From here, the highway parallels the river up to the Nass River Bridge, a few kilometers north of the Nass/Meziadin confluence. From here, the upper river is only accessible by helicopter.

The lower river is accessed from a series of logging roads that head northwest off the Nass Forest Service Road. This road is found 53 km north of the junction of the Yellowhead and the Cassiar Highways. There is a mess of logging roads here and a copy of the Northern British Columbia Backroad Mapbook is recommended.

Facilities

There are no real facilities along the Nass River. There are a few recreation sites nearby, like a four unit site at Jigsaw Lake. And you are only a couple hours from Terrace or from Stewart, where you will find food and lodging and gas.

Location: 450 km (280 miles) north of Terrace
Elevation: 811 m (2,660 ft)
Surface Area: 144 ha (357 ac)
Maximum Depth: 12 m (39 ft)
Mean Depth: 3.5 m (12 ft)
Way Point: 57° 28′ 54″ N, 130° 14′ 50″ W

Natadesleen Lake

Area Indicator

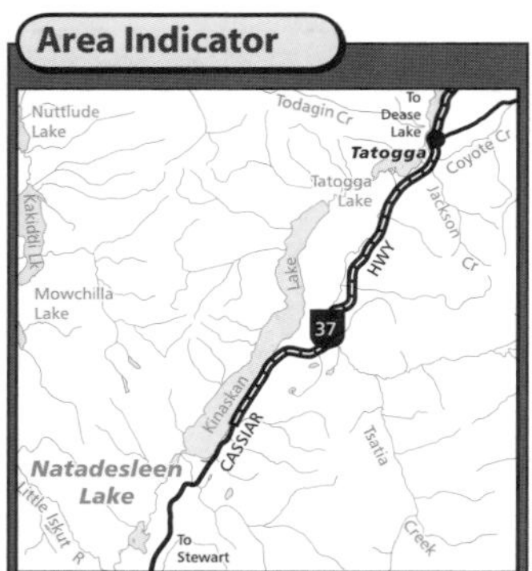

Fishing

Not a lot of people have ever fished Natadesleen Lake. That's because those who do never ever talk about it, hoping to keep the secret all to themselves. Regardless, the remote location helps keep it a quiet destination to visit.

To get to Natadesleen, you must first drive 450 km north of Terrace to Kinaskan Lake Provincial Park. Once there, you must hike about a kilometre to the lake. If you want to fish the lake properly, you're going to want to bring in a float tube or a canoe, which means carrying that tube or canoe all the way to the lake and back.

All in all, the lake is too much trouble for the average person to worry about, so, if you're the average person, you will probably want to stop reading now.

They gone? Good. Okay, so Natadesleen? One of the prettiest lakes you've ever laid eyes on. A crystal clear gem surrounded by towering mountains. And the fishing? Wow. There are faster lakes and there are lakes that hold bigger rainbow trout, but when you hit the lake at the right time, the fishing is fast enough to keep your heart racing. And the cold, glacier-fed lake stays productive throughout the ice-off season.

The fish can get up to 65 cm (26 in), although that is a rare catch indeed. Usually you are pulling them out of here at about 35–40 cm (14–16 in).

The lake is a fly angler's dream lake. Sure, there are no regulations against fishing the lake with spinners and spoons, but the lake screams to be fished with a fly.

What pattern should you use? Take your pick. This is the sort of lake that you can cast most anything at and you will get a bite. Whichever way you fish it, note that it is single barbless hook only. This is important, as you will probably be releasing most of the fish you catch here. The trick is not catching a fish; the trick is trying to attract the attention of one of the larger fish. As a general rule, you will need to fish deeper to find them. If you are dry fly-fishing, wait until evening, when the sun is no longer striking the lake and the bigger fish are more willing to rise.

Chances are you will be snagging something every few casts. The trout are acrobatic and put up a great fight, even the small ones.

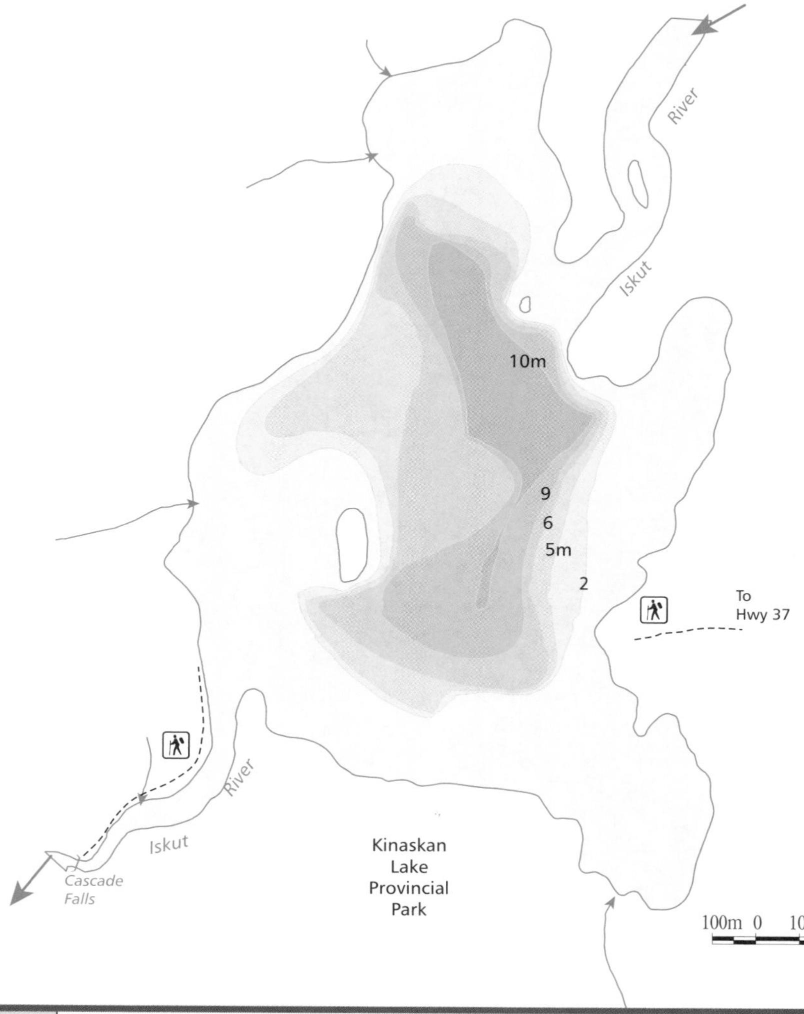

Directions

To get to Natadesleen Lake, you first need to take the Yellowhead Highway (Highway 16) to Kitwanga. From here, the Cassiar Highway (Highway 37) heads north towards Dease Lake and ultimately Alaska. From the junction, it is 364 km north to the Kinaskan Lake Provincial Park. About 10 km before the park, you will see the trail to the lake on the west side of the highway.

Facilities

Outside of the 1 km trail leading to the lake from the highway, there are no facilities on the lake. Those looking to camp in the area can venture to nearby Kinaskan Lake where there is a 50 unit campsite and good access to that lake. For the more adventurous, it is possible to paddle downstream to Natadesleen Lake, although the river has some Class III whitewater to worry about. You can also paddle across the lake to a trail that leads down to Cascade Falls, a 60 metre (200 ft) waterfall only about half a kilometre downstream.

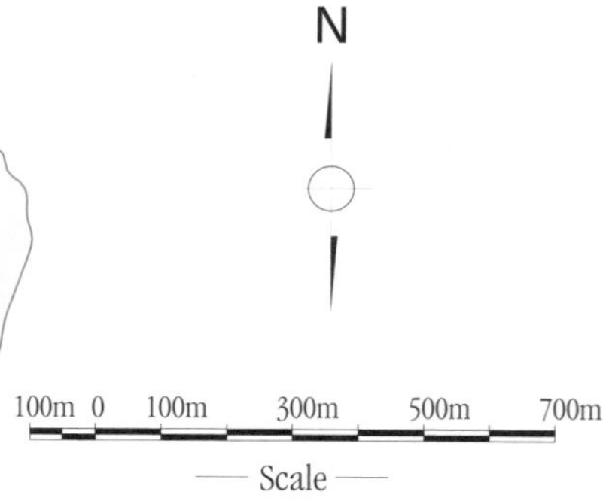

River
Iskut
10m
9
6
5m
2
To Hwy 37
Iskut River
Cascade Falls
Kinaskan Lake Provincial Park
N
100m 0 100m 300m 500m 700m
Scale

Needa Lake

Location: 42 km (26 mi) east of 100 Mile House
Elevation: 1,118 m (3,668 ft)
Surface Area: 188 ha (465 ac)
Maximum Depth: 40 m (131 ft)
Mean Depth: 9.7 m (32 ft)
Way Point: 51° 36' 34" N, 120° 43' 0" W

Fishing

Needa Lake is a popular lake found in a mess of great fishing lakes north of Highway 24. It offers a promising fishery next to the Windy Mountain Forest Service Road.

Anglers looking for trophy rainbow will not find them here as the trout rarely get bigger than 0.5 kg (1 lb). The lake, which has never been stocked, has a number of creeks that flow into it, offering great spawning grounds for the rainbow trout. As a result, there are more trout than the lake's food source can support comfortably. This creates too much competition for the food. Adding to the food problem are the hungry longnose suckers that are also found in the lake.

However, all that competition for food means the trout are ravenous and will hit most anything you throw at them. This means the fishing on Needa Lake can be fast and furious, making it the perfect place to bring a family for a fishing adventure. While most kids aren't willing to put the hours in casting for a 4.5 kg (10 lb) trout, they also don't care as much about the size of the fish. For them, the joy is in the catching and you will catch fish here.

The mid-size lake is mainly a trolling lake, although some anglers visiting the lake cast a spinner or a fly. The lake is separated into two bays by a shallow channel. Either bay is deep enough to troll.

Spincasters and fly fishermen should try working the deeper water off the shallow channel or the inflow and outflow creek areas. Spincasters can work small spoons and spinners, such as Apex Trout Killer spoons, Mepps spinners or other lures such as a Rapala Fat Rap.

Fly casters can match the hatch, if there is one happening. If not, they can work an attractor pattern like a Carey Special or Woolly Bugger. Nymph patterns also work well throughout most of the year.

Some people, especially those with small children, may choose to still fish for trout. This entails dangling a worm or other bait on a hook below a bobber. The trick is to suspend the bait just off the bottom where the trout like to hang out.

The lake is best fished in May to the early part of July, although the water is deep enough that fishing remains somewhat active throughout the summer months. At this time, it is best to troll deep (in the 12–18 metre/40–60 foot range) or fish during dawn or dusk. The fall is also a good time to fish.

Area Indicator

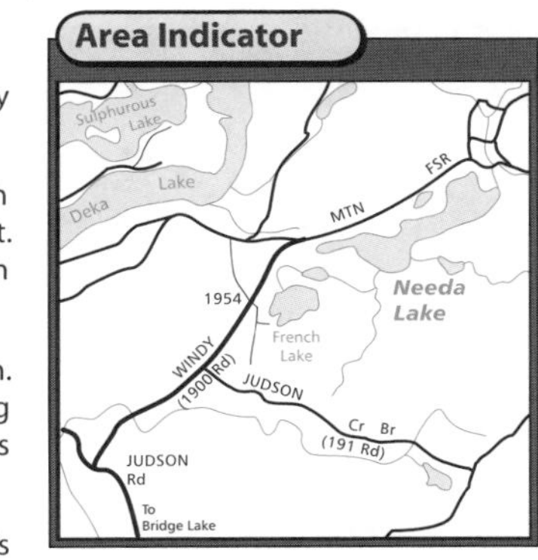

Directions

Needa Lake is situated north of Bridge Lake. From the Bridge Lake North Road you will need to access Judson Road. Follow that road and then take the first major logging road to the right (north), which is called the Windy Mountain Forest Service Road (1900 Road). Continue past French Lake to about the 1960 km mark where the signed Needa Lake Recreation Site side road leads down to the lake.

Facilities

The **Needa Lake Recreation Site** is found at the very eastern end of the lake off a side road leading from the Windy Mountain Forest Road. The site has six camping units ideal for small trailers or campers and a steep cartop boat launch onto the lake. The site also has a number of picnic tables for day-use.

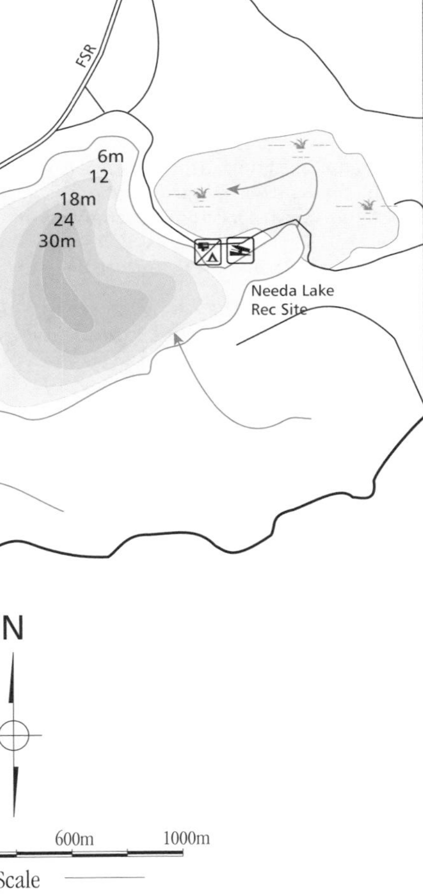

Nimpo Lake

Location: 290 km (180 mi) west of Williams Lake
Elevation: 1,120 m (3,675 ft)
Surface Area: 988 ha (2,441 ac)
Maximum Depth: 24 m (80 ft)
Mean Depth: 12 m (39 ft)
Way Point: 52° 20′ 18″ N, 125° 11′ 44″ W

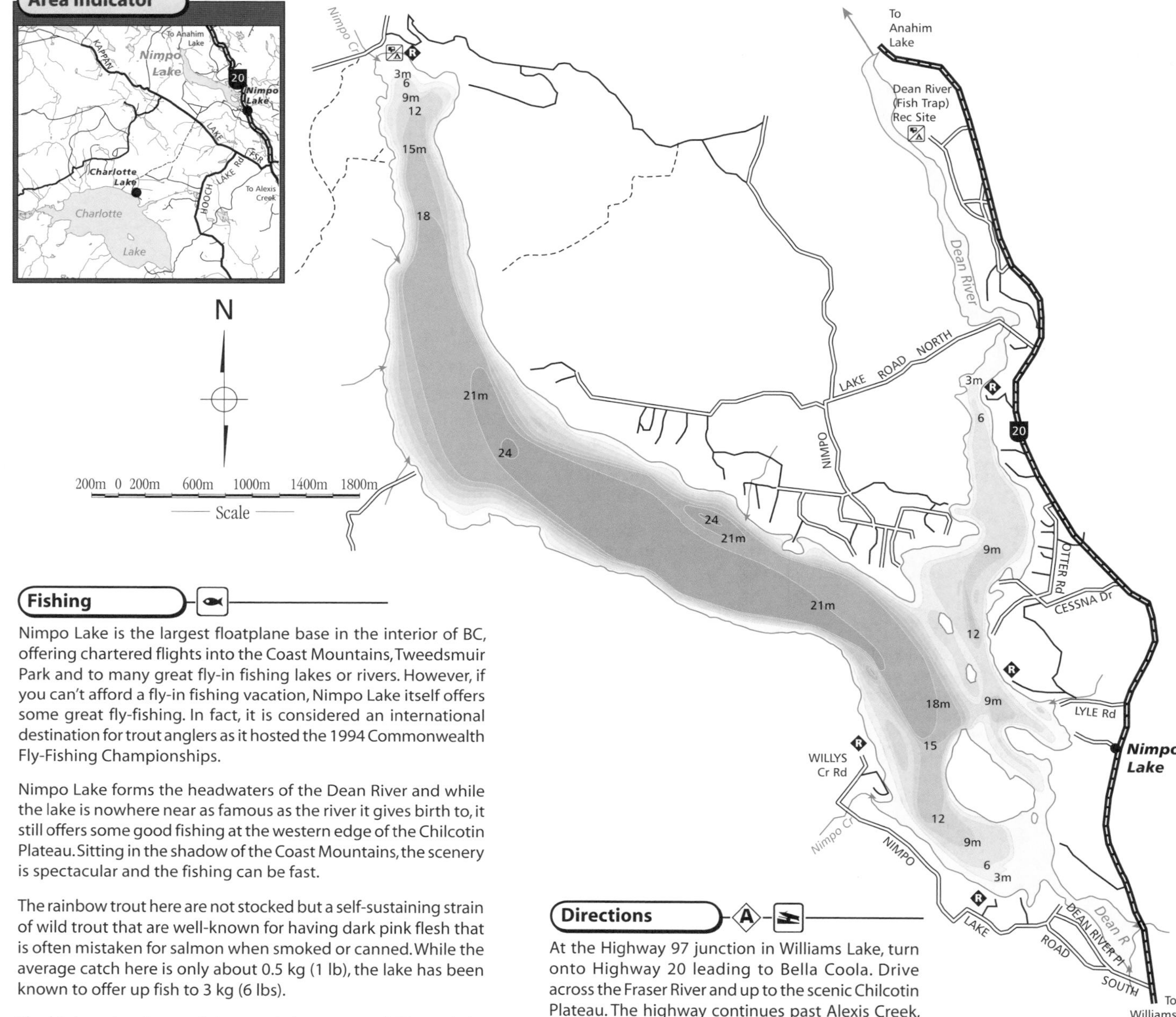

Fishing

Nimpo Lake is the largest floatplane base in the interior of BC, offering chartered flights into the Coast Mountains, Tweedsmuir Park and to many great fly-in fishing lakes or rivers. However, if you can't afford a fly-in fishing vacation, Nimpo Lake itself offers some great fly-fishing. In fact, it is considered an international destination for trout anglers as it hosted the 1994 Commonwealth Fly-Fishing Championships.

Nimpo Lake forms the headwaters of the Dean River and while the lake is nowhere near as famous as the river it gives birth to, it still offers some good fishing at the western edge of the Chilcotin Plateau. Sitting in the shadow of the Coast Mountains, the scenery is spectacular and the fishing can be fast.

The rainbow trout here are not stocked but a self-sustaining strain of wild trout that are well-known for having dark pink flesh that is often mistaken for salmon when smoked or canned. While the average catch here is only about 0.5 kg (1 lb), the lake has been known to offer up fish to 3 kg (6 lbs).

The higher elevation and deeper, darker waters of Nimpo Lake provide excellent fishing from ice-off in late April to mid-July, when the water warms. The fishing picks up again in September and ice fishing is also good during those chilly months.

Fly-fishers can work the shallows among the lily pads with black Doc Spratleys, green Carey Specials, damselfly nymphs and mayfly nymphs as the season dictates. In June, work Tom Thumbs and Mikaluk sedge patterns along the lily pads and reeds. When trolling flies, use a sinking fly line and a red or black Spratley, black leech or Muddler Minnow.

The best spot to troll is over deep water, past the island towards the main body of the lake. Work a green, black, gold or silver Flatfish, with a five to six metre, six pound test leader and a Hot Shot flasher. Lake trolls, such as a Ford Fender, with a worm or a Wedding Band and worm also works well.

Spincasters should fish from a boat with a Blue Fox Vibrax or Mepps Aglia in gold or silver.

Directions

At the Highway 97 junction in Williams Lake, turn onto Highway 20 leading to Bella Coola. Drive across the Fraser River and up to the scenic Chilcotin Plateau. The highway continues past Alexis Creek, Tatla Lake and Kleena Kleene stretching about 290 km (180 mile) before reaching the western side of the Chilcotin and Nimpo Lake. The scenic grasslands of the plateau give way to the Chilcotin River Valley and it's pine forests before the eastern foothills of the majestic Coast Mountains rise above you.

Facilities

With horseback riding, mountain biking, numerous hiking trails and good fishing, this is truly a family destination. There are a number of lodges available just off of Highway 20, along the eastern arm or the south and north end of Nimpo Lake. Seasonal and full-time residences also dot the shoreline. The community has a store, service station and small restaurant, while a few rough dirt roads provide access points to the north and west shore. There are no developed public camping facilities.

Nulki & Tachick Lakes

Location: 15 km (9 mi) southwest of Vanderhoof

Fishing

This pair of lakes could lay claim to being the centre of fishing activity in British Columbia. Not because they are so popular, though they certainly are that, but because the two lakes are found just a few kilometers southwest of the geographic centre of the province. Of the two, Nulki gives up more fish and is the more popular destination.

The lakes are very pretty and if the fish aren't biting, there's usually some wildlife–moose, deer, or birds, including trumpeter swans or white pelicans–to distract you. But the fish are usually biting and these two lakes are considered the most productive and popular lakes around Vanderhoof. In fact, both lakes host a number of fishing derbies over the course of the year.

A lot of their popularity has to do with the size of the fish. Both lakes produce good sized rainbow trout. In Nulki Lake, trout can get up to 2 kg (4 lbs) while in nearby Tachick Lake, the rainbow get up to 3 kg (6 lbs). While the average in both lakes is much smaller, there's always a chance of catching one of these good sized rainbow. Both lakes are stocked quite heavily with the Blackwater strain of rainbow, which feed on the redside shiner and other small course fish that inhabit the lakes.

Nulki is 8 km (5 miles) long and Tachick is 13 km (7.9 miles) long. Both lakes are very deep and they fish quite similarly. They are too big to be worked from a float tube, but a cartopper or bigger boat will serve you just fine. Most anglers prefer to troll using a Willow Leaf and Wedding Band tipped with bait, or a small Flatfish or Apex.

While fly-fishing is not popular at either lake, some people do bring a fly rod and gear along to Nulki. Fly fishers will find that trolling a Doc Spratley, Woolly Bugger or nymph works as well as anything else. Some people will stop and cast towards the drop off, but most people troll the lakes and almost nobody dry fly fishes here.

Similar to the open water season, Nulki sees more fishing pressure. The lake has a good population of burbot which are hard to catch in the summer but are quite active in the cold winter waters. They are usually caught in shallower water using (smelly) bait suspended just off the bottom.

Area Indicator

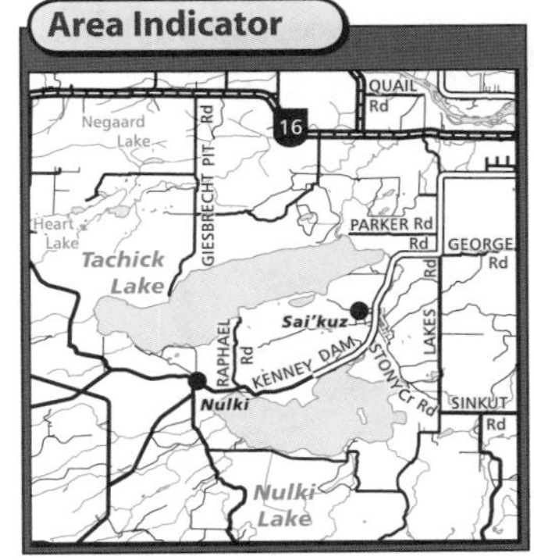

Nulki Lake

Elevation: 719 m (2,359 ft)
Surface Area: 1,656 ha (4,092 ac)
Max Depth: 7.6 m (25 ft)
Mean Depth: 4.4 m (14 ft)
Way Point: 53° 54'35"N, 124° 8'15"W

Nulki Lake Fish Stocking Data			
Year	Species	Number	Life Stage
2008	Rainbow Trout	10,000	Yearling
2007	Rainbow Trout	10,090	Yearling
2006	Rainbow Trout	10,000	Yearling

Tachick Lake Fish Stocking Data			
Year	Species	Number	Life Stage
2007	Rainbow Trout	40,176	Yearling
2006	Rainbow Trout	40,000	Yearling
2005	Rainbow Trout	40,000	Yearling

Tachick Lake

Elevation: 712 m (2,336 ft)
Surface Area: 2,208 ha (5,456 ac)
Maximum Depth: 7.6 m (25 ft)
Mean Depth: 4.4 m (14 ft)
Waypoint: 53° 57'22"N, 124° 11'27"W

Directions

Found southwest of Vanderhoof, these lakes are easily accessed from the Yellowhead Highway off the Kenny Dam Road. The best access to Nulki Lake is found about 15.5 km from the highway at Sai Kuz Park. Tachick Lake is found on the north side of the Kenny Dam Road off a series of side roads. The most westerly leads to a boat launch site.

Facilities

Sai Kuz Park is a full service resort on Nulki Lake that offers camping and cabin rentals along with a boat launch. A couple cabins are open year round for ice anglers who come to the lake. There is even a Potlatch house on site, a large building with space for 250 people, big enough for weddings, dances and conventions. Those looking to access Tachick Lake should continue to the west end where a boat launch is found.

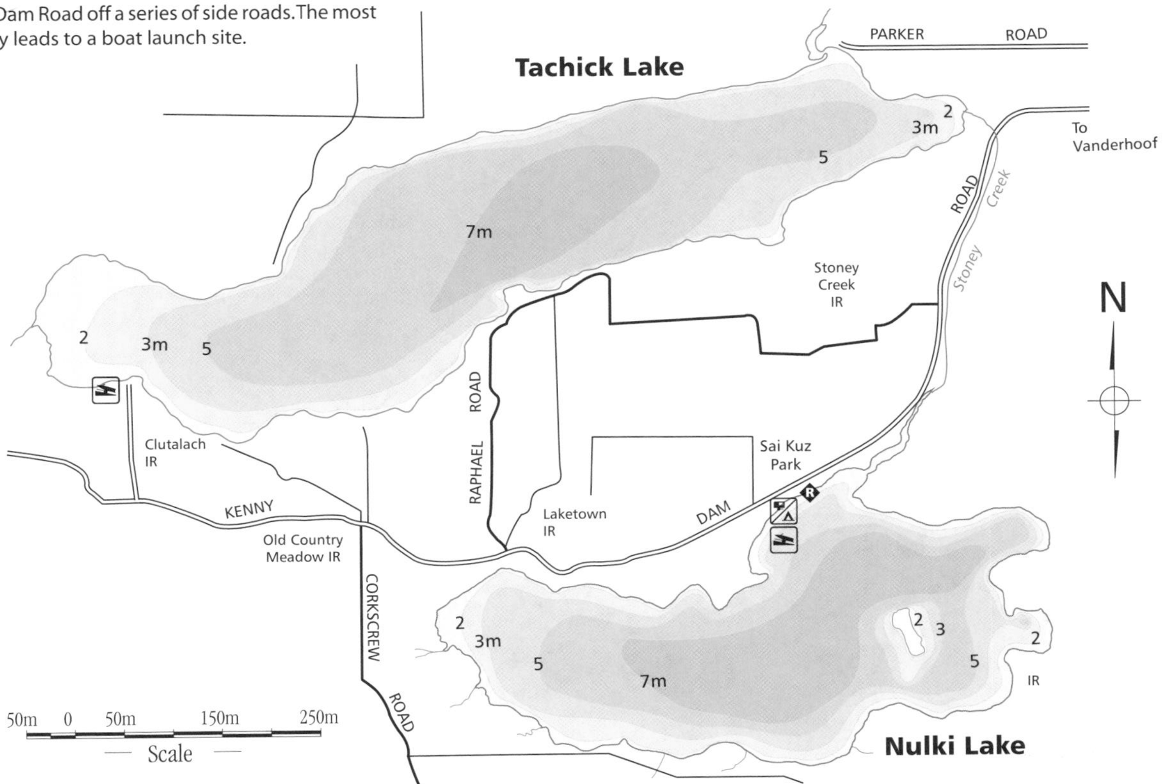

Location: 240 km (150 mi) west of Williams Lake
Elevation: 915 m (3,001 ft)
Surface Area: 487 ha (1,203 ac)
Maximum Depth: 15 m (49 ft)
Mean Depth: 7.8 m (25 ft)
Way Point: 51° 58′ 10″ N, 124° 53′ 54″ W

One Eye Lake

Area Indicator

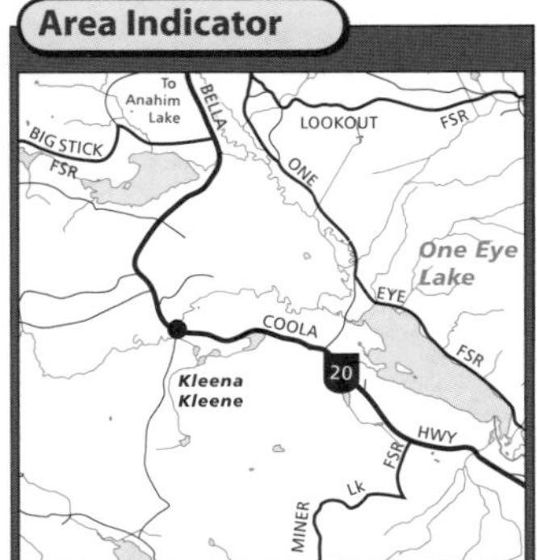

Fishing

One Eye Lake is one of the last lakes found on the Chilcotin Plateau before the plateau gives way to the Coastal Mountains. While it isn't tucked up right against the mountains it is on the west side of the Chilcotin Divide: the Klinaklini River flows through One Eye Lake and west on its way to the coast, while water from nearby Tatla Lake drains east via the Chikano River into the Chilcotin and ultimately the Fraser.

While the Klinaklini flows through One Eye Lake, salmon are unable to migrate this far upstream. Instead, the lake has good fishing for rainbow trout to 1.5 kg (3 lbs) and Dolly Varden to 4.5 kg (10 lbs). The lake has plenty of course fish, too, which explains the large dollies. Unlike rainbow trout, Dolly Varden feed on other fish and there are plenty of course fish in the lake for them to feed on. This reduces the amount of competition for the food, allowing the rainbow trout to grow larger than they might otherwise.

The lake is a mid elevation lake and is generally ice free around the same time as most of the Chilcotin Plateau lakes are, which is usually around the end of April or early May, depending on snowpack. Unlike many of the other lakes in the Chilcotin, One Eye Lake doesn't turn over. This phenomenon occurs in many lakes as the surface of the lake warms in spring and cools in fall. When the temperature of the top water is the same as the temperature as the deeper water. This allows the water to start to mix, turning up rotting vegetation and carbon dioxide from the lower reaches of the lake. While it ultimately results in more oxygen in the water, the week or two when this is happening means that the fishing is basically non-existent.

Because the lake is basically a widening of the Klinaklini River, there is too much water flowing through the lake to allow it to stratify. This means the fishing is pretty much steady from ice-off to ice on. Even during summer, anglers can usually find trout willing to bite.

The best fishing is usually around the inflow of the Klinaklini River, as the water is cool and well oxygenated and food washes into the lake from the river. The usual Chilcotin rainbow fly patterns will work on the lake.

Some fly anglers try a Muddler Minnow for the dollies, but these char are best caught on a spoon or lake troll with a baited hook. Jigging a bucktail and flasher near the inflow of the river can also be quite effective.

Directions

While you will find One Eye Lake referred to as a "remote fly-in lake" by some people, it doesn't need to be. In fact, the lake is one of the easiest lakes to access in the Chilcotin, situated just north of Highway 20. It is about 240 km (150 miles) from Williams Lake to the lake, which will be on your right, just past Tatla Lake. If you hit Kleena Kleene, you have gone too far.

Facilities

Because it is so easily accessed along Highway 20, the **One Eye Lake Recreation Site** is fairly busy throughout the year. While most of the use comes from anglers, there are a fair number of people just coming to camp at the seven unit site, too. There is a cartop boat launch.

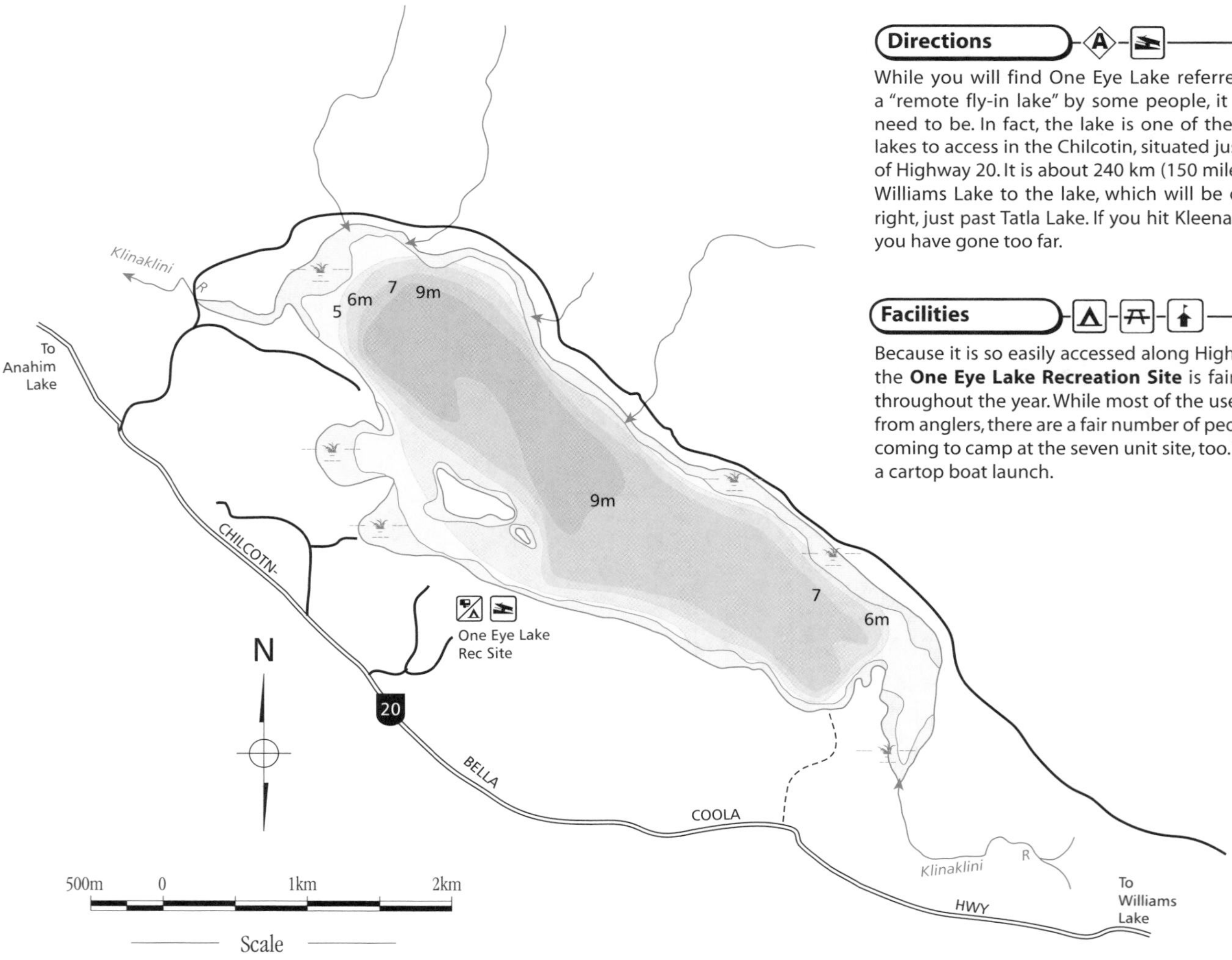

Klinaklini R
To Anahim Lake
CHILCOTIN-BELLA COOLA HWY
20
One Eye Lake Rec Site
To Williams Lake
5 6m 7 9m 9m 7 6m
N
500m 0 1km 2km
Scale

One Island Lake

Location: 52 km (32 mi) southeast of Dawson Creek
Elevation: 897m (2,942ft)
Surface Area: 158 ha (390 ac)
Maximum Depth: 10.7 m (35 ft)
Mean Depth: 3.5 m (12 ft)
Way Point: 55° 18′ 15″ N, 120° 17′ 36″ W

Fishing

Rainbow trout, the fisheries biologist will tell you, gain about half a kilogram (about a pound) a year. That means that even the biggest strain of rainbow, with a lifespan of about seven years, should get to a maximum of 5 kg (10 lbs).

So why do so many people who fish One Island Lake claim to have caught fish to 6 kg (12 lbs) and larger? Heck, the biggest fish to come out of this lake, people claim, weighed 10 kg (22 lbs). Even if these are just fishing stories, the fact remains that lots of big fish have been caught here.

This is a result of the lake having lots and lots of freshwater shrimp, which the fish gorge on. There are also some course fish that the larger fish eat, too, but the primary food is the shrimp. In fact, there is so much shrimp that the trout have a pinkish flesh that has often been confused with salmon on the plate.

The lake is stocked annually with 5,000 rainbow and 5,000 brook trout annually. Even the brookies reach great sizes with regular reports of fish in the 3.5 kg (7 lb) range. The brook trout help make this a decent place to fish in the winter.

There are about 50 cabins on the shores of the lake and the place can be quite busy in summer. While the fishing is best in spring and fall, it sees heavy use year round.

Most people who fish the lake do so trolling a Willow Leaf. Locals say that one of the best ways to fish the lake is to head towards the southwest end of the lake and just jig or cast a bobber and worm there.

The lake is also a good fly-fishing lake. As mentioned, there are plenty of shrimp in the lake and tying on a shrimp pattern can work. However the lake is one of the few lakes in the area that has leeches and a leech pattern can work well, too. Other popular patterns include Muddler Minnows or other streamers.

The island on One Island Lake lies across from the provincial park, where you will see at least one nesting pair of bald eagles. The lake is also on the flight path for migrating swans in the fall and there is plenty of wildlife in the area. However, there is also plenty of oil and gas development in the area. While the area around the lake has been heavily impacted, the lake itself is still a prime producer.

Area Indicator

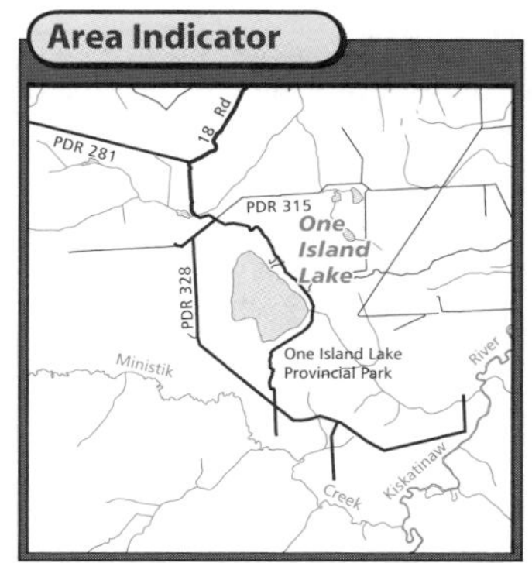

One Island Lake Fish Stocking Data			
Year	Species	Number	Life Stage
2008	Brook Trout	5,000	Fingerling
2008	Rainbow Trout	5,000	Yearling
2007	Brook Trout	4,275	Fingerling
2007	Rainbow Trout	5,000	Yearling
2006	Brook Trout	5,000	Fingerling
2006	Rainbow Trout	5,000	Yearling

Directions

To get to the lake, head southeast of Dawson Creek for 30 km on Highway 2. Turn right onto Highway 52 or Boundary Road, which weaves its way towards Tumbler Ridge. After about 10 km watch for the road to One Island Lake (Road 18) splitting off to the right. While there is a mess of oil and gas roads back here, the road to the park is well signed and fairly easy to drive. It was recently rebuilt as heavy industrial traffic was destroying access to the lake for cottage owners. While it still sees a lot of heavy industrial traffic and caution needs to be exercised when driving back here, the actual road is well maintained and can be driven with most vehicles.

Facilities

One Island Lake Provincial Park is a former recreation site turned into a provincial park that hasn't outgrown its roots. If you are looking for a front country camping experience, forget it. There is, however, a gravel boat launch, suitable for full sized boats.

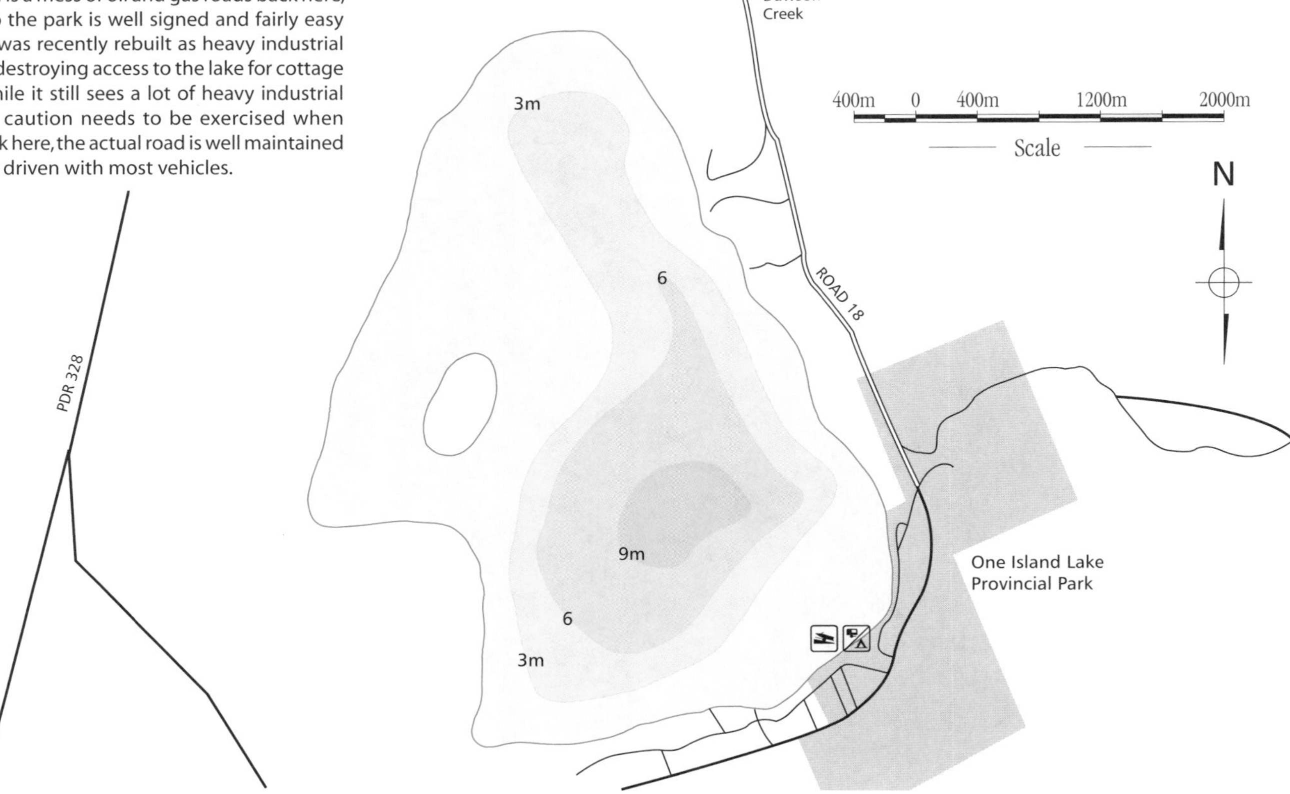

Location: 50 km (31 mi) north of Dawson Creek
Stream Lenght: 170 km (105 miles)
Geographic: 56°11′00″N, 120°50′00″W

Peace River

Fishing

The Peace River is one of Western Canada's great rivers, draining an area of about 302,500 square kilometers and flowing for 1,923 km (1,195 miles) from the head of Finlay River to Lake Athabasca. It is the longest river and has the largest watershed of any river originating in BC.

However, unlike the Fraser or the Skeena, the Peace is not a uniquely BC river. It flows east out of the province and into Alberta. Most of the river's BC portion is trapped behind the WAC Bennett Dam, where it springs fully formed out of Williston Lake. It flows past Hudson Hope and Fort St. John before crossing out of the province. This stretch of river offers about 170 km (105 miles) of fishable water.

The Peace River holds a wide variety of fish, as befits such a large river. Species include northern pike, walleye, bull trout, rainbow trout, lake trout, mountain whitefish, lake whitefish, Arctic grayling and burbot. The best fishing usually happens around the inlets of feeder streams, including the Kiskatinaw, Pine and Halfway Rivers.

Shore fishing can be done at a variety of places along the river, but with mixed success. The river is broad and there is no guarantee the fish will be near shore. However, in late spring there are a variety of caddis and mayfly hatches near shore that brings the trout in. Fly-fishing from the banks on evenings when the insects are hatching and the trout are rising can be magical. Dry fly-fishing the Peace around Hudson's Hope at the right time can rival rivers like the Bow in Alberta. Rainbow to 5 kg (10 lbs) have been pulled out of the water.

Pike and walleye are the most common targets in the big river and are usually caught by vertical jigging or spincasting crankbait or spoons along current seams. These predatory fish will hold in slower moving water, waiting to ambush prey.

The river is big and broad and sometimes fishes more like a lake than a river. This includes a tendency for winds to pick up down the valley and create dangerous conditions for boaters. Waves up to 2 metres (6 feet) high can be a problem.

Directions

The Peace River can be accessed from a few locations along its route in BC. From Chetwynd and Highway 97, turn north onto Highway 29. Continue past Moberly Lake and on to Hudson's Hope, where the river and highway course east towards Fort St. John. Highway 29 parallels the river for about 65 km before the highway climbs out of the valley. Another popular place to access the river is at the town of Taylor, northeast of Dawson Creek on the Alaska Highway.

Facilities

In addition to launches at **Taylor Landing Provincial Park** (little more than a boat launch and toilets) and **Peace Island Regional Park,** there are boat launches below the Hudson's Hope Museum. Access can also be found off of D.A. Thomas Road and just beside the Lynx Creek Bridge as you head north of Hudson's Hope on Highway 29. You can find accommodations, food and gas in Taylor, Hudson's Hope or Fort St. John, while random camping is allowed along the river.

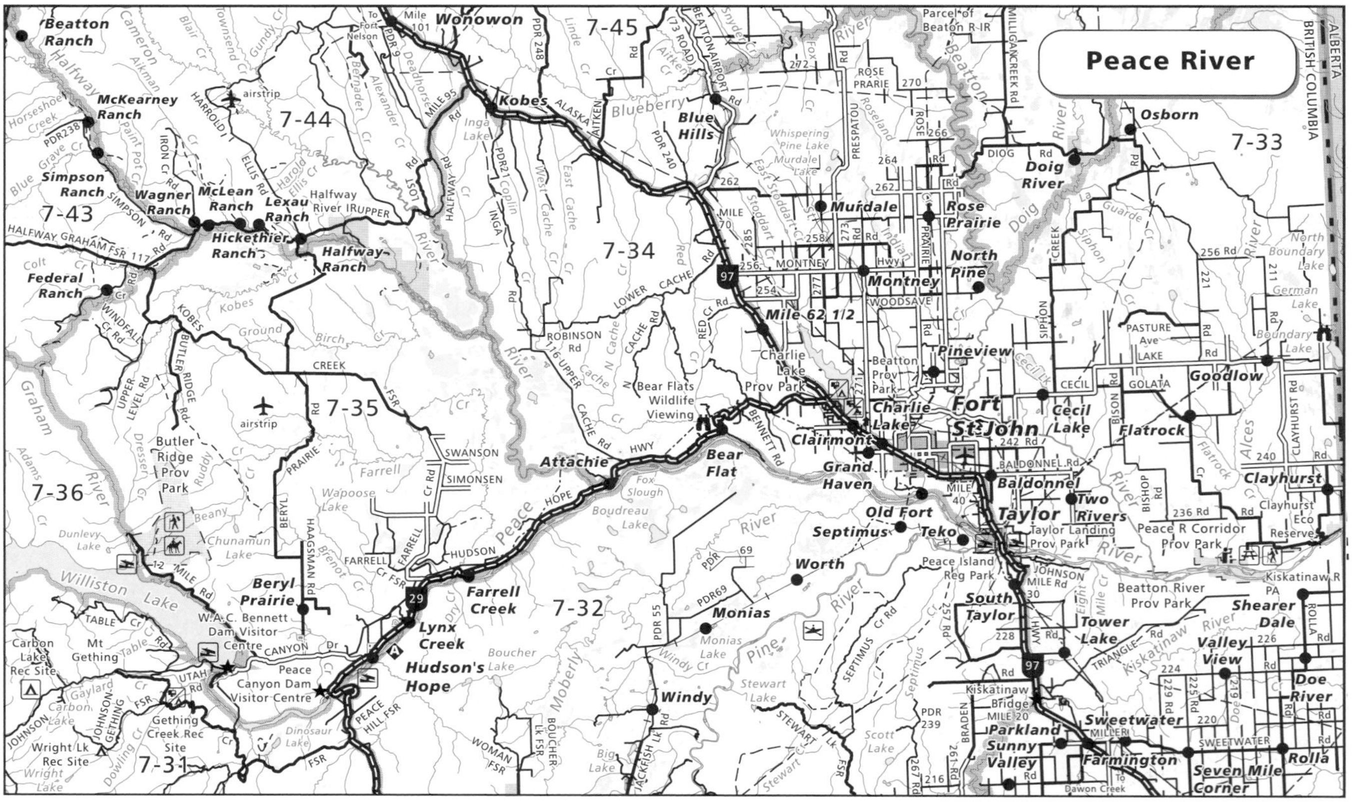

Peace River

Pinkut Lake

Location: 20 km (12.5 miles) north of Burns Lake
Elevation: 919 m (3,014 ft)
Surface Area: 575 ha (1,352 ac)
Maximum Depth: 32 m (104 ft)
Mean Depth: 10.4 m (34 ft)
Way Point: 54° 23′ 21″ N, 125° 39′ 57″ W

Fishing

Pinkut Lake is a mid sized lake found north of Burns Lake. Like it's companion lake, Augier, Pinkuit offers good fishing for rainbow trout and lake trout.

The lake is known for its sandy beach and for being a great family lake. It is a pretty lake and a popular weekend get-away for folks in Burns Lake. While it is only about twenty minutes from town, it is far enough away to have a sense of wilderness.

The lake is usually trolled. For rainbow trout, any of the traditional trolling techniques work. The old faithful is a Wedding Band, with or without a worm. However, little Flatfish are also a popular choice.

There is some fly-fishing that happens here, but not much. People have tried fishing from the shore near the recreation site with some success.

Near the Ethel F. Wilson Provincial Park is a creek that flows into the lake. People who have a canoe or float tube can quite easily get out onto the lake and work around this area. Some popular fly patterns include nymphs, Woolly Buggers and a small beetle-like terrestrial pattern. This latter is an attempt to emulate the pine beetle, as the fish have discovered these tasty (to a fish) treats. During certain times, pine beetles are a staple of the fish's diet and even trollers have reported catching fish that were full of these little black beetles.

Most of the trout that come out of the lake aren't big but there are quite a few of them and it is a rare day that someone is completely skunked.

For the larger lake trout, you will need a bigger lure. You will also need to get it right down to the bottom of the lake where the lake trout hang out. The standard is a T50 Flatfish in a darker colour. The go-to lure is usually black with silver flecks, but having a touch of green or yellow on the underbelly of the lure is also quite popular. A dark-coloured Swim Whiz is another popular choice.

Some people will jig a big spoon for lake trout, but more often than not they will troll, either using a leadcore line or a downrigger. People who are fishing for lakers tend to stay down near the south end of the lake, as the lake is deeper there.

The lake also holds burbot. Occasionally, you will find someone fishing for burbot on a set line, but generally, most people fish for rainbow or lake trout.

There is some ice fishing that happens for lake trout and burbot. For lakers, using a spoon is the most popular, while the burbot go wild for a baited hook, using a very smelly bait.

Area Indicator

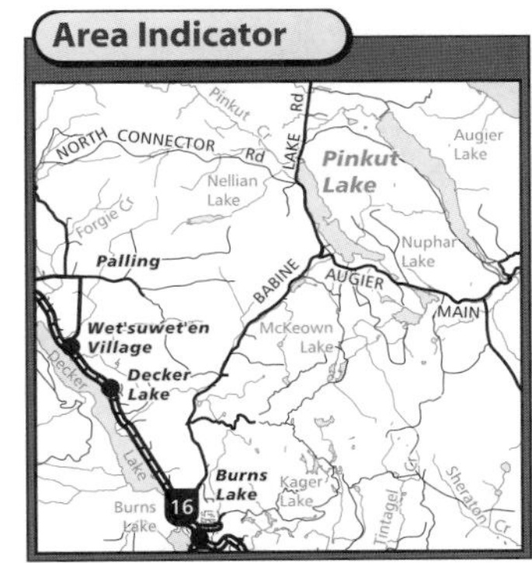

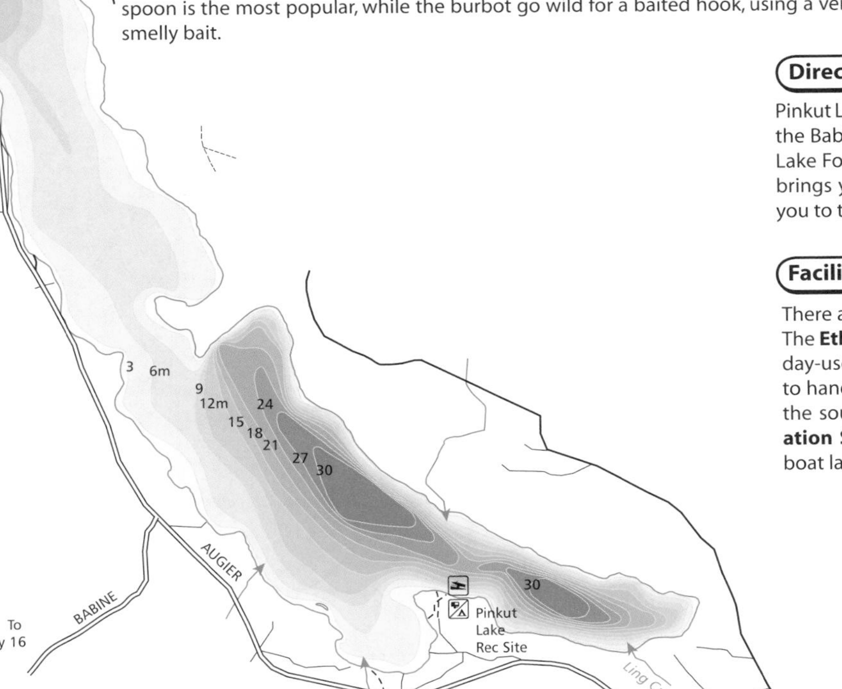

Directions

Pinkut Lake is north of the town of Burns Lake along the Babine Lake Road. At the junction with Augier Lake Forest Service Road, you have a choice. Right brings you to the recreation site, while left brings you to the provincial park.

Facilities

There are two public access points on Pinkut Lake. The **Ethel F. Wilson Memorial Provincial Park** is a day-use site only that offers little more than a place to hand launch. Early in spring, it can be buggy. To the south, the more popular **Pinkut Lake Recreation Site** offers five camping sites and a gravel boat launch. It is usually full on weekends.

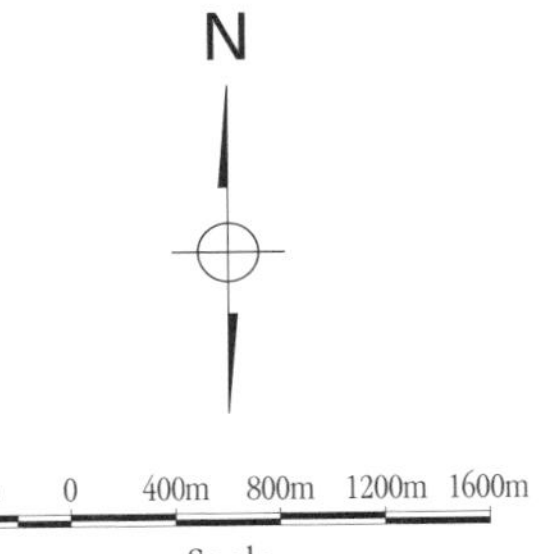

Location: 60 km (37 mi) northeast of Williams Lake
Elevation: 921 m (3,022 ft)
Surface Area: 453 ha (1,120 ac)
Maximum Depth: 35 m (115 ft)
Mean Depth: 18 m (59 ft)
Way Point: 52° 33′ 14″ N, 121° 36′ 23″ W

Polley Lake

Area Indicator

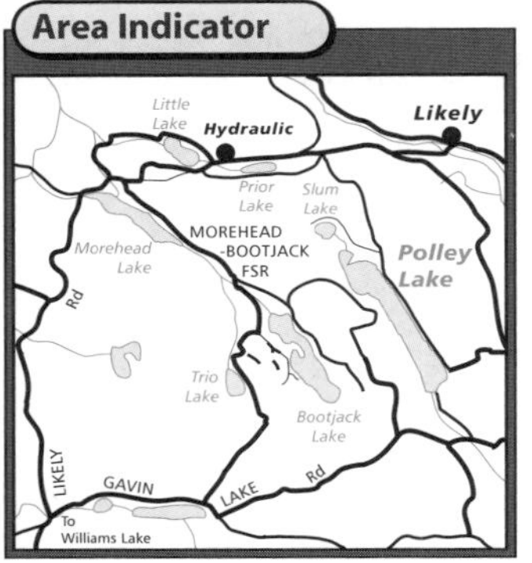

Fishing

Polley Lake is found south of Likely to the east of Quesnel Lake. This is a land of rolling hills covered by forests. Nearby Polley Mountain, the tallest in the area, is only about 500 metres (1,640 feet) above the lake.

The lake gets its name from one "Mr. W. Polley" a local prospector who held placer leases in the area. These days, the area is still known for an odd magnetic anomaly, suggesting the presence of a higher than normal concentration of magnetic minerals in the underlying rock of the region, which suggests that there is still gold in them there hills.

However, most people visiting the area are more likely to come bearing a rod and reel as opposed to a gold pan, searching for the silver flash of a rainbow trout, not the dull gleam of gold. The lake has rainbow up to 2 kg (4.5 lbs) caught by trolling, fly-fishing and spincasting.

The lake is fairly low in elevation (less than 1,000 metres) and is best fished in the spring. The summer doldrums hit the lake by mid July and the fishing is quite slow in the summer. By October, the fishing is very good again.

Since the lake is deep (35 metres or 115 feet) it is easily trolled. There is a prominent drop off surrounding most of the lake so troll just off the drop off area with a lake troll or small lure tipped with a worm. Shore casting is also fairly easy as the water drops off rapidly from shore. However, spincasters and fly anglers are best to anchor 8–15 metres (25–50 feet) from shore and work the near shore area with a lure tipped with a worm or with a dragonfly nymph, chironomid or damselfly nymph depending on the hatch.

There is some top water fishing on the lake during the mayfly and damselfly hatches, but don't go expecting great surface fishing. Still, it would be a shame to get there without a dry fly or ten in your box and miss all the excitement if there is a hatch. The most used fly in the area is the always reliable Tom Thumb, but it is best to have a wider selection like an Adams as well as mosquito or even beetle patterns.

In the fall, working a nymph pattern on a sinking line can work well. Other attractor patterns such as a Woolly Bugger or Doc Spratley are also popular.

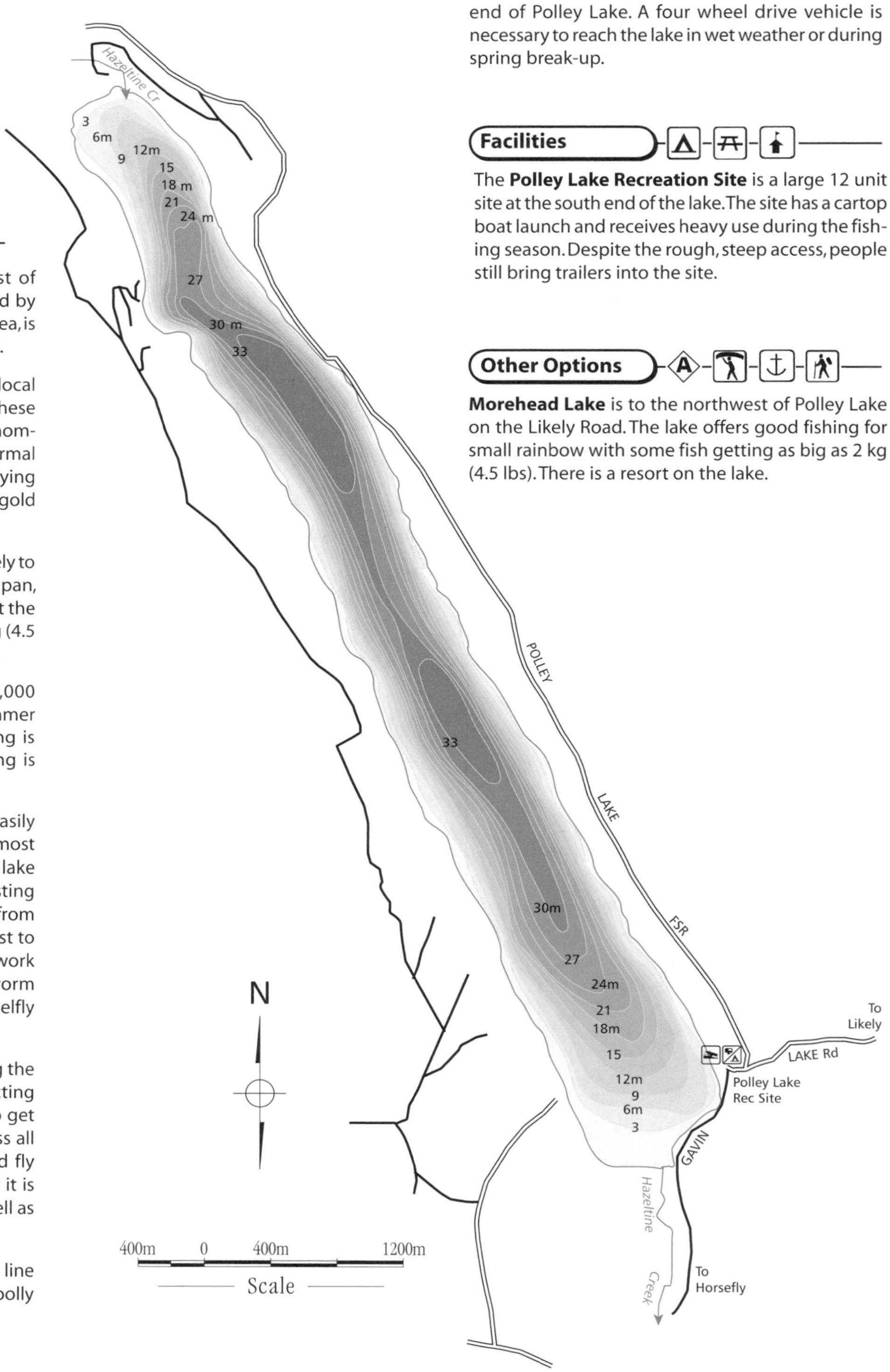

Directions

From Likely, follow the rough, cross-ditched Horsefly-Likely Forest Service Road south. About 10 km later, the Polley Lake Forest Service Road branches right (west). This road climbs out of the valley and it is about 4.5 km to the recreation site at the south end of Polley Lake. A four wheel drive vehicle is necessary to reach the lake in wet weather or during spring break-up.

Facilities

The **Polley Lake Recreation Site** is a large 12 unit site at the south end of the lake. The site has a cartop boat launch and receives heavy use during the fishing season. Despite the rough, steep access, people still bring trailers into the site.

Other Options

Morehead Lake is to the northwest of Polley Lake on the Likely Road. The lake offers good fishing for small rainbow with some fish getting as big as 2 kg (4.5 lbs). There is a resort on the lake.

Hazeltine Cr
POLLEY LAKE FSR
To Likely
LAKE Rd
Polley Lake Rec Site
GAVIN
Hazeltine Creek
To Horsefly
N
400m 0 400m 1200m
Scale

Puntzi Lake

Location: 135 km (84 mi) west of Williams Lake
Elevation: 958 m (3,143 ft)
Surface Area: 1,706 ha (4,216 ac)
Maximum Depth: 44 m (144 ft)
Mean Depth: 23 m (75 ft)
Way Point: 52° 11′ 42″ N, 124° 2′ 22″ W

Fishing

In the 1950s, the Pinetree Radar Line was built as a joint Canadian and US effort to detect a Soviet air threat against North America. A radar station and airstrip were built near Puntzi Lake and was operational from 1952 to 1966. The lake is also one of the best sites in the Chilcotin to see American white pelicans and trumpeter swans.

Oh, yeah, the lake also offers some of the best fishing in the Chilcotin. The lake is 11 km (7 miles) long and up to 5 km (3 miles) wide at its widest. In the 1980s, the lake was heavily stocked in an effort to rehabilitate the rainbow trout population. Since then other measures have been taken to improve the quality of fishing here. And it has worked. The lake has a healthy stock of rainbow as well as kokanee, both of which can get up to 1.5 kg (3 lbs).

Both kokanee and rainbow fish very similar, but, because the kokanee have a very soft mouth, a rubber snubber should be used. Even if you are not deliberately fishing for kokanee, chances are you are going to catch some.

The best time to fish here is in May and June, although the fishing is fairly steady through to October. Try trolling a Ford Fender or a Willow Leaf, generally with a baited hook, or spincasting a small spoon, spinner or Flatfish. Fly anglers can troll an attractor fly like a Doc Spratley or Carey Special.

Fly-fishing is quite effective in the spring, when the hatches are on, although success does tend to fall off in the summer. In fall the fly-fishing can pick up.

A popular time to visit the lake is during the first weekend in July, when the Puntzi Lake Fishing Derby happens. While the fishing can be a bit of a gong show, it can be a great time of getting together with other anglers and trading stories over the fire.

Once the lake is frozen, the fishing doesn't stop. Since it can get bitterly cold, folks fishing through the ice won't have much success for rainbow trout, especially after the ice has been on for a few months. But kokanee will still be biting, as will the whitefish.

Ice fishing gear can be as simple or as complex as you want to make it. All you really need is a length of line and a baited hook. A baited jigging lure is also a good option.

Fish are rarely found deeper than 3 metres (10 feet), so you don't need a rod or reel. Oh and an ice auger would probably be a good thing to bring along, too. Some people bring fish finders, but it is easy enough to peer through the hole and see the fish.

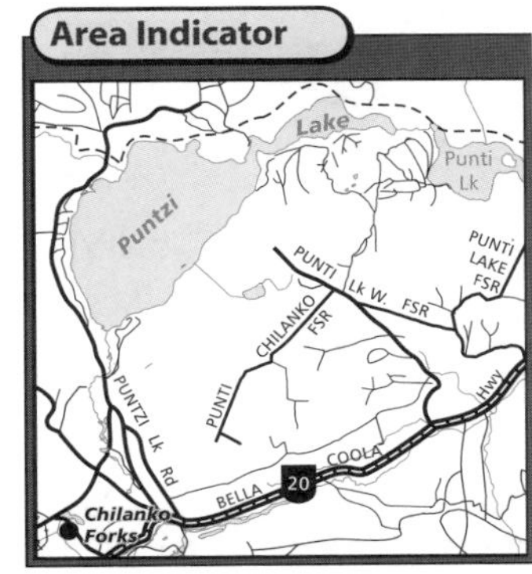

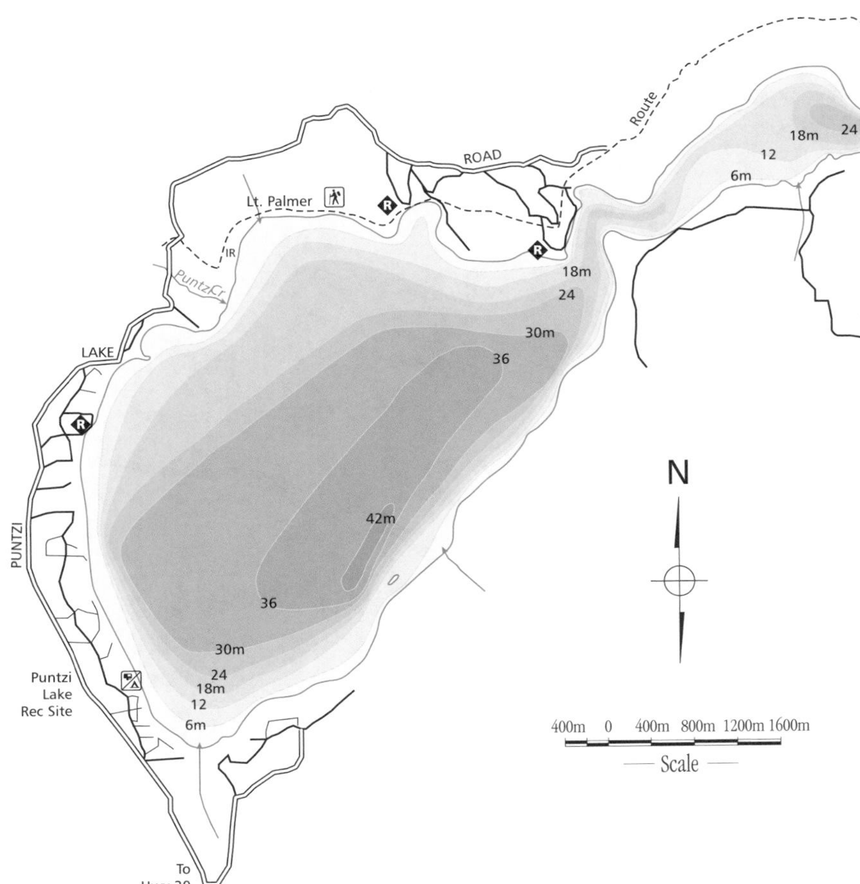

Directions

Puntzi Lake is just north of Highway 20. If you are coming from the east, watch for the Puntzi Lake Road a 'few' kilometres past the Redstone Gas Station. This good gravel road will take you past the resorts and the recreation site.

Facilities

The **Puntzi Lake Recreation Site** is a five unit site on the western shore of the lake. It is possible to launch a cartopper, but many people choose to stay at one of the resorts on the lake. These include **Howdy's Lakeside Resort**, **Barney's Lakeside**, **Puntzi Lake Resort**, **Kokanee Bay Resort** and the **Poplar Grove Resort.**

Location: 64 km (39.7 mi) east of Prince George
Elevation: 773 m (2,536 ft)
Surface Area: 836 ha (2,065 ac)
Mean Depth: 26 m (85 ft)
Max Depth: 48 m (157 ft)
Way Point: 53° 54′ 58″ N, 121° 54′ 56″ W

Purden Lake

Area Indicator

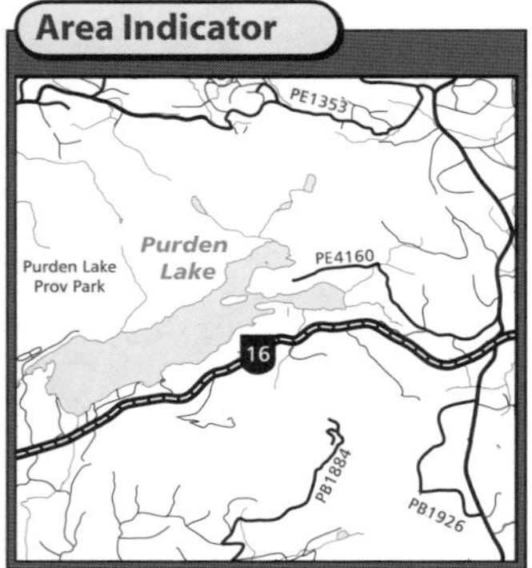

Purden Lake			
Fish Stocking Data			
Year	Species	Number	Life Stage
2008	Rainbow Trout	10,000	Yearling
2007	Rainbow Trout	10,000	Yearling
2006	Rainbow Trout	10,000	Yearling

Fishing

Nestled in the rolling mountains east of Prince George Purden Lake is a pretty lake to visit. The Cariboo Mountains rise in the south, while the McGregor Range is seen in the north. The lake is surrounded by a dense forest, but anglers will find a few open areas near the shore, especially in the park area found on the lake's southern shore.

The lake is an extremely popular summer getaway from Prince George and people come here to camp, hike, swim and water ski in summer. There are plenty of cabins on the south shore of the lake, while a provincial park protects the rest of the shoreline.

People also come here to fish, but the fishing can be frustratingly slow. This is despite the fact that the Freshwater Fisheries Society of BC stocks the lake with 10,000 rainbow trout annually. However, if you do find one, chances are it's going to be a good sized trout. While there are certainly small fish here, you stand a good chance of landing a rainbow in the 1 kg (2 lb) range. The trout can get up to about twice that size, but those fish are a bit rarer.

Because the lake is so big, trolling is the preferred method of fishing, using the traditional Willow Leaf and Wedding Band or trout lure or spoon. Work around the edges of the lake, near the drop offs. The best fishing usually happens at the east end of the lake, opposite the provincial park. Here you will find an island and a sort of sheltered bay north of the island. Try working the channel on the north side of the island and into the bay. There are also good drop offs along the north and south shores of the lake, about halfway down.

Speaking of wind, the lake can get quite rough when the winds blow up. As a result, a bigger boat is preferable. Another concern for anglers is all the boat traffic during the summer. All the noise and splashing tends to make the fish a bit skittish. At this time, it is best to fish early in the morning or later at night.

In addition to stocked rainbow trout, Purden Lake also holds plenty of burbot. Burbot can be hard to find from spring through to fall, as they tend to hang out in the deepest points of the lake. In order to find them in summer, it is best to tie on a jig and fish down in the deepest points of the lake.

However, in winter, the cold-water-loving burbot are much more active and can be caught in shallower water, usually 5 metres (25 feet) or less. Burbot love bait…anything smelly like chicken liver or cut herring. Usually you need to fish within a few feet, preferably a few in, of the bottom. Do note, however, that the lake is spring fed and the ice can be very thin.

Directions

Purden Lake is found 64 km east of Prince George on the Yellowhead Highway (Highway 16). Watch for the signed turnoff into the provincial park on the west side of the lake.

Facilities

The **Purden Lake Provincial Park** offers 78 campsites, including seven double units and twelve tent only sites. There is a concrete boat launch and a separate beach for boaters and water skiers.

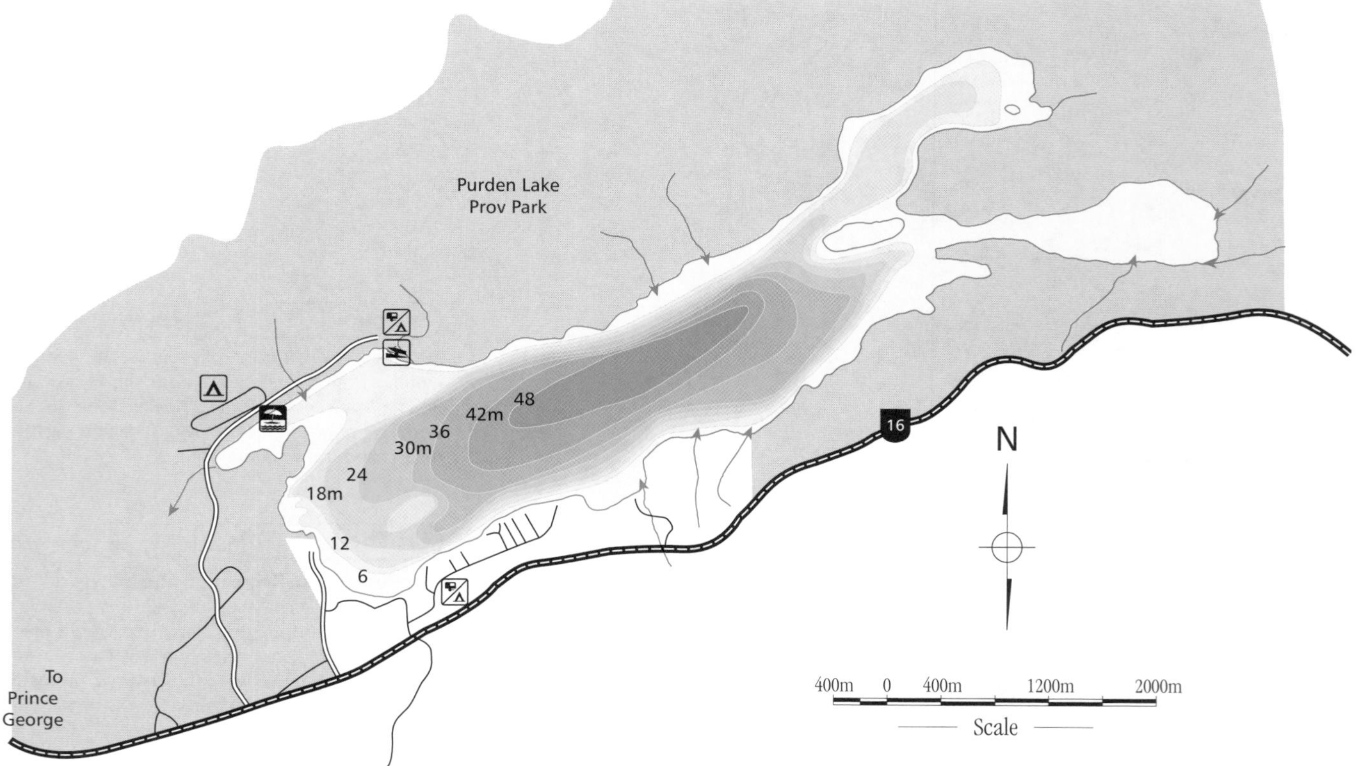

Quality Lake

Location: 7 km (4.3 mi) east of Tumbler Ridge
Elevation: 1,056 m (3,464 ft)
Surface Area: 20 ha (49 ac)
Maximum Depth: 6.2 m (203 ft)
Mean Depth: 2.1m (6.9 ft)
Way Point: 55° 5′ 55″ N, 120° 53′ 37″ W

Fishing

In the last few years, there have been a few reports of a grizzly bear, who thinks he owns the place, chasing anglers away from this lake. You have been warned.

That said, people who do make the trip will find great fishing for all skill levels. Catch rates for good sized rainbow trout are quite high.

The lake is quite shallow, with crystal clear water and has a history of winterkill. But it is stocked annually with catchable sized rainbow. Because the waters here are so nutrient rich, the fish are usually a good sized by late summer and early fall. While spring and early summer will net you a lot of hungry, small fish, it's best to wait until later in the year. By September, the fish have usually grown to 35–40 cm (12–16 in). On years the lake does not winterkill, you will find rainbow trout over 60 cm (24 in) in size.

Quality Lake has large areas of shoal, which produce an abundance of dragonfly nymphs, shrimp, caddisflies and leeches. Fly anglers can do quite well here; however there are times when there are so many insects that the fish just won't rise for anything. Black, green or red Doc Spratleys are a consistently reliable fly for Quality's rainbow and an excellent pattern to use for trolling. So, too is the Carey Special, which can represent a range of aquatic insects, from leeches to dragonfly nymphs. Trolling a leech pattern is almost always tempting to rainbow. Slowly travel the contours of the lake just on the outskirts of the reed beds, focusing your attention towards the back or south end of the lake. Other rainbow favourites are mayfly nymphs, dragonfly nymphs, bloodworms (the larva of a chironomid/midge) and shrimp patterns.

Dick Nites and Flatfish, in a variety of colours, are well worth trying in this lake. On sunny days, select bright coloured lures. On overcast days, you will have better luck with darker colours. Trolling is a great way to start a youngster out as line tangles and snarls are few and far between. The lake is ideally suited to small boats, canoes or belly boats as shore fishing opportunities are limited.

The lake also provides a strong early-season ice fishery before the affects of oxygen depletion and winterkill sets in. Natural baits, such as insects and earthworms, or an artificial variety such as Berkley's Power Bait, all work well, with or without a spoon, jig or spinner. Hang the bait below a bobber at the appropriate depth and then wait for the fish to nibble. To attract fish you can try jigging your offering up and down occasionally.

Facilities

There are no facilities at Quality Lake. There is camping in nearby Tumbler Ridge, as well as a trio of hotels and a couple bed and breakfasts to stay at.

Directions

From Tumbler Ridge, drive 7 km north towards Dawson Creek on the Heritage Highway/Feller's Heights Road. Turn right on the Bearhole Lake Road, just before crossing Quality Creek, and starting the long climb up the so-called Happy Face Hill. Drive for 6 km on this gravel road to the culvert crossing at the lake's outlet. Access from here is by a 100 m (300 ft) walking trail to the north end of the lake. Road access in winter is dependent on local industrial activity.

Area Indicator

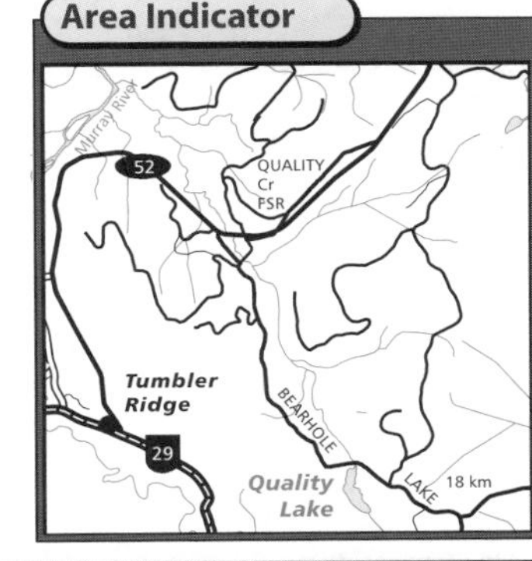

Quality Lake			
Fish Stocking Data			
Year	Species	Number	Life Stage
2008	Rainbow Trout	1,523	Spring Catchable
2007	Rainbow Trout	1,500	Spring Catchable
2006	Rainbow Trout	1,750	Catchable

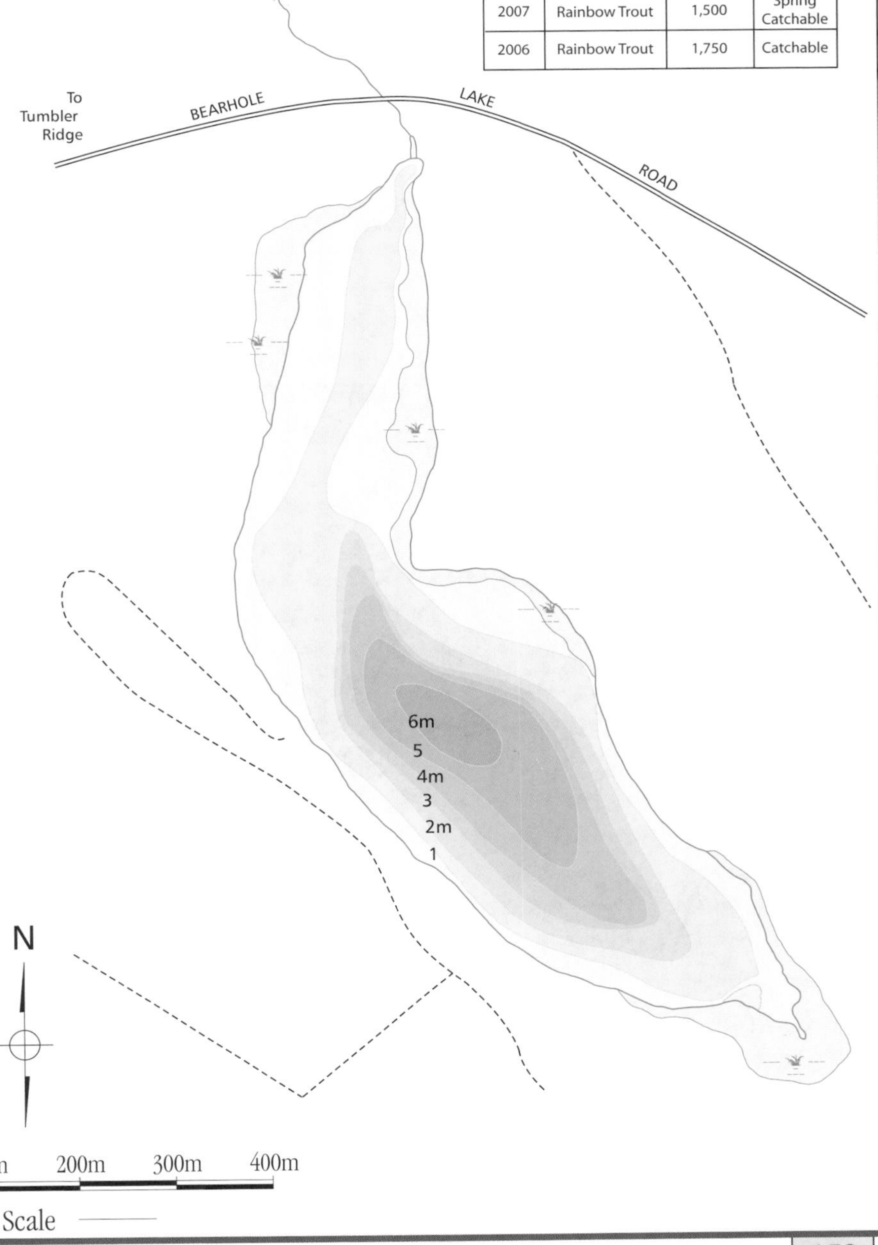

Location: Flows through Quesnel
Stream Lenght: 110 km (66 mile)
Geographic: 52° 50′ 1″ N, 122° 12′ 46″ W

Quesnel River

Fishing

The Quesnel River is one of a handful of great fishing rivers that are attached to Quesnel Lake. However, this river flows out of the lake, draining into the Fraser River.

The Quesnel is a 110 km (66 mile) long river and is accessed by one road or another for nearly its entire length. The river is divided into two sections; above the Cariboo River confluence it is open to fishing from June 16–February 28. The lower section is open July 1–March 31.

The river holds dozens of fish species, including runs of Chinook, Coho, pink and steelhead. But the river is best known for its rainbow trout and Chinook fishing.

The Chinook start moving into the river right around the time it opens for fishing and are present in the river until August. The Chinook here aren't huge, but pulling a 15 kg (30 lb) fish out of here is fairly common. Try cast or drift fishing with cured roe into deep holes. If trout are cleaning the hook of bait, switch to lures, wool (white, red or pink) or flies. Lures of choice include a Kitimat spoon and Spin-N-Glos.

Heavy gear and fast sinking lines with short strong tippet are what the fly angler needs to get down to the deep holes. Shooting heads allow increased line control and help maintain a drag-free drift. Patterns mixing bright and dark colours seem to be most effective. Woolly Buggers, Egg Sucking Leeches or Marabou Eggs dead drifted are equally good.

There is excellent dry fly-fishing on the river in the last half of June, with some prodigious mayfly and big stonefly hatches. In addition to native rainbow, some big trout (up to 5 kg/10 lbs) come downstream from Quesnel Lake to feed. Fishing an imitation stonefly or mayfly pattern will work well, as will an all-purpose dry fly like a Tom Thumb.

The fishing for rainbow slows over summer, but picks up again in the fall when the sockeye return. The rainbow love feeding on the sockeye eggs and a single egg pattern works wonders at this time. The best fishing is closer to Quesnel Lake.

Directions

The Quesnel flows into the Fraser at Quesnel. Highway 97 crosses the river just before downtown Quesnel, while a series of logging roads follow the river upstream. The lower stretches of the river can be accessed from the north along Quesnel Canyon Road, while the middle stretches of the river are best accessed from the south side, along the Quesnel Hydraulic Road. Between Likely and Quesnel Forks, the river is best accessed along the north side of the river. A good map, like the Cariboo Chilcotin Coast Backroad Mapbook is useful along the maze of roads.

Facilities

The river can be accessed from the north or the south end. There is a boat launch at **Beavermouth Recreation Site**, about 40 km east of Quesnel. There is also camping for about ten groups here. There are also a number of boat launches on Quesnel Lake, including one at **Cedar Point Provincial Park** that provide access to the lake.

There are private campgrounds and lodges in the area, or you can stay in Quesnel, where there are a variety of options for lodging, dining and other services.

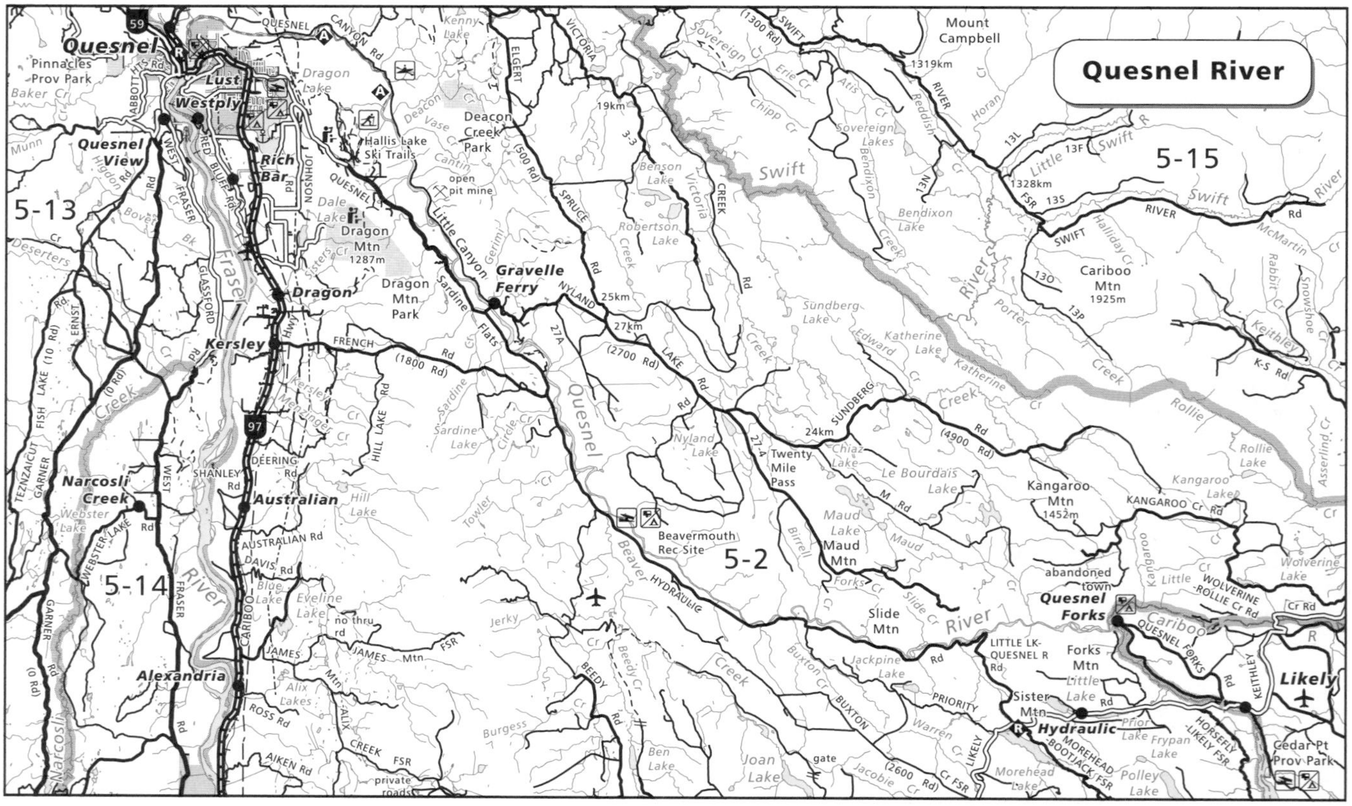

Quesnel & Horsefly Lakes

Location: 60 km (37 mi) northeast of Williams Lake
Elevation: 729 m (2,391 ft)
Surface Area: 27,196 ha (67,173 ac)
Max Depth: 365 m (1,198 ft)
Mean Depth: 158 m (518 ft)
Way Point: 52° 31′ 32″ N, 121° 0′ 44″ W

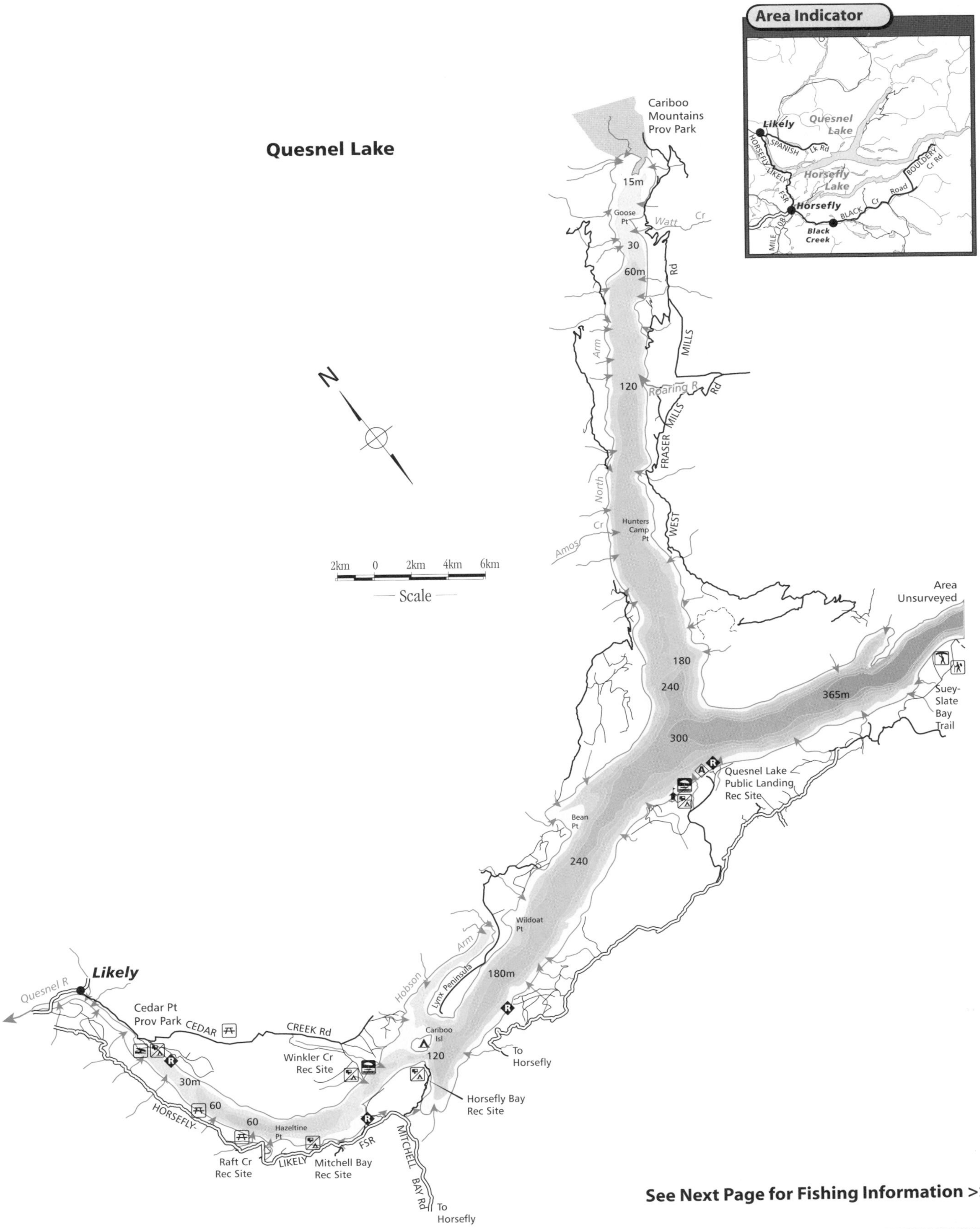

Area Indicator

Likely
Quesnel Lake
Horsefly Lake
Horsefly
Black Creek
SPANISH Lk Rd
HORSEFLY-LIKELY FSR
BOULDERY Cr Rd
BLACK Cr Road
MILE 108

Quesnel Lake

Cariboo Mountains Prov Park
15m
Goose Pt
Watt Cr
30
60m
MILLS Rd
North Arm
120
Roaring R
FRASER MILLS WEST Rd
Hunters Camp Pt
Amos Cr
180
240
Area Unsurveyed
365m
Suey-Slate Bay Trail
300
Quesnel Lake Public Landing Rec Site
Bean Pt
240
Wildoat Pt
Hobson Arm
Lynx Peninsula
180m
Cariboo Isl
120
To Horsefly
Horsefly Bay Rec Site
Likely
Quesnel R
Cedar Pt Prov Park
CEDAR CREEK Rd
Winkler Cr Rec Site
30m
60
60
Hazeltine Pt
HORSEFLY-LIKELY FSR
Raft Cr Rec Site
Mitchell Bay Rec Site
MITCHELL BAY Rd
To Horsefly

2km 0 2km 4km 6km
Scale

See Next Page for Fishing Information >>

Location: 68 km (42 mi) northeast of Williams Lake
Elevation: 787 m (2,582 ft)
Surface Area: 5,868 ha (14,500 ac)
Maximum Depth: 182 m (600 ft)
Mean Depth: 66 m (216 ft)
Way Point: 52°25′ N, 121°0′ W

Quesnel & Horsefly Lakes

Fishing

It's always tough to say that a lake has the best fishing in a given area, because best is such a subjective term. For some people, the best lake is one where they can pull out twenty fish in as many minutes. For others, it isn't worth considering unless it has the biggest fish. Others are looking for scenic qualities, while still others are looking for remote experiences.

That said, there are many people who would argue that Quesnel Lake would qualify as one of, if not the, best fishing lakes in the Cariboo. The lake has plenty to recommend it. The glacier lake is an astounding half a kilometre (1,640 feet) deep, making it the third deepest lake in North America, the second deepest lake in Canada and the single deepest lake in BC. It is also the deepest glacial lake in the world. The lake is 120 km (75 miles) long and is shaped like a slingshot.

The fishing is phenomenal, the scenery is great and the lake is big enough that you can usually find a place to fish that isn't too crowded. If you need a break, there are some amazing, secluded beaches to visit.

Nearby Horsefly Lake may not be as big or as deep as Quesnel Lake, nor does it have quite as big of fish, but the lake has gin clear water and some great fishing for rainbow trout, lake trout and kokanee.

Like most big lakes, these lakes produces big fish. In Quesnel Lake, rainbow trout to 7 kg (15 lb) are not unusual and lake trout to 18 kg (40 lbs) are an annual catch. In addition, the lake holds bull trout, kokanee and whitefish. Horsefly Lake sees rainbow trout to 6 kg (12 lb) and lake trout to 7 kg (15 lbs).

While these are the noteworthy catches, an average size fish here is still much bigger than most anywhere else in the region. It gets better. While the lakes are excellent trolling lakes, fly anglers and spincasters will have great luck here, too. The most common method of trolling is using Apex lures with a downrigger. **Continued >>**

Horsefly Lake (East)

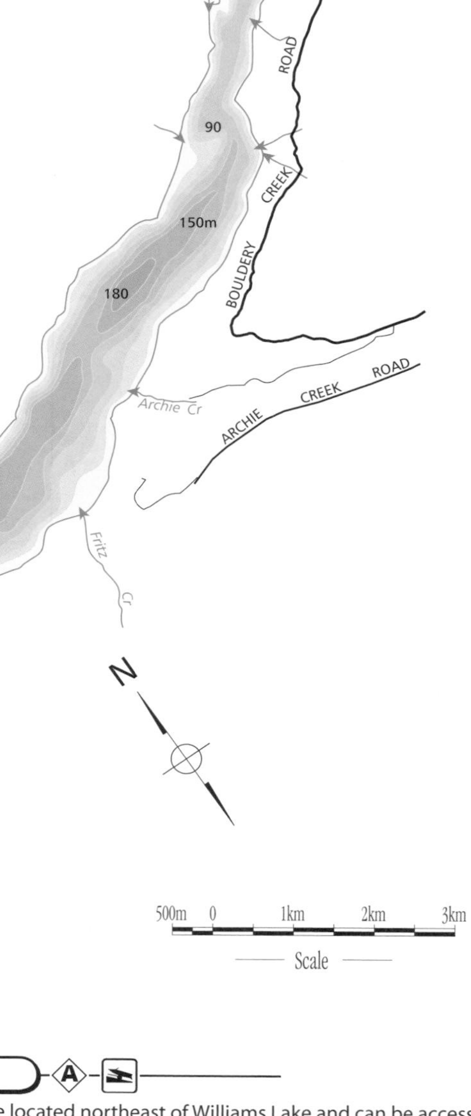

Directions

These two lakes are located northeast of Williams Lake and can be accessed from a variety of roads that head east off the Cariboo Highway (Highway 97). The best access is from 150 Mile House, east of Williams Lake. From here, you can take the signed and paved Horsefly-Likely Road, which splits 4.5 km north of 150 Mile House. Left on the paved Likely Road takes you to the settlement of Likely. Just east of town, the Cedar Creek Road takes you to Cedar Point Provincial Park. This is, of course, just one of many possible access points onto the lake. For more options, we recommend a copy of the *Cariboo Chilcotin Coast Backroad Mapbook*.

To get to Horsefly Lake, take the Horsefly Road at the Y intersection noted above. Follow the paved Horsefly road to the town of Horsefly. East of town, the Horsefly Lake Road goes past Horsefly Lake Provincial Park.

Quesnel & Horsefly Lakes

Location: 68 km (42 mi) northeast of Williams Lake
Elevation: 787 m (2,582 ft)
Surface Area: 5,868 ha (14,500 ac)
Maximum Depth: 182 m (600 ft)
Mean Depth: 66 m (216 ft)
Way Point: 52°25'N, 121°0'W

Fishing Continued

Big lakes and fly anglers don't typically go together, but Quesnel Lake, in particular, offers some spectacular fly-fishing. Fly-fishing starts in the middle of May and continues through October. Typically the best fishing is around creek mouths and catches of more than two dozen trout a day are not uncommon, although after a while it can be physically exhausting playing these giant fish.

As the salmon fry head out of the creeks and rivers and into the lakes, they are herded into "bait balls" by large trout, which slash into these pulsing masses of fry to feed. A well placed streamer pattern can result in a hard, fast strike from a 5 kg (10 lb) trout. Playing these beasts is another matter, as they fight hard and determined and have stolen more than a few flies in their time.

Early in the year, few people are around to fish. Rainbow trout spawn in late April and early May and just like during the salmon spawn other fish–bull trout, kokanee and even other rainbow trout–feed on floating eggs. Salmon fry begin making their way down the lake, too and big fish can be spotted in the clear water hanging around creek mouths and on the shoals.

By June the run off starts to wash silt into the lake, making the water murky and high. Still, the salmon fry are moving through the lake and if you can find the fry, you will find the trout.

The hatches reach full swing in June, too and there can be some great dry-fly-fishing.

As summer rolls into July, there are some spectacular mayfly and stonefly hatches on the rivers that flow into the lake; anglers can usually pick up a bit of action round the river mouths, but fishing the big lakes is usually done by trolling, as the trout are not usually congregated around the river mouths as they are earlier in the spring. Summer fishing conditions extend through to the end of August, when Sockeye salmon enter into the lakes on their way to their spawning streams. This is the start of the best fishing you can find. Not for sockeye, but for rainbow trout. As the salmon spawn, eggs wash down the streams and into the lakes. The fishing is absolutely amazing, both on the rivers and at the mouths of the river. Add to this salmon fry feeding in the big lakes and you have a perfect storm of fishing conditions.

If that wasn't enough, lake trout spawn in September. Later in the evenings, these massive fish begin to gather on the shoals near creek mouths.

The fishing continues into October. In addition to fishing egg patterns around creek mouths, there are salmon and kokanee fry feeding on plankton, which again creates quite a stir for the rainbow trout and bull trout. By October, the fishing pressure has dropped and there are few other people out on the water. While the weather can be hit and miss, there are usually a number of perfect fall days in October and the colours are awesome.

By November, the fishing tails off for the winter, only to begin again in May.

While Quesnel Lake has been called one of the top ten trout lakes in North America, Horsefly is not as well known. Of course, anglers looking for a bit more of a remote experience will find the lake less busy than Quesnel Lake. It fishes similar, but the fish are not as big or prevalent.

Do note that the lakes are big and high winds can prove dangerous to small and sometimes large boats.

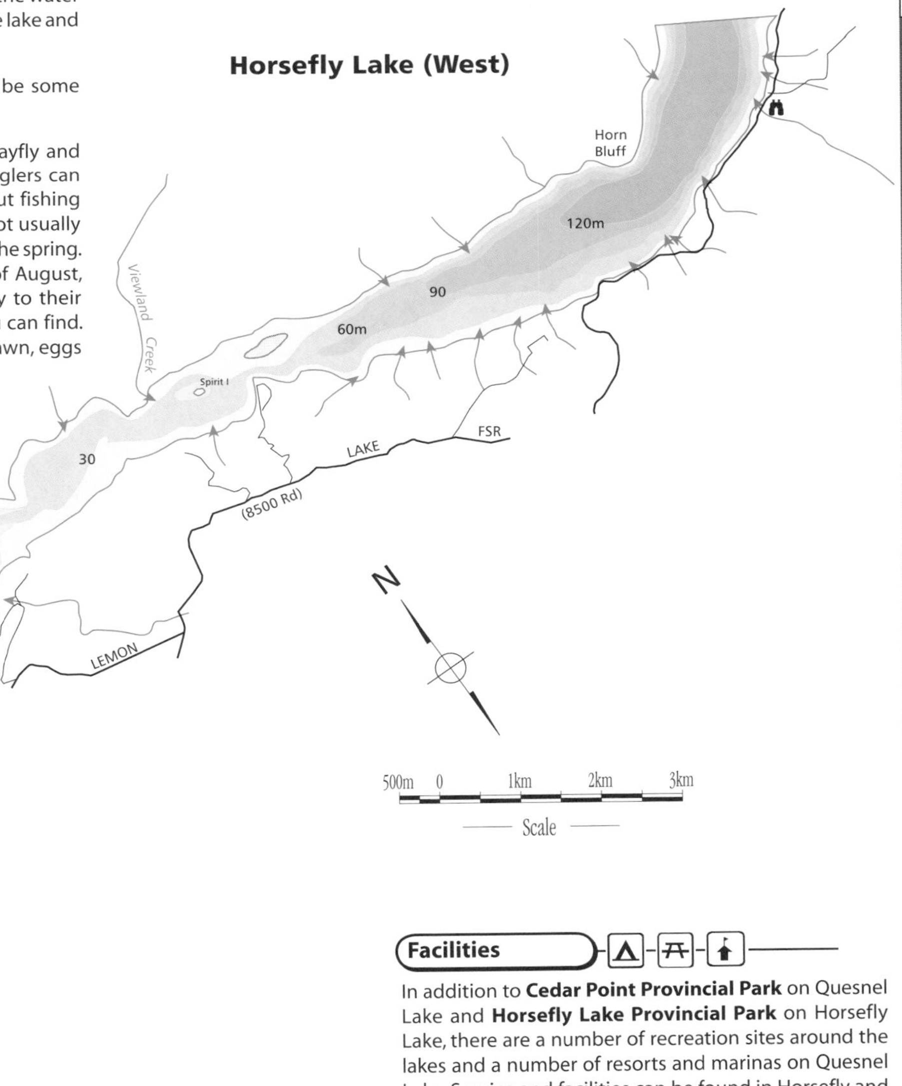

Facilities

In addition to **Cedar Point Provincial Park** on Quesnel Lake and **Horsefly Lake Provincial Park** on Horsefly Lake, there are a number of recreation sites around the lakes and a number of resorts and marinas on Quesnel Lake. Service and facilities can be found in Horsefly and Likely.

Location: 50 km (31 mi) southeast of Williams Lake
Elevation: 1,094 m (3,589 ft)
Surface Area: 230 ha (568 ac)
Maximum Depth: 21 m (68 ft)
Mean Depth: 6 m (20 ft)
Way Point: 51° 56′ 48″ N, 121° 28′ 13″ W

Rail Lake

Area Indicator

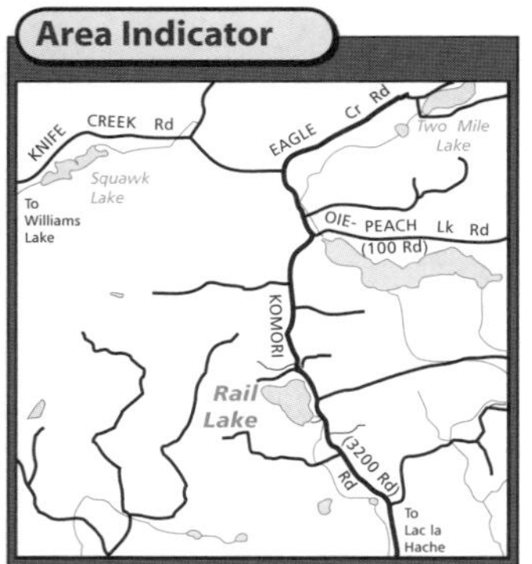

Rail Lake			
Fish Stocking Data			
Year	Species	Number	Life Stage
2008	Rainbow Trout	30,000	Yearling
2007	Rainbow Trout	30,000	Yearling
2006	Rainbow Trout	25,780	Yearling

Fishing

Rail Lake is a mid-sized lake found in the low, rolling hills north of Lac La Hache. The lake is surrounded by a mostly lodgepole pine forest and is home to some good numbers of rainbow trout as well as some burbot. The lake also has some course fish including squawfish and chub, which returned to the lake after a rehabilitation program.

To help counteract the course fish, anywhere from 25,000 to 30,000 rainbow are stocked in the lake each year. These are the Blackwater strain of rainbow, which grow to nice sizes feeding on these course fish. When you consider the stocking level and the fact that the lake doesn't receive heavy fishing pressure, it makes a great fishing lake.

Despite being Blackwater strain, you are not going to find trophy-sized trout here. The rainbow average 25–35 cm (10–14 in) in size, with some of the fish growing to 1.5 kg (3 lbs). However, because the lake is so heavily stocked, you usually don't have to wait long for the first bite. Or the second. Or the third. As a result, the lake is a great place for beginners and especially young children who will appreciate the fact that the fish take to the lure so willingly.

The lake is a mid elevation lake and is usually ice free by the end of April or early May. If you are in the area around that time, it is worth a stop to see. The first couple of weeks after ice-off can be a fun time to fish the lake, as the rainbow trout cruise the shallows near shore looking for food. This is because the oxygenated water is at the top of the lake and the first few tentative hatches happen in the shallow water. Sight fishing for rainbow can be lots of fun at this time.

However, all good things must come to an end and by early to mid-May the lake starts its annual turnover. Fishing is at a standstill until about the end of May. Fishing is good in the spring and again in the fall until ice over in the early part of November.

The deepest part of the lake is at the northeast end. Trollers should work a lake troll, Flatfish or other trout lure around the fringe area of this deep hole. Those looking to cast a fly or small spinner will find extensive shoals at the southern end of the lake. Remember to match the hatch looking for early season chironomids followed by mayflies, caddisflies and dragon and damselflies. Dry fly-fishing can be quite fun during the caddis hatch as can tossing a beetle imitation during the annual beetle flight.

Spincasters can use the usual assortment of spinners, like a Mepps Black Fury or Panther Martin. However, nothing beat the ol' bait and bobber, especially for the kids.

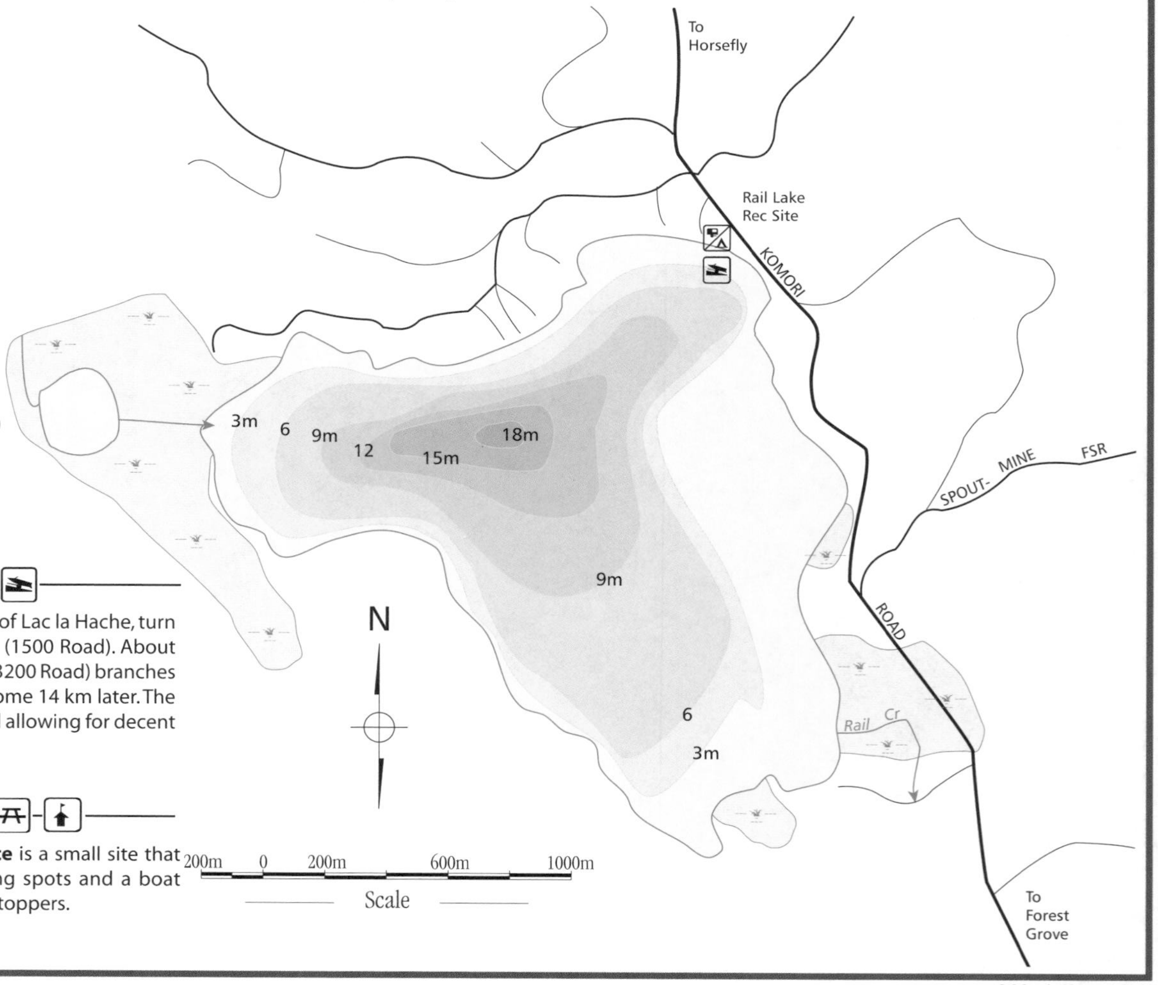

To Horsefly
Rail Lake Rec Site
KOMORI ROAD
SPOUT-MINE FSR
Rail Cr
3m 6 9m 12 15m 18m 9m 6 3m
N
200m 0 200m 600m 1000m
Scale
To Forest Grove

Directions

From Highway 97 at the town of Lac la Hache, turn off on the Timothy Lake Road (1500 Road). About 6.5 km later, the Komori Road (3200 Road) branches north. You will find Rail Lake some 14 km later. The roads in are usually quite good allowing for decent access.

Facilities

The **Rail Lake Recreation Site** is a small site that offers four lakeshore camping spots and a boat launch for small trailers or cartoppers.

Raven Lake

Location: 54 km (33.5 mi) west of Williams Lake
Elevation: 1,255 m (4,117 ft)
Surface Area: 28 ha (69 ac)
Max Depth: 23.2 m (76 ft)
Mean Depth: 13 m (42 ft)
Way Point: 52° 2′ 19″ N, 122° 52′ 49″

Fishing

Raven Lake is stocked annually with both rainbow and eastern brook trout, which provide for great year round fishing. There are usually 15,000 of each species stocked annually, although stocking amounts do fluctuate.

While the average catch here is usually about 1 kg (2 lbs), it isn't unusual to pull out a much bigger brook trout. Raven is an insect-rich lake and the fish are well fed.

Years ago, the water in Raven Lake was raised, which resulted in a ring of submerged trees and stumps around the shore. This structure, along with aquatic plants in two to three metre deep water, provides cover for fish searching for the aquatic insects and scuds sheltered there. Fly casters are successful when they place a dragonfly, damselfly, mayfly, leech or scud imitation in this structure, let it sink and retrieve slowly. This can be challenging when the sunken trees take the fly before the fish or the hooked fish decides to head for shore and tangles the leader in the process.

Trollers work the edges and in the middle of the lake with a Willow Leaf or 50/50 Ford Fender and worms, Hot Shots, Kwik Fish, or Flatfish in gold, black and silver, green and skunk. Spincasters are limited to a couple of open spots by the boat launches for casting.

Just be wary of tree remnants in the water. Better yet, bring a boat and cast Rooster Tails, a Mepps Aglia or Blue Fox in black or silver or gold towards (but not too close) shore. Suspending a worm or Powerbait just off bottom below a bobber can also be quite fun.

Because the lake is stocked with brook trout, it offers great ice fishing opportunities. Brook trout are hardier than rainbow and are much more active when the water temperature is cold and the oxygen level is low. This means that the ice fishing remains good, even later in the season when the rainbow trout start swimming around like drunken fools because of oxygen deprivation.

Early in the ice fishing season, the rainbow are still active and like krill or worms on a jig, while the brook trout love maggots or shrimp. You will usually find them in shallow water (less than 3metres/10 ft) in winter, looking for food. The best strategy is to drill a series of holes at a variety of depths and locations. If one hole is not producing, move onto the next one.

Area Indicator

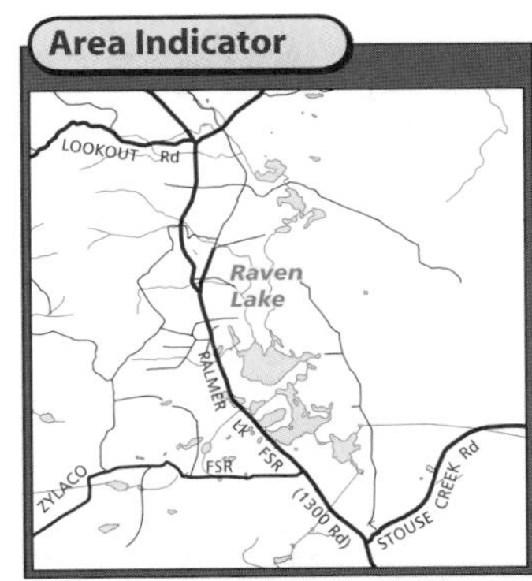

Raven Lake
Fish Stocking Data

Year	Species	Number	Life Stage
2008	Rainbow Trout	15,000	Fry
2008	Brook Trout	15,000	Fingerling
2007	Rainbow Trout	15,000	Fry
2007	Brook Trout	15,000	Fingerling
2006	Rainbow Trout	15,000	Fall Fry
2006	Brook Trout	19,000	Fingerling

Directions

From Williams Lake, turn south onto Highway 20 and go west across the Fraser River and up Sheep Creek Hill. Continue past Riske Creek to the Palmer Lake/Raven Lake sign (Alex Graham Road) and turn north (right) on the good gravel road. This road is about 68 km west of Williams Lake.

Once you pass the 16 km marker of the Palmer Lake Forest Service Road, the Raven Lake Recreation Site will be on your right-hand side. Watch for industrial traffic when travelling down the gravel roads.

Facilities

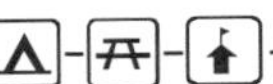

The **Raven Lake Recreation Site** was recently cleared of beetle-killed pine. There is a main site to the south and an overflow site to the north offering 13 spaces with tables. Both sites are RV friendly and have gravel boat launches. The north site is more suitable for trailered boats.

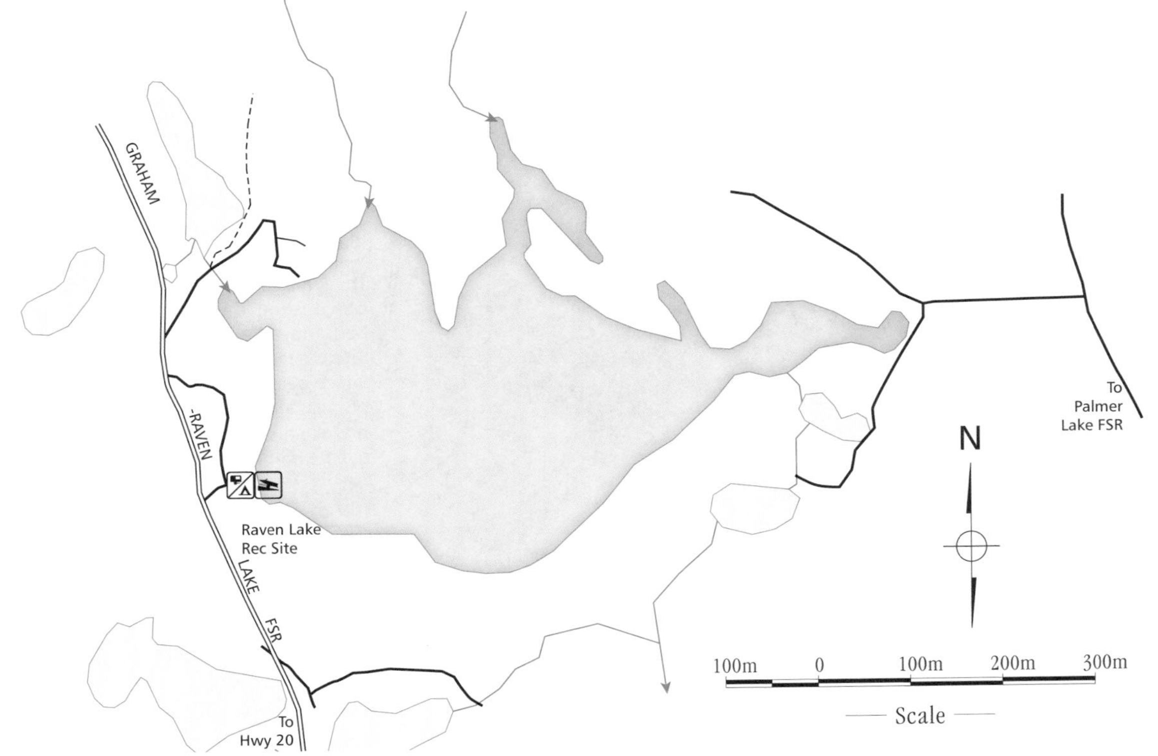

Location: 26 km (16 miles) north of Terrace

Redsand & Treston Lakes

Redsand Lake

Elevation: 146 m (479 ft)
Surface Area: 39 ha (96 ac)
Maximum Depth: 15 m (48 ft)
Mean Depth: 5.4 m (17 ft)
Way Point: 54° 42' 22.4" N, 128° 46' 48.0" W

Treston Lake

Elevation: 143 m (469 ft)
Surface Area: 90 ha (222 ac)
Maximum Depth: 34 m (111 ft)
Mean Depth: 8.8 m (29 ft)
Way Point: 54° 41' 42" N, 128° 46' 31" W

Area Indicator

Directions

To get to these lakes from Terrace, take the Yellowhead Highway (Highway 16) over the Kitsumkalum River and turn onto the Kalum Forest Service Road about 200 metres past the bridge. From the turn-off it is about 26 km to the Redsand Demonstration Forest. The road is two-wheel drive accessible.

Fishing

Redsand Lake is at the heart of the Redsand Demonstration Forest north of Terrace near Kitsumkalum Lake and while it is the titular feature in the area, it is an underappreciated and underutilized fishing resource.

That is to be expected when the Kitsumkalum River offers some fine steelhead and salmon fishing, with four distinct runs of steelhead to keep anglers occupied. The phenomenal river fishing to be had spoils people up here and because the fish just keep coming there's not many times in the year when people will say "Hey, there's nothing running in the rivers right now. Wanna go fish Redsand or Treston Lake?"

Which is funny, considering that the lakes are basically a blip on the Kitsumkalum. Still, there are a few people in the area who appreciate lake fishing and who do come to Redsand Lake to partake of the good cutthroat and Dolly Varden fishing to be had.

The lakes produce well for spincasters and trollers, as well as fly anglers. People trolling the lakes could do worse than a traditional Wedding Band. These can be undressed, or you can use a worm or maggot to bait the hook.

Redsand Lake is also a good lake for fly-fishing. Try working a chironomid or bloodworm pattern, especially early in the spring. Fishing a minnow pattern can also be productive, especially when salmon and steelhead smolts are returning down the Kitsumkalum River to the ocean. Working an emerging minnow pattern near the bottom of the lake can imitate a fry emerging from the gravel. During the spawn, you can also work an egg or egg pattern near to the inflow of the river.

There aren't a lot of hatches, meaning there aren't a lot of opportunities for dry fly-fishing, but a small surface chironomid pattern can sometimes work.

Do note if you are planning on fishing near the eastern side of the lake, you will need a boat, as the current from the Kitsumkalum can wash folks in belly boats downstream. However, if you stick to the west/northwest side of the lake, you should be fine in a float tube or pontoon boat.

Facilities

There are three campgrounds located in the Redsand Demonstration forest, though only one is located on Redsand Lake itself. The **Redsand Lake Recreation Site** is a large, open site with space for 25 groups and a nice beach. **Hart Lake Recreation Site** is the other popular alternative here. The demonstration forest is a popular hiking destination, with a number of interpretive trails in the area.

Other Options

The 800 lb gorilla in the room is the **Kitsumkalum River,** which offers some great steelhead and salmon fishing and is written up earlier in the book. Also found earlier in the book is **Kitsukalum Lake**.

Richmond (Priestly) Lake

Location: 35 km (21.7 mi) east of Burns Lake
Elevation: 715 m (2,345 ft)
Surface Area: 31 ha (77 ac)
Maximum Depth: 36 m (118 ft)
Mean Depth: 14 m (46 ft)
Way Point: 54° 8' 11.5" N, 125° 18' 21.1" W

Fishing

Also known as Priestly Lake, Richmond Lake is a picturesque fishing spot surrounded by forested hills and rolling countryside. Its deep, spring-fed, crystal-clear waters, supports a quality fishery for large rainbow trout.

The lake is stocked annually by the Freshwater Fisheries Society of BC with 3,000 yearling rainbow. These beautiful trout can reach 3 kg (6.5 lb) and may get bigger now that the lake is being stocked with sterile, all-female Blackwater rainbow trout.

The lake is quite deep–about 80 percent is more than 9 m (30 feet)–which extends the fishing action through the warmer days of summer. It can be covered well with a small boat, canoe, pontoon or belly boat. Much of the lake's foreshore is fairly steep, rocky and wooded, which limits the areas one can fish from shore. Fished by boat, the shoals at the north and south end of the lake can be very productive.

Anglers report considerable success trolling with Wedding Bands tipped with worms; Apex Trout Killers, Kamloopers and Krocodile spoons; as well as Mepps, Panther Martins, Vibrax and Gibbs spinners cast at different depths around the drop off. Vertical jigging with spoons or jigs using scented bait, such as one of the Berkley Powerbaits, will also work well.

Fly anglers can't go wrong in mooching along slowly with a Doc Spratley, or a leech pattern, such as a black marabou leech or a beadhead micro leech. Damsel nymphs like the '52 Buick, a marabou damsel or a dragonfly nymph, are other good bets. Butler's Lake Dragon or Kaufmann's Lake Dragonflies can also be great. Even though rainbow can be selective feeders, they often can't pass up the full meal deal the above flies provide.

Many times a lake has multiple hatches and the insect you see the most, is not what the fish are actually taking. This is particularly true in lakes like Richmond where the fish didn't get big by gulping everything in front of them. Swallows skimming flies off the surface can clue you into insect hatches. Check the water for nymph cases. If nothing is showing, go deeper with your offerings.

Ice fishing can also be quite rewarding on Richmond Lake. Because of the lake's depth, the best winter fishing is fairly close to shore in 1.5–3 metres (5–10 ft) of water. Berkley Powerbaits in nuggets, maggots or worms–either by themselves or on a small jigging spoon–are tough to beat.

Directions

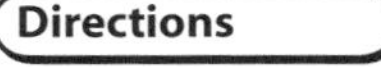

Despite its close access to the highway, the rough road and confusing nature of roads makes this lake somewhat difficult to find. Look for the Priestly Road about 31 km east of Burns Lake. This leads to the Priestly Railroad Station, where you turn right onto a gravel road and travel 4 km to the lake. There is a fork in the road 1 km from the highway; keep left. Follow a detour around a deep mud hole at 2.9 km and then keep right at the fork at 3.3 km. The stream crossing at 3.5 km is very difficult to pass; a winch is recommended.

Facilities

The **Richmond Lake Recreation Site** is a day-use site where it is possible to launch a cartopper. Some people do camp at the small site.

Area Indicator

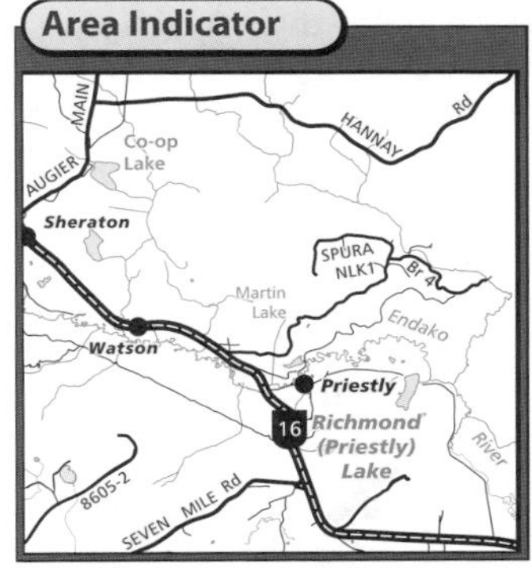

Richmond Lake Fish Stocking Data			
Year	Species	Number	Life Stage
2008	Rainbow Trout	3,000	Yearling
2007	Rainbow Trout	3,000	Yearling
2006	Rainbow Trout	3,000	Yearling

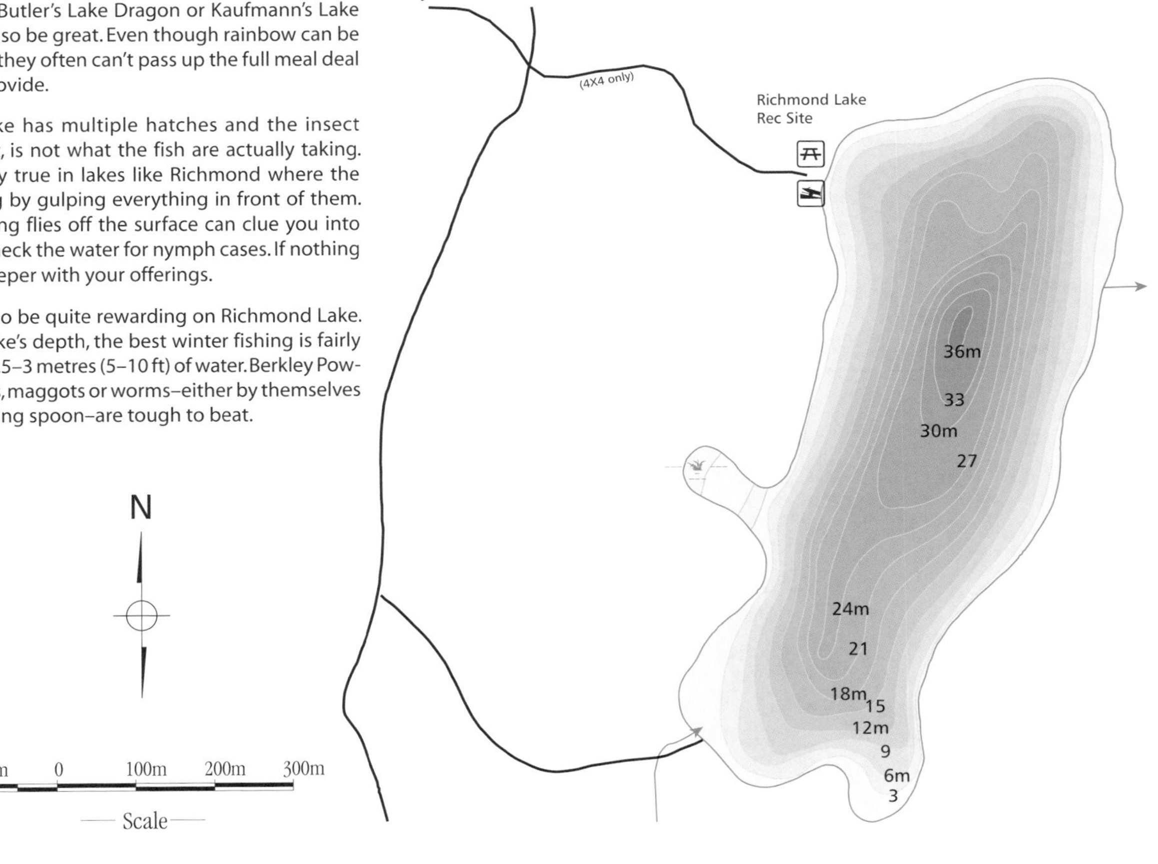

Location: 72 km (44.7 mi) northeast of Williams Lake
Elevation: 1,245 m (4,084 ft)
Surface Area: 29 ha (71 ac)
Maximum Depth: 11 m (36 ft)
Mean Depth: 5 m (16 ft)
Way Point: 52° 44' 42.6" N, 121° 32' 56.8" W

Rollie Lake

Area Indicator

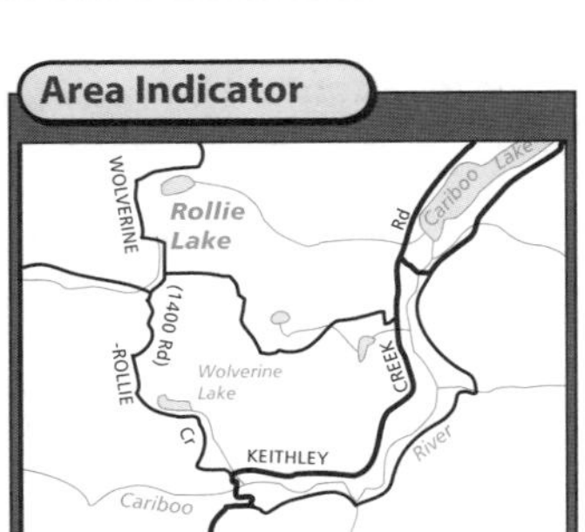

Fishing

Rollie Lake is a small lake situated north of Likely. It is one of a series of small lakes found north of the small town in a group that includes Wolverine, Kangaroo, Five Mile and Six Mile Lakes. There are only a handful of small lakes north of Quesnel Lake (the exception is Cariboo Lake) until you hit the Bowron Lakes, much farther north.

Rollie Lake is a small lake that rests slightly higher in elevation than many Cariboo Chilcotin Coast lakes, so don't expect it to be ice free until early to mid-May.

The lake was stocked with rainbow trout in the late 1970s and early 1980s, but the fish have since established a self-sustaining population. These wild fish average just under 0.5 kg (1 lbs), but some people have caught fish here to 1 kg (2 lbs). While these are not the trophy sized fish as you will find in nearby Quesnel Lake, Rollie Lake is a nice little lake for people looking to avoid the weather and waves and the endless searching for fish you will find in the big lake.

The lake has a maximum depth of 11 metres (36 feet), but averages less than half of that. It is a perfect lake to fish from a float tube or other small watercraft. Anglers usually fly-fish or cast small spoons or spinners, but people have been known to troll here, too. Working the drop offs along the north and south of the deep hole with searching patterns or light trolling gear will provide the best chance for success.

Spincasters and fly anglers will probably want to work these same areas. There are a trio of inflowing creeks on the north and west shores of the lake that can be fished as well. Fly casters will find the usual Cariboo flies–Spratleys, Careys, Woolly Buggers, nymphs and leeches, as well as a variety of insect patterns–will do well on the lake.

Directions

To access the lake from the south, travel to 150 Mile House on the Cariboo Highway (Highway 97). Take the paved road to Likely avoiding the turn-off to Horsefly. Continue north past Likely on what is now called the Keithley Creek Road. After crossing the Cariboo River, look for the Wolverine-Rollie Creek Road (1400 Rd) branching left (west) about 5 km later. This road leads past Wolverine Lake before climbing the hill to the junction with Kangaroo Creek Road. A right here should take you past Kangaroo Lake, to the rough side road leading to Rollie Lake.

Access to this lake is challenging, a copy of the *Cariboo Chilcotin Coast Backroad Mapbook* along with a GPS and a 4wd vehicle are recommended.

Facilities

There are no developed facilities at the lake, however people do camp and hand launch small craft at the lake. If you are looking for something a bit more developed, nearby Wolverine Lake has a forest recreation site to stay at.

Other Options

Wolverine Lake is found en route to Rollie Lake and contains rainbow trout as well as some lake chub. The lake does not receive a lot of fishing pressure despite the fact that it regularly produces rainbow in the 2 kg (4-5 lb) category. The Wolverine Lake Recreation Site offers lakeshore camping as well as a cartop boat launch.

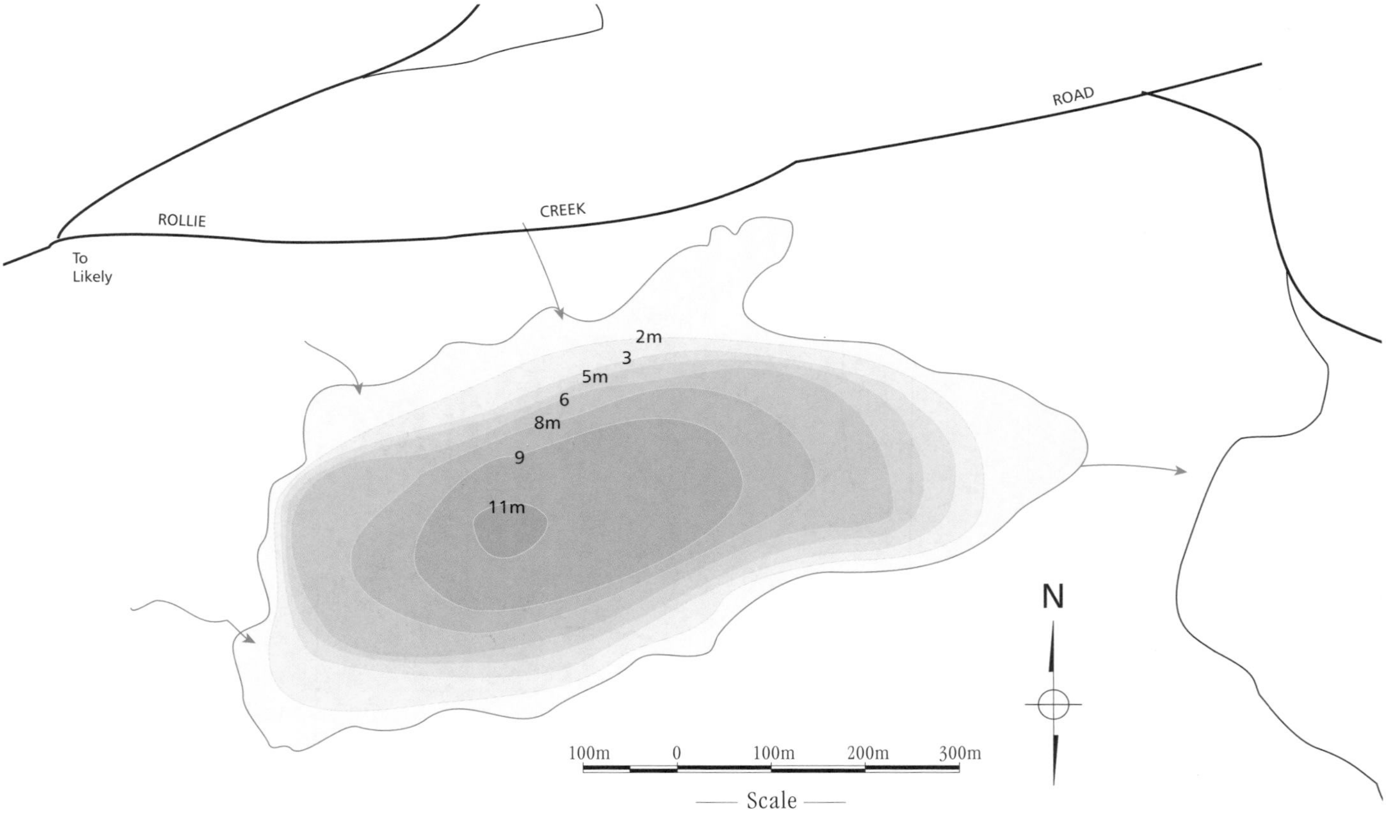

ROAD
ROLLIE
CREEK
To Likely
2m
3
5m
6
8m
9
11m
N
100m 0 100m 200m 300m
Scale

Rose Lake

Location: 28 km (17.4 mi) east of Williams Lake
Elevation: 984 m (3,228 ft)
Surface Area: 237 ha (586 ac)
Maximum Depth: 18 m (58 ft)
Mean Depth: 6 m (20 ft)
Way Point: 52° 14' 42" N, 121° 45' 40" W

Fishing

Rose Lake has both rainbow and kokanee. The rainbow are stocked annually at a rate of 25,000 to 30,000 fish per year meaning that the fishing should stay productive. However, this also means the fish tend to be on the small side, although some do reach 1 kg (3 lbs) in size. There are also a number of non-game species in the lake such as squawfish, redside shiner, suckers and peamouth chub.

The lake can be fished from the beginning of May into the early part of July. After the typical summer slowdown, the fishing picks up again in September and October with ice over occurring in November. The lake is deepest near to the center of the lake, but there is also a deeper hole at the east end of the lake. It is at the fringe of those two areas that you should either troll or work a fly.

Although the lake is lined with water lilies and shore casting is somewhat difficult, fly anglers are always intrigued by aquatic vegetation. These lilies are a prime area to find the trout feeding in, as they are perfect habitat for insects and invertebrates. Casting a damselfly or dragonfly nymph towards the lilies works very well in late June to early July. During non hatch times, scuds or freshwater shrimp patterns are also effective.

Fishing techniques for kokanee are quite similar to rainbow trout. While smaller kokanee do not eat bigger foods and so are not interested in lures, once they hit a certain size, kokanee begin feeding on leeches, insects and other larger food sources. You will find that you will catch a mixture of both.

To catch them, try a slow troll using a Willow Leaf, Wedding Band and worm or maggot fished near the surface with up to a 1 oz weight. Trolling in an "S" pattern results in better success as the lure is gaining and losing speed as the boat rounds the corners. This entices the fish to bite.

The biggest difference is that kokanee are much more sensitive to the temperature of water and prefer to spend their time in a narrow band of water, although they will dart into shallower (or deeper) water to feed. Kokanee are known for their soft mouths and whether trolling, spincasting or fly-fishing, it is advisable to attach some form of shock absorber, to prevent the hook from tearing through the soft flesh. Kokanee are strong, determined fighters and often do damage to themselves when trying to escape.

Similarly, the rainbow take well to a lake troll or a small Flatfish when trolling. Fly anglers can also try working a mayfly, damselfly nymph or caddisfly imitation in the spring and a water boatman or dragonfly nymph in the fall.

Area Indicator

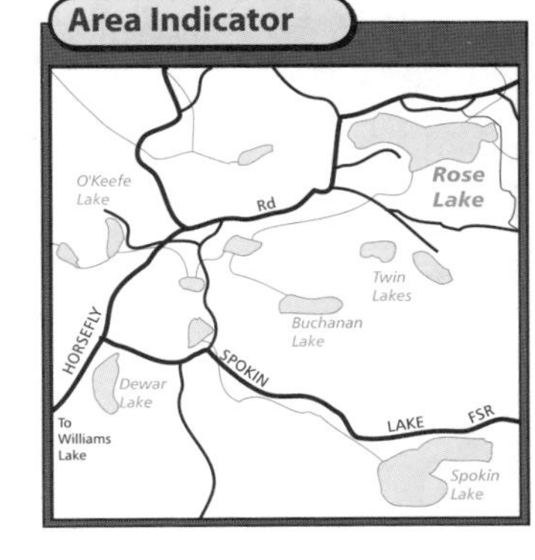

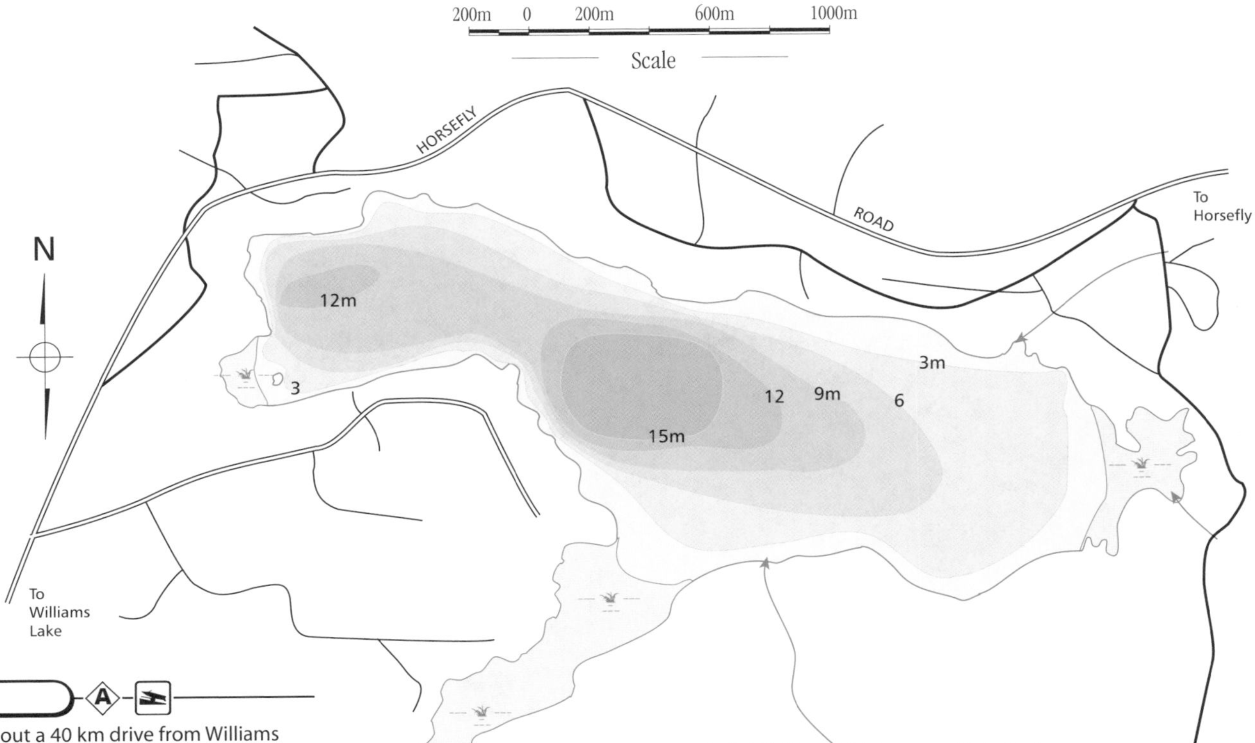

200m 0 200m 600m 1000m
Scale
HORSEFLY
ROAD
To Horsefly
N
12m
3
3m
12
9m
6
15m
To Williams Lake

Directions

Rose Lake is about a 40 km drive from Williams Lake along the paved Horsefly Road. From 150 Mile House, turn east from the Cariboo Highway (Highway 97) and head north on the Likely Road. At the 4.5 km intersection, turn right along the paved Horsefly Road. Continue past Dugan and then Dewar Lake before reaching Rose Lake.

Facilities

Although there are many lakeshore residences at Rose Lake, it is possible to launch a small boat at the lake. Those looking to camp can head south to Dewar or Dugan Lakes.

Location: 5 km (3 mi) east of New Hazelton
Elevation: 404 m (1,324 ft)
Maximum Depth: 8.2 m (27 ft)
Way Point: 55° 15′ 34.0″ N, 127° 31′ 7.7″ W

Ross Lake

Area Indicator

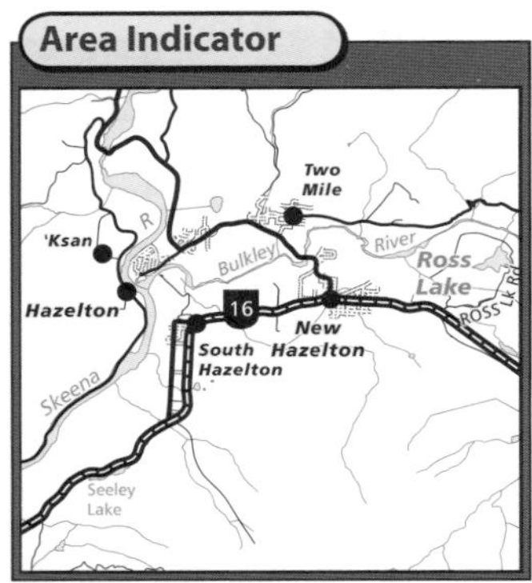

Ross Lake			
Fish Stocking Data			
Year	Species	Number	Life Stage
2008	Brook Trout	3,000	Fingerling
2008	Rainbow Trout	3,110	Fingerling
2007	Brook Trout	6,000	Fingerling
2006	Brook Trout	3,000	Fingerling
2006	Rainbow Trout	3,000	Yearling

Fishing

Ross Lake is a beautiful, popular lake. It is unique in that it offers easy access, great facilities, a family atmosphere and good sized rainbow and brook trout. There is something here for the novice, as well as the committed fly-fishing fanatic.

The lake is stocked each year with 3,000 yearling rainbow trout and 3,000 fingerling brook trout by the Freshwater Fisheries Society of BC. The fish experience rapid growth due to an abundance of food sources.

Restricted to electric motors only, the lake is perfectly suited to fish with a canoe, float tube or pontoon boat. It also has a few spots where anglers can fish from shore.

The brook trout tend to inhabit different areas of the lake than the rainbow. Look for the brookies in the shoreline zone, close to cover, during the spring fishing season. As the water warms, they seek cooler temperatures and go deeper. Brook trout often swim in schools and action can be frantic, followed by a wait until they return or you find them again.

Wedding Bands tipped with worms or one of the various Powerbaits from Berkley, often work well. Spinners and spoons allowed to sink and then slowly retrieved, will often get a bite. Brook trout also go after flies. Mayfly and caddis nymphs, Woolly Buggers, damsel, dragon micro leeches and shrimp patterns will usually tempt a brook trout. Some of the lake's brookies have been caught weighing up to 2.5 kg (5.5 lbs).

Rainbow are the more willing biters in Ross. The odd rainbow has been caught up to 65 cm (25 in) in size here. A bobber with a worm suspended just off the bottom can be quite successful. A torpedo bobber with a fly is an easy rig to cast and enables you to cover a wide area for the cruising rainbow.

Vertical jigging in deeper water during the warm days of summer is very effective for both species. Small light spoons such as Triple Teasers, Dick Nites and Needlefish are always good producers. These lighter weight spoons will need a split shot or small rubber-core weight attached 2 metres (6 feet) above the lure.

Ross Lake is also the most popular ice-fishing spot in the area. A wide range of baits, lures and flies can be used to catch trout under the ice. Berkley's Powerbait maggots or mealworms, krill and shrimp (even the canned, grocery-store variety) fished in 1.5–3 metres (5–10 ft) are good choices. The baits can be fished with or without an attractor spoon, jig or spinner. Hang the bait below a bobber at the appropriate depth and wait for the fish to nibble. Try jigging your offering up and down occasionally to attract the fish.

Directions

From New Hazelton head east (towards Smithers) on the Yellowhead Highway for 2 km. A left on Ross Lake Road will bring you to the lake after about 4 km of well-maintained gravel road.

Facilities

There is a boat launch, gravel swimming beach and a day-use area with fire rings at **Ross Lake Provincial Park**. The Rainmaker Trail circles the lake providing access to the lake and a chance to spot wildlife.

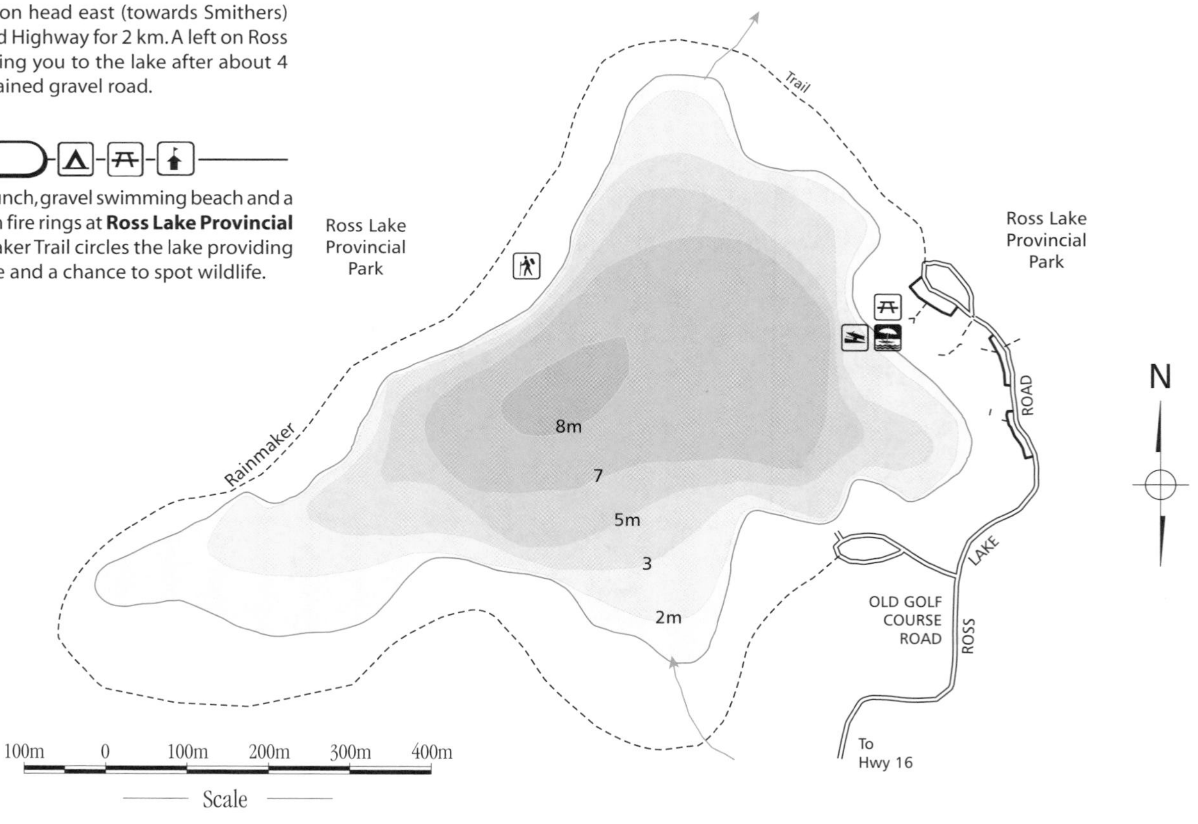

Ross Lake Provincial Park
Trail
Rainmaker
Ross Lake Provincial Park
8m
7
5m
3
2m
ROAD
LAKE
ROSS
OLD GOLF COURSE ROAD
To Hwy 16
N

100m 0 100m 200m 300m 400m
Scale

Round (Lacroix)Lake

Location: 22 km (13.7 miles) south of Smithers
Elevation: 585 m (1,919 ft)
Surface Area: 182 ha (450 ac)
Maximum Depth: 20 m (67 ft)
Mean Depth: 9.6 m (32 ft)
Way Point: 54° 39′ 29.3″ N, 126° 55′ 18.6″ W

Fishing

Round Lake's easy access and well-stocked waters make it an excellent place to introduce newcomers to freshwater fishing. With some basic gear and a few tips, novice anglers can successfully troll or still fish from a boat, spin a lure from the shore, or jig for dinner through a hole in the ice.

Round Lake is also home to a lively roster of other recreational activities–swimming, hiking, biking, water skiing, cross-country skiing and skating among them.

Due to its popularity with anglers, Round Lake, which is also known as Lacroix Lake, is stocked with 3,000 yearling cutthroat trout each year by the Freshwater Fisheries Society of BC. Reports up to 50 cm (20 in) are common, although a recent biological assessment showed the average cutthroat size was 28 cm (11 in). Northern pike minnow are also present and should not be overlooked when teaching children how to fish.

The simplest way to introduce novice anglers to lake fishing is using a technique known as still fishing. When still fishing from the shore, the angler casts out and waits for a bite. A commonly used bait is the good old worm, although at times, scented baits such as Berkley's Powerbait will out fish the worm. Some anglers attach a float (bobber) to the line so the baited hook stays suspended in the water. The depth can be adjusted by simply sliding the float up or down the line. If the float is removed, the bait can be fished on or near the bottom of the lake. When "bottom fishing" additional weight should be added so the line can be tightened and the hook and bait remain anchored in one location.

Small spinners or spoons such as Mepps or Krocodiles in the 1/8 ounce size work well if you are casting and retrieving. If you are trolling try a Needlefish or Triple Teaser with a small split shot to weigh it down. While trolling vary the speed and depth and troll in lazy "S" curves to cover the most water in search of fish. Be sure to note the lake is restricted to electric motors only.

Fly anglers do well on chironomids, damsels, dragons, beadhead micro leeches, Woolly Buggers and minnow imitations. Round Lake has heavy weed growth and is best fished early in the season before the summer algae bloom. Fishing picks up again in the fall.

Easy access also makes Round Lake a popular ice-fishing destination. Jigs tipped with Berkley's Powerbait–the ones smelling looking like maggots or mealworms–are a tried-and-true method. Holes should be drilled far enough out to avoid the heavy weed growth close to shore. Try to position your hole in 1.5–3 metres (5–10 ft) of water.

Directions

Round Lake is located next to the Yellowhead Highway (Highway 16) in the Bulkley River Valley, 11 km south of Telkwa. To reach the public-access site, turn north on Round Lake East or Round Lake West Road.

Facilities

The community hall on the northwest corner of the lake has a dock/boat launch, kitchen shelter, picnic area and swimming beach. Cottages, boat rentals, tackle and an all-season complement of family activities are available at the privately owned Round Lake Resort. A Bed and Breakfast is also located at the lake.

Area Indicator

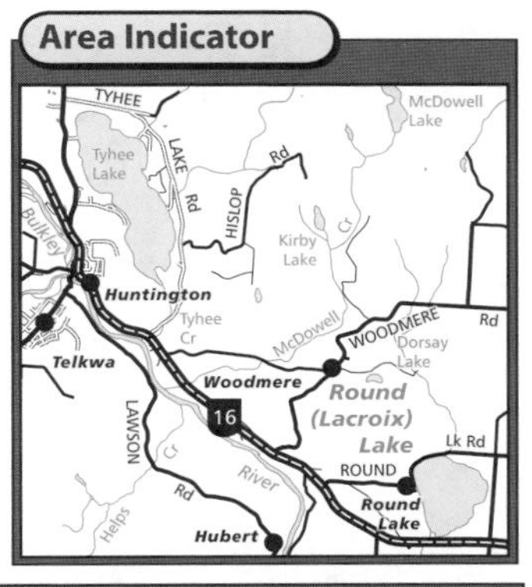

Round Lake Fish Stocking Data			
Year	Species	Number	Life Stage
2008	Cutthroat Trout	3,000	Yearling
2007	Cutthroat Trout	3,000	Yearling
2006	Cutthroat Trout	3,000	Yearling

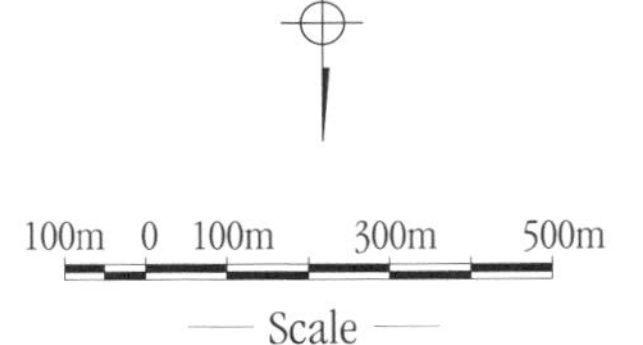

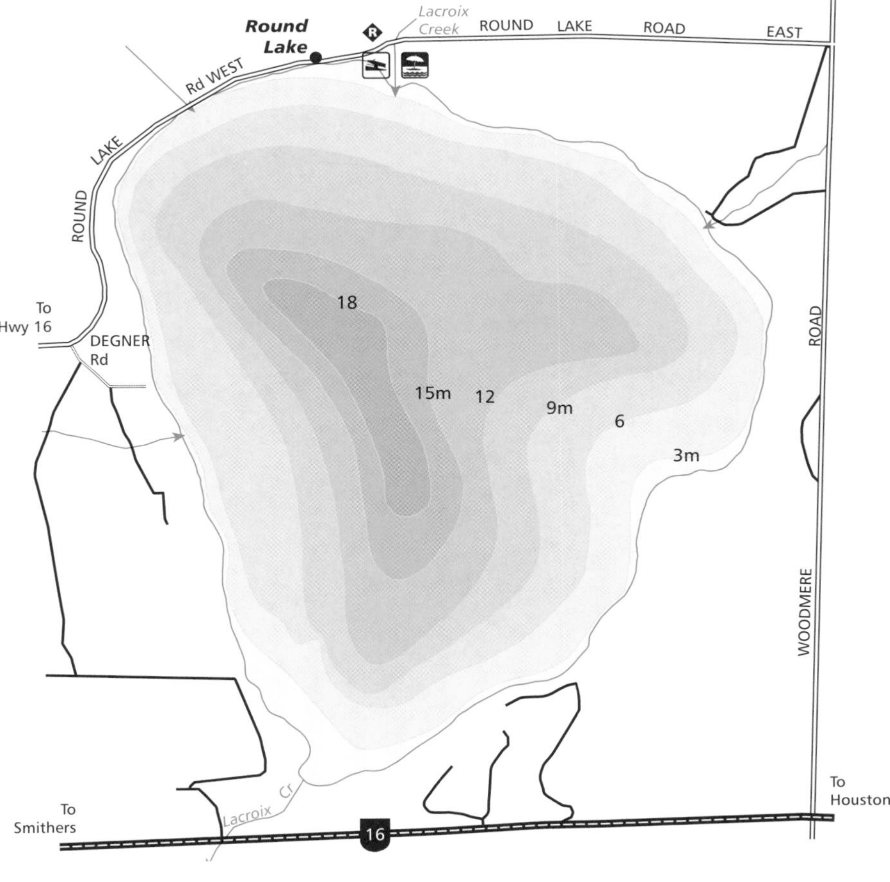

Location: 27 km (16.8 mi) northeast of 100 Mile House
Elevation: 863 m (2,831 ft)
Surface Area: 284 ha (702 ac)
Maximum Depth: 21 m (68 ft)
Mean Depth: 7.3 m (24 ft)
Way Point: 51° 49′ 40″ N, 121° 3′ 32″ W

Ruth Lake

Area Indicator

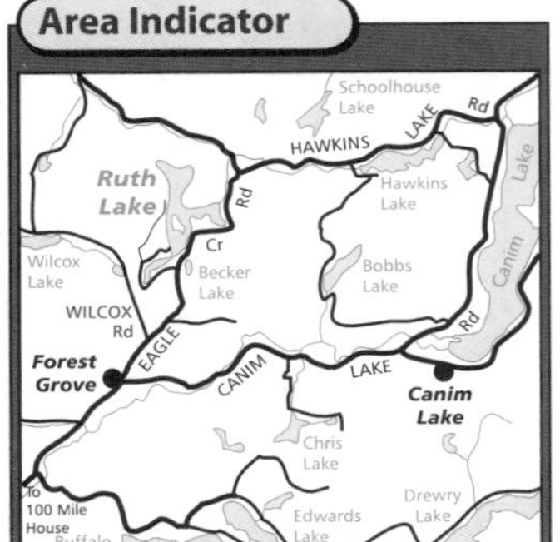

Directions

To get to Ruth Lake from the Cariboo Highway (Highway 97), head northeast on the Canim Lake Road, which is found just north of 100 Mile House. When you reach Forest Grove, turn left (north) on the Eagle Creek Road. Park signs will direct the way.

Ruth Lake Fish Stocking Data			
Year	Species	Number	Life Stage
2008	Rainbow Trout	29,999	Yearling
2008	Kokanee	20,000	Fry
2007	Rainbow Trout	30,000	Yearling
2007	Kokanee	20,000	Fry
2006	Rainbow Trout	30,000	Yearling
2006	Kokanee	20,000	Fingerling

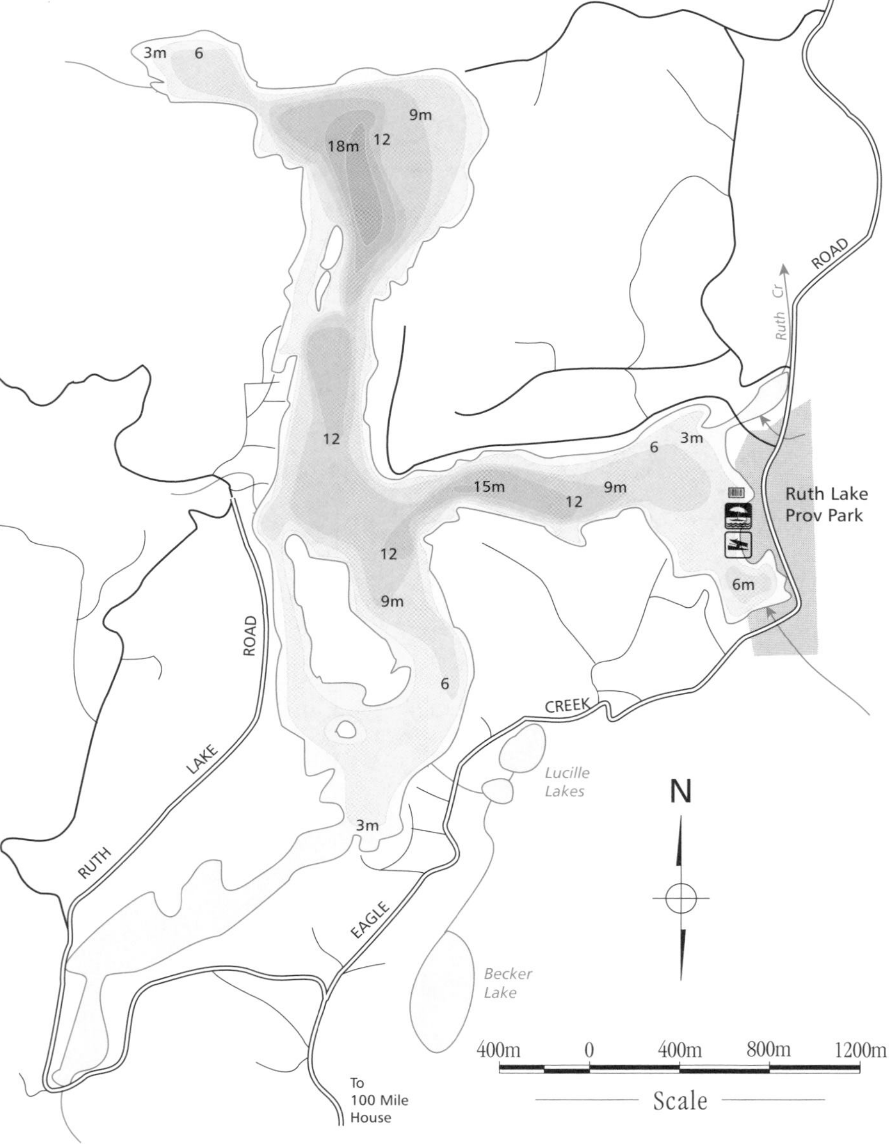

Fishing

Ruth Lake is an odd shaped, picturesque lake situated northeast of 100 Mile House. If you squint, the lake looks a bit like someone running, but only just a bit. The lake has three arms emanating from an island at the middle of the lake.

It was named after Ruth MacDonald, one of the few single women in the Cariboo round the turn of the twentieth century. As you might expect, it was named by some guy trying to woo her: "And ah named a lake after you, my purdy lady…"

The lake contains good numbers of rainbow and kokanee and is annually stocked with both. The Freshwater Fisheries Society of BC stocks about 30,000 rainbow and 20,000 kokanee here each year to help maintain the popular fishery.

The rainbow trout are the fish eating Blackwater strain rainbow, which feed on the course fish in the lake, which include squawfish, suckers, peamouth chub and redside shiner. As a result, the trout can get up to about 1 kg (2 lbs), while the kokanee are usually a little smaller.

The ice is off the lake a little earlier than other lakes in region, usually by late April to early May. After the water turns over, the fishing picks up and is pretty good until the early summer. By September, the fishing picks up again.

The lake is deep enough to troll if you stick around the deeper parts of the lake. In fact, the lake is best fished from a boat, whether trolling or spincasting. Most choose to troll. There are three distinct holes, one in the middle, one at the north end and one in the eastern bay. The southwestern arm of the lake is quite shallow (typically less than 3 metres/10 feet). Several islands mark the location for some nice, productive drop off areas where you can troll or cast a fly or lure tipped with a worm.

Because kokanee have similar feeding habits to rainbow trout, chances are you will hook some as they are attracted to much the same patterns and lures as a rainbow trout. However kokanee have very soft mouths and if they are your intended target, it is best to have a rubber snubber to reduce the damage to the fish's mouth when they take the lure. This is not good for the fish and not a good way to fish, period, so a snubber is recommended.

The standard method of trolling is with a lake troll, usually followed by a Wedding Band tipped with a lure. Trolling in a slow S curve will cause the lures to move erratically, which makes them much more interesting to the fish. Kokanee are very particular about water temperature and will usually be found in a very narrow band of water. And while rainbow trout are loners, kokanee tend to school; if you find one, chances are you've found a bunch.

Facilities

The **Ruth Lake Provincial Park** is a lovely park, which provides day-use area together with a cartop boat launch. In addition to a small beach area, there is also a floating dock here.

Sapeye & Bluff Lakes

Location: 190 km (118 mi) southwest of Williams Lake

Fishing

Sapeye and Bluff Lakes, along with nearby Horn Lake, are among the most storied lakes in the Chilcotin. In addition to great fishing for wild rainbow trout, the two lakes hold Dolly Varden and squawfish. The lakes are a mid-elevation lake and are usually ice free and fishable by early to mid May.

Sapeye has been regulated as fly-fishing only. It is the larger of the two and one of the best times to be here is during the mayfly hatch in late may or early June. Try working the far bay across from the campsite or around the island near the south end of the lake.

Unlike Sapeye Lake, which is long and narrow, Bluff Lake is a rounder lake with a pair of pronounced bays, which provide shelter from the nearly constant wind that blows in the area. It is connected to Sapeye Lake by a stream and it is possible to canoe from one lake to the other.

Catching dollies on the fly is a challenge, as they are much easier to take using bait. Still, a Muddler Minnow or other streamer pattern can sometimes fool them into striking, but most people who fish Sapeye stick to the rainbow trout.

Bluff Lake gets its name from a series of high, rocky bluffs that surround the lake.

Between the inflow of the stream and the boat launch is a huge weedy area where the insects hatch and where you will probably have the most success. The lake has shockingly clear water and it is possible to sight fish for trout. Of course, that also means the trout are easily spooked by things like, oh, the shadow cast by a float tube or small boat. They can also see your line a lot easier, so make sure you use the lightest gear possible.

Bluff Lake does not have as pronounced of hatches as Sapeye, but has a good population of freshwater shrimp. Fishing a scud pattern, a nymph, or even a chironomid can work when the hatches aren't happening.

Directions

Follow Highway 20 west from Williams Lake to just before the small settlement of Tatla Lake. Where the highway makes a sharp right hand curve, watch for the Tatlayoko Lake Road heading southwest. Follow this road for about 4 km to the Y intersection with the Bluff Lake Road (6000 Rd). Stay right and around 9 km you will come to the turn-off to the Horn Lake Recreation Site. About 2 km past that, you will come across the narrow road to Sapeye Lake, a nearly 180 degree corner back to your right. Five kilometres past this corner will bring you to the shores of Bluff Lake.

Facilities

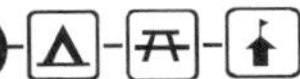

The **Sapeye Lake Recreation Site** offers space for eight groups. The access road into the lake is good, but very narrow, so trailers and large RVs are not recommended. There is no boat launch as such, but people with four wheel drive vehicles and good reverse skills can launch a trailered boat on the lake. Just be prepared to back up a fair ways as there is no room to turn around at the bottom.

Bluff Lake, on the other hand, has no campsite and very little parking at the launching site. Most of the surrounding land is privately owned. If there is no space at Sapeye, check out nearby Horn Lake, which is the largest site in the area.

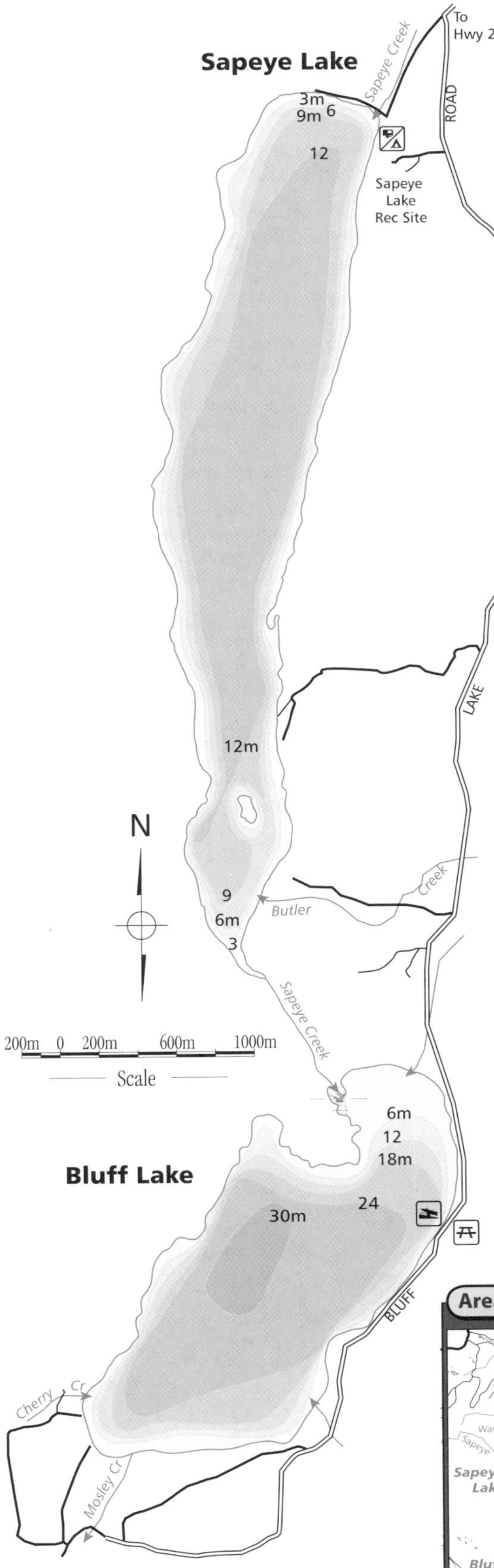

Sapeye Lake

Elevation: 895 m (2,936 ft)
Surface Area: 273 ha (674 ac)
Maximum Depth: 15 m (48 ft)
Mean Depth: 9.3 m (30 ft)
Way Point: 51° 47'26"N, 124° 43'44"W

Bluff Lakes

Elevation: 883 m (2,896 ft)
Surface Area: 183 ha (452 ac)
Maximum Depth: 31 m (100 ft)
Mean Depth: 19 m (61 ft)
Way Point: 51° 45'5"N, 124° 43'21"W

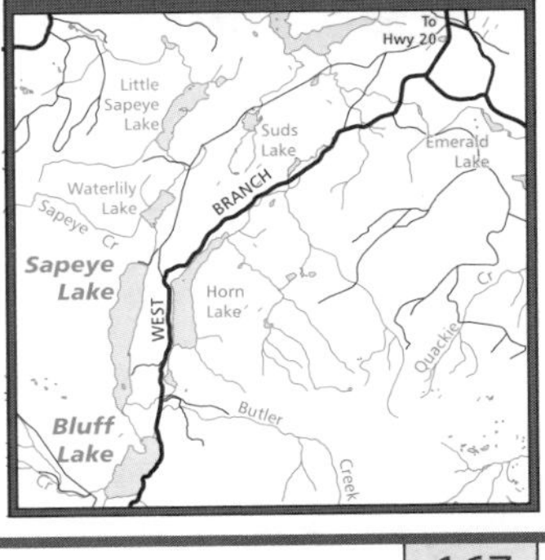

Location: 10 km (6 miles) southwest of Hazelton
Elevation: 306 m (1,004 ft)
Surface Area: 20 ha (49 ac)
Maximum Depth: 2.7 m (8.9 ft)
Mean Depth: 1.9 m (6.3 ft)
Way Point: 55° 11′ 50.8″ N, 127° 41′ 2.3″ W

Seeley Lake

Area Indicator

Fishing

Seeley Lake is a small, shallow lake found in the shadow of the towering peaks of the Hazelton Mountains. The best time to fish here are before mid-June and after the end of August, when the water is cooler and the fish are more active. Because the lake is so small and so shallow, it suffers from the summer doldrums.

The lake holds good numbers of good sized cutthroat trout, which can get up to 2 kg (4 lbs), although the average catch is about half that. In addition to cutthroat, the lake holds rainbow trout and Dolly Varden.

Cutthroat trout are much more aggressive feeders than rainbow trout and are piscivorous if given the choice, meaning they eat smaller fish. Fly anglers should work gold or silver bodied Muddler Minnows or some other streamer pattern on a sinking line with a short leader.

They can also try working a scud (freshwater shrimp) pattern, as these seem to be well received by the fish. Patterns like damselfly and dragonfly nymphs are always good standbys. If the fish aren't biting, an attractor pattern such as a Doc Spratley, Carey Special or a black broadhead leech can be worked around the drop offs and other potential areas until you get a bite. A throat pump will be helpful in determining what the fish are eating that day.

Spincasting Kitimat lures, Panther Martin spinners or trolling Willow Leafs/Ford Fenders can also be effective, especially when tipped with a worm. Also effective is a Needlefish or Triple Teaser with a small split shot to weigh it down. For kids a worm and bobber can often do the trick using light test and a small hook. Cast around the drop off areas as the cutthroat tend to cruise near shore areas in search of food.

Cutthroat are fairly voracious and it is easy enough to fish here using a bobber and bait, using a worm, a maggot or Powerbait. These are best still fished just off the bottom of the lake, near a drop off. The cutthroat trout cruise from the deeper water into the shallow to feed and the shorter the distance they have to swim into the dangerous shallow water, the more likely they are to take the literal bait.

The lake relies on natural recruitment to keep the trout populations up, but beaver dams on the spawning creeks can make it difficult for the fish to spawn, so the cutthroat population is not as strong as it could be. While the lake has no gear restrictions or catch limits (other than the regional catch limit of 5 per day), we encourage you to practice catch and release here to protect the trout population.

Directions

Seeley Lake is accessed from Seeley Lake Provincial Park along the Yellowhead Highway (Highway 16). Look for the park signs 10 km west of Hazelton.

Facilities

Seeley Lake Provincial Park is a small park found on the shores of the lake. The park has 20 campsites, a picnic area and a place to hand launch a boat. It is possible to swim in the lake, but it is cold. There is also a wildlife viewing platform on the edge of the lake designed for bird watching.

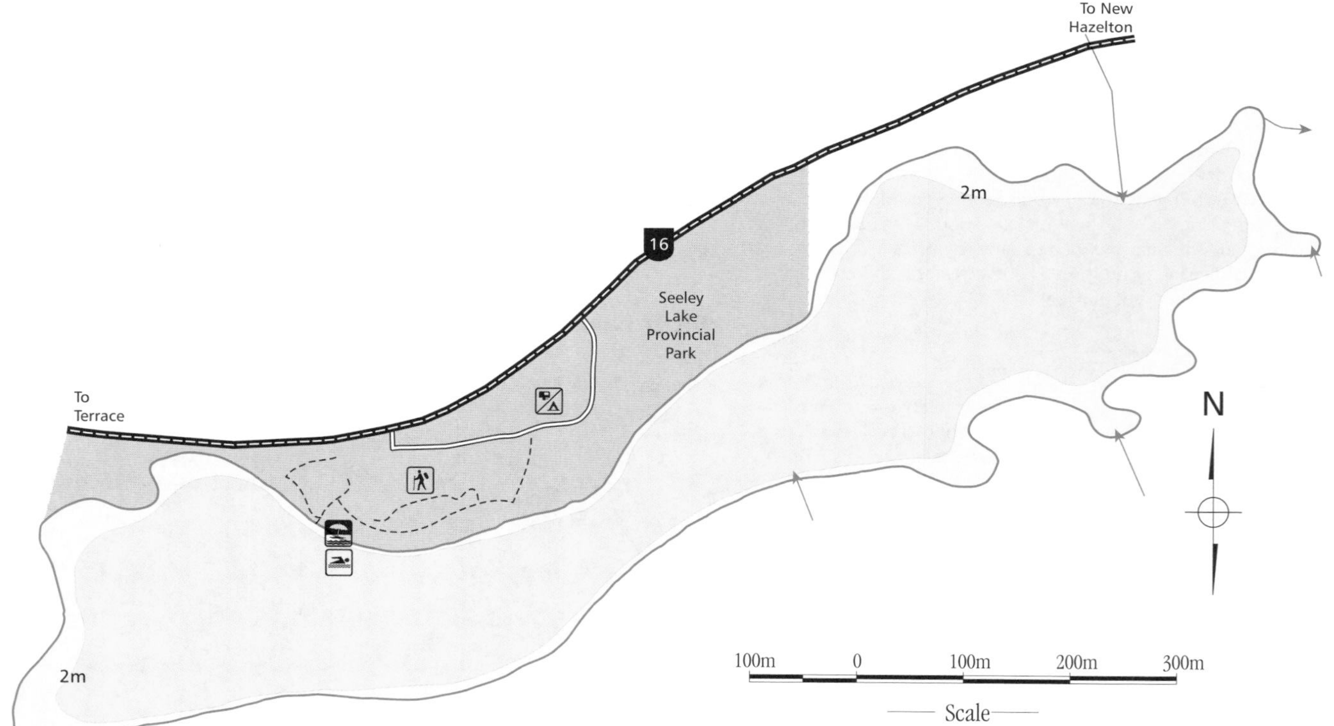

Sheridan Lake

Location: 30 km (18.6 mi) southeast of 100 Mile House
Elevation: 1,117 m (3,665 ft)
Surface Area: 1,659 ha (4,100 ac)
Maximum Depth: 35 m (115 ft)
Mean Depth: 7.3 m (24 ft)
Way Point: 51° 31′ 14″ N, 120° 53′ 47″

Fishing

Sheridan Lake is one of the province's premier trout lakes and receives heavy fishing pressure. The highly productive lake has an abundance of freshwater shrimp (scuds) that allow the rainbow to grow to nice sizes. It is also well stocked to help maintain the fishery.

The lake is more than 14 km (9 miles) long, with over 42 km (26 miles) of shoreline winding its way into bays and around peninsulas and islands. People from around the world come here, hoping to land one of the monster rainbow trout that lurk in the depths. How big? Well, the average catch is around 1 kg (2 lbs), a good catch is about 5 kg (10 lbs), but the biggest fish pulled out of here have grown to more than 8 kg (17 lbs). Tales of huge silver slabs leaping clear of the water and snapping lines or spooling reels circulate at the resorts. While it can be challenging to fish this lake at times, even a bad day should net you a couple good-sized trout.

The ice is usually off the lake by early May and fishing is very good just after ice-off before the lake turns over. Fishing slows again until mid June to mid July when the lake is at its best. Early morning and late evening can produce a fish of a lifetime. During the spring, troll or cast around the shallows. In the summer time, you should troll deep (over 14 metres/45 feet). By the fall, the fish return to the shallows and fishing is very good right up to the last week of November when the ice starts to form.

Trolling is the best method of fishing the lake. Apex, black and silver speckle Flatfish and Lyman plugs work very well. The trick is to troll fairly slowly.

For fly anglers, the evening caddisfly (sedge) hatch beginning in July can provide fantastic top water action. There is also a good evening mayfly hatch in mid June to late June and the chironomid hatches throughout the early spring are strong. Also, plenty of damselflies and dragonflies hang out around the weed beds that line the lake. Two popular flies used by locals are the Horsehair Nymph and the Slim Pickin's. Others that work are Tom Thumbs, a variety of shrimp imitations (#8–10 size), Muddler Minnows, chironomid pupae (#6–10) and sedge imitations.

The southwest bay of the lake is probably the best fly-fishing area. This is because the bay is relatively sheltered and full of weeds which together results in a prolific insect rearing area. While float tubes and pontoon boats are good near the shore, a cartopper or larger boat and motor is necessary to cover the entire lake water and get off in a hurry in the event of a summer squall.

Area Indicator

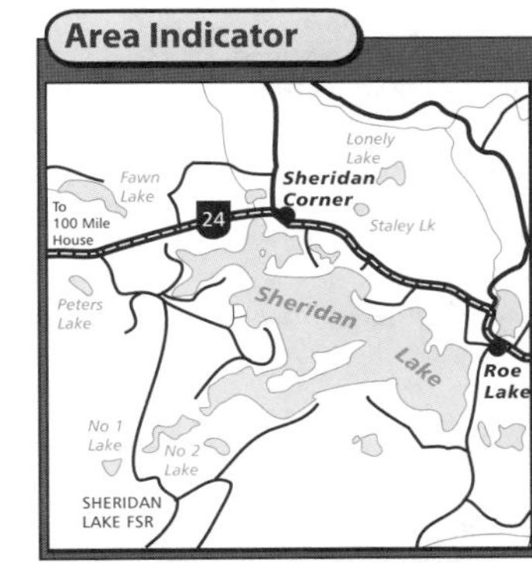

Sheridan Lake
Fish Stocking Data

Year	Species	Number	Life Stage
2008	Rainbow Trout	137,138	Yearling
2008	Rainbow Trout	150,183	Fry
2007	Rainbow Trout	137,911	Yearling
2007	Rainbow Trout	156,825	Fry
2006	Rainbow Trout	120,000	Yearling
2006	Rainbow Trout	24,999	Fry
2006	Rainbow Trout	150,000	Fall Fry

Directions

Sheridan Lake is located right next to the Fishing Highway (Highway 24), 36 km east of the Highway 97 junction. There are several launch sites around the lake.

Facilities

Resorts scattered around the lake include: **Sheridan Lake Resort**, **Sheridan Park Resort**, the **Piney Point Resort** and **Loon Bay Resort**. There is no public camping, but there are day use areas around the lake.

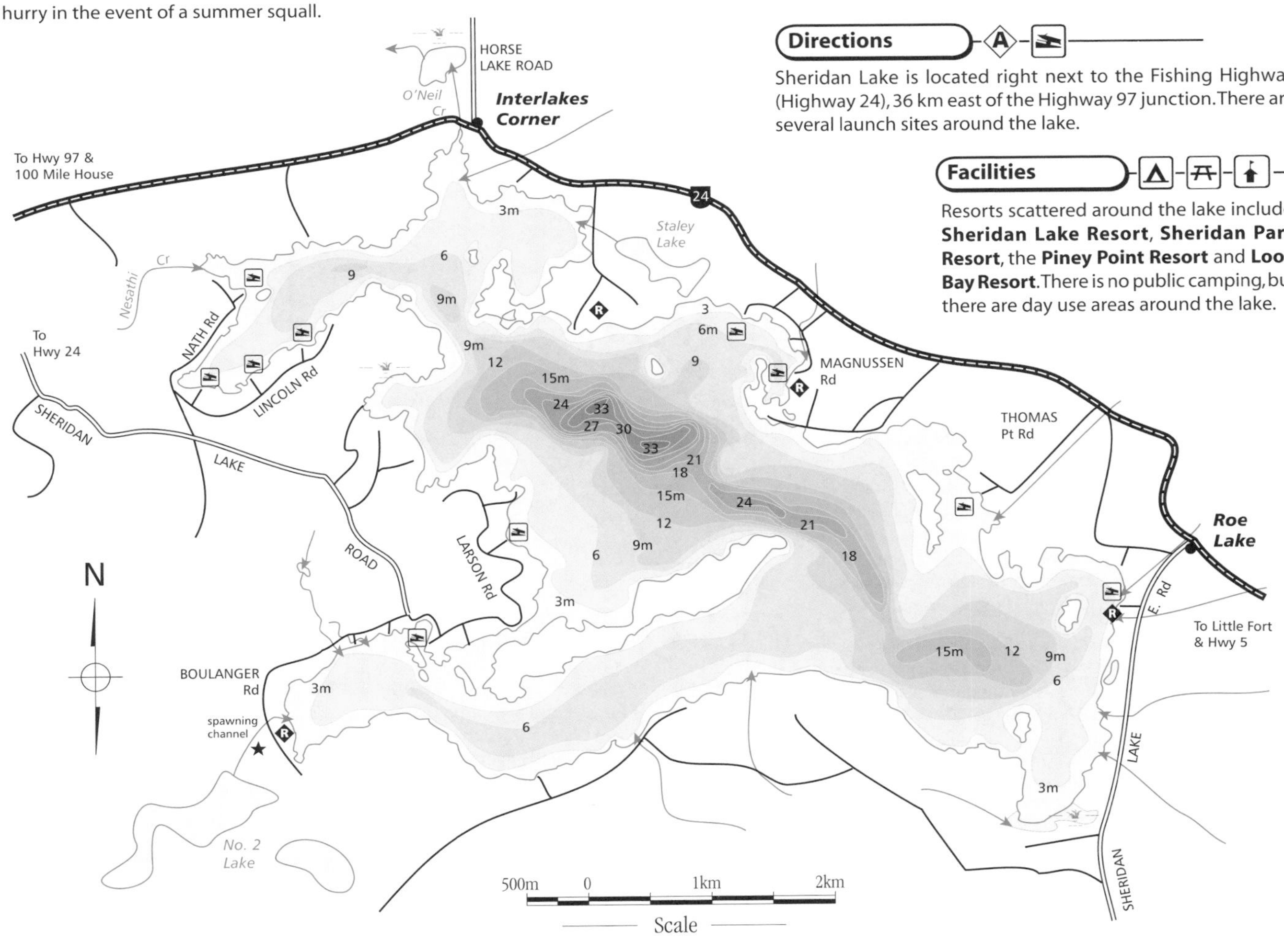

Location: Flows through Terrace
Stream Length: 619 km (385 mi)
Geographic: 54° 57′ 47″ N, 128° 23′ 40″ W

Skeena River

Fishing

One of Canada's great rivers, the Skeena is famed for the quality of its fishery. It is the second largest river entirely in BC and produces some of the biggest steelhead and salmon runs in the country. The river flows hundreds of kilometers inland twisting and winding its way to the Pacific Ocean near Prince Rupert. The river is the base for several guides and lodges in the region, providing fishing opportunities that are truly once in a lifetime in quality.

The Skeena feeds dozens of smaller rivers and a handful of larger ones, each with its own unique characteristics for fishing. All tolled, there are at least 32 rivers and streams attached to the Skeena that have steelhead runs. The top five steelhead rivers in the world (depending on who you talk to, of course) are all Skeena River tributaries. The thing is each and every one of those fish passes through the Skeena first.

While the river is home to fantastic runs of all five salmon species, it is best known for its steelhead runs. The steelhead here are legendary in both quantity and size. Anglers can literally fish for steelhead year round. Around mid-March spring runs begin to join the winter holdovers and are often very aggressive. By mid-May the run slows before the famous summer run. These big, feisty fish appear in late July and continue into August. Steelhead continue to enter the river and its tributaries throughout the fall and remain in the river in good quantities well through the winter. Steelhead in the Skeena average 4.5 kg (10 lbs), with 9 kg (20 lb) or bigger fish not uncommon. It should also be noted that all the fish in the Skeena are wild fish. Neither it, nor any of its tributaries have been stocked with hatchery fish.

Although steelhead runs number in the tens of thousands, anglers still can get skunked. Weeks can go by without a single day on the river because the water is too high, or too dirty. Even expert anglers rarely hook more than a few fish a day. However, if you were to ask them if it was worth all the waiting for that one single strike, they would respond unequivocally yes. There is a magic to steelhead fishing that other anglers just don't understand. For thousands of anglers who come here from all over the world as a pilgrim would travel to Mecca, that one single Skeena steelhead that they landed is the memory of a lifetime.

Fly anglers usually use a 7- or 8-weight, 9.5- or 10-foot single-handed rod or an 8- to 10-weight, 12- to 15-foot spey rod. A spare rod (or two) and lots of spare line is important, as steelhead are famous for stripping reels and snapping rods. As for flies, Skeena steelheads aren't particular. As long as they are in the mood, they will go for most any common steelhead pattern. Popsicles, Skunks, Silver Hiltons, black marabou for fishing deep and a variety of surface flies if you're fishing here in the summer.

Gear anglers can use Colorado Spinners, silver Krocodiles, Corkys, Spin-N-Glos, Gooey Bobs and even plastic worms. Drift fishing with a float suspending pencil lead above a short leader of about 30-50 cm (12-20 in) with 1/0 to #4 hooks or bar fishing using an eight ounce pyramid weight and a large Spin-N-Glo are common. Some anglers bottom bounce using wool (pink or orange) and a single egg.

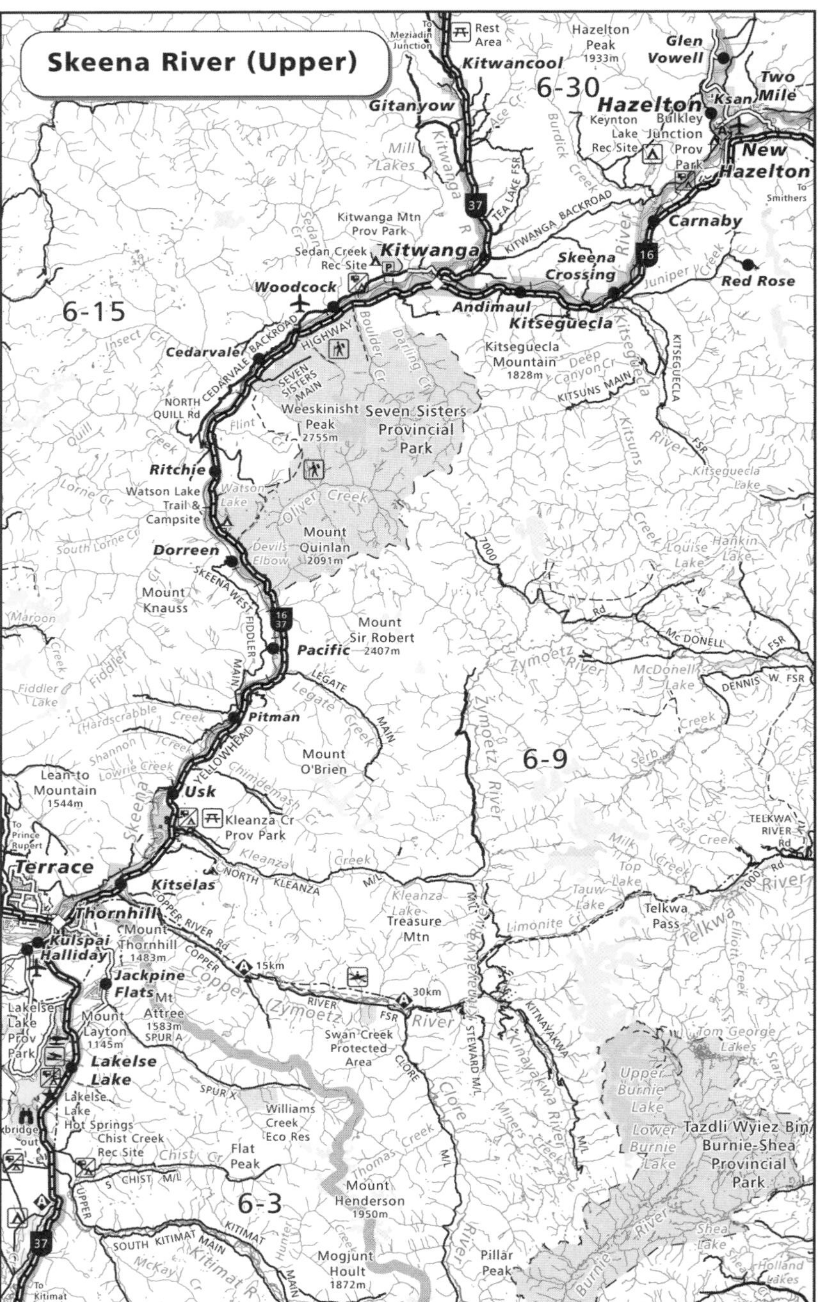

The other main sportfish that anglers pursue in the Skeena are salmon, with Chinook and Coho receiving the main attention. Chinook are the 'kings' of the river, hence their nickname and average 9-18 kg (20-40 lbs) with the odd fish breaking the 27 kg (60 lb) class. In fact, in 2001 a record 45 kg (99 lb) Chinook was caught and released on the river. While Chinook show up in late May, the best time for the giants is in July and early August. Coho average about 4.5 kg (10 lbs) and begin running in early August and are found in the river well into fall. Sockeye and chum salmon can also be found in the system from the beginning of July to mid-September while pinks usually show up a little later, but only every other year. Fishing can be very good for salmon since every year over two million salmon migrate up the Skeena. Although we recommend guides to help land a trophy Chinook or Coho, the river is quite accessible and can be fished from shore in many areas by experienced anglers.

Continued >>

Skeena River

Location: Flows through Terrace
Stream Length: 619 km (385 mi)
Geographic: 54° 29′ 51″ N, 128° 36′ 48″ W

Fishing

Continued

With all the attention focused on the steelhead and salmon, many anglers forget the fact that the Skeena also offers resident rainbow, Dolly Varden and sea-run cutthroat trout. Resident rainbow are, of course, much smaller than their sea-faring cousins, the steelhead. However, some quality-sized rainbow can be found throughout the entire river. Dollies like to hold in deep pools and feed on sculpin and other fry, so a good streamer fly or minnow imitation lure can be deadly worked off the bottom. Cutthroat also feed mainly on fry and are often quite aggressive and can put up a great fight when using a lightweight rod.

Directions

The Yellowhead Highway (Highway 16) picks up the main stem of the Skeena at Hazelton and follows it all the way to Prince Rupert, a distance of 287 km (178 miles). Most of the fishing happens in this stretch as with each tributary, the Skeena loses thousands of fish. But it also loses volume and for many people, the lower Skeena is intimidating. From Hazelton, the Salmon River Road follows the Skeena north for dozens of kilometres. When the road runs out, a railbed follows the river for many more miles. The upper river is only accessible by air.

Facilities

Facilities vary depending on where you are. The river passes through Prince Rupert and Terrace where you can find all services. There are two jet boat launches at the west end of Terrace and another one on Queensway Drive plus a few others elsewhere along the river. There is camping at the **Lakelse River Recreation Site**, at **Kleanza Creek,** the **Sedan Creek Recreation Site** and at a variety of private campgrounds along the river. Impromptu tent cities also form near some of the most popular fishing holes. While it is possible to do it yourself, a guide will help you make the most of your time. Noel Gyger (www.noelgyger.ca) acts as a booking agent for many of the guides in the area and is a wealth of knowledge on fishing the Skeena system.

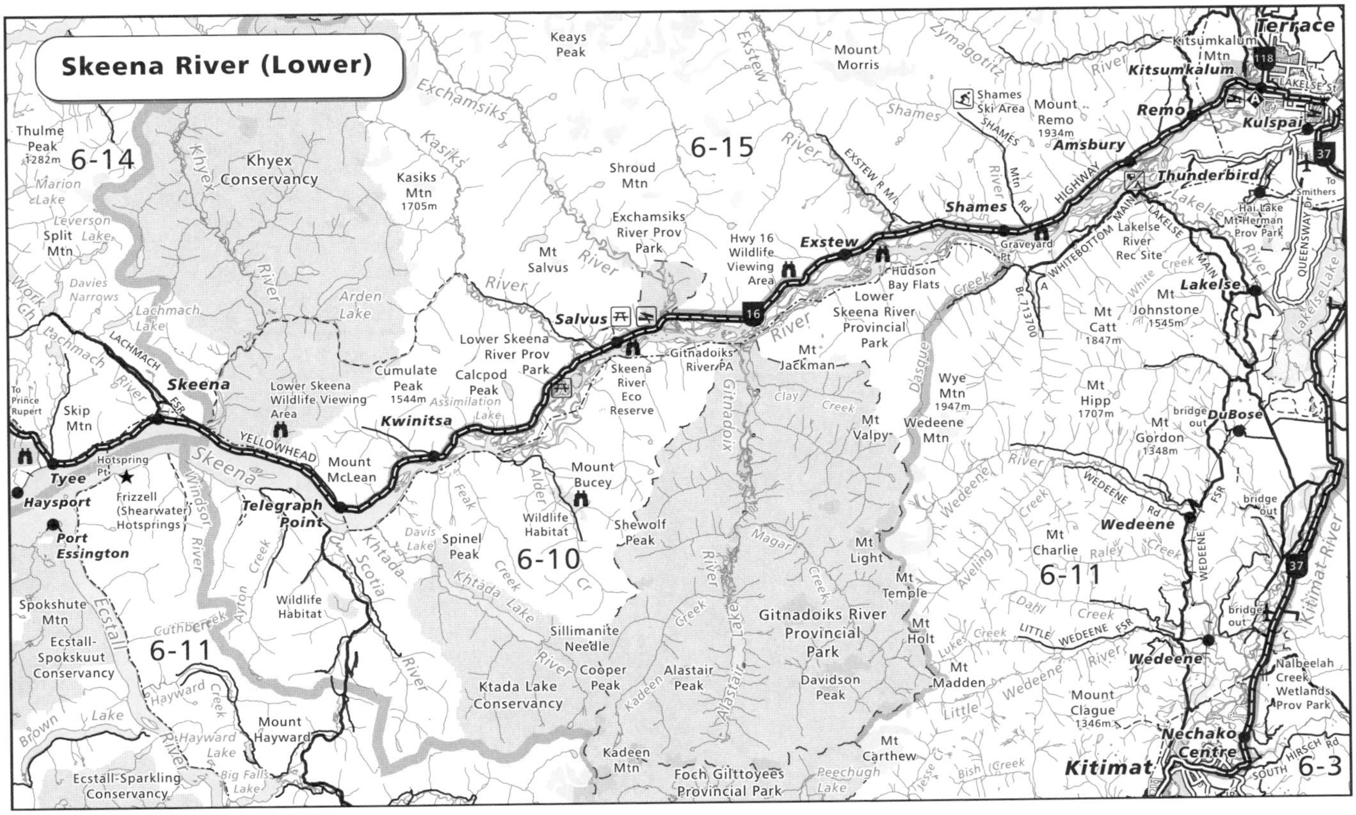

Skeena River (Lower)

Location: 25 km (15.5 mi) northeast of Williams Lake
Elevation: 1,048 m (3,438 ft)
Surface Area: 38 ha (94 ac)
Maximum Depth: 7 m (23 ft)
Mean Depth: 2 m (6.6 ft)
Way Point: 52° 18′ 31.0″ N, 121° 53′ 59.1″

Skulow Lake

Area Indicator

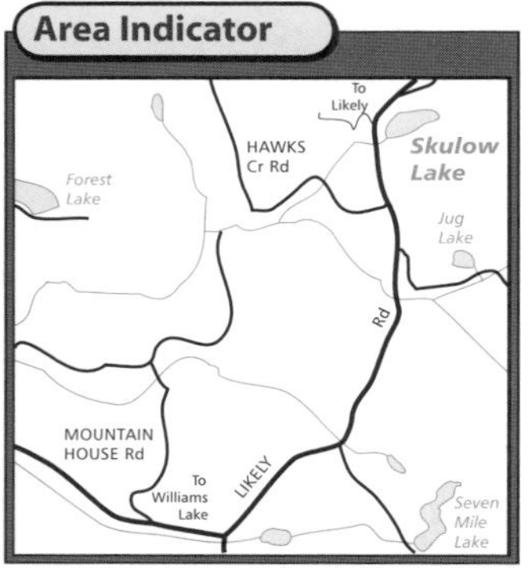

Skulow Lake Fish Stocking Data			
Year	Species	Number	Life Stage
2008	Rainbow Trout	5,000	Yearling
2008	Brook Trout	3,000	Fingerling
2007	Rainbow Trout	5,000	Yearling
2007	Brook Trout	5,000	Fingerling
2006	Rainbow Trout	7,000	Yearling
2006	Brook Trout	5,000	Fingerling

Fishing

Skulow Lake is located to the northeast of Williams Lake just off the Likely Road.

The lake is just over one kilometre above sea level, which puts it slightly above the average elevation for lakes in the area, but only just. Expect it to be ice free and fishable a couple of days later in May than lower elevation lakes.

Skulow Lake is stocked with both brook and rainbow trout. The Freshwater Fisheries Society of BC maintains these fisheries by dumping approximately 5,000 of each into the lake each year. The Blackwater strain of rainbow help control the redside shiner population in the lake. These trout also grow rapidly feeding on the smaller course fish and finding trout to 1 kg (2 lbs) is not uncommon.

The lake is quite shallow so it is better suited for spincasting and fly-fishing in the spring and fall. The deepest part of the lake is right in the middle with the water depth gradually declining from shore.

Brook trout are renowned for being a fickle and difficult fish to catch. One of the best times of year to catch brook trout is in the spring just after the ice comes off the lakes and into early June. Once the ice retreats, the oxygen content and cool temperatures of the water means the trout feed near the surface and in the shallows.

After a long winter brookies readily feed off new insect larvae and small minnows. Brookies have been known to be quite aggressive at this time of year and can be caught readily from shore with small spinners or even fishing with a hook and worm. Once the heat of summer sets in, brookies head down into the thermocline layer. At this time they can still be caught, but it is definitely much more challenging.

Fly-fishing in spring can be very productive for both brook and rainbow trout, as the bulk of their diet in the spring is insects such as chironomids and other insect larvae. For spincasters, try small spinners or trolling small spoons. Some proven brook trout spoons include the Little Cleo, smaller sized Williams Fishlander, Luhr Jensen Diamond King or Gibbs Gypsy. As for spinners, almost anything with a smaller profile can work well in silver or gold, such as a Blue Fox or Panther Martin. Small spinners can be deadly for both brook and rainbow trout when they are tossed along banks and beside sunken logs. You can potentially increase success by adding a worm or small dead minnow to the end of your presentations.

An aeration system is in place at the lake to reduce the winterkill problem of the past. As a result, the lake is not well suited for ice fishing as the ice is thin.

An electric motor only restriction applies at the lake.

To Likely
ROAD
6
5m
3
2m
3
LIKELY
LAKE
ROAD
SKULOW

Directions

South of Williams Lake at 150 Mile House, turn north from the Cariboo Highway (Highway 97) onto the Likely Road. Stay left at the junction of the Likely and Horsefly Roads and continue north on the Likely Road. Skulow Lake is on the right hand side of the Likely Road a couple of kilometers north of the Hawks Creek Road junction. The lake is about 24 km from the highway junction and easily reached by car.

Facilities

There are no developed facilities at the lake.

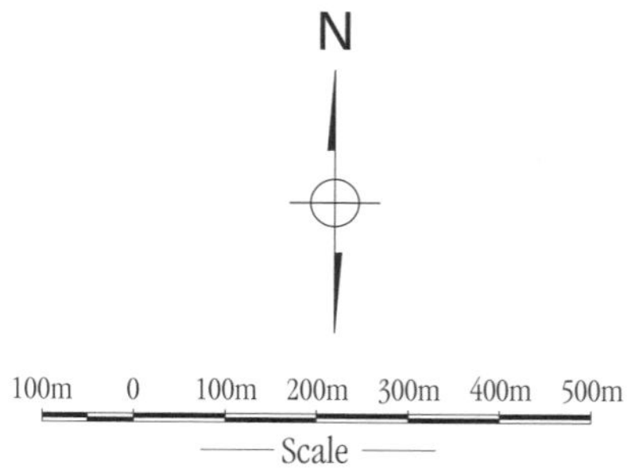

N

100m 0 100m 200m 300m 400m 500m
Scale

Snag Lake

Location: 30 km (18.6 mi) east of 100 Mile House
Elevation: 1,171 m (3,842 ft)
Surface Area: 91 ha (225 ac)
Maximum Depth: 7.3 m (24 ft)
Mean Depth: 2.6 m (8.5 ft)
Way Point: 51° 39′ 46″ N, 121° 44′ 35″ W

Fishing

Snag Lake is a shallow weedy lake that offers surprisingly good fishing for stocked brook trout. In fact, many consider this the best brook trout fishing in the Cariboo, with brookies getting to 2 kg (4 lbs) on a fairly regular basis.

To help boaster the brook trout population, the Freshwater Fisheries Society of BC stocks the lake with 20,000 trout each year. This attests to the popularity of the fishery.

The lake is located in a fairly dense forest and is neither a low nor high elevation lake. It is usually ice-free and ready to fish by mid to late May. The shallow nature of the lake means the summer doldrums hit with a vengeance and fishing here is an exercise in futility during July and August. It is best to come back again after mid-September.

Because of the dense forest, shallow bottom and prolific weed growth, fishing from the shore is difficult. Further, the weedy bottom makes trolling here difficult, but it can be done down the middle of the lake with a floating or slow sinking fly line. Most simply anchor just off the drop off and cast.

Fly anglers report good success casting large black dragonfly, damselfly or mayfly nymphs on a floating line towards the shallows. Use a slow but variable retrieve until you match the feeding preferences for that day. Black or maroon leeches can be fished in the same manner, but let them sink to the bottom before retrieving them. Tom Thumbs are also productive on the surface or just under when boatman or backswimmers are about.

In the spring, a unique lure to try is the Rattletrap. For some reason, brookies are attracted to the sound it makes during the retrieve. Mepps Aglia, Blue Fox Vibrax or Rooster Tail spinners can also take these aggressive feeders.

The fall is the best time to fish for the brook trout as the males are very aggressive just before spawning and strike at most anything. Also, the brook trout congregate in the shallows before spawning, making them fairly easy to find.

Brook trout remain active in the winter and ice fishing is possible if the roads in are ploughed or you have a snowmobile. Use shrimp, krill, salmon eggs and worms. These baits can be fished on a plain or glow hook and jig combination. The key to success is locating the fish. Remember to drill multiple holes in the 3 metre (10 foot) range, preferably near structure.

Snag Lake			
Fish Stocking Data			
Year	Species	Number	Life Stage
2008	Brook Trout	20,000	Fingerling
2007	Brook Trout	20,000	Fingerling
2006	Brook Trout	20,000	Fingerling

Directions

To get to Snag Lake, take Exter Road west from 100 Mile House. Follow it for a few kilometres until you reach Gustafsen Lake Forest Service Road (1100 Road), a good gravel road used by industrial traffic. Keep right at the 8 km and 20 km markers, as the road turns into the Gustafson-Dog Creek Forest Service Road.

At the 37 km marker, just past the cattle guard, take the first right and drive for another 3 km before turning right again. Drive for 8.1 km and turn right on a small indistinct road. About 50 metres later you should reach Snag Lake.

Area Indicator

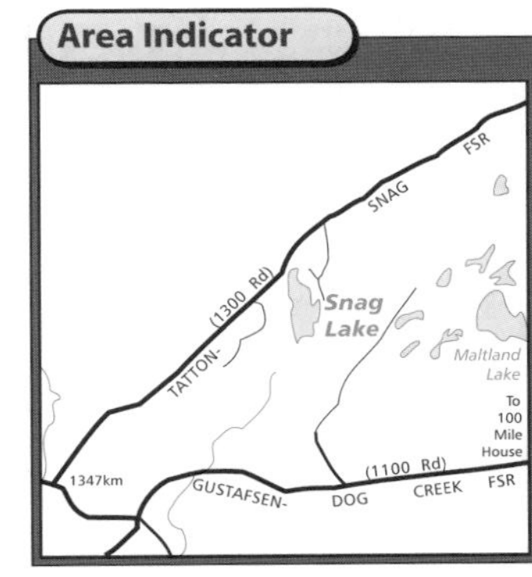

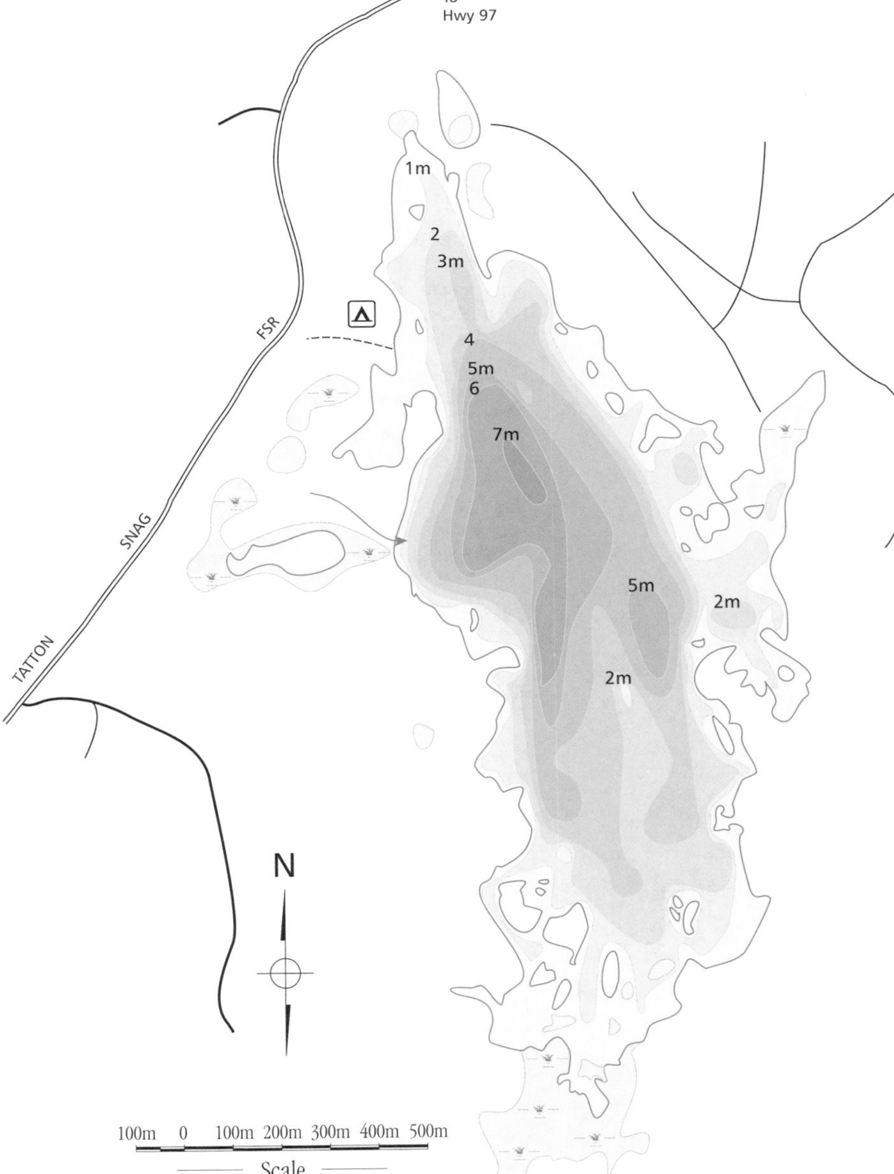

Facilities

There is a rustic camping area next to the western shoreline. You can launch a small boat from that location.

Location: 72 km (50 mi) northeast of Williams Lake
Elevation: 915 m (3,002 ft)
Surface Area: 454 ha (1,122 ac)
Maximum Depth: 72 m (236 ft)
Mean Depth: 29 m (95 ft)
Way Point: 52° 34′ 47″ N, 121° 23′ 22″ W

Spanish Lake

Area Indicator

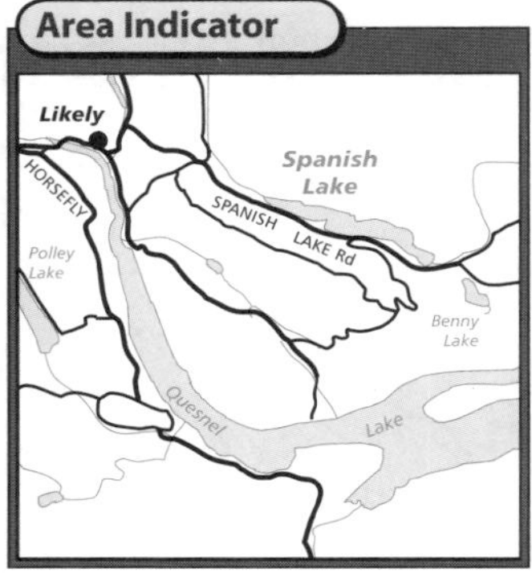

Fishing

In 1906, a pair of huge steam shovels were brought in to dig a channel connecting Spanish Lake to the Bullion Mines. The monster shovels were hauled up to Spanish Lake by wagon, not a small feat considering each shovel weighed about 10,000 kg (22,000 lbs). The shovels were assembled and a channel was started to connect the lake to the mine, but a year later operations were suspended and the shovels were left to rust. One shovel has been restored and is on display in Quesnel, while the other still rests in Cedar Point Park on nearby Quesnel Lake. The mine itself is about 7 km from Spanish Lake and is worth a visit. The 3 km (1.8 mile), 121 metre (400 foot) deep pit looks like more like a chasm than a mine, with about 200 million tonnes of material having been removed.

The mining pit is a sideshow to the real attraction to the area, which is the fishing. While nearby Quesnel Lake gets all the glory, Spanish Lake is also worthy of note, too. It doesn't have the sockeye returns and the great fishing during the spawning season, but it has good number of wild rainbow and bull trout and the occasional lake trout.

The rainbow are rarely over 0.5 kg (1 lb), but there are plenty of them. Maybe too many of them for the amount of food that is in the lake. As a result, the fish grow slowly. But they are almost always hungry. This means that whatever you throw at them that looks like food will usually get eaten.

Because the trout are so willing to take what you're offering, it is a great place to take the family fishing. The fishing is often fast enough to keep young hands and minds occupied…for while at least.

Trolling a lake troll is the most common way of fishing the lake. For rainbow trout, a popular choice is a Willow Leaf used in conjunction with just about any lure or bait. The most common is a spinner like a Wedding Band, but you can also use a small spoon (Needlefish, Super Duper or Midge Wobbler), small plug (Hot Shot or Kwikfish) or just a hook and a worm.

Don't troll too fast. Many expert trollers refuse to use a motor because it causes the boat (and therefore the lures) to move too fast. They use oars instead. The other trouble with engines is they create a constant rate of motion. Varying your speed will cause the lure to move more erratically, giving it a more lifelike behaviour, making it more appealing to the trout. Trolling in an S-Curve will also help randomize the motion of the lure. When it is on the inside of a curve, it will slow down, when it is on the outside, it will speed up.

Directions

To get to Spanish Lake, you must first get to Likely. The paved Likely Road is found off Highway 97 south of Williams Lake at 150 Mile House. It is about 80 km (54 miles) along this scenic backroad to Likely. Continue past Likely on the road to Keithley Creek and then turn right onto the Spanish Lake Road. Watch for the signs to the lake.

Facilities

The **Spanish Lake Recreation Site** offers half a dozen sites in a scenic forest next to the south side of the lake. There is no boat launch, but you can launch a cartopper.

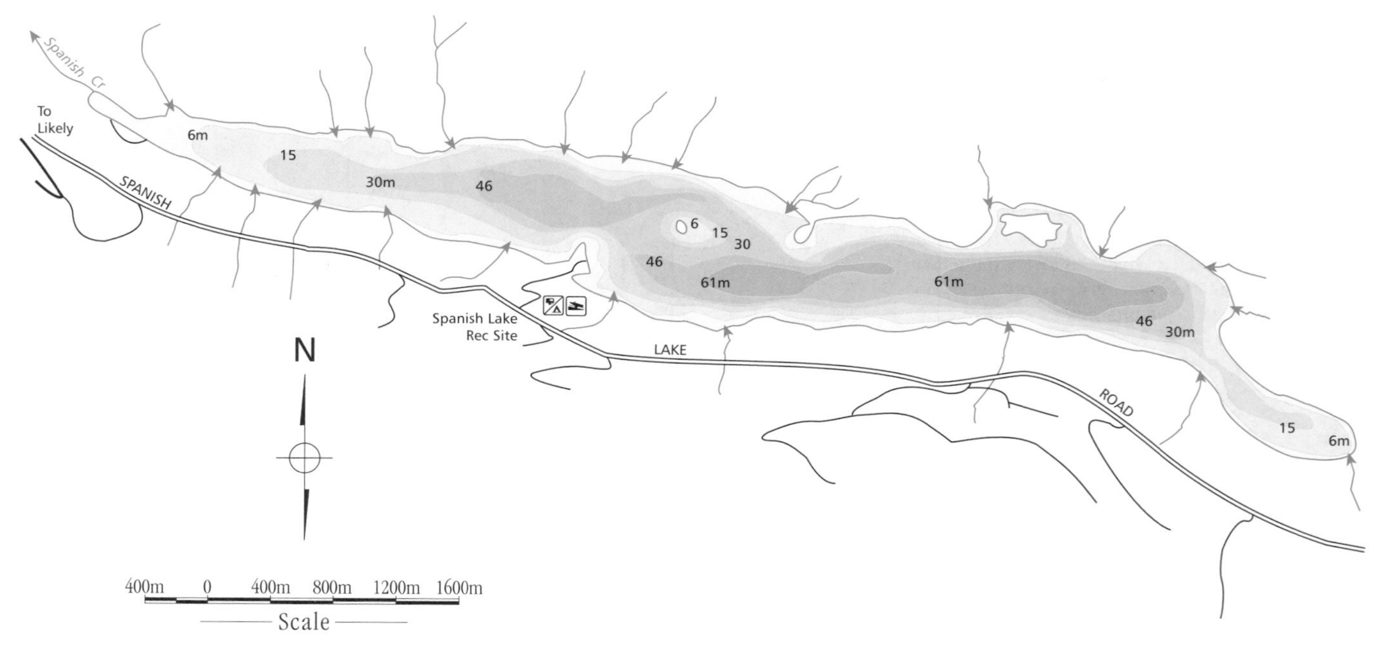

Square (Squaw) Lake

Location: 70 km (43.5 mi) northeast of Prince George
Elevation: 710 m (2,329 ft)
Surface Area: 13 ha (33 ac)
Maximum Depth: 10 m (32 ft)
Mean Depth: 4.4 m (14 ft)
Way Point: 54° 28′ 53.4″ N, 122° 41′ 56.6″ W

Fishing

Formerly known as Squaw Lake, this small lake is actually more circular, or at least oblong, than the new name implies. It is about 500 m (1,500 ft) by trail from the nearest road-accessible point. While that isn't much of a walk, it is enough to keep most people out and chances are if you fish here, you will be the only one here, especially in summer.

Because of the walk in and because of the no powerboat restriction on the lake, most people who fish here do so from the shore, or more preferably, from a float tube.

There are some reports of big fish here, but not many. The average catch is usually less than 0.5 kg (1 lb), but the fish are usually quite hungry and willing to chase after most anything you toss at them. The Freshwater Fisheries Society of BC stocks the lake annually with about 2,500 rainbow, which is a good number for the size of lake.

While the fishing can be quite brisk, the lake is like a giant bowl. There are really no obvious drop offs, points or outcroppings where the fish will hang around. The bottom of the lake slowly slopes to the middle, making it a bit of a crapshoot as to where you will actually find the fish. This is especially true in the summer, when the small, relatively shallow lake tends to heat up. At this time the fishery is pretty slow.

The lake can be fished from shore using a worm and bobber, but it is probably best to get onto the lake with a float tube or, if you really want to carry it in, a canoe. You can still toss a worm and bobber or you can use small spinners and spoons and for fly anglers, nymphs, leeches and attractor patterns. You don't have to get fancy here. As in football, 80% is just showing up.

However, what the lake is best known for is for its ice fishing. It is the only lake in the park open to ice fishing and attracts a lot of attention in the winter due to the proximity to the highway. The best time to fish is early in the season, once the ice is solid enough to bear weight (usually about 15 cm/6 in). Rainbow trout are not only susceptible to heat, but to the cold and more importantly, to declining oxygen levels in the water. By late winter, they begin to get sluggish and offer little fight.

The best way to catch rainbow trout through the ice is with a jigging lure with or without bait. Rainbow are often found just below the ice, where the oxygen levels are highest and in close to shore, where they don't have to dive too deep to find food. Start fishing right below the ice and work your way down to the bottom with the hook until you find the level that the fish are at. Some people will even sprawl out on the ice and look down through the hole, sight-fishing for the trout.

Directions

Square Lake is found in Crooked River Provincial Park, 70 km northeast of Prince George on Highway 97. It is a 500 m (1,500 ft) hike in to the lake from the parking lot at the west end of Bear Lake.

Facilities

Crooked River Provincial Park offers 90 campsites on nearby Bear Lake. The park can be busy and reservations are recommended.

Area Indicator

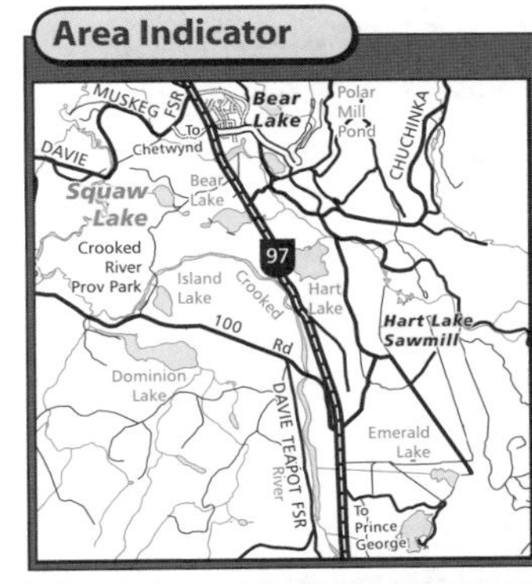

Square (Squaw) Lake			
Fish Stocking Data			
Year	Species	Number	Life Stage
2007	Rainbow Trout	2,500	Fry
2006	Rainbow Trout	2,576	Fall Fry
2005	Rainbow Trout	2,500	Fall Fry
2005	Rainbow Trout	1,500	Yearling

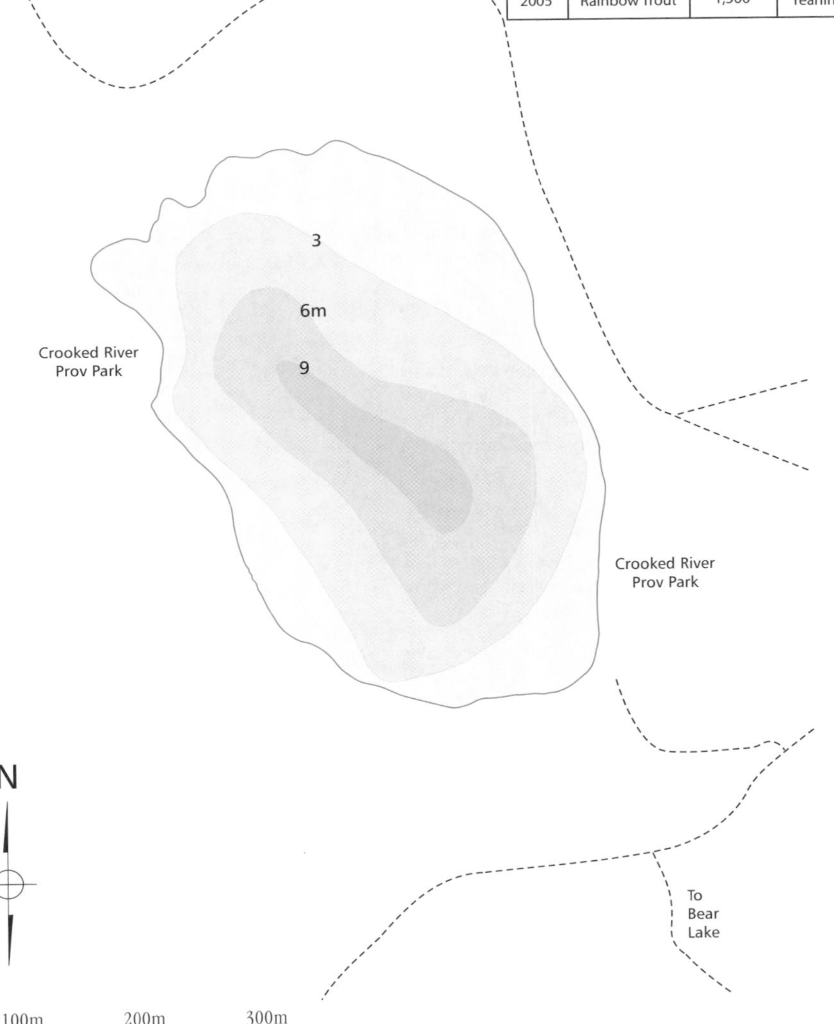

Location: 30 km (18.6 mi) northwest of Dawson Creek
Elevation: 889 m (2,916 ft)
Surface Area: 28 ha (70 ac)
Maximum Depth: 7.5 m (25 ft)
Mean Depth: 3.8 m (12 ft)
Geographic: 55° 57′ 47.7″ N, 121° 10′ 0.7″ W

Stewart Lake

Area Indicator

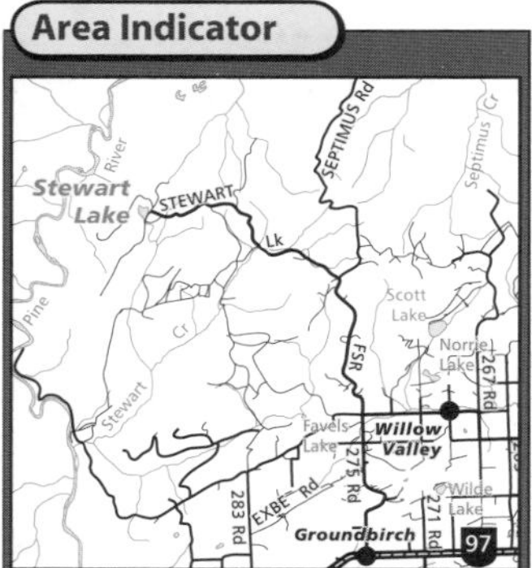

Fishing

Stewart Lake is a small lake set in the rolling hills and dense boreal forest found north of Goundbirch between Highway 97 and the Pine River. Even though the lake isn't managed as a trophy lake, the chance of pulling out a trophy sized trout is actually quite good here.

About 2,500 fish are stocked here annually. While the fish average about 35 cm (14 in) or so, there are a few monsters lurking here. Pulling out a 3.5 kg (7 lb) rainbow, while not a daily occurrence, does happen occasionally. This is mostly due to the fact that the shallow lake has a tendency to produce muddy tasting fish. As a result, most anglers tend to release the fish they catch allowing the fish the chance to grow quite large.

The deepest hole in the lake is about 7.5 metres (22 ft) deep and the fish retreat here in the heat of summer. While some people do fish here in summer, the fish become sluggish and provide little fight. Add to that the muddy taste and few people fish here during the heat of summer.

In spring and fall, however, the fishing can be fast and furious and catching 30 or more fish in a day is a very real possibility. The small lake is best fished from a float tube or small boat. If you do bring a boat, note the 10 hp power restriction.

Gear anglers will find that working a spinner like a Panther Martin, Mepps or a Roostertail will work well. Tolling will produce good results as long as you are aware that it is not a big lake. A Willow Leaf, small spinner and worm is probably the best option for trolling.

Fly anglers will find only a few hatches on the lake, including caddis or mayflies, but there is little dry fly action to speak of. Instead, working a Muddler Minnow, a Woolly Bugger, a bead head nymph or other emerger pattern will get the best results.

The lake is also a popular ice fishing lake and the access here in the winter (by snowmobile) is usually better than it is in summer. Rainbow trout are best fished through the ice early in the season, as soon as the ice is thick enough to support your weight. As the winter wears on, the oxygen levels in the water drop and the fish once again become sluggish and put up little fight.

Directions

Stewart Lake is found north of Groundbirch near the Pine River. It is 33 km north of the highway from the turnoff, just west of the Groundbirch store, which is found west of Dawson Creek. From the highway, follow Road 275 through the mixed farm and forestland around Groundbirch before heading into the rolling forested hills that the lake is set in. Beyond Willow Valley, the road name turns to Stewart Lake Forest Service Road. There are a number of side roads that fall off the main road, but you should be able to puzzle out which route to follow, though the farther you get from the highway, the rougher the road becomes. If not, a copy of the new Northern BC Backroad Mapbook book will certainly help..

Facilities

There is a day use recreation site at Stewart Lake, though people have been known to spend the night here. It is a popular ATV and snowmobile riding area.

Stewart Lake Fish Stocking Data			
Year	Species	Number	Life Stage
2008	Rainbow Trout	2,500	Yearling
2007	Rainbow Trout	2,500	Yearling
2006	Rainbow Trout	2,500	Yearling

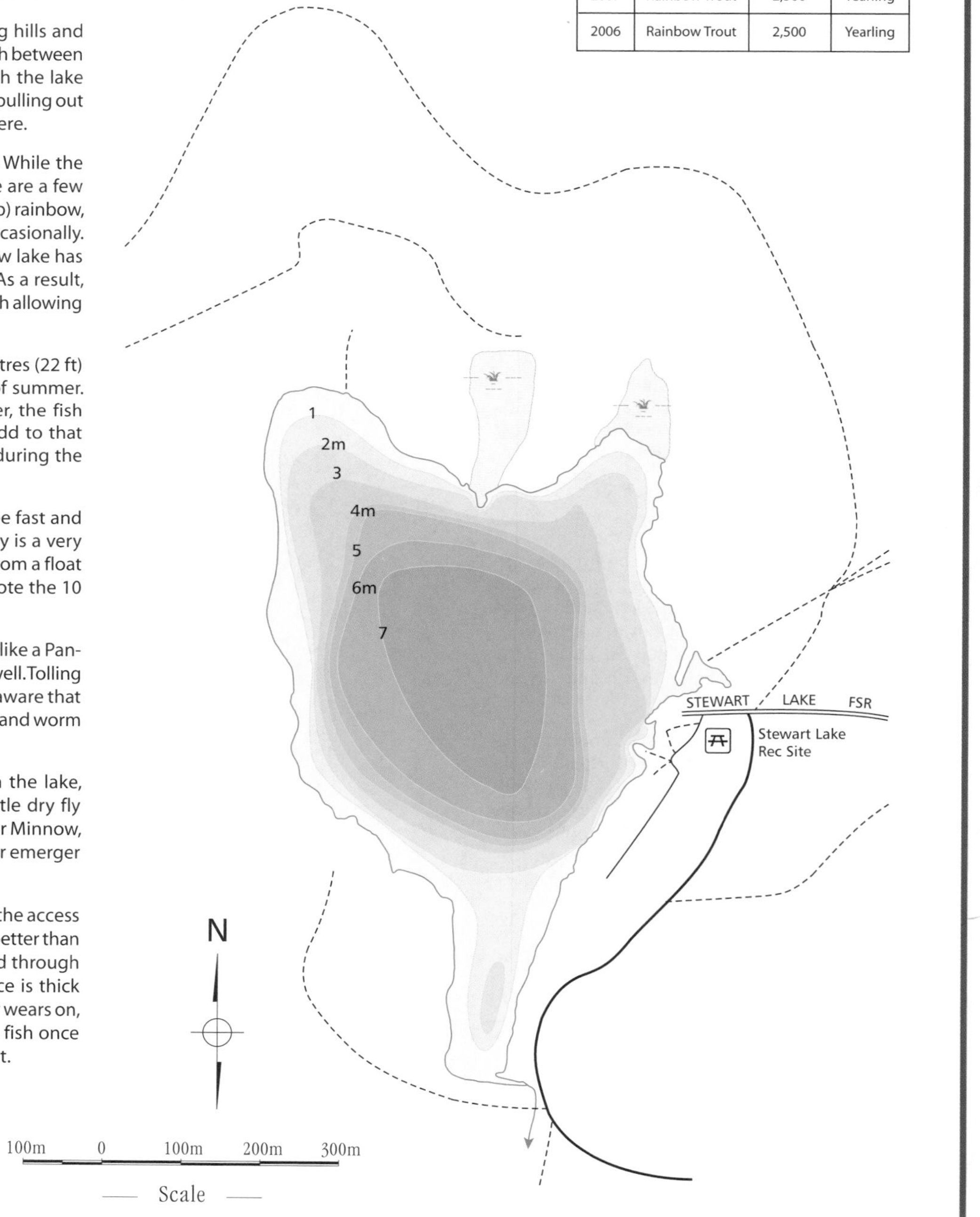

1
2m
3
4m
5
6m
7

STEWART LAKE FSR
Stewart Lake Rec Site

N

100m 0 100m 200m 300m

Scale

Succour Lake

Location: 40 km (25 mi) northeast of 100 Mile House
Elevation: 977 m (3,205 ft)
Surface Area: 94 ha (232 ac)
Maximum Depth: 42 m (136 ft)
Mean Depth: 12 m (38 ft)
Way Point: 51° 54' 17" N, 120° 49' 38" W

Fishing

Succour Lake is situated about 10 km northeast of the community of Eagle Creek, which in turn is situated on the shores of Canim Lake. The lake is fairly small, at just less than 100 hectares, and it doesn't see as much use as it might otherwise due to its proximity to the much larger Canim and Mahood Lakes.

Succour Lake is an average to slightly higher than average elevation lake. This is only an issue in the early part of the year, when the ice may be a day or two behind lower elevation lakes in coming off.

The lake offers a fairly good fishery for wild rainbow beginning in late May until late October. Since the lake is deep (over 40 metres or 135 feet) the water does not warm significantly during the summer months allowing for decent fishing throughout the ice-free season. The rainbow trout are usually quite small but some fish grow to 0.75 kg (1.5 lbs).

Given the depth of the lake, the lake can easily be trolled. Troll around the lake staying 50 to 100 metres (15-30 feet) off shore. Most people use a Willow Leaf lake troll or something like it (the 50/50 Ford Fender is also quite popular), usually followed by a Wedding Band or a small spoon. Small Flatfish are also extremely popular.

Spincasters and fly fishermen should work the near shore area especially off the northeastern shoreline. There is a drop off where fish hide before cruising the shallows in the evening in search of food.

The lake features fair to good hatches of the typical Cariboo insects. The most prolific insects are chironomids. These begin hatching almost as soon as ice is off. If you are in the area before turn over, there can be some fast fishing using a chironomid or bloodworm pattern in the shallows around the edge of the lake. Most likely, though, you will find the hatches happening in 3 to 10 metre (10 to 35 feet) of range.

Shore casting is difficult around the lake so it is best to use a float tube or pontoon boat and cast towards shore.

Facilities

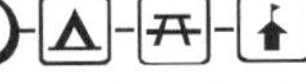

The **Succour Lake Recreation Site** is found on the southeastern shoreline and has three treed camping pads as well as a cartop boat launch and picnic tables.

Other Options

Hotfish Lake is situated northeast of Succour Lake. To reach the lake involves a 2 km hike up a fairly steep grade from the Spanish Creek Road (7000 Road). The hike into the lake is worth it as the fly-fishing and spincasting are excellent for most of the ice-free season. The rainbow are usually small but can grow to 1 kg (2 lbs).

Directions

To gain access to the lake, head northeast on the Canim Lake Road from just north of 100 Mile House. Once you reach the west end of Canim Lake, continue north on the shore of the lake to the community of Eagle Creek. The main road becomes the Hendrix Road (6000 Road), which continues northeast. About 5 km later turn left on the small road leading to Succour Lake. If you reach Christmas Lake on the Hendrix Road, you have gone too far.

A 4wd vehicle is recommended for the journey, as the final access road is rough.

Area Indicator

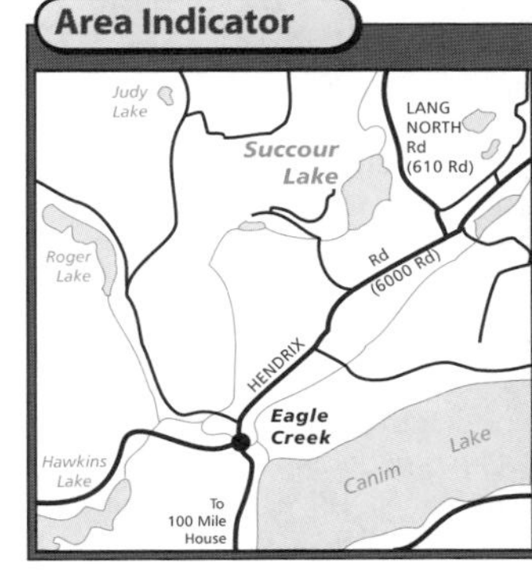

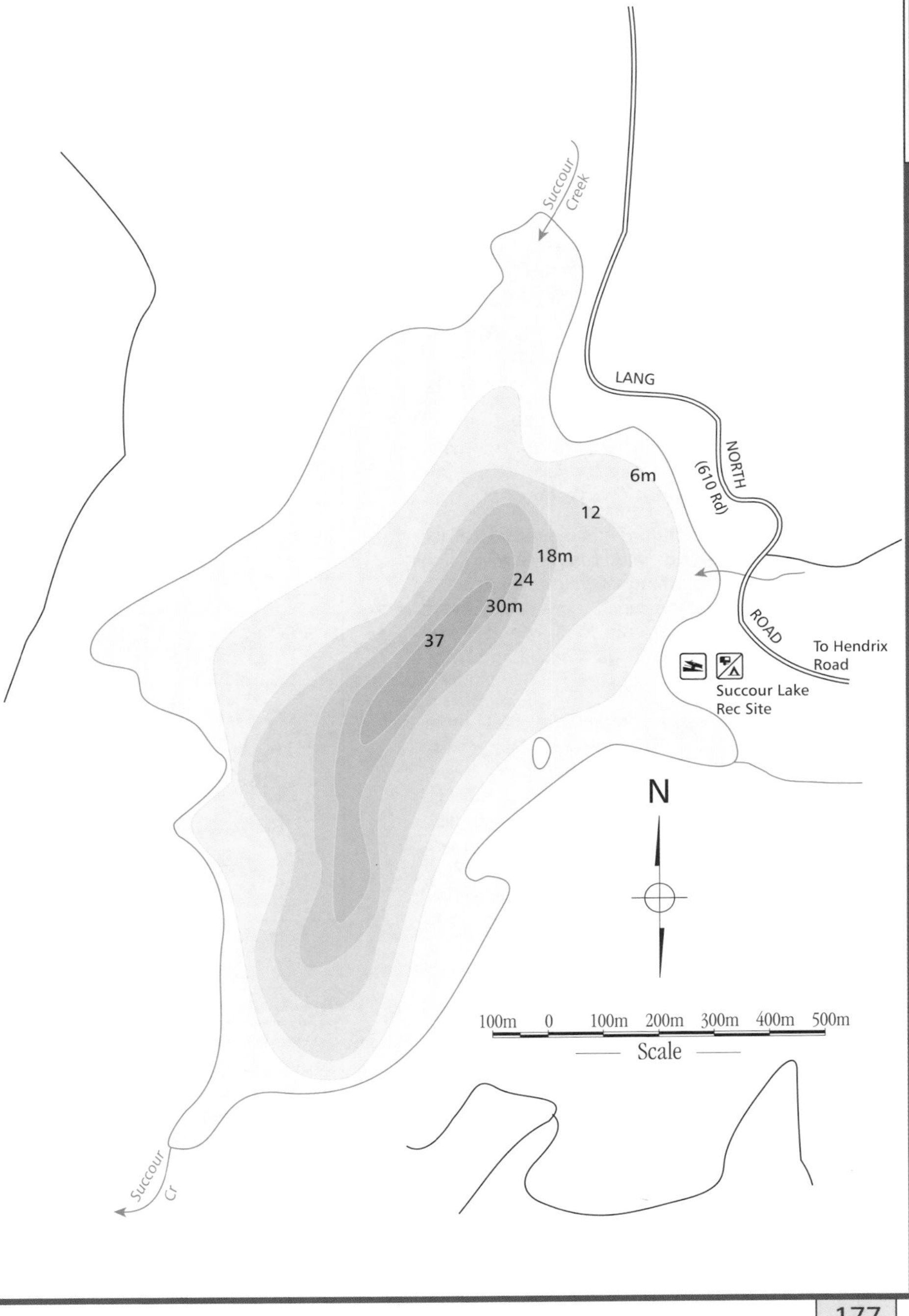

Succour Creek
LANG NORTH (610 Rd) ROAD
6m
12
18m
24
30m
37
To Hendrix Road
Succour Lake Rec Site
N
100m 0 100m 200m 300m 400m 500m
Scale
Succour Cr

Location: 5 km (46.5 mi) south of Chetwynd
Stream Length: 145 km (90 mi)
Geographic: 55° 13′ 28″ N, 121° 41′ 52″ W

Sukunka River

Fishing

Gunning for the title of most embarrassing name of a river, the Sukunka is a popular fishing river located just south of Chetwynd. The river is home to whitefish, bull trout and Arctic grayling. Of these, grayling is the most popular catch.

The river is usually accessed in one of two locations. Jet boaters will put in on the Pine River, near the Pine/Sukunka confluence, and boat upstream, stopping to sample some of the fishing holes along the way. People without a jet boat, or perhaps those with a canoe, usually go up to the Sukunka River Falls and fish the holes below the falls. It is possible to make your way downriver on foot, stopping to fish in a variety of locations.

There are other places to access the river, indeed, probably too many to point out. Another popular spot is near Little Prairie, where Highway 29 passes quite close to the river. Above Sukunka Falls, the river stretches deep into the Rocky Mountains. This area is little fished, but there are many nice fishing holes where the fish may never have seen a lure.

The river is quite popular with fly anglers and offers some great places to fish, either on the fly or using small spinners or spoons. While the northeast is not known for its great fly-fishing (or for its large fly-fishing community), the Sukunka is a notable exception.

The river doesn't have any pronounced hatches, but there are some, and in a year when there are lots of mosquitoes (which is most every year), fishing a mosquito pattern can be quite good.

In the early part of the year, most fly anglers fish patterns in blacks and dark greens. Later in the year, there seems to be a trend towards more brown patterns.

Fly-fishing techniques for grayling are similar to those used for trout. However, grayling can be easy to catch as they will eat most anything. Of course when food is plentiful, they can become much more finicky. Arctic grayling are quite willing to rise for a fly, and dry fly patterns like an Adam or a Royal Coachman can be quite effective.

Spincasters will find working tiny spinners like Panther Martins, Mepps and Blue Fox productive. The best way to fish is to cast out a bit upstream and allow the river to push the lure downstream, pulling in line just fast enough to keep the lure off the bottom. As with flies, stick with natural bug colors of gray green or brown that mimic native insects. The more common silver spinner also works great as it mimics the local baitfish. Keep them as small as you can cast on ultra light 3 to 6 pound test line.

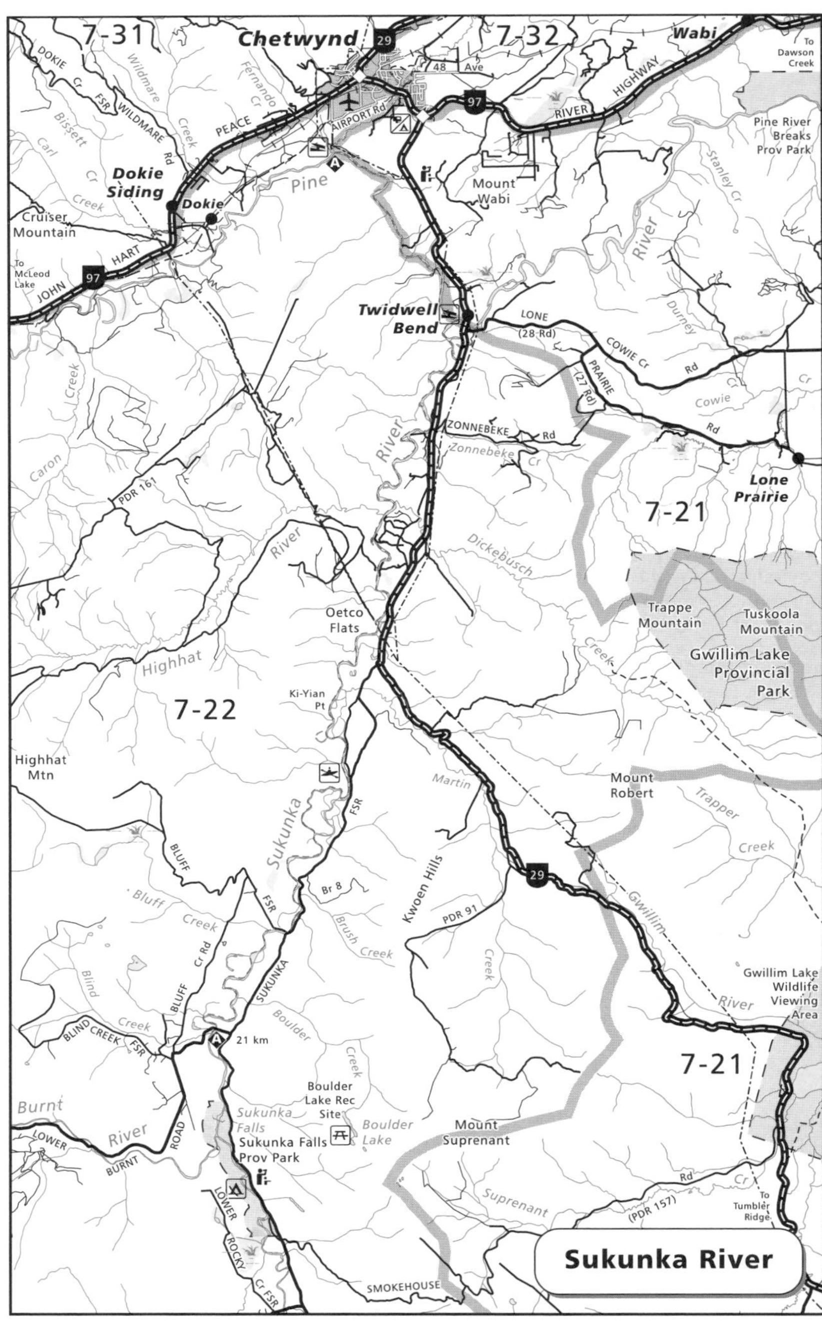

Facilities

There are no facilities at **Sukunka Falls Provincial Park**, although tenting is allowed. There is a recreation site farther up the road at Windfall Creek, while **Hole-in-the-Wall Provincial Park** also offers informal camping. Chetwynd offers lodging, food and other services.

Directions

The Sukunka River flows out of the Rocky Mountains draining into the Pine River south of Chetwynd. To get to the river from the junction of Highways 97 and 29, head east of Chetwynd to the turnoff to Tumbler Ridge and turn right. The bridge over the Pine River is 9 km from the junction. Jet boaters usually put in here. Highway 29 follows the Sukunka Valley for about 13 km where the Sukunka Forest Service Road continues south along the valley. It is about 20 km to Sukunka Falls Provincial Park along the good, but extremely busy industrial road.

Sulphurous Lake

Location: 32 km (20 mi) east of 100 Mile House
Elevation: 1,115 m (3,658 ft)
Surface Area: 381 ha (941 ac)
Maximum Depth: 47 m (154 ft)
Mean Depth: 15 m (51 ft)
Way Point: 51° 38′ 3″ N, 120° 49′ 29″ W

Fishing

Despite its name, Sulphurous Lake has clear water that holds a variety of sportfish, most notably kokanee. In addition to kokanee, the lake also holds rainbow trout and is one of a handful of lakes in the region that hold lake trout. If you happen to catch a laker, it must be released. There are also suckers, redside shiners and squawfish roaming the lake. The rainbow and kokanee can get to 1 kg (2 lbs), although rainbow are usually the bigger of the two.

The easy access and good fishing ensures a steady stream of anglers visit the lake. To help offset this, the Freshwater Fisheries Society of BC maintains an aggressive stocking program. Over 30,000 kokanee and 10,000 Blackwater strain rainbow are deposited annually.

Trolling is the best method to take kokanee, which prefer lures such as the Kokanee King, Needlefish or Apex in a variety of colours. Use a downrigger, leadcore line or fast sinking fly line. Kokanee tend to go deeper during the day, so it is crucial to present the offering in 6 to 9 metres (20 to 30 ft) of water. The best way to attract their attention is to troll in an S-pattern, sometimes speeding up or giving a quick pull on the line. Kokanee are famous for trailing a lure up and down the lake, but never striking. A quick burst of speed can often trigger a strike.

The rainbow stocked here are Blackwater strain, which feed on course fish like redside shiner, controlling their population. Because they like the baitfish, using a lure that resembles these fish is usually a good idea. Lake trolls such as a Willow Leaf or Ford Fender in silver or prism, with a Wedding Band and worm work well. Others to try include a size 70 Hot Shot or F-4 to F-5 Flatfish or Kwik Fish in perch scale, black and silver, or fire tiger colours. Troll along the drop offs before testing the middle of the lake where the water is deeper.

The island in the centre of the lake is a hotspot for fly fishers using leech or Doc Spratley patterns. Spring offers good chironomid hatches in the shallow areas. The key is locating the fish and presenting a black, green or chromie pattern to them.

Spring and fall are the best seasons for rainbow, while kokanee fishing peaks during the warmer months. However, ice fishing for kokanee is also very popular. This fishery is usually very good right after Christmas. Most of the action is found off the #2 and #3 access roads. Use a spoon like the Ruby Eye Wiggler, a dodger with a short leader and glow jig tipped with a bit of krill or a maggot.

Area Indicator

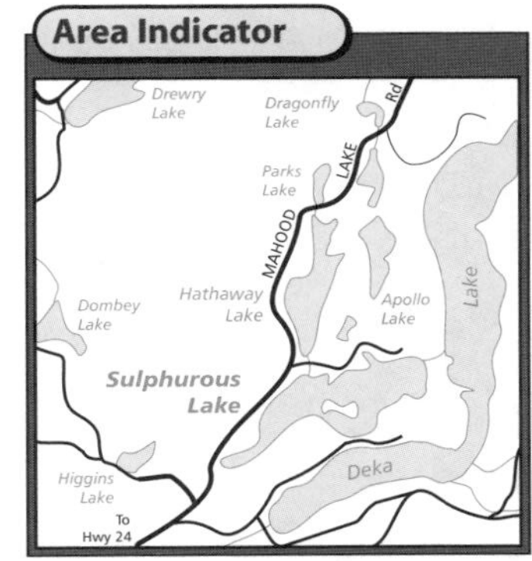

Sulphurous (Sulphurus) Lake
Fish Stocking Data

Year	Species	Number	Life Stage
2008	Rainbow Trout	10,000	Yearling
2008	Kokanee	40,000	Fry
2007	Rainbow Trout	10,000	Yearling
2007	Kokanee	30,000	Fry
2006	Rainbow Trout	10,000	Yearling
2006	Kokanee	30,000	Fingerling

Directions

Sulphurous Lake is located 11 km north of Highway 24 and Sheridan Lake. The lake is best reached by traveling along the Fishing Highway (Highway 24) to Interlakes Corner. The Horse Lake Road heads north from the highway and leads to the Mahood Lake Road. The first big lake after this junction is Sulphurous Lake.

Facilities

There is a public boat launch found at the north end of the lake off Pettyjohn Road. Those looking to stay a few nights will find the **Sulphurous Lake Resort** offers both cabins and a campsite as well as boat rentals and a small store.

Sundance Lakes

Location: 15 km (9 mi) east of Chetwynd
Elevation: 720 m (2,335 ft)
Surface Area: 9.9 ha (24ac)
Maximum Depth: 5m (16 ft)
Mean Depth: 2m (6 ft)
Way Point: 55° 42′ 50.3″ N, 121° 22′ 43.2″ W

Area Indicator

FABRICK Rd
Wabi
97
Sundance Lakes
To Dawson Creek
River
To Chetwynd
Pine

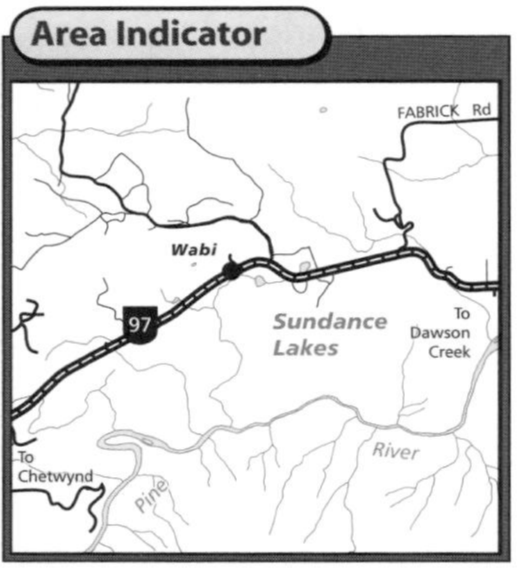

Sundance Lakes (West) Fish Stocking Data			
Year	Species	Number	Life Stage
2008	Rainbow Trout	2,500	Yearling
2007	Rainbow Trout	2,500	Yearling
2006	Rainbow Trout	2,500	Yearling

Fishing

These lakes should more accurately be called War Dance Lakes, as it was here where the local Beaver First Nations would hold tribal councils when taboos were broken. Twice in recorded history these councils were held, once, to determine the fate of a white man who was reportedly stealing furs from a First Nation trap line (he disappeared without a trace before he was tracked down) and once to determine the fate of a white man who was reportedly stealing from First Nations grave houses. Again, the man in question disappeared before he was tracked down, though in this case it is probable that the police whisked him away.

Despite their auspicious history, the lakes are fairly non-descript, found alongside Highway 97 east of Chetwynd and west of the Pine River Bridge. The east lake, confusingly, is found on the north side of the highway, while the west lake is found on the south side.

Only the west lake, on the south side of the highway is stocked, although trout do swim up the stream that connects the two together. The west lake is also aerated, in an effort to prevent winterkill in the shallow lake.

Up until about ten years ago, the lake was stocked with both brook trout and rainbow trout, but these days, you will only find rainbow in the lake. A variety of strains have been stocked in an attempt to find which species does best in the lake. The Freshwater Fisheries Society of BC seemed to have settled on the Pennask strain, which are a smaller trout, but extremely feisty. They are also famous for their acrobatic jumps in their attempts to shake the hook and one of the most fun fish to fish for, especially on light gear.

The lakes can be fished from shore, but a float tube or pontoon boat is a helpful addition. There are no boat launches on the lake and even a small cartopper is probably a bit ostentatious in these small lakes.

Gear anglers can toss the usual small spinners and spoons at the lake–Panther Martins, Mepps and the like. Fly anglers can use nymphs, leeches, Woolly Buggers and Doc Spratleys.

While the lakes are not closed to ice fishing, the aerators make ice fishing here extremely dangerous.

Directions

The lakes are located alongside Highway 97 about 15 km east of Chetwynd. If you cross the Pine River, you've gone too far. The east lake is visible from the highway; just look for a large beaver dam. There is a pullout on the north side of the highway. The west lake is not visible from the highway and is on the south side of the road. There is an access road back to the lake; it is about 500 metres before the pullout.

Other Options

There are not many lakes near these two lakes, which explains their popularity with local anglers. However, the lakes are only about 15 km from the **Pine River**, where you will find great fishing for grayling, bull trout, burbot, Dolly Varden, whitefish, rainbow and walleye.

Facilities

There are no facilities at the lakes. The closest accommodations are in Chetwynd to the west.

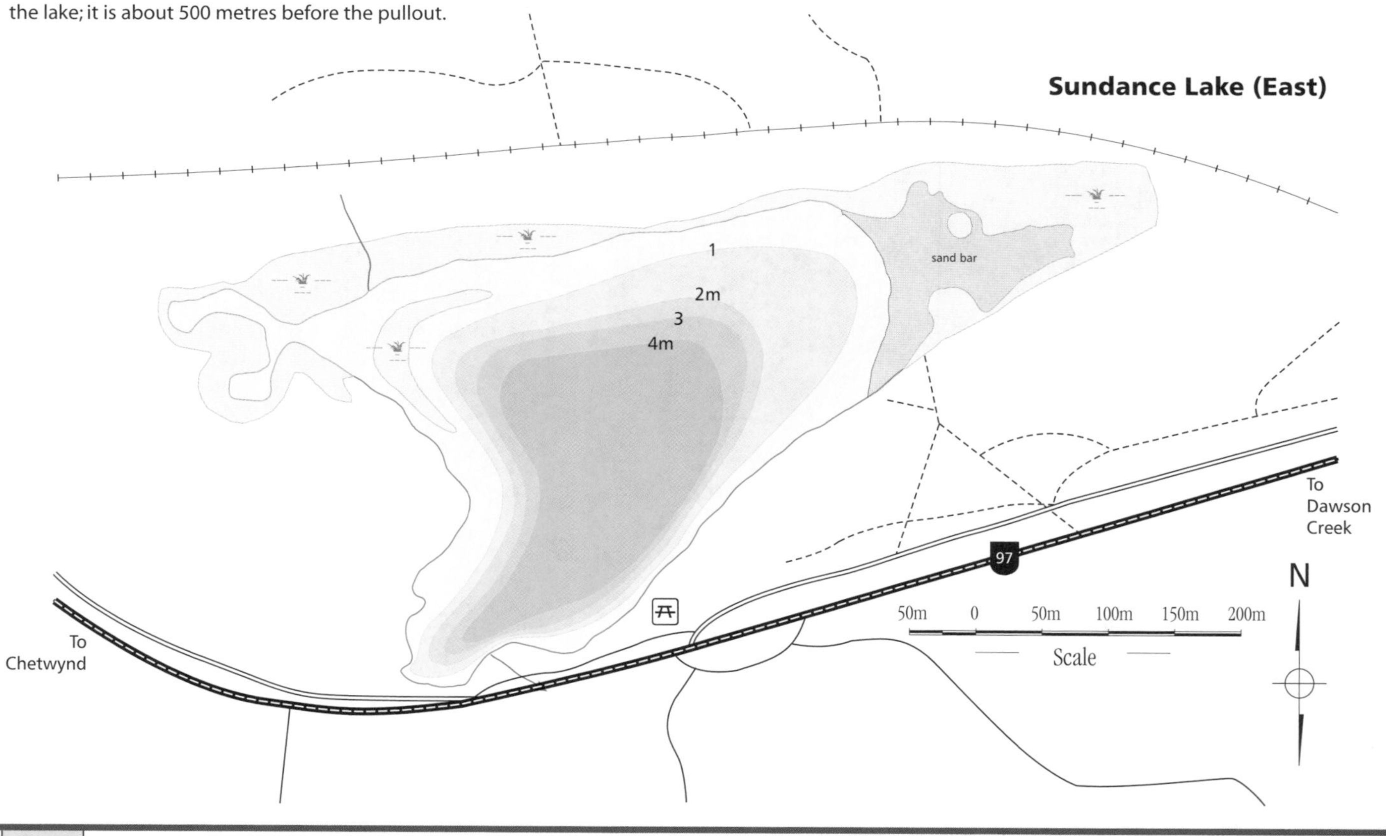

Sundance Lake (East)
1
2m
3
4m
sand bar
To Dawson Creek
97
To Chetwynd
N
50m 0 50m 100m 150m 200m
Scale

Suskwa River

Location: 12 km (7.5 mi) east of New Hazelton
Stream Length: 53 km (33 mi)
Geographic: 55° 17′ 9″ N, 127° 11′ 58″ W

Fishing

The Suskwa River is a Bulkley River tributary, which in turn is a tributary of the Skeena. While many of the rivers that flow into the Skeena are extremely popular, the Suskwa does not see the same pressure from anglers as the other, bigger rivers in the area.

There are a few reasons for that. The land around the Suskwa is mostly private, so accessing the river can be difficult. The river is difficult to drift and there are a few canyon sections that should only be attempted by people who know what they are doing. And the banks of the river are not conductive to walk and wade fishing. If you find a place you can access the river, you are limited in how much you can move up and down stream. The low volume river (indeed, it is little more than a creek) is not characterized by big runs, but by a pool here and a pool there. Finding a place where you can access the river and there is a pool where the fish hold…well, now you see why the river isn't fished that much.

There should be an entire class of anglers whose collective ears should have metaphorically perked up. Because for these people, the chance to fish a Skeena River tributary that sees little pressure, but still features good returns of steelhead, Chinook and other salmon, as well as resident trout is too much to pass up. Of course, you will need to be self-reliant and know what they are doing out there. Be sure to talk to locals and always scout ahead.

The spring run of Chinook gets here in July, which is when the river opens to fishing. The river is Class II water all year (that's a classified water rating requiring a special license, not a whitewater rating) and steelhead stamps are required from September 1 to October 31, which is when the steelhead are moving through this system. Casting or drift fishing with cured roe into deep holes seems to be the most effective method for Chinook, while steelhead like slow presentations so the quicker the water, the bigger the lure.

The Suskwa River is also a great place to spot wildlife. Moose, brown and black bear and deer are all seen around the river during the summer. If you are lucky, you may see some of the shyer residents like cougar, wolf, coyote, lynx and wolverine.

Directions

The Suskwa flows into the Bulkley at Bulkley Canyon. The turnoff onto the Suskwa Forest Service Road is just over 10 km east of New Hazelton. There are two main places to access the river along this road. At about the 4 km mark on the Suskwa Road, there is a major intersection with the Suskwa-Moricetown Forest Service Road. Turning left will bring you to a bridge over the Suskwa. At about the 15 km mark, there is a second bridge and access point. Intrepid explorers will find a few other places to climb down to the river.

Facilities

Near the second bridge over the Suskwa, you will find the **Suskwa (Bear) River Recreation Site.** There are a few small camping spots here, as well as good access to the river. There is lodging, food and other services in nearby Hazelton and New Hazelton.

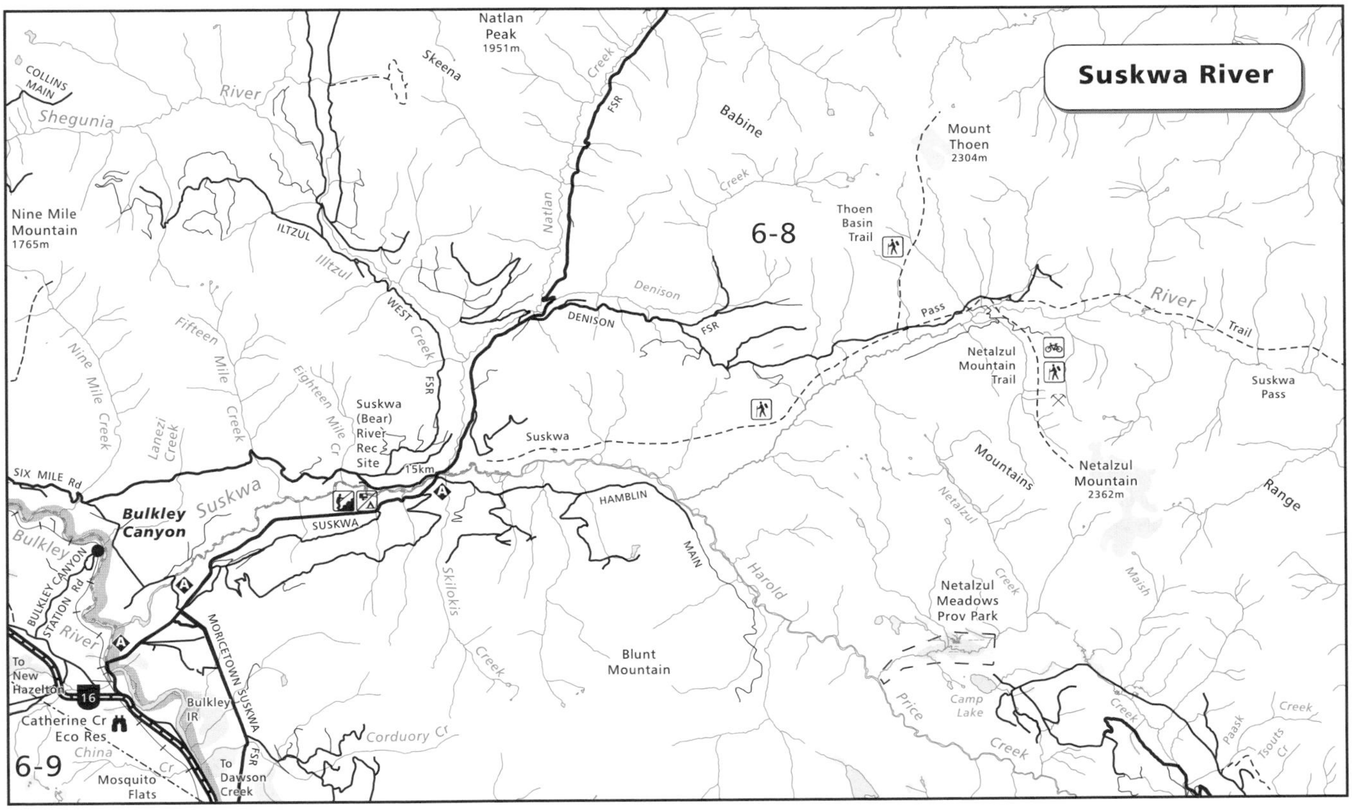

Suskwa River

Location: 35 km (22 mi) southeast of Dawson Creek
Elevation: 726 m (2,382 ft)
Surface Area: 600 ha (1,483 ac)
Max Depth: 7.6 m (25 ft)
Mean Depth: 3.1 m (10 ft)
Geographic: 55° 31′ 3″ N, 120° 0′ 55″ W

Swan Lake

Area Indicator

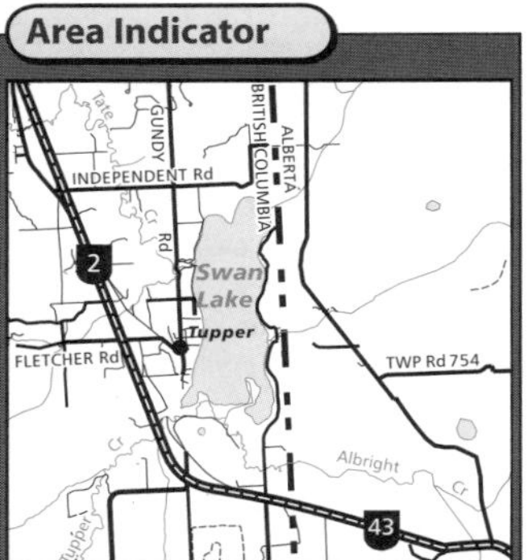

Fishing

Found on the Alberta Plateau, near the Alberta Boundary, Swan Lake is one of the larger lakes in the area. It is too shallow and too warm in summer to support trout, but offers great fishing for walleye. Northern pike, yellow perch and burbot also roam the lake.

In fact, the lake is quite productive and produces a lot of smaller fish, averaging less than 30 cm (12 in). However, there are also a good number of larger fish here, too.

But small walleye aren't necessarily a bad thing; walleye are a member of the perch family and offer some of the finest eating around, especially when under 1.5 kg (3 lbs). Although perch are not as popular fish to try catching due to their small size, they are also quite tasty. As an added bonus, they can keep youngsters busy for hours as they try bobbing off the dock or casting from shore.

Hammer handle sized northern pike are also quite prevalent. These predatory fish tend to fall in the 20–60 cm (8–24 in) range, though some have been known to get up to 9 kg (20 lbs).

One of the most popular areas to cast from is in fact off the dock. There is also good fishing from shore in the area around the boat launch as well as in the Tupper River area. By late spring, though, there is usually fairly heavy weed growth and casting from shore becomes quite difficult.

A small or mid sized boat will serve you quite well here. Pike are usually found in the shallows at the north and south ends of the lake. Northern pike are quite aggressive and like to chase anything that moves. Trolling larger spoons, plugs, crankbaits, spinnerbaits or buzz baits all do well. It is also possible to catch pike by stopping the boat and casting towards the shallows, while some people have taken to fishing for pike with large dry flies.

When the water is cooler, walleye tend to be sluggish and will rarely chase after moving lures. Instead, try slowly jigging a rubber jig tipped with a worm. As the water warms up, the walleye become more active and are willing to chase a spinner and crawler harness or crankbait. Try trolling along the shoals. Walleye can be found in shallower water in dawn and dusk, but usually retreat into deeper weed beds during the day.

Every spring, a fish ladder is in operation and allows fish to move back and forth between the lake and the stream. A footbridge crosses the stream here and provides excellent opportunities to view the fish in the shallow water.

Directions

To get to Swan Lake from Dawson Creek, travel south towards Grande Prairie on Highway 2 for 35 km. Look for the signs to Swan Lake Provincial Park and follow the gravel road leading east. At the first four-way stop, turn right and continue for about 4 km (2.5 mi) to the park. The road is accessible by most vehicles.

Facilities

Swan Lake Provincial Park protects the western shores of the lake and offers a boat launch, floating dock, beach swimming, day-use picnic area, a grassy 42 site campground, baseball diamonds, playground and a fish cleaning station. The park is open year round but services are not available after the snow falls.

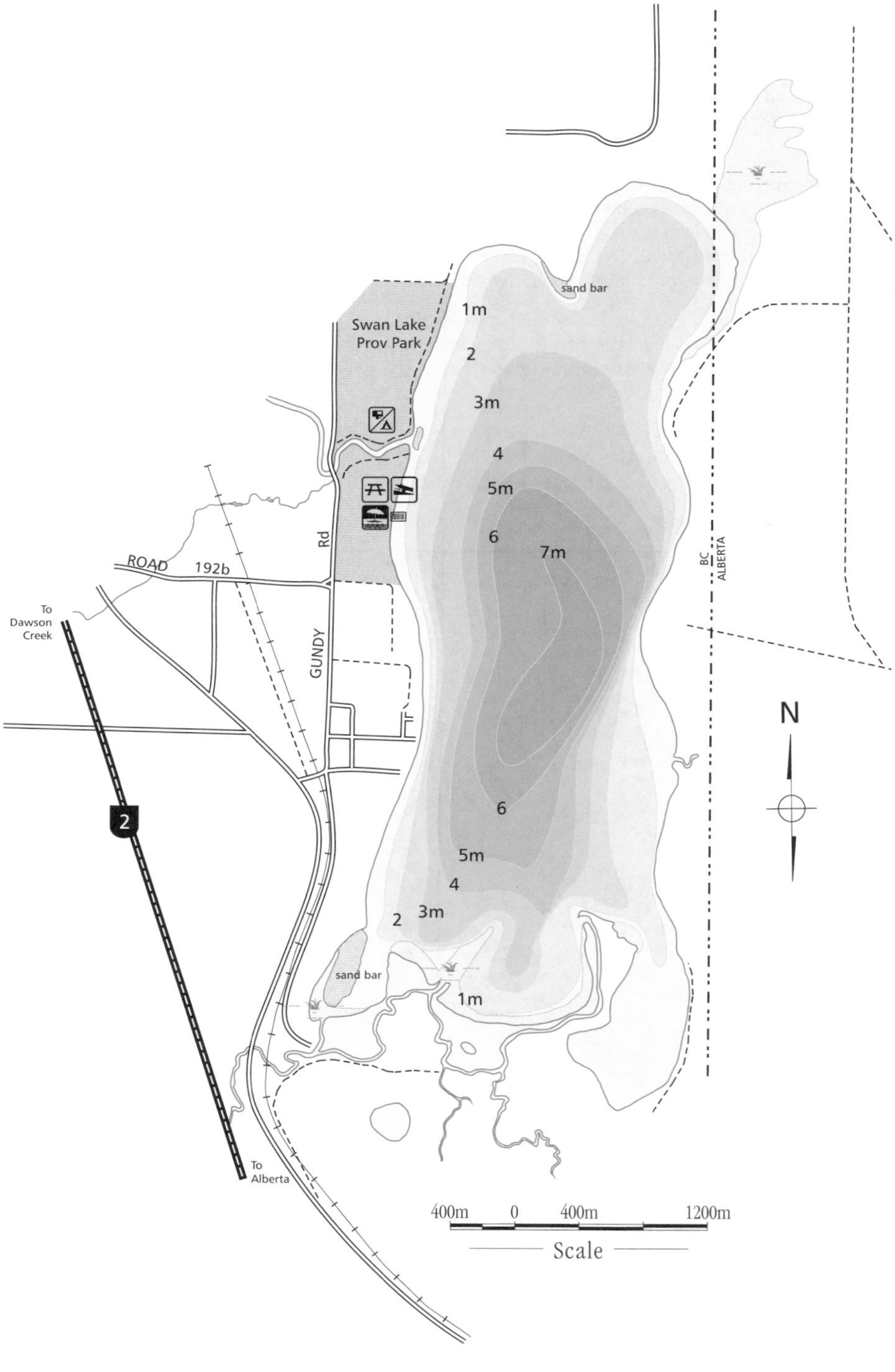

Swan Lake Prov Park
sand bar
1m
2
3m
4
5m
6
7m
ROAD 192b
GUNDY Rd
To Dawson Creek
To Alberta
BC
ALBERTA
N
400m 0 400m 1200m
Scale

Tatogga & Eddontenajon Lake

Location: 475 km (295 miles) north of Terrace
Elevation: 826 m (2,709 ft)
Surface Area: 321 ha (793 ac)
Maximum Depth: 18.3 m (60 ft)
Mean Depth: 8.8 m (28.7 ft)
Way Point: 57° 42′ 52″ N, 130° 0′ 37″ W

Fishing

These are not well known lakes. That is not to say that there is not great fishing here. The trouble is the lakes are 450 km north of Terrace and not a lot of people ever visit the area.

However, those who have fished here say that these lakes offer some of the best fishing in the world. That pound for pound (or more accurately, ounce for ounce, as the average size trout is about 30–35 cm/12–14 in) there are few fish that fight harder, they say. They also say that chances are you will be snagging something every few casts. People who fish Eddontenajon say it is not unusual to catch up to 100 rainbow in an hour. The trout are acrobatic and put up a great fight, even the small ones.

These lakes are part of the Upper Iskut Monoculture, an area of over 1,000 square kilometres, where the only fish you will find are rainbow trout. While there appear to be a few different strains of rainbow with different marking patterns, they are all rainbow trout. These trout can get up to 65 cm (26 in), although that is a rare catch indeed. Usually you're pulling them out of here at about 35–40 cm (14–16 in).

And there is an air of mystery here, too. The lakes are supposed to only hold rainbow, but what are those blips that show up on the depth sounder at nearly 60 metres (200 ft) deep, far deeper than rainbow trout ever go? Are these just fishing tales, told around a campfire, or is there something to the rumours? No one, of course, has ever pulled one of these mystery fish (if that's what they are) out. But maybe, just maybe, you will be the first.

The usual way to fish these lakes is with smallish spinners and spoons, especially a red and white pattern. Although, Eddontenajon Lake is shockingly deep, Tatogga Lake has a shoal area that covers about one third of the lake. The shallows are a good place to focus on during the spring and fall and cool summer evenings. The fishing can also be great where the Iskut River flows into the lake.

Directions

These two lakes are located about 400 km north of Kitwanga along the Cassiar Highway (Highway 37). The lakes are found on the east side of the road. Eddontenajon has a few roadside options with the best place being found at the south end of the lake, though it can get quite windy here. There is another rustic place to get onto the lake at the north end as well as a highway pullout about halfway down the lake where an angler could access the lake. Getting onto Tatogga is best done through the Tatogga Lake Resort. Some canoe the short stretch of the Iskut River between the two lakes. In fact, a canoe route links the entire chain of lakes from Kluachon Lake to the north to Natadesleen Lake in the south. Paddling and fishing the chain will take about two days, but you can take more time if you like.

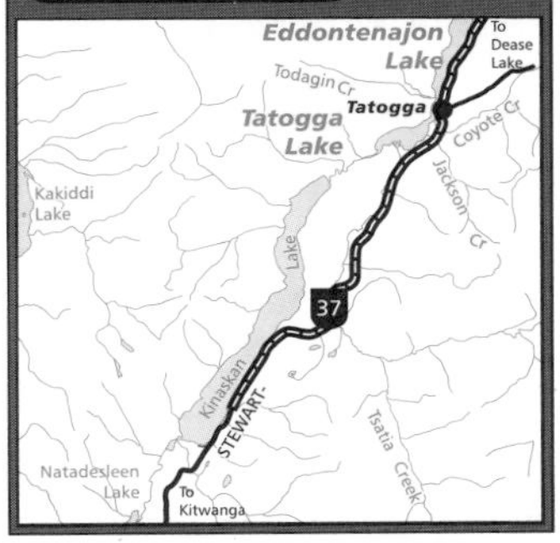

Facilities

For people wishing to stay on Eddontenajon, check out **Red Goat Lodge**. Folks looking to stay on Tatogga Lake can stay at the **Tatogga Lake Resort**. Nearby **Mountain Shadow RV Park** or **Kinaskan Lake Provincial Park** are other camping options in the area.

Area Indicator

Eddontenajon Lake
To Dease Lake
Todagin Cr
Tatogga Lake
Tatogga
Coyote Cr
Jackson Cr
Kakiddi Lake
Lake
37
Kinaskan
STEWART-
Natadesleen Lake
Tatia Creek
To Kitwanga

Tatogga Lake

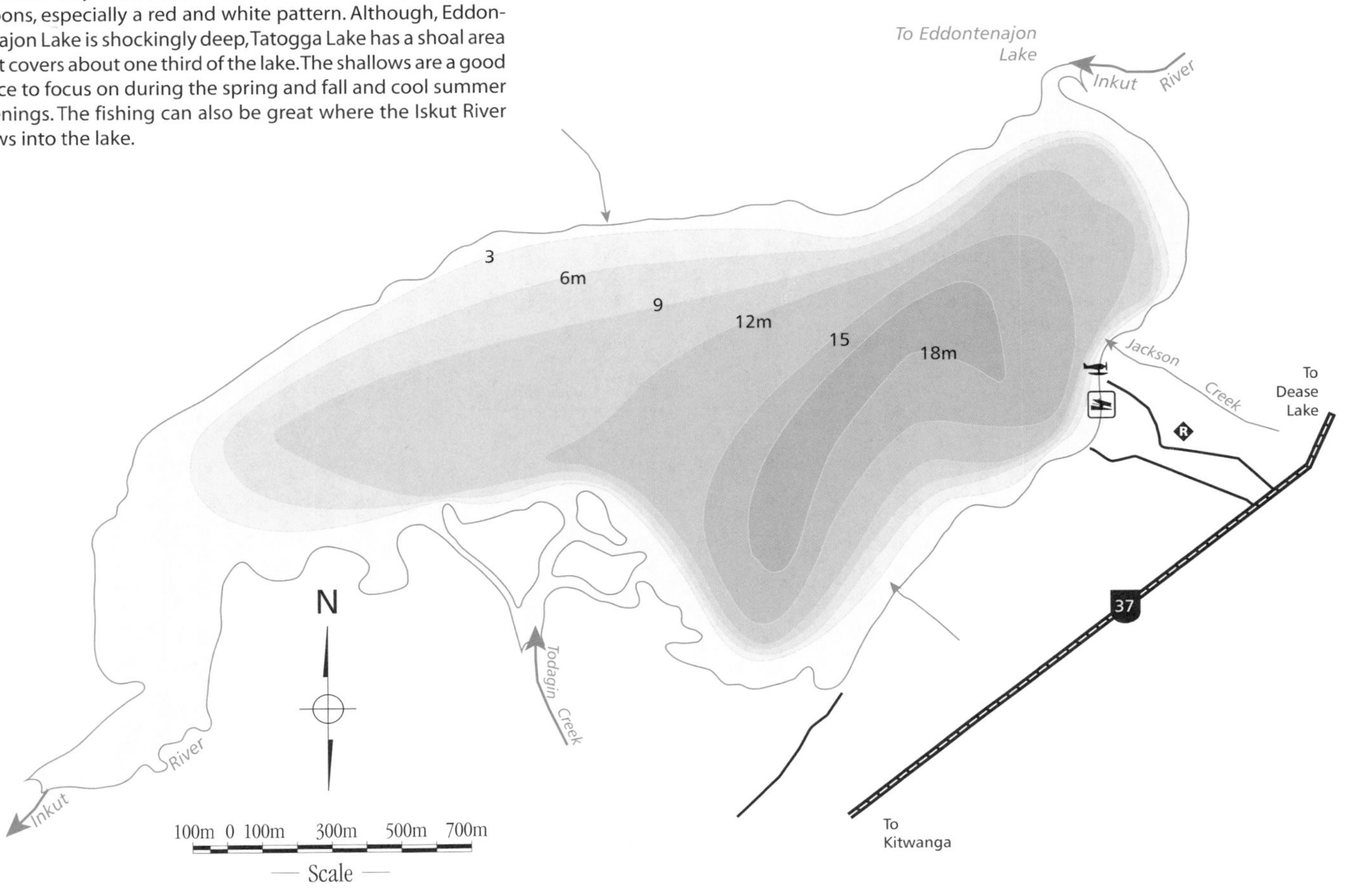

To Eddontenajon Lake
Inkut River
3
6m
9
12m
15
18m
Jackson Creek
To Dease Lake
N
Todagin Creek
River
Inkut
37
100m 0 100m 300m 500m 700m
Scale
To Kitwanga

Location: 17 km (10.5 mi) south of 100 Mile House
Elevation: 1,164 m (3,819 ft)
Surface Area: 103 ha (255 ac)
Max Depth: 5 m (16 ft)
Mean Depth: 1 m (3.3 ft)
Way Point: 51° 29′ 22.6″ N, 121° 15′ 17.3″

Taylor Lake

Area Indicator

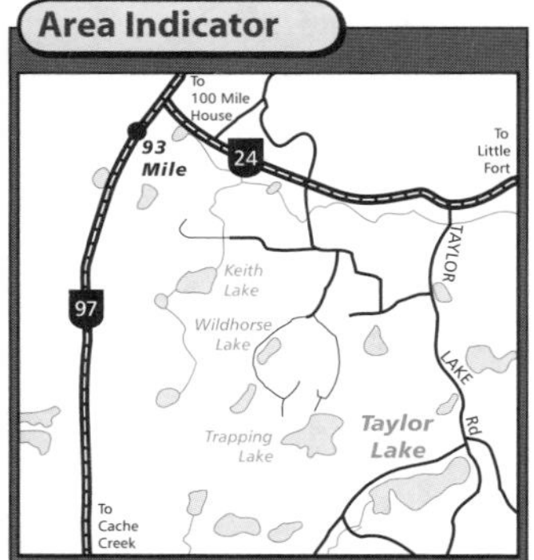

Fishing

Taylor Lake was first stocked beginning in the 1920s and periodically until the 1970s. Today, the lake maintains a self-sustaining population of trout allowing anglers to find decent numbers of wild rainbow that grow to 1 kg (2 lbs). However, the lake is prone to winterkill during long, cold winters. It always a good idea to check with the local tackle shops before heading to this lake.

The lake is virtually one large shoal area. In fact, the only part of the lake that is more than a few feet deep is the eastern end of the lake. Even at its deepest, the water only drops off to a mere 5 metres (16 feet) deep.

Of course when you mention shoals, fly anglers ears perk up. And so they should. The expansive shoals on the lake allow for some good insect rearing and the lake has good-sized hatches of chironomids, mayflies, dragon and damselflies as well as caddis. Although they generally hatch in that order, fly anglers should spend a few minutes figuring out what is currently hatching. Also remember that hatches sometimes overlap and it can be difficult figuring out what the fish are currently feeding on. If you aren't having much luck, try tying on an attractor pattern like a Doc Spratley or Carey Special. Once you do manage to find a fish, using a throat pump to determine what they are eating will certainly help improve your success.

The best fishing happens subsurface using things like a chironomid or nymph pattern, depending on, of course, what is hatching. Rainbow trout spend 90% of their time feeding within about a metre or so (3 feet) of the bottom and it is best to get your presentation down to them.

Since this is the Cariboo, it is always good to have at least a few Tom Thumbs or similar topwater pattern in your box for when the fish start rising to the surface. Another popular pattern specific to the area is a beetle pattern. When these take flight in early June the trout often feast on the critters. Like most dry fly-fishing, the action is best in the evening right before dusk.

Taylor Lake is slightly higher in elevation and holds its ice a few days longer than other lakes in the Cariboo. However, the shallow nature of the lake also means it will heat up quickly. All of this means that fishing this lake is best done from late May through early July and again in early October.

Directions

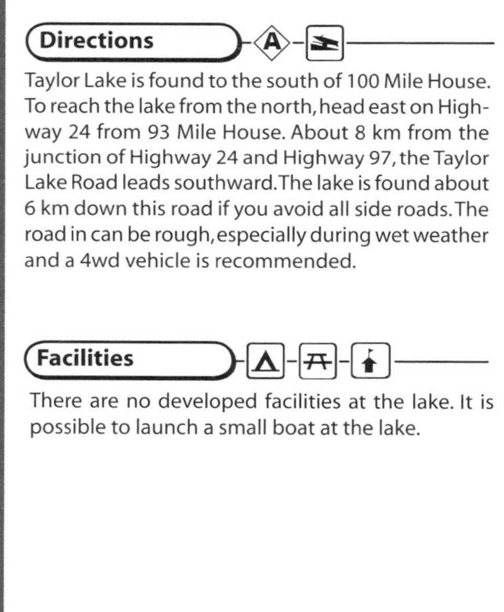

Taylor Lake is found to the south of 100 Mile House. To reach the lake from the north, head east on Highway 24 from 93 Mile House. About 8 km from the junction of Highway 24 and Highway 97, the Taylor Lake Road leads southward. The lake is found about 6 km down this road if you avoid all side roads. The road in can be rough, especially during wet weather and a 4wd vehicle is recommended.

Facilities

There are no developed facilities at the lake. It is possible to launch a small boat at the lake.

Other Options

Gracy and **Dundon Lakes** are a couple small lakes found to the south. They are connected to Taylor Lake via branches off Taylor Creek. Small trout can be found in both lakes in the spring and fall.

Tchesinkut Lake

Location: 15 km (9.3 mi) south of Burns Lake
Elevation: 743 m (2,437 ft)
Surface Area: 3,382 ha (8,359 ac)
Maximum Depth: 149 m (489 ft)
Mean Depth: 61.5 m (208 ft)
Way Point: 54° 5′ 39″ N, 125° 37′ 48″ W

Fishing

Between Burns Lake and the giant Francois Lake, lies the large-but-nowhere-near-as-large-as-Francois Tchesinkut Lake. Still, it is a good sized lake and quite pretty.

Somewhere in the last few decades, word got out that Tchesinkut was a great fishing lake. Lake trout to 15 kg (30 lbs)! Rainbow to 3 kg (6 lbs)! Kokanee beyond count!

And people came. People came from far and wide and fished and fished and fished. And they discovered that what they had heard was true. There were giant lake trout. There were what appeared to be an infinite number of kokanee in the lake. And so they fished some more.

And they kept what they caught. Some people even went so far as to bring nets in to catch all those kokanee, which at the time weren't protected as a sportfish.

But as time went on, people started noticing that there weren't as many fish to catch. That finding a lake trout bigger than 6 kg (15 lbs) was something that happened only rarely. That you could fish all day for kokanee and not catch any. That there weren't as many rainbow trout.

And so people stopped fishing the lake as much. Regulations were put in place to protect the slow growing lake trout. And because you couldn't retain lake trout except for in February and in July and single barbless hooks were mandatory, most of the catch and keep crowd stopped coming.

And you know what? The fishing is starting to improve. Slowly. But there are rumours of lake trout to 10 kg (22 lbs) being caught for the first time in nearly 15 years. Anglers are starting to catch rainbow and kokanee with fair regularity.

Part of that has to do with the regulations. Also the new breed of anglers who no longer fish to fill the freezer have had a positive effect.

Lake trout are still the big draw here and there's a reason they're popular with the catch and keep crowd. They have pink, firm flesh and are quite tasty. They can be found at a depth of between 18–30 metres (60–100 feet) and are best taken on blue and silver T50 or T60 Flatfish at the end of a leadcore or weighted line. Green frogs also work well, as do FST #7 half brass and half silver or a Gibbs Ruby Eye spoon.

As soon as the ice is off the lake, the best fishing for rainbow happens at the east end of the lake, near the marshy area. By mid-July, though, the fish are distributed evenly around the lake. Trolling a traditional Willow Leaf or Ford Fender with a Wedding Band and bait is the best way to fish.

The kokanee, which might get to 0.5 kg (1 lb) if you're lucky, are fished the same way as rainbow, just add a rubber snub to protect the fish's mouth. They don't start biting until mid-June.

Area Indicator

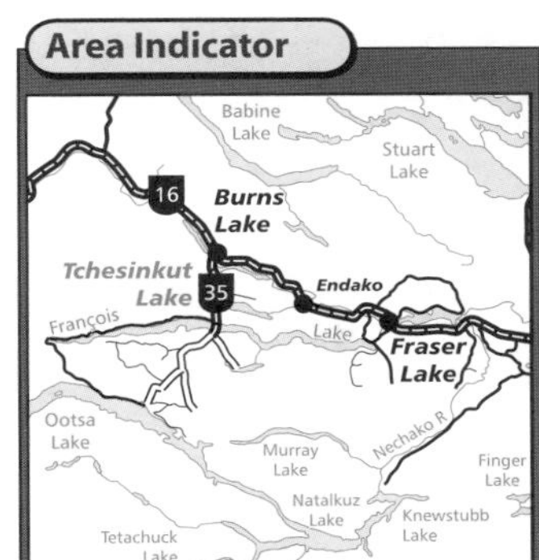

Directions

The lake is found alongside Highway 35 between Burns Lake and Francois Lake. To get to Agate Point Recreation Site, turn east onto the Tchesinkut Lake/Agate Forest Service Road.

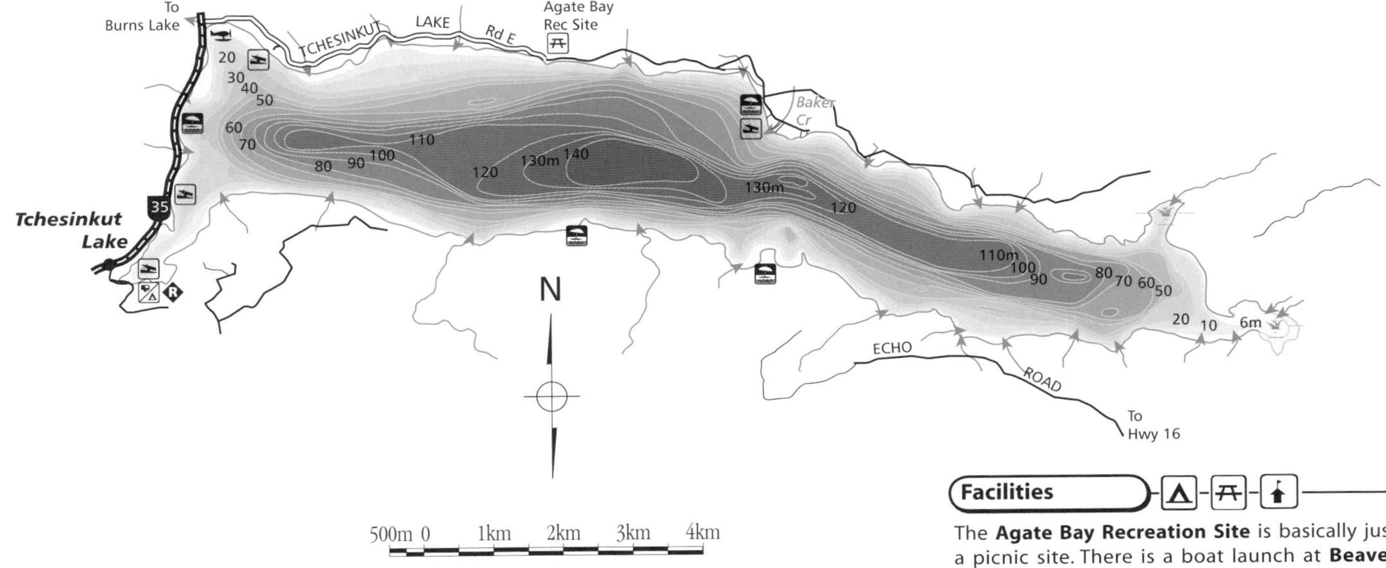

Facilities

The **Agate Bay Recreation Site** is basically just a picnic site. There is a boat launch at **Beaver Point Resort** as well as cabins and a large 40 unit campground.

Location: 11 km (6.7 mi) north of Quesnel
Elevation: 707 m (2,320 ft)
Surface Area: 243 ha (600 ac)
Maximum Depth: 21 m (69 ft)
Mean Depth: 8 m (26.2 ft)
Geographic: 53° 5′ 4″ N, 122° 27′ 18″ W

Ten Mile Lake

Area Indicator

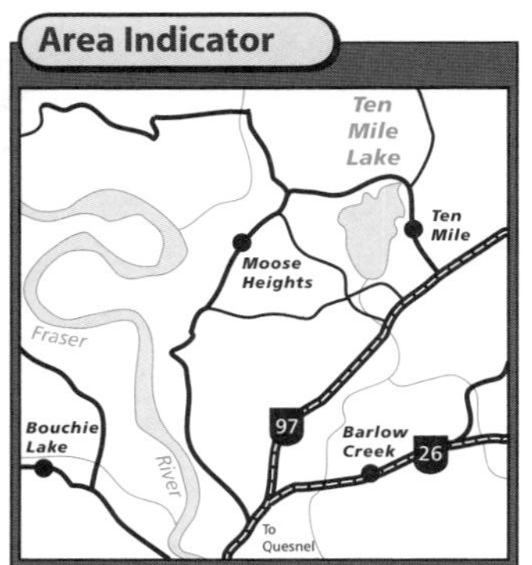

Ten
Mile
Lake
Ten
Mile
Moose
Heights
Fraser
River
Bouchie
Lake
97
Barlow
Creek
26
To
Quesnel

Ten Mile Lake Fish Stocking Data			
Year	Species	Number	Life Stage
2008	Kokanee	25,000	Fry
2008	Rainbow Trout	54,500	Fry
2007	Kokanee	25,000	Fry
2007	Rainbow Trout	50,000	Fry

Fishing

The Pacific Great Eastern Railway line built around the turn of the Twentieth Century passed by this lake. The mileage board near the lake was the 10 Mile board and people started calling the lake Ten Mile Lake. Even after the railway was abandoned and removed, the name stuck.

The lake is stocked with kokanee and rainbow. It is one of the heaviest stocked lakes in the region with an average of 50,000 rainbow and 25,000 kokanee stocked each year. The lake also holds some mountain whitefish and some course fish.

The rainbow here can get up to 2 kg (5 lbs) or more, although the average catch is much smaller than that. For anglers itching to get out on the water in spring, Ten Mile is a low elevation lake and is usually one of the first lakes to be ice free–usually by mid to late April. The best fishing comes shortly after ice-off to mid-June and again in September–October. Both trolling and fly-fishing can be productive.

The deepest part of the lake is towards the northwest end of the lake. Try trolling around the fringe of the deep water for best success. Rainbow prefer worms on a Willow Leaf lake troll or Wedding Band. If you prefer light tackle, troll a black or green Apex, Hot Shot or F-5 Flatfish.

For fly fishermen, the shallows contain lilies and other weeds, which make for good hiding spots for the trout. Try casting a leech, damselfly or dragonfly pattern towards the lily pads, reeds or bulrushes on the shore. Tom Thumbs are also productive when the mayflies and caddis flies are emerging.

The heavily treed, reedy shoreline presents little opportunity for spincasters, but there are beaches and a float to fish from. Try a black or yellow Rooster Tail, Mepps Black Fury or

Aglia or Blue Fox Vibrax in silver or gold.

The kokanee action can be quite good here in spring, summer and winter for fish that can get up to 1 kg (2 lbs). The best open water action usually occurs from June to August. Trollers targeting kokanee should go deep with leadcore lines or downriggers and a Wedding Band tipped with a worm or maggot. Use lures like Triple Teasers, a Macs Imperial Spoon in pink, red, orange, chartreuse or silver and a Dick Nite or needlefish in silver or 50/50 silver-orange.

Ice fishers target kokanee in deep water with FST wobblers, a leader with a teardrop

jig in pink or red tipped and a maggot. Rainbow found in shallower water can be fooled with a bit of shrimp and roe on a jig or plain hook. The lake also offers some ice fishing for whitefish.

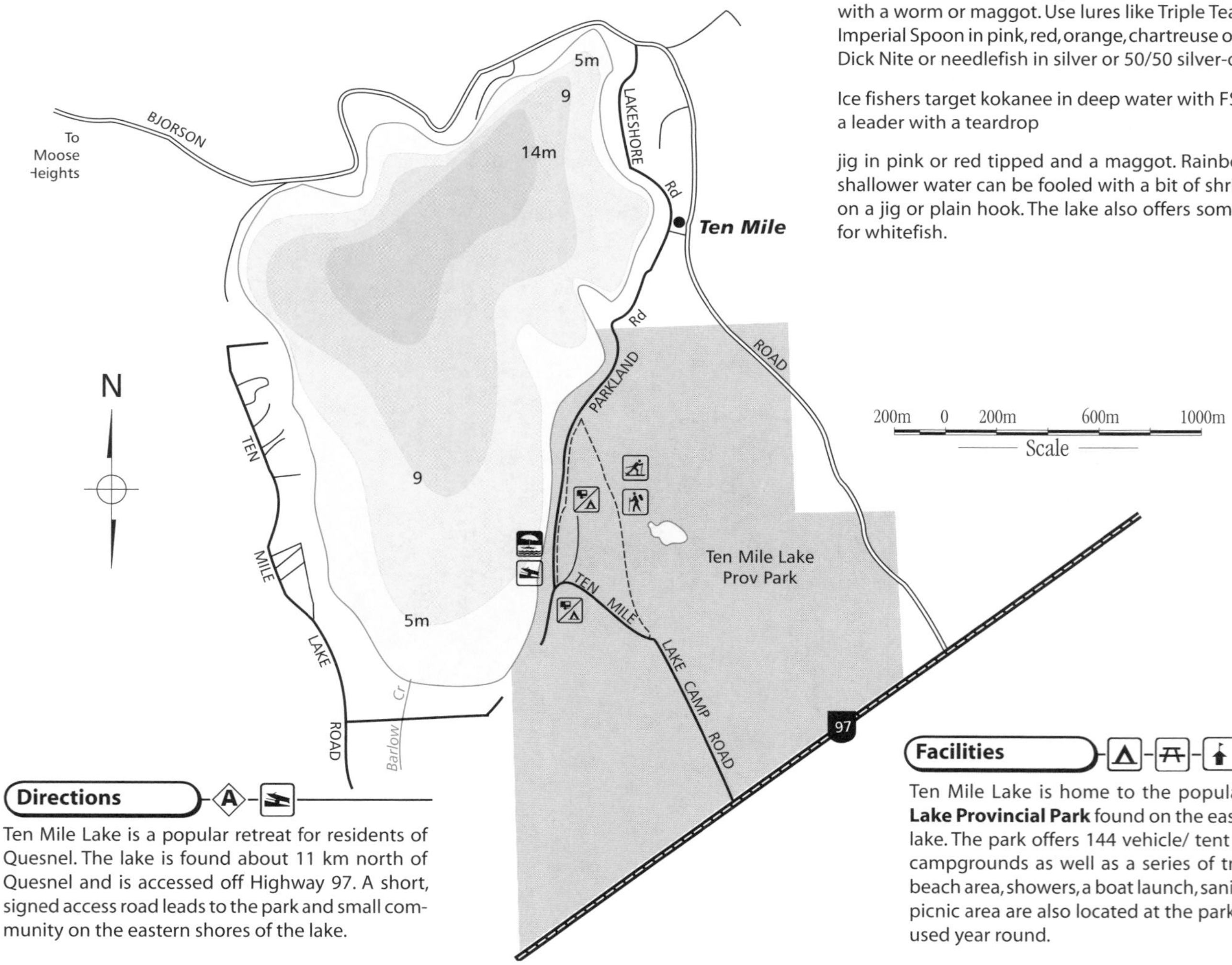

To
Moose
Heights
BJORSON
5m
9
14m
LAKESHORE
Rd
Ten Mile
Rd
PARKLAND
ROAD
N
TEN
MILE
LAKE
ROAD
9
5m
Ten Mile Lake
Prov Park
TEN
MILE
LAKE
CAMP
ROAD
Barlow
Cr
97
200m
0
200m
600m
1000m
Scale

Directions

Ten Mile Lake is a popular retreat for residents of Quesnel. The lake is found about 11 km north of Quesnel and is accessed off Highway 97. A short, signed access road leads to the park and small community on the eastern shores of the lake.

Facilities

Ten Mile Lake is home to the popular **Ten Mile Lake Provincial Park** found on the east side of the lake. The park offers 144 vehicle/ tent sites in two campgrounds as well as a series of trails. A large beach area, showers, a boat launch, sani-station and picnic area are also located at the park. The park is used year round.

Till Lake

Location: 20 km (12.4 mi) west of Williams Lake
Elevation: 872 m (2,860 ft)
Surface Area: 79 ha (194 ac)
Maximum Depth: 20 m (65 ft)
Mean Depth: 8 m (26 ft)
Way Point: 52° 2′ 45″ N, 122° 21′ 45″ W

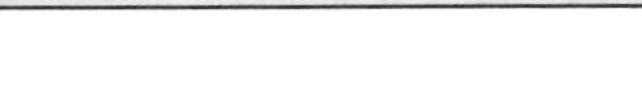

Fishing

Although the name and the turquoise water might lead you to suspect that this was a glacial lake, it's not. Instead, the lake is situated on a sandy plateau near Williams Lake, surrounded by a thick interior forest. The lake provides fairly good fishing for decent size rainbow. The odd trout is reported to reach 3 kg (6 lbs).

Each year, the lake is stocked with 10,000 Blackwater strain rainbow. Kokanee were stocked in the lake about a decade ago and brook trout nearly thirty years ago, but there have been no recent reports of any catches. Like most lakes stocked with Blackwater trout, Till Lake holds redside shiners. These small, course fish were introduced as a food fish for the rainbow, but most strains of rainbow prefer to eat insects. Blackwater trout, on the other hand, love eating shiners and in so doing, control the population.

Till Lake is often subjected to winterkill, so check with local sporting goods stores in Williams Lake before heading out. Early spring to mid-June and again in the fall are the best times to fish this lake. Fly fishers frequent the shoals on the north end and use scud, leech or Carey patterns. The deep water out from the boat launch and farther down the lake is very productive in the spring when using a floating line, long leader and chironomid pattern. A strike indicator is good at suspending the fly at the right depth.

Local trollers use a Willow Leaf and worm, with or without a Wedding Band. For lighter fare, go with a F-4 or F-5 Flatfish or size 70 Hot Shot in silver, gold, black or green. Toll flies, like a green Doc Spratley or Carey Special, or a black and blue Woolly Bugger.

With limited room along the shoreline, spincasters should fish from a watercraft. Use spinners like Mepps Aglia, Black Fury, Rooster Tail or Blue Fox in various colours. When the fish are on the surface, cast a bubble and Tom Thumb or leech pattern. Also try a bobber and worm or Powerbait drifted along the drop offs.

Ice fishers use a black and blue with a silver streak or silver and purple marabou jig or small blue Apex spoon. Worms, shrimp or roe are also effective in water up to 4 metre (12 feet) deep. As oxygen levels beneath the ice deplete, the rainbow become more and more torpid, putting up little fight. The best time to head to the lake is as soon as the ice is thick enough to safely support your weight.

Facilities

The **Till Lake North Recreation Site** is a large, RV friendly site that rests at the north end of the lake. It has space for 17 groups, although there are only eight tables and 11 fire rings. The lake has a rough boat launch suitable for a trailered boat.

Directions

From Highway 97 in Williams Lake, turn west onto Highway 20 towards Bella Coola. After crossing the Fraser and climbing Sheep Hill, look for the Meldrum Creek Road branching north (about 32 km west of Williams Lake). Follow this good all-weather road for about 13 km before the Till Lake Forest Service Road branches west. Follow this rougher road for another 1.7 km to the turn off to the recreation site. The lake is found about another kilometre or so down this side road.

Area Indicator

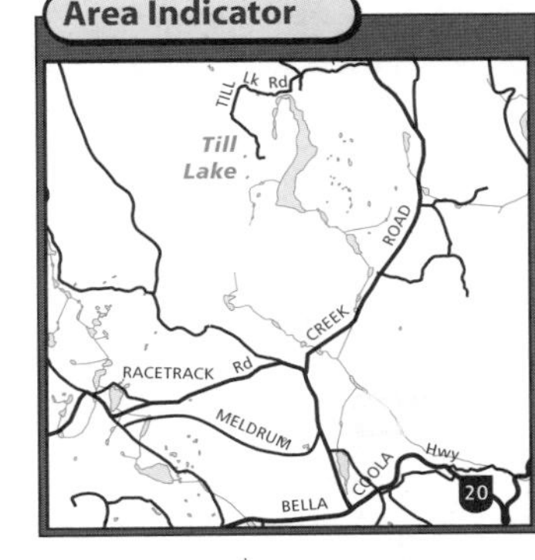

Till Lake			
Fish Stocking Data			
Year	Species	Number	Life Stage
2008	Rainbow Trout	10,000	Yearling
2007	Rainbow Trout	10,000	Yearling
2006	Rainbow Trout	10,000	Yearling

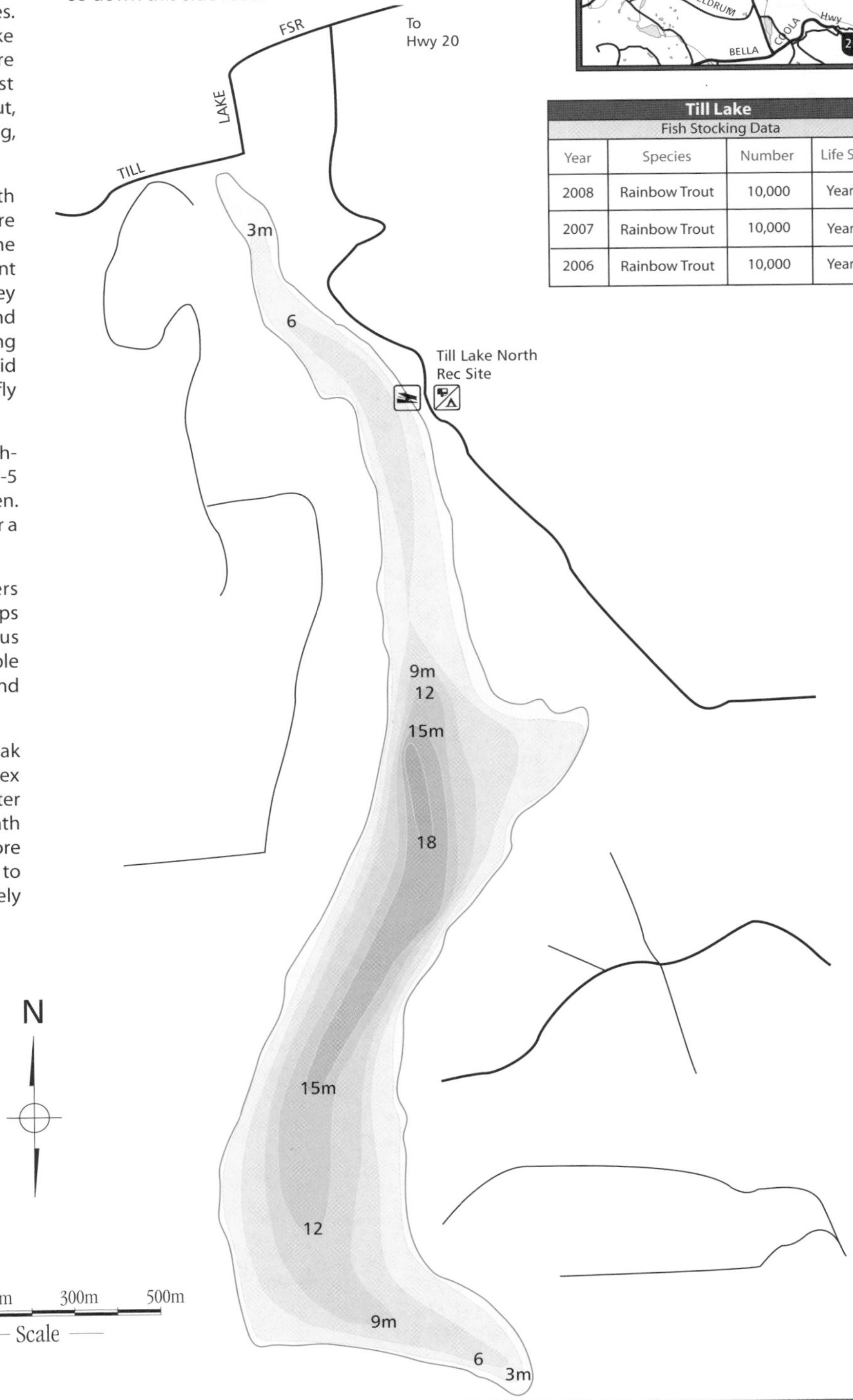

Location: 17 km (10.5 mi) south of 100 Mile House

Timothy & Dempsey Lakes

Dempsey Lake

Elevation: 929 m (3,048 ft)
Surface Area: 133 ha (3289 ac)
Maximum Depth: 28 m (92 ft)
Mean Depth: 10.1 m (33 ft)
Way Point: 51° 49' 50.4" N, 121° 13' 57.3" W

Area Indicator

Timothy Lake
Greeny Lake
Itautso Lake
Dempsey Lake
TIMOTHY (1500 Rd)
LAKE
Rd
Lac la Hache
97
SPRING
LAKE
Chub Lake
Soda Lake
Tubbs Lake
108 Mile Lake
Simon Lake
To 100 Mile House

Fishing

Timothy and Dempsey Lakes are a pair of good trout fishing lakes found east of Lac La Hache. The lakes are usually ice free by mid-April, but the fishing doesn't really start for most people until after turnover, which is usually done by mid to late May. Fishing remains steady through the fall.

Timothy is the larger and more popular of the two. The lake is stocked with 10 to 20,000 rainbow trout each year to help maintain the healthy population of trout. Despite the heavy fishing pressure, catching a 1.5 kg (3 lb) trout in Timothy is not uncommon. The lake does have a large number of course fish–redside shiners, squawfish, suckers and chub. The Blackwater strain rainbows feed on the redside shiners especially, which allows them to get nice and big.

Dempsey Lake is not stocked, but it is separated from Timothy Lake by a short channel and so there is probably some migration of fish from one lake to the other. While the lake is smaller, people have reported catching bigger fish here than in Timothy, with catches to 2 kg (4.5 lbs) reported. There are also suckers and squawfish at the lake.

Both lakes are deep enough to troll and the water drops off rapidly from shore. Trollers should circle the lake just off the drop off. If you can see the lighter coloured bottom on one side of your boat and the darker deep water on the other, you are doing it right.

Shore casters are able to cast towards the deeper water on Timothy if they work around the brushy shoreline. On Dempsey, spincasters and fly anglers should try working the inflow area at the north end of the lake. Fly-fishing is at its best in the early spring. Cast towards the shallows and weed beds that line the lakes.

Timothy Lake Fish Stocking Data			
Year	Species	Number	Life Stage
2006	Rainbow Trout	10,000	Yearling
2005	Rainbow Trout	20,000	Yearling
2004	Rainbow Trout	20,000	Yearling

Directions

While these two lakes are located next to each other, the access into each lake is different. Timothy Lake is found off the Timothy Lake Road (1500 Road) at Lac la Hache. It is about 14 km from the highway along the good gravel road to the west end of the lake. Resort signs will direct your way.

Dempsey Lake, on the other hand, is accessed from the Spring Lake Road south of Lac La Hache. Follow that road until it turns into Lake of the Trees Road. A series of side roads, including Dempsey Lake Road lead north to the lake. Please do not trespass on private property.

Timothy Lake

Elevation: 928 m (3,044 ft)
Surface Area: 444 ha (1,097 ac)
Maximum Depth: 23 m (75 ft)
Mean Depth: 14 m (44 ft)
Way Point: 51° 51' 12" N, 121° 15' 47" W

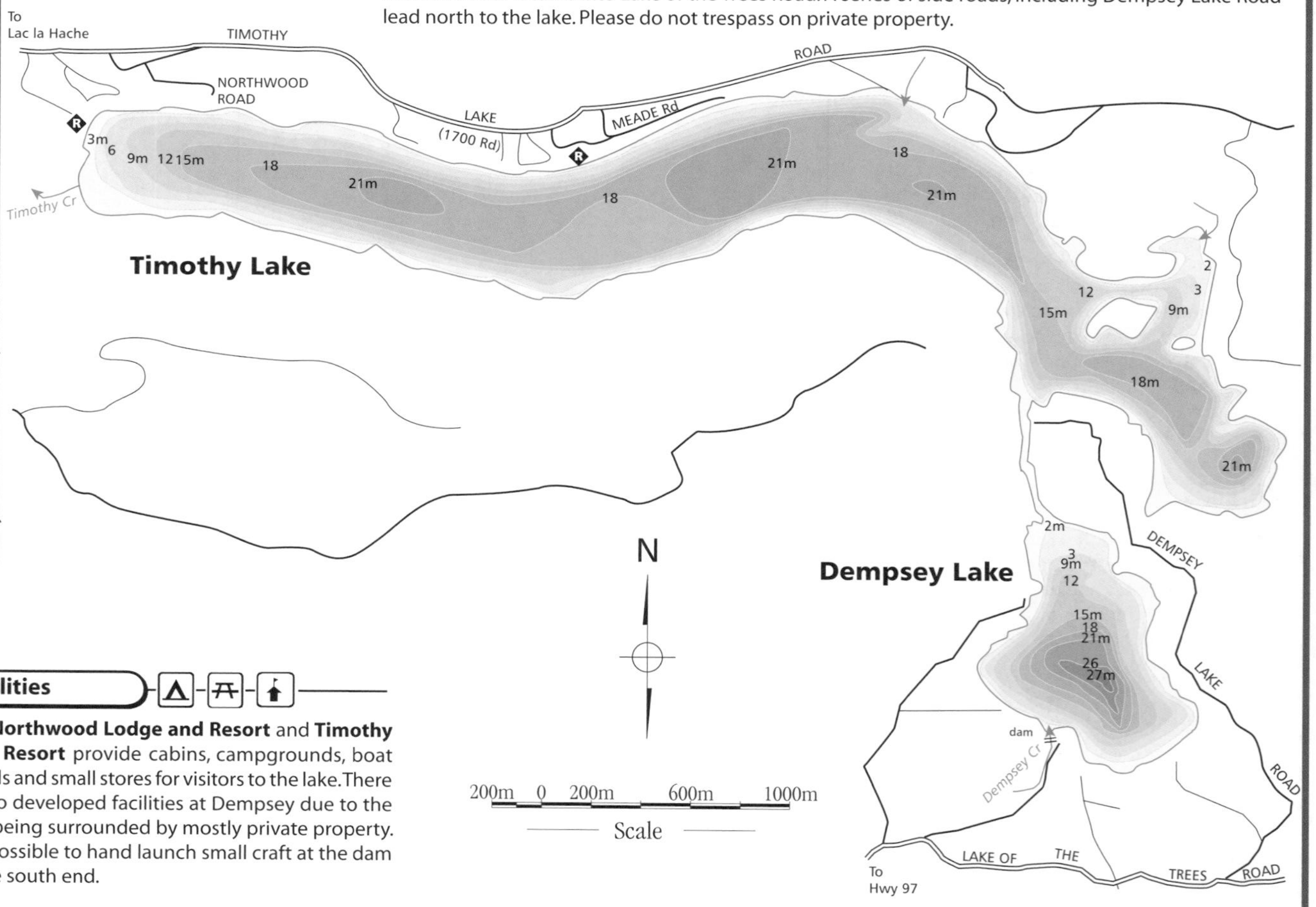

To Lac la Hache
TIMOTHY
ROAD
NORTHWOOD ROAD
LAKE (1700 Rd)
MEADE Rd
Timothy Cr
Timothy Lake
Dempsey Lake
DEMPSEY LAKE ROAD
dam
Dempsey Cr
LAKE OF THE TREES ROAD
To Hwy 97
N
200m 0 200m 600m 1000m
Scale

Facilities

The **Northwood Lodge and Resort** and **Timothy Lake Resort** provide cabins, campgrounds, boat rentals and small stores for visitors to the lake. There are no developed facilities at Dempsey due to the lake being surrounded by mostly private property. It is possible to hand launch small craft at the dam at the south end.

Tisdall Lake

Location: 80 km (50 mi) northeast of Williams Lake
Elevation: 957 m (3,140 ft)
Surface Area: 502 ha (1,240.5 ac)
Maximum Depth: 36 m (118 ft)
Mean Depth: 18 m (59 ft)
Way Point: 52° 14' 18" N, 121° 0' 49" W

Fishing

Tisdall Lake is a popular fishing lake located well east of Highway 97 in the Horsefly Lake area. The lake is known to have a very good population of wild rainbow trout, which tend to be in the 30–40 cm (12–16 in) range. The trout provide fast action for anglers using a fly or trolling.

The lake is usually ice-free by the end of April, but isn't fishable until mid to late May once turnover is finished. If you are in the area, there are often a few weeks just after ice-off when the fishing can be great. It is a bit of a crap shoot when the lake starts to turn over and the road can be dicey to drive in spring. Best stick to a lake closer to where you are.

Because there are so many rainbow trout and because they are so willing to be caught, it is a great place to take young families or people just starting to fish. The trout will usually chase anything that looks edible and most people can catch quite a few fish in a day's fishing here. Small spinners or a worm and bobber set-up are popular with those new to fishing.

Tisdall Lake is easily trolled except in the northeastern bay of the lake. Since the water drops off rapidly from the shore, it is best to circle the main body of the lake while trolling, sticking to the edge of the drop off. If you can see the lighter coloured bottom on one side of your boat and the darker deep water on the other, you are doing it right. Of course, you don't want to just troll in a straight line, but make slow S curves back and forth across the drop off. You will want your lure to be close to the bottom as trout spend most of their time feeding within a metre or two (3 to 6 feet) of the bottom and when they aren't feeding there, they are feeding at the top. They rarely feed mid-water.

Fly anglers and spincasters should work the near shore area or the outflow to Tisdall Creek. Just off the channel to the northeastern bay is also a good location to try casting a fly.

Directions

To reach Tisdall Lake involves a long drive from Highway 97. The road conditions for the entire journey are considered good except during spring break up or in wet weather. However, it is recommended to bring a copy of the *Cariboo Chilcotin Coast Backroad Mapbook* and a GPS to help guide you to the lake.

From the highway, follow Horsefly Road all the way to the small town of Horsefly. Just before entering the town, cross the bridge over the Horsefly River and begin the drive on the Black Creek Road. That logging road is a well maintained road, which a car can travel along without much trouble. Continue past Black Creek and the airport and then take the first right onto the McKinley Lake Road (500 Road). The first major right on the McKinley Lake Road is the Tisdall Lake Road (1000 Road). A couple kilometers later, a short access road leads to the recreation site at the east end of Tisdall Lake.

Facilities

The **Tisdall Lake Recreation Site** is a popular camping area due to the good fishing at the lake. It is not unusual for the 15 campsites to be full on a summer weekend. There is also a rustic launch for visitors to use.

Area Indicator

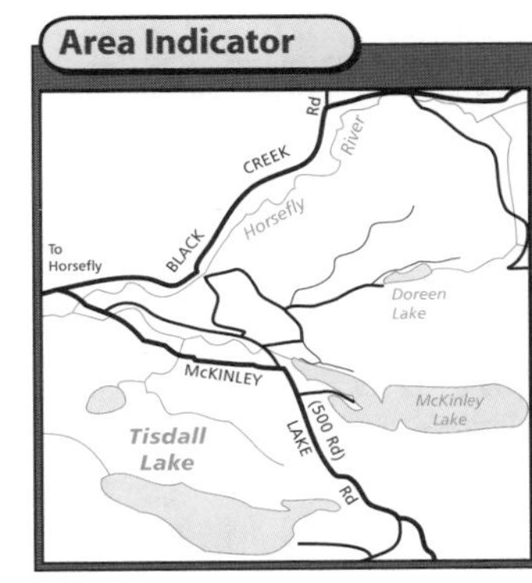

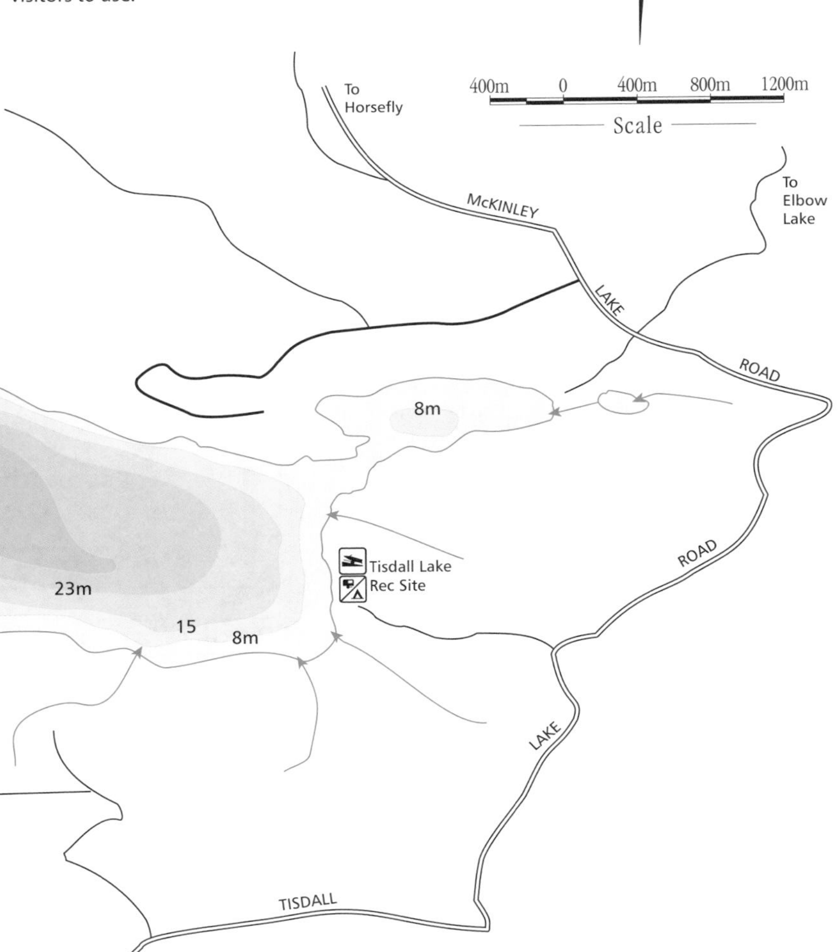

Location: 75 km (46.5 mi) west of Dawson Creek
Stream Length: 23.2 km (14.4 mi)
Geographic: 55° 10′ 50″ N, 129° 2′ 16″ W

Tseax River

Fishing

Salmon and steelhead arrive later in the Tseax, a Nass River tributary than they do in the Skeena. By mid-August, for instance, the Chinook have basically stopped running in the Skeena, but in the Tseax, the fishing is just reaching its peak.

While the area does not attract many tourists (mostly because there are no guides who operate on the river), the Tseax attracts plenty of attention from local anglers, who haven't had enough action on the Skeena.

The river flows through the Nisga'a Lavabeds, which are impressive in their own right; a barren landscape of rock and ash. There is a very short stretch of fishable water on the Tseax, maybe about a 2 km (a mile and a bit) upstream from the confluence with the Nass. Well travelled trails lead down from the bridge that crosses the river and along the river.

The river is a low flow river with lots of boulders so it isn't conducive to drift fishing from a boat. The boulders also make it a bit hard to walk up and downstream. Rather, most people fish from the bank, since the river is only about 15 metres (50 feet) wide across or so at its widest point.

There are basically only two good places to fish here, at the so-called Halfway Hole (because it is halfway between the bridge and the river) and at the river mouth itself. But, oh, what fishing there is to be had. The river has runs of Chinook, Coho, chum and steelhead and the fishing can be incredible.

The bears think so, too. Oh. That's another reason not a lot of people fish here. There are lots and lots of grizzly bear. While there haven't been any human-bear conflicts, there is something a little disconcerting about having a grizzly bear fishing the same pool as you. Make lots of noise, bring a bell, bear bangers and bear spray and possibly someone who runs slower than you….

The best fishing is in mid-August, when the Chinook and chum come into the river. However, if the water is too clean, the fish are easily spooked and won't bite, no matter what you throw at them. But if there is just a touch of colour in the water, it usually reassures the fish and they will hit most anything you throw at them. Conversely, if there is too much rain, the river will blow out. Fortunately, it is a low volume river and tends to recover quickly.

Chinook take to cured roe, Kitimat spoon, Spin-N-Glos or wool cast or drifted into deep holes. Chum are often caught by float fishing with pink worms or bottom bouncing wool or lures with pink in them. The fly angler can try Woolly Buggers or Egg Sucking Leeches for the Chinook or a '52 Buick or a bigger Marabou fly for chum.

In fall there is a great run of Coho and some steelhead.

It can be hard to tell where the Tseax ends and the Nass begins. There are boundary signs located along what was formerly known as the Nass Back Channel. These signs designate the mouth of the Tseax.

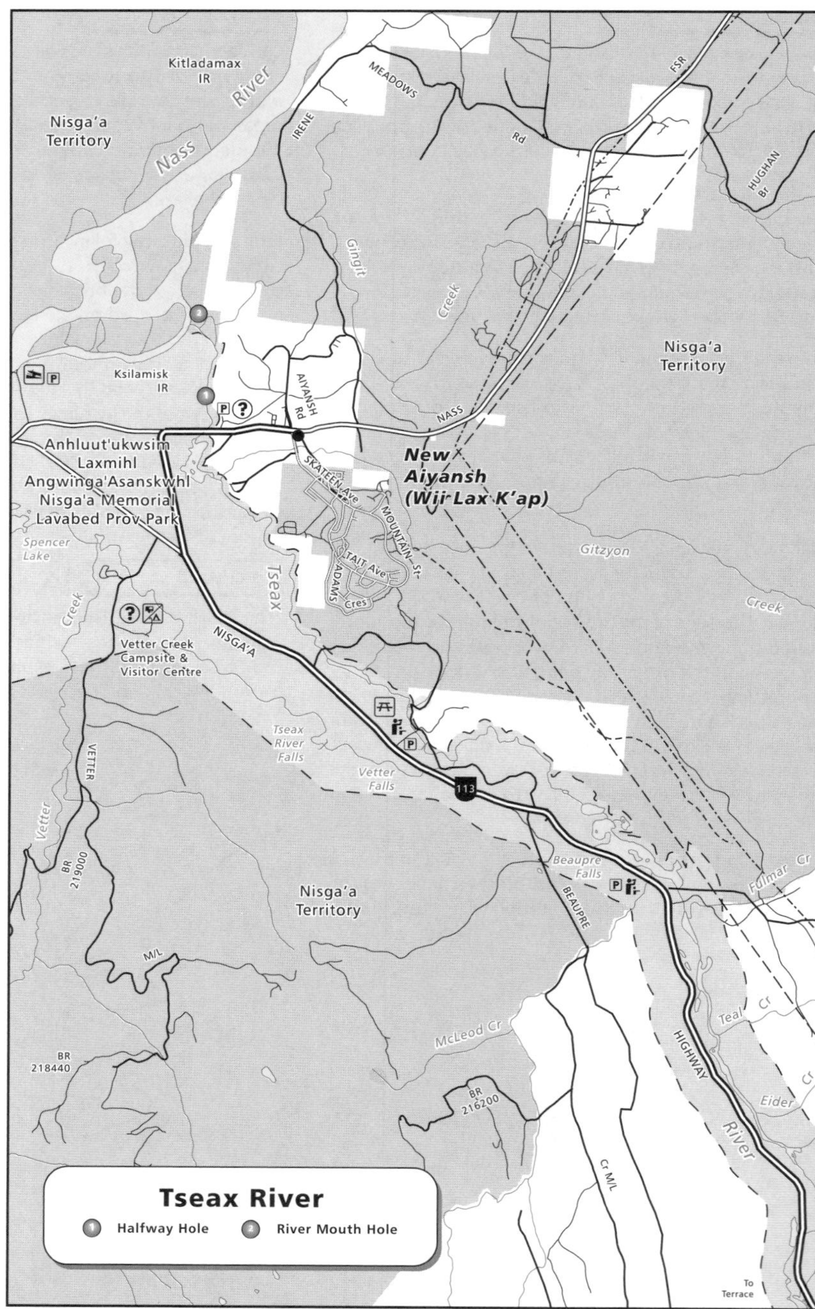

Directions

The Tseax River is found alongside the Nisga'a Highway, which runs between Terrace and New Aiyansh (or Wii Lax Cap, as it is also known as). The Kalum Lake Road (Highway 18) leaves Terrace and turns into the Nisga'a Highway.

Facilities

The river flows through the **Anhluut'ukwsim Laxmihl Angwinga'asanskwhl Nisga'a Memorial Lavabed Provincial Park.** There is a boat launch onto the Nass, as well as 16 campsites. There are some services, including food and lodging in nearby New Aiyansh, but many people head back to Terrace.

Tsuniah Lake

Location: 160 km (100 miles) southwest of Williams Lake
Elevation: 1,223 m (4,012 ft)
Surface Area: 1,080 ha (2,668 ac)
Maximum Depth: 40 m (130 ft)
Mean Depth: 17 m (55 ft)
Way Point: 51° 44′ 59″ N, 124° 43′ 32″ W

Fishing

Tsuniah Lake is set in a spectacular valley, between peaks that tower more than 2,400 metres (8,000 feet) on each side of the lake. The most notable peak is Mount Nemaia, which rises 2,613 metres (8,572 ft) above sea level. The lake is just one of a series of great fishing lakes in the region, found between Chaunigan to the east and Chilko to the west.

The lake covers just about 1,100 hectares and is over 1,220 metres (4,000 feet) above sea level. This puts it at a slightly higher elevation than other lakes in the plateau, but not as high as some of the other lakes in the valley, like Chaunigan. The extra elevation means that the lake isn't ice-free until a few weeks later after lower elevation lakes. Giving the lake time to turn over means that the fishing doesn't really get going until late May or early June.

The lake has seasonal hatches as are common to many of the Chilcotin Lakes–chironomids, caddis, mayflies and dragon and damselflies–but none of the large hatches that draw anglers from around the world. Instead, there is a steady stream of insects that hatch here.

The hatches occur later than they would at a low elevation lake. Most people who fish the lake troll the lake, dragging around a Doc Spratley or Carey Special, or your typical gadget bag of gear: Wedding Bands with or without a worm, Flatfish, and small spoons and spinners.

However, while trolling is usually the order of the day, people can have good luck stopping and casting. Patterns that work well on the lake include Pheasant Tail Nymphs, Hare's Ears and leech patterns.

The shoreline of the lake is open and people have been known to fish from near the recreation site, but a boat would definitely improve success.

Nearly directly across the lake is an island that makes a great place to fish. However, getting across in a small boat can be difficult when the wind kicks up. A good alternative on windy days is a sheltered bay just south of the recreation site. Fly anglers especially should try working around the mouth of the creek that flows into the lake here.

Directions

Getting to Tsuniah Lake involves a long drive from Williams Lake, the nearest major centre. Take Highway 20 past the Bull Canyon Provincial Park and watch for Young Road, which becomes the Chilko-Newton Forest Service Road. This is one of a number of roads that can be taken to the lake. Stay on the main road to the Chilko Airstrip Road, and then turn left, and left again to cross the Chilko River at Henry's Crossing. The Tsuniah Lake Road continues south to the lake.

Facilities

One of the oldest lodges in the area, the **Tsuniah Lake Lodge** has been a destination for anglers, horseback riders and pilots (the lodge has its own airstrip). It is a popular place to stay and is located at the north end of the lake. Further south, the **Tsuniah Lake Recreation Site** is an eight unit recreation site about a quarter of the way down the western shore of the lake. There is no boat launch, but you can get a cartopper onto the water.

Area Indicator

Chilko Lake
Tsuniah Lake
Nemaiah Valley

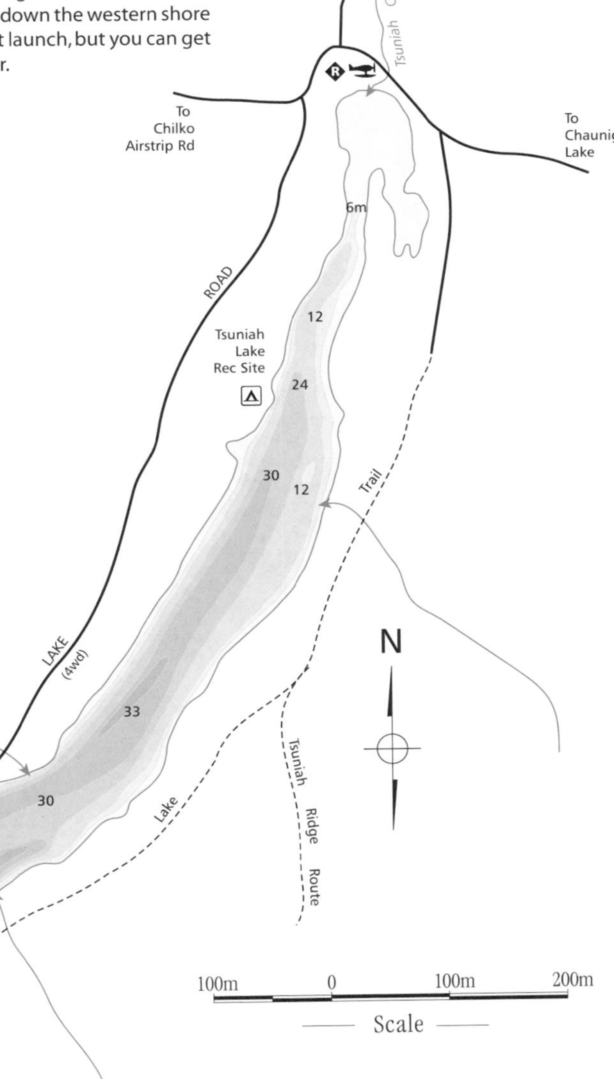

Location: 50 km (30 mi) north of Williams Lake
Elevation: 897 m (2,943 ft)
Surface Area: 309 ha (762 ac)
Maximum Depth: 43 m (142 ft)
Mean Depth: 20 m (64 ft)
Way Point: 52° 22' 40" N, 122° 4' 42" W

Tyee Lake

Area Indicator

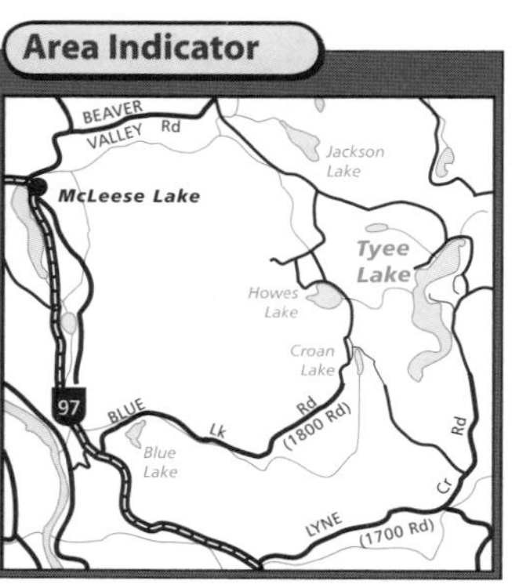

Tyee Lake Fish Stocking Data			
Year	Species	Number	Life Stage
2008	Rainbow Trout	26,476	Yearling
2007	Rainbow Trout	25,860	Yearling
2006	Rainbow Trout	25,000	Yearling
2005	Kokanee	10,000	Fingerling
2005	Rainbow Trout	25,000	Yearling

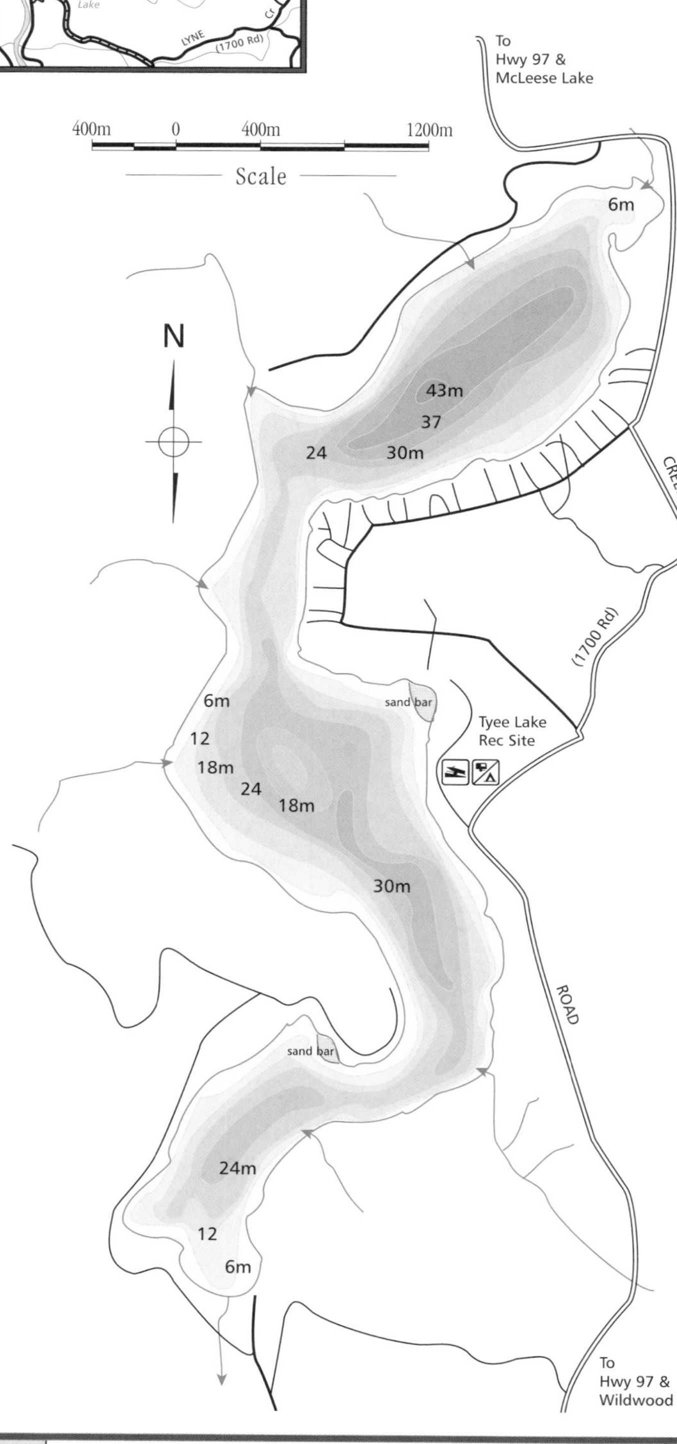

Fishing

For most anglers, the word "Tyee" is synonymous with 15 kilogram (30 pound) plus Chinook salmon. There are, however, no Tyee to be found in Tyee Lake.

However, the word also means a king or a chief, or "anything of superior order". And while it isn't the best fishing lake in the area, it does offer some great fishing for stocked rainbow and kokanee.

Each year the Freshwater Fisheries Society of BC stocks 20,000 rainbow and kokanee in the lake to ensure that the fishing remains good at the lake. The rainbow stocked here are a mix of some of BC's most famous trout. There are different strains and subspecies of trout in the lake. One of the most famous is the Gerrard strain, which are famous for the size they can get to. Like the Blackwater strain (which are also stocked in the lake) the Gerrard trout eat smaller course fish and kokanee, which helps them get bigger faster. In their home waters, Gerrard rainbow are the biggest trout in the world. In Tyee Lake, the Gerrard don't get to 10 kg (22 lbs) like they do in Kootenay Lake, but can get up to 2.5 kg (5 lbs) or more.

On the other hand, the kokanee are usually small with a monster being 1 kg (2 lbs). These popular sportfish provide good fishing in both the summer and winter. Several course fish species (suckers, squawfish and chub) are also found in the lake.

Tyee Lake is an ideal trolling lake. It is quite deep with the water dropping off rapidly from shore. As a result, you can troll most of the shoreline and get results. And since the trout and kokanee have similar eating habits, you can use virtually the same gear. Lake trolls are most popular, but chironomids, dragonfly or damselfly nymphs and even leeches should not be ruled out. The inflow and outflow creeks are good areas to try casting a fly or lure.

The ice is off the lake in early May and the better fishing begins towards the end of May. During summer there is better action for the kokanee if you can find where they are holding. By the fall, the fish move back to the shallower water and a shallow troll works.

Ice fishing is also good here, particularly for the kokanee. This fishery is usually very good right after Christmas. Use a spoon like the Ruby Eye Wiggler, a dodger with a short leader and glow jig tipped with a bit of krill or a maggot.

Directions

Tyee Lake is found north of Williams Lake on a decent gravel road. North of town, just past the Deep Creek Indian Reserve, the Lyne Creek Road (1700 Rd) branches east. It is about 17 km to the recreation site from the highway. An alternate access is available of the Beaver Valley Road to the north. A copy of the *Backroad Mapbook for the Cariboo Chilcotin Coast* can direct you in that way.

During wet weather, a truck may be necessary to reach the lake.

Facilities

Tyee Lake Recreation Site is a large, popular 25 unit site on the eastern shores of the lake. Sporting a boat launch, the site receives heavy use in the summer months by anglers as well as water skiers. There are numerous private cabins that line the lake.

Tyhee Lake

Location: 12 km (7.5 mi) southeast of Smithers
Elevation: 522 m (1,712 ft)
Surface Area: 318 ha (785 ac)
Maximum Depth: 22 m (73 ft)
Mean Depth: 11 m (36 ft)
Way Point: 54° 42′ 54″ N, 127° 2′ 12″ W

Fishing

Tyhee, or Tyee, Lake is an excellent all-around family camping and fishing destination in the Bulkley Valley. Numerous farms, private homes, a couple of bed and breakfasts, private camps and a seaplane base border this large lake.

The lake is home to many nesting loons and their lonely, wavering call is special to all who love the outdoors. In May, Sandhill cranes also come through the Bulkley Valley on their way to nesting grounds in Alaska, returning again in September.

It is a great place for birdwatchers, but the lake is also a great place for anglers, too. The lake takes its name from the Chinook word for a king salmon or Chinook, which aren't actually found in the lake. The lake is stocked each year with 20,000 yearling rainbow trout by the Freshwater Fisheries Society of BC. The Blackwater strain rainbow can exceed 3 kg (6.5 lb). Cutthroat trout, giant pygmy whitefish, burbot and a number of non-sportfish, including chub and dace, are also present.

Tyhee can get busy on summer weekends, so anglers should respectfully share their fishing space. The lake is heavily weeded around the shoreline so shore fishing is limited to the park area. In this area, young or novice anglers alike can have fun catching various non-game fish. Keep it simple; a hook and worm or Powerbait.

If fishing in a boat try using a lake troll, tipped with bait, trolling around the weed beds and lily pads. If that method doesn't work you can try trolling a leech, a spoon or a Rapala minnow. Tyhee's rainbow are opportunistic feeders and the bigger fish prefer bigger morsels–particularly small fish. Towards dusk, these larger fish can often be seen coming in to the shallows to feed. Fishing closer to the surface can be rewarding at this time of the day. In the spring, the fish feed heavily on the lake's prolific chironomid hatches.

The non-sportfish (chub and dace) are commonly seen in the shallows of the swimming area. They love chironomids just as much as the rainbow. For most kids, it really doesn't matter what they hook on the end of the line, as long as they catch something and have fun.

During winter, Tyhee is a popular, easy to access destination. Young anglers will pick up the basic techniques of ice-fishing in no time and, with some good bait and a bit of luck, pull a fish up out of the hole for dinner. Jigs tipped with an artificial mealworm or maggot from the Berkley's Powerbait line are a good starting point. Holes should be drilled far enough out to avoid the weed growth close to shore.

Facilities

The **Tyhee Lake Provincial Park** offers a host of amenities including a concrete boat launch and a campground with well over 50 sites. The park has flush toilets, showers, a sani-station, playground, volleyball courts, horseshoe pits, hiking trails and a swimming beach. The campground gate is locked when the snow begins to fall.

Directions

Tyhee Lake Provincial Park is located just east of Telkwa. Turn off the Yellowhead Highway (Highway 16) onto the Tyhee Lake Road in Telkwa, drive to the top of the hill and turn right.

Tyhee Lake
Fish Stocking Data

Year	Species	Number	Life Stage
2008	Rainbow Trout	20,077	Yearling
2007	Rainbow Trout	20,070	Yearling
2006	Rainbow Trout	20,000	Yearling

Area Indicator

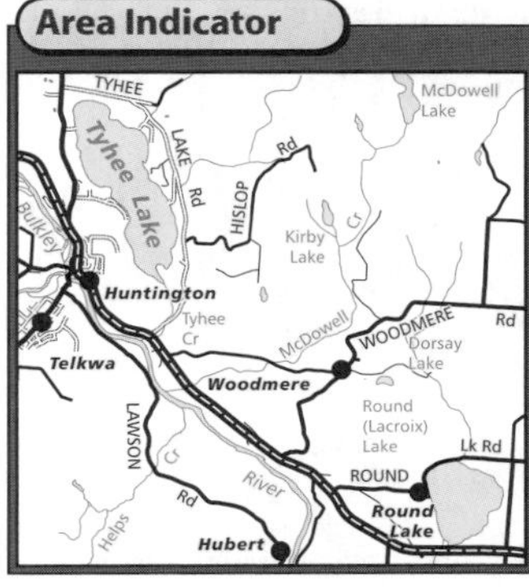

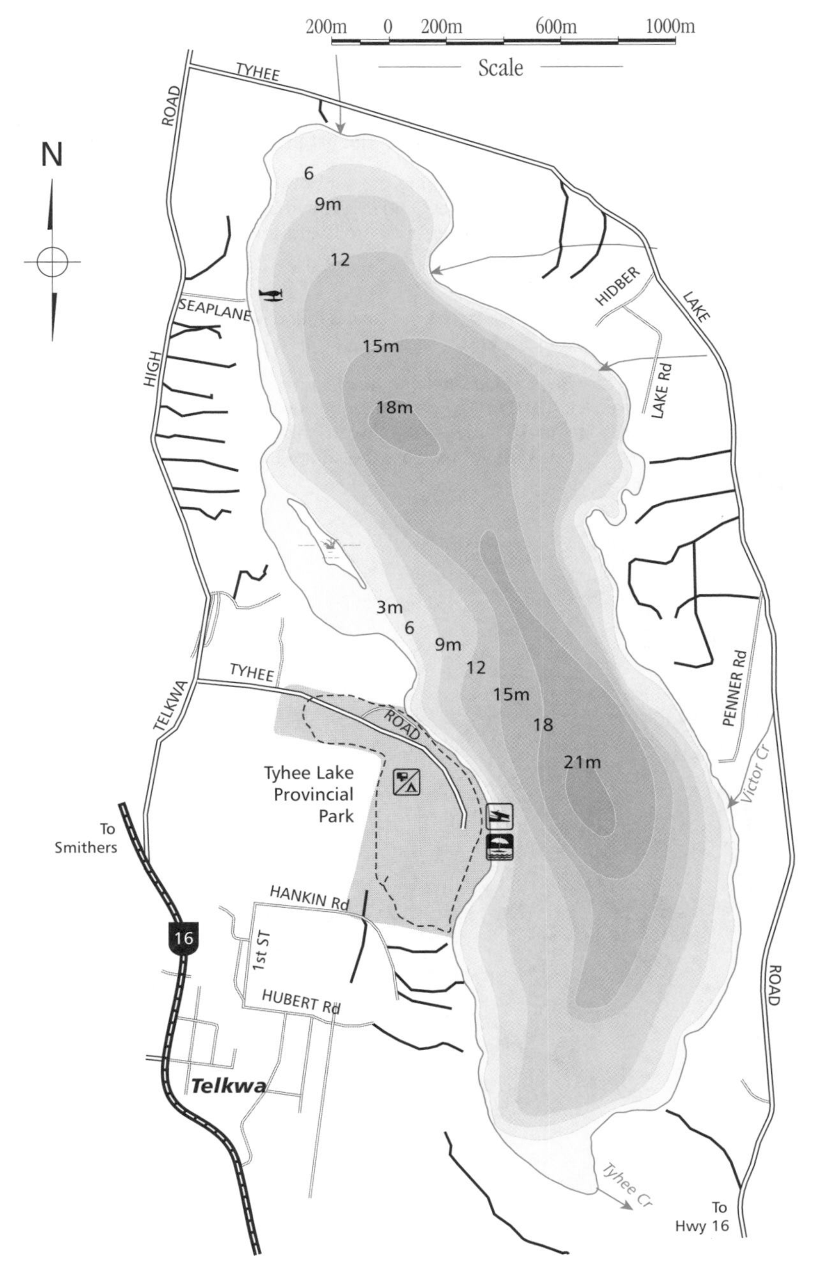

Location: 45 km (30 mi) southwest of Quesnel
Elevation: 1,143 m (3,750 ft)
Surface Area: 761 ha (1,881 ac)
Maximum Depth: 12 m (38 ft)
Mean Depth: 8 m (26 ft)
Way Point: 52° 39′ 7″ N, 122° 50′ 34″ W

Tzenzaicut Lake

Area Indicator

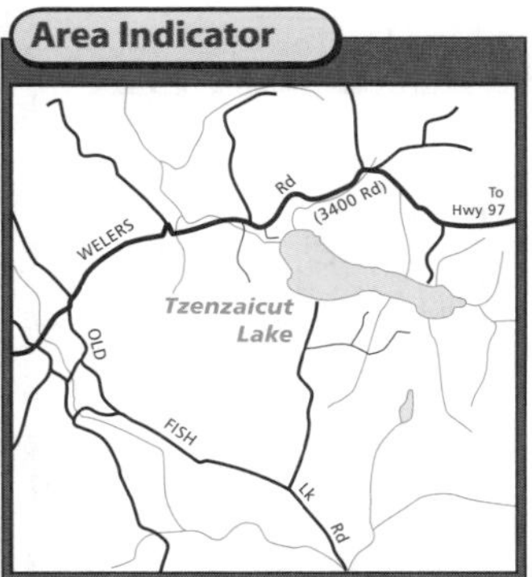

Fishing

While you may not have ever fished Tzenzaicut Lake, there is a good chance you have caught a Tzenzaicut trout. Eggs from this lake are used to stock many of the lakes in the region.

The lake has great natural spawning grounds, which means the fish are extremely prolific in the lake. The word Tzenzaicut actually means fish in the Carrier language and locals still call the lake Fish Lake, possibly because they can't wrap their mouths around the actual name of the lake.

The rainbow trout are so prolific, in fact, that there is too much natural competition in the lake. Not just with each other but with course fish such as suckers and redside shiners. As a result, the rainbow tend to a bit smaller. Fish in the 25–38 cm (10–15 in) range a possible, with a 1 kg (2 lb) fish being a big catch.

With all of these fish, Tzenzaicut Lake is a perfect family fishing lake because it is nearly impossible to not catch a fish here. As long as you know even a modicum about fishing (attach hook to line; put hook in water), chances are you will be able to catch a fish here.

The rainbow are abundant in the lake making the fishing good throughout most of the ice-free season. The fishing season does not begin until the end of May and slows around the beginning of July when the summer doldrums hit. By late September, the good fishing returns. Ice over begins early on in November.

Tzenzaicut Lake is unique because the water drops off rapidly from shore to an expansive, relatively flat bottom. Therefore, the best area to work is right around the drop off either on a shallow troll or by casting a fly or lure. A boat with a motor is almost a necessity if fishing the 760 hectare lake. Stretching over 11 km (7 miles) long and up to 1 km wide, there is a lot of territory to cover on the lake.

If fly-fishing, the rainbow trout seem to like bright patterns. Fly anglers will have great luck with scud patterns, green Spratleys and most anything with orange or yellow in it. Most Mepps, Blue Fox or Panter Martin spinners will for gear chuckers. Lake trolls and smaller Flatfish are preferred by trollers.

Directions

Located about 50 km southwest of Quesnel, Tzenzaicut Lake is found on a good gravel road that is suitable for most vehicles. The Tzenzaicut Lake Resort signs direct the way.

To reach the lake, cross the Fraser River at Quesnel and head south on the West Fraser Road and then turn right (west) on Marsh Road. A left of Camille Road will bring you to the gravel Garner Road (0 Road). Follow this road south to the 36 km marker, where a right (west) takes you to the Tzenzaicut Lake Forest Service Road (3400 Road). The resort is found just past the 48 km marker, while the recreation site is found about 10 km past that.

Facilities

The **Tzenzaicut Lake Resort** offers rustic cabins and RV friendly campsites as well as a boat launch. Further west, the **Tzenzaicut Lake Recreation Site** provides several user maintained campsites next to the northwest side of the lake. There is a graveled beach and a boat launch at the site.

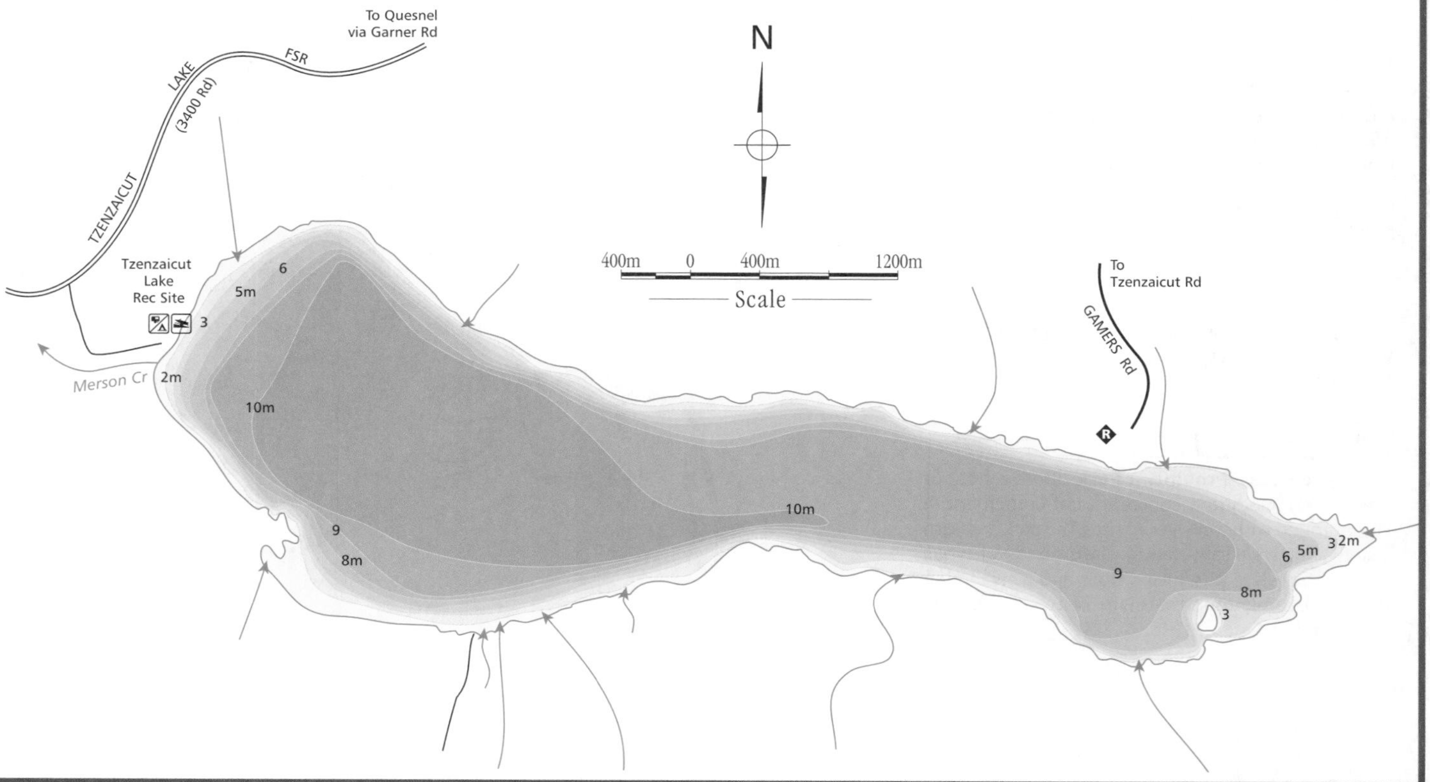

To Quesnel via Garner Rd
TZENZAICUT LAKE FSR (3400 Rd)
N
400m 0 400m 1200m
Scale
Tzenzaicut Lake Rec Site
Merson Cr
To Tzenzaicut Rd
GAMERS Rd
5m 6 3 2m 10m 9 8m 10m 9 6 5m 3 2m 8m 3

Valentine Lake

Location: 12 km (7.5 mi) southwest of 100 Mile House
Elevation: 1,243 m (4,078 ft)
Surface Area: 56 ha (138 ac)
Maximum Depth: 15 m (48 ft)
Mean Depth: 5 m (16 ft)
Way Point: 51° 35′ 8.2″ N, 121° 26′ 56.6″ W

Fishing

Valentine Lake is a popular, fly-fishing only destination found southwest of 100 Mile House. The Freshwater Fisheries Society of BC stocks the lake with 10,000 rainbow trout annually, each year ensuring a healthy trout population.

The lake is considered a trophy lake as it is nutrient rich and the fish grow rapidly. Trout over 4 kg (8 lbs) are reported on occasion. Of course, the average catch is much smaller than that. It should also be noted that in dry years the lake (and fishery) suffers because it becomes too alkaline.

The lake rests a bit higher than the average Cariboo lake, meaning the fishing doesn't really get going here until late May to early June. And just to rub it in, the lake is quite shallow and the lake water warms in the summer months so fishing becomes rather slow by late July and into August. By late September to early October, the fishing begins to improve again. This leaves a relatively small window of opportunity to find one of the lake's trophy trout on the fly.

But be forewarned, the big fish are rather difficult to trick and fishing here can be rather slow. The lake is deep enough to drag around a Doc Spratley or Carey Special or other attractor-type fly. Green or darker colours work best. The northwestern bay is a good area to fish as it is sheltered from the winds and working the fringe near the deep hole at this end of the lake can be productive.

The same holds true for anglers planning on casting from shore or their belly boat. When the sun is high or the water is warm, these fish hold up in the deeper holes (also the one at the southwest bay and at the south end) as they feel safer. They can then cruise into the shallows in search of food.

Fly fishers concentrate on the shallow areas around these holes and present black or green chironomid patterns on floating lines and long leaders or strike indicators to fool fish. As the water warms and the fish move to deeper water, fish leech or dragonfly patterns along the drop offs. When the fish are on the surface, a Tom Thumb or beetle pattern can be a lot of fun. As always, it is best to check with the local tackle shop on what is working before heading out.

In addition to the aforementioned artificial fly only regulation, there is an electric motor only restriction at the lake and an ice fishing restriction.

Area Indicator

Exeter
FSR
Exeter Lake
100 Mile House
GUSTAFSEN
LAKE (1100 Rd)
97
Edmund Lake
Valentine Lake
900 Rd
93 Mile
Keith Lake

Valentine Lake			
Fish Stocking Data			
Year	Species	Number	Life Stage
2008	Rainbow Trout	10,000	Yearling
2007	Rainbow Trout	10,000	Yearling
2006	Rainbow Trout	9,000	Yearling

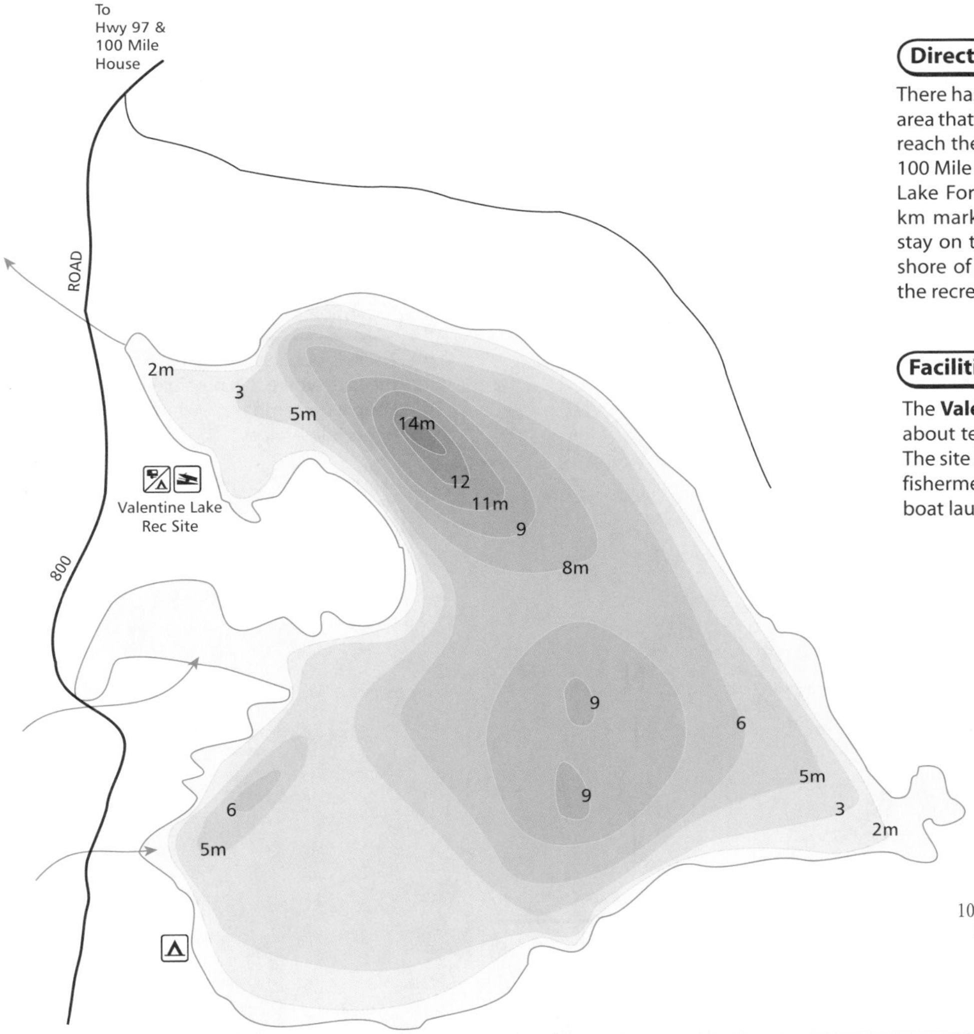

To Hwy 97 & 100 Mile House
ROAD
800
Valentine Lake Rec Site
2m
3
5m
14m
12
11m
9
8m
9
6
9
5m
3
2m
6
5m
N
100m 0 100m 200m 300m
— Scale —

Directions

There has been some recent logging activity in the area that has altered the access route somewhat. To reach the lake head west on the Exeter Road from 100 Mile House. That road turns into the Gustafsen Lake Forest Service Road (1100 Rd). At the 1108 km mark, head south onto the 800 Road. If you stay on the main road, it will lead by the western shore of the lake, providing fairly good access to the recreation site.

Facilities

The **Valentine Lake Recreation Site** has room for about ten campsites in the forest next to the lake. The site is popular with hunters in the fall as well as fishermen throughout the spring and fall. A cartop boat launch and picnic tables are found at the site.

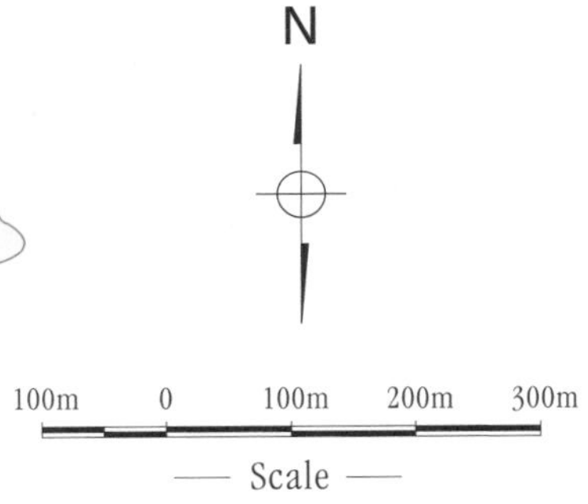

Location: 15 km (9 mi) north of Houston
Elevation: 803 m (2,634 ft)
Surface Area: 1.5 ha (3.7 ac)
Maximum Depth: 4 m (13 ft)
Mean Depth: 1.7 m (5.6 ft)
Way Point: 54° 28′ 49.8″ N, 126° 45′ 11.5″

Vallee (Johnson) Lake

Area Indicator

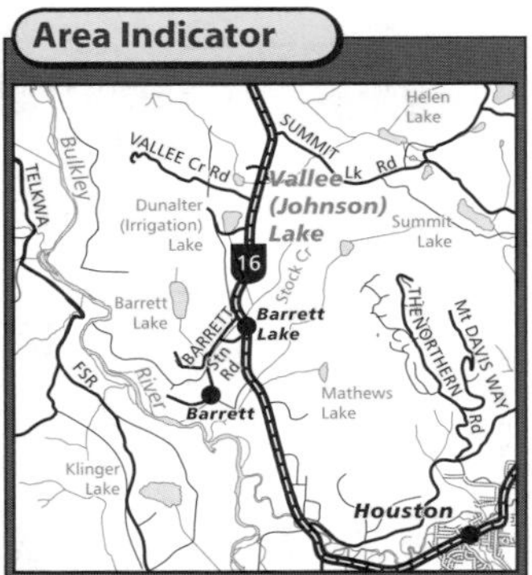

Vallee (Johnson) Lake			
Fish Stocking Data			
Year	Species	Number	Life Stage
2008	Rainbow Trout	2,000	Fingerling
2007	Rainbow Trout	2,000	Fingerling
2006	Cutthroat Trout	2,000	Yearling

Fishing

Vallee Lake, also known as Johnson Lake, sports a consistent track record of giving up fish for anglers. Up until 2006, it was stocked with 2,000 yearling cutthroat trout each year by the Freshwater Fisheries Society of BC, but as of 2007, the lake is now being stocked with rainbow trout. There is also a small population of non-sportfish.

The largest cutthroat captured in a recent biological assessment was 42 cm (16 in), while the average size was 30 cm (12 in). It is hoped that by planting sterile Fraser Valley rainbow trout that these trout will grow to similar sizes.

Vallee's small surface makes it a good lake for trolling, spincasting and fly-fishing. Dense aquatic vegetation around the lake's perimeter virtually eliminates the possibility of fishing from shore, but trolling using Apex Trout Killer, Triple Teaser and Needlefish spoons, in addition to Wedding Bands or the small Gibbs Willow Leaf trolls is effective. Fly anglers will find that leeches are perhaps the best searching pattern when exploring a new lake or fishing during non-hatch periods. Black, brown, olive green or maroon leeches, tied in many of the common commercial patterns found in tackle shops, are good choices at Vallee. One tried-and-true imitation is a No. 10 beadhead micro leech in black with a touch of red. Leech patterns work particularly well in the evenings, during the spring immediately after ice-off and again in the late fall as fish prowl the shallows before winter.

Yet even in the high heat of summer, a leech pattern worked slow and deep can provide steady action. Some fly anglers use a fairly slow hand-twist retrieve to imitate the leech's natural, undulating swimming motion.

A chironomid imitation on a floating line and a long leader can be very effective early in the season and again in the fall. In June, caddis, mayflies, damsels and dragons start to hatch and some great fishing can be had using an intermediate or full-sink line. A selection of gold-ribbed hare's ear, sparkle caddis pupa, damsel and dragonfly nymphs, Doc Spratleys, '52 Buicks and some shrimp patterns will take care of most of your sub-surface opportunities. Be sure to have a few dries ready for top-water action and include the world's best-selling dry fly, the Adams, among them. Tom Thumbs and elk-hair caddis, in a variety of colours and sizes, will complete the dry fly selection.

Ice fishing is a popular winter activity at Vallee. Most anglers use smaller ice-fishing jigs tipped with a Berkley Powerbait grub or worm. The lake is very shallow around the edge, so make sure you drill your hole in at least 1.5–3 metres (5–10 feet) of water.

Directions 

From Houston, drive northwest on the Yellowhead Highway (Highway 16) for about 15 km towards Smithers. Turn left (west) on Barrett Hat Road and follow this road for 800 metres to the unmarked road branching right. Access to the lake is 100 metres down this road.

Facilities 

There is public access area at the southeast end of the lake where it is possible to launch small boats. People do camp here, while Houston to the south offers full services.

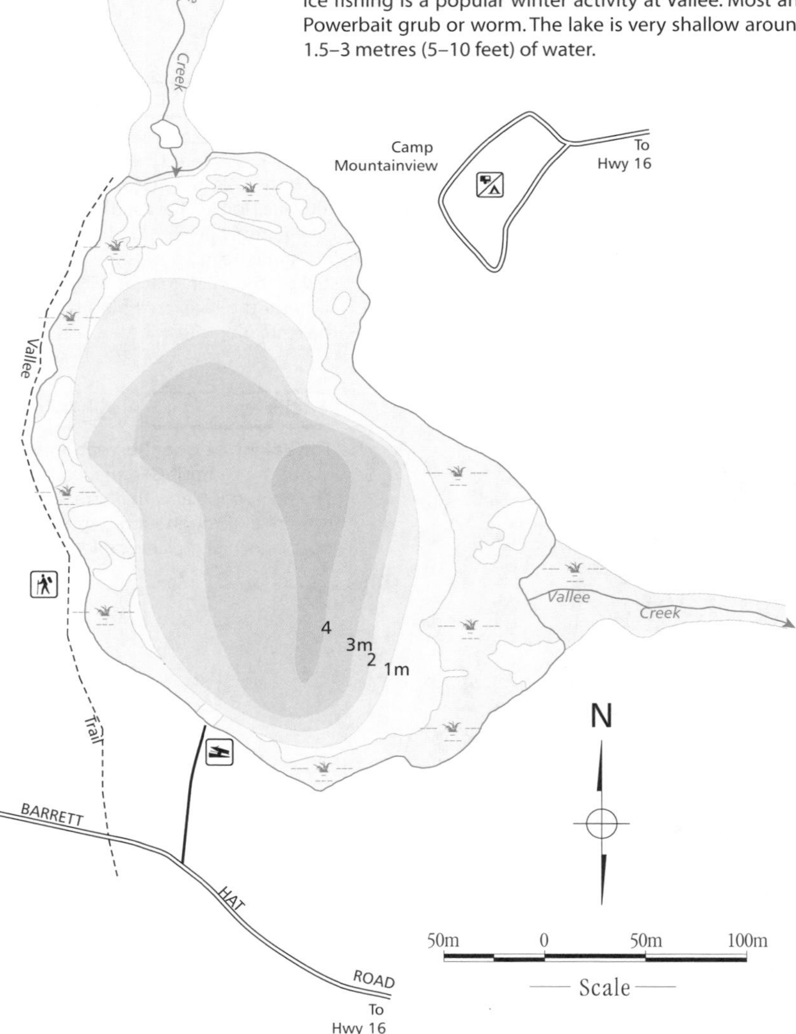

Wartig Lake

Location: 120 km (74.5 mi) northeast of Williams Lake
Elevation: 1,163 m (3,816 ft)
Surface Area: 51 ha (127 ac)
Maximum Depth: 30 m (97 ft)
Mean Depth: 8.3 m (27 ft)
Way Point: 52° 33′ 16″ N, 120° 34′ 46″ W

Fishing

As far as Cariboo lakes are considered, they do not get much further out there than Wartig Lake. The lake is found a long ways from civilization and does not see the crowds other lakes do. This helps the lake maintain a good population of naturally reproducing rainbow trout. It was last stocked in the early 1980's.

The success of the rainbow has to do with the good spawning found in a pair of creeks on the west side of the lake. The lake is also not infested by the course fish common to many of the other lakes in the Cariboo.

Visitors will find this is a surprisingly deep lake (in areas), making it a good trolling lake. As usual, most people who troll use a lake troll, followed by a Wedding Band or something similar. For lighter trolling, use flies, a Hot Shot, or Flatfish. Troll slowly along the edge of the drop off, keeping the deep water on one side of your boat and the shallow water on the other side. You will want your lure down into the thermocline, where the fish hang out and near the bottom as rainbow trout usually feed within a few metres (a few feet) of the bottom.

The southern part and the middle of the lake are both very shallow and ideal areas for insects and aquatic invertebrates rearing. This is where most fly anglers focus. The lake features traditional Cariboo hatches, starting with Chironomids and moving towards Dragon and Damselflies. As a general rule, the earlier in the year you're fishing, the shallower the hatches will occur, as the hatches occur when the sun warms the bottom of the lake up to a certain temperature.

Two deeper holes are found in the lake, one at the southwestern end and one at the northeastern end. The drop off areas around the deeper water are good spots to troll or cast small trout lures. Spincasters should try perennial favourites like a Mepps, Panther Martin, Vibrax or Gibbs spinner. The drop offs around notable structure or feeder and outlet streams are idea as these areas usually provide good food source for the opportunistic trout.

Facilities

The **Wartig Lake Recreation Site** is found on the southern shores of the lake. It offers several lakeside camping spots together with a cartop boat launch.

Directions

To reach Wartig Lake involves a long drive from Highway 97. Drivers should be alert for industrial traffic as the last portion of the road is narrow and rough in places. A copy of the *Cariboo Chilcotin Coast Backroad Mapbook* a GPS and four wheel drive vehicle will be a boon on the backroads.

From the highway follow the paved Horsefly Road to the small town of Horsefly. Just before entering the town of Horsefly, cross the bridge over the Horsefly River and begin the drive on the Black Creek Road. That logging road is a well-maintained road so a car can travel along it without much trouble.

Continue past Black Creek and the airport and past the Crooked Lake Road turn-off. Towards the end of the Black Creek Road, the Bouldery Creek Road (6100 Rd) heads northwest. Continue along that road past Horsefly Lake and Bouldery Creek to Wartig Lake.

Area Indicator

Quesnel Lake
Wartig Lake
(6100 Rd)
CREEK
BOULDREY
To Horsefly

Location: 24 km (15 mi) southeast of 100 Mile House
Elevation: 1,077 m (3,534 ft)
Surface Area: 261 ha (645 ac)
Maximum Depth: 10 m (33 ft)
Mean Depth: 4.3 m (14 ft)
Way Point: 51° 27′ 39″ N, 121° 6′ 14″ W

Watch Lake

Area Indicator

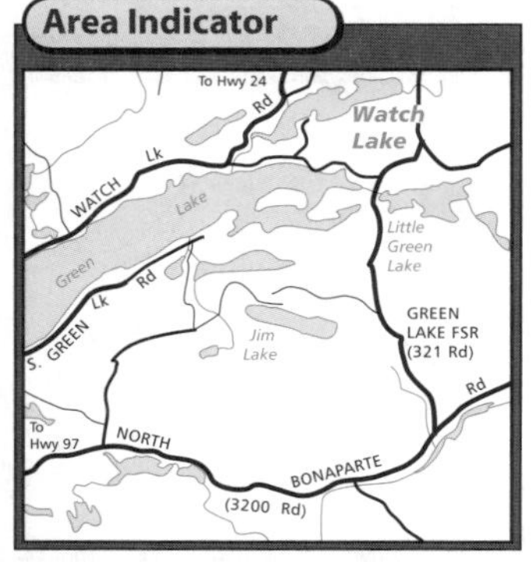

Watch Lake Fish Stocking Data			
Year	Species	Number	Life Stage
2008	Rainbow Trout	40,000	Yearling
2007	Rainbow Trout	40,000	Yearling
2006	Rainbow Trout	40,000	Yearling

Fishing

Watch Lake is found at the heart of an extremely popular recreation area that bears its name (along with nearby Green Lake). The lake has good numbers of rainbow in the 0.5 kg (1 lb) range caught by fly-fishing or spincasting. While that is the average sized catch, rainbow are occasionally caught to 3.5 kg (7 lbs). The record catch in the lake was 5.5 kg (12.25 lbs).

Being such a popular destination, the lake is stocked annually with 40,000 rainbow trout by the Freshwater Fisheries Society of BC. These trout have come from a variety of strains or sources over the years, from Blackwater to Green to Badger to Tzenzaicut. For the last few years, the lake has been stocked with Pennask strain trout, which are famous for their hard fighting ways and their acrobatic leaps into the air as they try to shake the lure.

The lake is fairly big and long, but not extremely deep. Because of the shallowness of the lake, the waters do warm up considerably in summer, meaning the best times to fish the lake are from the early part of May until mid July and then mid August to October. The lake freezes over by the end of November and the ice comes off around mid-April.

If you pick your lanes, the lake can be trolled. There are two distinct holes on the lake, one at each end. The trout usually inhabit a narrow band of water just below the warm water on the surface called the thermocline and where the thermocline and the bottom of the lake intersect is where you are most likely to find the trout, especially if there is a good food source. Working the edge of the drop off around the shoals with a lake troll or common trout lure will prove to be productive.

The lake has numerous bays meaning that fly anglers can find a sheltered area from the prevailing winds to use a belly boat. Work the near shore area with a chironomid imitation in the early spring or a damselfly or dragonfly nymph later in the spring. The two sunken islands nearby to the west end of the lake are particularly good spots to try.

The lodges boast that the lake is a quiet lake with no water skiers or speedboats. There is a speed restriction at the lake of less than 8 kph (5 mph) and a motor restriction of 9.9 hp.

Directions

Watch Lake is a popular recreation lake found to the southeast of 100 Mile House. The lake is accessed in several directions via paved roads. From the Cariboo Highway (Highway 97) at 70 Mile House, the Green Lake Road leads to the bigger lake to the south. Continue along the north shore of the big lake until you reach the Watch Lake Road. From Highway 24 at Lone Butte, turn south onto the Watch Lake Road and follow that road to Watch Lake.

Facilities

There are a trio of resorts on the lake, including **Aces High Resort**, the **Tall Timbers Resort** and **Watch Lake Lodge.** These three resorts offer a variety of services, including cabins to rent, RV/camping spots, boats to rent and more. For folks looking to stay at a provincial park, there are a number of campsites at nearby Green Lake.

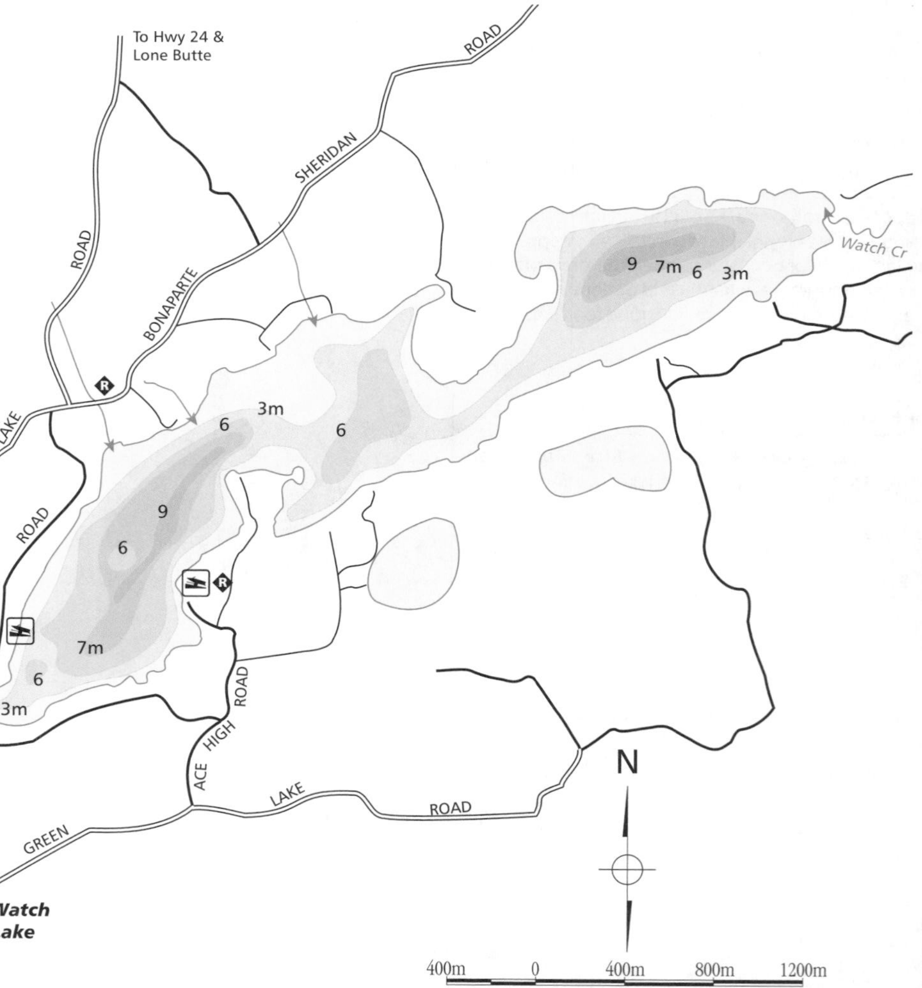

Wavey Lake

Location: 50 km (31 mi) east of 100 Mile House
Elevation: 1,223 m (4,013 ft)
Surface Area: 91 ha (225 ac)
Maximum Depth: 35 m (115 ft)
Mean Depth: 11 m (34 ft)
Way Point: 51° 32′ 28″ N, 120° 34′ 59″ W

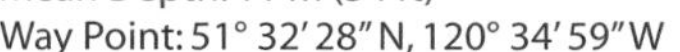

Fishing

Wavey Lake is another in a series of great fishing lakes found off Highway 24, the so-called Fishing Highway. Found due north of Lac des Roches, Wavey is much smaller than the bigger lakes along the highway. It also sits at slightly higher than average elevation. This means that the ice isn't off the lake until a week or two later than the average Cariboo Lake. Give the lake a few more weeks to turn over and you have a fishing season that starts on the lake as late as early June, but usually late May.

However, the elevation and the deepness of the lake means the fishing in the summer months is better at this lake than most others. Wavey Lake is about 35 metres (83 feet) deep and contains close to 30 hectares of shoal area. These shoals are ideal rearing habitat for the rainbow's food source, insects. And while the lake doesn't have any singular hatch, it does feature good insect hatches through the ice off-season.

One of the best ways to fish the lake is with a chironomid or bloodworm pattern. The bloodworm is the larva of the chironomid and is a favorite food with the trout. Most people fish chironomids with a full sink line and a strike indicator set so that the pattern hangs a few feet above bottom. The line is then retrieved extremely slowly, or even let out to allow the wind to push it around. Chironomids are not fast movers and chironomid fishing can be about as exciting as watching paint dry when the fish aren't biting, but it is a very subtle form of fishing that can be very rewarding.

Besides, the trout are usually biting, as the lake offers fast fishing for smaller rainbow with a 1 kg (2 lb) trout being a trophy. The lake also has some course fish (suckers, squawfish and redside shiners).

The trolling is best at the southern end of the lake as the water is deepest in that location. Try circling the drop off area around the inflow and outflow creeks. Towards the summer months, focus out from shore in the deeper water.

Spincasters and fly anglers should work the near shore areas. Just off the shoal areas near the north and south ends of the lake look particularly inviting.

Facilities

Wavey Lake Lodge is a rustic resort with both cabins and a lodge to enjoy. It is also possible to launch a small boat at the lake and to camp off the roadway.

Other Options

Around Wavey Lake there are numerous small fishing lakes. Each of the lakes offers good fishing for rainbow. The fish tend to be quite small in spring but they fatten up nicely over the year. Float tubes are well suited for most of the lakes.

Directions

Wavey Lake is found to the northeast of Bridge Lake. To reach the lake, travel along the Fishing Highway (Highway 24) eastbound past Bridge Lake to Lac des Roches. The Wavey Lake Forest Service Road (2000 Rd) leads north. About 7 km later, you will come to the access road leading to the lakeshore. A truck is recommended to reach the lake, especially after spring break-up.

Area Indicator

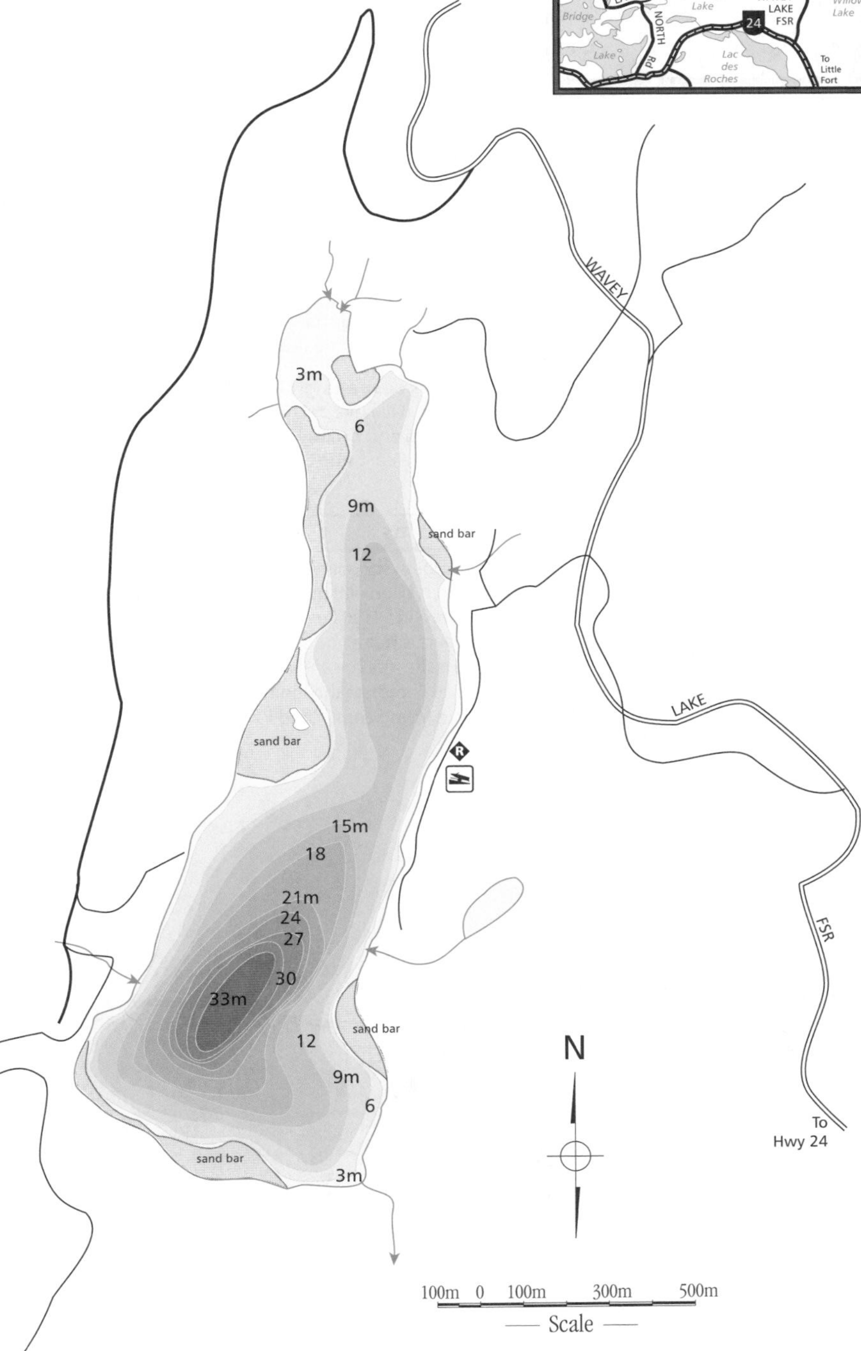

Location: East of Williams Lake
Elevation: 571 m (1,873 ft)
Surface Area: 723 ha (1,787 ac)
Maximum Depth: 24 m (79 ft)
Mean Depth: 12 m (39 ft)
Way Point: 52° 7′ 3″ N, 122° 4′ 5″ W

Williams Lake

Area Indicator

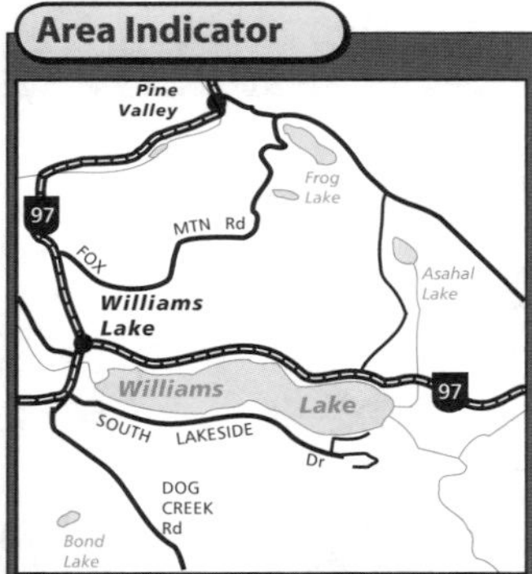

Fishing

Williams Lake is the large lake next to Highway 97 as you drive into the town that bears the same name. It is one of the easiest lakes to access in the Cariboo and as a result is one of the most popular.

Williams Lake is also one of the lowest elevation lakes in the Cariboo, at 567 metres (1,860 ft) above sea level. As a result, it provides one of the earliest fisheries in the Cariboo. The lake becomes clear of ice as early as late April and fishing begins by May.

The early spring is the best time to fish the lake, as the fish are most active then. By the summer months, the fishing is very poor and it is not until late in the fall that there is activity again

Williams Lake contains a few kokanee, burbot, whitefish and rainbow. There are also plenty of course fish such as suckers, redside shiners and squawfish. The rainbow have been stocked in the bigger lake periodically since the 1920s. Kokanee were stocked in the lake in 1987 and again in 1998, which is the last time anything was stocked in the lake.

The lake is 24 metres (79 feet) deep so it is well suited for trolling. In fact, since the fish are rather sparse, your best bet is to troll to help cover some area. Wind can also deter from the float tube or canoe experience.

Most people who fish the lake are looking for rainbow or kokanee and both fish rather similar. The best way to catch either is using a lake troll followed by a Wedding Band tipped with a worm. Because there is a good chance you will catch a mix of both fish, a rubber snubber is a good thing to use. This helps reduce the shock of setting the hook when you catch a kokanee. Kokanee have soft mouths and it is far too easy to tear the hook right out when setting the hook. This is, needless to say, quite hard on the fish and should be avoided.

Kokanee, unlike rainbow trout, tend to school. If you find one kokanee, chances are you've found a whole bunch, so working the same area can often be productive.

The lake is deepest right in the middle with the shallow areas being at the west and east end of the lake. Shore fishermen will have a difficult time finding a good place to cast given the private property that surrounds the lake. Spincasters and fly anglers should stick around the shallows at the west and east ends of the lake. A good place to try is off the east side of Scout Island, near the west end of the lake.

Directions

The northern shoreline, where Highway 97 passes by the lake, is filled with private residences. The southern shoreline is accessed by the South Lakeside Drive and is not as populated. The west end of the lake is quite marshy and offers a nice park while the east end is part of the Indian Reserve. Most access the lake from Scout Island Park at the west end.

Facilities

The city of Williams Lake, at the west end of the lake, has full facilities ranging from tackle shops to gas stations to motels. **Scout Island Park** is also found on the west end of the lake. It is a popular waterfowl viewing area and beach. The park provides picnic tables, toilets and access to the lake.

400m 0 400m 800m 1200m 1600m
Scale

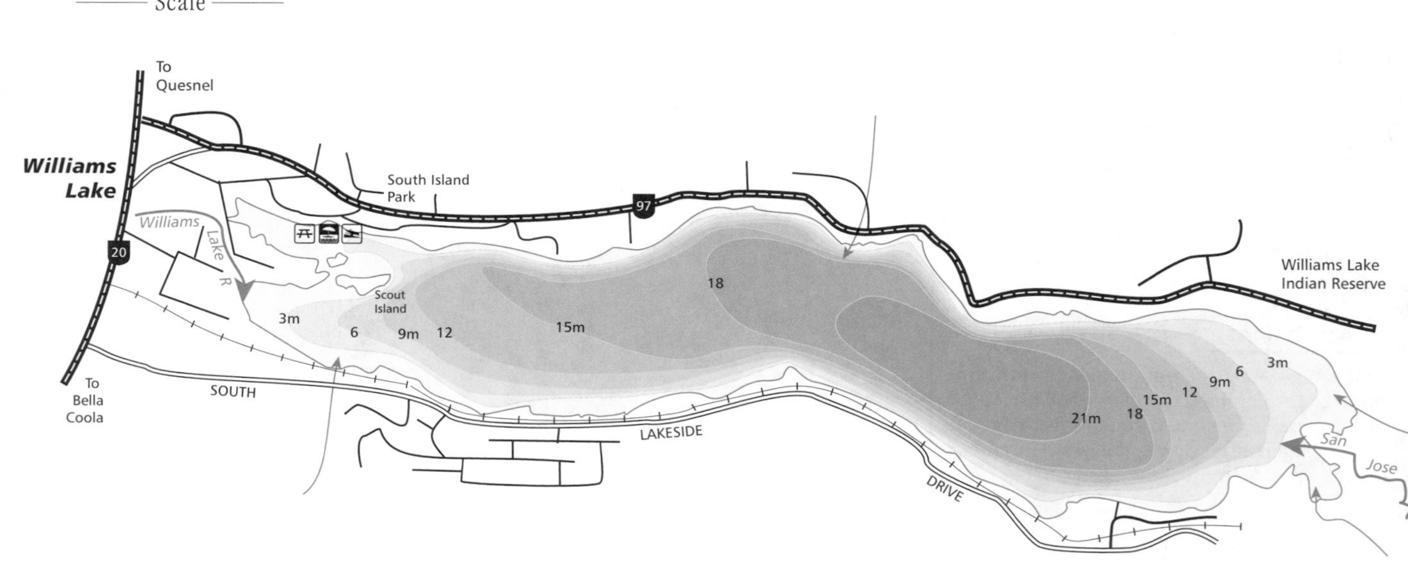

Fishing Tips & Techniques

In addition to the tips under each fish species, we have provided more tips and techniques below. This section is designed to give you a better understanding of the various types of fishing styles as well as a much more elaborate breakdown on fly-fishing. Whether new to the sport of fishing or a wily veteran, we recommend reading through this section to pick a few tricks. We also recommend stopping in at the local tackle shop before heading out. They are the ones that know the local tricks and what has been producing well recently.

Bait (Still) Fishing

Probably the simplest way to catch fish and introduce young people or novice anglers to sport fishing is by a technique known as still fishing. When still fishing from the shore or a boat, the angler casts out and waits for a bite. Still fishing can be done with or without the use of float. Floats (bobbers) can be attached to the line so the baited hook stays suspended in the water. The depth can be adjusted by simply sliding the float up or down the line.

In smaller lakes, a one metre (3–5 ft) leader with a size 8–12 hook is recommended. Weights should be avoided if possible, as they tend to scare off the fish. Most fish tend to bite on worms and a single egg or roe. Other effective baits include maggots or artificial bait such as powerbait. Use the lightest line and smallest hook possible for the size of fish you are trying to catch.

Ice Fishing

Many of the large, low elevation lakes do not ice up, and many high elevation lakes are not accessible. However, there are still quite a few places to try ice fishing in the area. Generally speaking, ice fishing is possible from the end of December through to early March as long as the ice is safe (there will need to be at least 15 cm/6 in of ice to bear weight safely). Jigging a small spoon or other attractant lure up and down has become one of the most popular fishing methods since live bait is not permitted in BC.

While rainbow slow down in cold water, burbot and eastern brook trout need less oxygen and remain active throughout the winter.

Jigging

Jigging can be an effective method of fishing if you can find where the fish are congregating. Jigging is essentially sitting in a prime location, such as near underwater structure and working a jig head and body up and down to entice strikes. Outside of the traditional jig head and (where permitted) bait set up, you will also see anglers jigging spoons and other similar type lures.

Spincasting

Spincasting is another popular and effective fishing method for all types of water. Essentially, spincasting is the process of casting a line from a rod with a spinning reel. The set up is quite simple making it easy for anyone to learn how to fish and have fun at it. The key is to have line light enough to cast and tough enough to withstand fighting and landing some fairly large fish. A good idea is to get an open face reel with removable spools. One spool could have light line (6 lb test or lighter) for small lakes and another have heavier line (8 lb or higher) for rivers and trolling.

Trolling

Trolling is the mainstay of bigger lakes, but also a popular alternative for many smaller lakes. Ideally you should use a longer, stiffer rod than traditional spincasting set ups. Eight-pound test is okay for small lakes but you will need heavier line for bigger lakes, especially if using a downrigger.

It is best to troll near structure, along the drop-off or near a mid-lake shallow, such as a sunken island. On larger lakes, trolling for rainbow is very effective. Concentrate on points, inflow creeks or bays. A depth chart or depth finder will help you pinpoint these locations.

Lake trolls are popular because of their effectiveness and ease of use on both big and small lakes. These usually consist of a Willow Leaf or Ford Fender with a short leader and a small lure like a Wedding Band or similar along with bait where allowed. There are many shapes, sizes and colours of lures that have proven effective trolling for trout and dollies. Some of the most common trolling lures include Flatfish, Krocodile or Little Cleo spoons. Fly fishers usually troll a leech pattern, particularly in murky water. Other all purpose trolling flies are Carey Specials, Woolly Buggers, and Doc Spratleys. Work the area just off the drop-off in

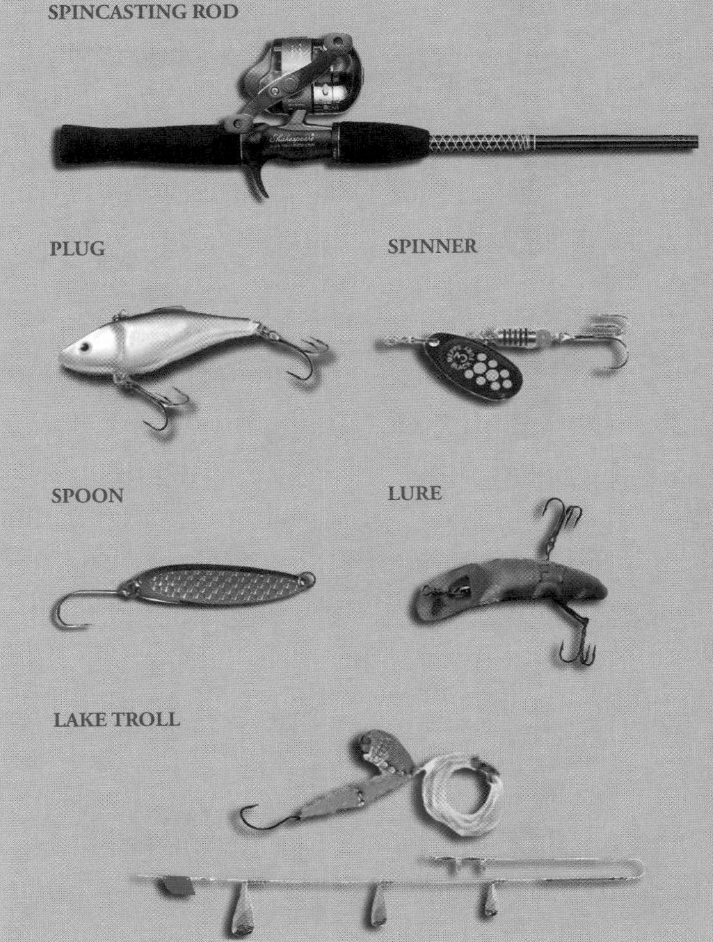

a figure-eight pattern to vary the direction, depth and speed of the fly.

When trolling for cutthroat, try a silver Muddler Minnow or other baitfish patterns. In the fall or winter, troll a streamer type fly pattern like a bucktail quickly behind the boat. As the water warms, try an Apex, Lyman plug or flasher with a hoochie in the 10–30 m (30–90 ft) depth for bigger fish.

On larger lakes, trolling for rainbow is very effective. Concentrate on points, inflow creeks or bays. In the fall or winter, troll a streamer type fly pattern like a bucktail quickly behind the boat. As the water warms, try an Apex, Lyman plug or flasher with a hoochie in the 10–30 m (30–90 ft) depth for bigger fish. For deep trolling, downriggers with the aid of a heavy weight will enable you to troll your lure deep enough to find holding areas. Alternatively, lead core line or similar set-ups allow you to get your presentation down deeper without having to use downrigging equipment.

Fishing Tips & Techniques

Fly-fishing is easily the most popular or at least most talked about fishing method of fishing in BC. It is also the hardest technique to master. Perhaps it is the challenge that attracts so many people to devote so much time. Or maybe it is the fact that once you have caught a fish on fly gear, everything else pales in comparison. Whether it is a small trout or an acrobatic salmon, the shear excitement of landing a fish with fly-fishing gear is exhilarating.

FLY FISHING ROD

BEAD-HEAD NYMPH

CAREY SPECIAL

CHIRONOMID

ELK HAIR CADDIS

DOC SPRATLEY

MUDDLER MINNOW

Fly-Fishing

Fly-fishing is easily the most popular or at least most talked about fishing method of fishing in BC. It is also the hardest technique to master. Perhaps it is the challenge that attracts so many people to devote so much time. Or maybe it is the fact that once you have caught a fish on fly gear, everything else pales in comparison. Whether it is a small trout or an acrobatic salmon, the shear excitement of landing a fish with fly-fishing gear is exhilarating.

Fly-Fishing Equipment

Basically, there are three parts to a fly-fishing outfit: the rod, the reel and the line. Rods come in a variety of lengths and weights, depending on your size and the size of the species you intend to fish. As an example, a 9 ft, 6-weight rod would be an ideal set up for everything from trout to salmon up to about 5 kg (11 lb) in size. Longer rods are helpful in casting and helping manipulate flies into position on streams, especially on rivers and streams.

To handle bigger fish, fly anglers need a much heavier rod such as an 8 or 9-weight rod. Many fly anglers will have at least two if not three or more rods of different size and weight in order to maximize their fishing experience. Essentially, a smaller size and weight rod would be used for fishing small trout or panfish, while the longer heavier rod would be used on rivers for big salmon.

When picking up a fly reel, the vast majority of reels (or any that are worth buying) will be weighted similar to the way rods are weighted. The reels are actually made to fit the appropriated rod. The difference in the weights of reels is mainly the size of the reel, since larger rods will be loaded with thicker line; therefore, the reel has to be a little larger to hold the increased line size. Also, the reel itself is often physically weighted to suit the rod weight so that the casting motion is balanced properly when casting your fly line.

When fly-fishing lakes, it is necessary to have a floating line in addition to a medium or fast sinking line. The floating line presents dry flies, as well as sub-surface wet flies. Dry line can also work well with weighted wet flies. However, a more popular subsurface option is using sink tip line, which is a combination of sinking and floating line where just the end of the fly line sinks. This type of line has a number of advantages, one being the ability to present subsurface flies while retaining the visibility of the fly line on the surface. This helps dramatically in spotting strikes, especially when fishing for trout. One of the best times to surface fish is during the mayfly and caddis hatches, however, trout usually prefer streamers and subsurface flies since they are very reluctant to strike the top of the water.

Medium sinking lines are ideal for fishing wet flies such as nymphs or chironomid pupae near the bottom. The medium sinking line offers the best control when attempting to fish a specific depth. If you do not have a medium sinking line, you can use a longer leader with some weight on your dry line. With a properly weighted fly or leader, this method can produce similar results. This type of presentation is ideal for working a particular depth, such as along a drop-off or along weed beds. Dragonfly, damselfly and even leech patterns can be worked quite effectively this way.

Fast sinking lines are ideal for trolling. If you are not familiar with the lake, trolling a fly is a good way to start. This allows you to cover a lot of distance searching for the ideal spot on the lake. Also, trolling is most effective on lakes with a low population of fish or during the summer doldrums. Woolly Buggers, streamers and leeches are all good all purpose trolling flies. Work the area just off the drop-off in a figure-eight pattern to vary the direction, depth and speed of the fly.

Regardless of which line you run with, you will also need backing and leader. The backing is designed to fill up the spool, as well as to act as reserve for when that fish goes on a 100 metre dash. Most people keep 100–150 metres of backing on their reel. The leader is a thinner monofilament line that attaches the thick fly line to the fly. Leaders have a thicker butt that tapers to a thin tippet.

Flies

There are numerous books on fly-fishing techniques and how to choose the best fly for the particular season; however, it is really quite simple. Match the hatch! What you want to do is use a fly that most approximates the insect or baitfish on which the sportfish are feeding.

To determine this, spend some time observing the aquatic insects at the lake and try to determine what the fish are rising to. If you cannot see the adult insect on the water surface then try using a small fine net to scoop up the insects. If you catch a fish, you can also use a throat pump to physically see what the fish are eating. Once you have discovered what type of insect the fish are feeding on, you should try to determine how the insect moves in the water so you can imitate it. For example, is the adult insect sitting motionless on the water or is it rapidly flapping its wings?

Here is a list of recommended flies to include in your fly box. By no means is this exhaustive, but rather a good base to work from:

Fishing Tips & Techniques

Beadhead Nymph is a variation of the halfback or pheasant tail nymph patterns, but is often a little more versatile. The fly is already weighted so it can be fished easily in streams and lakes with either sinking or floating line. The bead head also is an attractant that often glistens in the water attracting attention of predatory fish.

Carey Special is versatile enough to be used in both lakes and streams. Try size 4-8 for trout or 6-12 for salmon in red, green or brown. One of the most popular lake patterns in BC, it is a great searching pattern that can simulate many insects, including dragonfly, mayfly and caddis nymphs, as well as leeches. Smaller flies using a simple strip retrieve with sinking line is best in lakes, while moving water requires a bigger fly that is drifted with quicker strips.

Chironomids or midges have become one of the most important flies in the fly box of a BC lake angler. Chironomids can be found in every lake in the BC and varies in size and colour depending on the lake and time of year. The fly must always be worked very slowly in the part of the water column that depends on what stage of the main hatch is taking place. During the spring, it is best to fucus just off bottom with a pupa imitation that matches the colour of the lake bottom.

Doc Spratley is a general-purpose fly that can imitate most insects and a number of leeches. Perhaps the most popular fly in BC, the large sizes can imitate the dragonfly or damselfly nymphs, while smaller versions are like chironomid pupae. Black is the most versatile, but red, green and brown work, too. Depending on what you want to imitate dictates the method of presenting this fly. If you are looking to imitate a dragonfly nymph, stripping the fly in a consistent manner would be appropriate. On the other hand if you are looking to imitate a smaller nymph pattern, a shorter stripping retrieve may be required.

Dragon and **Damselfly Nymphs** vary in size and colour and are a great alternative when other hatches are not on. Black or light green patterns worked deep and even off bottom seem to be the norm for dragonflies, while damselflies are better still fished. Favourites include a '52 Buick.

Elk Hair Caddis is a fly that revolutionized top water caddis fly fishing. Depending on the time of year your presentations will vary with this type of fly. In the early part of the season, hatching caddis will often flap along the surface attempting to break away. Later in the season when caddis are laying eggs, they will literally smack the water and trout will pounce on them. Your presentation should imitate the look and what the fly is doing.

Leeches are a definite must in every fly box since they are found in virtually all lakes in BC. Leech patterns are versatile and great for searching lakes on the troll, especially murky lakes with lilly pads. Even if trout are feeding on something else, they will rarely pass up a well-presented leech.

Mayfly patterns vary dramatically in size and colour. During a hatch, trout can sometimes be so picky that they will literally pass up your mayfly if it is a size or two too small or a wrong colour. However, the mayfly hatch is a big part of the open water season and a good variety of this fly is needed in your box, especially early in the season.

Muddler Minnow imitates a minnow in distress and is the ideal meal for a wide variety of fish. In general, larger fish seem to like bigger presentations of this fly. The fly is mainly worked below the surface although some anglers have been known to put floatant on them and work them on or just below the top of the water for big aggressive fish.

Scud (Shrimp) patterns, similar to chironomids, vary greatly in size and colour depending on the lake. A good rule of thumb is to use whatever colour the lake bottom is (usually green or olive). Working the fly needs patience. It should be allowed to sink close to the bottom and retrieved with slow short strips followed by a short pause. Working closer to shore is better, since shrimp are most often found frolicking here in the evening.

Salmon and steelhead prefer bigger and bolder patterns. Although the names may be the same as those used for trout, it is often just the size that changes. Of course adding a bit of sparkle or brighter colours never hurts as many of the streams run murky.

Terrestrials like flying ants, grasshoppers and more recently the pine beetle are a lot of fun to fish during the summer. Work a dry fly on the surface that resembles the shape, size and colour of those flying around you.

Tom Thumb is one of the more popular dry flies in British Columbia. Size is very important to match the current hatch, especially if surface fishing. While the fly can imitate a number of different insects, it is most commonly used as a caddis imitation.

Waterboatmen or water bugs looks like beetles. Smaller flies are best during mid-day just after ice-off to mid-May. Try larger flies in September. Using a weighted fly on a dryline try to work the fly in an up & down movement. A dry fly on the surface can also work.

Woolly Bugger is a good versatile pattern for salmon, steelhead and trout. This fly imitates larger meals such as a baitfish or leeches and can be effective in both streams and lakes. The most popular colours are olive and black, with or without a beadhead.

Fishing Tips & Techniques

Northern BC Hatches: From ice-on to ice-off, fly patterns of choice should coincide with these major hatches. Remember that hatches are weather and location dependant. Hatches occur later the further north and the higher in elevation the lake is. But as a general rule, chironomid hatches start in April, peak in mid May and continue through June before returning at the end of September and through October. The next insect to hatch is the mayfly, which traditionally runs from May through to fall. Damselfly patterns are effective in June to August while dragonfly patterns can be used from May to the end of September. Evenings from mid-June to early July can produce some exciting top water action for caddisflies, while terrestrials, such as ants, grasshoppers and beetles, hatch through the summer. Water boatman are best right after ice-off and again in September and October. Finally, shrimp and leech patterns can be productive all year round, as there is not a set hatch period for them. Big dragon and damselfly nymphs can also be effective if there is not another hatch on.

April:
- •Chironomid larvae
- •Damselfly nymph
- •Dragonfly nymph
- •Leeches
- •Shrimp
- •Water boatman

May:
- •All chironomid stages
- •Dragonfly nymph
- •Mayfly nymph
- •Leeches
- •Shrimp
- •Water boatman

June:
- •All chironomid stages
- •Caddisfly pupae
- •Damselfly nymph
- •Dragonfly nymph
- •Mayfly nymph
- •Leeches
- •Shrimp
- •Terrestrials

July:
- • All chironomid stages
- •Caddisfly
- •Damselfly
- •Dragonfly
- •Mayfly
- •Leeches
- •Shrimp
- •Terrestrials

August:
- •Caddisfly
- •Damselfly
- •Dragonfly
- •Mayfly
- •Leeches
- •Shrimp
- •Terrestrials

September:
- •All chironomid stages
- •Damselfly nymph
- •Dragonfly nymph
- •Shrimp
- •Leeches
- •Water boatman

October:
- •Chironomid larvae
- •Damselfly nymph
- •Dragonfly nymph
- •Shrimp
- •Leeches
- •Water boatman

Fishing Small Lakes

On smaller lakes, the predominant fish species are rainbow, brook and cutthroat trout. If you are looking for more success and less size on your day out on the water, small lakes are a good bet as there is less water to cover. Fishing near structure such as logs and weeds, shoals or at the edge of a drop-off produces the best results. Food sources also congregate around weeds and inflow or outflow streams and in the thermocline. The thermocline is the area of the lake between the warm surface water and the cold water. Concentrate your efforts in these areas to improve your chances of angling success.

A good way to explore a new lake is to use searching type lures or flies and work them near the subsurface structures. Along with your depth chart map, it is a good bet to invest in a depth finder. Depth finders can give even more detail to the underwater structure that maps simply cannot provide. Another tool that can help when fishing lakes or streams is a good pair of polarized glasses. Polarized lenses will help you spot fish or underwater structure that may not show up on a map or depth finder.

A universal set up that will attract all species is a lake troll with a short leader and a Wedding Band or similar with bait. Flatfish, Krocodile or Little Cleo spoons are trolled, while fly fishers usually troll a leech pattern, particularly in murky water. Other all purpose trolling flies are Carey Specials, Woolly Buggers, and Doc Spratleys. Work the area just off the drop-off in a figure-eight pattern to vary the direction, depth and speed of the fly. When trolling for cutthroat, try a silver Muddler Minnow or other baitfish patterns.

If you are fishing from shore, try casting along the shore or towards a fallen log, weed bed or drop-off. Use the countdown method to find where the fish are holding. Casting almost any small spinner or spoon with some bait (worms are preferred) can prove successful, but watch for bait restrictions. Favorites are the Panther Martin (silver or black), Mepps Black Fury or Blue Fox. As for lures, a Deadly Dick, small Dick Nite, Flatfish or Kamlooper also work well. The good ol' fashion bait and bobber can be very effective, while fly anglers should pay attention to the current hatch.

As the water warms up and the fishing slows during the late spring, move to a higher elevation lake. By continually moving to higher elevations you can continue to fish the first few weeks of prime time period right until the lakes begin to cool down in the fall. And as the water gets too cold up high, begin moving down to the lower elevations. Most of the high elevation walk-in lakes offer good fly-fishing during their limited season, which lasts from late June until October. Another nice thing about these lakes is the fish are more active when the light penetrates the water. This makes an 11 o'clock arrival a good thing. If the water is murky, you might as well move on, as the lake is experiencing turnover and the fish will rarely bite.

Many of the lakes in the northern interior feature gin clear water. This means that insect life happens deeper, and that the fish are much easier to spook. Fly anglers in this region use long leaders (up to 7 m/35 feet) to get chironomid and other patterns down to where the action is happening.

Fishing Bigger Lakes

Big lakes can be intimidating. This is where the map comes in really handy. Study your map for structure and devise a game plan prior to arrival. Once at your spot, use your depth finder to hone in on those really unique structure areas and work them hard before heading on to another area.

On larger lakes, trolling for rainbow is very effective. Concentrate around creek or river mouths. Fish seem to hold around the drop-offs in these areas because of the large amount of feed available. Drop-offs near cliffs or rock walls are also good areas to focus your efforts. In spring, fall or winter, trolling a streamer type fly pattern quickly behind the boat so they skim off the surface can produce some big trout. Muddler Minnows, Polar Bear or bucktails are popular choices. As the water warms, try an Apex, Lyman plug or flasher with a hoochie in the 10–30 m (30–90 ft) depth. For deep trolling, downriggers with the aid of a heavy weight will enable you to troll your lure deep enough to find holding areas.

If fishing from shore, working the drop-off around creek mouths is your best bet. Bait balls (a large cluster of worms or eggs and a hook) can be fantastic for Dolly Varden and sometimes rainbow. During the summer a float with a grasshopper can also land you a nice trout.

Fishing Streams & Rivers

Rivers and streams can be a challenge to fish, but at the same time they offer other opportunities that lakes do not. Most notably, hot spots in rivers can be very easy to find as they are often at the bottom of a small waterfall, or the slack water next to the fast water. The main problem with bigger rivers is getting your presentation out far enough from shore to where the fish are holding. The easiest way to overcome this problem is to use a boat if possible. This way you can find seams and pools where fish are holding and get your presentation to where the fish are instead of fighting the current with your cast from shore. You can also access some of the more remote areas that shore anglers are not fishing to find some of the more productive holes.

Of course getting a boat onto smaller streams is often not possible. In these cases, a good set of waders and river shoes can make a big difference in being able to get to the good holes. To work these streams effectively, you need to sneak up on holes to avoid being detected by trout. Work every pocket, pool or seam no matter the size. Some of the biggest fish are hiding in the most unlikely places. Many of the smaller rivers in the area run quite warm in summer and wading can be a refreshing break from the heat of the day. Bring along a hat that you can dip in the water, too.

Please Note: There are regulations imposed for many of the lakes and streams in order to preserve the quality of the resource. Always check the regulations before fishing!

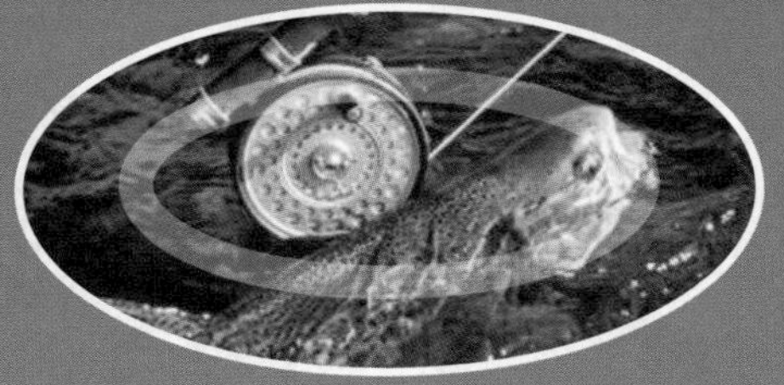

Fishing Tips & Techniques

Releasing Fish - The Gentle Way

There is a growing trend among anglers to catch and release, unharmed, a part of their allowable catch. As well, more restrictive regulations on specific waters can severly limit the angler's allowable harvest.

A fish that appears unharmed may not survive if carelessly handled, so please abide by the following:

1- Play and release fish as rapidly as possible. A fish played for too long may not recover.

2- **Keep the fish in the water as much as possible.** A fish out of water is suffocating. Internal injuries and scale loss is much more likely to occur when out of water.

3- Rolling fish onto their backs (while still in the water) may reduce the amount they struggle, therefore minimizing stress, etc.

4- Carry needle-nose pliers. Grab the bend or round portion of the hook with your pliers, twist pliers upside down, and the hook will dislodge. Be quick, but gentle. **Single barbless hooks are recommended**, if not already stipulated in the regulations.

5- Any legal fish that is deeply hooked, hooked around the gills or bleeding should be retained as part of your quota. **If the fish cannot be retained legally, you can improve its chances for survival by cutting the leader and releasing it with the hook left in.**

6- If a net is used for landing your catch, it should have fine mesh and a knotless webbing to protect fish from abrasion and possible injury.

7- **If you must handle the fish, do so with your bare, wet hands (not with gloves).** Keep your fingers out of the gills, and don't squeeze the fish or cause scales to be lost or damaged. It is best to leave fish in the water for photos. If you must lift a fish then provide support by cradling one hand behind the front fins and your other hand just forward of the tail fin. Minimize the time out of the water, then hold the fish in the water to recover. If fishing in a river, point the fish upstream while reviving it. When the fish begins to struggle and swim normally, let it go.

Index

Index

Important Numbers

Fish and Wildlife

BC Fishing Information ... www.BCFishing.com
... www.sportfishing.bc.ca
Freshwater Fisheries Society of BC ... www.gofishbc.com
Department of Fisheries and Oceans ... www.pac.dfo-mpo.gc.ca
Current salmon and steelhead regulations ... www.env.gov.bc.ca/fw/
... www.pac.dfo-mpo.gc.ca/recfish/default_e.htm
E-Licensing ... www.fishing.gov.bc.ca
BC Wildlife Federation ... www.bcwf.bc.ca
Observe, Record and Report ... 1-877-952-7277

General

Enquiry BC ... 1-800-663-7867
B.C. Ferries ... www.bcferries.com , 1-800-223-3779
Private Barges (Tahtsa Reach & Babine Lake) ... 1-250-845-2322
Highways Report ... www.drivebc.ca , 1-800-663-7867 (Enquiry BC)
To Report Forest Fires ... 1-800-663-5555, *5555 (cellular phones)
Weather Conditions ... www.weatheroffice.ec.gc.ca
Tourism BC ... www.hellobc.com , 1-800-435-5622
Cariboo Chilcotin Coast Tourism Association ... www.landwithoutlimits.com
... 1-800-663-5885
South Cariboo Tourism ... http://www.southcaribootourism.com/
... 1-877-511-5353
West Chilcotin Tourism ... www.visitthewestchilcotin.com
Northern BC Tourism Association ... www.northernbctravel.com
... 1-800-663-8843
Updates ... www.backroadmapbooks.com

B.C Forest Services (Road Conditions)

Northern Interior Forest Region ... 250 565-6100
... www.for.gov.bc.ca/rni
Southern Interior Forest Region ... http://www.for.gov.bc.ca/rsi/
... 250-828-4131
- 100 Mile Forest District (100 Mile House) ... 1-250-395-7800
- Central Cariboo Forest District (Williams Lake) ... 1-250-398-4345
- Chilcotin Forest District (Alexis Creek) ... 1-250-394-4700
- Columbia Forest District (Revelstoke) ... 1-866-837-7611
- Headwaters Forest District (Clearwater) ... 1-250-587-6700
- Kalum Forest District (Terrace) ... 1-250-638-5100
- Kamloops Forest District (Kamloops) ... 1-250-371-6500
- Nadina Forest District (Burns Lake) ... 1-250-692-2200
- North Coast Forest District (Prince Rupert) ... 1-250-624-7460
- Prince George Forest District ... 1-250-614-7400
- Quesnel Forest District ... 1-250-992-4400
- Vanderhoof Forest District ... 1-250-567-6363

Parks

B.C. Parks ... www.bcparks.ca
Park Reservations ... www.discovercamping.ca
... 1-800-689-9025

Advertisements